MW01008900

THE FOURTH TURNING IS HERE

WHAT THE SEASONS OF HISTORY TELL US ABOUT HOW AND WHEN THIS CRISIS WILL END

NEIL HOWE

Simon & Schuster

New York London Toronto Sydney New Delhi

Simon & Schuster
1230 Avenue of the Americas
New York, NY 10020

First Simon & Schuster hardcover edition July 2023

SIMON & SCHUSTER and colophon are registered trademarks of Simon & Schuster, Inc.

For information about special discounts for bulk purchases, please contact Simon & Schuster
Special Sales at 1-866-506-1949 or business@simonandschuster.com.

The Simon & Schuster Speakers Bureau can bring authors to your live event.
For more information or to book an event, contact the Simon & Schuster Speakers
Bureau at 1-866-248-3049 or visit our website at www.simonspeakers.com.

Manufactured in the United States of America

1   3   5   7   9   10   8   6   4   2

Names: Howe, Neil, author. | Strauss, William Fourth turning.
Title: The fourth turning is here : what the seasons of history tell us
about how and when this crisis will end / Neil Howe.
Other titles: 4th turning is here
Description: First Simon & Schuster hardcover edition. | New York : Simon & Schuster,
2023. | Original work "The Fourth Turning" written by William Strauss and
Neil Howe in 1997. | Includes bibliographical references and index. | Summary: ·
"The visionary behind the bestselling phenomenon 'The Fourth Turning' looks once
again to America's past to predict our future in this startling and hopeful prophecy
for how our present era of civil unrest will resolve over the next ten years—
and what our lives will look like once it has"—Provided by publisher.
Identifiers: LCCN 2023007927 (print) | LCCN 2023007928 (ebook) |
ISBN 9781982173739 (hardcover) | ISBN 9781982173753 (ebook)
Subjects: LCSH: United States—History—1945- | United States—Forecasting. |
Twenty-first century—Forecasts. | Cycles.
Classification: LCC E839 .H68 2023 (print) | LCC E839 (ebook) |
DDC 303.4973—dc23/eng/20230224
LC record available at https://lccn.loc.gov/2023007927
LC ebook record available at https://lccn.loc.gov/2023007928

ISBN 978-1-9821-7373-9
ISBN 978-1-9821-7375-3 (ebook)

To Bill
And to all the years we trekked together across faraway decades—
some in the past, and others yet to be

Contents

Preface

This book presents a theory of modern history and a forecast of America's future that have been in development for many decades. Bill Strauss and I began working on both the theory and the forecast back in the late 1980s, while writing *Generations: The History of America's Future*, which was published in 1991. We released our most recent book-length exposition of both in *The Fourth Turning: An American Prophecy*, published in 1997. That was twenty-six years ago.

Remarkably, over all those years, readers' interest in our approach has steadily increased and the number of our readers has grown in episodic leaps. Many have been persuaded that the recent course of American history has vindicated the map of the future we originally laid out back in the 1990s.

One surge of new interest came in 2008, when the Global Financial Crisis inaugurated the worst global economic downturn since the Great Depression. This happened at approximately the time we foresaw that America would enter its "Crisis era" or winter season. Another came in 2013, when national media proclaimed the arrival of a new "Millennial" generation which, as we emphatically foresaw, would not be a mere "Gen Y" clone of the generation that preceded it. Still others came in 2016 (Donald Trump's startling takeover of the Republican Party) and in 2020 (the global pandemic), years roiled by the growing populism, partisanship, distrust, and dysfunction that we had suggested would prevail early in the Crisis era.

Over the last several years, I have been showered by requests to reapply our theory to the future from the perspective of where America finds itself today. This book is my effort to do just that. I am authoring it alone. My longtime collaborator Bill Strauss passed away in the fall of 2007, just on the eve of the Crisis era that we had long foreseen.

In writing this book, my key objective was to answer the questions today's readers most want answered: When did our current Fourth Turning (or Crisis era) begin? How has it evolved? Where is it going? And how will it end? In order to draw historical parallels, I review the history of earlier Fourth Turnings and examine the range of possible scenarios for how America and the world will be different when this one is over. In keeping with our generational method, in which objective events and subjective perceptions interact, I also narrate how each of today's generations is likely to experience the Fourth Turning. While history may shape generations early in life, so too do generations, as they grow older, reliably shape history.

Older readers may be mostly focused on how today's Fourth Turning will end. But younger readers will surely care a great deal about what comes afterward—and what it will feel like to mature and take charge in a post–Fourth Turning world. So I pay considerable attention as well to the First Turning which—about a decade from now—will follow today's Fourth Turning. Before this book is over, I will be asking readers to imagine a plausible future for America that will stretch deep into the twenty-first century.

For readers who are new to our work, I include a concise introduction to our theory of generations and history. You the reader are of course invited to read our earlier works. But you don't have to read them to understand this book. For readers who are familiar with our paradigm, I incorporate much new historical and social science research that was unavailable when our earlier books were written. I also investigate issues that we earlier left unaddressed. These include how the saeculum can be understood as a complex natural system; why the length of a phase of life, and therefore of a generation, has gradually changed over time; and when and where the modern global saeculum (that is, the synchronized generational rhythm outside America) first began to emerge.

The authorial "we" that I use throughout the book is meant to be ambiguous. This is for convenience. In the first few chapters, where I introduce the seasons of time and generational archetypes, I often intend it to refer to both Bill Strauss and myself. Later in the book, I usually intend it to refer to myself only.

With these preliminaries, you the reader are good to go.

Yet to help you on your journey, let me offer a few words of counsel.

The first have to do with crisis. This book proposes that America is midway through an era of historical crisis, which—almost by definition—will lead to outcomes that are largely though not entirely beyond our control. The prospect of such radical uncertainty may fill us with dread. All too often in the modern West we fear that any outcome not subject to our complete control must mean we are heading toward catastrophe.

Over the course of this book, I hope to persuade you of a more ancient yet also more optimistic doctrine: that our collective social life, as with so many rhythmic systems in nature, requires seasons of sudden change and radical uncertainty in order for us to thrive over time. Or, to paraphrase Blaise Pascal: History has reasons that reason knows nothing of.

The other words of counsel have to do with generations. This book suggests that generations are causal agents in history and that generational formation drives the pace and direction of social change in the modern world. Once people understand this, they are often tempted to judge one or another generation as "good" or "bad."

This temptation must be resisted. In the words of the great German scholar Leopold von Ranke, who weighed so many Old World generations on the scales of history, "before God all the generations of humanity appear equally justified." In "any generation," he observed, "real moral greatness is the same as in any other." In truth, every generation is what it has to be. And, as you will soon learn, every generation usually turns out to be just what society needs when it first appears and makes its mark.

Marcel Proust wrote that "what we call our future is the shadow that our past projects in front of us." It's easy to understand that our future must somehow be determined by our past. What's harder to understand is exactly how. The secret is to get out of the "shadow"—to escape the slavish habits and delusive hopes of "what we call our future"—and to recognize deeper patterns at work.

At first glance, these deeper patterns may strike us as grim and unforgiving. Yet once we take time to reflect on them, we may come to a different conclusion: that they are corrective and restorative. They may even save us from our own best intentions.

1

WINTER IS HERE

History never looks like history when you are living through it.

—JOHN W. GARDNER

The old American republic is collapsing. And a new American republic, as yet unrecognizable, is under construction.

Little more than a decade ago, the old America, while not in robust health, still functioned. In the mid-2000s, most voters still read the same news and trusted their government, the two parties still conferred on big issues, Congress still passed annual budgets, and most families remained hopeful about the nation's future.

Then came the Global Financial Crisis (GFC), the rise of populism, and the pandemic. These were three hits that a healthy democracy could have withstood but that caused ours to buckle and give way, revealing pillars and beams that had been decaying for decades.

Pollsters are struggling to catch up with the depth of Americans' dismay across the political spectrum. Seventy-nine percent of voters agree that "America is falling apart." Seventy-six percent worry about "losing American democracy." Sixty-two percent say "the country is in a crisis" (only 25 percent disagree). Measures of national happiness and national pride ("very proud to be an American") have fallen to record lows.

At its worst, the recent collapse has exposed our aging republic's staggering incompetence at carrying out even basic tasks. We can't keep the electricity turned on or baby formula stocked in stores. We can't recall how to enforce laws on the streets or at the border. We can't ensure minimal care for homeless families or minimal compliance from tax-evading oligarchs. We can't conduct a peaceful military withdrawal from an allied democracy or a peaceful transfer of power from one president to the next.

Public health, once a basic task that America took for granted, has become an insuperable challenge. Despite our riches and our science, America ended up with Covid deaths-per-capita on par with many of the poorest and least stable countries of the world. U.S. life expectancy, already declining since 2014, fell further in 2020 than in any single year since 1943, when America was suffering major battle casualties in Africa, Europe, and the Pacific. It fell again by seven months in 2021.

Such incompetence, in turn, has exposed other more troubling changes. One is the steep decline in Americans' trust both in one another and in their leaders. No public trust means no public truth, or at least nothing more substantial than what TV pundit Stephen Colbert calls "truthiness." Conspiracy theories rush in to fill the void, and the nation's unifying narratives are replaced by a mingle-mangle of warring anthems.

What America has experienced over the last decade, writes social psychologist Jonathan Haidt, is aptly captured in the biblical story of the tower of Babel: As if the Almighty had flipped a switch, everyone began speaking different languages and refusing to cooperate on common projects.

Another change has been the abject failure of leaders to govern as if outcomes matter. Leaders who can't identify objectives, exercise authority, and get results—who are forever redefining what they are there to do—invite contempt for their office. Institutions struggling to fulfill their core function are taking on vast new tasks at which they have zero chance of success: The Pentagon now attends to climate change, the Fed to racial equity, the CDC to parenting toddlers.

Other agencies, perversely, are prohibited from fulfilling their core mission. The U.S. Bureau of Alcohol, Tobacco, Firearms, and Explosives cannot maintain a national firearms registry, even though guns now kill more children annually than automobiles (an astonishing predicament America shares only with Yemen). Because Medicaid cannot reimburse doctors for providing routine health care to poor people who don't qualify for the program, Americans end up paying anyway for such care in the costliest manner conceivable. In order to slow the rising cost of college tuition, the federal government initially subsidized student borrowing and then forgave much of what had been borrowed. Both measures are guaranteed to make tuitions rise much faster than they would have otherwise, while saddling America's future middle class with debt. They also transfer billions from future taxpayers, most of whom will never earn college degrees, to big-name universities, many of which already possess endowments worth billions.

"How Dumb Can a Nation Get and Still Survive?" asks one national newspaper headline. Yet another headline directs readers in a more instructive direction: "How to Tell When Your Country Is Past the Point of No Return."

Incompetent governance, ebbing public trust, and declining public compliance all feed on one another in a vicious circle. One symptom is the rise of free-floating anger in public venues. Airlines, restaurants, hospitals, and police report an epidemic of unruliness. Road-rage traffic deaths are up, as are random mass shootings. Over the last two decades, Gallup's "negative experience" or sadness index for Americans has been rising. So has the share of popular song lyrics that include synonyms for "hate" rather than "love." And so, for that matter, has the share of all newspaper headlines denoting fear, disgust, and especially anger.

Even at its best, America's response to its recent collapse has revealed a distressing preference for policies that exacerbate longer-term challenges. Yes, the bipartisan monetary and fiscal response to the 2007–2009 financial crash and the 2020–21 pandemic did protect the have-nots and averted more serious recessions. Yet it did so largely through trickle down: pumping up the asset valuations of the wealthy by flattening the yield curve and smothering market volatility. It did so as well through massive deficit spending, sending federal debt up to levels previously seen only in times of total war. Like addicts acquiring tolerance, policymakers have backed themselves into a corner: The public braces itself for the dark hour when the Fed can no longer ease and Congress can no longer borrow no matter how badly the economy founders.

Along the way, the dysfunction deepens. Debt pyramids grow. Savings get funneled into speculation. Markets concentrate through consolidation. Competition weakens. Productivity growth ebbs. Widening income and wealth inequality, once something Americans merely worried about in the abstract, is now generating what economist Anne Case and Nobel Prize–winner Angus Deaton call an epidemic of "deaths of despair"—rising midlife mortality among lower-income Americans due to opioids, alcoholism, and suicide.

What's more, despite doubling down on an all-hustle, no-fringe-benefits gig economy, younger workers are losing hope of upward generational mobility. Barely half of Millennials and Gen-Xers (that is, anyone born after 1960) are out-earning their parents at age thirty or age forty. Less than half of young men are out-earning their fathers. And even fewer of any of these groups *think* they are doing as well economically as their parents. Many of the poorest give up and never leave home. The most affluent—bidding against one another for a fixed number of the best schools, the best jobs, and the best lifestyles—work themselves to Sisyphean exhaustion.

Not long ago, to be an American was to be a rule-breaking, risk-taking individualist who believed that flouting convention somehow made everything better over time. That still describes many older Americans. It doesn't describe many young adults. Today's rising generation, shell-shocked by the pervasive hollowing out of government, neighborhood, workplace, and family, is looking for any safe harbor it can find. Millennials seek not risk, but security. Not spontaneity, but planning. Not a free-for-all marketplace, but a rule-bound community of equals.

Older generations have for decades exulted in their unconstrained personal growth and in a government that doesn't ask much of them. They are very attached to "democracy," a word which (to them) denotes an obstacle-prone vetocracy: Everything gets discussed, but nothing much happens. Gridlock, lobbies, regulatory review, and lawsuits ensure that comprehensive policy change always gets vetoed. The old, who benefit most from stasis, thereby keep what they have.

Younger generations, meanwhile, are souring on democracy. At last count, Americans today in their thirties are less than half as likely as Americans over age sixty to agree that "it is essential to live in a democracy." A small but rapidly rising share of the young (about a quarter, twice as large as the share of the old) say democracy is a "bad" or "very bad" way to run the country. Most of these would prefer military rule. The young increasingly associate democracy with sclerosis and incapacity. For most of their lives, they've understood that the only organizations America still trusts to get things done are the Pentagon and Google. So many of them wonder: Isn't it time we just get on with it?

The generational contrast is stark. Today's older generations, including most of America's leaders, were raised amid rising abundance. For them, the middle class was always growing and mostly accessible. One word they heard frequently was "affluence." They have few memories of any great national crisis, but grew up enjoying strong institutions built by adults haunted by such memories. Today's younger generations were raised amid declining abundance. For them, the middle class was always shrinking and mostly inaccessible. Coming of age, one word they have heard frequently (its use has skyrocketed since 2008) is "precarity." They cannot recall the presence of strong institutions and have grown up fearing—even expecting—another crisis in their absence.

In every sphere of life, this new mood of contracting horizons has been creating a new and different America.

Globally, America has grown more alarmed about its enemies, less generous toward its friends, more wary of everybody. The Global Financial Crisis in 2008 was the pivot point. Until then, "globalization" seemed inexorable and global trade expanded (as a share of global production) almost every year. Since then, global trade has been shrinking, trade barriers have proliferated, and onshoring has replaced offshoring. Until 2008, the number of democracies around the world was still expanding. Since then, the number of autocracies has been expanding. Four of these (China, Russia, Iran, and North Korea) are gathering into a nuclear-armed and explicitly anti-Western "axis." One (Russia) recently launched the first major European land invasion since World War II.

At home, Americans are also turning inward. We are building walls around our immediate perimeter—to protect our town, our tribe, our kin. The old are spending more money and time investing in their own children and grandchildren. The young, hedging their bets, move less, stay closer to their families, mortgage their future to buy a credential rather than a home, and increasingly marry both later in life and only within their own class.

Income is becoming more correlated with education (though less with race or ethnicity). Education in turn is becoming more correlated with health and longevity. Among Americans born in 1930, the wealthiest fifth could expect to live five years longer than the poorest fifth. Among those born in 1960, the longevity gap has expanded to thirteen years. Everyone knows which side of that divide they want to be on. And as best they can they act accordingly.

Our time horizons too are contracting. Young Americans are deferring or canceling their aspirations. Over the last decade, we have witnessed a declining birth rate and falling home ownership among young adults—and fewer business start-ups either by or for young adults. Yet even as youth grows less hopeful of a better future, the old grow more attached to a better past. Hollywood produces endless oldie sequels. Advertisers bury the Super Bowl in nostalgia ads. Congress dares not touch the growing share of federal outlays dedicated to "earned" senior benefits. And famous tycoons celebrate perpetual monopolies: Warren Buffett looks to invest in "castles protected by unbreachable moats"; Peter Thiel says "competition is for losers."

Personal identity is likewise balkanizing into self-referential fortresses such as ethnicity, gender, religion, region, education, and (of course) political party. Each identity invents narratives for itself according to its own "lived reality." Feeling increasingly isolated and vulnerable as individuals, Americans find it harder to bear genuine diversity. We seek to surround ourselves with our like-minded tribe, canceling or censoring outsiders. Corporations now cultivate their consumer brand tribes, celebrities their "Stan" fan tribes. Immersing ourselves in truthy news feeds, most of us have succumbed to Will Ferrell's seductive proposal in *Anchorman 2*: "What if we didn't give people the news they *needed* to hear, but instead gave them the news they *wanted* to hear." Acknowledging few objective, society-wide standards, we only grudgingly tolerate those deputized to enforce national rules.

As for America's civic life, this is where the old republic has disintegrated beyond recognition.

Our politics are now monopolized by two political parties that represent not just contrasting policies, but mutually exclusive worldviews.

These are "megaparties," to use political scientist Lilliana Mason's powerful term, which attract supporters first and foremost through their emotional brand identities and only secondarily through their positions on issues. Pundits aptly refer to them by simple colors, blue and red, to call attention to the visceral group loyalties they evoke. Each faction espouses different values, adopts different lifestyles, buys different brands, and (in a growing trend) resides in different communities. Electoral choices are becoming ever-more lopsided, one way or the other, by state or county. Elected leaders from the two parties hardly talk to each other, much less socialize or discuss ideas. At this point, there is really nothing left to talk about.

At the national level, Congress remains gridlocked so long as both parties remain competitive. Compared to earlier decades, few major new laws are enacted. The normal budget process has been abandoned. Only vast tax-and-spend packages, permitted under special "reconciliation" rules, get enacted, under protest. What passes for national leadership is the issuing of executive orders from the White House. At the state level, whichever side takes over the governorship and legislative assemblies gets to do pretty much anything it wants. Watching ever-more states succumb to these takeovers, partisans on both sides brood over what could happen nationally if the wrong side gains full control at the federal level.

Every election, no matter how local, has thus become a national election. And every national election is regarded as a do-or-die turning point for America. Overwhelming majorities of voters on both sides say that victory for the wrong side will do lasting damage to the country. Half say that politics is a struggle between right and wrong. A third say that violence may be justified to achieve political goals, and two-thirds *expect* violence in response to future election results.

After each presidential election, the victors zealously prepare the nation for a makeover. The vanquished declare fraud, orchestrate national demonstrations, prepare a "resistance," or (in one notorious instance) attempt a putsch. Legitimacy is not graciously sought by the former, or magnanimously granted by the latter. Each side's most energized partisans claim to represent the unmediated popular will. Unlike the career mandarins who managed the old republic, populists make no pretense of rule-making neutrality: Justice requires a whole new set of rules to usher in a whole new definition of how the national community should think or feel.

We may want to believe these disquieting trends are unique to America—national flukes that will disappear as mysteriously as they appeared. But they are not.

The same trends are now coursing through most of the world's developed and emerging-market nations: growing economic inequality; declining generational and social mobility; tighter national borders; and intensifying ethnic and religious tribalism, weaponized through portable social media. Electorates are demanding, and getting, more authoritarian government. Charismatic populists are ascending to power—or have already gained power—in southern and central Europe, in Latin America, and in southern and eastern Asia.

Global surveys indicate a growing dissatisfaction with democracy itself—what academics call a "global democratic recession"—led in most countries, as in America, by the rising generation of young adults. After conducting a comprehensive analysis of global survey data, the Cambridge University Centre for the Future of Democracy recently concluded: "We find that across the globe, younger generations have become steadily more dissatisfied with democracy—not only in absolute terms, but also relative to older cohorts at comparable stages of life." Affluent nations, especially anglophone affluent nations, appear to be at the forefront of this generational trend.

Americans certainly stand out in one respect. Perhaps because they once expected better, Americans have grown grindingly pessimistic about the prospects for their old republic on its current course. Less than a quarter say their country is heading in the right direction. Only a third say its best years are still ahead. Two-thirds say that their children, when they grow up, will be financially "worse off" than they are. Two-thirds also agree that America shows "signs of national decline," up from only one-quarter twenty-five years ago.

Yet as Americans witness the old civic order collapse, they are moving beyond pessimism. They are coming to two inescapable conclusions.

First, in order to survive and recover, the country must construct a new civic order powerful enough to replace what is now gone. And second, the new order must be imposed by "our side," which would rescue the country from its current paralysis, rather than by "the other side," which would plunge the country into inescapable ruin.

In this dawning climate of hope and (mostly) fear, every measure of political engagement is surging. U.S. voter turnout rates are now the highest in over a century. Individual donations and volunteering for political campaigns are exploding. Civic literacy, such as people's understanding of the Constitution, has been climbing steeply after decades of decline. Measures of partisanship (feeling strongly about an issue) and sorting (partisans all feeling the same way across all issues) are reaching the highest levels in living memory.

In our political behavior, we are becoming less a nation of detached individualists and more a nation of all-in tribal partisans, ready to move collectively in one direction or the other. In our public remarks, we are replacing layered irony with bland sincerity, because ambiguity could be misinterpreted: What we say now commits us to one side or the other. Our preferred leadership style is moving from the elite technocrat to the plainspoken everyman (or everywoman), who talks less about options and fine gradations than about ultimatums and flat guarantees.

Abraham Lincoln, observing in 1858 that America was a "house divided," prophesized that it would remain so until "a crisis shall have been reached, and passed"—after which "this government . . . will become all one thing, or all the other." Today, as then, America is torn by a struggle between two great political tribes, each trying to reshape the new republic toward its own goals and away from its adversary's. Today, as then, both the rhetoric of violence and the threat of violence against political leaders is rising. Today, as then, few are in the mood to compromise.

This may be the most ominous signal of all: To most Americans, the survival of democracy itself is not as essential as making sure their side comes out on top. Just before the 2022 election, while 71 percent of voters agreed that "democracy is under threat," only 7 percent agreed that this was the biggest problem facing the country.

Sensing that the price of failure is permanent marginalization, partisans on each side are girding for a crisis in which they are ready to break any guardrails to prevail. Everything is now on the table: gerrymandering, tilting election rules, subpoenas, impeachments, nuking the filibuster, packing the Supreme Court, and—in extremis—mobilizing mobs in support of state refusal to follow federal rules (nullification) or in support of outright state independence (secession).

However the struggle plays out, America is getting ready for a gigantic makeover of its national governing institutions. Newspaper editorials focus mostly on the wrong question. They ask which side will win. The Democrats or the Republicans? The blue zone or the red zone? The puritanical left or the populist right? But this is not the most important question. In fact, the new regime will necessarily combine elements of both. The most important question is whether Americans are prepared for the trauma that will accompany the collapse of one regime and the emergence of another.

All the pieces are in place. Few voters still think the status quo is sustainable. Few centrists still rouse much enthusiasm within their parties. And during recent emergencies (especially the pandemic) America's central government has already road-tested many of the policies it may employ to begin reconstruction. It can now issue universal incomes to households and firms, block interest due on loans, freeze ("sanction") individual bank accounts, stop cross-border trade, and compel firms to stay open or closed. Through the Fed, it can now allocate credit by firm or industry and convert any amount of public or private credit into U.S. dollars. Even censorship of social media "disinformation" now seems to be within the ambit of its powers.

Very soon, something will trigger this makeover to exit its destructive phase and enter its constructive phase. What will this trigger be? Almost any new emergency could suffice. And almost any will soon be forthcoming. In 2022, the Collins English Dictionary added the word "permacrisis" to its lexicon, meaning "an extended period of instability and insecurity, especially one resulting from a series of catastrophic events."

Perhaps the trigger will be another financial crash or recession or pandemic—followed by policy paralysis or partisan upheaval.

Perhaps it will be a great-power adversary who, sensing our domestic turmoil, will doubt America's resolve to fulfill its treaty obligations—and put it to the test.

Or perhaps America will simply fragment from within, a catastrophic failed-state scenario that could put anything else into play, from an economic crash to global chaos. Back in the year 2000, the very possibility seemed unthinkable. Now it seems all too thinkable. Ever since the 2020 election season, close to half of Americans have been telling pollsters they believe a civil war is imminent.

Yes, in the face of adversity, the old America is disintegrating. But at the same time, America is moving into a phase transition, a critical discontinuity, in which all the dysfunctional pieces of the old regime will be reintegrated in ways we can hardly now imagine.

The civic vacuum will be filled. Welcome to the early and awkward emergence of the next American republic.

Back in 1997, in *The Fourth Turning*, Bill Strauss and I wrote that America was then traversing an "Unraveling" era of exuberant individualism amid collective apathy and political drift. That era, we predicted, had another ten years to run. Beyond that? We wrote that Americans in the late Clinton years suspected they were "heading toward a waterfall"—an assessment we agreed with.

Roughly on schedule, in the fall of 2008, with the arrival of global economic mayhem, the "Unraveling" era came to an end. And the generation-long era of the waterfall commenced. Only now that Americans are in it, they realize that it feels more like a series of punctuated cataracts. They had better get ready. History, like any good movie director, saves the most vertiginous plunges for last.

Only when this collective rite of passage is complete, sometime in the mid-2030s, will Americans be able to assess exactly where the cataracts have taken them, what they have gained or lost along the way, and how as a people they have been remade. Yet even from today's vantage point, it is possible to foresee the approximate direction of our trajectory.

THE SEASONS OF HISTORY

The reward of the historian is to locate patterns that recur over time and to discover the natural rhythms of social experience.

At the core of modern history lies this remarkable pattern: Over the past five or six centuries, Anglo-American society has entered a new era—a new *turning*—every two decades or so. At the start of each turning, people change how they feel about themselves, the culture, the nation, and the future. Turnings come in cycles of four. Each cycle spans the length of a long human life, roughly eighty to one hundred years, a unit of time the ancients called the *saeculum*. Together, the four turnings of the saeculum comprise history's periodic rhythm, in which the seasons of spring, summer, fall, and winter correspond to eras of rebirth, growth, entropy, and (finally) creative destruction:

- The *First Turning* is a *High*, an upbeat era of strengthening institutions and weakening individualism, when a new civic order implants and an old values regime decays.

- The *Second Turning* is an *Awakening*, a passionate era of spiritual upheaval, when the civic order comes under attack from a new values regime.

- The *Third Turning* is an *Unraveling*, a downcast era of strengthening individualism and weakening institutions, when the old civic order decays and the new values regime implants.

- The *Fourth Turning* is a *Crisis*, a decisive era of secular upheaval, when the values regime propels the replacement of the old civic order with a new one.

Each turning comes with its own identifiable mood. Always, these mood shifts catch people by surprise.

In the current saeculum, the First Turning was the *American High* of the Truman, Eisenhower, and Kennedy presidencies. As World War II wound down, no one predicted that America would soon become so confident and institutionally muscular, yet also so bland and socially conformist. But that's what happened.

The Second Turning was the *Consciousness Revolution*, stretching from the campus revolts of the mid-1960s to the tax revolts of the early 1980s. In the months following John Kennedy's assassination, no one predicted America was about to enter an era of personal liberation and cross a cultural watershed that would separate anything thought or said afterward from anything thought or said before. But that's what happened.

The Third Turning was the *Culture Wars*, an era that began with Reagan's upbeat "Morning in America" campaign in 1984, climaxed with the dotcom bubble, and ground to exhaustion with post-9/11 wars in the Mideast. Amid the passionate early debates over "the Reagan Revolution," no one predicted that the nation was entering an era of celebrity circuses, raucous culture wars, and civic drift. But that's what happened.

The Fourth Turning—for now, let's call it the *Millennial Crisis*—began with the global market crash of 2008 and has thus far witnessed a shrinking middle class, the "MAGA" rise of Donald Trump, a global pandemic, and new fears of a great-power war. Early in Barack Obama's '08 campaign against John McCain, no one could have predicted that America was about to enter an era of bleak pessimism, authoritarian populism, and fanatical partisanship. But that's what happened. And this era still has roughly another decade to run.

Propelling this cycle are social generations, of roughly the same length as a turning, which are both *shaped by* these turnings in their youth and later *shape* these turnings as midlife leaders and parents. Ordinarily, each turning is associated with the coming of age (from childhood into adulthood) of a distinct generational archetype. Thus there are four generational archetypes, just as there are four turnings:

- A *Prophet* generation (example: Boomers, born 1943–60) grows up as increasingly indulged post-Crisis children, comes of age as defiant young crusaders during an Awakening, cultivates principle as moralistic midlifers, and ages into the detached, visionary elders presiding over the next Crisis.

- A *Nomad* generation (example: Gen X, born 1961–81) grows up as underprotected children during an Awakening, comes of age as the alienated young adults of a post-Awakening world, mellows into pragmatic midlife leaders during a Crisis, and ages into tough post-Crisis elders.

- A *Hero* generation (example: G.I.s, born 1901–24, or Millennials, born 1982–2005?) grows up as increasingly protected post-Awakening children, comes of age as team-working young achievers during a Crisis, demonstrates hubris as confident midlifers, and ages into the engaged, powerful elders presiding over the next Awakening.

- An *Artist* generation (example: Silent, born 1925–42, or Homelanders, often called Gen Z by today's media, born 2006?–2029?) grows up as overprotected children during a Crisis, comes of age as the sensitive young adults of a post-Crisis world, breaks free as indecisive midlife leaders during an Awakening, and ages into empathic post-Awakening elders.

Each turning is therefore associated with a similar constellation of generations in each phase of life. (In an Unraveling, for example, the Artist is always entering elderhood and the Nomad is always coming of age into adulthood.) During each turning, most people pay special attention to the new generation coming of age—because they sense that this youthful archetype, alive to the future's potential, may prefigure the emerging mood of the new turning.

They're right. This rising generation does prefigure the emerging mood. Yet like the mood of the turning, the personality of the rising generation always catches most people by surprise.

By the time of the 1945 VE and VJ Day parades, at the start of the First Turning or High, Americans had grown accustomed to massive ranks of organized youth mobilizing to vote for the New Deal, build dams and harbors, and conquer half the world. No one expected a new generation of polite cautionaries who preferred to "work within the system" rather than change it. But with the Silent Generation, that's what they got.

When Martin Luther King, Jr., led his march on Washington, DC, at the start of the Awakening, Americans had grown accustomed to well-socialized youth who listened to doo-wop music, showed up for draft calls, and worked earnestly yet peaceably for causes like civil rights. No one expected a new generation of rule-breakers who preferred to act out their passions, cripple "the Establishment," and reinvent the culture. But with the Boom Generation, that's what they got.

A year after *The Big Chill* appeared, when Apple was loudly proclaiming that "1984 won't be like *1984*," Americans at the start of the Unraveling had grown accustomed to moralizing youth who busily quested after deeper values and a meaningful inner life. No one expected a new generation of hardscrabble free agents who scorned yuppie pretention and hungered after the material bottom line. But with Generation X, that's what they got.

Flash forward twenty years to the peak year of the *Survivor* TV series, near the onset of the Great Recession and the beginning of the Millennial Crisis. Americans by now had grown accustomed to edgy and self-reliant youth who enjoyed taking personal risks and sorting themselves into winners and losers. No one expected a new generation of normcore team players aspiring to build security, connection, and community. But with the Millennial Generation, that's what they got—or, perhaps we should say, are getting.

IT'S ALL HAPPENED BEFORE

So much for the shifts in national mood and generational alignment over the last saeculum, stretching back to the end of World War II. Have shifts like these ever happened before in earlier saecula? Yes—many times.

Let's first conjure up America's mood near the close of the most recent Third Turning or fall season: the Culture Wars. Most readers will be old enough to recall personally much of what happened between the end of the Cold War (1991) and the Global Financial Crisis (2008). They may have fond memories of that era's new sense of personal freedom and diversity, less fettered either by laws or regulation ("The era of big government is over," declared President Clinton in 1996) or by scolding prudes ("Just Do It" was Nike's iconic slogan of the 1990s). They may have more anxious memories of that era's wilder and meaner trends, such as terrifying rates of violent crime, a darkening pop culture (unless Public Enemy and Nirvana remain at the top of your oldies list), and the rapid erosion of unions and public programs that once protected the middle class.

At the cutting edge of it all was an undersocialized rising generation whose favorite new motto ("works for me") celebrated a self-oriented pragmatism and whose favorite generational nonlabel ("X") was meant to deflect the canting moralism of former hippies hitting midlife. Meanwhile, adults of all ages did their best to shelter a new generation of "babies on board" who were now aging into grade-schoolers located in carefully marked "safe zones."

As highlighted by such bestselling authors as John Naisbitt (*Megatrends*) and Alvin Toffler (*Powershift*), our world in that era was becoming more complex, diverse, decentralized, high-tech, and self-directed. It was a freer, coarser, less-governed America in which no one really took charge of any big issue—from globalization and deficits to poverty-level wages and haphazard wars. Most Americans went along with the open-ended mood and voted for the leaders who provided it. Only a minority mounted a fierce resistance and denounced those whom they held responsible. But, as time went on, it's fair to say that most Americans had serious misgivings about where a leaderless nation would eventually find itself.

If we want to find a historical parallel, we need to go back roughly one long lifetime (eighty to one hundred years) before the end of this Third Turning to the end of the last Third Turning.

Elders in their eighties in the early 2000s could have recalled, as children, the years between Armistice Day (in 1918) and the Great Crash of 1929. Euphoria over a global military triumph was painfully short-lived. Earlier optimism about a progressive future succumbed to jazz-age nihilism and a pervasive cynicism about high ideals. Bosses swaggered in immigrant ghettos, the KKK in the Heartland, the Mafia in the big cities, and defenders of Americanism in every Middletown. Unions atrophied, government weakened, voter participation fell, and a dynamic marketplace ushered in new consumer technologies (autos, radios, phones, jukeboxes, vending machines) that made life feel newly complicated and frenetic.

"It's up to you" was the new self-help mantra of a rising "Lost Generation" of barnstormers and rumrunners. Their risky pleasures, which prompted journalists to announce it was "Sex O'Clock in America," shocked middle-aged decency brigades—many of them "tired radicals" who were by then moralizing against the detritus of the "mauve" decade of their own youth (in the 1890s). During the Roaring Twenties, opinions polarized around no-compromise cultural issues like alcohol, drugs, sex, immigration, and family life. Meanwhile, parents strove to protect a Scout-like new generation of children (who, in time, would serve in World War II and be called the "Greatest Generation").

Sound familiar?

Let's move backward another long lifetime (eighty to ninety years) to the end of the prior Third Turning.

Elders in their eighties in the 1920s could easily have recalled, as children, the late 1840s and 1850s, when America was drifting into a rowdy new era of dynamism, opportunism, violence—and civic stalemate. The popular Mexican War had just ended in a stirring triumph, but the huzzahs over territorial gain didn't last long. Immigration surged into swelling cities, triggering urban crime waves and driving voters toward nativist political parties. Financial speculation boomed, and new technologies like railroads, telegraph, and steam-driven factories plus a burgeoning demand for cotton exports kindled a nationwide worship of the "Almighty Dollar." First among the votaries was a brazen young "Gilded Generation" who shunned colleges in favor of hustling west with six-shooters to pan for gold in towns fabled for casual murder. "Root, hog, or die" was the new youth motto.

Unable to contain this restless energy, the two major parties (Whigs and Democrats) were slowly disintegrating. A righteous debate over slavery's territorial expansion erupted between so-called Southrons and abolitionists—many of them middle-aged spiritualists who, in the more utopian 1830s and early '40s, had dabbled in moral reform, born-again spiritualism, utopian communes, and other youth-fired crusades. An emerging generation of children, meanwhile, were being raised under a strict regimentation that startled European visitors who, just a decade earlier, had bemoaned the wildness of American kids.

Sound familiar?

Run the clock back the length of yet another long life, to the 1760s. The recent favorable conclusion to the French and Indian War had brought a century of conflict to a close and secured the colonial frontier. Yet when Britain tried to recoup war expenses through mild taxation and limits on westward expansion, the colonies seethed with directionless discontent. Immigration from the Old World, migration across the Appalachians, and colonial trade arguments all rose sharply. As debtors' prisons bulged, middle-aged people complained about what Benjamin Franklin called the "white savagery" of youth. Aging orators (many of whom were once fiery young preachers during the circa-1740 Great Awakening) awakened civic consciousness and organized popular crusades of economic austerity. The children became the first to attend well-supervised church schools in the colonies rather than academies in corrupt Albion. Gradually, colonists began separating into mutually loathing camps, one defending and the other attacking the Crown.

Sound familiar again?

As they approached the close of each of these prior Third Turning eras, Americans celebrated a self-seeking ethos of laissez-faire "individualism" (a word first popularized in the 1840s), yet also fretted over social fragmentation, distrust of authority, and economic and technological change that seemed to be accelerating beyond society's ability to control it.

During each of these eras, Americans had recently triumphed over a long-standing global threat—Imperial Germany, Imperial New Spain (alias Mexico), or Imperial New France. Yet these victories came to be associated with a worn-out definition of national direction—and, perversely, stripped people of what common civic purpose they had left. Much like the fall of the Soviet Union in 1991, early in our most recent Third Turning, they all unleashed a mood of foreboding.

During each of these eras, truculent moralism darkened the debate about the country's future. Culture wars raged; the language of political discourse coarsened; nativist feelings hardened; crime, immigration, and substance abuse came under growing attack; and attitudes toward children grew more protective. People cared less about established political parties, and third-party alternatives attracted surges of new interest.

During each of these eras, Americans felt well rooted in their personal values but newly hostile toward the corruption of civic life. Unifying institutions that had seemed secure for decades suddenly felt ephemeral. Those who had once trusted the nation with their lives were now retiring or passing away. Their children, now reaching midlife, were more interested in lecturing the nation than in leading it. And to the new crop of young adults, the nation hardly mattered. The whole res publica seemed to be unraveling.

During each of these previous Third Turnings, Americans felt like they were drifting toward a waterfall.

And, as it turned out, they were.

The 1760s were followed by the American Revolution, the 1850s by the Civil War, the 1920s by the Great Depression and World War II. All these Unraveling eras were followed by bone-jarring Crises so monumental that, by their end, American society emerged wholly transformed.

Every time, the change came with scant warning. As late as November 1773, October 1860, and October 1929, the American people had no idea how close the change was—nor, even while they were in it, how transformative it would be.

Over the next two decades or so, society convulsed. Initially, the people were dazed and demoralized. In time, they began to mobilize into partisan tribes. Ultimately, emergencies arose that required massive sacrifices from a citizenry who responded by putting community ahead of self. Leaders led, and people trusted them. As a new social contract was created, people overcame challenges once thought insurmountable and used the Crisis to elevate themselves and their nation to a higher plane of civilization. In the 1790s, they created the world's first large democratic republic. In the late 1860s, decimated but reassembled, they forged a more unified nation that extended new guarantees of liberty and equality. In the late 1940s, they constructed the most Promethean superpower ever seen.

The Fourth Turning is history's great discontinuity. It ends one epoch and begins another.

Yet as we reflect today on America's entry into yet another Fourth Turning era, we must remember this: *The swiftness and permanence of the mood shift is only appreciated in retrospect—never in prospect.* The dramatic narrative arc that seems so unmistakable afterward in view of its consequences was not at all obvious to Americans at the time.

During the American Revolution Crisis, General George Washington early on believed his army would likely be crushed. Even as late as the mid-1780s, nearly all the founders lamented the incapacity of their feeble confederation to govern a vast, scattered, and willful citizenry.

During the Civil War Crisis, despite the rapid crescendo of deaths in major battles that each side hoped would be decisive, no clear victor emerged. Shortly before his 1864 re-election, President Abraham Lincoln (along with many of his advisors) predicted that he would likely "be beaten badly" at the polls and that his accomplishments would thereafter be dismantled by his opponents.

As for the Great Depression–World War II Crisis, there is a reason why this depression is called "Great": At the end of 1940, after a decade of economic misery and New Deal activism, most Americans believed the depression had not yet ended. Unemployment was still in the double-digits; deflation still loomed; and bond yields were hitting record lows. Looking back, we see President Franklin Roosevelt's political achievements as monumental. But at the time, no one had any idea what his legacy would be until after the climax of World War II—that is, like Lincoln, not long before his death.

Similarly, as we look at our current Crisis era, we cannot yet presume to know what America will or will not accomplish by the time this era is over. Yet basic historical patterns do indeed recur.

Let's take another look at the opening decade of our current Fourth Turning, the 2010s. And let's compare it to the opening decade of the prior Fourth Turning, the 1930s. The parallels are striking.

Both decades played out in the shadow of a massive global financial crash, followed by the most severe economic contraction in living memory. Both were balance-sheet depressions, triggered by the bursting of a debt-financed asset bubble. Both were accompanied by deflation fears and the chronic underemployment of labor and capital. Both failed to respond to conventional fiscal and central-bank policy remedies. Terms often used to describe the 2010s economy, like "secular stagnation" and "debt deflation," were in fact resurrected from celebrity economists (Alvin Hansen and Irving Fisher) who first coined them in the 1930s.

Both decades began with most measures of inequality hitting record highs, ensuring that social and economic privilege would move to the top of the political agenda. In both decades, leaders experimented with a multitude of new and untested federal policies. During the New Deal, Americans lost count of all the new alphabet-soup agencies and programs (AAA, NRA, WPA, CCC, TVA, PWA)—as they did again during the Great Recession and the global Covid-19 pandemic (ARRA, TALF, TARP, QE, QT, CARES, PPP, ARP). The policy measures of the 1930s were sometimes just as head-scratching as those we are subjected to today: killing pigs and plowing under cotton to "save" farmers (under the AAA), for example, or fixing wages to "boost" spending (under the NRA).

In both decades, populism gained new energy on both the right and the left—with charismatic outsiders gaining overnight constituencies. In both decades, partisan identity strengthened, the electorate polarized, and voting rates climbed. Where a decade earlier partisans had focused on winning the "culture war," by the mid-1930s and mid-2010s their focus had grown more existential—winning decisive political power.

In both decades, marriages were postponed, birth rates fell, and the share of unrelated adults living together rose. In both decades, families grew closer and multigenerational living (of the sort memorialized in vintage Frank Capra movies) became commonplace. In both decades, young adults drove a decline in violent crime and a blanding of the popular culture—along with a growing public enthusiasm for group membership and group mobilization.

"Community" became a favorite word among the twenty-somethings of the 1930s, as it became again among the twenty-somethings of the 2010s. Other favorite words in both decades were "safety" and synonyms like "security" and "protection." New Deal programs advertised all three, as have the costliest government initiatives in recent years. During the 2010s, firms began offering "feeling safe" as a benefit to their customers. "Stay safe" became a common farewell greeting. Political parties worldwide issued ever more slogans promising economic security and ever fewer promising economic growth. (Preceding the EU parliamentary elections in 2019, the universal motto of mainstream parties was "a Europe that protects.") And in both decades, an ancient truth revealed itself: When people start taking on less risk as individuals, they start taking on more risk as groups.

Around the world, in both decades, authoritarian demagogy became a sweeping tide. The symbols and rhetoric of nationalism galvanized ever-larger crowds in real or sham support. (By 2017, governments in thirty nations were paying troll armies to sway public opinion online.) In both decades, intellectuals lent their support to grievance-based political movements based on religious, ethnic, or racial identity. Fascist language and symbols gained (or regained) popular traction in Europe—and, in Russia, Joseph Stalin gained (or regained) his reputation as national savior. In both decades, patriotism came to be equated with the settling of scores. *Wolf Warrior 2*, released in 2017, became the highest grossing film ever released in China largely by living up to its marketing tagline: "Anyone who offends China, wherever they are, must die."

In both decades, meanwhile, economic globalism was in rapid retreat. Dozens of nations began or extended border walls. The grand alliances by which large democratic powers had earlier governed global affairs were weakening. Autocrats, their political model now gaining popular appeal, had widening room to maneuver. And maneuver they did, with terrifying impunity.

Above all during these decades, social priorities in America and much of the world seemed to shift in the same direction: from the individual to the group; from private rights to public results; from discovering ideals to championing them; from attacking institutions to founding them; from customizing down to scaling up; from salvation by faith to salvation by works; from conscience-driven dissenters to shame-driven crowds.

WHAT LIES AHEAD

History is seasonal, and winter is here. A Fourth Turning can be long and arduous. It can be brief but stormy. The icy gales can be unremitting or be broken by sizable stretches of balmy weather. Like nature's winter, the saecular winter can come a bit early or a bit late. But, also like nature's winter, it cannot be averted. It must come, just as this winter has.

America entered its most recent Fourth Turning in 2008, placing us fifteen years into the Crisis era. Each turning is a generation long (about twenty to twenty-five years), and it is likely that this turning will be somewhat longer than most. By our reckoning, therefore, we have about another decade to go.

What can we expect during the remainder of this era? And what will follow it? In this book, we will try to answer such questions. And our method will be to draw evidence from the historical track record, consisting of four earlier saecula in American history, another three prior saecula in America's ancestral English lineage, and other saecula in several modern societies outside of America.

Here let's offer a preview.

What typically occurs early in a Fourth Turning—the initial catalyzing event, the deepening loss of civic trust, the galvanizing of partisanship, the rise of creedal passions, and the scramble to reconstruct national policies and priorities—all this has already happened. The later and more eventful stages of a Fourth Turning still lie ahead.

Every Fourth Turning unleashes social forces that push the nation, before the era is over, into a great national challenge: a single urgent test or threat that will draw all other problems into it and require the extraordinary mobilization of most Americans. We don't yet know what this challenge is. Historically, it has nearly always been connected to the outcome of a major war either between America and foreign powers, or between different groups within America, or both.

War may not be inevitable. Yet even if it is not, the very survival of the nation will feel at stake. The challenge will require a degree of public engagement and sacrifice that few Americans today have experienced earlier in their lives. Remnants of the old social and policy order will disintegrate. And by the time the challenge is resolved, America will acquire a new collective identity with a new understanding of income, class, race, nation, and empire. For the rising generation of Millennials, the bonds of civic membership will strengthen, offering more *to* each citizen yet also requiring more *from* each citizen.

In any case, sometime before the mid-2030s, America will pass through a great gate in history, commensurate with the American Revolution, the Civil War, and the twin emergencies of the Great Depression and World War II.

The risk of catastrophe will be high. The nation could erupt into insurrection or civil conflict, crack up geographically, or succumb to authoritarian rule. If there is a war, it is likely to be one of maximum risk and effort—in other words, a *total* war—precisely because so much will seem to rest on the outcome.

Every Fourth Turning has registered an upward ratchet in the technology of destruction and in humanity's willingness to use it. During the Civil War, the two capital cities would surely have incinerated each other had the two sides possessed the means to do so. During World War II, America enlisted its best and brightest young minds to invent such a technology—which the nation swiftly put to use. During the Millennial Crisis, America will possess the ability to inflict unimaginable horrors— and confront adversaries who possess the same.

Yet Americans will also gain, by the end of the Fourth Turning, a unique opportunity to achieve a new greatness as a people. They will be able to solve long-term national problems and perhaps lead the way in solving global problems as well. This too is part of the Fourth Turning historical track record.

The U.S. Civil War, for example, reunited the states, abolished slavery, and accelerated the global spread of democratic nationalism. The New Deal and World War II transformed America into a vastly more affluent and equitable society than it had been before—and into a nation powerful enough to help many other countries grow more prosperous and democratic themselves throughout the rest of the twentieth century.

In about a decade, perhaps in the early or mid-2030s, America will exit winter and enter spring. The First Turning will begin. The mood of America during this spring season will please some and displease others. Individualism will be weaker and community will be stronger than most of us recall from circa-2000. Public trust will be stronger, institutions more effective, and national optimism higher. Yet the culture will be tamer, social conscience weaker, and pressure to conform heavier. If the current Fourth Turning ends well, America will be able enjoy its next golden age, or at least an era that will feel like a golden age to those who build it. Come this spring, America's chief preoccupation will be filling out and completing the new order whose rough framework was only hastily hoisted into place at the end of the winter.

Inevitably, that completion will in time generate new tensions and move America into yet another (summer) season by the 2050s. But all this takes us far ahead of the central focus of our story, which remains the outcome of winter.

"There is a mysterious cycle in human events," President Franklin Roosevelt observed in the depths of the Great Depression. "To some generations much is given. Of other generations much is expected. This generation has a rendezvous with destiny."

This cycle of human events remains mysterious. But we need not stumble across it in total surprise or remain ignorant of why it arose, what drives it, how it behaves, or where it's going. Indeed, we must not. For today's generations have their own rendezvous with destiny.

MEMORIES OF TOMORROW

"The farther backward you look, the farther forward you are likely to see," Winston Churchill once said. He understood that events never keep moving in a straight line, but rather turn around inevitable corners. And to figure out how events are likely to turn in the future, there is no alternative but to learn how this has happened before.

One central purpose of this book is to make sense of these turnings by distilling them into a recognizable pattern. Another is to apply this method to the next few decades and describe some likely future scenarios for America and the world.

Along the way, we don't want to look at events only from the outside in or from the top down. We also want to look at them from the inside out, that is from the perspective of each generation experiencing them. You, the reader, surely belong to one of these generations. And your children and parents surely belong to others.

The book is organized into three parts.

Part One explores our cyclical perspective and explains our method and terminology.

In Chapter 2, we introduce readers to the modern cycle of seasonal history—when it arose, who first noticed it, and how it works. In Chapter 3, we look at the generations and generational archetypes that propel this cycle of history forward through "saecular time." In Chapter 4, we delve into many other "long cycles" uncovered by historians and social scientists—for example, cycles in politics, in the economy, in population, in migration, in crime, and in the culture—and explain how most of these are remarkably synchronous with the seasonality of the saeculum. In Chapter 5, we examine the saeculum as a complex social system—that is, from the perspective of complexity theory—and grapple with such issues as contingency in history, the appearance of anomalous cycles, and growing evidence of a "global saeculum" outside of America.

Part Two covers what can be expected to happen over the next decade or so.

In Chapter 6, we survey the history and common chronology of earlier Fourth Turnings. In Chapter 7, we take a close look at the Fourth Turning that is now unfolding in America—the Millennial Crisis—and speculate on how it is likely to reach its climactic "Ekpyrosis" and then its resolution. In Chapter 8, we lay out the dramatic changes in social mood and social direction we are likely to witness in the years to come. In Chapter 9, we switch our perspective and view the next decade through the eyes of each generation experiencing it. We also look at the role or "script" awaiting each generation by the late 2020s. Our main focus will be on the four generations that make up the completed Fourth Turning constellation: Boomer elders, Gen X in midlife, Millennial rising adults, and Homelander children.

Part Three pushes further ahead in time, past the winter and into the spring season of the saeculum.

In Chapter 10, we speculate on how America is likely to change during the First Turning and on how each generation is likely to handle its next phase of life in the late 2030s, 2040s, and early 2050s. We close by pausing at the edge of the coming summer season and asking a question that may then seem as controversial as it today seems outlandish: Will America, and perhaps the world, attain a new golden age? In the Epilogue, we reflect on some basic lessons we can draw from the seasons of history.

We're now almost ready to proceed to Part One, where we lay out the central thesis of this book: that social change in the modern world follows a strong cyclical dynamic. Before moving on, however, we first need to step back and rethink some deep preconceptions about how we see time and history.

Most of us who live in the modern world routinely make sense of social change by seeing it as more or less unidirectional and progressive over time. We find it difficult to think about history any other way. This is remarkable, because progress as a paradigm for understanding history is in fact a very recent innovation. Before this innovation, during nearly all of the millennia that humanity has (to our knowledge) thought about time at all, a very different paradigm was dominant: the cycle.

Let's pause here to recount the history, as it were, of how people look at history. One important lesson we will draw from this recounting is that civilization began to behave in a recognizably cyclical pattern precisely when civilization began to assume that history should be understood as progressive.

This points to something of a paradox. As a description of social *belief*, the wheel of time has powerful primordial origins. Strong among the ancients, its appeal has steadily weakened among us moderns. Yet as a description of social *behavior*, this wheel, weak among the ancients, has become increasingly consequential in the modern world. We will return to this paradox at the end of the chapter.

THE MODERN WHEEL OF TIME

From the Grim Reaper of the Christians to the blood-drenched Kali of the Hindus, humanity has traditionally viewed time darkly. Time, we realize, must issue in our dissolution and death. Its passage is destined to annihilate everything familiar about our present—from such trivial pleasures as a morning cup of coffee to the grandest constructions of art, religion, or politics. "Time and his aging," observed Aeschylus, "overtakes all things alike."

Over the millennia, people have meditated on this anxiety over time and change, and they have addressed it by developing three ways of understanding time: *chaotic*, *cyclical*, and *linear*. The first, chaotic, has never been popular outside of a handful of sophists and sages. The second, cyclical, was the dominant view of all ancient civilizations and is still commonplace in premodern societies. The third, linear, has become ascendant relatively recently—over just the last several centuries in the modern West, especially in America.

In *chaotic time*, history has no pattern. Events follow one another randomly, and any effort to impute order to their whirligig succession is pointless. This may be the first intuition of a small child, for whom change in the natural world seems utterly beyond control or comprehension. It may be the insight of the jester who wants to puncture our complacency about the future. Patternless time has even become a supreme spiritual goal, the "knowing beyond knowing" of many Eastern religions. Buddhism teaches that a person reaches nirvana by ritually detaching him- or herself from any connection to the meaning of space or time or selfhood.

The weakness of chaotic time, of course, is that it doesn't address our anxiety about time's destructive blindness. We all understand that much of what happens to us is unpredictable. What we want to know is: In what ways can we reasonably *expect* the world to change over time? Society could hardly function without some consensus about its common future. We need some certainty about what will happen—and also about what is supposed to happen. For this reason, no society or religion has ever fully endorsed chaotic time—not even Buddhism, in which all who fail to reach nirvana remain subject to the orderly reign of karma.

Enter *cyclical time*, whose prehistoric origins are informally rooted in the countless rhythms common to virtually all traditional societies: chanting, dancing, sleeping, waking, planting, harvesting, hunting, feasting, gestating, birthing, and dying. Cyclical time took formal shape when the ancients first linked these rhythms to cycles of planetary events (diurnal rotations, lunar months, solar years, zodiacal precessions).

Cycles conquered the fear of chaos by repetition and example, by the parent or hunter or farmer performing the right deed at the right moment in the perpetual circle—much as an original god or goddess performed a similar deed during time's mythical first circle. Eventually, great cycles came to mark the duration of kingdoms and prophecies, the coming of heroes and shamans, and the aging of lives, generations, and civilizations. Cyclical time is endless, yet also endlessly completed and renewed, propelled by elaborate rituals resembling the modern seasonal holidays.

Unlike chaotic time, cyclical time is both descriptive and prescriptive. It furnished ancient societies with a fixed moral standard, a measure by which each person or generation could compare its behavior with that of its ancestors. Those who believed in cycles could engage in what anthropologist Lévy-Bruhl calls a "participation mystique" in the divine re-creation of nature's eternal round.

The power of this concept is conveyed by the colossal monuments to recurring time (the obelisks, pyramids, ziggurats, sunstones, and megaliths) left behind by so many archaic societies. It is also conveyed in the linguistic roots of our very words for time. Etymologically, the word "time" derives from the Indo-European root for shining heavenly beings (cognates include *deity, divine, day,* and *diurnal*), almost certainly linking it to regular celestial cycles. *Period* originally meant "orbit," as in "planetary period." *Annual* comes from *annus*, whose root meant "circle." *Hour* comes ultimately from the common ancient Greek root *horos*, meaning "solar period." *Year* is cognate with *horos*. *Month* derives from *moon*.

Without reference to cycles, time would literally defy description. Or even measurement. The twenty-first-century physicist still possesses no other means of quantifying time except by reference to a natural cycle—such as the regular orbit of a planet around the sun or the regular vibration of an excited cesium atom.

Clearly, cyclical time continues to shape our lives today. With electronic apps, we still monitor (more accurately than ever) the daily rhythms of our lives. We still pay attention to the calendar, celebrate annual religious and civic holidays, and upon occasion thoughtfully compare our own life cycles with those of our parents and grandparents.

Yet none of us takes cyclical time as seriously as the ancients. And for a very simple reason: The sacred cycle would strip those of us who live in the modern world of our most treasured privilege—a free and open-ended future in which we can aspire to be different from or better than our ancestors. It would leave little room for what we think of as originality, creativity, and progress.

"For the traditional societies, all the important acts of life were revealed *ab origine* by gods or heroes. Men only repeat these exemplary and paradigmatic gestures *ad infinitum*," explains religion scholar Mircea Eliade. "This tendency may well appear paradoxical, in the sense that the man of a traditional culture sees himself as real only to the extent that he ceases to be himself (for a modern observer) and is satisfied with imitating and repeating gestures of another." Bronze Age warriors aspired to nothing higher than emulating Hector or Achilles. We moderns do aspire to something higher, or at least something different.

So what's the alternative? Enter the third option: *linear time*—time as a unique, directional, and (usually) progressing story with an absolute beginning and an absolute end.

This option, which arose upon occasion in the ancient world, had both secular and spiritual origins. In the secular realm, we can think for example of the Athenian homage to Prometheus, the god of fire and forethought who brings progressive civilization to humanity—or of the Roman imperial dream of a future one-world cosmopolis. Even more decisive was the rise and spread of the Western monotheistic religions, which inspired the hope that we are all destined for more than a life tied to fortune's wheel. The Judaic, Persian, Christian, and Islamic cosmologies all embraced the radically new concept of personal and historical time as a unidirectional drama. For humanity, time begins with a fall from grace; struggles forward in an intermediate sequence of trials, failures, and divine interventions; and ends with redemption and re-entry into the Kingdom of God.

Linearism required hundreds of years to catch on, but when it did, it changed the world. In medieval Europe, unidirectional time as outlined by the early Christian theologians remained a relatively arcane idea, fully understood by only a clerical elite. But in the sixteenth century, the Reformation and the spread of the printed Gospel ushered in a new urgency (and popular involvement) to linear history. For the first time, ordinary people throughout Europe began speculating about the historical "signs" of Christ's second and final "coming"—and inventing new sects according to their expectations about when and how this would happen. Two centuries later, the Enlightenment took Christian linearism and used it to undergird a complementary secular faith, what historian Carl Becker called "the heavenly city of the 18th-century philosophers"—the belief in indefinite scientific, economic, and political improvement.

By the late nineteenth century, with the industrial revolution roaring at full throttle, the Western dogma of history as progress reached its apogee. Either as a religious credo, a positivist dogma, or an evolutionary science, it was not to be questioned. The 1902 edition of *The Cambridge Modern History* explained: "We are bound to assume as a scientific hypothesis on which history is to be written, a progress in human affairs. This progress must inevitably be towards some end." "Providence was progress," was how Lord Acton later described the prevailing Victorian view. "Not to believe in progress," he wrote, "was to question the divine government."

England's first New World settlements began as outposts of radical Calvinism and the radical Enlightenment. Not surprisingly, America has come to embody the most extreme expression of progressive linearism. The first European explorers often saw in this fresh landmass—this New Atlantis, El Dorado, or Utopia—an authentic opportunity to remake humanity and therein put an end to history. Successive waves of immigrants likewise saw themselves as builders of a millennial "New Jerusalem," in-augurators of a revolutionary "Age of Reason," defenders of "God's cho-sen country," and pioneers in service of a "Manifest Destiny." Thus arose the dogma of American exceptionalism, the belief that this nation and its people had somehow broken loose from any risk of cyclical regress.

Along the way, linear time's signal achievement has been the sup-pression of cyclical time. Ages ago, cyclical time conquered chaotic time. In recent centuries, the conqueror has in turn been chained and shack-led. The suppression began with the early Christians who rooted out calendrical paganism, denounced classical cycles, and tried to suppress entire branches of nonlinear learning, such as the "hermetic" fields of alchemy and astrology. Only "the wicked walk in a circle," warned Saint Augustine. At the dawn of the modern era, the assault grew more fierce. The Reformation not only triggered a renewed attack on pagan holidays (chopping down Maypoles), but also popularized the calibrated clocks, calendars, and diaries that enabled people to employ time as a rational means to a linear end—be it discovery, riches, holiness, or power.

Along the way, the West began employing technology in an effort to flatten every physical manifestation of the natural cycle. With artificial light, we believe we can defeat the sleep-wake cycle; with climate con-trol, the seasonal cycle; with refrigeration, the agricultural cycle; and with high-tech medicine, the rest-recovery cycle. Triumphal linearism has shaped the very style of Western and (especially) American civili-zation. Before, when cyclical time reigned, people valued patience, rit-ual, the relatedness of parts to the whole, and the healing power of time within nature. Today, we value haste, iconoclasm, the disintegration of the whole into parts, and the analytic power of time outside nature.

Cyclical time tended to interpret change in a fourfold pattern corre-sponding to the seasons. Linear time prefers to interpret it in a threefold pattern of progress, opposition, and triumph. The quaternity reconciled us to what must always be. The triad prepares us for what is yet to be. Triadic progress still rules the Western imagination. Five centuries ago, Reformation preachers wielded it (innocence, wickedness, redemption) to herald an imminent "apocalypse"—literally, a time-ending revela-tion of all secrets. Twenty-first-century pundits still do the same today, though they call it the "end of history," "Homo Deus," or the transhuman "singularity."

Let's now assess the track record of all these exertions to transcend the cycle. Surprisingly, given all the effort and resources expended, *we would have to judge them a failure*. By means of advanced technology and ever-more rational forms of social organization, modernity promises to flatten all the age-old natural and social cycles that once afflicted us. At best, however, what modernity ends up doing is substituting several new cycles for each one it eliminates. Often—for example, when we channel a river or industrialize a society—we don't even eliminate the natural cycle of floods or wars. We simply ensure that the original cycle is both less frequent and more devastating.

As a rule, in fact, "progress" succeeds in generating a proliferating variety of entirely new cycles. Just ponder them all: business cycles, financial cycles, building cycles, electoral cycles, fashion cycles, opinion cycles, budget cycles, crime cycles, power cycles, traffic cycles, and so on.

The ancients knew none of these things. They simply observed the calendar, and if, after watching nature, they chose to modify their behavior, they typically did so in incremental ways that had been passed down from ancestors. When the days grew longer, they were accustomed to rising earlier in the morning. When the climate shifted, they were accustomed to migrating.

Modern believers in linear time have abandoned such habits of natural readjustment. And they have done so eagerly. After all, that's what is so appealing about modernity: *not* having to readjust continually to the natural world. Yet by disabling their capacity to achieve day-to-day homeostasis with their environment, moderns have created entirely new cycles or have deepened existing ones. We build a car or factory or city or state that works perfectly—until it doesn't work at all.

The most consequential of modern cycles are those that are driven by periodic shifts in the public mood. Unfortunately, because of their long duration, we have been slow to recognize them. We are much quicker to tag and clock short-term fluctuations like a news cycle or a housing cycle. They're like regular waves crashing on the shore: You can't miss them. Recognizing long-term public mood shifts, on the other hand, requires patience. They're more like the waxing and waning tides: You can easily overlook them among the splashing waves even though they propel currents that gradually reshape continents.

Why should the public mood be so consequential? Because modern societies are as a rule democratic (much more so, at least, than ancient societies). In order to progress as a nation, modern polities have little choice but to harness the voluntary participation of citizens who also see their own lives as progressing. As Alexis de Tocqueville first explained after his tour of America in the 1830s, a popular consensus in a democratic republic exerts a compulsive power that absolute monarchs can only dream about.

And why should such shifts be periodic? Because they are governed, at the deepest level, by the relatively invariant human life cycle.

To see how this works, consider what happens in a modern society whose newest members are impressed at an early age by some important but neglected collective priority: Maybe it's a desire for peace—or war or justice or affluence or sanctity. After a predictable period, perhaps twenty or thirty or forty years, this group will assume governing roles as leaders and parents. In that role, they will feel entitled or at least be expected to shift their society's direction according to their new priority, that is, in a new linear trajectory. That trajectory will prevail until, of course, another cohort group displaces them and chooses to amend or reverse it.

Such a dynamic, in which society's emerging members are initially *shaped by history* and subsequently *shape history*, may have several moving parts. As younger groups are arriving, older groups are departing. At any given moment more than one group probably share governing tasks. Other complications are possible. But there's nothing complicated about how this dynamic can generate a regular long-term cycle of action and reaction, of innovation and compensation.

We introduced this long-term cycle earlier. We call it the *saeculum*. It is roughly eighty to one hundred years in length—the duration of a long human life—and it naturally divides itself into four basic moods or seasons. As for the "new social groups" that push this dynamic forward, these of course are *generations*, each of which is roughly eighteen to twenty-five years in length.

There is, accordingly, something paradoxical about history's long cycle. It is almost entirely *ancient* in its terminology and perspective. Yet it is almost entirely *modern* in its behavioral consequences.

As we shall see, the term *saeculum* dates back over two millennia. *Generation*, as both a word and concept, dates back even earlier, to the very dawn of civilization. Most ancients were entirely at home with the notion of long-term recurring periods (the Mayan *baktun* or *pictun*, the Hindu *yuga*, or the *annus magnus* of the Babylonians, Greeks, and Romans). Almost always, this giant calendar was depicted as a circle (*yantra*, *chakra*, or *mandala*), sometimes divided into dualities (*yin/yang*) but most often into a quaternity of four seasons (or elements or temperaments). This circle was punctuated by one or two breaks (solstices), moments of discontinuity, at which time the priests or gods would need to restart the cycle over again.

Yet however familiar the ancients were with the concept of a "great year," mostly because it seemed so analogous to every other cycle in their lives, they were unlikely to witness any dramatic evidence of one. The constraint of tradition was too strong. Even if a new generation happened to come of age with new and different aspirations (say, due to some major triumph or disaster), ancient mores would tend to suppress their expression. As often happened after any unnatural intervention (such as a solar eclipse or an untimely royal death), society would engage in purification rites to push the distended circle back to its natural groove, after which time was presumed to keep turning as before.

Among moderns, the situation is reversed. For many of us, the concept of a long-term cycle of history is unfamiliar and exotic. We are supremely skeptical of historical cycles despite the reality that our world, unlike the ancients', is overrun by cycles of our own making that we neither understand nor control. Most importantly, we are distressed, as the ancients were not, by the likelihood that the society to be inherited by our children and grandchildren will be very unlike our own. And we don't have an inkling how or why.

The society that believes in cycles the least, America, has fallen into the grip of the most portentous cycle in the history of mankind. Many

Americans might prefer to believe that their nation only moves in the direction we want it to move. Or, when it doesn't, we imagine that history forks in radically different directions due to mere accidents—a slim electoral margin, a barely won battle, an improbable invention, an assassin's fateful bullet.

In order to move beyond this fixation on the intentional and accidental, we moderns—and we Americans especially—need to explore the possibility that deeper and simpler forces may be at work. Such exploration is the heart and soul of the scientific method.

In this spirit, let us hear from the late historian Arthur M. Schlesinger, Jr., who (along with his father, another eminent historian) saw strong evidence that American political moods shift according to a cycle that is driven by generational turnover. He rightly points out that a cycle thesis only makes sense so long as the cycle itself is, for the most part, causally independent of the phenomena it is trying to explain.

> A true cycle . . . is self-generating. It cannot be determined, short of catastrophe, by external events. War, depressions, inflations, may heighten or complicate moods, but the cycle itself rolls on, self-contained, self-sufficient and autonomous. . . . The roots of this self-sufficiency lie deep in the natural life of humanity. There is a cyclical pattern in organic nature—in the tides, in the seasons, in night and day, in the systole and diastole of the human heart.

Schlesinger thereby joins a long and rich tradition of historians, philosophers, writers, and poets who have seen in politics and war rhythms similar to what Schlesinger has seen in "the natural life of humanity."

We will begin to meet these historians, philosophers, writers, and poets in the next few chapters, where we explore our cyclical perspective and explain our method and terminology.

Part One

SEASONS OF HISTORY

2

SEASONS OF TIME

Peace makes plenty, plenty makes pride,
Pride breeds quarrel, and quarrel brings war;
War brings spoil, and spoil poverty,
Poverty patience, and patience peace
So peace brings war, and war brings peace.

—JEAN DE MEUN (FL. 1280–1305)

In the pre-Roman centuries, Italy was home to Etruria, among the most mysterious of ancient civilizations. The Etruscans' origins are unknown. Because they were unrelated to other Italic peoples, many ancient Romans supposed they had migrated from elsewhere, perhaps from Lydia, in present-day Turkey. Though their written language used the Greek alphabet, many Etruscan words remain untranslatable and most of their literature has perished. To understand their rituals, modern historians puzzle over comments in ancient chronicles and pore over artifacts dug from tombs. From these clues, they have concluded that the Etruscans looked upon time as the playing out of an unalterable destiny. According to legend, an old sibyl issued a prophecy that their civilization would last for ten lifetimes, at which time *finem fore nominis Etrusci*: Etruria was doomed.

Around the time this prophecy was issued, perhaps in the ninth century BCE, the Etruscans invented the ritual by which they would measure the duration of their prophecy. No one knows its Etruscan name, but by the time the Romans adopted the ritual, it was known as the *saeculum*. The word had two meanings: "a long human life" and "a natural century," each approximating one hundred years. The word's etymology may be related to the Latin *senectus* (old age), *serere* (to plant), *sequor* (to follow), or some lost Etruscan root. Much of what we know about the saeculum comes from Varro (a prolific scholar and Augustus's librarian) via Censorinus, a Roman historian of the third century CE. By then, Etruria had become a distant memory to a Rome that was itself weakening.

In *De Die Natale*, Censorinus described "the natural saeculum" as "the time span defined by the longest human life between birth and death"—and explained how the Etruscans measured it. They would identify all the people born during the year a new city was founded. Of these people, the one who lived the longest completed, with his death, the end of the first saeculum. Then, of all who were born in that end year, once again the death of the oldest survivor marked the end of the second saeculum. And so on.

Although he furnished the traditional numbers for the first six Etruscan saecula (which averaged 107 years in length), Censorinus admitted these calculations must have encountered practical difficulties. Who kept track of "the one who lives the longest"? Were women or slaves counted? How did the various Etruscan cities agree on a common system of reckoning? Censorinus reported that the Etruscan priests somehow confirmed the dates by watching for "certain portents" such as lightning or comets. We know little for certain except that the Etruscans considered the natural human life span to be the central unit of their history and destiny. Censorinus sometimes identifies the saeculum with what the ancients called their "great year" (*annus magnus*).

In the end, as chance would have it, Etruria's ten-saeculum prophecy proved alarmingly accurate: The last vestiges of their culture were buried under the advance of Rome during the reign of Augustus, nearly one full millennium after the Etruscan year zero.

The Romans had their own mythical prophecy. When Romulus founded Rome, he supposedly saw a flock of twelve vultures, which he took to be a signal that Rome would last twelve units of time. Eventually, the early Romans (who turned to Etruscan learning on such matters) came to assume that the twelve vultures must refer to twelve saecula. This assumption was confirmed by a set of prophetic books presented by an old sibyl to Tarquin the Proud, the last king of Rome and himself an

Etruscan. Thereafter, these Sibylline Prophecies were kept under close guard in the Temple of Jupiter, to be consulted only at moments of crisis and doubt.

As their city prospered and conquered, the Romans became obsessed with the saeculum as a rhythmic measure of their destiny. At some early date, perhaps not long after Rome's legendary founding in 753 BCE, Rome instituted the tradition of "saecular games." This three-day, three-night extravaganza combined the athletic spectacle of a modern Olympics with the civic ritual of an American July Fourth centennial. Held about once per century, these *ludi saeculares* were timed to give most Romans a decent chance of witnessing them at some point in their lives. By the second century BCE, the first Roman historians routinely employed the saeculum (or saecular games) to periodize their chronicles, especially when describing great wars and new laws.

When Augustus established the empire in 27 BCE, after decades of violence and civil war during the late republic, popular hope for a better future expressed itself in Virgil's poetic promise that an aging Rome could "reestablish its youth" and give birth to a new *saeculum aureum*—a new "age of gold." After Augustus, later emperors occasionally claimed that their ascendancy would herald a new saeculum—a dawning age that would rejuvenate a vast empire gradually shuddering into decadence and ruin. During the early empire, writers explicitly referred to their own era as Rome's eighth saeculum. A century later, after a round of civil wars, the satirist Juvenal assumed he was living in the ninth.

Why were the Romans so fascinated by the saeculum? It wasn't just an odd way of groping toward one hundred years as a convenient round number. Censorinus himself raises and dismisses this possibility, noting that the Romans always distinguished between a "civil" saeculum (a strict hundred-year unit of time) and a "natural" saeculum (the stuff of life and history).

A more probable explanation is that the Romans were impressed by a strong 80-to-110-year rhythm that seemed to pulse through their history. During the republic, this rhythm appeared in the timing of Rome's greatest perils and its subsequent renewals: the founding of the republic; the wars against the Veii and the Gauls, in which Rome was nearly overwhelmed; disastrous defeats in the Great Samnite War, which sent Rome officially into mourning; the near catastrophe of Hannibal's invasion; and Rome's desperate campaign against invading Germanic tribes, the Cimbri and the Teutones. Rome did not soon forget these near-death experiences. The consuls who led the republic during two of them—Marcus Furius Camillus (against the Veii and the Gauls) and Gaius Marius (against the Germans)—became known in the annals as Rome's "second" and "third" founders.

During the empire, the saecular pattern resumed, with periodic renewals after civil wars or invasion: the founding of the Augustan principate; the late first-century recovery under Trajan; the late second-century recovery under the Severii; and the late third-century recovery under Diocletian and Constantine. The first emperor to be baptized a Christian (on his deathbed), Constantine notably *declined* to hold another saecular games in the early 300s. The ritual was never renewed.

Unusually for an ancient people, the Romans embraced a dynamic and aspirational vision of their imperial destiny. And they were willing to innovate endlessly in its pursuit, assimilating new peoples and borrowing freely from other cultures along the way. The result may have been a very early appearance of the modern cycle of history.

At last, even the "eternal city" was fated to meet a crisis from which it could not recover. In one of history's more bizarre coincidences, Romulus's vulture augury proved to be even more accurate than the original Etruscan prophecy. The city of Rome was sacked by the Gothic chieftain Alaric in 410 CE, exactly thirty-eight years before the twelve hundredth anniversary of its legendary founding, ninety-seven years for each of the twelve vultures seen by Romulus. A few years later, Augustine, bishop of Hippo, launched his "City of God" attack on the cyclical futility of the imperial "City of Man." Futile indeed it was. The last Western emperor of Rome formally abdicated in 476 CE, just twenty-eight years after Rome's twelve hundredth anniversary.

Yet even if the Etruscan and Roman empires vanished from history, the saeculum did not.

THE SAECULUM REDISCOVERED

After Rome fell, the idea of the saeculum lay dormant in the Western world for roughly a thousand years. While the notion of linear time remained implicit in Christian dogma, the medieval clergy and nobility do not appear to have thought much about worldly progress. In the Augustinian lexicon, the word "saeculum" lost its meaning as a specific length of time and came to refer to unbounded biblical time, as in *saecula saeculorum*, or "endless ages."

All this changed during the Renaissance, when European elites began to see themselves as rational and self-determining architects of their own future. With the rediscovery of classical texts, humanists became reacquainted with the lofty civic aspirations of the Greco-Roman world. With the advent of the Reformation, laypeople felt the rush of events as a preliminary to Christ's return. Prior to that millennial event, they had reforms to fight for, fortunes to work for, ideals to be martyred for, and signs of grace to pray for. As time became more directional, history became more urgent.

Right at this threshold of modernity—when Columbus was voyaging, da Vinci painting, and Ferdinand and Isabella nation-building—the saeculum re-entered Western culture. In the romance languages, the word became vulgarized into the derivatives still used today: the Italian *secolo*, Spanish *siglo*, and French *siècle*. From *centurio* (the rank of a Roman officer who commanded one hundred soldiers), humanists invented an additional word: *centuria*. Initially, it meant one hundred years, but soon it acquired a life-cycle connotation as well.

The 1500s became the first hundred-year period to be proclaimed a century—and the first to be affixed a century number. In 1517, Desiderius Erasmus exclaimed "Immortal God, what a century I see opening up before us!" Following the Gregorian calendar reform of the 1580s, Protestant historians began to categorize Western history into centuries. During the seventeenth century, essayists and diarists began referring to such "natural" centuries as the prior "century of Spanish gold" or the current "grand century of Louis XIV." At the century's end, poetic celebrations of time's rebirth were observed in courtly circles—as with John

Dryden's "Secular Masque" of 1700 ("'Tis well an old age is out, / And time to begin a new"). On the eve of the French Revolution, the prospect of another century's end triggered fanatical optimism and grim pessimism. It was time for a decrepit *ancien régime* to be replaced, in the words of English political philosopher William Godwin, by a new age of "perpetual improvement"—including (Godwin hoped) the eventual attainment of human immortality.

After Napoleon, ruminations on the meaning of the historical century assumed romantic overtones. German pedagogue Gustav Rümelin wrote that the word itself had come to mean "a mystical, sublime, almost natural measure of formidable distances of years." Ralph Waldo Emerson described each century as "loaded, fragrant." A fresh wave of historians now strove to bring to life the unique interior logic or spirit or *Zeitgeist* of each century as though no one could be compared to any other. For many, this "mood" of a century took precedence over any exact number of years. As the French academic Antoine Augustin Cournot observed during the 1870s, "The ancient Romans did not fix the return to their secular games with such a degree of precision; and when we talk of the *siècle* of Pericles, of the *siècle* of Augustus, of the *siècle* of Louis XIV, we mean that it has to do with *siècles* in the Roman sense, not with centuries." Cournot's *siècle*, of course, was the saeculum.

As the nineteenth century itself seemed to grow old, the phrase *fin de siècle* (popularized in 1888 when a play with that title opened in Paris) was often joined to words like "decadence" and "degeneration." Pundits began yearning for a new source of energy, what the popular French philosopher Henri Bergson would call *élan vital*, to release them from time's prison. Once again, the Western world began to talk about restarting its saecular calendar. The French essayist Remy de Gourmont attributed this 1900 deadline to modernity itself: "We think by centuries when we cease to think by reigns."

Europeans did not have to wait long. Most soon came to regard the quiet months of 1914 as the *fin* of one *siècle* and the assassination of the Austrian Archduke as the *commencement* of the next. Before long, the word started marching forward again, now dressed in the uniform of collective action—whether as Benito Mussolini's "century of fascism,"

Henry Luce's "American Century," or Henry Wallace's "century of the common man." Decades later, by the year 2000, as people watched the modern mass man of that century's dawn transform into the postmodern de-massified man of that century's twilight, many wondered if yet another epoch of civilization might be growing old.

Meanwhile, starting around the middle of the twentieth century, the saeculum began to reveal itself as more than just a long and largely amorphous era of social time. In the hands of historians and social scientists, it began to take shape as a clearly definable cycle of historical behavior—initially, as a *cycle of war and peace*. Nearly five hundred years had passed since the climax of the Italian Renaissance. By now, perhaps, enough repetitions had occurred for a pattern to be recognized.

The first to contribute was Quincy Wright, a historian at the University of Chicago, who earlier in his life had crusaded in vain for the U.S. Senate to ratify the League of Nations. Wright hoped international peacekeeping agencies might someday make war obsolete. But he also realized that, before anyone could end war, scholars needed to understand its dynamics. He therefore undertook his epic *Study of War*, a consortium of more than fifty separate research projects that he completed in 1942—just as America was entering a second world war that soon proved to be even more devastating than the first.

In his *Study*, Wright observed that war-waging occurred "in approximately fifty-year oscillations, each alternate period of concentration being more severe." Wright uncovered this pattern not only in modern American and European history, but also in Hellenistic and Roman times—and noted that others had glimpsed it before him. He attributed this pattern mainly to generational experience. "The warrior does not wish to fight again himself and prejudices his son against war," he observed, "but the grandsons are taught to think of war as romantic." While Wright ruminated over many other topics, from the psychology of war to international law, his saecular rhythm has drawn the most interest from later scholars.

Despite his discovery of war's persistent periodicity, nothing could shake Wright's conviction that it could be avoided through rational decision-making. By the time he died in 1970, however, his hopes were crumbling under the powerful insights of his scholarship. The most rational decision makers any war scholar could hope for, "the best and the brightest" technocrats who assisted Presidents Kennedy and Johnson, could not prevent America from plunging into a demoralizing conflict in Vietnam. That happened right on the cusp of the "minor war" quadrant of Wright's cycle. And the United Nations (whose creation he had encouraged) had become a helpless bystander.

Only a few years after his book appeared, Wright's timetable was corroborated by a famous British historian and contemporary, Arnold J. Toynbee. In *A Study of History*, best known for its grand theory of the rise and fall of civilizations, Toynbee identified an "alternating rhythm" in a "Cycle of War and Peace." Punctuating this cycle were quarter-century "general wars" that had occurred in Europe at roughly one-century intervals since the Renaissance. Toynbee identified and dated five repetitions of this cycle, each initiated by the most decisive conflicts of its century:

- The *overture* began with the Italian Wars (1494–1525), fought between France, Spain, and the Holy Roman Empire over the wealthy principalities of northern Italy.

- The *first cycle* began with Philip II's "Imperial Wars" (1568–1609), marking the expansionary high tide of Hapsburg Europe and of the Spanish *Siglo de Oro*, as well as the rise of the Dutch Empire.

- The *second cycle* began with the War of Spanish Succession (1672–1713), featuring the tireless campaigns of Louis XIV of France to dominate Europe.

- The *third cycle* began with the French Revolutionary and Napoleonic Wars (1792–1815), which shaped world politics for the rest of the nineteenth century.

- The *fourth cycle* began with World Wars I and II (1914–1945), ultimately settled by the global agreements that still shape geopolitics today.

In addition to these five modern centuries, Toynbee identified similar cycles spanning six centuries of ancient Chinese and Hellenistic history, all situated in what he called mature "break up" eras of civilization. Everywhere, he found the span of time between the start of one "general war" and the start of the next to have averaged ninety-five years with a "surprising degree of coincidence" across the millennia.

Underlying this periodicity, noted Toynbee, were "the workings of a Generation Cycle, a rhythm in the flow of Physical Life," which had "imposed its dominion on the Spirit of Man." Like Wright, he linked this rhythm to the gradual decay of the "living memory of a previous war." Toynbee elaborates: "The psychological resistance to any move towards the breaking of a peace that the living memory of a previous war has made so precious is likely to be prohibitively strong until a new generation that knows war only by hearsay has had time to grow up and to come into power." War will then be favored "until the peace-bred generation that last light-heartedly ran into war has been replaced, in its turn." Also like Wright, Toynbee diagnosed lesser "supplementary wars" at the midway point of each cycle.

Toynbee did something more. He subdivided the war cycle into four periods and identified a "breathing space" after a bigger war and a "general peace" after a smaller war. He sometimes seemed to imply that no wars occur during these intervening quarter-century eras. Plainly, that is wrong. Some wars, at least minor wars, have occurred during practically every quarter century of European (and American) history. To account for these, historian L. L. Farrar, Jr., reconstructed Toynbee's four-phase war theory and replaced the "breathing space" and "general peace" eras with what he calls "probing wars." Historian Richard Rosecrance similarly posited a four-part war cycle that alternates between bipolar eras of "war" and multipolar eras of "power vacuum." He notes that "one of the tragedies of western international history has been that this cycle has been repeated time and time again."

Several other historians and social scientists have since broadened the Toynbeean cycle beyond war and peace into a more general thesis about global "long waves" of social behavior. Terence Hopkins and Immanuel Wallerstein believe the cycle reflects the wavelike economic dynamics of the Western capitalist "world system" as it developed after the fifteenth century. George Modelski and William R. Thompson agree that this "long cycle system" encompasses economic trends, but they insist its "regularities and repetitions" are driven primarily by power struggles between nation states to determine global dominance.

Modelski divides this cycle into four quarter-century phases, each succeeding the last in a natural entropic progression. In the first *world power* phase, both the (social) demand for order and the (political) supply of order is high. In the *delegitimizing* phase, the demand for order declines. In the *deconcentration* phase, the supply of order declines. The cycle culminates when the demand for order rises again—leading to an order-producing era of *global war*. Like Schlesinger, he stresses that the cycle's regularity is endogenous to the system—Modelski calls this property "closure"—and that its particular timing is regulated by generational change: "It is not difficult to see how a concatenation of four generations might also determine the wave-length of the war-peace cycle."

The final major-war phase, writes Modelski, is distinguished not by the mere scale of human destruction, though this will likely be high, but rather by a universal perception that an old global structure of politics has perished and a new one has been born. This global rite of passage is myth-generating in its scope: "The major event clusters of the cycle, the global war campaigns and the celebrated settlements, the ceremonial observances of the great nations, and the passing into obscurity of others, these make up the rituals of world politics. They are the key markers of world time." The new winner, able to "set the rules," may now enjoy "a golden age" and become "an object of respect, acclaim, and imitation."

William Thompson presents the most recent (2020) and thorough presentation of the global long cycle thesis. His major dates, powers, phases, and wars all match those of Modelski and Toynbee. But he adds earlier cycles before 1500 (going back to the tenth century) involving China, the Mongols, Genoa, and Venice. He also gives ample room to complementary cycles—in demography, technology, and commerce. "Long waves," he writes, "transform economies, culture, and geopolitics at the same time."

Notice the similarity between these modern long cycles and the ancient wheels of time. The dualistic alternation between war and peace, or between civic growth and decay, resembles the endless struggle between yin and yang in ancient Chinese thinking or between Love and Strife in ancient Greek thinking. The fourfold rotation of phases resembles the ritualized seasons of nature: a springlike era of growth followed by a summerlike era of jubilation, and an autumnal era of fragmentation followed by a wintery death—and regeneration. The final phase evokes the Stoics' Ekpyrosis (or *kataklysmos*), the purifying and time-ending fire (or flood) that marks the great discontinuity: the end of one circle and the beginning of the next.

What is at work here? What did Quincy Wright proclaim in his youth and resist in his old age? What rhythm did Arnold Toynbee see rippling through the "modern" age of every mature civilization he studied? It's the unit of history the Etruscans discovered: the natural saeculum, history turning to the beat of a long human life.

The culminating phase of the saeculum is a quarter-century era of war, upheaval, and turmoil. Early humanist scholars called this the *revolutio*, a word derived from the Copernican *revolutiones orbium cælestium*—implying, in some manner, a predictable moment of astro-

CHART 2-1

The Modern Saeculum of War and Politics

	FIRST QUARTER	SECOND QUARTER	THIRD QUARTER	FOURTH QUARTER
Wright (1942)	Peace	Minor Wars	Peace	Major Wars
Toynbee (1954)	Breathing Space	Supplementary Wars	General Peace	General War
Rosecrance (1973)	Decreased Involvement	Power Vacuums	Increased Involvement	War
Farrar (1977)	Probing Wars	Adjusting Wars	Probing Wars	Hegemonic Wars
Hopkins-Wallerstein (1982)	Hegemonic Maturity	Declining Hegemony	Ascending Hegemony	Hegemonic Victory
Modelski (1987) & Thompson (2020)	World Power	Delegitimization	Deconcentration	Global War
NATURE	Spring	Summer	Autumn	Winter

nomical return. With the Reformation, the word "revolution" connoted a path back to a (Christian) golden age, to paradise, to justice. A century later, the English political philosopher Thomas Hobbes linked it to politics, a meaning that took on vast new weight with the British "Glorious Revolution" in the late seventeenth century and the Atlantic revolutions (including those in America and France) in the late eighteenth century.

Yet a better word is *Crisis*. Its Greek root, *krisis*, refers to a decisive or separating moment. In disease, the *krisis* is when physicians know whether a patient will recover or die; in war, it's the moment in battle that determines whether an army will win or lose. Thomas Paine attached the word to political revolution in 1776, when he published his ragingly popular pamphlets, *The American Crisis*. From Jacob Burckhardt to Klemens von Metternich to Friedrich Nietzsche, nineteenth-century thinkers applied it to the periodic total wars that Karl Marx called "express trains of history." By World War I, historian Gerhard Masur explains, "crisis" was widely understood to mean "a sudden acceleration of the historical process in a terrifying manner," sufficient to "release economic, social, and moral forces of unforeseen power and dimensions, which often make return to the status quo impossible."

The Crisis ends one saeculum and launches the next. Yet if this denotes the cycle's maximum moment of yang or Strife, a curious asymmetry arises: What denotes the cycle's opposite extreme—the maximum moment of yin or Love? If we can locate and describe history's winter solstice, we should be able to do likewise with its summer solstice.

An important clue lies in Modelski's description of his second-quarter "delegitimizing" phase, which he describes as the season of "internal renovation" and "revitalization of the system's normative foundations"— that is, the system's understanding of right and wrong. Just as a fourth-quadrant era serves to remake the outer-world framework of political and social institutions, a second-quadrant era serves to remake the inner-world framework of culture and values.

What defines these eras? Forty years ago, religious anthropologist Anthony Wallace drew upon worldwide research to offer a suggestion. A "revitalization movement," he wrote, is a "deliberate, organized, conscious effort by members of a society to construct a more satisfying culture." In origin, these movements are a collective response to "chronic, psychologically measurable stress." When successful, they generate an entirely new "cultural mazeway," a transformed understanding of "nature, society, culture, personality, and body image." After categorizing such movements (as nativistic, revivalist, millenarian, messianic, and so forth), Wallace hypothesized that all of today's established religions are the ossified remains of the "prophetic and ecstatic visions" of past revitalization movements.

Wallace did not say how often these movements arise, but he did note that "they are recurrent features in human history" and—hinting at the saeculum—that "probably few men have lived who have not been involved in an instance of the revitalization process."

Until recently, scholars seldom inquired into the periodicity of these "prophetic and ecstatic" eras of modern history. In a provocative essay announcing that, "against all the predictions of nineteenth-century sociologists, religious movements have survived and flourished in the modern world," Princeton sociologist Robert Wuthnow reported that revitalization movements "have been distributed neither evenly nor at random in space and time." In fact, at least since the Renaissance, their timing is quite regular. The movements are listed here, along with their two-decade spans of peak enthusiasm. The lifeless phrase "revitalization movement" is dropped in favor of a gnostic trope long popular among Westerners—the image of an "awakening of the spirit," or simply *Awakening*:

- The Reformation Awakening (1530s–40s), famously ignited by a young Augustinian cleric, Martin Luther, and leading to religious division and social upheaval throughout Western Europe.

- The Puritan Awakening (1630s–40s), featuring the armed clash of Protestants against Catholics and ushering in the violent high tide of the seventeenth-century European "wars of religion."

- The Pietist Awakening (1740s–50s), an anti-Enlightenment "turn to experience" and, in some regions, the beginning of revivalism (including the Great Awakening in America).

- The Evangelical-Utopian Awakening (1830s–40s), the first Awakening in the Western world that inspired idealism and anarchism entirely outside the boundaries of organized religion.

- The New Age Awakening (1960s–70s), a cultural watershed that shaped the early lives of most people, in most regions of the world, who are today in their late-40s or older.

These movements had much in common. All gave rise to passionate and moralizing attacks against cultural and religious norms that felt "old" at the time. All were spearheaded by young people. All set forth new normative priorities (what today we call "values"). And all followed a predictable timing: Each was separated from the last by the approximate length of a saeculum, and each occurred roughly halfway between two neighboring Crises.

An Awakening is the other solstice of the saeculum: It is to Crisis as summer is to winter, Love to Strife. Within each lies the causal germ of its opposite. In the second quarter of the saeculum, the confidence born of growing security triggers an outburst of Love that leads to disorder; in the fourth quarter, the anxiety born of growing insecurity triggers an outburst of Strife that re-establishes order. An Awakening thus serves as a cycle marker, reminding a society that it is halfway along a journey traversed many times by its ancestors. Wuthnow observes that "periods of religious unrest . . . have, of course, been regarded as portents of change—as historical watersheds—at least since Herodotus."

If Awakenings are the summers and Crises the winters of human experience, transitional eras are required. A springlike era must traverse the path from Crisis to Awakening, an autumnal era the path from Awakening to Crisis. While the two saecular solstices are solutions to needs eventually created by the other, the two saecular equinoxes must be directional opposites of each other. Where the post-Crisis era warms and lightens, the post-Awakening era chills and darkens. Where the cyclical spring brings consensus, order, and stability, the autumn brings argument, fragmentation, and uncertainty.

As the wheel turns from Crisis to Awakening and back again to Crisis, modern history shows a remarkable regularity. In Europe, every cycle but one ranges from 80 to 105 years. The conspicuous anomaly is the interval between Waterloo and VJ Day, a Toynbeean cycle that lasted a full 130 years.

The exceptional length of this interval in Europe may be just that—an anomaly. Or it may raise the possibility that the Toynbeean template has wrongly conflated two cycles into one. What historians call the "long nineteenth century," from 1815 to 1914, was a period of extraordinary peace among the great powers. But the peace was broken by one major disruption: an explosion of European nation-building wars fought between the mid-1850s and mid-1870s (involving Germany, France, Italy, England, Russia, and the Balkans)—not counting major wars outside Europe, including the U.S. Civil War. If this were deemed another Crisis era, and if the turn of the century were regarded as another Awakening era, the result would be one anomalously short cycle (1815 to about 1870) followed by another of nearly the usual length (1870 to the circa-1950 origins of the Cold War). Replacing one unusually long cycle, therefore, would be a foreshortened cycle followed by another of the typical recent length. Later in this chapter and in Chapter 5, we will suggest that this interpretation may be preferable to Toynbee's.

Either way, the presence of irregular cycles is hardly surprising. Looking at global history, after all, means looking at many different societies. Like the various Etruscan towns, each could be running on its own somewhat different saecular cycle, and each could be interfering (politically or culturally) in the affairs of its neighbors. Societies that are less modern than others may be more resistant to the rhythm of the saeculum. Amid all this noise of history, perfect periodicity can hardly be expected.

If you wonder how history can become regularly seasonal, you might want to test the following hypothesis. Imagine a scenario in which most of history's "noise" is suppressed. Imagine a single large society that has never had a powerful neighbor and that, for centuries, has remained relatively isolated from foreign interference. Imagine that this society was born modern on a near-empty continent, with no time-honored traditions to restrain its open-ended development. Imagine, finally, that this thoroughly modern society has acquired a reputation for pursuing linear progress—and for suppressing the cycles of nature—unequaled by any other people on earth. From what you know about the saeculum, wouldn't you suppose that its history would be governed by a cycle of astonishing regularity? Indeed you would.

But of course this society is no hypothesis. This society is America.

THE SAECULUM IN AMERICA

Inspect the left-hand seal on the back of a U.S. one dollar bill. It's a circle enclosing a four-sided pyramid, above which hovers an eye—perhaps the Eye of Providence that sees all of history at one glance. Read the inscription above the pyramid: *annuit coeptis* ("God favored the creation"), words borrowed directly from Virgil's praise of the Augustan *saeculum aureum*, Rome's new "age of gold." Read also the inscription underneath: *novus ordo seclorum* ("the new order of the centuries").

When the Founders designed the Great Seal, they put the saeculum right on the money, though the implied message was left ambiguous: Were they celebrating the saeculum—or, alternatively, announcing their triumph *over* the saeculum?

The circle of time was not something the Europeans had to bring to America. At least a hundred saecula had been witnessed by the American ancestors of the native people who first glimpsed white sails on the horizon. These New World ancients were intimately familiar with the same astral and seasonal circles that preoccupied their Old World counterparts—as suggested by the abundance of crosses, swastikas, tetramorphs, and squared mandalas used in their ritual art. The rhythm of human life, often expressed in terms of generations, was regarded as a sacred link between ancestors and posterity.

Indeed, the circle of time was the one thing Europeans expressly left behind—the one piece of baggage missing among all the nails, axes, Bibles, and contracts they hauled out of their longboats. Columbus's "discovery" of America, coinciding with the very birth of modernity in the West, inevitably gave rise to a European image of America as the ultimate destination of time's circle—a fabled Cathay or godly New Jerusalem. When the newcomers first met the natives, they chose to see either golden-age "Indians" or infernal devils—static images of the end of history. When they began carving towns out of the Atlantic forests, what they sought were final answers to mankind's perennial "wheel" of deprivation. What these migrants did not seek—indeed, what they were fleeing—was a pagan resignation to the seasonality of nature.

For Native Americans, this invasion by linear time had tragic consequences. It created an insurmountable barrier between the newcomers' culture and their own—a barrier which would doom any opportunity for peaceful coexistence. For the world, this invasion set in motion the most remarkable experiment in modern history: a society "born new," hostile to tradition, obsessed with improvement, and surrounded by boundless natural resources. Both Europeans and Americans sensed that something epochal was underway. Georg W. F. Hegel described America as "the land of the future where, in the ages that lie before us, the burden of the world's history will reveal itself." As the Founders intuited, a "new order of the saecula" had been created.

Until the eighteenth century, the saeculum in America and Europe beat to a similar rhythm. Ever since, the American saeculum has shown a timing that is more regular and even better defined than the European cycles chronicled by Toynbee.

Anglo-American Crises

To see the pattern best, start with the present and move backward. Eighty years passed between the attack on Pearl Harbor and the attack on Fort Sumter. Eighty-five years passed between Fort Sumter and the signing of the Declaration of Independence. Add two years (to Gettysburg), and you reach President Lincoln's famous "fourscore and seven years" calculation. Back up again and note that 87 years is also the period between the Declaration and the climax of the colonial Glorious Revolution.

Add another decade or so to the length of these saecula, and you'll find this pattern continuing through the history of the colonists' English predecessors. Exactly 100 years before England's Glorious Revolution was Queen Elizabeth's memorable triumph over the Spanish Armada, and 103 years before that was Henry Tudor's dynasty-securing victory in the War of the Roses.

Not just in retrospect, but even as these events occurred, people understood they were participating in historical recurrences of legendary proportions. In 1688, supporters of England's Glorious Revolution rallied crowds by reminding them that the year was, providentially, the centennial of Queen Elizabeth's "Great '88" victory. In 1776, Thomas Paine fired up the colonists by reminding them of the fate of the last Stuart king. At Gettysburg, Lincoln moved the nation by evoking what "our forefathers brought forth upon this continent." FDR's funeral near the end of World War II brought to mind, for millions of Americans, Walt Whitman's valedictory to Lincoln ("O Captain! my captain! our fearful trip is done").

Over time, American historians have built a nomenclature around these successive dates. In the winter of 1861, when war loomed, both the Union and the Confederacy announced that this confrontation would constitute a "new revolution" and a "new declaration of independence." In the 1930s, Charles and Mary Beard declared the Civil War to be the "Second American Revolution"—a label since reused countless times, most recently by James McPherson. Similarly, in the 1970s, historian Carl Degler called the New Deal "The Third American Revolution." He pointed out that the Democratic Party, for decades afterward, successfully reminded voters of the "lessons of the Great Depression"—just as the Republican Party "waved the bloody shirt" for decades after the defeat of the South. In his magisterial history of the American Constitution, Bruce Ackerman identifies "not one, but three 'founding' moments in our history: the late 1780s, the late 1860s, and the mid-1930s."

Counting forward from the 1780s, then, we are now living under America's third republic. Should we be preparing for another? More than twenty years ago, political scientist Walter Dean Burnham predicted "that the present politics of upheaval may lead to a fourth American republic." In recent years, others across the political spectrum have echoed this "fourth republic" prediction. Now that the Millennial Crisis has begun, we can point to the probable timing of its arrival: sometime shortly before or after the Millennial Crisis comes to an end.

The list of Anglo-American Crises is a familiar one. There can be little argument about the dates, except of course for the Millennial Crisis, since we cannot yet tell how long it will last.

The War of the Roses Crisis (1455–1487; climax 1485) began with an irrevocable break between the ruling House of Lancaster (red rose) and the powerful House of York (white rose). After mutual recriminations, declarations of treason, and opening skirmishes, the rival houses plunged England into an unparalleled quarter century of internecine butchery—in which dozens of the highest nobility were slaughtered, kings and princes murdered, and vast landed estates expropriated. The Battle of Towton (1461), at which the Yorkists triumphed, was the bloodiest battle ever fought on English soil. At the Battle of Bosworth Field (1485), dynasty-founding Henry Tudor defeated and killed Richard III, the last English king ever to die in combat. England entered the Crisis a tradition-bound medieval kingdom; it emerged a modern "monarchical" nation state.

The Armada Crisis (1569–1597; climax 1588) began when newly Protestant England felt the encircling global threat of the mighty Catholic Hapsburgs. A spectacular crescendo soon followed: repeated efforts to assassinate Queen Elizabeth, Francis Drake's voyage around the world in a ship loaded with pirated Spanish treasure, and Philip Sidney's heroic battle death in the Lowlands. Then came England's "Great Fear," the summer of the Spanish Armada invasion—which ended in a naval victory so miraculous that church bells pealed annually for decades in its remembrance. England entered the Crisis a strife-ridden "heretical" nation; it emerged a rapidly growing commercial power at the heart of a nascent global empire.

The Glorious Revolution Crisis (1675–1706; climax 1691) began for England's Atlantic colonies with two simultaneous catastrophes: Bacon's Rebellion, a violent insurrection in Virginia, and King Philip's War, New England's genocidal struggle with the Algonquin Indians whose per-capita casualties mark it as the deadliest conflict ever fought by

Americans. Afterward, the colonists slid into further political upheavals: resistance against the absolutist designs of the Duke of York, the Stuart heir to the English throne; the pan-colonial Glorious Revolution in favor of King William; and finally a further decade of war against Canadian New France. The ordeal ended with England's European victories over King Louis XIV, which ensured that Catholic Stuarts would never again rule the colonies. In the New World, observes historian Richard Maxwell Brown, "it would be no great exaggeration to call the years 1670 to 1700 the first American revolutionary period." English-speaking America entered the Crisis a rude and fanatical colonial backwater; it emerged a stable provincial society of learning and affluence.

The American Revolution Crisis (1773–1794; climax 1788) began when Parliament's response to the Boston Tea Party ignited a colonial tinderbox that Sam Adams's "committees of correspondence" had carefully prepared. The line of no return—from the arming of militias, to the first battle deaths, to the signing of the Declaration of Independence—was quickly crossed. During the dark 1777 winter after General George Washington's retreat from New York, the Patriots feared that the rebellion might fail and its leaders be hanged as traitors. The war ended in triumph with the American victory at Yorktown. But the mood of emergency did not calm until after the ratification of the Constitution in 1788, which assured citizens that their "United States" would not dissolve into anarchy. By the mid-1790s, the new republic had at last achieved stability and prosperity. British America entered the Crisis as loyal if disunited colonists; it emerged the most ambitious experiment in republican democracy the world had ever seen.

The Civil War Crisis (1860–1865; climax 1864) began with Abraham Lincoln's election, which several Southern states immediately interpreted as an invitation to secede. So they did, triggering the most violent national conflict ever fought on New World soil, with greater casualties than all other U.S. wars combined. The stakes of the conflict were raised in 1862 with the Emancipation Proclamation, which made clear to both sides that Union victory meant the end of slavery. The climax was not reached until September of 1864, when crushing Union victories spelled imminent victory—and Lincoln's reelection. The following April, Robert E. Lee surrendered on Palm Sunday. Lincoln was assassinated five days later, on Good Friday. The outcome was laden in religious symbolism. But was it worth the suffering? "In 1865," observes historian James McPherson, "few black people and not many northerners doubted the answer." Unlike other Crises, the Civil War ended less with optimism than with a sense of tragedy having run its course. America entered the Crisis a sectionally divided agrarian republic; it emerged an industrializing dynamo, battle-scarred yet newly dedicated to the principle of equal citizenship.

The Great Depression–World War II Crisis (1929–1946; climax 1944) began with the Black Thursday stock market crash, followed by Hoovervilles, bank closures, and breadlines. During his first term, FDR buoyed his own partisan majority—and made bitter enemies—by engineering a "New Deal" expansion of federal power in order to renew prosperity. By the end of his second term, however, the economic depression lingered. Then came the Japanese attack on Pearl Harbor, which galvanized and reunited the nation. Within months, America was planning, mobilizing, and producing on a scale having no historical precedent. After peaking with heroic naval assaults on two distant continents, the mood of emergency wound down with the capitulation of the Axis powers and with America's unexpected postwar prosperity. The U.S. entered the Crisis an isolationist, industrializing also-ran; it emerged a global "superpower," whose economic and military prowess, democratic institutions, and Marshall Plan generosity became the wonder of the free world—and the envy of its new Soviet rival.

The Millennial Crisis (2008–2033?; climax 2030?) began with the Global Financial Crisis and the Great Recession. Thus far it has witnessed stagnating living standards, ebbing global trade, the rise of populism, and the most extreme political polarization since the eve of the Civil War. Beset by the prospect of national breakup, of great-power aggression, and of serial recessions, Americans sense that the crisis is still gathering energy—and that its climax has yet to arrive.

Anglo-American Awakenings

While a Crisis rearranges the outer civic world, an Awakening rearranges the inner spiritual world. While a Crisis elevates the group and reinvents public space, an Awakening elevates the individual and reinvents personal space. While a Crisis restarts our calendar in the "secular" realm of the political order, an Awakening does something similar with society's culture. When Americans today speak of elections or alliances, we tend to begin by saying, "Postwar" or "Since World War II (or the 1940s) . . ." When we speak of music or religion, we are more likely to say, "Since the 1960s (or 1970s) . . ." In a Crisis, older people give orders while the young do great deeds; in an Awakening, the old remain the deed-doers and the young come of age as order-givers.

Just as World War II prompted historians to study war cycles, the Consciousness Revolution sparked new interest in the periodic recurrence of cultural upheaval. The defiance, idealism, and autonomy of youth during late 1960s and '70s brought renewed attention to similar episodes in America's past. Some observers recalled the muckrakers, missionaries, and militant feminists of the 1890–1910 decades. Others, coining the term "New Transcendentalist," harkened back to the youth rebellions of the 1830s. In 1970, when historian Richard Bushman summed up the Great Awakening of the 1740s, he likened this "psychological earthquake" to "the civil rights demonstrations, the campus disturbances, and the urban riots of the 1960s combined."

All the turmoil on campus inspired several prominent scholars to reflect on earlier Awakenings in American history. Berkeley sociologist Robert Bellah points out that they have periodically renewed "a common set of moral understandings about good and bad, right and wrong." The Brown religious historian William McLoughlin, who borrows directly from Wallace's theory, describes them as eras of "culture revitalization" that extend "over the period of a generation or so" and end with "a profound reorientation in beliefs and values." McLoughlin identifies five American Awakenings: first, the "Puritan Awakening" in the seventeenth century; then, the "Great Awakening" in the eighteenth; and next, the "Second," "Third," and "Fourth" Awakenings starting in the 1820s, 1890s, and 1960s, respectively.

American Awakenings, he notes, have a symbiotic relationship with national Crises: Each Awakening was nourished by the security and affluence of the very "old order" it attacked, and each gave birth to the normative foundations upon which the next "new order" was founded. In 2000, the late Nobel laureate economic historian Robert Fogel wrote a book in support of McLoughlin's four-awakenings thesis. Fogel observes that, from one awakening to the next, "the typical cycle lasts about 100 years" and notes that the "Fourth Great Awakening" (which "began around 1960") had passed its "revival" phase yet was still shaping public attitudes.

Like McLoughlin, Fogel emphasizes the direct impact of each Awakening on the civic regime change that occurs about forty to fifty years later. Several American historians have come to similar conclusions—that deep within the revivalist or utopian upheavals of America's periodic Awakenings lies the ideological energy of the American Revolution, Civil War, and New Deal. "Few would doubt that the piety of the Awakening," writes religious historian Nathan Hatch of the 1740s, "was the main source of the civil millennialism of the Revolutionary period." Few would doubt, as well, the profound impact of 1830s-era revivalism and abolitionism on the rise of Lincoln's Republican Party or the influence of the 1890s-era "social gospel" on FDR's reform coalition.

The Consciousness Revolution, America's fourth Awakening, is now history. We cannot yet know if it will have the same formative influence on America's fourth republic. Already, however, the stage is set: Today's pundits routinely point to the "sixties" or "seventies" as the birthplace of nearly every ideological driver that is pushing America's politics toward dysfunction and breakdown. For conservatives, that era spawned a generation of hate-America leftists and postmodern critical theorists who later took over academia, think tanks, and mainstream media. For progressives, it spawned a generation of born-again evangelicals and greed-is-good libertarians who later took over churches, business lobbies, and the military. Political scientists agree that most measures of political polarization, both in the electorate and in Congress, began rising in or just after the 1970s.

It is therefore hard to imagine that the resolution of the Millennial Crisis—whatever that may be—can avoid being interpreted as history's judgment on how the contradictory values agendas unleashed by the

Consciousness Revolution are ultimately resolved. According to political philosopher Francis Fukuyama, who calls the sixties "the Great Disruption," such eras of de-norming and values upheaval are historically resolved only after several decades of "social reconstruction." The Fourth Turning, in effect, puts the institutional capstone on the terms of that reconstruction.

The exact dates of Anglo-American Awakenings may vary, but most historians would broadly agree on the following eras.

The Reformation Awakening (1525–1551; climax 1537) began in England when Martin Luther's novel doctrines energized young religious reformers at Cambridge University. Thus began a quarter century of religious and social upheaval. On the Continent, it touched off peasant uprisings, fanatical heresies, the sack of Rome, and the disintegration of Catholicism throughout much of Western Europe. In England, the enthusiasm seethed until King Henry VIII's formal break with the Papacy in 1533, and then peaked with the publication of William Tyndale's Bible and the suppression of Catholic rebellions. After stalling in Henry VIII's final years, the Awakening picked up a riotous second wind under Henry's evangelical son, Edward VI. It only subsided when, late in his short reign, Edward slowed the pace of reform in the face of royal bankruptcy, rampant inflation, and social chaos. The Awakening transformed England from a loyal supporter of the Roman Church to a nation possessing its own fully Protestant clergy, doctrine, and liturgy.

The Puritan Awakening (1621–1649; climax 1640) began as a resurgence of radical Protestant fervor throughout Europe. On the Continent, it ignited in Bohemia and touched off the Thirty Years' War. In England, it boiled over with the House of Commons' 1621 "Protestation" denouncing the arbitrary rule of King James I. When the growing reform fervor found itself thwarted under James's son, John Winthrop led a "saving remnant" to America—touching off the Great Migration to New England. At home, Puritan enthusiasm led inexorably to the English Civil War, the beheading of King Charles I, and Cromwell's short-lived Commonwealth. In the colonies, the excitement subsided when the new Puritan settlements stiffened their moral orthodoxy. Entering the Awakening, England regarded the American colonies as mere high-risk commercial ventures. It emerged having transplanted large and educated communities across the Atlantic— most notably a Calvinist New Jerusalem to Massachusetts—where the faithful in the New World could be free of the corruption of the Old.

The Great Awakening (1727–1746; climax 1741) began as a series of isolated religious revivals in New Jersey and Pennsylvania. Led by the young theologian Jonathan Edwards, the revivals moved to the Connecticut Valley in the late 1730s. The Awakening soon spread throughout the colonies—and, in the South, among African slaves (who thereby often acquired reading skills) as well as among their owners. It reached a peak in 1741 during the rousing American tour of the English-born evangelist George Whitefield. As "new light" challenged "old light," the revival split colonial assemblies and pitted emotional young believers in "faith" against stolid older defenders of "works." After mass gatherings and "concerts of prayer" in the early 1740s, the fervor receded. Before the Awakening, colonial America adhered to what young people called their elders' "Glacial Age of Religion"; it emerged liberated by itinerant preachers from European habits of class deference and geographic immobility.

The Transcendental Awakening (1822–1844; climax 1831) was triggered by Denmark Vesey's slave revolt, the evangelical preaching of Charles Finney, and Andrew Jackson's decision to run for president—soon foiled by John Quincy Adams's "stolen election." Often merging with Jacksonian populism, it peaked with Nat Turner's violent rebellion, the founding of abolitionist and other reform societies, and the Democrats' ultimate triumph over the "monster" National Bank. After inspiring a transcendentalist school of philosophy and literature, this tide of idealism—what one historian calls a "heyday of sectarianism"—spawned a profusion of "movements": new prophetic religions (including the Latter Day Saints, Adventism, and Christian Science), spiritualist clubs, utopian communes, temperance reform, dietary faddism, and conspiratorial parties like the Antimasons and the Locofocos. The excitement faded after the Millerites' predicted apocalypse failed to appear and a revived economy refocused popular interest in westward expansion. America entered the Awakening a staid temple of natural-law rationalism; it emerged riding a tidal swell of romantic idealism and evangelical piety.

The Third Great Awakening (1886–1908; climax 1896) began with the Chicago Haymarket Riot and the launching of the global student missionary movement. Agrarian protests and labor violence sparked the tumultuous 1890s, a decade that Henry Steele Commager calls a "cultural watershed" and that Richard Hofstadter describes as a "searing experience" to those who lived through it. Following William Jennings Bryan's revivalist run for president, a cadre of inspired youth turned America upside down—as "settlement workers" uplifting the poor, "muckrakers" blasting immoral industrialists, and feminists hailing the "new woman." With the economy's quick recovery from the Panic of 1907, the national mood stabilized. Before it was over, the Awakening had launched fundamentalism, the Pentacostals, and Christian Socialism; "progressive" reform, the Chautauqua Circuit, and Greenwich Village; the NAACP, the Wobblies, and renewed crusades for women's suffrage and temperance. America entered the Awakening gripped with the steam-and-corset mentality of the Victorian twilight; it emerged with the vitalism, idealism, and modernism of a dawning century.

The Consciousness Revolution (1964–1984; climax 1980) began with urban riots, campus protests, anti-Vietnam demonstrations, and fiery denunciations of America's military-industrial "Establishment." The fervor grew amid a drug-and-hippie "counterculture," before broadening in the seventies into a New Age transformation of lifestyles and values—which included a dramatic revival (led by "Jesus freaks") of evangelicalism. Over time, the early political idealism was worn down by Watergate, stagflation, rising drug use and crime, foreign-policy debacles, and a pessimistic zeitgeist known as "malaise." Hopes then turned to the economic liberation of the individual from the "system"—inspiring, by the late seventies, growing antitax and antiregulatory movements. The climax arrived, and the mood broke, with Reagan's defeat of Carter in 1980. The awakening ended with Reagan's era-changing "Morning in America" victory in 1984. Onetime hippies reached their yuppie chrysalis. America entered the Awakening with a global reputation for institutions that could build anything but a culture that could imagine nothing. America emerged with that reputation reversed.

History from the Inside Out

In the combined lists of Crises and Awakenings, you can recognize the rhythm of the natural saeculum coursing through Anglo-American history. When it was part of Britain, America completed three full saecula. The present-day American nation is now late in its sixth full saeculum— just over forty years past the climax of the Awakening and fifteen years into the final Crisis turning.

Notice the powerful two-stroke pendularity in American history. At 103, 103, and 97 years, the spans of the first three cycles (from one Crisis climax to the next) roughly match the saeculum of the ancient Romans. The fourth, at 76 years, is the shortest—and it includes a greatly truncated Crisis turning, only five years long. We will discuss what happened to the Civil War Saeculum in later chapters. Its peculiar timing represents the one true anomaly in the Anglo-American saeculum. Still, it is long enough to approximate Censorinus's definition of a natural saeculum—a long human life. The fifth saeculum is 80 years long. And the length of the sixth, estimated here at 86 years, is simply our best guess.

In Chapter 5 we will explain why the American saeculum tended to grow somewhat shorter from the early 1700s to the mid-1900s—and *why it may be growing longer again today.* In any case, we should not expect exact periodicity in any complex social or natural system. The saeculum is not like the orbiting of a planet. It is more like the recurrence of seasons or the rhythm of respiration: Its periodicity can only be approximate.

In Chapter 7 we will discuss plausible dates for the end of the Millennial Crisis. The early 2030s (best guess 2033) represents our estimate of the resolution of the Crisis era—with the climax occurring several years earlier (perhaps in 2030).

These dates are roughly consistent with the timetable suggested by the "world system" and "long cycle" theories we examined earlier. Thompson, in his extensive 2020 examination of the global long cycle,

CHART 2-2

The Anglo-American Saeculum

SAECULUM	Time from Climax of Crisis to Climax of Awakening		Time from Climax of Awakening to Climax of Crisis		Time from one Crisis Climax to next Crisis Climax
		(climax year) AWAKENING (full era)		(climax year) CRISIS (full era)	
LATE MEDIEVAL				(1485) War of the Roses (1455–1487)	
TUDOR	52 years ⟶	(1537) Protestant Reformation (1525–1551)	51 years ⟶	(1588) Armada Crisis (1569–1597)	103 years
NEW WORLD	52 years ⟶	(1640) Puritan Awakening (1621–1649)	51 years ⟶	(1691) Glorious Revolution (1675–1706)	103 years
REVOLU-TIONARY	50 years ⟶	(1741) Great Awakening (1727–1746)	47 years ⟶	(1788) American Revolution (1773–1794)	97 years
CIVIL WAR	43 years ⟶	(1831) Transcendental Awakening (1822–1844)	33 years ⟶	(1864) Civil War (1860–1865)	76 years
GREAT POWER	32 years ⟶	(1896) Third Great Awakening (1886–1908)	48 years ⟶	(1944) Great Depression— World War II (1929–1946)	80 years
MILLENNIAL	36 years ⟶	(1980) Consciousness Revolution (1964–1984)	50 years? ⟶	(2030?) Millennial Crisis (2008–2033?)	86 years?

concludes that the current "United States global system" is likely to enter its closing "global war" phase in 2030. Joshua Goldstein, another much-published scholar of long cycles, would put the highest likelihood of great-power war "in the late 2020s." These are close to the crisis climax target dates forecasted by the earliest global-system theorists back in the 1980s: 2025 or 2030. In other words, the target dates haven't shifted much.

Thus far we have been presenting these seasons of history entirely in terms of repeating patterns and abstract social processes—like cycles of war and peace, the dynamics of a "world system," or recurring "revitalization movements." This approach may be sufficient to explain what the saeculum is. But it does little to explain what motivates it. Why, at a personal level, do people feel compelled to drive history forward in this manner? The approach also does little to explain its timing. Why couldn't the saeculum have a periodicity of fifty years—or two hundred years?

To understand not just what the saeculum is, but how it feels to those people who live in it, we need to connect objective history with subjective experience. We need to move beyond the saeculum's external timing and learn about its internal dynamics. We need to look at history from the inside out.

"History is the memory of states," Henry Kissinger famously wrote. Taken literally, of course, this makes no sense: Only individuals have memories, and one person's memory does not constitute history. Yet what about the collective memories of all people who similarly interact with the same history at roughly the same age? What about people grouped into social generations? We might dynamically rephrase Kissinger thus: Each new generation, as it assumes leadership, redefines a nation's history according to its own collective experience.

We turn next to examine the social generations that push the seasons of history forward and ultimately govern their timing. Modern history does not beat to a rhythm invented by great statesmen, with all their flush treasuries, strong armies, and powerful laws. It beats instead to the cycle of life, dictated by biology and society and experienced by each person.

3

SEASONS OF LIFE

All our lives we remain a prisoner of the generation we
belonged to at age twenty.

—CHARLES AUGUSTIN SAINTE-BEUVE

Ibn Khaldun, a renowned polymath of the fourteenth-century Islamic
world, was a contemporary of the poet Petrarch and of Italy's early Renaissance. He flourished during the twilight years of Al-Andalus, as
the last Muslim dynasties were getting pushed out of Spain by Christian armies. Khaldun read widely, traveled extensively, conversed with
emirs and princes, and beheld the horrors of his times. As a teenager,
he witnessed the depopulation of his Tunisian homeland by the Black
Death. As a mature philosopher, in the early 1400s, he traveled through
the Mideast and met personally Timur the Great, even as this ambitious
Mogul conqueror was besieging and massacring city after city.

Based on his learning and firsthand experience, Khaldun wrote
the *Muqaddimah* ("Introduction to History"), a stunningly original
and unified theory of politics, sociology, economics, and history. Khaldun's theory is strictly cyclical: The security and prosperity of a kingdom, he says, rise and fall in lockstep with the growth and decline of
its *'asabiyya*—Arabic for "group feeling" or "social cohesion." And what
drives this cycle of *'asabiyya*? A regular and predictable schedule of generational replacement.

According to Khaldun, a new dynasty typically lasts 100 to 120 years.
He compares its life cycle to that of a person, whose vital trajectory can
be divided into five stages. First, the dynasty is born in a crisis moment of
invasion or rebellion; second, it grows and strengthens; third, it reaches

its zenith of generosity and power (a "midpoint" he compares to a person's peak functional age); fourth, it weakens and declines; and fifth, it perishes. The early stages of strong social cohesion are marked by coarse (pastoral) manners, simple laws that are obeyed, a thirst for reputation, and modest affluence, equally shared. The late stages of withering 'asabiyya are marked by refined (urban) manners, complex laws that are evaded, a thirst for money, and great riches, hoarded by a few.

In its duration and cadence, Khaldun's repeating dynastic cycle unmistakably reflects the rhythm of the saeculum. It matches the duration of a long human life. Its seasonal rotation begins and ends in crisis. And midway through it reaches a sort of solstice at which the rate of change switches from positive to negative.

Yet Khaldun goes further. He claims that the regular timing of this cycle is driven by a predictable succession of generations. The first generation "founds and builds." The second generation, too young to participate as adults in the founding, nonetheless matures into leaders who can "imitate" their elders and improve on their foundations. The third generation is the first to lose any contact with the founders' experience. Its heart is no longer in the project. While its leaders try to invent "rules and traditions" to keep things going, the dynasty begins to decline. The fourth generation, in its turn, no longer cares about the dynasty and may even "despise" the founders' collective spirit. Its members look after themselves and brace themselves for whatever comes next, for a world in which 'asabiyya has vanished. They are "the destroyers," writes Khaldun: They preside over the dynasty's collapse.

The *Muqaddimah* is a vast tapestry, brimming with insights into the pace and direction of social change. It may have influenced seminal later thinkers, from Machiavelli to Hegel. Modern scholars praise its all-inclusive scope; Toynbee called it "a philosophy of history which is undoubtedly the greatest work of its kind that has ever been created by any mind in any time and place." Central to Khaldun's outlook is a cycle of social beliefs and behavior. And driving that cycle is a dynamic of generational aging—which helps to explain history's underlying regularity.

Once again, historical cycles and generations seem to go together. While Khaldun never talked about a "self-sufficient pattern"—as Schlesinger did—his reasoning was essentially the same. Generational rhythms are self-generating and independent of random events because they beat in time with the human life cycle.

But how exactly are generations created? And what rules govern their two-way interaction with history?

GENERATIONS AND HISTORY

Before generations can be created, one essential requirement must be met. A society must have social roles for every phase of life, and each role must be distinct and reasonably well defined. Most societies have no problem meeting this requirement. Almost all possess such phase-of-life roles. And across societies, these roles typically have much in common.

Let's start at the beginning of the life cycle. For children, biology ensures that everywhere their social role, up into their teens at least, will be *growth* (receiving nurture, acquiring values). After a rite of passage, youths enter a new life phase, young adulthood, with a new social role, *vitality* (serving institutions, testing values). Then comes midlife, the age range in which adults are deemed capable of leadership. Here the role is *power* (managing institutions, applying values). Still later comes elderhood, associated with decreasing activity yet increasing mentorship. The elder role is likely to be *authority* (stewarding institutions, transferring values).

An astonishing variety of civilizations have embraced this basic four-part schema of life phases. It holds for the Hindus (the four *ashrama*) no less than for the ancient Romans, whose last transition from midlife to elderhood (from *virilitas* to *senectus*) inspired the venerable name *senatus* for an authoritative council of state.

These life phases also tend to be evenly spaced in their accepted age boundaries. In today's America, for example, each life phase is a bit more than twenty years in length. Adulthood arrives, legally at least, shortly after age twenty. Midlife arrives in the early forties. (Age forty-three is the youngest any American has been elected president.) Elderhood is signaled in the mid-sixties by an initial Social Security check, today sent out at a median age of sixty-four, along with the title (welcome or not) of "senior." And contrary to widespread belief, many people have always lived well past their mid-sixties. Even in high-mortality premodern societies, at least one in ten of all the people who reach their mid-twenties will go on to survive into their mid-eighties.

The universality of this overall life-cycle pattern has inspired comparison, once again, to the seasonal wheel of time. Carl Jung described the "arc of life" as "divisible into four parts." According to sociologist Daniel Levinson, "Metaphorically, everyone understands the connections between the seasons of the year and the seasons of the human life."

This growth-and-decay seasonality makes the rhythm of the human life cycle seem a lot like the rhythm of the saeculum, history's "natural century." Only there's this important difference. Whereas the life cycle represents the wheel of time experienced by each person, the saeculum represents the wheel of time experienced by an entire society or nation. *Generations are created precisely through the intersection of these two seasonal cycles, one personal and the other collective.*

To see how this works, let's imagine a traditional society in which, as expected, all four phases of life are clearly defined and strictly prescribed. Each new phase-of-life group tries to perform its social role—growth, vitality, power, or authority—exactly as it has always been performed. There are no distinct "generations" to speak of.

Now imagine that the society is suddenly hit by a Great Event (what sociologist Karl Mannheim called a "crystallizing moment"), some emergency, perhaps a war, so consequential that it transforms all of society's members yet transforms them differently according to their phase-of-life responses.

For children, this response might be an awestruck respect for adults (and the desire to stay out of their way); for young adults, taking up arms and risking death to meet the enemy; for midlifers, organizing the troops and mobilizing society for maximum effort; for elders, setting strategy and clarifying the larger purpose. The experience leaves a different emotional imprint according to the expected social role—differences reinforced by social interaction within each group. Children mirror one another's dread, youths one another's valor, midlifers one another's tenacity, seniors one another's wisdom.

If the Great Event is successfully resolved, its enduring memory imparts to each group a unique location in history—and a distinct generational persona. It may mark young adults as collective heroes, around whom grand myths later arise. When this hero generation reaches midlife, its leaders show greater hubris than their predecessors. As elders, they may issue more demands for public reward. Meanwhile, the generation following them—the trembling children of the Great Event—bring a more deferential persona into later life-cycle phases. The generation born just after the Great Event may be seen in hopeful colors as the golden age children for whom the triumph was won.

To make this illustration more up-to-date and personal, today's Americans need only recall World War II.

World War II left a massive impression on everyone alive at the time. And it did so by phase of life. It cast Missionary elders as champions of long-held visions, stamping the peers of Henry Stimson, George Marshall, Douglas MacArthur, and Albert Einstein as the "wise old men" of their era and separating them, in America's memory, from the prior Progressive Generation.

The war enabled the middle-aged Lost to get a big job done, spotlighting the gritty exploits of a George Patton or a Harry Truman and rooting a peer group that had earlier been slow to settle down.

The victory empowered young-adult G.I.s as world conquerors, enhancing their reputation for "ask not" civic virtue and Great Society teamwork and later earning them the longest presidential tenure of any U.S. generation.

The war bred caution and sensitivity among Silent children, lending them a persona that produced a lifelong preoccupation with process, fairness, and artistic expression.

So powerful was the social impact of World War II that it came to define the very cohort boundary lines between generations. The G.I.s include nearly everyone who saw combat in this war. The Lost, by contrast, include all the combat-eligibles of the prior world war—and the Silent those children and teens who remember the war personally but typically saw no combat. The initial Boomer birth cohort of 1943 includes the first "victory babies," just too young to recall the war themselves.

CHART 3-1

American Generations and World War II

GENERATION	Birth Years	Famous Member	Generational Connection to World War II
Progressive	1843–1859	Woodrow Wilson	*Prewar Elders* *(Unsuccessful Multilateralists)*
Missionary	1860–1882	Franklin Roosevelt	**Elder Leaders:** Principled Visionaries
Lost	1883–1900	Dwight Eisenhower	**Midlife Generals:** Pragmatic Managers
G.I.	1901–1924	John F. Kennedy	**Rising-Adult Soldiers:** Can-Do Heroes
Silent	1925–1942	Michael Dukakis	**Sheltered Children:** Deferential Helpmates
Boom	1943–1960	Bill Clinton	*Postwar Children* *(Victory Babies)*
Gen X	1961–1981	Barack Obama	*Postwar Children* *(Symbol of Lost Direction)*
Millennial	1982–2005?	Pete Buttigieg	*Postwar Children* *(Last Adult Memory of G.I.s)*
Homeland	2006?–?	Priah Ferguson	*Postwar Children* *(History Only)*

Among generations born afterward, the symbolic memory of that epic war kept resonating, but with dampened echoes. By the time most G.I.s had passed into retirement, during the 1980s and '90s, Generation X was coming of age amid adult criticism for having forgotten the war-era sense of community. Meanwhile, families, schools, churches, and the media were again emphasizing those old civic virtues in the raising of Millennial children, who later came of age as the last Americans to have any adult contact with G.I. Joe or Rosie the Riveter. For today's Homeland Generation of children, World War II is becoming pure history, as distant from them as the Civil War was for the child Silent.

What happens as a Great Event and its echoes fade with the passage of time? In a traditional society, nothing. Absent another Great Event, generations gradually disappear. Twenty-one years afterward, only three generations shaped by the event remain alive; after forty-two years, only two; and after sixty-three years, only those who were then children can recall it. By then, social inertia will have nudged everyone back to the traditional life cycle. People will still have different phase-of-life roles according to their age, but they will no longer show striking generational differences in how they fill those roles. In ancient epics, this is where the falling curtain of time ends the saga.

In a modern society, however, new Great Events keep occurring, and they do so with great regularity. These are the solstices of the saeculum: Crises and Awakenings. Through five centuries of Anglo-American history, no span of more than fifty years (the duration of two phases of life) has ever elapsed without the occurrence of a Crisis or an Awakening. Every generation has thus been shaped by either a Crisis *or* an Awakening during one of its first two phases of life—and has encountered both a Crisis *and* an Awakening at some point through its life cycle.

This has clearly been the case for twentieth-century America since the last Crisis. (See Chart 3-2.)

From the climax of World War II, shift your attention ahead roughly forty years to the end of the next Great Event of the saeculum, the postwar "Consciousness Revolution." From the early 1940s to the early 1980s, each generation had aged by two phases of life. Two generations that were earlier active (Lost and Missionary) had by now departed, and two new generations that were earlier unborn (Boom and Gen X) had by now arrived.

This Awakening—this society-wide obsession with breaking rules, celebrating the spirit, and shedding social discipline—again defined generations, but in ways entirely unlike the earlier Crisis. Back in World War II, sixty-five-year-olds were moralistic visionaries; now, in the Consciousness Revolution, they were stolid defenders of the Establishment. Before, forty-five-year-olds were hardscrabble midlife pragmatists; now they were polite navigators of midlife "passages." Before, twenty-five-year-olds were uniformed soldiers; now they were free agents "doing

CHART 3-2

Recent Generations and Their Locations in History

ERA	1908–1929	1929–1946	1946–1964	1964–1984	1984–2008
		(CRISIS)		(AWAKENING)	
KEY EVENTS	Four Freedoms World War I Prohibition Scopes Trial	Crash of '29 New Deal Pearl Harbor D-Day	Levittown McCarthyism "Affluent Society" Little Rock	Woodstock Kent State Watergate Tax Revolt	Perestroika Culture Wars Dotcom Bubble 9/11 Wars
Entering ELDERHOOD Age 63–83	Progressive Woodrow Wilson John Dewey	Missionary Franklin Roosevelt Douglas MacArthur	Lost Dwight Eisenhower Norman Rockwell	G.I. Lyndon Johnson Ronald Reagan	Silent Nancy Pelosi Colin Powell
Entering MIDLIFE 42–62	Missionary Herbert Hoover Andrew Volstead	Lost George Patton Humphrey Bogart	G.I. John Kennedy Walt Disney	Silent Ralph Nader Woody Allen	Boom G. W. Bush Oprah Winfrey
Entering RISING ADULTHOOD Age 21–41	Lost Al Capone F. Scott Fitzgerald	G.I. Robert Oppenheimer Jimmy Stewart	Silent Martin L. King, Jr. Elvis Presley	Boom Angela Davis Jim Morrison	Gen X Michael Dell Kurt Cobain
Entering YOUTH Age 0–20	G.I. Jackie Cooper "Pollyanna"	Silent Shirley Temple "Little Rascals"	Boom Jerry Mathers "Dr. Spock Babies"	Gen X Tatum O'Neal "Rosemary's Baby"	Millennial Hilary Duff "Barney's Gang"

their own thing." And the children? Gone were the sheltered "goody two-shoes"; in their place were latchkey kids.

Every forty years or so, the persona of each phase of life becomes nearly the opposite of that established by the generation that had once passed through it. This rhythm has been at work since the dawn of modernity. English children born early in Queen Elizabeth I's forty-five-year reign came of age as ambitious empire builders. Children born late in her reign came of age obsessed with holiness. Two generations later, the American youth of the Glorious Revolution preferred teamwork over conversion; the youth of the Great Awakening preferred the reverse. In the Transcendental Awakening, young adults tried to fire the passions of the old; in the Civil War Crisis, young adults doused old men's fires.

When we first notice a generational difference, we often interpret it as a mere phase-of-life difference. "If you aren't a liberal when you're young, you have no heart, but if you aren't a conservative when you're middle-aged, you have no head," goes the old saying—which (in its various wordings) has been attributed to Edmund Burke, François Guizot, Benjamin Disraeli, and Winston Churchill. Here we interpret the perspective of youth as nothing more than deviance, something young people will "grow out of." And there is something to this: When we are young, because we are young, we are able to reimagine the world with a freedom that we no longer possess as we grow older. It is by means of this very freedom that the rising generation is able to strike out in a new direction and keep the saeculum moving forward.

Yet this new direction, as a rule, never leads the rising generation to follow the path of its parents as it grows older. Far from it. Liberal parents often end up raising conservative kids. And even when their kids also regard themselves as liberal, we can bet that it will be a species of liberalism alien to their parents'. It is therefore wrong to suppose, as some do, that children regularly will come of age with attitudes (toward life, elders, politics, culture) similar to those that midlife leaders had when they were young. Dating back centuries to the birth of modernity, this has not happened.

By focusing on the *direction* of these peer-personality reversals, we can begin to appreciate the *cause* of their regular timing. Ask yourself: In a modern society, how would we expect youth to behave in a nation run by complacent rationalists focused on overhauling the outer world? Exactly: They would compensate by becoming discontented moralists focused on overhauling the inner world. Or vice versa.

Generational aging is what translates the rhythm of the past into the rhythm of the future. It explains why each generation is not only *shaped by* history, but also *shapes* later history. It regulates the velocity and direction of social change. It connects life in its biographical intimacy to history writ large with its social or political trends.

If the connection between generations and history is so powerful, why haven't people always known about it?

People have. At the dawn of recorded history, the *generation* (not the year) was the universal standard of social time. When translating Hellenic myths into verse, Greek poets used sequential "generations" to mark the successive appearance of Gaea, Uranus, Cronus, and Zeus. In the Hebrew Bible, "Genesis" measures time with a chain of generations, each begetting and raising the next.

The ancients were often vague about what they meant by the word. The Indo-European root, *gen-*, means (as a verb) nothing more specific than "to come or bring into being" or (as a noun) anything new "brought into being." Applied to people, it can assume alternative meanings. One meaning is the *family generation*: everyone brought into being by the same biological parent—used in such phrases as "fourth-generation" heir. The other meaning is the *social generation*: everyone brought into being by nature or society around the same time. Social generations refer to entire peer groups, as when the New Testament speaks of "a faithless and perverse generation" or the poet Hesiod of "generations" of gold or silver or bronze.

Ancient authors seldom bothered to define "generation" with any more precision than this. Many liked to conflate the social generation of a tribe or nation with the personal generation of that nation's leader, which naturally led to a confusion of social and family generations. Also, they typically regarded distinct social generations as an episodic phenomenon: something that happened once in their mythical history, but perhaps was not expected to happen again.

With the arrival of modernity, however, this changed. Just when the West began to talk about centuries, so too did it begin to talk self-consciously about new peer groups. Intellectuals no longer confused leaders with the people they led. And they began to expect new generations to appear. Shortly before the French Revolution, social generation theories exploded on the scene—with every salon in Paris buzzing with talk (some of it from Thomas Jefferson) about how to define the length and natural rights of each new generation.

Over the next 150 years, many of the best minds in the West struggled to enlarge and refine this concept. Most agreed with Auguste Comte that generations had become, in the modern world, the master regulator of the pace of social change. John Stuart Mill formally defined a generation as "a new set of human beings" who "have been educated, have grown up from childhood, and have taken possession of society." Wilhelm Dilthey described a generation as "a relationship of contemporaneity... between those who had a common childhood, a common adolescence, and whose years of greatest vigor partially overlap."

In the aftermath of World War I, Karl Mannheim, José Ortega y Gasset, François Mentré (who coined the term "social generation" in a book by that name), and many others produced an extraordinary body of generations theory. As the twentieth century progressed, social scientists began routinely to weigh "generational effects" (or "birth-cohort effects") as an explanation for changes in behaviors or beliefs. In recent decades, corporations have learned to practice "generational marketing." Generational references appear incessantly in TV ads, political speeches, movies, and pop-culture vernacular. Pundits now compete hard to name each new generation—not just in America, but around the world.

Yet even as this flood of generational self-consciousness expands, its breadth has grown faster than its depth. Just as we shun the concept of a cycle the more we actually encounter regular social cycles, so do we trivialize the concept of a generation the more we find ourselves talking about how pop music has changed from Jim Morrison to Kurt Cobain to Taylor Swift. Each generation's link with pop music, social media, and technology has become far better understood (and accepted) than its profound connection to nature and history.

Why do we moderns celebrate endless generational novelty? Because it indulges our expectation of unbounded progress. Why do we resist the wheel of time? Because it undermines that illusion. While modernity is all about controlling the future, generations in fact tie us to our past and to age-old dynamics of social behavior. Time and again, generational change explodes in the face of those who claim to know which way progress lies. In the modern world, each generation of new leaders is trying to escape the imagined shadows of its own parents' errors. The last thing it expects, or wants, is for its own children to try to return to those shadows.

When the leaders are utopian ideologues, they may be so certain they possess the key to unlimited progress that (like the French revolution-aries or the Italian fascists) they will restart the civic calendar at Year One (in 1792 and 1922, respectively). And they may feel so threatened by memories of the past that, like Stalin or Pol Pot, they will try to liqui-date the elite of any generation that came of age before their revolution began. "Who controls the past controls the future," runs Big Brother's party slogan in George Orwell's *1984*, and "Who controls the present controls the past."

Most of us moderns do believe, either tentatively or ardently, in some definition of progress. Yet it is fair to say that most of us find that our hopes for progress are routinely disappointed by events.

Only with a better understanding of generational change can we avoid being blindsided by it. Only then can we appreciate the judgment of William and Mary historian Anthony Esler that "the generational ap-proach may, in fact, provide one of the royal roads to total history." But first we need to take a closer look at social generations themselves. How exactly do we define, describe, and recognize them?

IDENTIFYING GENERATIONS

"You belong to it, too. You came along at the same time. You can't get away from it," Thomas Wolfe wrote (in *You Can't Go Home Again*) about his own "Lost Generation." "You're a part of it whether you want to be or not." To Wolfe, as to F. Scott Fitzgerald, Ernest Hemingway, Malcolm Cowley, and other writers of the 1920s, membership in that generation reflected a variety of mannerisms: weary cynicism at an early age, risk-taking, binge-like behavior, disdain for a pompous "older generation." Wolfe's young-adult peers stood across a wide divide from moralistic midlifers and across another divide from a new batch of straight-arrow kids. To "belong to it," you had to come of age not long before World War I. No one formally defined it that way; people just *knew*.

What's more, as time passed, everyone recognized that the members of this generation were growing older. By the time Wolfe's novel was posthumously published (in 1940), they were no longer the rising generation. "If there is such a thing as a Lost Generation in this country," Wolfe wrote by then, "it is probably made up of those men of advanced middle age who still speak the language that was spoken before 1929, and who know no other. These men indubitably are lost." By referring to his generation, in other words, Wolfe was not using a shorthand to refer to any fixed phase of life. He was referring rather to *a particular group of people* who, over time, aged *through* every phase of life. Wolfe's Lost Generation literati never explained exactly how they identified their "generation." But the question must be raised: In a world in which people are born every minute, how can social generations be located and their birth year boundaries defined?

To answer it, you must first determine the *length* of a generation. As the Great Event scenario showed, history puts a different stamp on different peer groups *according to their age-determined social roles.* Thus the length of a generation (in birth years) should approximate the length of a phase of life (in years of age). Since the early nineteenth century, this implies that it should average about twenty-one years, although the length may vary somewhat for each generation depending on the noise of history and the precise timing of Great Events.

Next, to apply these lengths to real birth years, you locate an underlying generational persona. Every generation has one. It's a distinctly human—and variable—creation, with attitudes about family life, gender roles, institutions, politics, religion, lifestyle, and the future. A generation can think, feel, or do anything a person might think, feel, or do. It can be safe or reckless, individualist or collegial, pious or worldly. Like any social category (race, class, nationality), a generation can allow plenty of individual exceptions and be fuzzy at the edges.

Unlike most other social categories, however, it possesses its own personal biography. You can tell a lifelong story about the shared experiences of the Silent Generation in ways you never could for all women, all Hispanics, or all Californians. The reason, to quote the Italian historian Giuseppe Ferrari, is that every generation "is born, lives, and dies." It can feel nostalgia for a unique past, express urgency about a future of limited duration, and comprehend its own mortality.

There is no fixed formula for identifying the persona of a real-life generation. But it helps to look for three attributes: first, a generation's *common location in history*; second, its *common beliefs and behavior*; and third, its *perceived membership in a common generation*.

Common location refers to where a generation finds itself, at any given age, against the background chronology of trends and events.

At critical moments in history, members of each generation tend to occupy a single phase of life. At the end of World War II, the Silent, G.I., Lost, and Missionary Generations each fit snugly into the age brackets of childhood, young adulthood, midlife, and elderhood. The same close fit between generations and phases of life occurred in the late 1920s (just before the Great Crash) and in the early 1960s and early 1980s (just before and after an era of cultural upheaval). These moments are generational crucibles, wherein members of a peer group share what Mannheim called "a community of time and space" and face "the same concrete historical problems." Ortega y Gasset refers to them as "zones of dates" which make members of a generation "the same age vitally and historically."

At any given moment, history inevitably touches a generation's oldest and youngest cohorts in different ways. The Vietnam War put more pressure on Boomers born in 1945 than on those born in 1955, for example, and World War II put more pressure on G.I.s born in 1920 than on those born in 1910. Yet within each generation, a few special birth cohorts can pull on older or younger people and gather them around a common location. Cheryl Merser observes in *Grown Ups* that for Americans born in the 1950s (like herself), their "sixties took place in the seventies." This "sixties" experience felt authentic enough to bind Merser and her peers to older Boomers. But no one could have their "sixties" in the 1950s or 1980s.

Generations can be separated at exact birth dates by paying attention to what philosopher Julián Marías defines as the "social cartography" of successive birth cohorts. "In this analogy," he suggested, "each generation would be the area between two mountain chains, and in order to determine whether a certain point belonged to one or the other, it would be necessary to know the relief." Sometimes the watershed is obvious, sometimes subtle. Occasionally, even a split second can be decisive in separating adjacent generations. In contemporary America, a one-minute delay in birth can mean the difference between kindergarten and first grade six years later. And still later, that can mean the difference between serving in a war or not—or getting laid off your first job or not.

Common beliefs and behaviors refer to objective traits that members of a generation share with one another (at a given age) more than with people born earlier or later. Such traits are fundamental to most generations theorists. Comte wrote that each generation develops a "unanimous adherence to certain fundamental notions." Dilthey points to a "generational *Weltanschauung*," a worldview that shapes a generation's lifelong direction.

To see how generational traits differ, consider shifts in political affiliation, such as the huge contrast between the Republican-leaning Lost (lifelong skeptics of big government) and the Democratic-leaning G.I.s (lifelong supporters of technocracy)—or between Republican-leaning Xers and Democratic-leaning Millennials. As far back as we can measure, indeed, people's lifelong voting behavior is heavily tilted according to which party was most popular when they reached their late teens and early twenties.

Consider also attitudes toward free agency, such as the young Silent's well-documented quest for marital and career "security" in the 1950s, versus Gen-Xers' nineties-era aversion to marriage and corporatism. Consider the gap between acceptable gender roles, a gap that G.I.s widened but that Boomers narrowed. Or consider overall life goals. Back in the late 1960s, Boomer college freshmen believed by a two-to-one majority that "developing a meaningful philosophy of life" was more important than "getting ahead financially." A decade later, Xer freshmen responded with a two-to-one majority *the other way*.

No trait ever appears uniformly across all cohorts of a generation. Indeed, major trends *within* a generation often help to define it. From first birth year to last, Millennials have trended strongly toward less risk taking and longer time horizons—as measured by rates of crime and substance abuse (falling) and educational attainment (rising). In this respect, they are like the G.I.s but very unlike Boomers, for whom these indicators (first birth year to last) moved in the opposite direction.

Common *perceived membership* refers to how a generation defines itself—and to its own understanding about which birth cohorts belong and which don't. Perceived membership gives a generation a sense of destiny. Marías once remarked that "to ask ourselves to which generation we belong is, in large measure, to ask who we are."

Perceived membership confirms what many pollsters have long suspected about Boomers—that their true boundaries (born between 1943 and 1960) should start and stop a few years earlier than the fertility bulge used by the Census Bureau to define this generation (between 1946 and 1964). Indeed, the term "Generation X" was a self-label first coined and popularized by young literati born between 1961 and 1964—and its central purpose was to disclaim any affiliation with Boomers.

Even when a historical generation can no longer be asked directly, it often leaves behind plenty of evidence about its perceived peer membership. This evidence is what links the famous circle of Lost Generation authors born in the late 1890s with writers just a bit older (Randolph Bourne, T. S. Eliot, Ezra Pound), but not with writers just a bit younger (John Steinbeck, Langston Hughes, W. H. Auden).

To say that you belong to your generation certainly does not mean that you think favorably of your generation. According to German literary historian Julius Peterson, every generation includes what he called "directive," "directed," and "suppressed" members. The "directive" members set the overall tone, the "directed" follow cues (and thereby legitimize the tone), and the "suppressed" either withdraw from that tone or, more rarely, spend a lifetime attacking it. Even in their resistance, of course, the suppressed confirm their generation's influence over their lives.

Perhaps the most important aspect of a generation's self-perception is its sense of direction. Ortega y Gasset once wrote that each generation is "a species of biological missile hurled into space at a given instant, with a certain velocity and direction" which gives it a "preestablished vital trajectory." Mannheim referred to each generation's sense of "essential destiny."

For some generations, this sense of destiny can be overwhelming. The cohesion of postwar G.I.s and of the post-Revolutionary peers of

Thomas Jefferson reflected a massive generational consensus about the kind of future they expected to build. Yet for other generations, this sense of destiny may be weak. Gen-Xers came of age expecting little of themselves as a generation—a fact which itself has become part of their collective persona. A similar sense arose among the peers of George Washington and of Dwight Eisenhower.

A generation can collectively choose its destiny. But you cannot personally choose your generation—any more than you can choose your parents, your ethnicity, or your native land. That much is fate, conditioning much about who you are. For Martin Heidegger, belonging to a generation "throws us into" the world at a single time and place, thereby shaping both our outlook and our options. "The fateful act of living in and with one's generation," he wrote, "completes the drama of human existence."

THE GENERATIONAL PANORAMA

In 2013, *Time* magazine put the Millennial Generation on its cover, joining an explosion of media commentary that year (as measured by Ngram) about America's newest wave of rising adults. Most of the stories depicted a "special" generation of "connected" youths, probably over-sheltered and over-pampered, who were trying to stay upbeat in a downbeat economy.

The last time America witnessed comparable attention paid to a new generation happened twenty-three years earlier, when *Time* put Generation X on its cover—though the label had not yet been invented. That happened a year later (in 1991) with the publication of Douglas Coupland's *Generation X*. The commentary this time was very different: These were "throwaway" kids, left to grow up by themselves, who responded to hard times with irony and indifference.

Rewind another twenty-three years to 1967 and the Summer of Love. America was again fascinated with a new generation, this time bold and idealistic young people whose "demands" were triggering a "generation gap." Predictably, *Time* put Boomers on its cover.

Rewind again, this time less than twenty years, for a flurry of anxiety over the gray-flannel young Silent. Or again back to the early 1930s and the radicalized young G.I.s. Or again back to Armistice Day and the alienated young Lost—only this time we notice them in Paris because (quipped composer Virgil Thomson) "I prefer to starve where the food is good."

Here's the point: Every twenty years or so, Americans are surprised to encounter a new rising generation. They are struck by some publicized event or situation in which youth seem to behave very differently than the youth who came just before. This typically happens when the oldest members of the new generation are in their late twenties or early thirties.

The average periodicity of these events is significant. At 21.5 years, it is very close to the average recent length of a phase of life—and of a

CHART 3-3

American Generations Coming of Age

GENERATION COMING OF AGE	YEAR WHEN GENERATION WAS FIRST NOTICED
Awakener	1734: Edwards's Northampton Revival
Liberty	1755: Washington at Battle of the Monongahela
Republican	1776: Jefferson's Declaration of Independence
Compromiser	1804: Lewis and Clark Expedition
Transcendental	1831: Turner's Rebellion & Garrison's *Liberator*
Gilded	1849: California Gold Rush
Progressive	1876: Edison & Westinghouse star at Centennial Expo
Missionary	1896: William Jennings Bryan's populist crusade
Lost	1918: Doughboys and literati in Paris
G.I.	1935: CCC & WPA youth teams
Silent	1951: Korean War-era young adults dubbed "Silent"
Boom	1967: Hippies celebrate Summer of Love
Generation X	1991: Publication of Coupland's sardonic *Generation X*
Millennial	2013: *Time* cover features recession-era "Millennial" youth

generation. Altogether, they reflect the rhythm of the most memorable generational "surprises" that America has encountered since the early eighteenth century. What happens between each of these twenty-two-year surprises? New cohorts are born and fill the child phase of life—and each older generation moves up a notch into a later phase of life. If we count forward another twenty-two years from the most recent surprise, Millennials in 2013, we can anticipate that the next surprise, for the rising Homeland Generation, will occur in the mid-2030s. We will have much to say about Homelanders—including why we date them differently from "Generation Z"—in subsequent chapters.

This list may point to mere events, but if you reflect closely on the events themselves, you will find that each gives expression to the youthful persona of a distinct generation—a generation with its own location in history, its own worldview, and its own sense of "essential destiny."

If you belong to America, you belong to an American generation. The same is probably true of most of your ancestors and heirs. All of history is nothing more than a sequence of collective biographies like yours and theirs.

The sequence of Anglo-American generations shown in Chart 3-4 is corroborated by historians who have written about American generations over the last century. Most have identified a similar sequence of generations situated at roughly the same dates.

How long are the generations shown here? The entire panorama divides 570 birth years into twenty-four generations, for a total average length of twenty-four years. For the fourteen generations born before and during the American Revolution, the average length was twenty-five years. Ever since, the average has shortened to twenty-one years—matching the recent duration of a phase of life.

The generational birth years also coincide with the saecular rhythm of alternating Crises and Awakenings. When you compare dates, you will find that the first birth year of each generation usually lies just a few years *before* the opening or closing year of a Crisis or Awakening. The leading edge of every generation thus emerges from infancy and becomes aware of the world just as society is entering one of these eras. Likewise, a generation's leading edge comes of age just before the next mood shift.

CHART 3-4

24 Anglo-American Generations

GENERATION	Birth Years	Famous Member (Man)	Famous Member (Woman)	Era in Which Members Came of Age	Archetype
Arthurian	1433–1460	King Henry VII	Elizabeth Woodville	War of the Roses Crisis	Hero
Humanist	1461–1482	Thomas More	Elizabeth of York	—	Artist
Reformation	1483–1511	William Tyndale	Anne Boleyn	Reformation Awakening	Prophet
Reprisal	1512–1540	Francis Drake	Queen Elizabeth I	—	Nomad
Elizabethan	1541–1565	William Shakespeare	Mary Herbert	Armada Crisis	Hero
Parliamentary	1566–1587	William Laud	Anne of Denmark	—	Artist
Puritan	1588–1617	John Winthrop	Anne Hutchinson	Puritan Awakening	Prophet
Cavalier	1618–1647	Nathaniel Bacon	Martha Corey	—	Nomad
Glorious	1648–1673	"King" Carter	Hannah Dustin	Glorious Revolution Crisis	Hero
Enlightenment	1674–1700	Cadwallader Colden	Mary Musgrove	—	Artist
Awakening	1701–1723	Jonathan Edwards	Eliza Lucas Pinckney	Great Awakening	Prophet
Liberty	1724–1741	George Washington	Mercy Warren	—	Nomad
Republican	1742–1766	Thomas Jefferson	"Molly Pitcher"	American Revolution Crisis	Hero
Compromise	1767–1791	Andrew Jackson	Dolley Madison	—	Artist
Transcendental	1792–1821	Abraham Lincoln	Elizabeth Cady Stanton	Transcendental Awakening	Prophet
Gilded	1822–1842	Ulysses Grant	Louisa May Alcott	Civil War Crisis	Nomad
Progressive	1843–1859	Woodrow Wilson	Mary Cassatt	—	Hero
					Artist
Missionary	1860–1882	Franklin Roosevelt	Emma Goldman	Third Great Awakening	Prophet
Lost	1883–1900	Harry Truman	Dorothy Parker	—	Nomad
G.I.	1901–1924	John Kennedy	Katharine Hepburn	Depression–WWII Crisis	Hero
Silent	1925–1942	Joe Biden	Sandra Day O'Connor	—	Artist
Boom	1943–1960	Newt Gingrich	Hillary Clinton	Consciousness Revolution	Prophet
Generation X	1961–1981	Jeff Bezos	Kamala Harris	—	Nomad
Millennial	1982–2005?	Mark Zuckerberg	Taylor Swift	Millennial Crisis	Hero
Homeland	2006?–?	Jacob Tremblay	Gianna Bryant	—	Artist

Finally, we notice the recurring pattern within each saeculum. The first generation comes of age with an Awakening, while the second has an Awakening childhood; the third comes of age with a Crisis, while the fourth has a Crisis childhood. Each of these four locations in history is associated with a generational archetype: *Prophet, Nomad, Hero,* and *Artist.* Throughout Anglo-American history, with only one exception (the U.S. Civil War, when the Hero was skipped), these archetypes have always followed one another in the same order.

Due to this recurring pattern, America has always had the same *generational constellation* during every Crisis or Awakening—that is, the same archetypal lineup entering the four phases of life.

But what *are* the archetypes that are so predictably created by their location in history? And why do they lie so near the heart of our personal interaction with history? Answering these questions means visiting the ancient doctrine of quaternal temperaments—and the great myths that arose alongside them.

ARCHETYPES AND MYTH

Most ancient cultures not only divided up time into four parts, giving rise to four *seasons,* but so too did they divide up most other forces in nature and man. This often gave rise to four basic *elements* or *gods* or *animals* or *diseases* or *personalities.* Each item in these quaternities was typically linked to a corresponding season. And, like the seasons, two-apart items were deemed to be opposites—at war with each other. Health or happiness was associated with some sort of balance between all four items.

The strict ordering of these patterns, when they were first fully investigated in the early twentieth century, gave structural anthropologists something of a field day. The ancient Greeks, for example, accepted four elements (fire, water, air, and earth), each of which was associated with a basic quality (hot, wet, dry, or cold) along with a matching season, god, humor or bodily fluid, and mood. These last two quaternities—humors and moods—were powerful enough to dominate European medicine well into the modern era. They've also given us such colorful words as *sanguine, choleric, melancholic,* and *phlegmatic.*

In the 1920s, a new generation of European psychologists discovered something else. These moods corresponded closely with the new theories of personality types and "mentality" types (*Denkformen*) they were developing. Most prominent was Carl Jung, who described his own quaternity (thinking, intuition, feeling, sensation) by acknowledging his debt to ancient poet-philosophers like Heraclitus. Several other European philosophers and linguists of that era, including Erich Adickes, Eduard Spranger, and Ernst Kretschmer, joined in with their own quaternities.

In recent decades, the Jungian quaternities have inspired a growing number of four-type psychosocial theories and therapies, including the well-known Myers-Briggs "personality type indicator." Today's bookstores overflow with self-help guides explicitly invoking Jungian archetypes, often in their titles (*King, Warrior, Magician, Lover* or *Awakening the Heroes Within*). Other writers interpret history by means of personality archetypes, as in William Irwin Thompson's suggestion that modern personas can all be traced back to four tribal archetypes: headman, clown, shaman, hunter.

Though archetypes are ordinarily applied only to individual personalities, they can also be extended to generations. Like an individual, a generation is shaped by the nurture it receives in childhood and the challenges it faces coming of age. When it assumes a persona, a generation, like an individual, can choose from only a limited number of available roles, each pre-scripted (as Jung would say) by a "collective unconscious." Hippocrates believed that a functional person must balance all four temperaments. So too must a functional modern society, immersed in directional time, experience the sequential unfolding of all four archetypes.

The ancient Greeks' sequence of four temperaments (and their associated seasons) corresponds with the historical order in which generations enter midlife—when a generation asserts maximum power over the direction of society. The Hero enters midlife in the saecular spring, the Artist in summer (an Awakening), the Prophet in autumn, and the

CHART 3-5

Temperaments and Archetypes

CLASSICAL TEMPERAMENT	*Sanguineus* (outer-driven, optimistic)	*Cholericus* (emotionally expressive)	*Melancholia* (inner-driven, pessimistic)	*Phlegmaticus* (emotionally reserved)
Associated Deity	Prometheus	Dionysus	Apollo	Epimetheus
Associated Season	Spring	Summer	Fall	Winter
Heraclitan Quaternity	Wet	Hot	Dry	Cold
Cardinal Virtue	*Temperentia*	*Prudentia*	*Iusticia*	*Fortitudo*
Adickes World Views	Traditional	Agnostic	Dogmatic	Innovative
Spranger Life Type	Theoretical	Aesthetic	Religious	Economic
Kretschmer Temperament	Anesthetic	Hyperesthetic	Melancholic	Hypomanic
Jungian Function	Reason	Intuition	Feeling	Sensation
Myers-Briggs Personality Type	Intuitive-Thinking	Sensation-Perception	Intuitive-Feeling	Sensation-Judging
Thompson Social Function	Headman (King)	Clown (Artist)	Shaman (Priest)	Hunter (Soldier)
Moore-Gillette Male Type	King	Lover	Magician	Warrior
GENERATIONAL ARCHETYPE	*Hero*	*Artist*	*Prophet*	*Nomad*

Nomad in the winter (a Crisis). Everything matches—temperaments, archetypes, seasons of the year, and seasons of the saeculum.

Yet a full archetype needs more than a personality and a season. It needs a story. Fortunately, the ancients had plenty of these as well.

Let's start with the plotline everybody knows. At the beginning is the miraculous humble birth, the sheltered childhood, and the early evidence of superhuman powers. Then comes the rise to fame with a triumphant struggle against the forces of evil. And finally, inevitably, the overweening hubris leading to a fall through betrayal—or through heroic sacrifice—and death. Maybe you recognize this as the saga of Hercules, Orpheus, Jason and the Argonauts, Beowulf, Roland, Superman, or the boys of Iwo Jima.

Jung saw this "hero myth" as perhaps the most potent expression of his archetypes, recurring in a wide range of eras and cultures. Some hero myths, like Superman, are pure fable; others, like our memory of World War II veterans, are rooted in historical reality. Yet as time passes the details that distinguish between fable and reality tend to fade until what's left is mostly myth, the raw outline of the archetype itself.

When we group all the heroes together, we quickly realize that they fall into two basic categories. As the contrasting stories of Hercules and Orpheus suggest, heroes can be secular or spiritual; they can be oriented toward the outer world or toward the inner. "There are two types of deed," insists Joseph Campbell in *The Power of Myth*. "One is the physical deed, in which the hero performs a courageous act in battle or saves a life. The other is the spiritual deed, in which the hero enters a supernatural realm, receives sacred insights, and then comes back with the message."

The secular hero-king and the spiritual hero-prophet often appear in the same myth. Yet when they do, they are never anywhere close to the same age. Typically, they are two phases of life apart. In legends where the young hero-king starts his perilous journey, his first encounter is often with a ritual elder, holy man, crone, or what Campbell calls a "shaman"—a person who has undergone a spiritually transforming rite of passage and, entering old age, can access secret powers. Sometimes he (or *she*) can be a lethal enemy—as is Darth Vader or the Evil Queen. But more often the elder prophet protects and looks after the young hero.

Recall all the classic Western pairings of the daring young hero and the wise elder prophet: Gilgamesh and Utnapishtim; Joshua and Moses; the Argonauts and the centaur Cheiron; Aeneas and the Sybil of Cumae; King Arthur and Merlin; Parzival and Gurnemanz. Outside the West, such pairings are nearly as common. In Hindu myth, the young king Rama meets the old hermit Agastya. In Egyptian myth, Horus, son of Osiris, is taught by the all-knowing Thoth. In Navajo myth, the questing young sun gods are told powerful secrets by the cronish Spider Woman.

The reason these young hero myths are so embedded in our civilization is because they explain what happens when the secular world (the domain of kings) is being redefined beyond prior recognition—in other words, during a Crisis era.

The other type of myth, of the young prophet and the old king, is much the opposite. These legends tell of the founding not of kingdoms, but of religions. They invoke memories not of a realm threatened by anarchy or peril, but of a realm suffocating under mighty soul-dead rule. They speak to the insight (not valor) of youth and the supremacy (not wisdom) of elders.

When we encounter sacred myths of young prophets (Abraham in Ur, Moses in Egypt, Jesus before the Roman magistrate), the image of the pivotal person roughly forty years older is typically one of expansive wealth and rationalism, resplendent in power but bereft of values (Hammurabi, the Pharaoh, Pontius Pilate). While the hero myth ends in the palatial city, the prophet myth *starts* there. In the Buddhist myth, young Siddhartha escapes the sumptuous pleasure dome of his royal father. In Persian myth, young Zoroaster defies the worldly *kavis* and *karpans*.

These prophet myths reveal what Jung called the "shadow"—the suppressed antithesis—of the aging hero archetype. The hero is seen not through his own eyes, but through the fresh vision of the young prophet. The recurring tone of these myths is one of stress and hostility across the generations. By teaching lessons about the conscience (or judgmentalism) of youth and about the power (or corruption) of the old, these young prophet myths speak of Awakening eras.

Myths evoking the Nomad and Artist are less grand and more personal, mainly because they happen at a less critical phase of life—childhood or entering midlife. Compared to the Hero and Prophet myths, these tales are more about human relationships than the rise and fall of dynasties or religions. This may explain why the ancients took less interest in them. Many were not written down until recent centuries, when they were often framed as fables or fairy tales for children.

Even so, these archetypes also embody "shadow" life cycles that mirror each other in reverse. Nomads start out as abandoned and left-alone children who later, as adults, strive to slow down, simplify, and brace their social environment. Artists start out as sheltered and sensitive children who later, as adults, strive to speed up, complicate, and adorn their social environment.

One story line features a Cinderella-like hated child, who must rely on wits and pluck first to survive, then to compete and succeed. These stories include "Aladdin," "Hansel and Gretel," "Pinocchio," and "Jack and the Beanstalk." The protagonists' prospects are binary: They either get destroyed or they get rich. Parental figures are typically ineffectual, needy, missing, or malevolent. This is, from the child's perspective, an Awakening era. When a story shows the Nomad in midlife, it tells of an aging adventurer, savvy, (still) going it alone, yet now up against big challenges. Think of classic adventure stories about the rootless ronin or mercenary—Han Solo in *Star Wars*, for example.

The opposing child myth is that of the sensitive, dutiful child growing up in a well-sheltered world. They appear in "The Little Dutch Boy," with the boy doing his small part to save the mighty dike, or in anthropomorphic tales of sweetly vulnerable creatures (Bambi, Peter Cottontail, Winnie the Pooh). Relations across generations are harmonious. Looking through a child's prism, we can recognize the possibility (Christopher Robin), if not the fact (the Little Dutch Boy), that the adult world is in Crisis. When a story shows the Artist in midlife, it features wellintentioned adults (still) trying to please others, yet now feeling trapped by social expectations. Flip the Cinderella myth around and consider, from the adult's perspective, the kindly fairy godmother or the distracted father.

In these four archetypal myths, we recognize two sets of opposing temperaments, as well as two sets of inverted life cycles. This same archetypal ordering arises repeatedly in different eras and cultures. Why? A culture will not elevate an event (or a story) into myth unless it illustrates enduring human tendencies.

This sequence also explains the oft-noted similarities between very old and very young generations, whose archetypal location lies a full cycle apart. If a generation's shadow is *two* phases of life older (or younger), then a generation's matching archetype is *four* phases of life older (or younger). The affinity between grandparent and grandchild is universal folk wisdom—as is the tension between parent and child.

Lewis Mumford sums up the pattern nicely: "The commonest axiom of history is that every generation revolts against its fathers and makes friends with its grandfathers."

What these archetypal myths illustrate is this: Your generation isn't like the generation that shaped you, but it has much in common with *the generation that shaped* the generation that shaped you. Or, put another way: Archetypes do not create archetypes like themselves; instead, they create the shadows of archetypes like themselves.

ARCHETYPES AND HISTORY

These myths suggest that for each archetype, an opposing archetype becomes a logical necessity. Each archetype emerges early in life in response to its shadow. And this requires that each generation exert a dominant formative influence on people who are *two phases of life younger*—that is, on the *second* younger generation.

This critical cross-cycle relationship it just what we see in most societies. It arises because a new child generation gathers its first impressions of the world just as a new midlife generation gains control of the institutions that surround a child. Even though a child's biological parents will be distributed about equally over the two prior social generations (assuming these average twenty to twenty-five years in length), the older parental group has the dominant role.

Boomers were parented by both G.I.s and Silent, but the G.I.s exerted greater power over fifties-era schools, curriculum, and media. Xers were parented by both Silent and Boomers, but starting in the 1970s, the Silent Jim Hensons, Robert Reeds, and Bill Cosbys set the tone for child Gen-Xers. Likewise for later generations. In the 1990s, Boomers like education secretary Bill Bennett, Hillary Clinton, and Steven Spielberg set the tone for child Millennials. And today midlife Gen-Xers are now orchestrating the rollout of cloying, family-friendly video programming to child Homelanders.

Move up one phase-of-life notch, and this pattern repeats. When a child generation comes of age, it does so just as that older generation, on the cusp of elderhood, is gaining political control of the young adult's world. A younger generation reaches military age just as its cross-cycle shadow reaches its maximum power to declare war.

In American history, a generation's dominance in national leadership typically peaks around the time its first cohorts reach age sixty-five—just as foot soldiers are on average about forty-two years (or two phases of life) younger. The G.I.s fought in (Missionary-declared) World War II, the Silent in the (Lost-declared) Korean War, Boomers in the (G.I.-declared) Vietnam War, Xers in (Silent-declared) Desert Storm, and Millennials in the (Boomer-declared) War on Terror.

This cross-cycle relationship has been true throughout American history. Benjamin Franklin's (Prophet) Awakening Generation set the tone for Jefferson's (Hero) Republicans, who in turn did so for Lincoln's (Prophet) Transcendentals. In between, Washington's (Nomad) Liberty Generation set the tone for Daniel Webster's (Artist) Compromisers, who afterward did so for Grant's (Nomad) Gilded.

The reaction of each archetype to its shadow can be supportive or antagonistic. Like Luke Skywalker's dual relationship with his father, it is usually some of both. As we have seen, each archetype, as it grows older and assumes power, leaves little room for youth to compete with its own strength. It also recognizes that society doesn't really need more of its own strength. Most parents thus enter midlife raising a new generation *whose collective persona they hope will complement, not mirror, their own.* Later on, however, the results of that nurture usually come as a surprise—and often not as a welcome surprise.

The G.I. pediatrician Benjamin Spock declared just after World War II that "we need idealistic children," and his peers raised Boomers accordingly—though many of his peers later voiced displeasure over the self-righteous product.

Silent Generation author Judy Blume wrote at the height of the Consciousness Revolution that "I hate the idea that you should always protect children," and her peers raised Xer children accordingly—though many of her peers later voiced anguish over the hardened product.

President Bill Clinton advocated school uniforms across America in his State of the Union message in 1996 in order to teach Millennial children "good values and good citizenship"—though many of his peers have since voiced dismay over the pro-social product.

A key consequence of these cross-cycle shadow relationships is a recurring pattern of *overprotection* and *underprotection* of children. During a Crisis, Nomad-led families overprotect Artist children; during an Awakening, Artist-led families underprotect Nomad children. Following a Crisis, Hero-led families expand the freedoms of Prophet children; following an Awakening, Prophet-led families curtail the freedoms of Hero children.

These powerful cross-cycle phenomena explain why, when myths depict multiple archetypes, they always depict them in one fixed order—the only order that is possible in the seasons of time: Hero to Artist to Prophet to Nomad. (See Chart 3-6, below.)

Now return to our earlier generational overview of modern American history. Give each generation an archetype label and an adjective describing how people in its age brackets were generally regarded by others at the time.

In Chart 3-7, we recognize the familiar life cycle personas of today's generations. As time advances, each generation ages—so each life story

CHART 3-6

Seasons of Life and Time

ERA	Year 0–20	Year 21–41 (CRISIS)	Year 42–62	Year 63–83 (AWAKENING)	Year 84–
Entering **ELDERHOOD** Age 63–83	Artist	Prophet	Nomad	Hero	Artist
Entering **MIDLIFE** Age 42–62	Prophet	Nomad	Hero	Artist	Prophet
Entering **RISING ADULTHOOD** Age 21–41	Nomad	Hero	Artist	Prophet	Nomad
Entering **YOUTH** Age 0–20	Hero	Artist	Prophet	Nomad	Hero

CHART 3-7

Recent Generations and Their Archetypes

ERA	1908–1929	1929–1946 (CRISIS)	1946–1964	1964–1984 (AWAKENING)	1984–2008
KEY EVENTS	Four Freedoms World War I Prohibition Scopes Trial	Crash of '29 New Deal Pearl Harbor D-Day	Levittown McCarthyism "Affluent Society" Little Rock	Woodstock Kent State Watergate Tax Revolt	Perestroika Culture Wars Dotcom Bubble 9/11 Wars
Entering ELDERHOOD Age 63–83	Progressive (Artist) *empathic*	Missionary (Prophet) *visionary*	Lost (Nomad) *tough*	G.I. (Hero) *powerful*	Silent (Artist) *empathic*
Entering MIDLIFE Age 42–62	Missionary (Prophet) *moralistic*	Lost (Nomad) *pragmatic*	G.I. (Hero) *confident*	Silent (Artist) *indecisive*	Boom (Prophet) *moralistic*
Entering RISING ADULTHOOD Age 21–41	Lost (Nomad) *alienated*	G.I. (Hero) *team-playing*	Silent (Artist) *sensitive*	Boom (Prophet) *defiant*	Gen X (Nomad) *alienated*
Entering YOUTH Age 0–20	G.I. (Hero) *protected*	Silent (Artist) *suffocated*	Boom (Prophet) *indulged*	Gen X (Nomad) *abandoned*	Millennial (Hero) *protected*

tracks a diagonal. This allows neighboring generations to overlap. In a wonderful turn of phrase, the French generations theorist François Mentré likened generational succession to "tiles on a roof."

You can read these diagonals as a sequence of generational archetypes. Notice that each diagonal archetype *shadows* its two-apart neighbor and *matches* its four-apart neighbor. Move four diagonals to the right from the Missionaries and find (in youthful Boomers) the first generation since then to which the labels "student radical" and "muckraker" have been applied. Move four diagonals to the right from the Lost and find (in Gen-Xers) nineties-era media references to a "New Lost" Generation.

As each generation ages, its persona must adjust itself to a new social role as it enters each successive phase of life. A Prophet or Hero generation in its mid-twenties remains in some sense outside society and is still preparing for adult roles. That same generation in its late sixties is running society as political and community leaders and as heads of families. How each archetype behaves and is perceived by others changes dramatically over those forty-odd years. What may be fresh and promising about an emerging archetype in its youth may well seem stale and oppressive after it has fully taken over.

Consider the contrast between the young Arthur and the mature Arthur or between the young Merlin and the mature Merlin. In maturity, a generation, just like a person, sees the world differently as its life transitions from potential to actual. It must confront its own collective failures and shortcomings—often, as we have seen, by encountering its archetypal shadow in its own offspring. The tendency of each archetype to trigger its shadow was called *enantiodromia* by the ancient Greeks. It is the tendency of all natural phenomena, when pushed to their extreme, to give rise to their opposite and thus to preserve an equilibrium across the cycle.

Yet the cycle only manifests itself across generations, not within generations. The underlying archetype of each generation endures unchanged. Sociologists J. Zvi Namenwirth and Richard Bibbee observe that "value orientations do not change much during a generation's lifetime. Committed during its early stages, a generation most often carries its value commitments into the grave."

When this rhythm is filled out with the full range of historical examples, a four-type cycle of generations emerges. They are listed here beginning with the Prophet archetype—the one born in the saecular spring.

- A *Prophet* generation grows up as increasingly indulged post-Crisis children, comes of age as the defiant young crusaders during an Awakening, cultivates principle as moralistic midlifers, and ages into the detached, visionary elders presiding over the next Crisis.

- A *Nomad* generation grows up as underprotected children during an Awakening, comes of age as the alienated young adults of a post-Awakening world, mellows into pragmatic midlife leaders during a Crisis, and ages into tough post-Crisis elders.

- A *Hero* generation grows up as increasingly protected post-Awakening children, comes of age as the teamworking young achievers during a Crisis, demonstrates hubris as confident midlifers, and ages into the engaged, powerful elders presiding over the next Awakening.

- An *Artist* generation grows up as overprotected children during a Crisis, comes of age as the sensitive young adults of a post-Crisis world, breaks free as indecisive midlife leaders during an Awakening, and ages into empathic post-Awakening elders.

Has anybody noticed this four-type cycle before? Yes—many times.

Even in the ancient world, the cycle is strongly suggested by several of the most enduring narratives recounted by priests and poets. Let's consider one from the Hebrew Bible and another from Homer, each referring to mythologized Bronze Age events that (perhaps) occurred in the thirteenth or early twelfth century BCE.

The Book of Exodus is, at root, the story of four generations: first, the prophetic peers of Moses and Aaron, who defy the pharoah and inspire their people; second, the worshippers of the golden calf, "men of little faith" whom God punishes with extra trials and tribulations; third, the dutiful soldier-peers of Joshua, who wage a successful invasion of Canaan; and fourth, a nondescript inheritor generation ("Judges") who enjoy "land for which ye did not labor, and cities which ye built not" and initiate an era of fragmentation and decline.

In the *Iliad* and the *Odyssey*, similarly, the key Greek protagonists embody four generational archetypes: first, the generation of Nestor, the expedition's "wise, white-haired" advisor; second, now past prime fighting age, the generation of Agamemnon, the able and shrewd (yet also cursed) commander; third, the generation of triumphant and hubristic young warriors Odysseus, Achilles, Ajax, and Diomedes; and finally, the generation of Telemachus, who later comes of age, with the help of "Mentor," as the deferential inheritor of his father's kingdom.

Classical literature abounds with provocative bits and pieces of generational cycles. The early poets and historians typically focused on political cycles launched by Heroes, while sacred myths focused on religious cycles launched by Prophets. Polybius, who wrote at the time of Rome's rapid expansion in the second century BCE, was perhaps the only ancient author to offer an explicit *theory* of political regime change regularly triggered by generational succession. But his idea attracted few immediate followers.

The full exposition of such a theory would have to wait for modernity— or, more accurately, for the last decades of the Islamic Renaissance. Ibn Khaldun, as we have seen, spelled it all out: a detailed model of social cohesion and dissolution driven by a four-generation rhythm. And he did so in a work of such analytical realism that he has been credited as an inspiring pioneer of sociology, demography, and economics.

In the nineteenth and twentieth centuries, just as the European fascination with natural centuries and generations intensified, newer versions of the four-part generational cycle appeared. The French philosopher Émile Littré created one in 1859. The Italian historian Giuseppe Ferrari laid out another in 1874. German philologist Eduard Wechssler took his theory of personality types and applied it to generational succession in 1930. Toynbee's four-stage "Physical Generation Cycle" appeared in 1954. And Julián Marías, a student of Ortega y Gasset, took his mentor's generational theories and distilled them into a four-part theory in 1968.

In the 1950s, the eminent Harvard sociologist Talcott Parsons proposed a four-stage theory of healthy social "function," widely known as the "AGIL" theory. In the A stage, society pursues economic exploitation (focus: commerce). In the G stage, it pursues public action (focus: political power). In the I stage, it pursues social cohesion (focus: reputation). And in the L stage, it pursues values commitment (focus: moral suasion). After that, the cycle repeats. While Parsons suggested no particular time frame in which this AGIL cycle occurs, its movement clearly reflects our succession of generational archetypes (starting with the Nomad) or the succession of turnings (starting with the Third Turning).

The late historian and political philosopher Samuel Huntington proposed a recurring four-part "IvI" (Institutions versus Ideals) cycle to describe social change in America history. Huntington's periodicity matches the saeculum—and though he does not explicitly identify generations, he directly implies them: The first generation *constructs institutions*; the second *perfects those institutions* while becoming aware of their moral failings (an attitude he calls "hypocritical"); the third *propounds new ideals*; and the fourth *tests those ideals* while becoming aware of their practical failings (an attitude he calls "cynical"). More recently, Modelski complemented his seasonal "long cycle" of war and peace with a four-stage model of social change. What Modelski calls the "generational mechanism" underlying his cycle runs from *constructive* to *adaptive* to *normative* to *competitive*.

In all these theories, models, and stories, a strikingly similar pattern emerges. The labels vary, but the archetypal order (Hero to Artist to Prophet to Nomad in both of the above examples) is always identifiable—and always the same.

Whatever the historical problem, Namenwirth observes that it takes "four whole and consecutive generations to traverse the complete prob-

CHART 3-8

Four-Type Generational Cycles

	PROPHET	NOMAD	HERO	ARTIST
Old Testament	Moses (prophetic)	Golden Calf (faithless)	Joshua (heroic)	Judges (administrative)
Homer	Nestor (sagacious)	Agamemnon (accursed)	Odysseus (hubristic)	Telemachus (deferential)
Polybius	populist	anarchic	kingly	aristocratic
Ibn Khaldun	ignoring	despising	founding	admiring
Ferrari	revolutionary	reactionary	harmonizing	preparatory
Wechssler	organic (myth, circle)	personal (epic, spiral)	mechanical (science, pyramid)	mathematical (rhetoric, cone)
Toynbee	war-declaring	too old to fight	war-fighting	too young to fight
Marías	reflective	anti-custom	initiating	conformist
Parsons	moral suasion	commerce	political power	reputation
Huntington	moralizing	cynical	institutionalizing	hypocritical
Modelski	normative	competitive	constructive	adaptive

lem solving sequence." He goes on to suggest that, for us moderns, "this generational succession might therefore well delineate our wheel of time." At no other region or era has the cycle of generations propelled this "wheel of time" with more force than in modern America. So that's where we now turn.

4

SEASONS OF
AMERICAN HISTORY

It is not worthwhile to try to keep history from repeating itself, for man's character will always make the preventing of
the repetitions impossible.

—MARK TWAIN

The Renaissance—what historians Jules Michelet and Jacob Burckhardt
both called "the rediscovery of the world and of man"—marked the Western threshold into modern history. It was an age of humanist art and architecture, demonstrating that "man" was now indeed "the measure of all
things." It was an age of autocratic nation building, when "new monarchs"
strengthened and centralized their authority, crushing their weaker rivals
by means of cannons, gunships, muskets, and massed infantry. It was an
age of buoyant commercial activity, accelerating population growth, and
stunning overseas explorations that gave rise to global empires.

Yet even with the sea route to Cathay and the innumerable *palazzi
ducali*, there remained a void. Yes, man and worldly things were now
in the foreground. But what about God and sacred things? The birth of
modernity remained only half-complete. The other half did not arrive
until forty to fifty years later.

That was when modernity's alter ego appeared in the righteous fire
of the Reformation and its attendant heresies, reforms, and persecutions.
The Reformation redefined the quest for holiness—a quest that no longer
interested worldly clerics and rulers—in terms of the individual. By clearing away intermediaries between the believer, his Savior, and the Word,

the Reformation gave birth to an entirely modern definition of faith and of conscience. Where the Renaissance shattered and reassembled the medieval secular order, the Reformation did likewise with the medieval religious order. Where the Renaissance redefined historical time as worldly progress toward wealth and happiness, the Reformation redefined it as spiritual progress toward holiness and salvation. Once both had run their course, the Western view of history and the future would never be the same.

Energizing these changes were two remarkable European generations. The first, embodying the Hero archetype, was born during the middle two decades of the fifteenth century. Its best-remembered names evoke rationalism, conquest, and practical invention: rulers like Lorenzo "the Magnificent" of Florence, Ivan "the Great" of Russia, Ferdinand and Isabella of Spain; artists like Sandro Botticelli, Leonardo da Vinci, and Donato Bramante; and explorers like Christopher Columbus, Vasco da Gama, and Amerigo Vespucci. The other generation, born about forty years later, embodied the Prophet archetype. In continental Europe, its best-remembered names—Martin Luther, John Calvin, Ulrich Zwingli, William Tyndale, Emperor Charles V, Ignatius Loyola, Teresa of Ávila— resonate with fervor, self-absorption, and judgmentalism.

Modernity was thus created out of a stunning clash of generational archetypes. While the first, the Hero generation, celebrated the outer splendor of man's power over nature, its Prophet shadow, repelled by the "stinking" immorality of this arrogant show (as Luther recounted of his coming-of-age visit to Rome), glorified the inner fire of God's power over man. Propelled by this original cycle, other cycles would follow— setting in motion the rhythm of modern history and a Western fascination with generational contrasts that has lasted to this day.

THE ORIGIN OF THE AMERICAN CYCLE

While the modern generational cycle can be said to originate—at least in its Western manifestation—in Western Europe during the late 1400s, the origin of the American generational cycle can be specified with greater precision.

The place was the British Isles, home to the society that long dominated the development of English-speaking North America. The date was 1485, when the army of a daring young noble named Henry Tudor defeated and slew King Richard III near the town of Market Bosworth. This event put an end to the War of the Roses and secured for England a dynamic "new monarchy." With his victory, the first Tudor began to transform England into a nation with modern principles of executive sovereignty. Forty-nine years later, Henry's son enlisted his peers' zeal for enthusiasm and reform to challenge the Church of Rome: He evicted its vast spiritual power and confiscated its immense temporal wealth. In so doing, he secured for England a "reformed" national church with modern principles of religious legitimacy.

As with the rest of Europe, England's launch out of the Middle Ages was propelled by two history-bending generations, each the archetypal shadow of the other. The first, the Heroic *Arthurian Generation* of Henry VII and explorer John Cabot, laid the political foundations. It sought to found a new dynasty in the imagined manner of the earliest king of the Britons. The second, the Prophetic *Reformation Generation* of Henry VIII and preacher John Knox, laid the religious foundations. It sought to found a new church in the imagined manner of the earliest Christians.

Over the next two centuries, an alternating sequence of Heroes and Prophets gestated a new American civilization:

- William Shakespeare's *Elizabethan Generation* produced the Heroes who founded (circa 1600) the first permanent English settlements on the Atlantic seaboard.

- John Winthrop's *Puritan Generation* produced the Prophets who summoned (circa 1640) the first "Great Migration" to America.

- Robert ("King") Carter's *Glorious Generation* produced the Heroes who transformed (circa 1690) a chaotic colonial backwater into a stable provincial society.

- Jonathan Edwards's *Awakening Generation* produced the Prophets who declared (circa 1740) the New World's social and cultural independence from the Old.

- Thomas Jefferson's *Republican Generation* produced the Heroes who created (circa 1790) the United States of America.

To observe that the American generational cycle has its roots in England is not, of course, to ascribe the family roots of most Americans to that one small corner of the globe. To trace the family lineage of tens of millions of Americans today, you would have to tell stories that mostly originate elsewhere.

For Native Americans, such a story would start thirty millennia ago, when the first Asiatic peoples trekked the land highway across the Bering Strait and founded tribal civilizations on the tracks of receding glaciers. For Black Americans, such a story would start five centuries ago among the kingdoms of central Africa and tell tales of capture, bondage, and sale, and of deadly "middle passages" to the New World. For countless later immigrants, such stories would crisscross over the earth—from potato farms along the Shannon to rice fields along the Yangtze; from the crowded shtetls of Ukraine to the barren *landskap* of Sweden; from the braceros of Mexico to the boat people of Indochina.

Notwithstanding the ethnic diversity of today's Americans, the *historical cyclicality* of American history originated with English immigrants— those who dominated the development of the colonial civilization that would later become the United States. For more than two centuries after the founding of Jamestown and Plymouth, Native Americans remained almost entirely outside the settled boundaries of that civilization. African Americans—living side by side with colonists in substantial numbers and amounting to nearly a fifth of the population by 1776—were a greater defining influence on American society. But the vast majority lived in four Southern colonies where their influence was strictly regulated by the institution of slavery.

The remainder of America's ethnic diversity is of relatively recent origin. Among White colonists, Anglo-Saxon immigrants were long dominant. By 1700, nearly a full saeculum after the Plymouth Plantation, an estimated 93 percent of free colonists had English, Scottish, or Ulster Scot ancestors. By 1790, two saecula afterward, this figure was still around 80 percent; and of the rest, more than half consisted of German or Dutch "stock"—peoples whose history and religion had been inter-twined with those of England. As late as the 1830s, the free population of the United States was almost entirely Northern European and Prot-estant. "American" political debates were waged largely in terms of Brit-ish precedents (think: common law, bill of rights, trial by jury), and the usage of the English language had become more standard in America than in England itself.

This ethnic mix began to change with the large waves of Gilded Gen-eration immigrants in the 1840s. These and other immigrants pushed and pulled on an Anglo-American generational cycle that had already acquired historical momentum. Like new moons caught in a planetary orbit, these new immigrant waves affected the social trajectories of all parties, arriving minority and resident majority.

Though not directly linked to the origin of the cycle, the stories of African Americans and non-Anglo immigrants are closely linked to the cycle's rhythm. From the Stono Uprising of 1739 to Nat Turner's Rebel-lion of 1831, from W. E. B. Du Bois's turn-of-the-century call to resist Jim Crow violence, to the long hot summers of the 1960s, America's largest outbreaks of racial unrest have coincided with Awakenings and the rising Prophet archetype. The growing influx of new ethnicities (Catholic Ger-mans and Irish in the 1850s; Jews, Italians, and Poles in the 1910s; His-panics and Asians in the 1990s) has coincided with the rise of the Nomad archetype. The most fateful inclusions—or exclusions—of minorities in a brand-new definition of citizenship have always coincided with Crises and the rising Hero archetype.

America's very existence as a favored destination for global migrants seeking religious, political, or economic freedom has played a crucial role in the emergence of the generation as a unit of history. In most of the Old World, Britain included, meaningful membership in generations tended to be limited to elites—that is, to those who were empowered to break from tradition and redefine social roles. Yet after Jamestown and the *Mayflower*, the New World offered much more freedom to anyone who could voluntarily buy or borrow passage. Ever since, the promise of gen-erational change helps explain why America has remained such a mag-net to would-be immigrants worldwide. In a series of stages—religious toleration, national independence, suffrage for free males, emancipation of slaves, full civil rights for women and minority races—America has gradually offered more people access to its "Dream" of generational advancement.

Nowadays everyone, no matter how disadvantaged or recently arrived, can share in the periodic redefinition of social roles—and, hence, join in what keeps the generational cycle turning. Partly because of the kind of society the earliest immigrants created here, but also because of the people drawn here ever since, America offers the world's clearest example of the generational cycle at work.

ARCHETYPES IN AMERICAN HISTORY

From the Arthurian Generation through today's Homeland Generation children, there have been twenty-five generations in the Anglo-American lineage. The first six were purely English. The next four were colonial, yet still heavily influenced by English society and politics. The eleventh (Awakeners, born 1701–1723) became the first distinctively American generation—the first whose name, birth years, and persona diverge significantly from its British peers. The Awakeners were also the first generation to be composed mostly of native-born Americans and— late in life—the first to know the U.S. nation and flag. Thus, although today's Homeland children are the twenty-fifth in our full lineage of post-medieval generations, they are fifteenth in the *American* line.

In the last chapter, we discussed how history shaped these generations. Now let's revisit these generations to explore how they have shaped American history. Recall that every generation belonging to the same archetype encounters a similar turning during the same phase of life. The only exception arose during the Civil War Saeculum, which produced no Hero archetype. During this anomaly, which we examine in Chapter 5, the Gilded Generation assumed a hybrid collective persona, starting out young as a Nomad archetype and transitioning (imperfectly) into a Hero archetype in midlife and elderhood.

Now, let's revisit these generations to explore how they have shaped

American history. To get a better grasp on the connection between archetypes and history, let's draw up a roster of prominent people who share each archetype and reflect on their common life-cycle narrative.

We remember **Prophets** best for their coming-of-age passion (the crusading pitch of Jonathan Edwards, Elizabeth Cady Stanton, William Jennings Bryan) and for their principled stewardship as elders (the sober pitch of Samuel Langdon addressing the troops at Bunker Hill, President Lincoln addressing the Union at Gettysburg, or FDR addressing the nation in his "fireside chats"). Indulged as children, they become protective as parents. Their principal endowments are in the domain of *vision*, *values*, and *religion*. Their best-known leaders include: John Winthrop and Sir William Berkeley; Samuel Adams and Benjamin Franklin; James Polk and Abraham Lincoln; Herbert Hoover and Franklin Roosevelt. These are principled moralists, summoners of human sacrifice, wagers of righteous wars. Early in life, few saw combat in uniform; late in life, most came to be revered more for their inspiring words than for their great deeds.

We remember **Nomads** best for their rising-adult years of hell-raising (Paxton Boys, Missouri Raiders, rumrunners) and for their midlife years of hands-on, get-it-done leadership (think of Daniel Morgan, Stonewall Jackson, George Patton). Underprotected as children, they become overprotective parents. Their principal endowments are in the domain of *liberty*, *survival*, and *honor*. Their best-known leaders include: Nathaniel Bacon and Benjamin Church; George Washington and John Adams; Ulysses Grant and Grover Cleveland; Harry Truman and Dwight Eisenhower. These are cunning, hard-to-fool realists—taciturn warriors who preferred to meet problems and adversaries one-on-one. They include the only two presidents who had earlier hanged a man (Washington by orders, and Cleveland personally), one governor who hanged witches (William Stoughton), and several leaders who had earlier led troops in do-or-die wars. Washington, Grant, and Eisenhower became of course the only two-term U.S. presidents to be elected on the basis of their military renown.

We remember **Heroes** best for their collective coming-of-age triumphs (Glorious Revolution, Yorktown, D-Day) and for their worldly achievements as elders (the Peace of Utrecht and colonial slave codes, the Louisiana Purchase and steamboats, the Apollo moon landings and interstate highways). Protected as children, they become indulgent as parents. Their principal endowments are in the domain of *community*, *affluence*, and *technology*. Their best-known leaders include: colonial governors Gurdon Saltonstall and Pieter Schuyler; Thomas Jefferson and James Madison; Alexander Hamilton and John Marshall; John Kennedy and Ronald Reagan. These are optimistic and rational institution builders. They were aggressive advocates of public works and material progress in midlife, and they maintained a reputation for civic energy and competence deep into old age.

We remember **Artists** best for their quiet years of rising adulthood (log-cabin settlers of 1800, prairie farmers of 1880, new suburbanites of 1960) and their midlife years of flexible, consensus-building leadership (think of Whig "compromises," Progressive "good government," post-Watergate "procedural democracy"). Overprotected as children, they become underprotective parents. Their principal endowments are in the domain of *pluralism*, *expertise*, and *due process*. Their best-known leaders include: colonial governors William Shirley and Cadwallader Colden; John Quincy Adams and Andrew Jackson; Theodore Roosevelt and Woodrow Wilson; John McCain and Joe Biden. These are champions of fairness, inclusion, openness, and a level playing field. They are renowned for their political deal-making skills—and are remembered less for overhauling the system than for trying tirelessly to improve whatever they inherited.

These four archetypes have lent balance and self-correction to the continuing story of America. If our ancestral legacy had much more or less of any of the four, we would today be poorer for it.

While each generational archetype is present in every decade, the effect of any generation on what happens during a given year or decade is critically dependent on its phase of life. The type entering elderhood will be dominant. The type entering midlife will be rising in influence. The type coming of age into young adulthood will be regarded, not always positively, as an early indicator of society's long-term direction. And the type moving beyond elderhood (and also entering childhood) will be

CHART 4-1

Archetypes in History

ARCHETYPE	HERO	ARTIST	PROPHET	NOMAD
Generations	Arthurian Elizabethan Glorious Republican — G.I. Millennial	Humanist Parliamentary Enlightenment Compromise Progressive Silent Homelander	Reformation Puritan Awakening Transcendental Missionary Boom	Reprisal Cavalier Liberty Gilded Lost Gen X
Reputation as Child	good	placid	spirited	bad
Coming-of-Age	empowering	unfulfilling	sanctifying	alienating
Primary Focus Coming-of-Age	outer world	inter-dependency	inner world	self-sufficiency
Young Adulthood	building	improving	reflecting	competing
Transition in Midlife	achieving to confident	conformist to experimental	detached to judgmental	risk-taking to exhausted
Leadership Style Entering Elderhood	collegial, expansive	pluralistic, indecisive	principled, judgmental	solitary, pragmatic
Reputation as Elder	powerful	sensitive	visionary	tough
Treatment as Elder	rewarded	liked	respected	abandoned
How It Is Nurtured	tightening	overprotective	relaxing	underprotective
How It Nurtures	relaxing	underprotective	tightening	overprotective
Positive Reputation	rational, selfless, competent	expert, open-minded, caring	principled, resolute, creative	perceptive, practical, effective
Negative Reputation	unreflective, duteous, hubristic	conformist, complicating, indecisive	narcissistic, willful, unyielding	desperate, uncultured, reckless
Endowments	community, affluence, technology	arts & letters, expertise, due process	values, vision, religion	survival, honor, liberty

waning in influence: Departing elders will be regarded, often with regret, as an early indicator of what society is losing and will miss.

The beliefs and behavior of each generation considered separately are therefore only part of the picture. What's historically more important is what happens to society as all these generations together age in place (to return to François Mentré's simile) like "tiles on a roof"—overlapping in time, corrective in purpose, complementary in effect. As generations age, they together form new archetypal *constellations* that alter every aspect of society, from government and the economy to culture and family life.

TURNINGS IN AMERICAN HISTORY

A *turning* is an era with a characteristic social mood, each era reflecting a new shift in how people feel about themselves and behave toward each other. It arises from the aging of the generational constellation. As we have seen, society enters a turning once every twenty years or so, when all living generations begin to enter their next phases of life. Like archetypes and constellations, turnings come four to a saeculum, and always in the same order.

Like the four seasons of nature, the four turnings of history are equally necessary. Awakenings and Crises are the saecular solstices; Highs and Unravelings are the saecular equinoxes.

When a society moves into an Awakening or Crisis, the new mood announces itself as an unexpected change in social direction. An Awakening begins when events trigger an upheaval in cultural life, a Crisis when events trigger an upheaval in civic life. An Unraveling or High announces itself as a consolidation of the new direction. An Unraveling begins with the perception that the Awakening has been resolved, leaving a new cultural mindset firmly in place. A High begins when society perceives that the Crisis has been resolved, leaving a new civic regime firmly in place.

The gateway to a new turning can be obvious and dramatic (like the 1929 stock market crash) or subtle and gradual (like 1984's "Morning in America"). It usually occurs two to five years after a new generation of

CHART 4-2

Turnings in the Anglo-American Saeculum

	FIRST TURNING (High)	SECOND TURNING (Awakening)	THIRD TURNING (Unraveling)	FOURTH TURNING (Crisis)
GENERATION ENTERING				
Elderhood	*Nomad*	*Hero*	*Artist*	*Prophet*
Midlife	*Hero*	*Artist*	*Prophet*	*Nomad*
Young Adulthood	*Artist*	*Prophet*	*Nomad*	*Hero*
Childhood	*Prophet*	*Nomad*	*Hero*	*Artist*
SAECULUM				
LATE MEDIEVAL			Retreat from France *(1435–1455)*	War of the Roses *(1455–1487)*
TUDOR	Tudor Renaissance *(1487–1525)*	Protestant Reformation *(1525–1551)*	Intolerance & Martyrdom *(1551–1569)*	Armada Crisis *(1569–1597)*
NEW WORLD	Merrie England *(1597–1621)*	Puritan Awakening *(1621–1649)*	Reaction & Restoration *(1649–1675)*	Glorious Revolution *(1675–1706)*
REVOLUTIONARY	Augustan Age of Empire *(1706–1727)*	Great Awakening *(1727–1746)*	French & Indian Wars *(1746–1773)*	American Revolution *(1773–1794)*
CIVIL WAR	Era of Good Feelings *(1794–1822)*	Transcendental Awakening *(1822–1844)*	Mexican War & Sectionalism *(1844–1860)*	Civil War *(1860–1865)*
GREAT POWER	Reconstruction & Gilded Age *(1865–1886)*	Third Great Awakening *(1886–1908)*	World War I & Prohibition *(1908–1929)*	Great Depression & World War II *(1929–1946)*
MILLENNIAL	American High *(1946–1964)*	Consciousness Revolution *(1964–1984)*	Culture Wars *(1984–2008)*	Millennial Crisis *(2008–2033?)*

children starts being born—or, equivalently, two to five years after the oldest members of older generations start to come of age, to reach mid-life, or to enter elderhood. Thereafter, throughout the turning, each new archetype is *moving into* its next phase of life. By the time they all entirely fill their new phases of life, the mood of the current turning grows stale and feels ripe for replacement with something new. And, in another two to five years, that replacement will begin.

The four turnings comprise a quaternal social cycle of growth, ful-fillment, entropy, and death (and rebirth). In a springlike High, a society fortifies and builds and converges in an era of promise. In a summerlike Awakening, it dreams and plays and experiments in an era of euphoria. In an autumnal Unraveling, it harvests and consumes and diversifies in an era of unease. In a hibernal Crisis, it focuses and struggles and sacri-fices in an era of survival. When the saeculum is in motion, therefore, no long human lifetime can go by without a society confronting its deepest worldly and spiritual needs.

Every twenty to twenty-five years (or, in common parlance, "once a generation"), society is surprised by the arrival of a new saecular season—just as it is surprised by the arrival of a new generation. It is similar to the unexpected way the beginning of summer is announced by the first oppressively humid day or the beginning of winter by the first ice storm. We keep forgetting that history, like nature, must turn.

In Chapter 2, we already looked at Second Turnings and Fourth Turnings—that is, at Awakenings and Crises. Here we summarize what happens in all four turnings so that we can track the social mood across the entire saeculum. The modern Anglo-American saeculum has thus far produced six or seven repetitions of each turning. From the record of history, we can construct the following typology.

The First Turning

A *High* brings a renaissance to community life. With the new civic order in place, people want to put the Crisis behind them and enjoy what they have collectively achieved. Any fundamental social issues left untouched by the Crisis will remain so.

The need for dutiful sacrifice has ebbed, yet society continues to demand order and consensus. The recent fear for group survival transmutes into a desire for strength, growth, and investment in the future—which in turn produces an era of broad economic prosperity, institutional trust, and political stability. The big public arguments are over means, not ends. Security is a paramount desire. Life tends toward the friendly and homogeneous; public spaces are bland yet safe. Shame as a social motivator (the feeling that I need not judge myself so long as others approve of me) reaches its zenith. Gender distinctions attain their widest point, and child-rearing becomes more indulgent. Wars are unlikely, except as unwanted echoes of the recent Crisis.

Eventually, civic life seems fully in control but devoid of any higher purpose. People worry that, as a society, they can *do* everything but no longer *feel* anything.

The post–World War II American High may rank as the all-time nadir in criminal violence and all-time apogee in national confidence. The post–Civil War surge into the industrial age was supported by Victorian family mores, symbolized by the multiple skirt bustles amid the massive turbines at the Centennial Exposition's Hall of Machines. In the early nineteenth century, geometric township grids projected a mood of ordered community that culminated in the Era of Good Feelings, the only time any U.S. president since Washington (James Monroe in 1820) was re-elected by acclamation. In the upbeat 1710s, poetic odes to flax and shipping heaped praised on "industry" and "diligence."

Many older readers recall America's circa-1963 optimism about the future: The moon could be reached and poverty eradicated, both within a decade. Walt Disney's original Tomorrowland welcomed visitors to a friendly future with moving skywalks, futuristic Muzak, and well-behaved nuclear families. During this "golden age" of space-opera science fiction, the future was all about high-tech rocket ships, intergalactic civilizations, limitless scientific progress, and peace and prosperity through social engineering—assuming, of course, nuclear war could be avoided.

The Second Turning

An *Awakening* arrives with a fiery protest against the High's moral complacency and its extreme regimentation of society and culture. The outer world now feels trivial compared to the inner world. Society begins to search for soul over science, meanings over things.

Initially, the youth-fired advocacy of the individual over the community may hardly slow the forward momentum of High-era institutions. Yet over time new ideals and agendas, often embodied in utopian experiments, steadily undermine society's trust in the established order. People stop believing that social progress requires social discipline. Citizens no longer coalesce around common goals. Euphoric enthusiasm over near-term personal transformation eclipses any caution about long-term social costs—contributing to a high tolerance for risk-prone lifestyles. Public order deteriorates, and crime and substance abuse rise. Gender distinctions narrow, and child-rearing reaches the point of minimum protection and structure. Coming-of-age youth focus their energy on reshaping values, leaving institutional leadership in the hands of the old. Wars are awkwardly fought and badly remembered afterward.

Eventually, the enthusiasm cools—leaving the old cultural regime fully discredited, comity shattered, institutions delegitimized, and politics riven by an incipient "values" divide.

Many Americans today can recall this mood on campuses and urban streets around 1970. Earlier Americans knew a similar mood in Greenwich Village around 1900, across the "burnt over" (that is, evangelized) districts along the Erie Canal around 1835, or in the Connecticut Valley nearly a century earlier. In all these eras, passionate "reformers" fought not so much to make people more secure or prosperous, but to liberate them from false idols, bad faith, immorality, and social oppression. Their goal was to overthrow the "technocracy" during the Consciousness Revolution, to smash the "conspiracy of trusts" during the Progressive era, or to destroy the "monster Masons" and the "monster Bank" during the age of Andrew Jackson.

Recall America's conception of the future during the last Awakening (1964–1984). Early in the era, with the memorable TV show *Star*

Trek, it hadn't evolved much beyond Tomorrowland. Then it started moving—to *2001: A Space Odyssey*, *A Clockwork Orange*, *Sleeper*, *Star Wars*, *Close Encounters of the Third Kind*, and *E.T.* These were mythic or supernatural futures in which individual consciousness triumphs over science, rationalism, state authority, and middle-class morality.

The Third Turning

An *Unraveling* begins with a society-wide embrace of the liberating cultural forces set loose by the Awakening. With the new moral agenda in place, people feel content in their newfound personal freedom. They settle on an ethos of pragmatism, self-reliance, and laissez-faire.

While individual satisfaction remains high, public trust ebbs under the assault of a fragmenting culture, market turbulence, weakening civic habits, and harsh debates over values. Me-first lifestyles thrive in public spaces that are perceived as more fun but less safe. Guilt as a social motivator (the feeling that others may not judge me so long as I approve of myself) reaches its zenith. Gender-role differences wane to their narrowest, families stabilize, and new protections are provided for children. As moral debates grow acrimonious, the big public arguments are over ends, not means. Decisive public action becomes nearly impossible, and community problems are deferred. Wars are fought with righteous fervor but without consensus or follow-through.

Eventually, cynical alienation hardens into a brooding pessimism. People can now *feel*, but collectively can no longer *do*.

The mood of the recent Culture Wars era, starting with Reagan and ending with G. W. Bush, seemed new to Americans at the time, but was not new to history. After World War I, America argued about temperance, women's suffrage, and fundamentalism amid a floodtide of crime, alcohol, immigration, political corruption, and circus trials. The 1850s likewise simmered with moral indignation, shortening tempers, and multiplying "mavericks." It was a decade, says historian David Donald, in which "the authority of all government in America was at a low point." Entering the 1760s, the colonies felt rejuvenated in spirit but reeled from violence, insurrections, and paranoia over official corruption.

Recall America's view of the future around the turn of the millennium: Think-tank luminaries pondered a future of unlimited personal choice in a world in which political and social authority—and with the World Wide Web, possibly materiality itself—had atrophied into irrelevance. People either celebrated all their new options or gathered their bug-out survivor gear. The future teemed with images of *Mad Max* anarchy, *Blade Runner* social collapse, *Terminator* punishments, *Matrix* conspiracies, and endless zombie apocalypses.

The Fourth Turning

A *Crisis* arises in response to sudden threats that previously would have been ignored or deferred, but which are now perceived as dire. Clear and present dangers boil off the clutter and complexity of life, leaving behind one simple imperative: The national community must prevail.

Initially, the new mood of urgency hardly affects the prevailing distrust and public paralysis of Unraveling-era society. Yet over time people come to support new efforts to wield public authority, whose eventual successes soon justify more of the same. Leaders govern, emergencies are declared, and laws and customs that resisted change for decades are swiftly scrapped. To each citizen more benefits are granted, and from each more sacrifices are expected. A preoccupation with national peril causes spiritual curiosity to decline. As the new civic order becomes more demanding, private risk-taking abates and crime and substance abuse decline. Families strengthen, gender distinctions widen, and child-rearing reaches a smothering degree of protection. The young focus their energy on worldly achievements, leaving values in the hands of the old. Wars are fought with determination and for maximum result.

By the end of the Fourth Turning, the mood shifts to exhaustion, relief, and pride in what the nation has accomplished. In repeated surveys taken since 1948, American historians nearly always rank the three leaders in charge during the climax of Fourth Turnings—Lincoln, FDR, and Washington (usually in that order)—as the three "most effective" presidents in U.S. history. Buoyed by a new-born faith in the group and in authority, leaders plan, people hope, and society looks forward to peace and security.

Only the Silent and G.I. Generations—less than 4 percent of today's Americans—have any personal recollection of the Great Depression and World War II. But the mood of this era has periodically recurred at every great gate of America's history, from the Civil War and the Revolution back into colonial and British history.

During its last Crisis, America's conception of the future shifted to visions of stronger community—enhanced by ideology, authority, and technology. While these powerful new worlds often had a dystopian dark side (*Brave New World, Animal Farm, 1984*), they also teemed with superheroes who defended the public from dire threats (Buck Rogers, Flash Gordon, Superman, Captain America, and Wonder Woman). Since the beginning of the Millennial Crisis, Americans have come full circle. Today they are again encountering powerful yet oppressive communities portrayed in novels and movies like *The Hunger Games, Elysium*, and *The Circle* or in award-winning TV series like *The Handmaid's Tale* and *Black Mirror*. Alienated anti-heroes have been replaced by a pantheon of Marvel- and DC-curated save-the-world superheroes—whose recent domination of pop fantasy has no parallel since the late 1930s.

Notice how each turning, like each generation, is balanced by an opposing archetype at the other end of the saeculum: Solstice balances solstice, and equinox balances equinox.

During an Awakening, individuals detach themselves from their community and turn society inward toward diverse and subjective goals. During a Crisis, individuals reattach themselves to their community and turn society outward toward a single and objective goal. During a High, obliging individuals serve a purposeful society, and even bad people get harnessed to socially constructive tasks. During an Unraveling, an obliging society serves purposeful individuals, and even good people find it hard to cooperate or lead.

Each turning made its own contribution to history. Each offered its own solutions—which, in time, created new problems and anxieties. Thus have the four turnings kept the great wheel of time in motion, periodically infusing civilization with new vitality, propelling the human adventure forward.

As we survey all of the mood shifts that characterize each of the four seasons, we may be prompted to ask: What would history be like if the saeculum did not exist?

In chaotic time, history would bear no pattern. Society would zigzag randomly. At any moment, it could accelerate, stop, reverse course, or come to an end. The mood of any one decade could follow the mood of

CHART 4-3

Four Turnings, by Social Mood

TURNING	FIRST (High)	SECOND (Awakening)	THIRD (Unraveling)	FOURTH (Crisis)
Families	strong	weakening	weak	strengthening
Child Nurture	loosening	underprotective	tightening	overprotective
Gap Between Gender Roles	maximum	narrowing	minimum	widening
Ideals	settled	discovered	debated	championed
Institutions	reinforced	attacked	eroded	founded
Culture	innocent	passionate	cynical	practical
Social Structure	unified	splintering	diversified	gravitating
Worldview	simple	complicating	complex	simplifying
Social Priority	maximum community	rising individualism	maximum individualism	rising community
Social Motivator	shame	conscience	guilt	stigma
Sense of Greatest Need	do what works	fix inner world	do what feels right	fix outer world
Vision of Future	brightening	euphoric	darkening	urgent
Supply of Social Order	rising	high	falling	low
Demand for Social Order	high	falling	low	rising
Wars	restorative	controversial	inconclusive	total

any other. Imagine, for example, the 1950s following the 1970s; or the 1940s following the 1960s. Crises or Awakenings might follow each other with no breathing space in between.

In linear time, history might bear a pattern, but it could only be a long-term and unidirectional trend. Each twenty-year segment would produce more (or less) of everything produced by the prior segment. If we drew a line from the 1920s through the American High, we might extrapolate a future of ever-growing political and social regimentation. If we drew a line from the American High through the 1990s, we might extrapolate the opposite: centrifugal forces fated to pull society to pieces. There would be no apogee, no leveling, no reversal.

In cyclical time, society always evolves in a correctional direction. Usually, the circle is a spiral of progress; sometimes, it is a spiral of decline. Always, people strive to mend the errors of the past, to correct the excesses of the present, to seek a future that provides whatever they believe to be most in need. Thus can a civilization endure and thrive.

PARALLEL RHYTHMS

In our first chapter, we introduced a paradox: Modernity, though predicated on the goal of eliminating natural cycles, has given rise to an ever-growing multitude of social cycles unique to modernity itself. Many of these are cycles that take decades to complete. Over the last century, a distinguished roster of historians and social scientists have joined the two Schlesingers, Sr. and Jr., in describing these cycles—what the younger Schlesinger called "patterns of alternation, of ebb and of flow, in human history."

What are these cycles *about*? They include all the intriguing trends and trend reversals that we often notice in our society from one decade to the next: in politics, war, community, crime, the economy, family, gender roles, fertility, and culture. What is the *timing* of these cycles? Very often, their duration is either a full saeculum or a half saeculum. Cycles that last a full saeculum are usually divisible into four seasonal phases. Cycles that last a half saeculum (such as the political realignment cycle or the economists' K-wave) are two-stroke cycles—meshing neatly, like a double-time beat, with the full saeculum. What *causes* these cycles? Many of these scholars aren't sure. Those who do discuss causation often, like Schlesinger, Jr., Toynbee, or Modelski, allude to generational change—even if they don't explain exactly how that works.

Perhaps the main reason these cycle theorists have failed to attract more attention is that mainstream academia evaluates each newly discovered cycle as an isolated curiosity. Most academics neither look for social cycles nor ponder the causes of those they stumble across. And so long as the experts aren't paying attention, it doesn't matter how insistently or eloquently the seasons of history may speak to them. The saeculum remains as unheard as if the only records of it were still lying in some Etruscan tomb, still etched in a language no one can decipher.

Here we summarize several of the best-known of these cycle theories. And we suggest that perhaps they are not unrelated after all. Perhaps they are all reflections of the seasons of the saeculum, modernity's Great Year, beating to the rhythm of the long human life.

Politics

The best-known cycle theory of American politics was first suggested by Arthur Schlesinger, Sr. Working off a casual remark of Henry Adams's about the pendular rhythm of politics, Schlesinger discerned a somewhat irregular oscillation between "liberal" versus "conservative" eras since the American Revolution. Later, the theory was more fully developed by his son, Arthur Schlesinger, Jr., who relabeled the eras as "public energy" versus "private interest."

The Schlesinger, Jr., cycle lines up with the saeculum as follows: The "public energy" eras overlap largely with Awakenings and Crises, the "private interest" eras with Highs and Unravelings. It is thus a two-stroke cycle. This should not be surprising: Crises and Awakenings both require a dramatic reassertion of "public energy"—the former to ensure social survival by building authority up, the latter to seek social justice by tearing authority down. No such need appears in Highs or Unravelings.

Schlesinger's match is not exact and would be closer if his cycle (about fifteen years per era) were not so rapid. But by identifying anomalous longer periods, Schlesinger kept his cycle close to the saecular rhythm through the 1980s. More recently, its rapid timetable again began to go awry. By his extrapolation, America in the 1990s was due for a major new dose of big-government activism. That didn't happen of course. Timing aside, though, Schlesinger is right about the fundamental rhythm of American politics. Authoritarian government wasn't dead; it was just hibernating, poised to return in a Crisis era, rested and refreshed.

The second-best known cycle theory of American politics is the party realignment cycle. Hatched in the early postwar era by a cluster of eminent political scientists (primarily V. O. Key, Jr., Walter Dean Burnham, and James L. Sundquist), this cycle coincides perfectly with the saeculum. Every forty years or so—always during a Crisis or Awakening—a new "realigning election" gives birth to a "new political party system." According to Burnham, these elections occurred in 1788 (Federalist-Republican), 1828 (Jacksonian Democrat), 1860 (Lincoln Republican), 1896 (McKinley Republican), 1932 (New Deal Democrat), and 1968/72/80 (Nixon-Reagan Republican). By this count, Burnham reckoned (in 1970) that "we are en route to a sixth party system." Today, indeed, many political scientists wonder if this "sixth" system may be overdue for a replacement.

Burnham emphasizes both the "remarkable regular periodicity" of this cycle and the implication that political change is discontinuous. "Four-fifths of the time," politics is in "system maintenance mode," he says, until "disruptive change" punctuates the equilibrium. Though these realignments don't coincide with his own cycle, Schlesinger conceded their regularity. "Over the last century and a quarter," he agreed, "each realignment cycle has run about forty years." What triggers these cycles? Political scientist Paul Allen Beck suggests generational causation. Children who grow up during realignments come of age shunning them, whereas children who grow up during eras of "normal" politics come of age seeking them. The result is *one* realignment every *two* phases of life.

Beck's insight points to the importance of coming-of-age Prophets and Heroes, children during eras of "normal politics," in driving political realignments during Awakening and Crises. These, we might say, are politically *dominant* generations—versus politically *recessive* Nomads and Artists. Later in life, it turns out, these dominant archetypes tend to be much more influential as national leaders. To illustrate this, consider all eighteen U.S. presidents born since 1861. They belong to six generations, three dominant (Missionary, G.I., and Boom) and three recessive (Lost, Silent, and Gen X). Thus far, fourteen presidents belong to dominant generations; only four belong to recessive generations. And these four (Truman, Eisenhower, Obama, and Biden) probably do not rank among America's most consequential.

The Schlesinger and Burnham cycles, along with the dominant-recessive cycle, both describe a two-stroke alternation, lasting half a saeculum. As such, both can be deepened by reinterpreting them within the seasonal quaternity of the full saeculum.

The "public energy" of an Awakening cannot be equated with that of a Crisis: sixties protests by "new left" radicals was hardly a reenactment of their parents' "old left" New Deal, nor was circa-1900 muckraking reminiscent of Lincoln's struggle to save the Union. One type of "public energy" weakens the authority of government; the other type strengthens it. Likewise, the "private interests" of a High cannot be equated with those of an Unraveling. In a High, private interests want to cooperate with public institutions that appear to be working; in an Unraveling, they want to flee from public institutions that appear to be failing.

The saeculum also deepens our understanding of voter behavior. Eras of rising partisan solidarity and voter turnout typically begin during a Crisis. High solidarity and turnout continue through the High, though the campaigning becomes less shrill and more mannerly.

Eras of partisan splintering and falling voter turnout, on the other hand, typically begin during an Awakening—trends which persist through the Unraveling as third parties gain support and campaigning becomes abrasive and vitriolic. The steep slide in voter participation from 1970 to 1990 resembles a similar decline between 1900 and 1920. Third parties tend to thrive in the disengaged Unraveling environment. Ross Perot's voter share in 1992 was the largest for a third party since the Bull Moose ticket in 1912, which was the largest since the Republicans in 1856—all Unraveling eras.

In an Awakening, voters seek to disconnect from civic authority they increasingly don't need and distrust. In a Crisis, by contrast, voters seek to rebuild civic authority they need and must rely on. Critical Awakening-era elections can be called *de*-aligning to the extent that they reflect a loosening of party discipline. Critical Crisis-era elections can be called *re*-aligning to the extent that they establish or reinforce one-party rule. These elections inaugurate sun-and-moon eras, according to political pollster Samuel Lubell's famous formulation, in which one energetic (and dominant) majority party behaves like the sun and the other reactive (and suppressed) minority party merely reflects the sun's light. Examples of sun parties: the Federalists in the 1790s, the Republicans in the 1860s, the Democrats in the 1930s.

America is currently well into a Crisis era, and the relevant indicators are shifting in the expected direction. Since 2016, voter participation has soared to rates not seen in over a century; national party partisanship is off the charts; and third parties are getting throttled, since (in today's polarized climate) any vote wasted on a third party raises the odds that your sworn enemy will take over the country. We will see in Chapter 7 that a political realignment, while not yet issuing in a decisive advantage to either party, may have already begun as well. And, if you're keeping count, the birth of America's *fourth* republic should coincide with the rise of America's *seventh* party system.

Foreign Affairs

We might suppose that nothing could be more random than changes in America's foreign policy. What pattern, after all, can possibly account for the global accidents of war and diplomacy? Most diplomatic historians supposed the same thing until 1952, when political scientist Frank L. Klingberg (himself a student of war scholar Quincy Wright's) discovered a "historical alternation of moods" in American foreign policy. He explained the clear difference between a mere *event* and society's *response* to that event. Whatever the provocation, he showed, America's response depends on whether the prevailing mood is ticking toward "introversion" or tocking toward "extraversion."

With each two-stroke alternation lasting about forty-seven years, Klingberg's cycle roughly matches the timing of the saeculum. In general, his "introversions" (which average twenty years) overlap with Awakenings and Crises; his "extraversions" (which average twenty-seven years) with Highs and Unravelings.

During an Awakening or Crisis, when people are absorbed with internal social change (the New Deal until Pearl Harbor; the Age of Aquarius after the Tet Offensive), America becomes an "introverting" society. During a High or Unraveling, when people can focus on external issues (either to engage in gunboat diplomacy, manifest destiny, or global coalition-building), America becomes an "extroverting" society. During the anomalous Civil War and Reconstruction eras, the Klingberg cycle deviates entirely from the normal rhythm of the saeculum.

Klingberg explains his cycle by pointing to "generational experience"—in particular to the desire of national leaders to correct for the foreign policy "failures" or "excesses" of their formative years.

In the 1920s and 1930s, for example, the midlife Lost Generation shunned any foreign policy that risked a repeat of America's senseless Wilsonian Crusade for Democracy. Yet the midlife G.I. Generation dismissed the Lost's caution. G.I.s built out an expansive postwar Pax Americana precisely in order to avoid the costly policy mistakes of the 1930s (trade wars, isolationism, appeasement). The midlife Silent were distressed by these imperial ambitions. When they surged into Congress in the early seventies, they were eager to corral the out-of-control "interventionism" of the Pentagon and CIA. The next generation, in turn, didn't think much of the Silent's restrictive Powell Doctrine. The Boomer diplomats and generals who chose to bomb Serbia in the mid-1990s and invade Afghanistan and Iraq after 9/11 were eager to erase their own memories of America's "Vietnam syndrome."

If we date the beginning of America's most recent veering back to introversion to 2005 or 2006 (when public approval of the Iraq War plummeted), we could infer from Klingberg's timetable that America may swing fully back to extraversion by the mid-2020s. As we have seen, this timing matches the expectations of global "long cycle" theorists. Even before Russia's invasion of Ukraine, recent surveys have shown that the American public is growing more interventionist.

Foreign policy often leads to war. And without question, every major war in Anglo-American history has been shaped by the turning in which it arose.

High-era wars have all been echoes of the prior Crisis—including the War of 1812 (reconfirming the American Revolution) and the Korean War (reconfirming the global post–World War II status quo). These wars tend to be standoffs. Patience is high, enthusiasm low.

Awakening-era wars have all been enmeshed in the creedal passions then gripping society—from the boozy revivalists assaulting Louisbourg in 1745 to the massive protests against the Vietnam War in the late 1960s. Most famously, the seventeenth-century English Civil Wars resulted in the judicial beheading of a king and the election of a (short-lived) "Parliament of Saints." Domestic turmoil drives military decisions, making each war controversial in its time and badly remembered afterward.

Unraveling-era wars typically end in spectacular victories and are momentarily popular—from the capture of Quebec to the capture of Ku-

CHART 4-4
Wars and Turnings*

FIRST TURNINGS	SECOND TURNINGS	THIRD TURNINGS	FOURTH TURNINGS
Queen Anne's War	*English Civil Wars*	French & Indian War	*Wars of the Roses*
War of 1812	Pequot War	Mexican War	*Anglo-Spanish War (Armada)*
Korean War	King George's War	World War I	King Philip's War
	Second Seminole War	Operation Desert Storm	Bacon's Rebellion
	Spanish-American War	Wars in Iraq/Afghanistan	King William's War
	Philippine Insurrection		Glorious Revolution
	Vietnam War		American Revolution
			American Civil War
			World War II

* After 1675, American wars only, and with estimated total deaths exceeding 1,500; before 1675 (in italics), English wars only, and with estimated military deaths exceeding 25,000.

wait. But they fail to alter the underlying social mood. Enthusiasm is high, patience low.

Crisis-era wars have all been costly in resources and decisive in results. They have all required maximum social consensus and exertion. They have also been deadly: Total casualties in these wars (as a share of the population) vastly outweigh casualties in all other wars combined. Home-front resolve is high, and the outcome contributes to a redefinition of the kingdom, nation, or empire.

One takeaway is this: During Awakenings and Crises, society is "introverting" most of the time. But when it is not—when instead society is "extroverting"—the wars tend to lie on either end of the spectrum. During Awakenings, they are wars of extreme convulsion; during Crises, they are wars of extreme efficacy.

Economy

In 1930, Stalin arrested the economist Nikolai Kondratieff and shipped him off to Siberia. His crime: daring to defy that most linear of modern ideologies—Marxism-Leninism—by suggesting that the long-term performance of market economies is cyclical. Soon after his death in the gulag, Kondratieff became a cult figure to many economic historians around the world. Today, his name is attached to a popular family of two-stroke economic "K-cycles," some traceable back to the fifteenth century and all having a periodicity of forty to fifty-five years.

According to Toynbee, Modelski, and Thompson, the K-cycle ordinarily moves in sync with the generational long cycle. K-cycle peaks occur near the ends of Highs and Unravelings, K-cycle troughs near the ends of Awakenings and Crises. This pattern implies that America today lingers in a long-wave downswing that began shortly before the 2007–2009 Great Recession and that is due to end sometime later in the 2020s.

Here again, a two-way pendulum doesn't do justice to the seasonality of the full saeculum. During a High, wage and productivity growth is typically smooth and rapid. During an Awakening, a soaring economy hits at least one spectacular bust (the mid-1970s, mid-1890s, late 1830s, mid-1730s) that is darkly interpreted as closing a golden age of postwar growth.

During an Unraveling, economic activity again accelerates, but now the growth is more leveraged, less balanced, and prone to speculative booms and busts. In the end, typically, an international financial crash triggers a spiral of debt deleveraging that helps push the nation into the Crisis era. This was certainly the case in 2008 and 1929. And the crashes of 1857, 1772, and the mid-1670s (touched off in London by King Charles II's multiple defaults) may have helped to catalyze the Crisis eras that soon followed those years. During a Crisis, the economy is rocked by some sequential combination of panic, depression, recovery, inflation, war, and mobilization. Early in a High, a new-normal economy is reborn.

In a parallel manner, the presence of public authority in the economy shifts from one turning to the next. During a High, government plays an intrusive planning and regulatory role. Witness the royal trading patents of the 1610s, the promotion of commerce and planned townships by Hamiltonians and Jeffersonians (respectively) circa 1800, the subsidizing of industrial and westward expansion by the Republicans in the 1870s, and the "military-industrial complex" of the 1950s. The rules of the game promote saving and investment, favor the young, and try to protect groups of producers (land-owning farmers, merchant companies, industrial trusts, unions).

During an Awakening, the popular consensus underlying this public role in the economy begins to disintegrate. During an Unraveling, public control recedes, while entrepreneurship, risk-taking, and the creative destruction of the market prevail. The new rules of the game encourage dissaving and debt, favor the old, and try to protect individual consumers. During a Crisis, a popular consensus around a more hands-on state role re-emerges.

Economic historians who study technological and financial innovation often see a cycle of similar timing. According to Carlotta Perez, perhaps the most respected scholar in this field, the entire innovation S-curve plays out over two consecutive K-waves. During the first wave comes acceleration: an "eruption" of new tech paradigms during the Awakening, followed by a "frenzy" of start-ups and experimentation during the Unraveling. During the second wave comes deceleration: monopoly, regulation, and "maturity" during the Crisis, followed by profitable if uncreative dominance on a vast scale during the High.

Since our most recent Awakening (in the 1960s), her obvious example is information and communications technology. Starting with the prior Awakening (in the 1880s), it was steel, electricity, autos, and mass production. Going back another saeculum (in the 1820s), it was steam engines and railways. Each long wave has generated vast progressive gains in our material standard of living. Yet time after time this wave has undulated in synchrony with a parallel rhythm of cultural, social, and political currents.

Inequality

In his bestselling 2013 book *Capital in the Twenty-First Century*, the French economist Thomas Piketty argues that modern market capitalism tends to raise inequality over time. He does concede, however, that this long-term trend was recently broken by one conspicuous exception: a forty- to fifty-year period from the 1930s to the 1970s when inequality *declined* in most of the Western world. The period is well known to economists, who refer to it as the "Great Compression."

It's not hard to identify causes of this decline in inequality. The era began with financial crashes, total wars, high taxation, punitive inflation, and financial repression, all of which were likely to strip wealth from the plutocrats. Later on, postwar governments enacted major labor, full-employment, and social welfare measures which tended to raise the incomes of the poor and working classes. In America, inequality of both income and wealth, after reaching twin peaks in 1914 and 1929, fell somewhat during the Great Depression, fell rapidly during the 1940s, and then kept falling gradually until sometime in the 1970s. Ever since, inequality has been steadily rising again. Today we sometimes refer to the Great Compression of the postwar High as the golden age of America's middle class.

Yet is this era, as Piketty suggests, an isolated exception? Stanford economic historian Walter Scheidel thinks not. Yes, Scheidel argues in *The Great Leveler* (2017), Piketty is correct that—once you strip out decades of catastrophe, war, and reconstruction—inequality almost always rises during eras of peace and uneventful prosperity. *Yet this has always been true,* he explains, not just since the advent of capitalism several centuries ago but since the rise of urban civilization itself several millennia ago.

So how, according to Scheidel, does inequality ever fall? Only during violent, traumatic, and (usually) deadly upheavals and the social reconstructions that inevitably follow them. In other words, if we look at the entire panorama of civilization since its early emergence in the fifth millennium BCE, going all the way from ancient Uruk and Jericho to modern-day Paris and Shanghai, we see one general rule at work: Inequality has been (gradually) rising most of the time and (rapidly) falling only at crisis-punctuated intervals. Scheidel's historical taxonomy of equalizers resembles the four horsemen in John's Book of Revelation: pandemic, revolution, state failure, and total war.

In the seasonal rubric of the modern saeculum, these are the Crisis and subsequent High eras. The U.S. Civil War, brief as it was, destroyed or devalued the wealth of the affluent and of course vastly reduced inequality in the South by emancipating slaves. During the twenty years following Appomattox, nationwide inequality stabilized despite the ongoing tide of immigration and industrialization. As for the American Revolution, economic historians Peter H. Lindert and Jeffrey G. Williamson conclude that the late 1770s and 1780s, while wreaking economic devastation at least on par with the Great Depression, also equalized living standards—even after growth resumed under President Jefferson. "As was true of the Civil War, World War I, and World War II," they write, "the higher-paid occupations suffered more than the lower-paid during the revolution and early nation-building."

Awakenings and Unravelings in America, on the other hand, have always been eras of rising urbanization, commercialization, litigation, international commerce, and rent-seeking. And in the late 1760s, the late 1850s, the late 1920s, and the early 2000s, such trends pushed inequality to peak or near-peak levels. Highs promote income and class equality, and Awakenings change that. Unravelings promote *in*equality, and Crises change *that.*

Thus far, during our current post-2008 Crisis era, inequality trends have been mixed. Among the affluent, the income shares of the top 1 percent or 5 percent continue to grow even larger than before, thanks largely to market-friendly Fed policies—policies that may now be changing. Among low-income households, on the other hand, expanded safety nets over the last decade, especially during the pandemic, have pushed the nation's poverty rate (after including all benefit income, as measured by the U.S. Census) to an all-time low.

Branko Milanovic, whose extensive research on inequality is as widely read among economists as Piketty's, has recently speculated that all one-way theories about the direction of inequality (always rising or always falling) are probably mistaken. Rather, he writes, "In a highly stylized way, what we expect to find when we consider inequality over time is a cyclical pattern." He goes on to explain: "Rising inequality indeed sets in motion forces, often of a destructive nature, that ultimately lead to its decrease. . . . A very high inequality eventually becomes unsustainable, but it does not go down by itself; rather, it generates processes, like wars, social strife, and revolutions, that lower it." In his own words, Milanovic is referring to the Fourth Turning.

Community

"Where were you in '62?" asks the famous poster for *American Graffiti*, the Lucas/Coppola 1973 blockbuster which millions of Americans today regard as a nostalgic farewell to a lost era of national innocence. But what is the special significance of the year 1962?

Sociologist Robert Putnam, who has written academic blockbusters of his own (most notably, *Bowling Alone*), believes he knows. According to his massive data archives, 1962 was the year when the average of his indicators on volunteering, trust in strangers, community engagement, political participation, and family togetherness—indicators stretching back to 1910—reached its all-time peak. By the mid or late 1960s, these social trust indicators were already starting to fall. In 1962, in other words, most Americans assumed the upward trend would continue; by 1973, when the movie appeared, everybody knew the trend had reversed direction.

This finding is hardly controversial among social scientists. The post-1965 decline in social trust, notes Walter Dean Burnham, is "among the largest ever recorded in opinion surveys." Where Putnam shines is in the inexhaustible variety of the indicators he tracks. They extend beyond the obvious (number of friends, time with family, membership in organizations), to the more illuminating: lawyers per capita (rising), the frequency of using the pronoun "I" instead of "we" (rising), agreeing that "most people are honest" (falling), coming to a full stop at stop signs when no one is looking (falling), staying informed about national politics (falling), and citing "money" or "self-fulfillment" as opposed to alternatives like "patriotism" as an important life value (rising).

Putnam also points out that the drivers behind these shifts have been largely generational. In other words, it's not that everyone at every age became more individualistic as we moved from the 1960s to the 1990s. Rather, it's mostly that younger, later-born cohorts started out and remained more individualistic than older, earlier-born cohorts were *at the same age*. And, as time has passed, the later-born cohorts gradually replaced the earlier-born cohorts in every age bracket. When asked, Boomers themselves tend to agree with Putnam's generational assessment. According to one 1987 survey, Boomers conceded by a margin of over two-to-one that their parents' generation did a better job in "being a concerned citizen, involved in helping others in their community." They also overwhelmingly agreed that the nation was worse off due to "less involvement in community activities."

As dramatic as the decline in social trust has been during the Awakening and Unraveling eras of the most recent saeculum, Putnam insists that its earlier rise from the late 1920s to the early 1960s (during the Crisis and High eras) was just as striking. His overall perspective is therefore cyclical. As he writes: "American history carefully examined is a story of ups and downs in civic engagement, *not just downs*—a story of collapse *and* renewal" (his italics).

Rising community, Putnam observes, was largely the work of what he calls America's "long civic generation," born roughly between 1910 and 1940—essentially, most of the G.I. and Silent Generations. Rising individualism has been largely the work first of Boomers and then of Xers, whom Putnam describes as America's "second consecutive generation of 'free agents.'"

So what are the earlier cycles of social trust and civic engagement? And which generations drove them? Putnam, hesitating to stray from his abundant twentieth-century data sources, rarely speculates on these questions. Yet he does observe that the need to build community at a time of crisis or war is probably part of the story. "The wartime Zeitgeist of national unity and patriotism that culminated in 1945 reinforced civic-mindedness," he observes, and this may have been true in earlier eras.

While the survey data for earlier eras are admittedly limited, there are telltale signs that similar earlier cycles of community building and dismantling did indeed pulse to the beat of the saeculum. According to sociologist Theda Skocpol, the rise of civic volunteerism and membership in nationwide fraternal organizations rose strongly during and just after the American Revolution and the Civil War.

It also helps to read what observers were saying and writing about America during earlier decades. The two most famous European overviews of American democracy published during the nineteenth century (Alexis de Tocqueville's *Democracy in America* and James Bryce's *The American Commonwealth*) followed the authors' tours of America in 1831 and in 1883–84, respectively. These dates were both near the cusp of a High and an Awakening. And both authors lauded America for its national optimism, its community spirit, and the absence of any important ideological conflict. In subsequent decades, however, both authors darkened their outlook—commenting in letters and essays on America's growing market-driven incivility and widening social and political divisions. One cannot imagine Tocqueville writing the same work in 1855, or Bryce writing his in 1910.

Paralleling the community cycle are the changing ideals or metaphors that Americans use to express their attitude toward society at large. In a High, people want to *belong*; in an Awakening, to *defy*; in a Unraveling, to *separate*; in a Crisis, to *gather*.

Among racial and ethnic minorities, these attitudes play a conspicuous role in shaping the dominant strategy for group advancement.

During the saeculum following Appomattox, the image of an effective Black leader progressed from Booker T. Washington (conformance) to W. E. B. Du Bois (defiance) to Marcus Garvey (separation). During the saeculum following VJ Day, cutting-edge African American organizations have retraced many of the same steps—from the Congress of Racial Equality (conformance) to the Black Panthers (defiance) to the Nation of Islam (separation).

These changes have important implications for religious, ethnic, and racial minorities. Awakenings, as we mentioned earlier, have been eras of Black protest (both before and after the end of slavery) and rising racial violence. Unravelings have been eras of separatism and anti-immigration parties and laws. Crises have been eras in which minorities are often included within a community-wide mobilization. Highs have been eras in which minorities may—or may not—be mainstreamed within a new "melting-pot" definition of community.

Each Crisis and High combination, therefore, may be described in terms of who is let in or shut out of the community's refreshed definition of equal citizenship.

During and after the Glorious Revolution, British White Protestants were let in; all others were shut out. During and after the American Revolution, other Western European White Protestants were let in. While Blacks were still shut out in the South, they rapidly gained emancipation in the North, in part due to service during the war. During and after the Civil War, Irish Catholics were let in. Blacks were emancipated everywhere—again, due in part to their wartime service—but greater civic participation in the South, robust in the 1870s and 1880s, was completely shut down during and after the 1890s.

During and after World War II, all European and many non-European "hyphenated Americans" were let in. Blacks gained entry economically during the war, mainly due to their new power to migrate out of the South and earn equal wages in federal jobs. They gained entry politically during the civil rights movement, which culminated at the very end of the American High with the Civil Rights Act of 1964. From 1940 to 1970, Black earnings, homeownership, and voting rates (relative to Whites) soared—and haven't risen much higher since then.

By Putnam's timetable, community should be changing direction right about now. And indeed, over the last decade, with America again in a Crisis era, there are signs that community indicators may again be gaining strength. Voting rates and political participation, for example, are surging as Americans flock to strengthening (if utterly partisan) party tribes. Activism at the local and state level is gaining traction, even if that is not—at least, not yet—happening at the federal level. Putnam sees hopeful signs that the Millennial Generation is volunteering at much higher rates than their parents did at the same age. He concedes, however, that "they will have their hands full if they are to make up for the impending departure of their highly civic grandparents and the long-time *incivisme* of their parents' generation."

Family and Gender

When Betty Friedan wrote *The Feminine Mystique* in 1963, at a trough in the public status of women, she observed that the history of women's rights is like a series of gathering tidal waves, each sweeping over American institutional life at discrete intervals before sweeping out again amid rips and eddies. The timing of these waves follows the saeculum. Feminism, as a popular outlook, bursts on the scene during an Awakening. During an Unraveling, the gap between acceptable gender roles shrinks to its narrowest point. The efficacy of masculine power (and feminine morality) is re-idealized during a Crisis. During a High, the gap between acceptable gender roles grows to its widest point, after which the cycle repeats.

As with turnings, so with life cycles. Prophet generations have always been top-heavy with impassioned, norm-breaking women who dare to rival male peers in public life. These have ranged from Anne Hutchinson (heretic) to Susan B. Anthony (social reformer) to Emma Goldman (anarchist) to Oprah Winfrey (inspirational celebrity). Hero generations favor a more masculine stereotype of rational leadership (a Thomas Jefferson or John Kennedy) which reasserts the public-private division of sexual labor.

Through the centuries, young Nomad women have displayed some variant of the "garçonne" look that hides gender differences, while young Artist women have flaunted the hoops and beehives that accentuate gender-role contrasts. In midlife, both archetypes have struggled to reverse course—Nomads to expand gender differences, Artists to shrink them. The unattached Lost flappers fictionalized in Samuel Hopkins Adams's novel *Flaming Youth* (published in 1923) later opted for marriage and "respectability" in the 1930s. The early-marrying Silent housewives fictionalized in *Peyton Place* (published in 1956) later opted for new careers in the 1970s, often after divorcing and switching from "Mrs." to "Ms."

Friedan implicitly had this seasonal rhythm in mind when she observed that just after World War II younger women had been steered out of public vocations and thrown "back" onto the domestic pedestal. Others have made similar observations about earlier Highs.

Seasonal shifts in gender roles are linked to shifts in the family as an institution. During a High, the family feels secure and child-rearing becomes more indulgent. Prior to the American High, the previous golden age of indulgent families was the 1870s—an era that family historian Mary Cable likens to the "Dr. Spock 1950s." During an Awakening, the fixed rules and roles of family and gender are attacked by the rising generation, and child-rearing becomes underprotective. (The terms "free love" and "open marriage" were first coined not in the 1960s, but in the utopian communes of upstate New York in the 1830s and 1840s.) During an Unraveling, the family feels endangered and child-rearing becomes more protective. Prior to the 1990s, the previous age of family pessimism was the 1920s, a decade whose shrill hysteria over "the lost family" has yet to be matched.

Today, the family is again on the ascendent as a cherished and trusted institution. An unprecedented share of today's Millennial young adults are today living in an extended family with their parents and asking them regularly for support and advice. Millennials overwhelmingly desire to start families themselves (over 70 percent say it's "extremely important" in high-school senior surveys), even if they concede they will probably do so several years later than they "ideally" would like. They are as likely as older generations to mention "family and children" as giving them "meaning in life." The prevailing style of child raising, having already become steadily more protective and time-intensive for Millennial children, is approaching suffocation for Homelander children. As for ideal gender roles within the family, youth surveys indicate that Millennials are separating them more than Xers and Boomers were at the same age.

Demography

The onset of war, plague, or famine causes birthrates to fall, and the onset of peace and prosperity causes birthrates to surge. In traditional societies, this pattern can be attributed to the iron laws of biology and the availability of natural resources (especially arable land). In modern societies, it is assisted by the rhythm of the saeculum—in particular, by the resurgent popularity of family life and the widening of gender role divisions that occur during Highs.

Over five centuries, every Fourth Turning has been marked by a fall in the birthrate relative to the prevailing trend. Thus, Artist generations are typically "baby bust" generations: This is true today of child Homelanders, who are the product of the lowest fertility rate in American history. And it was true of child Silents in the 1930s, who were similarly the product of an unprecedented birth dearth. On the other hand, every High has been marked by a relative rise in the birthrate, which means that Prophet generations are typically "baby boom" generations. During the last High, Boomers were of course the product of a striking "boom" in the birthrate. And in the nineteenth century, when birthrates generally fell decade over decade, Missionaries and Transcendentals were the product of remarkably stable birthrates.

Awakenings (when Nomads are born) and Unravelings (when Heroes are born) show a less pronounced bust-and-boom pattern. During the late 1960s and '70s, the total fertility rate plunged—giving the "baby buster" label to Generation X. Yet fertility rebounded sharply in the early 1980s with the arrival of Millennial babies-on-board—giving them the "echo boom" or "baby boomlet" label.

Immigration to America has also followed a saecular rhythm: It tends to climb in an Awakening, peak sometime during an Unraveling, and then fall during a Crisis. The climb coincides with quickening geographic mobility, rising public tolerance, pluralist-minded leaders, and loosening social controls. A large influx of low-skilled labor also helps to widen wage inequality and enrich employers during these eras. The Unraveling-era reversal is often triggered by a sudden nativist backlash (in the 1850s, 1920s, and 2000s). The subsequent fall coincides with aggressive new efforts to "protect" the nation—and by the time a Crisis hits, immigration is often regarded as both less desirable by American voters and less attractive to foreigners seeking new opportunities. The 1930s—to cite an extreme example of a Crisis decade—remains the only decade in American history in which average yearly net immigration was negative.

Across the centuries, most immigrants to America have been teens or young adults when they arrived. Thus, a Nomad archetype that comes of age during an Unraveling always becomes a relatively large immigrant generation. This was true of the Liberty (with the Scotch-Irish wave), the Gilded (Western European and Irish Catholic), the Lost (Southern and Eastern European and Chinese), and Generation X (Latin American and East Asian).

Xers, like the Lost, are likely to remain throughout their lives more immigrant at every age than Americans older or younger than themselves. In 1960, the typical immigrant was elderly: Americans aged fifty-five to seventy-four had a higher immigrant share than any younger age bracket. Those were mostly Lost. By 2010, the typical immigrant was young: Americans aged twenty-five to forty-five had the highest immigrant share. These were mostly Xers.

Following the Lost came the G.I.s, who became a generation of sharply declining immigrant share—due to the closing of America's immigration door in the early 1920s and the Great Depression of the 1930s. Following Xers came the Millennials, who likewise are becoming a generation of declining immigrant share. Since the Great Recession, the U.S. net immigration rate has fallen sharply to just over half of its per-capita rate over the two decades prior to 2008.

At the opposite extreme, an Artist archetype that grows up during a Crisis and comes of age during a High typically becomes a small immigrant generation. The Silent Generation, for example, remains to this day the *least* immigrant generation in American history. Throughout their lives, members of this great civil-rights generation have themselves always occupied an age bracket of striking ethnic homogeneity—that is, mainly White and native-born—from their split-level suburban young adulthood in the 1960s to their assisted-care elderhood in the 2020s.

It's too early to tell whether today's young Homelanders, the newest Artist arrivals, will also become a small immigrant generation. But if the net immigration rate remains low, or falls further, that future is certainly possible.

Social Disorder

Rates of crime and worries about social disorder rise during Awakenings, reach a cyclical peak during Unravelings, and then fall during Crises.

"It seems to be now become dangerous for the good people of this town to go out late at night without being sufficiently well armed," the *New York Gazette* lamented in 1749. Many echoed this complaint during later Unravelings, each of which has given birth to a mythic American image of violent crime—from the roaring forty-niner gold towns to Al Capone's gangland Chicago to the "Miami Vice" of Pablo Escobar's heyday. Each time, the crime peak has coincided with equally memorable public efforts to suppress it: The term "lynching" dates from the 1760s, "vigilante" from the 1850s, the "G-Man" from the 1920s, "three-strikes-you're-out" from the 1990s. Ultimately, the public reaction has its desired effect. Late in an Unraveling or early in a Crisis, indicators of violence and civic disorder fall—and these typically stay down through most of the following High.

Historian Randolph Roth, perhaps the leading authority on levels and trends in American criminality and codirector of the Criminal Justice Research Center at Ohio State, has identified a pattern that closely matches this saecular rhythm.

In his quantitative historical overview of murders by unrelated adults, *American Homicide* (2009), Roth points out that over the centuries the general trend in criminal violence has been downward. During the seventeenth century, for example, Americans were on average several times more murderous than at any time during the twentieth century. On top of this downward trend, however, Roth also points out huge swings up and down. The downswings generally coincide with post-Crisis decades that we would call Highs: the 1720s–30s, the 1810s–20s, the 1880s–90s, and the 1940s–50s. And the upswings generally overlap with post-Awakening decades we could call Unravelings: the 1750s–60s, the 1840s–50s, the 1910s–20s, and the 1970s–80s.

What causes these swings? When he examines them carefully in each locality, Roth observes that they seem to be inversely correlated with basic indicators of social trust. (He credits this insight, in part, to University of Maryland criminologist Gary LaFree.) When people believe their government is stable and legitimate and their social hierarchy is fair, they commit fewer murders—and vice versa. Simple patriotism turns out to be a pretty good proxy measure of social trust, which prompts Roth's best-known indicator: *the share of all new counties named after national heroes.* In decades when this share was rising, the homicide rate fell; in decades when it was falling, the homicide rate rose.

Trends in substance use and abuse typically mirror and slightly precede these crime trends. In fact, indicators of per-capita alcohol consumption follow an astoundingly regular cycle: They begin rising during a High, peak near the middle or end of the Awakening, and then begin to decline during the Unraveling amid growing public disapproval. The sharpest drop in alcohol consumption in American history occurred near the end of the Second Great Awakening, when it fell from an all-time U.S. peak in 1830 (four gallons per person per year) down to less than one-third of that level by the eve of the Civil War. The second-sharpest drop occurred between 1900 and 1910, near the end of the next Awakening, followed by a further decline during Prohibition.

During the current saeculum, per-capita alcohol consumption began rising around 1960, peaked around 1980, and fell until the early 2000s. For other mind-altering substances (including most stimulants, narcotics, and hallucinogens), the trends are similar. Remarking on this eighty-year cycle, Yale medical historian David Musto notes that "a person growing up in America in the 1890s and the 1970s would have the image of a drug-using, drug-tolerating society; a person growing up in the 1940s—and perhaps in the 2000s—would have the image of a nation that firmly rejects narcotics."

While not all abused substances follow this pattern, those that don't are typically introduced at a time when they are deemed harmless. This happened with tobacco: Cigarette smoking prevalence rose sharply among all age brackets during the Great Depression and peaked during the American High, though (on schedule) it began falling after the harms were known. The recent opioid epidemic has followed a similar pattern: It caused rising mortality from legal prescriptions among all age brackets in the late 1990s before spilling over catastrophically into illegal use and synthetic fabrication in the 2010s.

In all generations, youth is the age in which most crime is committed and most known-to-be-risky drug abuse begins. Yet some generations of youth show a much larger rise in both crime and drug abuse rates than others. In general, young Prophets pioneer the dysfunctional rise while indulgent elder Heroes look on. Young Nomads, habituated to this rise as children, later suffer a reputation as *under*-socialized. Young Heroes bring these rates down while moralizing elder Prophets threaten. Young Artists, habituated to this reversal as children, later gain a reputation as *over*-socialized.

Religion and Culture

In its orientation toward values, the saeculum regularly oscillates between a focus on inner spirit or faith (in an Awakening) and a focus on worldly uplift or works (in a Crisis). Eminent historians have long noticed this pattern in American history—as when Edmund Morgan observes: "In the 1740s America's leading intellectuals were clergymen and thought about theology; in 1790 they were statesmen and thought about politics."

Metaphorically, this is a shift from the inner to the outer. The 1930s was an outer-focused decade; its culminating expression, the 1939 New York World's Fair, was a celebration of technology on a vast scale and of humanity's power to reshape the environment. Americans were meanwhile losing interest in church sermons, and enthusiasm for missionary work plummeted among young G.I.s (very unlike their parents)—in what clergy were calling "the religious depression of the '30s." The only other period that historians often call a "religious depression" is the era alluded to by Morgan, the 1780s and 1790s. During these revolutionary years of nation-building, writes religious historian Sydney Ahlstrom, "churches reached a lower ebb of vitality . . . than at any other time in the country's religious history."

The 1970s, by contrast, was an inner-focused decade, in which New Age guru Marilyn Ferguson urged America to embark on a "Voyage to the Interior," the first step toward a "Higher Consciousness." The charismatic Jesus Movement was also thriving, signaling the new and growing appeal of "born again" religion. But enthusiasm for technology? Not so much. In the spring of 1970, on the very first Earth Day, young Boomers publicly celebrated "thinking small" by putting an automobile formally on trial, declaring it "guilty," and then pounding it to pieces with sledgehammers. Two years later, the Apollo moon launches were discontinued amid declining public interest and shifting federal budget priorities.

During an Awakening, the culture is reshaped by young Prophets' defiance of political and family authority. Once each saeculum, for example, an Awakening ushers in a dramatic surge in the number and fury of collegiate protests. This was true when Thomas Hobbes (born in the same year as John Winthrop) denounced universities as "the core of rebellion" against the English crown in the 1640s. So it has happened ever since—with memorable waves of campus unrest later in the 1740s, 1830s, 1880s, and 1960s.

Another telling indicator is the founding of countercultural utopian communes. This pattern in American history is so overwhelmingly clustered in Awakening years (especially around 1840, 1900, and 1970) that political scientist Michael Barkun claims it "strongly suggests the existence of a utopian cycle with a moderately predictable rhythm."

Yet if we move a half saeculum forward or backward, we typically see Hero youth pushing the culture in a very different direction. Go back that far from the back-to-nature Wheeler Ranch hippies (1970s) and we arrive at the dam-building CCC Youth Corps (1930s). Go back that far from the frenzied "vanity" bonfires of young preacher James Davenport (1743) and we arrive at the sober efficiency of young Cotton Mather (1689) in organizing a revolution in Boston against the Stuart crown. Or go forward that far from the optimistic young rationalists who wrote *The Federalist Papers* in the late 1780s (using the pseudonym "Publius") and we arrive at those whom Ralph Waldo Emerson described in the 1830s as "young men born with knives in their brain . . . madmen, madwomen, men with beards, Dunkers, Muggletonians, Come-Outers, Groaners, Agrarians, Seventh-Day Baptists, Quakers, Abolitionists, Calvinists, Unitarians, and Philosophers" who gathered not to reason or build but "to chide, or pray, or preach, or protest."

This alternation between inner versus outer goals, especially among youth, certainly affects other saecular trends. During an Awakening, the defiance of family and political authority helps initiate the dissolution of community bonds and favors looser norms and higher levels of social disorder. Later on, during the Unraveling, law-breaking becomes harshly regarded as an individual failing to be punished with more severity. During a Crisis, the strengthening of family and political authority helps restore community bonds and favors tighter norms and lower levels of social disorder. Later on, during the High, law-breaking becomes leniently regarded as a social failing to be punished with less severity.

Throughout their lives, Prophets tend to believe that good guilt-driven personal choices (the right lifestyle or values) create a better world. Heroes tend to believe that good shame-driven social choices (the right community or system) create a better world. According to sociologist Ruth Engs, the last three Awakenings have coincided with peaks in what she calls "a cycle of clean-living movements": conscience-driven lifestyles regarding food, drugs, dress, language, sex, and leisure. Originating in youth-founded reform and millenarian sects, these movements grow more demanding as their founders mature. During Crises these movements begin to decline, and during Highs they wane to minimal influence on younger generations.

Such regular shifts in the social mood reveal how society periodically rejuvenates and replenishes its culture. A Crisis, by the time it's over, entirely alters the social framework for the expression of thought and feeling. In a High, the culture optimistically if blandly reflects the public consensus about the fledgling civic order. New currents arise only on the romantic or "beatnik" fringe, where their subtle criticisms seldom challenge the consensus head-on.

Come the Awakening, the civic order feels sufficiently secure and prosperous to encourage or at least allow radical cultural experiments— according to the dictum of the Chinese revolutionary playwright Cao Yu that "art for art's sake is a philosophy of the well-fed." New norms, styles, and directions first assault and then push aside conventions that now seem exhausted. In an Unraveling, the new culture flourishes, liberates, splinters, and diversifies. Over time, as the habits and institutions of the post-Crisis order weaken, the now-ascendant cultural themes begin to feel less original and more like parodies and plagiarisms.

Early in the next Crisis, cultural innovation is no longer taken seriously (least of all by youth) except as sheer entertainment. Instead, cultural messages find themselves hijacked by partisan political and economic agendas of growing urgency. What does this art say to me? becomes less important than Whose side does this art say that I'm on? Today, this question can be policed on social media through canceling, flaming, or doxing. Later in the Crisis, cultural messaging is cleansed, censored, and harnessed to new public goals. Society's most talented artists are enlisted to create propaganda—in support of a new civic order.

After the Crisis, the new regime creates a fresh slate upon which cultural activity can (again) serve benign and decorative ends. Yet as the years pass, those ends will grow subversive—establishing the beachhead on which a fresh Awakening vision will ultimately land.

All forms of culture reflect these patterns. Consider musical styles over the past three saecula. The seasonal sequence is from protesting to transgressing to gravitating to harmonizing. With Awakenings came spirituals and gospel songs; then ragtime and early blues; more recently soul, rock, and protest folk. With Unravelings came minstrels; then blues and jazz; more recently country, rap, grunge, and alt rock. With Crises came camp songs and marches; then swing and big bands; and, very recently, cross-genre melding and social media participation. With Highs came ballads and piano sheet music; more recently, crooners, musicals, band stands, and vintage rock.

Consider architecture and fashion. A High produces styles that are expansive yet functional, while featuring romantic revivals that combine confident masculinity (and large constructions) with yielding femininity (and standardization). An Awakening returns to natural, folk, rural, and primitive motifs, always starting with a thaw in conventional social discipline combined with a new lifestyle asceticism. An Unraveling is the most eclectic era, with a deliberate mixing and ironic crossing of styles, periods, and genders. A Fourth Turning ultimately ushers in a new interest in the rational and classical, in balance and decorum.

While every turning can lay claim to cultural innovation, some shine more in certain media than in others. In music, Awakenings have been eras of special creativity. In literature, Highs and Unravelings have clearly come out ahead ever since William Shakespeare and John Milton. During the last three saecula, Unravelings have been eras in which American culture has exercised a profound influence over the rest of the world. Why? Perhaps because this is when migration to America is highest and when America can export the fruits of its recent Awakening. No other decades match the 1850s and 1920s for the dazzling reputation enjoyed by American authors in Europe, and surely none matches the 1990s for the rising global appetite for American popular culture of every variety (books, journals, news, film, software, and electronic games). During the Millennial Crisis, on schedule, the global appeal of American pop culture appears to be losing its edge.

More broadly, as Americans look ahead to the rest of this Crisis era, they can expect cultural trends to continue to follow the saecular pattern. Over the last decade, church-going and religious affiliation have entered a steep decline—by some measures, an unprecedented decline— signaling yet another "religious depression." Transforming humanity through technology and politics, on the other hand, is attracting growing interest, especially among the rising generation. On college campuses, STEM majors are rapidly displacing liberal arts majors. Half a saeculum ago, ambitious youth admired celebrity humanities professors who taught philosophy and linguistics; today, they admire celebrity tech CEOs who build rocket ships and behavioral algorithms.

The late scholar of sociology and religion Robert Bellah once famously observed that the history of the American experiment can be described as an oscillation—and tension—between the personal "conversion" and the public "covenant." That oscillation remains with us still.

These parallel rhythms—in politics, society, culture—never stop beating. And, so long as we keep extrapolating along straight lines, they never stop taking us by surprise.

When each new generation comes of age, its members assume they have the future trajectory of their society entirely figured out. So they do, for a while. Yet as they grow older and as newer generations come of age, they come to understand that this trajectory inevitably bends with the saeculum. They discover that the straight line they extrapolated in their youth did not lead to the future after all. It turned out be, instead, just one tangent to a great arc whose curvature requires the distance of time to appreciate. And with that discovery, each generation grows wiser as it grows older.

5

COMPLEXITY, ANOMALIES, AND GLOBAL HISTORY

> There are decades when nothing happens. And there are weeks when decades happen.
>
> —ATTRIBUTED TO LENIN (V. I. ULYANOV)

"The fox knows many things, but the hedgehog knows one big thing." So wrote Isaiah Berlin, quoting an ancient Greek poet, in a 1953 essay about Russian literature. The essay has since become celebrated, not so much because many people care about Tolstoy or Pushkin, but rather because they are fascinated by the fundamental divide Berlin observes in how people think.

Is it better to organize the world around one central idea? Or to remain open to a plurality of unrelated ideas? Is it better, like the hedgehog, to see all the links between things that seem different? Or, like the fox, to see each thing clearly for what it really is?

This divide has been debated since the beginning of time. It is also a convenient way to frame the questions readers often ask when they encounter any general theory of history. Our "Great Year" cycle, offering a unifying explanation of a wide variety of social trends, undeniably takes the perspective of the hedgehog. So it is only fair that those who see the world like a fox will want to dig deeper to understand how it all actually works.

After Franklin Roosevelt declared that there is a powerful "cycle in human events," he made two further observations—that this cycle is powered by "generations" and that it is "mysterious." In earlier chapters, we've discussed the generations. In this chapter, we try to clarify a few of the mysteries.

Specifically, we explore the following questions:

- *Free Will and Contingency.* How is a historical cycle compatible with free will—or, more seriously, with the obvious importance of random accidents and episodic technological discoveries?

- *Seasonal History as a Complex System.* The saeculum is a living "complex system"—meaning that it conforms to a growing body of theoretical research on complexity in nature. How do complex systems work? How do they come to be? What purpose do they serve?

- *Cycle Length and Anomalies.* What governs the timing or periodicity of the saeculum? How has this timing changed in the past, and how might it change in the future? What gives rise to saecular anomalies like the Civil War Crisis era?

- *Generations and Global History.* While America may have been the first generationally "modern" society, many other societies are becoming modern as well. If global history is gradually adopting the saecular timetable, what will that mean for the future of the world—including America?

FREE WILL AND CONTINGENCY

Those of us who live in the modern West instinctively resist the insights of predictive social science. We like to think we are masters of our own destiny, free to choose whatever we desire. It follows, we often feel, that our future behavior must be essentially unpredictable.

There's just one problem with this intuition, strong though it may be. It is fatally undermined by all the actual choices we end up making—which, when measured statistically across populations, reveal overwhelming predictability. To be sure, we may persuade ourselves that we are free to act on our whimsical desires. But are those *desires themselves* unpredictable? Corporations and political parties don't think so. They spend billions to uncover predictive patterns that govern when people will want to buy certain kinds of products or vote for certain kinds of candidates. They know, for example, that most of us will buy swimming trunks in June and snowmobiles in December; vacation less (but buy more lipstick) at the end of a recession; and swing for the out-of-office political party after a presidential election.

It's not just professionals who possess this sort of predictive knowledge. We all do. Most of us would agree that we can predict with a fair degree of accuracy how our family, friends, and neighbors will respond to most situations. In fact, we often equate predictability with good character—the notion that we can "count on" someone to do something. Does this predictability deny people their freedom? Hardly. Indeed, the prospect of a person or society that is truly "free" in the sense of being truly unpredictable would be terrifying. The very morality of reward and punishment for good or bad actions, the philosopher David Hume once argued, *contradicts* freedom of the will. The administration of justice presupposes instead that our actions are tied to predictable personalities and that each of us will respond to rewards and punishments in a predictable manner.

In short, a cycle that predicts how society's mood or behavior is likely to change ten years from now in no way nullifies anybody's freedom. Or at least it doesn't do so any more than the prediction that such things will *not* change ten years from now—which is probably most people's default assumption in the absence of predictive social science.

Even if a cycle of history does not violate free will, many troublesome questions remain: They go by the name of fortune, chance, or accident. Perhaps the most evocative word is *contingency*, which refers to the multitude of events that "touch upon" every other event. How can the saeculum coexist with contingency? Who could have predicted the steamship and locomotive? Or the stock crash on Black Thursday? Or the surprise attack on Pearl Harbor? Or the accuracy of Lee Harvey Oswald's bullet? Or the invention of the microchip? All these contingencies have had an enormous impact on our lives. How can any theory of social change predict such things?

The answer is straightforward: The saeculum neither predicts them nor denies them. History is forever begetting random accidents. All the saeculum insists is that what matters most is not the accidents themselves, but rather society's *response* to the accidents. To understand how this works, select a critical "accident," transport it to the opposite end of the saeculum, and try to consider its effect. Move the Watergate break-in back forty years: Would circa-1934 America have been receptive to a pair of twenty-something reporters eager to bring down a powerful president recently elected by an enormous landslide? Not a chance. Or move the Great Depression forward forty years: Would circa-1974 Boomers have coped with economic depression by cheerfully donning uniforms, joining paramilitary public works programs, and building colossal dams and bridges for the federal government? Again, not likely.

History always produces sparks. But some sparks flare briefly and then vanish, while others touch off firestorms out of any proportion to the sparks themselves. The propensity of sparks to act one way rather than another is what we mean when we talk about changes in social mood.

As Frank Klingberg noticed, the history of American reactions to foreign provocations is filled with such contrasts. Compare, for example, America's involvement in World War I and World War II. Both wars were preceded by acts of foreign aggression causing massive loss of life (the sinking of the *Lusitania*, the bombing of Pearl Harbor). In one case, Congress waited two years—and patiently endured further provocations—before declaring war amid significant political opposition. In the other case, Congress declared war the next day, and did so with only a single dissenting vote. In one case, the war helped inflame divisive issues like Prohibition, labor violence, and sedition trials. In the other, the nation mobilized with no distractions. Both wars ended in total victory. In one case, soldiers came home to moral nagging and vice squads; in the other, to generous benefits and ticker-tape parades. Both wars strengthened America's influence overseas. In one case, that influence was quickly squandered; in the other, it was consolidated over the next two decades.

Late in a Fourth Turning, generational forces tend to funnel exogenous events toward a concerted national response. When Adolf Hitler and Hideki Tojo became global threats, America was poised for decisive action. With self-oriented Prophets in power and team-oriented Heroes coming of age, the archetypal order-givers were in charge and the archetypal order-takers were on the battlefield. The result, once the emergency started, was maximum *cooperation* between generations. Elder Prophet leaders do not back down from confrontation. Indeed, Sam Adams, John Brown, Jefferson Davis, and FDR have all been plausibly accused of helping to foment or stage a crisis for the express purpose of galvanizing their nation.

Halfway across the saeculum, no war can escape the crosscurrents of a youth-fired Awakening. During the Vietnam War, the archetypal order-takers were old, the order-givers young. Young Prophets challenged the moral emptiness of the institutions directing them. Meanwhile, elder Heroes did everything they could to pre-empt the need for sacrifice—if necessary, by means of sheer affluence and technology (the nation could have "guns *and* butter"). The result was maximum *antagonism* between generations. During the late sixties, both generations were ill at ease in their war-waging roles, each displeasing the other with its behavior.

History teaches, as we have seen, that wars tend to reflect the mood of the current turning. Wars in a Fourth Turning find the broadest possible definition and are fought to unambiguous outcomes. This suggests that, had the Japanese not attacked Pearl Harbor, the U.S. would have found some other provocation to declare total war against the Axis powers. Whether a different provocation would have led to a better or worse outcome (say, victory in Europe without the concessions at Yalta) is impossible to say. The saeculum does not guarantee good or bad outcomes.

Another source of historical randomness, we imagine, is technology. No one can deny that technological discoveries regularly change our lives. Yet we are often mistaken about the direction of causation. While many assume that a new technology shapes a new decade or generation, the true causal arrow may point more in the reverse direction: *Every new decade or generation shapes how that technology gets put to use.*

To illustrate, let's return to the American High. Back then, the slow and bulky "mainframe computer" conjured up images of military or corporate control. For the G.I. Generation then in charge, that's how computers were supposed to function: They helped leaders process information, after which clear directives could be issued to everybody else. Ever since the Great Depression, the G.I.s had always approached information and communication according to this A-frame schema: Somebody at the top came to a decision, and then society would get its "marching orders." Even as late as the 1960s, most technologists could not imagine that America would ever need more than a handful of such machines.

During the Awakening, of course, all that changed. With Boomers coming of age in the 1970s, it seemed inevitable that the so-called microchip revolution would *individualize* society. In 1977, Apple began marketing the "personal computer," one for each person. By 1984, the new information paradigm was summed up by an advertisement showing a lone yuppie athlete throwing a hammer into his or her father's Orwellian telescreen. Over the following decade, Boomers would empower "personal choice" via the worldwide web. For the next quarter century, with Xers coming of age, every U.S. president would regularly sermonize about how the microchip and the Internet were empowering the individual—and would soon topple dictators and authoritarian institutions everywhere.

During the most recent decade, with still another (Millennial) generation coming of age, America seems to have come full circle. Once again, the tide has mysteriously turned. "Social media," enabling everyone to stay 24/7 connected on a handful of monopoly platforms, is now widely seen as *collectivizing* society. Infotech's emerging toolkit—big data and artificial intelligence linked to ubiquitous sensors and "smart" censorship—seems to pose, once again, the threat of centralized control. As for dictators and authoritarians abroad, they no longer fear digital tech. To the contrary, they have fallen in love with its top-down capabilities of total surveillance, "lockdown" repression, and orchestrated hysteria.

This pattern should make us wonder: Do these new technologies really change us—or do they just give us *what we want when we want it?* More often than not, technology tailors itself to the national mood.

When automobiles, telephones, and radios were still new during the 1910s and 1920s, they were regarded as inventions that would individualize and fragment American life. They would separate rich from poor, facilitate privacy, and allow people to travel and vacation anywhere. And so they did—for a while. Then, with the army convoys and propaganda machines of World War II, these same technologies symbolized unified civic purpose. By the 1950s, they helped standardize a middle-class lifestyle. And by that time they were joined by television, broadcasting the soothing consensus messages of Walter Cronkite and Ed Sullivan.

In the 1970s, on schedule, all these technologies found themselves attacked as symbols of dehumanizing conformity. In the 1990s, during the Unraveling, the attacks stopped. Instead, Americans began using them to break away and "be yourself." Witness the growing popularity, in that era, of "off-road" SUVs, cellular phones, and cable TV with hundreds of channels. And today, with a new turning, these technologies are once again adapting themselves to a new paradigm. Cars are hooking up to centralized grids, and virtually every electronic technology, from cars to phones to TV, is connecting to a single digital network. We trust AI to plot our route and to select our entertainment and our vacations—and our ads—all on the basis of monitored speech or behavior. Careful what you say or do: Alexa may be tracking it.

To sum up: Technological discoveries may themselves defy prediction. They are, in this sense, randomly exogenous, if you will. But how such discoveries are harnessed by the devices and infrastructures that change our lives is neither random nor exogenous. This depends critically on society's priorities. We thus return to the cycle. If a society's priorities are susceptible to prediction, so too is the manner in which technology will be invited into the lives of society's members.

SEASONAL HISTORY AS A COMPLEX SYSTEM

Since the seventeenth century, any reference to a natural cycle or period has always brought to mind a simple physical system, like the orbit of a planet around the sun. Its timing is exact, and its gravitational cause can be precisely identified and described. A cycle of social behavior, by contrast, possesses only approximate timing. And what causes it typically isn't understood at all. So in what sense can we talk about any sort of cycle in history? History is part of nature, isn't it?

Systems theory offers a helpful perspective on such questions. It suggests that there are four basic types of natural systems: simple, complicated, complex, and chaotic. Yes, everything is part of nature. But we understand nature in different ways depending on what we're looking at.

To explain these different types of systems, let's use the following analogy (which we gratefully borrow from the financial journalist Michael Lewis). A car key is *simple*. I can easily grasp how it works, and I know exactly when it works—instantly. The car itself is *complicated*. It has thousands of parts. While I don't know exactly how they all work, I know that engineers and mechanics do—and when the car doesn't respond to my commands, I know that they know exactly how to fix it.

The daily traffic cycle in New York City, on the other hand, is *complex*. No one really understands the tangled causal dynamic behind it: We know that the congestion in any one block is connected to the congestion in every other block, but we don't exactly understand how. Also, the timing of the cycle is only approximate. As a result, we can only make guesses about how to "fix" a traffic cycle that we don't like. Finally, there's the traffic in Miami just after a hurricane warning. We might call this a *chaotic* system. Here, both the causes and the timing are unknown. To the extent this chaos degrades into pure randomness, in fact, it is no longer a "system" at all.

Applying this analogy, we may conclude that a cycle of history is best understood as a special type of complex system. In general, for a system to be complex, it needs to have two basic characteristics. First, the system must be composed of multiple parts that interact according to nonlinear rules. Lots of nonlinear interaction means it is impossible to predict the system's future simply by knowing what's happening now to all of its parts. Second, despite this analytic unpredictability, we can observe approximate but stable patterns, such as cycles, in how the entire system behaves. In complexity science, these stable patterns are sometimes called "attractors" because they tend to show up regardless of the exact starting conditions. They are deemed to be an "emergent property" of the system.

The loftiest cycle of history, accordingly, has much in common with the lowliest cycle of traffic. It has a periodicity that is *approximately known* in a complex system determined by nonlinear and interactive drivers in a manner that is *largely unknown.*

Complexity theorists, who employ machine-learning algorithms to study such systems (from meteorology to species evolution), are generally comfortable in a world of mysterious predictability. Most of the rest of us are not. But we ought to be. In our natural environment, complex systems are everywhere. Consider the beating of a heart, the budding of a flower, the molting of a sparrow. The mere act of breathing involves hundreds of physiological feedbacks involving blood chemistry, neuronal signals, hormonal balance, and muscular proprioception. No one can calibrate or predict its timing with exact precision. But every phase of breathing must follow another in the proper order and at roughly the right moment, or a person would quickly die.

Likewise with the saeculum. History flows in a progression of ebbs and flows whose schedule is regular yet not precisely fixed. George Modelski likened the study of long cycles (what he calls *chronomacropolitics*) to the study of natural cycles (*chronobiology*). Even when winter arrives a bit early or late, it is still possible to foretell in what order the leaves will fall, the birds will migrate, and the streams will freeze. The ancients seldom searched analytically for causes. They didn't try to identify, as modern biologists do, each of the biochemical reactions causing leaves to start to bud. Instead, they thought about the recurrent motions of nature and society holistically, as a complex system, which often made them better able than moderns to intuit what was likely to happen next.

When we think about familiar complex systems, processes of natural life come most easily to our minds. Recall the *nonhuman* automobile as our example of a system that is merely complicated. A traffic cycle, on the other hand, will always be a complex system because it is composed of many automobiles each having a *human* driver.

Complexity theorists believe there's a good reason we think this way. Most nonliving complex systems are temporary. They appear briefly and then disappear. Consider, for example, the circulating convection bubbles in a pot about to boil. Yes, these loops of bubbles form a gorgeously complex system. But left to themselves, this system won't last long. It will quickly degenerate into total randomness (all the water boils away and becomes vapor) or total inactivity (somebody turns off the heat, causing the water to cool and the bubbles to vanish).

But now consider a complex system composed at all levels of living creatures. This might be a single cell made up of organelles; an animal made up of cells or organs; or an entire society made up of animals. Living complex systems possess a remarkable ability: They can *self-adjust* in order to maintain their complexity as their environment changes. Theorists call this ability "self-organized criticality." It makes sense that living systems would acquire it: For anything alive, total randomness or total inactivity ordinarily means death.

As we look around at the world of living complex systems, including human societies, we can't help but be impressed by the omnipresent balance between order and change. Living systems actively seek this criticality or balance. Too much randomness and the system disintegrates; too much order and it fails to adapt. All learning and creativity in living systems is accomplished in between, in a sort of dance "at the edge of chaos," to use a phrase coined by chaos theorist Norman Harry Packard. It's why animals have sex: Genes replicate, but in new random combinations. It's why a few people always insist on taking idiotic risks: In some situations, these could be adaptive. And it's why teenagers argue with their parents and agree with their peers: Societies unable to form new generational communities are doomed to failure.

As this last example suggests, the saeculum itself can be regarded as a complex living system that seeks a similar balance between order and disorder. This balance is dynamic in the sense that it self-adjusts over the duration of the saeculum. The saeculum typically veers closest to freedom and disorder at the end of a Third Turning and closest to solidarity and order at the end of a First Turning. Throughout this rhythm the system always maintains within itself a capacity for recovery and self-adjustment—for example, through the process of generational aging and replacement.

What role does *progress* play in the saeculum's dynamic pursuit of balance? To understand the role of progress, we need to appreciate that human social systems are very unlike other systems in the natural world—simple or complex, nonliving or living. Humans can intuit and act on ideas. And societies can institutionalize these ideas as shared systems of morality, religion, law, political authority, and commerce. Since the dawn of modernity, one very important idea is the conviction that people can deliberately change these systems in ways that improve their societies over time. To be modern is, as we have seen, to believe that history is linear and progressive.

Modern ideologies of progress generally fall into two great camps, idealist and materialist. The modern idealist tradition (most famously represented by the Italian philosopher Giambattista Vico or the German philosopher Georg W. F. Hegel) has always been popular among those inclined to religion or faith. It holds that all historical processes, including "cycles of history," are guided by God or Spirit. These will, at the end of time, inevitably lead all or some portion of humanity to eternal salvation or perfection. A second materialist tradition (represented, most recently, by technologist Ray Kurzweil or historian Yuval Noah Harari) has always been popular among those inclined to technocracy or works. It urges societies themselves to remake nature, perhaps even human nature, in ways that will usher all or some portion of humanity toward permanent security and fulfillment.

In certain ways, these two schools have much in common. The basic message of both, idealist and materialist, hasn't changed since the earliest proselytes of revolution and reformation. The message is this: Humanity is on the brink; it's all our fault; we must do something big now; and if we do it right, we will be saved forever. In both its idealist and materialist forms, the message pushes forward the seasonal rhythm of the saeculum. It not only confirms our modern belief in the possibility of progress, it reinforces our modern sense of urgency in its pursuit. It makes each generation determined to correct what one or more of its predecessors got wrong in this quest.

Yet in other ways, these two schools are very different. The goal of those who subscribe to the first school is to be *individually worthy or righteous enough* to be saved. The goal of those who subscribe to the second is to be *collectively smart or powerful enough* to be saved. Here we can easily recognize two of our generational archetypes: Prophet and Hero, respectively. And we can locate the season in which each of these schools reaches maximum influence. Enthusiasm for the "inner world" definition of progress typically peaks at the end of a Second Turning or Awakening. And enthusiasm for the "outer world" definition peaks at the end of a Fourth Turning or Crisis.

If we pause and reflect on all of the seasonal extremes that seem to appear in the saeculum, we see two pairs of seasonal opposites. One pair, reaching its extreme at the solstices, is solidarity (end of First Turning) and freedom (end of Third Turning). The other pair, reaching its extreme at the equinoxes, is idealism (end of Second Turning) and materialism (end of Fourth Turning). The result is a quaternity of both social moods and generational personalities that resemble those we examined in Chapter 3. Carl Jung, for example, proposed two dominant axes or spectrums for thinking about personality types. The first corresponds to our solstices: thinking (objective and public) versus feeling (subjective and personal). The second corresponds to our equinoxes: judging (or intuiting) versus perceiving (or sensing).

To this point, we have been examining modernity's aspirations for progress. What about modernity's actual achievement of progress? In some respects, modern societies have undeniably changed in ways that nearly all of us would regard as progress—better health and longer lives, for example. And the achievement of progress is entirely compatible with the saeculum: We may think of history, if we wish, as a progressing spiral.

However—and this must be emphasized—*progress is not the purpose of the saeculum.* If the saeculum has a purpose, it is rather to push a society that always anticipates something better into phases of creative self-adjustment where it must, from time to time, confront something worse. It is to steer a people resolved to avoid cycles into participating in a cycle that will spare it from dissolution or stasis and therefore from social death. The saeculum contributes to long-term progress only to the extent that it keeps society alive and adaptive. In this sense, its purpose resembles that of natural evolution: The saeculum may or may not make us better, but it does foster our survival. It may not give any generation what it wants. But, over time, it usually gives society what it needs so that more generations will follow.

Let's move on to perhaps the most natural question we always want to ask whenever we encounter a complex social system: What exactly makes it work?

Unfortunately, as we have seen, this question can never be fully answered. Therein lies the mystery of complexity. Although a complex social system may reveal a cycle that can be known, at least approximately, it is typically driven by a vast multitude of nonlinear and interactive causes that cannot be summarized in any single causal story. Imagine, for example, asking a biochemist what causes your blood pressure to rise and fall every twenty-four hours. Or an epidemiologist what causes influenza to arrive in periodic waves. These scientists will probably pause, ask you to sit down, give you a very long and complicated explanation—and then admit there is a great deal they still don't understand.

Just so with the saecular seasons of history. This cycle depends on the functioning of social systems and human psychology at every level of aggregation—in other words, it depends on practically everything. It is linked to the dynamics of family life, of friendship networks, of social and political institutions, and of ancestral moral reasoning. It is also linked to the biology of human development and reproduction and possibly to hormonal or epigenetic rhythms within human physiology that few have yet investigated.

This last possibility is intriguing. An estimated two-thirds of all mammalian species exhibit multi-year cycles of population expansion and contraction. These range from roughly four years for lemmings and voles to ten years for snowshoe hares to thirty-eight years for moose. Most of these cycles appear to be unrelated to climate, predators, or anything else in the environment. More intriguingly, many are linked to a matching behavioral pattern—for example, cycles of aggression, herding, migration, mating, and stress. In effect, these animals act differently depending on when, during this repeating calendar, they are born.

While biologists aren't sure what drives these cycles, some have speculated that they may be triggered by periodic changes in the animals' production of hormones and neurotransmitters and that these changes may be synchronized by pheromones and behavioral cues. No one has any idea whether this triggering does happen or could happen in humans. Research on this question, even for small mammals, remains in its infancy.

If the full range of possible or contributory causes of the saeculum seems impossibly broad, we may do better by focusing on a simpler question. Which cultural or social dynamics appear to be most fundamental in setting the saeculum into motion?

Based on historical observation, we can highlight three.

The first dynamic is cultural, and we can observe its emergence in history. It is the idea of social destiny or collective improvement. If a society has no expectation of progress, then the inertia of tradition will prevail and the long cycle will remain dormant. To be sure, this outcome is paradoxical: While moderns are driven to seek progress, it is their desire for progress that sets up the generational polarity that gives rise to cycles.

The second dynamic is the generational polarity itself, which always pits two-apart archetypes against each other: Heroes versus Prophets or Nomads versus Artists. During its childhood, every generation is raised to become the complement or "shadow" of the archetype currently in midlife. Later, when this generation comes of age, the polarity heightens the potential for both conflict and cooperation with the two-apart archetype then entering elderhood.

The third dynamic is the presence of clear phase-of-life roles—without which generations cannot form. All societies possess phase-of-life roles. Yet most modern societies further stimulate generational consciousness by creating a special adolescent "borderline" phase of life between childhood and adulthood. This is when peer bonds are forged in a mighty youth-culture cauldron—a time when, as parents know full well (and as researchers confirm), peer pressure strongly competes with family influence. Modern adolescence stimulates strong peer bonding. And only through peer bonding does a generation acquire a sense of its own destiny. As Yale developmental psychiatrist John Schowalter puts it: "Going from child to adult, you go over a bridge of your peers."

CYCLE LENGTH AND ANOMALIES

Every wave has a *wavelength*. And every social cycle has a *periodicity*. To know what it is, we can simply measure it across multiple cycle peaks. But to understand why the cycle has any given length or periodicity— and what may make it change over time—we need to know something about what determines it.

While a complex social system may not reveal its own causes, the natural framework of a behavioral cycle may suggest explanations for its length. Let's return to the example of the New York City traffic cycle. To be sure, most questions about why the congestion rises and falls at certain hours or at certain intersections may be impossible to answer. But we can bet that the overall periodicity of this traffic cycle beats to the alternating pattern of day versus night. And for an obvious reason. That is the cycle's natural framework: Because people are still tied to a diurnal rhythm, most people will tend to drive during the day and to sleep during the night.

The saeculum has its own natural framework. As we observed in Chapter 3, each saeculum requires four consecutive turnings or genera- tions. And each turning or generation has the length of a phase of life, the most critical of which is childhood, extending from birth to the begin- ning of adulthood. By defining social roles, especially the child's depen- dency role, a phase of life becomes the vital crucible for the formation of generational identities and boundaries. The length of a phase of life, therefore, ought to approximate the length of a generation.

For simplicity in that discussion, we illustrated the pacing of gener- ational formation by imagining phases of life fixed at twenty-one years, which would generate a saeculum of eighty-four years. Yet this length has not remained fixed since the dawn of modernity, at least not in the Anglo-American context. For the six pre-American generations, born through the late sixteenth century, the length of a generation averaged twenty-six years. For the seven American generations born before the founding of the United States, it averaged twenty-five years. Yet for the next ten U.S. generations, through Millennials, it has averaged just over twenty-one years. As the length of a generation has shrunk, so too has the length of a saeculum, from just over one hundred years to just over eighty years.

The demographic data, spotty as they sometimes are, make it clear that this shortening trend in the length of a generation has roughly tracked a similar long-term shortening in the length of a phase of life.

In England from the 1500s to the mid-1700s, as in nearly all of early modern Western Europe, the average age at which men married—and thus were able to set up their own households—was relatively high, around twenty-seven or twenty-eight. Late marriage age was compelled by low living standards and scarce arable land. Poor nutrition meant that most girls did not complete puberty until their late teens. Births out of wedlock were (by today's standards) quite rare. In the late 1700s, as living standards began to rise, average marriage age began to fall in Britain. It fell even faster in the American colonies, especially on the frontier, thanks to higher real wages and an abundance of available land. By 1800, the average U.S. marriage age was at least two years younger than in Europe.

Over the next century, the pervasive democratizing of society shortened the effective length of a phase of life at a still faster pace. Until the late 1700s, in both Britain and America, social power lay overwhelmingly in the hands of wealthy male landowners, who often secured their independence and their inheritance (with the death of their fathers) even later than when they married. Starting in the early 1800s, however, that domination rapidly weakened. Suffrage expanded to all free males. Women, who typically leave home (with marriage) at a younger age than men, began to exercise more influence in politics and the culture—and in the early twentieth century they gained the vote. The spread of public schooling and a media-propagated "youth culture" further accelerated the pace of each generation's collective self-awareness.

Since 1904, after the eminent psychologist G. Stanley Hall popularized the word "adolescence," Americans have grown accustomed to the idea that everyone transitions from childhood to adulthood at a similar age, ordinarily no later than their early twenties. They have also come to accept Hall's description of this transition as a brief period of parental rebellion, moodiness, and separation from society. About the same time,

young Americans began to examine and discuss their unique generational identity in novels and essays. Starting with the "Lost Generation,"
no generation has come of age in America without inspiring a recognizable collective label.

For the first four generations to come of age during the twentieth
century, from the Lost through the Boomers, average generational
length shortened to an all-time low of just under twenty-one years. Over
the same period, marriage ages for both men and women also sank to
their all-time low, especially from the mid-1940s to mid-1970s. Rapid
real wage increases, excluding only the decade of the Great Depression,
ensured that sons substantially outearned their fathers at the same age
and could therefore leave home earlier. In 1969, near the peak of this
gathering economic optimism, Americans were suddenly talking about a
new "youth generation" of teenagers. Four years later, Congress saw fit to
lower the national voting age from twenty-one to eighteen.

So let's summarize the long-term trend. Over the two centuries from
the late 1700s to the late 1900s, we witnessed a significant shortening
of generations and turnings. And over the same period, we witnessed a
roughly equivalent shortening in the time required to move from birth to
adulthood—which is a good proxy for the length of a phase of life. This
finding should offer us some confidence that the length of a phase of life
is indeed the natural framework for the rhythm of the saeculum.

Yet this close correspondence raises an important question. If generational length has tracked phase-of-life length in the past, shouldn't it
continue to track it in the future? And if it does, can we anticipate future
trends in generational length by looking at how phase-of-life length is
now changing?

The answer is probably yes. What's more, when we look at what has
happened since the early 1970s in the time required to move from birth
to adulthood, we confront a significant trend reversal: *Over the last fifty
years, this time span has no longer been contracting. It has been rapidly
expanding.*

The magnitude of the reversal is dramatic by just about every measure. Consider rising marriage age. After reaching its historic low of
just over age twenty-one in the early 1960s, the median U.S. age of first

marriage for both men and women has climbed steeply and has today reached a historic high of twenty-nine. That's a gain of eight years. Or consider the rising average age of mothers at the birth of their first child, from barely twenty-one in the late 1960s to a historic high of twenty-seven today. That's a gain of six years.

Young people who once started full-time careers in their late teens or early twenties are now doing so in their late twenties. And despite their longer years of training and education, they are no longer out-earning their parents. A record-high share of people aged twenty-five to twenty-nine—today about one-third—are living with older family members (usually parents). This share is highest, and has been growing the fastest, among non-college youth, an alarming number of whom now find themselves unable to start a self-sufficient career at *any* age.

Developmental psychologist Jeffrey Arnett, observing this slowing developmental clock, proposed in 2000 that his field invent a new term to describe Americans from age eighteen to twenty-four: "emerging adulthood." He also proposed that the next phase of life, "young adulthood," start around age twenty-five and extend from there until sometime in the mid- to late forties. Arnett's concept of delayed young adulthood has gained considerable traction among his academic peers.

At the same time, we are witnessing later ages at which older adults are assuming leadership roles in business and politics—which may point to later age thresholds for midlife and elderhood. Over the last fifty years, for example, the average age of all members of Congress and state governors has risen by about six years, from fifty-three to fifty-nine. The average age at which people first get elected to these posts has risen by about three or four years. Presiding over the White House (President Joe Biden), Senate (Minority Leader Mitch McConnell), and House (Speaker Nancy Pelosi) as of the end of 2022 were three octogenarians—an extraordinary and of course unprecedented development.

It's too early to tell how much of this slowdown in the phase-of-life timetable will still be with us three or four decades from now. The trend may be in part transitory. Indeed, some of it may be reversed by the seasons of history themselves. With the completion of the Millennial Crisis and the advent of the First Turning, we may well see generational forces trigger an abrupt *lowering* in the age of economic independence and political leadership.

Even so, at least some of the recent dilation in life-cycle time likely constitutes a new long-term trend that will extend deep into the twenty-first century. Early in Chapter 9 we will briefly explore one consequence of this trend: the possible emergence of a "late elderhood" phase of life to reflect the growing social influence of people in their late seventies and beyond.

In Chapter 8 we will consider a more direct effect: the possibility that, as phases of life grow longer, so too may generations and turnings. Instead of expecting future generations and turnings to last just over twenty years, we should expect them to last perhaps twenty-two or even twenty-three years. As we shall see, this dilation in phase-of-life duration will extend our best guess about exactly when the Millennial Crisis—and the Millennial Saeculum—will come to an end. Four twenty-year turnings point to an eighty-year saeculum; four twenty-three-year turnings point to a ninety-two-year saeculum.

If it is true that the natural framework of the seasons of history is now getting longer, we may also need to rethink some of our common assumptions about historical change. Time and again, we are told that the pace of current events is accelerating. Really? In fact, the underlying saecular rhythm of social change may be *decelerating* somewhat. We also hear that generations are getting shorter and new generations are arriving more often. In fact, the logic of phase-of-life timing suggests the opposite—that generations are getting *longer* and new generations are arriving a bit *less* often.

This matters every time we try to identify the appearance of new generations of children. Marketers and pollsters are naturally inclined to cut the current generation of young adults short and start a new generation so that they have something fresh to talk about. In time, after realizing their mistake, they have to readjust their dates. This happened with Millennials back in 1993, when marketers (starting with *Ad Age*), defined "Generation Y" (the next generation after Xers) as anyone born in 1974 or after. This would have chopped Generation X down to roughly a decade in length. Years later, this definition was abandoned. Today everyone born through the end of the 1970s, by just about anybody's definition, is deemed to be an Xer. "Generation Y was a placeholder until we found out more about them," admits a former *Ad Age* writer.

Something similar is today happening with "Generation Z" (the next generation after Millennials). The Pew Research Center has defined these post-Millennials as starting in 1997—thus cutting Millennials down to only 16 birth years. Pew also defines Generation Z as only 16 years in length. Neither Pew nor the marketers advance any social or historical theory of generational formation that would justify these early cutoff points. We are confident that the perspective of time will again push observers to redraw their generational dividing lines. Rather than thinking of Millennials and post-Millennials as growing somewhat *shorter* than their parent's generations, we should actually be expecting the opposite— that they will be growing somewhat *longer* than their parents' generations.

Longer phases of life and a slower pace of social change may also persuade us to re-examine the common assumption that the lives of youth are becoming more rushed than ever. Consider young people today who are looking forward to full adult independence perhaps by their early thirties. And compare them with their counterparts sixty years ago— married with a full-time career and their own home and first child by their early twenties. If today is rushed, what do we call that?

Today's high-school grads, with their vague expectation of an eventual "capstone" marriage around age thirty, are actually experiencing a pace of life that has less in common with youth in 1960 than with early-modern youth around 1650 or 1750. Today, as then, young people are coming of age in a slow-growth economy that cannot easily make room for new entrants. Today, as then, they need to spend most of their twenties patiently acquiring the skills and capital (it used to be tools or land) before being able to live independently without parental support. To be sure, this way of life may be stressful. But rushed it is not.

Thus far, we've been considering gradual *trends* in the seasonal and generational cycle. Let's now move on to another timing issue: large and conspicuous *anomalies* in the cycle.

In Anglo-American history, there has been only one such anomaly: the U.S. Civil War. Its saeculum had normal First and Second Turnings, but greatly abbreviated Third and Fourth Turnings which together spanned only twenty-one years (1844–1865), the usual length of one turning. Only thirty-two years elapsed between the climax of the Transcendental Awakening and the climax of the Civil War. Also, that saeculum produced no generation of the Hero type, making this the only time in five centuries that the cycle of four archetypes has been disrupted.

Why did this anomaly happen? We cannot know for certain. One reason suggests itself, however. The three adult generations alive at the time (elder Compromisers, midlife Transcendentals, and young-adult Gilded) let their worst instincts prevail. As a result, the Civil War Saeculum did not end as other saecula have. It did not, to the same degree, unify society and strengthen national political institutions. Even less did it forge the coming-of-age generation into dominant civic leaders. Instead, the Civil War Saeculum culminated in a catastrophically destructive conflict that sent massive generational shock waves well into the next saeculum.

Well before the Civil War started, America's senior leaders understood the threat of rising North-versus-South sectionalism. But following the failure of the Compromise of 1850, pushed so hard by Henry Clay and Daniel Webster before their deaths, the aging Compromisers of the Buchanan era simply ran out of viable solutions. Few were able to rise above empty process and moral confusion—from Chief Justice Roger Brooke Taney, who wrote the disastrous *Dred Scott* opinion, to Kentucky Senator John Crittenden, whose last-gasp "Crittenden Compromise" in the winter of 1861 was greeted with contempt by both sides. Meanwhile, a large share of the midlife Transcendentals who began to assume top leadership posts during the 1850s regarded the very notion of compromise as an abomination. America proceeded to split into two self-contained societies that could not resist waging war (and, later, peace) with ruthless finality. The young-adult Gilded never outgrew an adventurer's lust for battle or an easily bruised sense of personal honor—until the war had devastated their own lives and future prospects.

Together, these three generations (Artist, Prophet, and Nomad) comprised a dangerous constellation. They accelerated the arrival of the Crisis, forced it to a swift climax, and pushed America into the most apocalyptic conflict that politicians, preachers, generals, and soldiers were jointly capable of achieving.

To be sure, this Fourth Turning utterly transformed America—as Fourth Turnings always do—in ways that most Americans today would regard as positive. The Civil War Crisis crushed sectionalism. It unleashed industrial production on a national scale. It abolished slavery. And it created, from the late 1860s to the late 1880s, a remarkable if turbulent era of biracial democracy in much of the South. All these outcomes were beyond the imagination of most Americans before the war.

Yet much of this progress failed to live up to its promise. Progress in the South was undermined as soon as the Union abandoned (in 1877) its military occupation of the South, and Congress finally gave up (in 1890) any effort to block Southern "redeemer" states from disenfranchising Black voters. Reconstruction thus collapsed into lynching, Jim Crow, and racial apartheid. The postbellum South thereafter entered a regime of one-party government, limited franchise (even for Whites), economic backwardness, and widespread rural poverty. Not until a full saeculum later, during the late 1960s, were basic civil rights restored to most Southern Blacks—or did income per capita in the South rise back up to a mere two-thirds of the U.S. national average.

The nationwide post–Civil War reaction against political reform not only changed the course of Southern history. It changed the overall course of American history. After Appomattox, the public pushed Congress to demobilize rapidly and to scale back the scope of governmental power. Governors did little about the corrupt machine bosses who took over large cities bursting with immigrants. Legislators routinely accepted bribes from massive corporations and trusts. Prominent social causes before the war (from urban planning and worker rights to female suffrage) withered until the 1890s, during the next Awakening, when they had to rise again virtually from scratch.

Postwar elections indicate that many Americans did indeed attribute the unusual suffering of the Civil War Crisis to the die-hard leadership of aging Transcendentals. Following the Civil War, voters tossed out older radicals in their sixties for younger (Gilded) realists in their forties. In the four elections from 1866 to 1872, the Transcendental share of Congress and state governors fell from more than two-thirds to one-third—the steepest decline in one generation's political power in U.S. history. The new Gilded generation of leaders avoided lofty crusades and governmental compulsion. They favored quick wits, smart deals, and personal loyalty. To use their own generation's parlance, they were "pragmatists" (William James) who believed in "the law of competition" (Andrew Carnegie) and "let the chips fall where they may" (Roscoe Conkling).

After the Civil War Crisis, therefore, no rising generation came forward to fill the usual Hero role of building public institutions to realize the Transcendentals' visions. The Progressives (a protected, "good child" generation even before the war) were next in line and could have become this. But because the Crisis congealed so early and so violently, most of this generation was still in childhood by the end of the war—and emerged more shell-shocked than empowered. Though many first-wave Progressives served as youngsters in combat, they left postwar politics in the hands of the "bloody shirt" Gilded. Asserting little collegial confidence, Progressives developed the ameliorative persona of the Artist archetype. As young liberal reformers in the 1880s, they were lampooned (according to one historian) as the "gelded men of the Gilded Age." As they later assumed power, many embraced racial segregation in both the North and the South as a modern and "progressive" tool of social management.

Filling the archetypal void, the Gilded Generation matured after the Civil War into a sort of hybrid of the Nomad and Hero. It presided over two decades of "Reconstruction" (1865 to 1886) in which manners were ruder, immigration larger, social unrest higher, and government weaker than in other post-Crisis eras. In no other High has politics been considered a disreputable profession—or has civic improvement rested so fully in the hands of wealthy tycoons. Later on, by the turn of the century, the Gilded were repudiated by an Awakening that vilified the old for their vulgarity and avarice. In no other Awakening have young reformers directed almost all their fury against "robber barons" and other despotic individuals and almost none against oppressive government. In all these ways, the absence of a Hero generation pushed the beginning of the Great Power Saeculum into a somewhat atypical trajectory.

The Civil War anomaly represents a singular deviation from the seasonal cycle. As such, it cannot tell us why or under what conditions other anomalies may arise in this complex system. Yet there are at least two important lessons we can draw from it.

The first is that while the saeculum does indeed determine the direction of the social mood, it does not determine good or bad outcomes. Nor does it determine whether the saeculum culminates in a milder or harsher Crisis era. Accordingly, it does matter what choices people make. Each generation may be compelled to play out an archetypal role, but it can play that role either well or poorly. To this extent, at least, the saeculum does leave room for human freedom.

The second is that, like all complex systems, the saeculum possesses the property of *dynamic stability*. Complex systems are always getting pushed and pulled by random events. But because they are dynamically stable, they usually respond to shocks in ways that pull them back to their central trajectory. What the Civil War anomaly demonstrates is that this stability can persist even after the seasonal cycle is severely disrupted—altered in its timing and deprived of one of its archetypal components. After the Civil War Crisis, the subsequent High and the Awakening may have been a bit atypical. But by the closing decades of the next saeculum, from the Roaring Twenties until VJ Day, the rhythm of generations and turnings seems to have returned to its equilibrium path.

GENERATIONS AND GLOBAL HISTORY

While the seasons of history may have found their earliest and most regular expression in England and America, they are recognizable in much of the rest of the world as well. And they are becoming ever-more recognizable with the passage of time. As many other societies become "modern" in the American sense—that is, individualistic, democratic, and progressive—their social moods increasingly fall under the rhythmic sway of generational archetypes.

"Among democratic nations each new generation is a new people" wrote Tocqueville (more than once) after touring America in the early 1830s. He presciently anticipated that as other societies became democratic, so too would they follow America's path, each steering its course according to the deepest convictions of whichever generation is presently in charge. No longer would people be constrained by the dead hand of their royal or aristocratic or clerical ancestors. In effect, Tocqueville was predicting that Jefferson's natural-law imperatives—"the earth belongs to the living generation" and "one generation is to another as one independent nation to another"—would ultimately prevail around the world.

It's hard to argue he got that one wrong. Since Tocqueville, it has become commonplace for rising generations to declare their intention to right the wrongs committed by their predecessors—not just in America, but in practically every nation on earth.

Over the last century, moreover, we can do more than observe generational cycles outside America. We can also begin to identify the basic periodicity of a *global* saeculum—that is, a world in which many societies are following roughly the same cycle.

It has always been true that neighboring societies are unlikely to follow a very different saecular calendar. Over time, through cultural exchange and political interaction, they will tend to gravitate toward a synchronous rhythm. As communication and transportation become cheaper and faster, moreover, this gravitational pull becomes ever-stronger and works at ever-greater distances. Many generational trends, from student protests to pop music genres, are now essentially global. So too is the impact of major political turning points, from World War II to the collapse of the Soviet Union. Even the movements we witness toward and away from "globalization" have become globally synchronized.

Imagine, by analogy, taking multiple mechanical clocks and gradually moving them closer to each other. They will soon tick in unison. To conserve energy on each vibration, the slow clocks will speed up slightly and the fast clocks will slow down slightly. This phenomenon, known as sympathetic resonance, is yet another dynamic property of most complex systems.

Let's briefly expand our view of the saeculum beyond the American lineage and try to identify just when (historically) and where (geographically) it makes sense to talk about a global saeculum that is driven by global generations. If the seasons of history are global, they will affect the world's future. And, to that extent, they will surely affect America's future as well.

From its earliest "modern" origins in the late fifteenth century, we've already seen that the saeculum was always a regional and more or less synchronized development. The region was Western Europe and its colonial dependencies. And the synchrony was apparent in the European "long cycle" of great wars alternating with durable peace settlements, of Crisis eras alternating with Awakening eras. Yet during these centuries, there was one particular moment when all four turnings of the cycle became much more clearly defined—and when each of the associated generations began to develop a distinct self-consciousness (often, along with a name) linked to its historical role.

That moment was the Crisis era known as the "Atlantic Revolutions" of the late eighteenth and early nineteenth centuries. This staggered quarter century of upheavals began with the American Revolution and then moved (roughly ten years later) to the French Revolution, before spreading to further revolutions and palace coups (often with the help of Napoleon and his armies) throughout much of the rest of Europe and the West Indies—and finally (roughly fifteen years after the French Revolution began) to most of Latin America. During this era, powerful new governments were established, a multitude of "old regimes" were pulled down, and democracy became a realistic hope for a growing class of liberal citizenry.

In many European nations, either through victory or defeat, a powerful Hero-like war generation emerged. In Britain, this was the generation of William Pitt the Younger and Horatio Nelson (born from the mid-1750s to the mid-1770s, roughly ten years later than the American Republican Generation). The Tory leaders of this generation, ruling with a heavy hand, established an extraordinary record for longevity in office. Their eight prime ministers ran Britain for just over half a century: 1783 to 1834. In France, this was the revolutionary generation of Robespierre and Danton, of Lafayette and Napoleon. After their final battle at Waterloo in 1815, all these combat-weary veterans of multiple European wars were ready to settle. They established a placid if repressive era of order and peace under the aegis of the Congress of Vienna, supervised on the Continent by their Austrian peer, Prince Metternich.

Six subsequent European generations developed in the wake of this civic earthquake.

First arrived the war-child Artist archetype that came of age from the early 1800s to the early 1820s, called the "generation of 1820" in France—known for its liberal reformers, its gushy romantic poets and artists, and its conventional mores. The generation included John Keats, Mary Shelley, Victor Hugo, Eugène Delacroix, Franz Schubert, and Heinrich Heine. These were the "sensible" young adults of Jane Austen novels. They produced few well-known leaders, except perhaps for Britain's Robert Peel and France's François Guizot, both moderate liberals.

Second was the Prophet archetype that came of age from the late 1820s to late 1840s, a crop of young utopians and radicals known everywhere on the continent as the "generation of '48." Their riotous revolutions of 1848, directed against their aging arch-enemy Prince Metternich, failed politically almost everywhere. But they did succeed, ideologically, in giving birth to new dreams—of utopianism, socialism, and nationalism. Their paradigmatic young narcissist is the fictional Frédéric Moreau in Gustave Flaubert's *Sentimental Education*. Late in life, many became senior "Gray Champions" of new nations or empires (Napoleon III in France, Otto von Bismarck in Germany, and Giuseppe Mazzini and Giuseppe Garibaldi in Italy). In Britain, they furnished the titanic elder duo of mid-Victorian prime ministers, William Ewart Gladstone and Benjamin Disraeli, and the queen herself, whom Disraeli delighted by making her "Empress of India."

Third was the Nomad archetype that came of age from the late 1840s to late 1860s, though in several war-gripped countries their members constituted the young champions of a Hero archetype. They were known as the "generation of 1871" in Germany, for their victories over Denmark, Austria, and France—as well as in France, for their defeat and their brutally crushed Paris Commune. Having grown up as children in "the hungry forties," they entered adulthood (the older Bismarck famously declared in 1862) knowing that the future of Europe would not be settled by lofty speeches, but by "blood and iron." They became a celebrated generation of pragmatists, positivists, and stunningly original artists (the first and greatest generation of Impressionist painters). As mature leaders in the late Victorian years, they were no-nonsense nationalists, increasingly drawn to social Darwinism and imperialist competition.

Fourth was the Artist archetype that came of age in the 1870s and 1880s as a protectively raised generation of "posts": as in post-war, post-reform, post-Realist, and even post-Impressionist. As young adults, they were little noticed at the start of the prosperous Victorian High. They rapidly professionalized governments, businesses, and universities, and they systematized all of the modern social sciences, from sociology to economics. Including Sigmund Freud, Henri Bergson, Joseph Conrad, and Oscar Wilde, they are reputed to be the nineteenth century's most sexually repressed generation. They furnished the cultivated, colorless, if sometimes eccentric senior leaders of the Edwardian era (the likes of Prime Minister Henry Asquith and Chancellor Bethmann Hollweg). Excelling at administration more than leadership, they led Europe, disastrously, into World War I.

Fifth was the Prophet archetype that came of age in the 1890s and early 1900s. The "naughty nineties" in Britain were a "Belle Époque" on the continent, an era of climaxing confidence and affluence, which these rising young adults challenged with avant-garde movements in thought and feeling. From Igor Stravinsky and Virginia Woolf to Pablo Picasso and Marcel Proust, they were a generation of "isms"—modernism, futurism, symbolism, cubism, and surrealism. In politics, many became radical feminists, socialists, and bomb-throwing anarchists. Their idealistic dreams blasted by the Great War, they adjusted with difficulty to an "older generation" role in the 1920s and '30s. Late in their lives, several became national inspirations during total war (Winston Churchill, Joseph Stalin), during revolution (Vladimir Lenin, Mahatma Gandhi, Muhammad Ali Jinnah), or during Europe's recovery from the rubble (German Chancellor Konrad Adenauer).

Sixth was the Nomad archetype that came of age with World War I and its chaotic aftermath, universally known afterward as "the generation of 1914," *la génération du feu*, a "sacrificed generation," or (as in America) a "lost generation." Acquiring a reputation as risk-takers and iconoclasts even before the war, these rising adults later became the disillusioned skeptics of the 1920s. And, by the Great Depression, many had become skeptical of democracy itself. Their intellectuals reconceived atomic physics (Erwin Schrödinger), philosophy (Martin Heidegger), and fiction (Franz Kafka). Their midlife military officers ultimately tore the world to pieces. Nearly all of their most aggressive war leaders and revolutionaries, along with their most infamous traitors, had been between ages twenty-one and thirty-one in 1914: Adolph Hitler, Benito Mussolini, Francisco Franco, Charles de Gaulle, Pierre Laval, Vidkun Quisling, Josip Broz Tito, Hideki Tojo, Mao Zedong, Chiang Kai-shek, and Ho Chi Minh.

In all seven of these generations, we notice an obvious correspondence with American generations. For different countries across Europe, of course, the generational birth-year boundaries will differ somewhat. And, until the late nineteenth century, the birth-year boundaries come a bit earlier in America than in Europe. But the close affiliation is unmistakable—and was recognized at the time on both continents. Jefferson and many of his friends regularly corresponded with Parisian *philosophes* about natural rights, republican virtue, and (of course) revolution. In the 1840s, the young utopian commune founders in upstate New York borrowed heavily from idealistic "'48" peers in Europe pursuing the same dreams. The sensitive and refined young elites depicted in the novels of Henry James only make sense when surrounded by Europeans of a similar temperament. Many of these Americans flocked to Germany to get serious "university" educations which (they felt) were unavailable at home.

The European experience also sheds further light on the U.S. Civil War anomaly. As happened in America, Europeans who reached adulthood in the 1860s and early 1870s developed a sort of hybrid archetype. In Germany, France, Italy, Spain, Hungary, Romania, and Bulgaria, major wars gave birth to new nations or new national regimes. In these countries, the youth generation came of age into a Crisis era and assumed a personality closer to the Hero archetype. In several other countries, most notably Britain, there was no comparable national challenge and the youth generation moved closer to the Artist archetype.

Either way, the European saeculum starting sometime between the battles of Trafalgar and Waterloo (1805 to 1815) and ending around 1870 resembled the Civil War Saeculum in America: It had only three generations and was roughly twenty years too short. The subsequent European saeculum, ending around 1950, would then last eighty years—within the normal range. As we observed in Chapter 2, "the long European nineteenth century" (1815 to 1914) may be something of a misnomer: That century was interrupted in the middle by multiple wars of national unification that reset the generational cycle.

The timing of these wars, moreover, is significant, because they coincided with the outbreak of similar national convulsions outside of Europe. Thus did the rhythm of the saeculum in Europe begin to synchronize itself with its rhythm in the rest of the world.

In Japan, the 1860s witnessed the Meiji Restoration, which propelled this new "rising sun" empire toward the domination of East Asia by the end of its first saeculum. In China, the 1850s and 1860s witnessed the Taiping Rebellion, led by Hong Xiuquan (a messianic Christian who was roughly the same age as the leaders of the U.S. Civil War). In absolute number of fatalities, the Taiping Rebellion probably ranks as the most violent civil war in human history. Though ultimately suppressed, it weakened the ruling Qing dynasty and set China up to become, eventually, Japan's largest victim. India, following the Sepoy Mutiny of 1857, itself became a formal nation the next year, the "British Raj"—a colonial regime that would last exactly eighty-nine years (until 1947).

In South America, meanwhile, the late 1860s witnessed the War of the Triple Alliance, fought between Brazil, Argentina, and Uruguay on one side and Paraguay on the other. It vies with the U.S. Civil War as the deadliest conflict ever waged in the western hemisphere (nearly exterminating the people of Paraguay). It gave rise in its aftermath to a decades-long "golden age" led by oligarchs in Brazil and Argentina—three or four decades of political stability, territorial expansion, and economic modernization. In Mexico, at about the same time, chronic political instability came to an end with the "Restored Republic," followed by a similar era of national development under the dictatorial authority of Porfirio Díaz. In all three nations, tragically, the brutal inequality of this development caused the last several decades of their first saeculum to be engulfed in social and political revolutions.

However this increasingly global saeculum may have begun in the mid-nineteenth century, there can be little question about exactly how and when it ended—with the Crisis era defined by the Great Depression and World War II.

The 1930s and 1940s witnessed total wars, national revolutions, and genocidal terror whose aggregate death toll almost defies comprehension. Estimates range from 50 to 100 million or possibly more. The Crisis era ended in the late 1940s with a series of global and durable political settlements. It began, in most countries, with a global economic depression and its accompanying political upheavals. It did not begin with World War I, which, destructive as it was for Europe, was followed by peace and prosperity in the 1920s. The leading exception may be Russia, which (along with much of the rest of Eastern Europe) endured a continuous and calamitous Crisis era lasting just over thirty years—from the outset of World War I in 1914 to the raising of a Soviet "iron curtain" across Europe in 1946.

This Crisis era certainly encompassed most of the world: all of Europe; the United States along with other anglophone nations; nearly all of East and South Asia; and much of Latin America. Here was a Fourth Turning that synchronized the generational clock, so to speak, across an unprecedented share of humanity.

On schedule, roughly forty years or so later, there arrived a Second Turning. From the late 1960s into the 1980s, a global Awakening arose—everywhere spearheaded by idealistic youth attacking a repressive Establishment. What Americans call their sixties youth protest movement had analogous waves elsewhere. In Western Europe, it was the era of New Left Euroterrorism—from the initial "May 68" strike in France to the "Baader Meinhof" bombings and assassinations in West Germany and the murderous "Years of Lead" (*Anni di piombo*) in Italy. In China, it was the Cultural Revolution, in which youth brigades tore down every "reactionary" vestige of ancestral Confucian culture. In capital cities around the world—from Prague, Tokyo, and Seoul to Mexico City, Buenos Aires, and Santiago—this Awakening featured massive protests by youth, who were often massacred by authorities in organized reprisals.

Starting with people born at the beginning of the twentieth century, we can identify six generations that have shaped—or have been shaped by—these two global turnings. Their exact birth-year boundaries naturally vary a bit by country. In particular, the slightly earlier timing of the Crisis and Awakening eras in America implies slightly earlier birth years for American generations than for their counterparts abroad. In America, the post–World War II economic boom was already underway by 1946; in most of Europe and Asia, postwar reconstruction was barely underway by 1950. Similarly, most of the Awakening-era youth trends that arrived in America in the mid-1960s came somewhat later to the rest of the world.

Overall, with these minor differences in timing, we can draw a portrait of six global generations that most readers will have no trouble recognizing.

Coming of age during the Crisis era, born from the early 1900s to the early 1920s, a global "G.I. Generation" (Hero) acquired a reputation as strong institution builders and defenders. Generational names: War or Soldier (Europe); Blitz (Britain); Resistance (France, Italy); Patriotic War (Soviet Union); Second or Long March (China); Independence (India). Sample leaders: Margaret Thatcher, François Mitterrand, Helmut Schmidt, Pierre Trudeau, Leonid Brezhnev, Indira Gandhi, Deng Xiaopeng.

Coming of age soon after the Crisis era, born from the mid-1920s to the mid-1940s, a global "Silent Generation" (Artist) acquired an early reputation as earnest technocrats—and, as they grew older, as open-minded liberal reformers. Generational names: Air Raid (Britain); War Child or Builder (Germany); Thaw (Soviet Union); Reconciliation (Spain); Third or Technocrat (China). Sample leaders: Jacques Delors, Mikhail Gorbachev, Helmut Kohl, Gerhard Schröder, Václav Havel, Lech Wałęsa, Mario Draghi, Wen Jiabao, Manmohan Singh.

Coming of age during the Awakening era, born from the late 1940s to the early 1960s, a global "Boom Generation" (Prophet) is acquiring a reputation as values-focused, ethnocentric senior leaders. Generational names: '68 or Boom (Europe); Protest or *Sponti* (Germany); *Brigate Rosse* (Italy); Post-1947 (India); Fourth or Red Guard or Sent Down (China). Sample leaders: Xi Jinping, Vladimir Putin, Angela Merkel, Viktor Orbán, Narendra Modi, Joko Widodo, Shinzo Abe, Andrés Manuel López Obrador, Benjamin Netanyahu.

Coming of age soon after the Awakening era, born from the mid-1960s to the mid-1980s, a global "Xer Generation" (Nomad) is acquiring an early leadership reputation as innovative outsiders and reactive populists. Generational names: Generation X (Europe, Asia); '90s or Berlin (Germany); '69 or *Bof* (France); Zippy (India); Fifth or Reform (China); Generation 386 (South Korea). Sample leaders: Emmanuel Macron, Marine Le Pen, Boris Johnson, Andrzej Duda, Giorgia Meloni, Matteo Salvini, Sebastian Kurz, Pedro Sánchez, Volodymyr Zelensky, Justin Trudeau, Scott Morrison.

Coming of age in the new Crisis era, born from the late 1980s to mid-2000s, a global "Millennial Generation" (possibly Hero) of young people will soon reach leadership age. Their generational names to date mostly reflect perceptions of their sheltered upbringing and delayed path to adulthood: Millennial or Generation Y or Z (Europe, Asia); *Bamboccioni* (Italy); Strawberry (China); *Satori* (Japan); *Sampo* (South Korea). Growing up as children in the new Crisis, born in the late 2000s to late 2020s, a global "Homeland Generation" (possibly Artist) may come of age after the new Crisis era. It is still acquiring generational labels, though the term "Generation Z" is sometimes used.

To be sure, this global saeculum is not yet, literally, global. We can still identify regions where it is not yet fully active, either because the inhabitants are not yet fully modern or because they have fallen into a somewhat different generational rhythm.

The latter possibility may describe the Muslim-majority societies of Africa and the greater Middle East. Most of these did not experience their most recent regime-founding Fourth Turning in the 1930s and '40s, but rather (with full national independence) in the 1950s and early '60s. As we might expect, their Second Turning also came later. Their "Muslim Awakening" suddenly exploded in 1979 (in Iran, Afghanistan, and Saudi

Arabia) and raged until well past the year 2000. The Awakening triggered violence and crackdowns throughout the region—and ghastly Jihadist terror episodes throughout the world.

The youthful Prophet archetype that spearheaded this Awakening was certainly younger than its counterpart in the West. Most of its members were born in the 1960s and '70s. (Osama bin Laden, born in 1957, counts as one of its very oldest members.) Yet even these Muslim Awakeners have by now moved well into midlife—which, they are finding, presents its own surprises. In their youth, they angrily rebelled against their own civic-minded parents, who had once joined secular, socialist parties like the Baathists (Arab nationalists). Today, they often skirmish with their own children, whom they find more materialistic and libertarian than they were at the same age. This emerging Prophet-Nomad friction is likely to shape the politics of the Arab, Turkic, and Persian Mideast well into the 2030s.

Across most of the world, however, the generational constellation is much closer to where it is in America. Each archetype is only a bit younger than it is in America. And each society is, at most, only slightly behind America on the saeculum's seasonal calendar. The most powerful nations of the world, like America, have already entered their own Crisis eras.

This development—this movement of the global Millennial Saeculum toward a largely synchronized culmination—is unlikely to lessen the severity of the global Millennial Crisis, either in America or in the rest of the world. Indeed, given America's deep geopolitical involvement in world affairs, it is likely to raise the stakes of the Crisis climax for all parties. We will return to this global convergence later on, in Chapter 7, and ponder its implications for how the rest of the Crisis era will ultimately unfold.

Part Two

CLIMAX OF WINTER

6

A WINTER CHRONOLOGY

December 23, 1776: THESE are the times that try men's souls. The summer soldier and the sunshine patriot will, in this crisis, shrink from the service of their country; but he that stands by it now, deserves the love and thanks of man and woman. Tyranny, like hell, is not easily conquered; yet we have this consolation with us, that the harder the conflict, the more glorious the triumph.

—THOMAS PAINE

"Something happened to America at that time," recalled U.S. Senator Daniel Inouye on VJ Day in 1995, in the last of the fifty-year commemoratives of World War II. "I'm not wise enough to know what it was. But it was the strange, strange power that our founding fathers experienced in those early, uncertain days. Let's call it the spirit of America, a spirit that united and galvanized our people."

Inouye went on to reflect wistfully on an era when the nation considered no obstacle too big, no challenge too great, no goal too distant, no sacrifice too deep. Today, nearly eight decades later, nobody under age ninety-five has any adult memory of what Inouye was talking about.

In the climactic years between Pearl Harbor and VJ Day, arguments were forgotten, ideals energized, and creaky infrastructure repurposed for urgent new goals. At home, at work, and in the military, teamwork and discipline were unusually strong. Shirkers and doubters drew scorn. Despite the risk of death or injury, soldiers fighting thousands of miles from home overwhelmingly agreed (in surveys taken after the war) that their efforts were positive for the world, positive for America, and positive for their own lives personally.

People were also hopeful, even in the face of terrible adversity. During the summer of 1940, with Germany conquering Western Europe and Japan advancing into China, a Roper poll found that a plurality of Americans, 36 to 43 percent, were optimistic about "the future of civilization."

With the people thus united, that era established a powerful new civic order replete with new public institutions, economic arrangements, political alliances, and global treaties, many of which have lasted to this day. That era also ushered in a grim acceptance of destruction as a necessary concomitant to human progress. It was a time when wars were fought to the finish; when a president could command a prized young generation to march off with the warning that one in three would not come home; when America's smartest young scientists worked 24/7 to build weapons of mass destruction; when imagined domestic enemies were rounded up in snowy camps; when enemy armies were destroyed, their leaders hanged. Indeed, while this beloved "Spirit of America" resonates with warm reminiscences from a distance of eighty years, it was also a time of brutal, even lethal forms of social reconstruction.

Today's older Americans, who may have grown up as children during that era or its immediate aftermath, often recall that era fondly but selectively: They would like to restore its unity and selflessness, but without the conflict or carnage. Yet how? The only way they can see is a way *back*, to an America stripped of the civic atrophy, institutional dysfunction, and pervasive ennui that have settled in over the intervening decades. Such a task feels hopeless because it is.

Like nature, history is full of processes that cannot happen in reverse. Just as the laws of entropy do not allow a bird to fly backward, or droplets to regroup at the top of a waterfall, history has no rewind button. Like the seasons of nature, time's arrow only moves forward. Starting from an Unraveling, society cannot move into a High (or into an Awakening) without a Crisis in between.

A Fourth Turning is a solstice era of maximum darkness, in which the supply of social order remains low—though the demand for order is now steeply rising. It is the saeculum's hibernal, its time of trial. In winter, writes William Cullen Bryant, "The melancholy days are come, the saddest of the year, / Of wailing winds, and naked woods, and meadows brown and sere." Nature exacts its fatal payment and pitilessly sorts out the survivors and the doomed. Pleasures recede, tempests hurt, pretense is exposed, and toughness rewarded—all in a season, says Victor Hugo, that "changes into stone the water of heaven and the heart of man." This is a time of fire and ice, of polar darkness and brilliantly pale horizons. What it doesn't kill, it reminds of death. What it doesn't wound, it reminds of pain. In Swinburne's "season of snows," it is "The light that loses, the night that wins."

Like natural winter, which reaches its solstice early, the Fourth Turning passes its nadir of public order near its beginning. Just as the coldest days of winter are days of lengthening sun, the harsh (and least hopeful) years of a Crisis are years of renascent community. Early on, amid popular unrest and government failure, this shift may be barely noticed. But it signals a critical negative-to-positive flip in the rate of change: Early in the Awakening, the removal of each civic layer brings demands for the removal of more layers; early in the Crisis, each new exercise of civic authority brings a perceived need for the *adding* of layers.

Further into the Crisis era, as the community instinct regenerates, people resolve to do more than just relieve the symptoms of trauma. Having rediscovered what is achievable through unity, teamwork, and social discipline, they go to work on larger social problems. More than they ever did before, people comply with authority, accept the need for public sacrifice, and—when necessary—shed any activity unrelated to the survival needs of their community. This is a critical threshold: People either coalesce as citizens of a single nation and culture—or rip hopelessly apart.

The "spirit of America" comes once a saeculum, accompanying what the ancients called *Ekpyrosis*, nature's fiery moment of death and discontinuity. The Ekpyrosis refers specifically to the culminating years of the Crisis era, when public events move at maximum speed—completing the combustion of the old saeculum and making room for the birth of a new.

Seasonal winters are how the natural world reverses entropy. Everything visible dies in a wreckage of decay, but underground new seeds germinate. Saecular winters are how a modern society reverses entropy.

Because these violent disruptions destroy mature institutions, they are feared. But because they give birth to rejuvenated institutions, they are necessary. Periodically, Vishnu must yield to Shiva. Forests need periodic fires. Rivers need periodic floods. Societies too. That's the toll humanity must pay for a new golden age.

For America and perhaps for much of the rest of the world, the Millennial Crisis is already underway. And the culminating Ekpyrosis will soon begin. What can we expect?

This is the first of four chapters that will try to answer this question—as always, by examining the rhythms of the past. In this chapter, we will look closely at the characteristic chronology of a Crisis era. In what order, historically, do events tend to happen? What does this timeline imply for where we are today and what is still to come?

In the following three chapters, we look specifically at the Millennial Crisis and speculate on how it will turn out; we look at how our society will change; and we look at how our lives will change, depending on our generation.

A CHRONOLOGY OF CRISIS ERAS

Fourth Turnings have furnished the great pivot points of the Anglo-American legacy. We are now in the seventh. Each of the six completed since the fifteenth century generated its own facsimile of the halcyon "spirit" that today's aging World War II veterans remember so vividly. From the similarities of these Crisis eras, a chronology of common phases can be constructed:

- During the prior Unraveling, the Crisis is usually foreshadowed by a *precursor*—an emergency that temporarily galvanizes society.

- A Crisis era begins with a *catalyst*—a watershed event that produces a sudden but lasting shift in the social mood.

- Once catalyzed, a society experiences at least one *regeneracy* (there is usually more than one)—which reunifies community and re-energizes civic life.

- The regenerated society eventually reaches a *consolidation*—when everyone understands that their new community is engaged in a true struggle for survival.

- The consolidated society propels toward a *climax*—a crucial moment that confirms the death of the old order and triumph of the new.

- The climax culminates in a *resolution*—a triumphant or tragic conclusion that separates winners from losers, resolves the big public questions, and establishes the new order.

According to this Crisis chronology, every phase except the precursor occurs over the span of one Crisis turning, which (except for the U.S. Civil War) means that around twenty-four years on average elapse between the starting catalyst and the ultimate resolution. All of the phases of the Crisis always occur in the same fixed order, but not according to any predictable schedule. The Crisis chronology therefore spells out a regularity in sequence, though not any regularity in timing.

The *precursor*, when it happens, always occurs at some time during the prior turning, an Unraveling. It briefly foreshadows the mood of the coming Crisis era by showing how a society aware of its own weakening civic instincts can still galvanize and rise up to meet a new challenge. Examples of precursors include the response to 9/11 before the Millennial Crisis; World War I before the Great Depression–World War II Crisis; or the French and Indian War before the American Revolution Crisis. Yet after the challenge is met, the mood reverts to its Unraveling norm. The generational constellation has not yet moved into the life phases that make a Crisis era possible.

The *catalyst* is an event that finally terminates the Unraveling mood and unleashes the Crisis mood. We've seen in Chapter 5 how sparks of history—sudden and startling events—can arise in any turning. Some sparks ignite nothing. Some flare briefly and then extinguish. Some have important effects but leave underlying problems unresolved. Others ignite epic conflagrations. Which ones ignite? Ignition is substantially determined by the season of the saeculum—in other words, by the turning in which the events are located. Sparks in a High tend to reinforce the impulse to gather; in an Awakening, the impulse to defy; in an Unraveling, the impulse to detach.

The catalyst can be one spark—or, more commonly, a series of sparks that ignite one another like the firecrackers traditionally used by the Chinese to mark their own breaks in the circle of time. Each of these sparks is linked to a specific threat about which society had been fully informed—but against which it had left itself poorly protected. Afterward, the fact that these sparks were foreseeable, even foreseen, generates a new mood of paralysis and pessimism. The catalyst thus marks the beginning of the Crisis.

Once the Crisis is underway, a society begins a process of *regeneracy*, a drawing together into whatever definition of community is available at the time. Out of the debris of the Unraveling—like nebulae precipitating into young stars—scattered individuals and households start congregating into ever-larger groups. These groups, which may sort themselves by politics, region, class, religion, ideology, or ethnicity, help like-minded people find shelter against risk, leverage over public policy, and a common agenda. Once a group or coalition gains sufficient power, it can begin to take on major challenges facing the entire people or nation. Collective action, the channeling and orchestration of popular passions on a vast scale, is now seen as vital to solving the society's most fundamental problems.

Society may experience a single regeneracy in which a single dominant group, after gathering strength, can successfully meet the ultimate challenge posed by the Crisis. This has happened once: in the Armada Crisis. A single regeneracy may also lead to society's mobilization into two exclusive and antagonistic groups and thence directly to deadly civil conflict. This has happened twice: in the U.S. Civil War and the English War of the Roses. In every other case, society's first regeneracy, after giving birth to two or more dominant groups, eventually weakens. These groups then fragment and reassemble during a second regeneracy.

During the entire regeneracy phase, the mood is a confusing mix of hope, fear, and dizzying uncertainty. There is the hope that one's own strengthening community will overcome its adversaries and the forces of

disorder. Conversely, there is the fear of defeat and failure. And throughout there is uncertainty—the terrifying prospect that, win or lose, the upheavals unleashed by the Crisis will come to no natural resting place or
stopping point. This is how Americans felt in the late 1930s, as the world
careened toward global war and the economic depression lingered despite
the "New Deal." This is how Americans felt in the mid-1780s, after their
new "confederation" appeared to be foundering in poverty and anarchy.

At some point after achieving its final regeneracy, society experiences
a *consolidation*, the moment when all members of the dominant new
community understand that they are engaged in an ultimate struggle for
survival. While hopes and fears mount, uncertainty subsides: Everything
rests on this one outcome. After the consolidation, the community unites
in maximum collective energy and efficacy. Most people who haven't yet
chosen sides must now choose. Leaders redirect every available institution toward a common goal. Thus invigorated, society starts propelling
itself in a trajectory that nobody foresaw before the catalyzing event. Social problems that earlier in the Unraveling posed insuperable challenges
now appear to have simple if demanding solutions. A new resolve about
urgent public ends crowds out qualms about harsh public means.

The *climax* of a Crisis determines whether the new order will or will
not prevail against its enemies and obstacles. Between the consolidation
and the climax—that is, during the Ekpyrosis—civic action reaches its
point of maximum power. Where the new values regime had once (a half
saeculum earlier) justified personal fury, now it justifies public fury. The
risk of an all-out struggle against a perceived external aggressor is high—
as is the risk of internal political revolution or civil war. Leaders, with
public support, become more inclined to define enemies categorically, to
disarm or confine them extra-legally, to censor news media, to rule out
compromises, and to turn down negotiated settlements. Near the end
of an Awakening, public action comes to a complete rest, seemingly im-
movable. Near the end of a Crisis, public action acquires a tsunami-like
momentum, seemingly unstoppable.

The Ekpyrosis is history's equivalent to nature's raging typhoon,
sucking all surrounding matter into a single vortex of ferocious energy.
Anything not lashed down goes flying; anything standing in the way

gets flattened. Always occurring late in the Fourth Turning, the climax gathers energy from an accumulation of unmet needs, unpaid debts, and unresolved problems. It then spends that energy on an upheaval whose direction and magnitude were beyond comprehension during the prior Unraveling. The climax shakes a society to its roots, transforms its institutions, redirects its purposes, and marks its people (and its generations) for life.

During the Great Depression–World War II Crisis, the Ekpyrosis corresponded to the emergence of the "Spirit of America" described by Senator Inouye. During these years, according to surveys, the vast majority of Americans wanted summary punishment meted out to Axis leaders without trial—and rejected a negotiated settlement with any of them (even as late as the Battle of the Bulge). Resolve is so strong that even calamitous reversals don't easily shake it. During the U.S. Civil War, shortly after the deadliest Union debacles, voting in counties suffering the most casualties showed sizable declines in support for Lincoln among Democrats. Yet voting in these counties showed no decline at all in support from Lincoln's more numerous Republican partisans, despite widespread rumors that Union generals had bungled on the battlefield.

The Ekpyrosis often directly precedes the outcome of total war, but not always. In the American Revolution and Glorious Revolution crises, the worst war violence came earlier. In those Crisis eras, the climactic outcome was settled politically, not militarily. However it happens, the climax determines the location and contours of the next great threshold of history. It signals the imminent birth of a new turning and a new saeculum, dividing everything "before" from everything "after"—just as a continental divide sends falling rain toward one ocean rather than another. The climax can end in triumph, or tragedy, or some combination of both. Whatever the outcome, society passes through a great gate of history.

Soon after the climax, this great gate is sealed by the Crisis *resolution*, when success (or failure) is acknowledged and when leaders choose (or are compelled) to rein in the pace of public action. In the resolution, victors are rewarded and enemies punished; nations or empires are forged or destroyed; treaties are signed and boundaries redrawn; peace is accepted, troops repatriated, and ordinary life begins anew.

One large chapter of history ends, and another starts. In a very real sense, one society dies—and another is born.

LOOKING BACK: PAST CRISIS ERAS

To understand the unfolding rhythm of today's Millennial Crisis, we need to examine the chronology of earlier Crisis eras.

As we've discussed, there have been six prior Crises in the Anglo-American lineage, dating back to the fifteenth century:

War of the Roses, 1455–1487 (Late Medieval Saeculum)

Armada Crisis, 1569–1597 (Tudor Saeculum)

Glorious Revolution, 1675–1706 (New World Saeculum)

American Revolution, 1773–1794 (Revolutionary Saeculum)

Civil War, 1860–1865 (Civil War Saeculum)

Great Depression–World War II, 1929–1946 (Great Power Saeculum)

With the partial exception of the U.S. Civil War (due to its short duration), the basic sequence of events in each of these eras is similar. Starting with the most recent and working back, we describe them here.

GREAT DEPRESSION–WORLD WAR II CRISIS: 1929–1946

The *precursor* to the Great Depression–World War II Crisis was America's formal participation in World War I (1917–18). This came late enough to spare America Europe's dreadful casualty rate, but early enough to be decisive—and to give America a leading role in the peace settlement. Very briefly, Americans rallied madly to the flag while President Woodrow Wilson and Congress agreed to impose conscription, crack down harshly on dissenters, and set up executive boards to manage wartime production and trade.

Yet even during mobilization, the war faced serious opposition. Socialists objected to killing workers, German-Americans to killing Germans, and Christian pacifists to killing anyone. Rural Democrats feared Wall Street just wanted more profits, while Republican businessmen feared government just wanted more power. Meanwhile, the war planning boards trained a new wave of industrialists in their thirties and forties like Bernard Baruch and Hugh Johnson in how to mobilize an economy. And the fight to reverse Germany's Ludendorff Offensive in 1918 became a bracing rite of passage to a new wave of U.S. army and navy officers in their twenties and thirties—including George C. Marshall, Douglas MacArthur, Bull Halsey, Harry Truman, Chester Nimitz, and George Patton.

Immediately after the Armistice came the Spanish influenza, back-to-back recessions, and the Red Scare—persuading most Americans that the critics had been right: The war had been a colossal blunder. The Senate turned down Wilson's high-minded League of Nations proposal, plunging America back into isolationism. President Warren G. Harding, elected by a landslide in 1920, promised a return to do-nothing "normalcy." Markets boomed. The Third Turning mood resumed, only now with a darker, more nihilistic tone than before the war.

By the late 1920s, America felt increasingly wild. Its daily life was propelled ever faster by the spread of autos, airplanes, telephones, and radio; its government was disregarded as weak and irrelevant; its culture was hopelessly cleaved between the Prohibitionist "booboisie" and the jaded pleasure seekers; and its public was captivated by what Hemingway called a "movable feast" of celebrities and trifles. "The restlessness . . . approached hysteria. The parties were bigger, the pace was faster, the shows were broader, the buildings were higher, the morals were looser, and the liquor was cheaper," wrote Fitzgerald of New York City in 1926. "The city was bloated, glutted, stupid with cakes and circuses, and a new expression, 'O yeah?' summed up all the enthusiasm."

By decade's end, historian Frederick Lewis Allen described the public spirit as having reached a low ebb. While everyone was fascinated by the "new era" business mergers and the ever-rising stock ticker (by one estimate, more than a million Americans owned stocks on margin), they also knew the fun and frolic couldn't last forever. The end had to come. But no one knew when.

The *catalyst* arrived on Black Thursday, October 24, 1929. A market comeuppance had been foreseen by many, but the public reaction caught everybody by surprise. In a mood shift Allen described as "bewilderingly rapid," Americans now realized that "an old order was giving place to new," that the 1930s "would not be a repetition" of the 1920s, that there would be no more "aching disillusionment of the hard-boiled era, its oily scandals, its spiritual paralysis, the harshness of its gaiety."

By 1932, the unemployment rate had risen to 24 percent and GDP had sunk 25 percent below its 1929 value—both numbers seemingly unthinkable. Bankruptcies multiplied. Cities and states ran out of relief funds. Hunger spread, and breadlines formed in the cities. President Herbert Hoover, elected before the crash in another Republican landslide, could not shift gears fast enough. While he eventually backed unprecedented federal measures to boost investment (the Reconstruction Finance Corporation) and reform banking (the first Glass-Steagall Act), his insistence on sticking to the now-suicidal gold standard doomed any recovery. It also doomed his re-election, especially once Democrats mocked him for offering subsidies to the rich while relegating the jobless to "Hoovervilles."

The 1932 national election was another landslide, this time in favor of a Democrat: Franklin D. Roosevelt, a twice-elected governor of New York about whom the public knew little—except that he was not Hoover. Despair deepened and bank runs spread everywhere in the winter of '33. On FDR's inauguration day, March 4, both the New York Stock Exchange and the Chicago Board of Trade had suspended trading, not a single bank was open in twenty-eight states, and millions had already lost their savings.

Nevertheless, the new president's address marked the first *regeneracy*. Observing that "the only thing we have to fear is fear itself," he appealed to timeless values, promised ceaseless experimentation, and declared he would "wage a war against the emergency" as though "we were in fact invaded by the foreign foe." In his first hundred days in office, FDR and his "brain trust" proposed vast new regulatory powers over banking, securities, agriculture, and business practices—plus requests to Congress for new spending on relief and public works (under names like the Civilian Conservation Corps, the Federal Emergency Relief Administration, the Public Works Administration, and the Tennessee Valley Authority). Many bills were presented, passed, and signed in less than a day.

While some newspapers called FDR a dictator (not always disapprovingly), the public took heart. Later that summer, the stock market rebounded. Production and income began to recover. Some new measures, like leaving the gold standard, proved very helpful. Many others, like the National Recovery Administration—whose blue-eagled uniforms were introduced in spectacular downtown parades—proved worse than useless. Either way, FDR hardly paused. In 1935 and '36, the administration pushed the "Second New Deal" through Congress. This included the National Labor Relations Board (regulating labor disputes), a corporate earnings tax, Social Security (including retirement, unemployment, and various poverty programs), and a new "works" program called the Works Progress Administration.

The New Deal coalition pushed hard in those years. And it did so in part because it feared the rising popularity of "share the wealth" demagogues on both the right and the left—the likes of Father Coughlin (the antisemitic radio priest), Huey Long (populist governor of Louisiana), Upton Sinclair (muckraker author and activist), and Francis Townsend (who advocated immediate federal payments to retired people). Taking advantage of rising production, Congress of Industrial Organizations leader John L. Lewis and United Auto Workers chief Walter Reuther led industrial workers in often-violent sit-down strikes. Tens of thousands of young Communists joined "popular front" agitators on the front lines of street battles. Running for re-election in 1936, FDR amped up his own radicalism as he inveighed against the "greed" and "avarice" of "economic royalists." "They are unanimous in their hate for me—and I welcome their hatred!" he told a roaring crowd in Madison Square Garden.

On Election Day, he showed that he had effectively coopted the populists and steamrolled the Republicans. He won by a 24 percent popular vote margin. The Democrats now utterly dominated Congress, by 76 to 16 in the Senate and 333 to 89 in the House. In his victorious inaugural address, FDR pointed to Americans still in desperate need ("I see one-third of a nation ill-housed, ill-clad, ill-nourished") and hoped most citizens would join him in pressing still further his progressive agenda.

But they didn't. In fact, the first regeneracy was already ebbing. And for most of the next three years the President was on the defensive. The initial reversal came after FDR's "court packing" scheme, which even loyal New Dealers repudiated (and in any event soon proved unnecessary). Then came a backlash against radical labor tactics like "sit-down strikes," for the first time swinging public sympathy toward business. Finally, a severe recession: In May 1937, the economy turned down again, not to recover until 1939. In the midterms, the GOP rebounded, winning back seven Senate seats and cutting the Democrats' huge House majority by nearly two-thirds.

Compounding the administration's frustration was growing Southern resistance. Because Southerners made up nearly half the Democrats in Congress and nearly all the critical committee chairmanships, FDR depended on their support. Most of them enthusiastically backed transferring income from the urban North to the rural South and even from rich Whites to poor Whites. But they dreaded disturbing the economic "color line" that kept Blacks dependent on Whites. To many Southern leaders, national union rules and federal legislation that equalized pay or hours did just that. Southern Democrats began voting more often with Northern Republicans. FDR campaigned heavily, but unsuccessfully, for liberal Democrats in the 1938 Southern primaries.

His domestic agenda stuck, the president turned his attention increasingly, and urgently, to foreign policy. Around the world, fascist dictatorships were on the march. And for several years, the response of America's public and leaders had been redoubled isolationism. With each new outrage—Mussolini's invasion of Ethiopia (1935), the Spanish Civil War (1936), Japan's full invasion of China (1937), and Hitler's takeover of Austria and Czechoslovakia (1938)—Congress responded with ever-tighter Neutrality Acts.

While FDR favored more spending on defense and more solidarity with allies, he dared not move too far ahead of public opinion. "All about us rage undeclared wars—military and economic," FDR warned Congress in January of 1939. But to millions of Americans, no danger seemed worth another "War to End All Wars." These isolationists ranged from college students who had signed the "Oxford Pledge," swearing never to fight in another war, to conservative small-town Republicans who began to form an "America First Committee." Even after the invasion of Poland in August, the mood shifted only enough for FDR to amend the Neutrality Act to allow cash-and-carry arms shipments to allies.

But in the spring and summer of 1940, with the fall of France and the Battle of Britain, the public mood began to shift rapidly—now supporting aid to Britain and, above all, military preparedness. It wasn't any longer just about world peace. It was about America being left alone in a world overrun by dictators. From June on, Congress passed vast new defense spending bills by near-unanimous votes. In September, it enacted America's first-ever peacetime conscription. Newly energized and motivated, FDR finally chose to run for a third term and defeated a Republican opponent (Wendell Willkie) who then pulled his party behind the president on the need to rearm.

This new consensus behind mobilization in mid-1940 marked the second *regeneracy*—this time different in purpose and backed by an altered constituency. Turning America into "an arsenal of democracy" lost the White House some pacifist Democrats and Lindbergh-leaning Republicans in the North. But it brought back on board nearly all the Southern congressman, whose pro-military voters quickly warmed to the new nationalism and whose districts looked forward to receiving a large share of the new armament spending.

In March of the next year, Congress overwhelmingly approved the Lend-Lease Act, which allowed America to "lend" unlimited war matériel to allies abroad. The president thereupon announced that "as a united nation, our democracy has gone into action." By early November, the nation was practically on a war footing: U.S. Navy ships were escorting supply convoys to Britain and the Soviet Union; sporadic hostilities had broken out in the North Atlantic; and Secretaries Stimson and Hull were girding for an imminent attack by Japan. A torrent of federal military spending was at last lifting America out of the Great Depression—

pushing up GDP at a blistering annual rate of 18 percent and bringing unemployment below 10 percent for the first time since 1929.

The December 7 aerial bombing of Pearl Harbor, triggering immediate declarations of war, was the *consolidation*. Most Americans, realizing that everything they had achieved was now at risk, felt (in Senator's Inouye's words) a "spirit of America . . . that united and galvanized our people." Columnist Walter Lippmann wrote, "Overnight we have become . . . at long last a united people . . . an awakened people—wide awake to the stark truth that the very existence of the Nation, the lives, the liberties, and the fortunes of all of us are in the balance."

From just under half a million in 1940, military personnel grew by another half million *every two months* for the next three years. Production of private homes, cars, and appliances practically ceased. Assembly lines retooled wholesale for the manufacture of aircraft, ships, and military vehicles—all to one end: total victory. The President explained he was no longer Dr. New Deal; he was now Dr. Win-the-War. And the outcome was no longer up to him, but up to the war planners, officers, soldiers, and factory workers.

The first year, 1942, was the darkest. German U-boats torpedoed hundreds of merchant ships, many within sight of eastern cities. Japanese fast-carrier and invasion fleets, though checked at Midway, roamed freely through most of the Pacific and Indian Oceans. By year's end, Americans had a toehold in the Solomon Islands and North Africa. In 1943, the tide shifted decisively in the Allies' favor—in Russia, the Mediterranean, and the North Atlantic. By the end of the year, the Allies were in Italy, and large new capital ships were at last giving the U.S. Pacific Fleet a clear advantage over Japan.

Yet Americans still had no idea how long the struggle would go on. The end became much clearer in June and July of 1944, with the Allies' breakout from the D-Day landings and the crushing U.S. victory over Japan's carrier-based air force at the Battle of the Philippine Sea. This was the *climax*. The outcome was now certain, and it was expected soon. VE Day for Europe came on May 8, 1945. VJ Day, delayed by stubborn Japanese resistance until after two war-ending atomic bombs, came on August 15, 1945.

At the war's climax, unemployment virtually disappeared while union membership spread and wages soared. Everyone seemed to be in motion: During the war, nearly one-quarter of Americans changed residences— either in the service under orders or as workers seeking better jobs. Millions of poor farmers found much better pay in the cities. These included Southern Black families after A. Philip Randolph pressured FDR to sign Executive Order 8802, ensuring equal pay for African Americans in war industries. (For many Black Americans, America's "V for Victory" became a "Double-V for Victory" campaign that included the acquisition of full citizenship rights.) In his 1944 message to Congress, FDR tied his New Deal back into the war by spelling out a Second Bill of Rights, guaranteeing basic economic security along with political liberty. Later that year, in the "G.I. Bill of Rights," Congress passed an extensive array of benefits for returning veterans, America's future middle class.

If 1945 and 1946 proved to be the *resolution* of the domestic legacy of the New Deal, so too did those years secure America's new position in the world. They saw signed treaties with the defeated Axis powers; the establishment of the United Nations, the World Bank, and the IMF; the Bretton Woods exchange-rate agreement; the post-Potsdam power-sharing with Joseph Stalin's Soviet Union; and diplomat George Kennan's first inkling of a coming "cold war." Altogether, for those "present at the creation" (like Undersecretary of State Dean Acheson), this resolution constituted the foundation of our "postwar" world.

Today's Americans often look back on the peace and prosperity created by this resolution as historically inevitable, like a giant sunlit plateau that has always been part of the landscape. But while the war still raged, it seemed merely visionary and highly unlikely—unlikely, that is, unless the nation exerted itself to the utmost.

In his wartime State of the Union addresses, FDR made frequent use of the word *total*: as in "total mobilization," "total war," "total victory," and "total peace." He argued that America must resolve not just to win the Second World War, but also—in order to prevent the chaos that followed the first war—to superintend postwar global norms on everything from commerce to human rights. When FDR explained his "four freedoms" (freedom of speech, of worship, from want, and from fear), he insisted that each must be observed "everywhere in the world." Even in his last address, delivered in January 1945, there was no letting up. "This war must be waged—it is being waged—with the greatest and most persistent intensity. Everything we are and have is at stake. . . . We have no question of the ultimate victory. We have no question of the cost. Our losses will be heavy."

This was hardly a message that pandered to its audience. But when Franklin Roosevelt died just three months later, Americans mourned him as they had no president since Abraham Lincoln.

CIVIL WAR CRISIS, 1860–1865

The *precursor* to the Civil War Crisis was the Mexican-American War (1846–48), in which the young United States waged a stunningly successful war against an even younger Mexican republic. With the signing of the Treaty of Guadalupe Hidalgo, the United States formalized its acquisition by force of roughly one-quarter of its present-day lower-forty-eight landmass. Just before the war, New York magazine editor (and Democrat) John O'Sullivan coined the term "manifest destiny" to express America's jubilant support for its Jacksonian president, James Knox Polk, and his single-minded expansionism.

The victory over Mexico thrilled many restless Americans ready to move westward. Yet it also soured many others, especially Whigs and New Englanders, who feared the growing political power of Southern Democrats. The war also gave a rising generation of military officers in their twenties, just out of West Point or Southern military academies, a chance to test their skills in places like Monterrey, Vera Cruz, and Chapultepec. Among them were Ulysses S. Grant, Stonewall Jackson, William Tecumseh Sherman, James Longstreet, George McClellan, and Ambrose Burnside.

The war had hardly been won before weak government, a surge of immigration, and rising violence pushed America back into its Third Turning. Above all, America was veering into a sectional quarrel over the future of slavery: Most Northern voters wanted no further spread of slavery to the territories and future states; most Southern voters wanted, and felt they needed, robust further expansion of their economic system and way of life.

There seemed to be no middle ground. Senior lawmakers managed to defer confrontation through patchwork work-arounds, but at the cost of inflaming tempers on both sides. The Fugitive Slave Act of 1850, which required Northerners to apprehend and return escaped slaves, triggered "resistance" agitation in Northern cities. The Kansas-Nebraska Act of 1854, which overruled the 1820 Missouri Compromise between the North and the South on admitting new slave states, touched off deadly clashes between Southern Bushwhackers and Free-Soil Jayhawkers west of the Missouri River. It also intensified the mood of violence on Capitol Hill, where (historian Joanne Freeman reports) shoving and fistfights, brandished pistols and bowie knives, canings, duel threats, and duels themselves became commonplace. According to two North Carolina Whigs, nearly a third of U.S. House members entered the chamber armed.

As an elder generation of "Great Compromisers" (led by Henry Clay, John C. Calhoun, and Daniel Webster) passed away, a more abrasive crop of public figures, more spiritual yet also more confrontational, began to take their place. "The age is dull and mean. Men creep, not walk," complained abolitionist John Greenleaf Whittier in a poem entitled "For Righteousness' Sake." In 1852, Harriet Beecher Stowe's *Uncle Tom's Cabin* sold an astounding six hundred thousand copies, polarizing both sides. Anger was further roused by the Supreme Court's *Dred Scott* decision in 1857 and by John Brown's suicidal raid on Harper's Ferry, Virginia, in 1859. After his execution, Brown, who had earlier ax-murdered pro-slavery supporters in Kansas, was likened by Northern abolitionist leaders to Jesus Christ Himself. During the prior decade, America's evangelical churches (Presbyterian, Methodist, and Baptist) had already split into Northern and Southern halves. During the 1850s, America's political parties did the same. The national Whig Party disintegrated in 1854, the national Democratic Party in 1858.

By 1860, Americans were interpreting events—and were voting—almost entirely along sectional lines. To Southerners, Northern leaders were coalescing into a "Black Republican" party determined to stunt the Southerners' future expansion and "degrade their honor" over the slavery question. To Northerners, Southern leaders were backing a "Slave Power Conspiracy" intent on dominating every branch of the federal

government and defying the electorate. In the fall election, the Republican candidate Abraham Lincoln ran on a "free soil" platform and won
every Northern and Western state. (His name wasn't even on the ballot
in most Southern states.) The Democrats' vote was split, but the candidate who won nearly everywhere in the South was John Breckinridge,
who ran on a radical pro-slavery platform.

On November 7, 1860, the nation learned that Lincoln had won
the presidency by gaining an electoral college majority, even though he
won only 40 percent of the popular vote. In response, Southern state
leaders swiftly organized secession conventions and voted for independence from the Union. By December 20, South Carolina had made it
official. And even before the new U.S. president could be sworn in on
March 4, 1861, all seven Deep South states had held conventions, voted
overwhelmingly for secession, and together formed a new "Confederate
States of America."

This Southern reaction to Lincoln's election, not the election itself,
was the *catalyst* of a new Crisis era, which was fated to unfold with terrifying speed. Had the South not seceded, ironically, it could have hoped
to maintain its peculiar institution for perhaps decades to come: After
his election, Lincoln reiterated the Republicans' promise not to interfere with slavery where it already existed; he was even willing to support
a constitutional amendment to that effect. In any case, the Democrats
still held a majority in the Senate. But with secession, the possibility of
another compromise evaporated. By Christmas, stock market prices,
which had barely recovered from the 1857 crash, fell by nearly a quarter.
"We are divorced, because we have hated each other so," explained Mary
Chesnut of South Carolina in her diary.

The nation held its breath as the new president declared his intent
to "hold and occupy" federal properties located in the South without
however firing the first shot. He succeeded: The rebels fired first. On
April 12, 1861, Charleston batteries began bombarding Fort Sumter.
This was the *regeneracy*. War was now a fact, and the two sides rushed
to rally for their respective causes. To fight for the Union, Lincoln immediately ordered the states to call up seventy-five thousand volunteers—a
request that pushed the wavering border states (Virginia, North Caro-

lina, Tennessee, and Arkansas) to join the Confederacy. In the North, fear of national disintegration inspired a wave of patriotic demonstrations in cities. Abolitionists who had earlier (in protest) flown the stars and stripes upside down turned the flag upside up again. "There are but two parties now, Traitors and Patriots. And I want hereafter to be ranked with the latter, and I trust, the stronger party," wrote Grant (a still-unknown colonel) to his father.

Two months later, both sides were shocked by the scale of casualties in the first large engagement, the First Battle of Bull Run, in which nearly five thousand soldiers were killed, wounded, or missing. By April 1862, they were shocked again: thirteen thousand at Shiloh. And again in September, following Lee's advance into Maryland: twenty-three thousand in one day at Antietam. Stories of dozens of lesser battles, each with lists of the fallen, filled newspapers. The exigency of mobilization invaded the lives of citizens. Both governments ordered conscription, new taxes, public borrowing, and money printing. Armies enforced price controls and freely requisitioned property, including factories, ships, and railroads. Both sides suspended habeas corpus. Lincoln arrested without charges many thousands of Northern Democrats he considered dangerous (the exact number is unknown). On one occasion, he rounded up and jailed dozens of Maryland legislators.

A week after Antietam, Lincoln chose to issue the Emancipation Proclamation, which declared that all slaves within states "in rebellion against the United States" shall be designated "forever free." The proclamation, made official on January 1, 1863, suddenly raised the stakes of the war and so became the *consolidation* of the Crisis.

To avoid offending War Democrats and moderate Republicans, Lincoln was careful to frame the proclamation as a war measure: The object was not to abolish slavery but to cripple the slave-based Confederate war effort. Yet Republican Radicals rejoiced because they knew, practically, that this would put a permanent end to slavery *if the Union could prevail.* The Confederacy knew this as well and declared "retaliation"—promising that any ex-slaves caught "serving" the Union might be summarily executed (a promise often fulfilled late in the war). General Lee called Lincoln's decree a "savage and brutal policy . . . which leaves us no alternative but success or degradation worse than death." The proclamation also re-cast the Union globally as a champion of republican liberalism. After Lincoln's announcement, Britain and France quietly abandoned any effort to recognize President Davis's government in Richmond.

The war raged on. Lee and his Army of Virginia continued to embarrass Union armies in the east, while multiple Union generals drove Rebel armies out of Missouri, Kentucky, Tennessee, Louisiana (after taking New Orleans), and northern Mississippi in the west. On July 4, 1863, the Union rejoiced after learning that Lee had been turned back at Gettysburg, Pennsylvania (casualties over three days: fifty-one thousand). On the same day, Grant took the Vicksburg citadel—effectively seizing control of the entire Mississippi River. Yet Rebel resistance grew the farther Union armies advanced. While they sensed the tide was turning, Northern voters had no idea how long the war would last or whether they could tolerate the escalating cost.

The *climax* came in September 1864. In the west, General Sherman finally took Atlanta and prepared for his scorched earth "march to the sea," while Admiral Farragut took Mobile, Alabama, the last Gulf port east of Texas still held by the Confederacy. In Virginia, Grant set in to besiege Lee around Petersburg and Richmond while General Sheridan drove the last Rebel forces out of the Shenandoah Valley.

All summer Lincoln had feared that Northern voters, staggered by the heavy casualties incurred during Grant's Overland Campaign, were ready to elect a "Peace Democrat" who would let the South go. But now, the end in sight, voters re-elected Lincoln by an impressive 55 percent popular majority and gave only 40 of 183 House seats to the Democrats. Half of the states in the Union did not elect a single Democrat. The administration took a big gamble in passing out ballots to war-weary Union soldiers at the front. But it paid off: Overwhelmingly, they voted to reelect their commander in chief.

Over the course of the war, Republicans in Congress enacted sweeping laws redirecting the future of the Union's parochial and agrarian states. With federal support, America was now to become an educated, industrial, and progressive republic—united around the founding principles of the Republican Party: "Free Soil, Free Labor, Free Men." In January 1865, buoyed by their election victory, Lincoln and the Radicals arm-twisted two-thirds of the House of Representatives into approving the 13th Amendment, henceforth prohibiting slavery in every state. Once ratified by three-quarters of the states (which happened in December), the once-impossible dream of a handful of abolitionists became the supreme law of the land. Together with Lee's surrender at Appomattox Courthouse ten weeks after the House vote, this was the *resolution*.

No doubt this resolution would have seemed bittersweet to Lincoln had he lived to see its fruits. Yes, the Union was preserved, the slaves emancipated, and the Industrial Revolution fully unleashed. But the Union's postwar authority quickly collapsed, its politicians fell into disrepute, and emerging social issues like labor violence and urban squalor remained unaddressed. The war left the South impoverished and in political exile. And neither two more Constitutional Amendments (ratified in 1868 and 1870) nor a far-reaching Civil Rights Act (in 1875) could prevent Reconstruction in the South from ending in Jim Crow by the late 1880s.

Nonetheless, the resolution transformed America—not just by reuniting the states but by guaranteeing, or at least promising to guarantee, certain universal human rights. As the war raged, its purpose had grown to that of *rededicating* "a new nation, conceived in Liberty . . . to the proposition that all men are created equal."

By committing the Union to this rededication, no matter what the cost, Lincoln began to sound less like the optimistic Whig than the brooding Calvinist. The war's very carnage, Lincoln darkly suggested in his second inaugural address, might be nothing less than God's bloody retribution for the injustice of "American slavery." If the dying must continue until "every drop of blood drawn with the lash shall be paid by another drawn with the sword . . . ," he declared, "so still it must be said 'the judgments of the Lord are true and righteous altogether.'"

During the Great Depression, just as many of the last Civil War veterans were passing away, Lincoln's popularity enjoyed a huge resurgence—in books, films, and music. At a time of national suffering, Americans sought inspiration in his leadership. Hoover-era Republicans rallied to Lincoln as a classic liberal, defender of individual rights. Franklin Roosevelt loved to quote him as well, and once said "it is time for us Democrats to claim Lincoln as one of our own." Early in World War II, in his famous "Century of the Common Man" speech, Vice President Henry Wallace announced that a "fight to the death between the free world and the slave world" had just begun. "Just as in the United States in 1862, we could not remain 'half slave' and 'half free,' so in 1942 the world must make its decision for a complete victory, one way or the other."

The president agreed. In his annual message to Congress in January 1944, which he read aloud to Americans on the radio, Roosevelt began as follows: "Ladies and Gentlemen: This Nation in the past two years has become an active partner in the world's greatest war against human slavery." Listeners understood that he was conjuring up the Great Emancipator himself.

AMERICAN REVOLUTION CRISIS, 1773–1794

The *precursor* to the American Revolution Crisis, the French and Indian War (1754–1763), was in fact the colonists' fourth war against the French in Canada. But this time it was one piece of a much broader global conflict, which persuaded Britain to dedicate serious manpower and resources to vanquishing New France once and for all. Britain succeeded with its stunning capture of Quebec in 1759 and Montreal in 1760. Eager for money, glory, and victory over the French, colonial militias and privateers excitedly joined the war effort.

The war briefly kindled a sense of pan-colonial unity after the Albany Congress (of seven colonies) in 1754. It was during this meeting, not later during the Revolution, that a forty-eight-year-old Pennsylvania representative, Benjamin Franklin, drew his famous "Join or Die!" cartoon. Yet the war also brought the colonists great suffering at the hands of the French, their native allies, and the colonists' own British officers. Here is where an entire generation of young adults—including George Washington, Daniel Morgan, Francis Marion, Daniel Boone, Robert Rogers, and Benedict Arnold—got their first taste of treachery and brutal combat.

By 1763, after the celebrations were over and most of the British officialdom had sailed home, the colonies reverted to their Third Turning mood. Only now the lawlessness and violence was worse than ever, fed by a new immigrant rush from Europe and a new westward rush into the now-"pacified" wilderness.

Frontier settlers fought with Native Americans. Colonial elites dealt harshly with frontier settlers. Colonies quarreled with one another, often over their geographical boundaries. British authorities meanwhile initiated some modest measures to raise revenue and bring order to colonial chaos. Two of these measures—the Stamp Act of 1765 and the Townshend Acts of 1767—did unite most colonists in brief and savage resistance. Yet each time few colonists objected to British rule in principle, only to the "unrightful" means by which Parliament was acting. And each time, Parliament brought closure by backing down.

In 1773–74, there were no more happy endings. A small network of radical Whigs (some calling themselves Sons of Liberty) organized to block imports of taxed tea, in most cases by intimidating ship captains in major ports. For these radicals, the actual *price* of the tea wasn't the issue (even including the tax, Britain had lowered the price of tea to below where it had been before); it was the *principle* of the tax that mattered. On December 16, 1773, Sam Adams persuaded several dozen followers to dump forty tons of this tea into Boston Harbor. No doubt they figured that Britain would back down again.

Not this time. Instead, an out-of-patience Parliament in 1774 issued the punitive Coercive Acts, dubbed the "Intolerable Acts" in the colonies. Parliament in effect agreed with the Sons of Liberty: Yes, what matters is the principle—that Britain may levy a tax if it wants to—and we're going to insist on it.

The Coercive Acts were the *catalyst*. In the spring and fall, the leading colonists drafted plans of union, organized politically and militarily, and convened a new "Continental" Congress. Among heavily indebted New England merchants and southern planters, the desperation was heightened by the global financial crisis of 1772, which prompted London creditors to call in their loans and demand payment in metal coin. Abigail Adams (who until then had been conciliatory) now agonized in her diary over whether "redress by the Sword" should sever the "threefold cord of Duty, interest and filial affection" binding the colonies to the throne. Late in 1774, Philadelphia lawyer Joseph Galloway suggested that the Congress could itself create a unified colonial government while still offering to share sovereignty with Parliament. That proposal, voted down 5–4, turned out to be the last compromise anyone took seriously. After learning about the Congress, King George III wrote to his prime minister that "blows must decide" whether the Americans "submit or triumph."

Next April, news of the British raid on colonial armories in Concord and Lexington, resulting in more than a hundred deaths, electrified the colonies. After what Adams in her diary termed "the terrible 19 of April," all hope for reconciliation was lost: "Tyranny, oppression and Murder," she wrote, had now "plunged her Sword into our Bosoms." The onset of open hostilities marked the first *regeneracy*—on both sides. "Patriots" embarked on a course of action that only a few years earlier would have been deemed blatantly treasonous by most Americans. And "Loyalists" became those Americans who still believed it was treasonous.

By 1776, while a new Congress was drafting and signing a Declaration of Independence, the Patriots whipped urban mobs into a revolutionary frenzy—hounding the remaining British officials out of office, pulling down vestiges of British rule (like statues of King George), and tar-and-feathering any "Tories" who publicly dared to resist the will of their neighborhood "committees of safety."

On the battlefield, however, the Patriots' militias and General George Washington's ragged Continental Army were routinely overmatched by the Redcoats. Through 1778, the Patriots managed only one major victory (at Saratoga in 1777), which ultimately persuaded the French to ally with them. Enduring starvation and desertion during the first three winters, Washington did his best to boost morale and instill regimental discipline. "These are the times that try men's souls," began Thomas Paine's wildly popular *The American Crisis*, which Washington read aloud to his troops.

Yet even if the Redcoats could take towns and hold them at will, they could not maintain any authority in them when they left. In the spring of 1778, the British decided they had been too conciliatory. Under the new command of General Henry Clinton, they chose to wage a more brutal war. They would invade the South, ally themselves with plentiful backcountry Loyalists, and strip the rich planters of their property—including their slaves, whom they promised to liberate. (Nineteen slaves escaped from Jefferson's Monticello estate alone.) The war thus entered its most violent phase, with murderous reprisal battles between Patriots and Loyalists, relentless guerilla tactics, and frequent refusal to give quarter to surrendered troops.

The British experienced initial success. By the fall of 1780, they had occupied Savannah and Charleston, taken thousands of prisoners, and were recruiting plenty of Loyalist allies. Again, however, the Patriots patiently wore them down. In October, Patriot militia overran and massacred hundreds of Loyalists at the Battle of Kings Mountain, with some hanged after the battle. It was the war's largest all-American fight, and it essentially put an end to British recruiting. Later that month, Washington appointed General Nathanael Greene to assume command of the regular army in the South. A brilliant tactician, Greene ceaselessly harassed and attritted the British regular army in the South, then under the command of General Charles Cornwallis.

In the summer of 1781, an exhausted army under Cornwallis moved to Yorktown, expecting to be evacuated by British ships. But after a swift march by Washington, who besieged him by land, and a blockade by a French fleet, besieging him by sea, Cornwallis surrendered.

At this point, Parliament was distracted by troubles at home and broader threats from France in Europe, India, and the West Indies. So Britain abruptly announced a cessation of hostilities. The war was over. In the fall of 1783, after the signing of the Treaty of Paris, the British military evacuated New York City—along with seventy-five thousand White and Black American Loyalists (equivalent, per capita, to the abrupt emigration of 8 million Americans today). After re-occupying the city, Washington resisted calls from his officers to seize national leadership. Abiding by the authority of the Continental Congress, he disbanded his army, resigned his command, and made his way back to his Mount Vernon estate in the winter of 1784.

Yet clearly the crisis was not over. Ports had been wrecked, towns had been depopulated, plantations were fallow, furloughed soldiers wandered the countryside, and thousands of merchants and professionals had gone into exile. According to historian Allan Kulikoff, "The war ended but the misery continued. . . . This depression seared the memories of all who lived through it." By 1790, American per-capita incomes had dropped an estimated 20 to 30 percent since 1774. Some of the new "states" printed paper currency, resulting in rampant inflation—while others repudiated their war debt, drying up new credit. States that tried to raise taxes to repay their creditors touched off armed rebellions by farmers. Several states feuded with one another over boundaries, and nearly every state enacted tariffs on other states. And since no one could protect America's export trade, some states discussed making separate agreements with Britain or Spain.

America, in short, suffered not only from sudden poverty, but from the absence of any effective national authority. In 1776, the colonies had merely declared their right to be "Free and Independent States." These sovereign states later agreed to Articles of Confederation. But the Articles established a toothless executive with no power to raise money and a weak legislature whose decisions states could easily veto or disregard. According to Benjamin Rush, "The Congress is abused, laughed at and cursed in every company." By the mid-1780s, few delegates to the Congress even bothered to show up for its meetings.

By 1786, a new cadre of leaders—nearly all veterans of the revolutionary struggle—came to agree on the urgent need for a stronger national government. With Washington's endorsement, they urged states to send delegates to Philadelphia the following spring "for the sole and express purpose of revising the Articles of Confederation." This marked the second *regeneracy*.

By September, after months of debate, thirty-nine of the fifty-five attendees signed the final draft of a new framework. As the delegates left Independence Hall, an excited crowd famously asked old Ben Franklin what sort of government they had come up with. "A republic," he replied, "if you can keep it."

After publication and distribution, this ambitious new constitution quickly divided Americans into two camps, those who approved and those who disapproved, *consolidating* the ultimate debate over what sort of national government the people would adopt. Favoring approval were the "Federalists," led in print by James Madison, Alexander Hamilton, and John Jay. Prominent Federalists tended to be better educated, more cosmopolitan, and more likely to have served in the Continental Army. They also tended to be young: Most, in their mid-forties or younger, belonged to the Republican Generation. Favoring disapproval were the "Anti-Federalists," led by local leaders with backcountry ties, like Patrick Henry, George Mason, and George Clinton. Most had been eager signers of the Declaration of Independence. But they were suspicious of any authority having "supremacy" over their own state. Most, in their late forties and older, belonged to the Liberty Generation.

Over the next year, while arguments and rebuttals came pouring out of the print shops, citizens elected delegates for ratification conventions in each state. One by one, these popularly elected conventions met. And one by one, they voted their approval. By mid-summer, eleven states had said yes, culminating with Virginia and New York in June and July of 1788. This was the *climax*. The rising generation had prevailed. The deal was sealed.

On paper, America was now to have an effective national government. It was a curious document: seven articles and twenty-one sections spelling out the passionless levers and wheels of federal government, yet with scarcely any reference to the spirit or higher purpose of this new regime. Many older clergymen asked the signers why there was no mention of "God" in the Constitution. In reply to one of these queries, thirty-two-year-old Hamilton is alleged to have said, no doubt in feigned astonishment, "Indeed, Doctor, we forgot it!"

With or without the invocation of the deity, of course, someone still had to demonstrate that the Constitution could work in practice. That was accomplished by President George Washington together with a youthful, Federalist-dominated Congress over the next six years. The United States stabilized the dollar, assumed the national debt, levied taxes, suppressed state border disputes, and commissioned an army and navy. As a concession to the Anti-Federalists, it agreed to add a "Bill of Rights" to the Constitution. In 1794, it proved it could put down a tax revolt (the Whiskey Rebellion), win on the battlefield (against a Native American confederacy, at Fallen Timbers), and negotiate a fresh trade agreement with Britain (Jay's Treaty). These actions weren't always popular, but they did instill long-term confidence.

Also by that year, news of the revolutionary terror in France reinforced the appeal of those who argued that the sober "Spirit of '87" was a necessary complement to the fervent "Spirit of '76." What's more, as the European powers plunged into general warfare, their hunger for food and raw materials caused U.S. exports to soar and national prosperity to return. The *resolution* was now at hand.

So Americans had their republic. But how long could they keep it? And how would it evolve? While in France, John Adams once mused on these questions in a letter home to his wife, Abigail. "I must study politics and war," he wrote, so that his sons could study science, architecture, and commerce—so that their children (Adams crossed out the word "sons" and wrote "children" for Abigail's sake) could study painting, poetry, and the arts.

Adams refused to speculate on what *their* children would do. But time would demonstrate that their learning would not continue in the direction of ever-more refinement. For these fourth-generation descendants would have their own founding moment to reenact—hailed in the South as a "Second Declaration of Independence" and embraced more earnestly in the North as the Union's "Second Revolution." Let the record show that, on the male side, two of John Adams's five great-grandsons were young Civil War officers—and one (Colonel Charles Francis Adams, Jr.) led a Union cavalry regiment into the smoking ruins of Richmond in April 1865.

GLORIOUS REVOLUTION CRISIS, 1675–1706

In 1675, nearly nine in ten colonists in British North America lived either in New England or the Chesapeake (Virginia and Maryland). In both regions, the vast majority were of English descent and most of these were still immigrants themselves. In the colonies, and back in England, memories of Puritan idealism and its convulsive national aftermath were starting to fade. A new "cavalier" reaction had set in, which gave rise to a new focus on "the main chance"—that is, on the personal acquisition of money, property, pedigree, fame, and title.

Both regions were ruled by closed oligarchies. In New England, this was a decaying Puritan theocracy fearful of the future (and of the reigning Stuarts). In the Chesapeake, it was an unstable Tidewater elite who dreaded the violence and land-hunger of newly arrived commoners. Under-governed and adrift, Americans of every rank viewed the future of their societies with foreboding.

In 1675–76, with few warnings and no precursor, both regions were engulfed in devastating wars between settlers and natives. The *catalyst* and the first *regeneracy* arrived almost at the same time.

In New England, King Philip's War (named after the Wampanoag chief who led the natives) quickly grew into a struggle of extermination. It left half of these colonies' towns destroyed or pillaged and ended up killing a stunning 10 percent of the regional population—one-third of them English, two-thirds native. Many of the northern and western towns were not resettled for another thirty years. In the Chesapeake, a similar war morphed into a popular revolt led by Nathaniel Bacon against the Virginia governor, William Berkeley. Bacon, championing the smaller settlers, favored a more aggressive policy against inland native tribes; Berkeley, favoring the tidewater grandees, wanted peace with the natives. Before it was cut short by Bacon's sudden death from dysentery, the revolt reduced Jamestown to ashes and granted new rights to commoners. While Bacon was still alive, his army issued a remarkable "Declaration of the People of Virginia" accusing the governor of various "unjust gains" and acts of "civil mischief and ruin . . . against the consent of the people."

By the late 1670s and early 1680s, the colonies had returned to an uneasy peace. But soon they were aroused again, this time against a new threat stoked by a growing "Whig" faction in the English Parliament who suspected that the Stuart monarchy was preparing all their subjects for Catholic absolutism. The second *regeneracy* dates to 1685, when James II, avowed Catholic and believer in "the divine right of kings," succeeded to the English throne. At about the same time, New England learned that new Stuart colonial governors were determined to strip them of their traditional powers of self-government.

The *consolidation* happened in the spring of 1689, after colonial leaders heard rumors that a political revolution was underway in Britain: King James II was abdicating in favor of the resolutely anti-Catholic William of Orange and his Protestant wife, Mary, the eldest daughter of James II. Popular rebellions thereupon broke out in the colonies against magistrates beholden to the "Great Scarlet Whore" (a common Protestant epithet for the Roman Catholic Church). Colonial militia officers deposed the powerful royal governors in Boston and New York, persuading other colonial assemblies to follow suit. The rebellion in Maryland permanently unseated the unpopular Catholic elite which had dominated that colony since its founding.

Colonial leaders were naturally apprehensive about how William and Mary and the "Glorious Revolution" Parliament back in London would respond to their homegrown revolution. They had to wait a couple of years to find out. William's immediate concern was defending himself against France after King Louis XIV publicly allied himself with the cause of the deposed James. Britain struggled to repel the French Navy and suppress French-supported "Jacobite" rebellions in Ireland and Scotland. The colonists finally got their answer in 1691—which marked the *climax*. In the end, the British crown could abide by colonial self-government (below royally appointed governors and councils, with limited powers). But in return Britain would need commercial and military support from the colonies in its coming global struggle against Louis XIV and his European allies.

This new arrangement suited the new rising generation of colonial leaders, though it did entail colonial mobilization for two long wars against New France lasting until 1713. The final outcome, to be sure, rested on the new regime's success in its European war: If Britain was defeated by France and if the old Stuarts were reinstated, it seemed certain that all their colonial liberties would be lost. But that fear was put to rest by the European victories of John Churchill, First Duke of Marlborough, at Blenheim (1704) and Ramillies (1706), which effectively extinguished the hopes of the French Sun King. For colonial America, this marked the *resolution*.

The crisis transformed the colonists' collective self-identity. Before, they had been neglected self-governing colonies with practically no connection to one another. After, they were still mostly self-governing—but within a Whig and firmly Protestant British empire whose basic mission they were all willing to share.

The resolution of the crisis achieved greater social stability by legitimizing a seismic shift in political authority from an older and wilder (Cavalier) generation to a younger and more cooperative (Glorious) generation. In New England, young adults ousted older militia commanders, set up revolutionary "public safety" committees, and broadened church and political membership. They supported the Salem witchcraft frenzy which erupted (in 1692–93) at a moment of maximum danger for New England's future—and which targeted unpopular old people who allegedly victimized children.

In the Chesapeake, a more acceptable distribution of power and land (and a decline in violence) was achieved by a very different sort of policy revolution. In effect, the Southern colonies shut down the large inflow of White indentured servants and replaced it with a large inflow of African slaves, now available from European traders who were already bringing them to sugar plantations in the West Indies. For the established gentry, Black slaves had the advantage that they would be thereafter excluded from competing for power or land. From 1680 to 1720, the Black share of the Southern colonial population expanded from one in twenty to nearly one in four. The young elite who came to power in those decades wrote the slave codes and created the stable planter oligarchy of Byrds, Randolphs, Fitzhughs, Carters, Lees, Taneys, and Carrolls that would shun outsiders and rule the South for generations to come.

Racial slavery, odious as it may seem to us in retrospect, was a solution to a social problem that made sense to Tidewater planters at the time. Thus did the resolution of one crisis push America on the tragic path toward a larger crisis nearly two centuries later.

During the eighteenth century, many leading Europeans praised Britain's "Glorious Revolution" for showing the world how to be modern—that is, how to progress from political absolutism toward liberalism and democracy. Most American colonists praised it as well. But the lessons they drew from the 1670s and 1680s had populist and millenarian overtones missing from the dominant British narrative. Four generations later, those lessons inspired Americans to champion self-government once again by staging another revolution, but this time *against* the regime they had once admired.

Thomas Jefferson, during his presidency, was determined to rehabilitate the reputation of Nathaniel Bacon. He was not an outlaw, insisted Jefferson. He was a revolutionary hero, championing "the will of the people" against tyrants "one hundred years exactly" before the heroes of 1776. A few decades later, Nathaniel Hawthorne wrote "The Gray Champion," a story about an elderly Puritan leader who periodically returns to rally America during its moments of trial. He was first seen on the streets of Boston during the city's 1689 rebellion, rousing the people to rise up against their hated English governor, Sir Edmund Andros. He was next seen in 1775, reports Hawthorne, urging on the Patriots digging the breastworks at Bunker Hill.

If Hawthorne had counted forward another eighty-six years, he could have written about yet a third reemergence in 1861—perhaps at Fort Sumter or at the First Battle of Bull Run. Hawthorne, writing this story in 1837, did not make this calculation. He simply concluded: "Long, long may it be ere he comes again! His hour is one of darkness, and adversity, and peril. But should domestic tyranny oppress us, or the invaders' step pollute our soil, still may the Gray Champion come."

ARMADA CRISIS, 1569–1597

The *precursor* to England's Armada Crisis was the five-year reign of Mary I (1553–58). For Catholics, Mary's rule was a moment to celebrate. But for young Protestants, especially for those who later called her "Bloody Mary," it was a moment to hide, flee, dissemble, conspire, or meet death with dignity. The survivors included Elizabeth Tudor, Robert Dudley, William Cecil, Francis Walsingham, Thomas Gresham, and Francis Drake. Many first met each other in exile or in prison.

In 1558, after Elizabeth succeeded to the throne following Mary's death, her subjects hoped for a new era of peace. Elizabeth was young.

She was a born leader. And she favored a pragmatic compromise between Puritans and Catholics. Under Elizabeth, the Church of England adopted a rigorous dogma acceptable to Calvinists and a rich liturgy acceptable to Catholics. "I will not make windows into men's souls," she reportedly wrote to her ministers. Elizabeth hoped that her "via media" would calm the waters.

Her hopes, and the hopes of her subjects, were short-lived.

In the fall of 1569 came the *catalyst*: sudden news of a Catholic uprising led by the Duke of Norfolk, the most powerful peer of the realm. Within months, the queen found herself excommunicated by the pope—and a year after that, the target of a Spanish assassination attempt. In the summer of 1572 in France, the Spanish-allied Catholic League slaughtered thousands of Protestants in the St. Bartholomew's Day Massacre. In the Netherlands, the Spanish Duke of Alba's troops crushed a Protestant revolt. Protestants around Europe reeled at the news. Spanish troops, ships, and gold seemed indomitable. Behind the mighty walls of El Escorial, King Philip II (the former husband of Queen Mary) began to regard the heretic Elizabeth as a removable annoyance.

Feeling themselves encircled by the armed might of a Catholic empire, members of the English Parliament convened late in 1572 to unite behind their queen. The mood was grim. Petty politics were forgotten, new taxes levied, new regiments raised, new trade laws enacted, and new punishments meted out to conspirators, real or supposed. The first (and only) *regeneracy* was underway. Through the next decade, mounting alarm gripped the royal council, driven in part by successive assassination plots linked to Elizabeth's cousin, Mary, "Queen of Scots." Mary, held under house arrest in England, was a committed Catholic and would succeed to the throne if Elizabeth was eliminated.

In 1585, England reached the point of no return, thus marking the *consolidation*. Elizabeth impounded Spanish ships in her ports, sent out all of her "sea dogs" to raid on the Spanish, and began ferrying troops abroad to help the Dutch and the Protestant French. She agreed to have Mary arrested for treason in 1586 and executed the next year. The kingdom then bravely girded itself for the invasion it knew was coming:

Philip II's 130-ship armada carrying seventeen thousand soldiers. The famous *climax* arrived in 1588, when the queen's small English Navy broke the armada in battle and the surviving ships were wrecked by storms on their way home. Thanksgiving services were held across England, and medals were struck to commemorate God's judgment against the unbelievers ("He blew, and they were scattered").

The war against Spain would grind on for years. The English kingdom, vastly smaller in population and wealth than Philip II's empire, was pushed to the breaking point. Elizabeth called frequent parliaments, kept taxes high and court expenses low, and through her county sheriffs eventually summoned over one in ten combat-age men for service (a staggering share in the sixteenth century). Mortality from disease rose steeply among soldiers, sailors, and the rural poor. And the brutality inflicted by English troops on the Irish, whose local nobility were regularly suspected of conspiring with Spain, became infamous.

A formal peace was not declared until 1604, after both Elizabeth and Philip II had died. But by 1597 all the kingdom's goals had been secured. The Netherlands had fended off the attacking Spanish armies. A new French king (Henry IV) had pushed the Spanish out of France. And England itself no longer feared another invading armada, though Philip eventually sent three of them. The *resolution* was at hand.

The larger-than-life imagery that came to surround Queen Elizabeth, even during her lifetime, was not due to her great power—during her reign, England was always weaker than its rivals—but rather due to her indominable spirit. "I know I have the body but of a weak and feeble woman," she told her small militia on the eve of the armada as she walked among them dressed in white and gold with an armor chest plate, "but I have the heart and stomach of a king." In moments of national peril, Britain has repeatedly commemorated Elizabeth and her fierce Tudor will. It did so in 1940 while awaiting Hitler's invasion during the Battle of Britain. And it did so in 1805 while awaiting Napoleon's invasion.

It did so as well during the Glorious Revolution of 1688, as England prepared to face off against mightier France. Everyone marveled that the flight of James II and the arrival of William and Mary had occurred on the exact centennial of the Armada year. No one is certain why this revolution was so quickly called "glorious." But we do know that radical Whigs were the first to use the term. And they no doubt recalled the last time England had been saved from a Catholic absolutist. It was in the reign of Queen Elizabeth, otherwise known as Eliza, Good Queen Bess, the Virgin Queen, Astraea, Cynthia, the Fairy Queen, and finally—after her victory over the Armada—as Gloriana.

WAR OF THE ROSES CRISIS, 1455–1487

For a quarter century before the onset of this civil war, during the 1430s and 1440s, England had become a late-medieval cauldron of misrule, corruption, and division. In recent years, the kingdom had lost virtually all of its territorial possessions in France. Armed and unemployed veterans returning from the mainland triggered a pandemic of social disorder. Some fueled popular rebellions against royal corruption. Others joined large armies or "affinities" in the service of several dozen independent barons.

The king, Henry VI, lapsed into periodic insanity. His rule was in any case dominated by his pro-French queen, Margaret of Anjou, immortalized by Shakespeare as the "she-wolf of France." This was the House of Lancaster (the red rose), founded in 1399 by Henry's grandfather, Henry Bolingbroke. The pro-English faction was led by Richard, the Duke of York, and later by his son Edward. This powerful House of York (the white rose) had its own plausible claim to the throne rivaling Lancaster's. The two houses feuded bitterly—at court, in Parliament, and on the streets.

With no *precursor*, the rift erupted into organized violence when the two houses clashed in open battle in 1455 over who should serve as lord protector during the king's latest lapse into madness. This Battle of St. Albans was the *catalyst*. Over the next four years, more small-scale battles followed, the two sides trading victories.

Then came a fateful acceleration of events, triggering a *regeneracy* for both sides. In November 1459, a Lancaster-packed "Parliament of Devils" condemned most of the Yorkist leaders for high treason. Fleeing England in December, these Yorkists now had no choice but to reorganize, return, and wage all-out war for the crown itself. Come the spring of 1460, the two sides had abandoned the medieval custom of parleying before battle. By autumn, fallen knights were routinely executed on the field. Early next spring, in a blowing snowstorm, the Yorkists routed the Lancastrians at the Battle of Towton, killing at least ten thousand soldiers. Incredibly, this toll amounts to about one in every fifty English males between fifteen and fifty. Towton almost certainly ranks as the deadliest single day of combat (as a share of total population) ever fought by the English people anywhere in the world.

After the victory, young Edward York, crowned Edward IV in 1461, reigned for most of the rest of the Crisis era. But his House of York did not rule in peace. Yorkists and Lancastrians continued to wage sporadic military campaigns over a crown that changed heads six times. The War of the Roses witnessed the judicial murder of nobles, the expropriation of vast landed wealth, the slaughter of royal family members, and the repeated intervention by foreign princes (the King of France and the Duke of Burgundy) on one side or the other.

The grim final twist came in 1483, after Edward IV died of natural causes following several years of relative calm. He left behind two young sons, who fell under the guardianship of their powerful Yorkist uncle Richard, Duke of Gloucester. Fearing his in-laws in what had by now become a deadly game of thrones, Richard acted preemptively. He had Parliament declare the young princes illegitimate and declare himself king. Months later Richard almost certainly had his nephews murdered. So began the brief and inglorious reign of Richard III.

So too did the *consolidation* arrive, with new competition from a long-lost relative of the House of Lancaster. This was the young expatriate, Henry Tudor, Earl of Richmond, who had been waiting in Brittany for a moment of Yorkist weakness. Now was the moment. Early in 1485, Henry requested and received aid from the French and from the late Edward's in-laws. Later that year, he landed in England, raised his standard, gathered his allies, and marched on London. The two armies met at Bosworth Field, where Richard was defeated and killed. This was the *climax*, decided during the battle when one of Richard's most powerful noble allies defected to Henry's side.

The new king, now crowned as Henry VII, deftly pacified many

Yorkists by marrying Elizabeth of York, sister of the two "Princes in the Tower" put to death by Richard. He thus succeeded in joining the lineages. Henry even designed his own special "Tudor rose," half-white and half-red, to symbolize reconciliation. The *resolution* came in 1487 when Henry put down the most serious rebellion against his rule. Thereafter, the new House of Tudor was secure.

Henry Tudor and his court had high hopes for the glory of his new dynasty. Moved by the great popularity of Thomas Malory's *Le Morte d'Arthur*, first printed around the time of his coronation, Henry named his first-born son Arthur and had Elizabeth give birth to him, in 1486, in the town of Winchester (believed to be the location of Camelot). Alas, Arthur died at age fifteen, before he could be crowned. He bequeathed to his younger brother Henry both the kingship and his young new wife, Catherine of Aragon. While Henry VIII would later preserve the Tudor lineage, he would not, by the time he died, lead England into anything resembling an Arthurian golden age.

As for the future direction of English politics, it may not have mattered which contender in the War of the Roses ultimately secured a lasting dynasty—Henry, Richard, or even Edward (had he lived longer). What mattered was that all were ruthless politicians and innovative managers. Their long-term plans were mostly the same: suppressing anarchy by weakening the great nobles, hiring their own loyal and literate administrators, and systematically consolidating their own executive power. This new type of ruler—what historians call the "new monarch"—was appearing throughout Western Europe in the late fifteenth century, wresting their societies across the threshold of modernity.

William Shakespeare, to be sure, cared very much that the winner was Henry Tudor. Shakespeare wrote most of his histories as a young man during England's next saecular winter—while Queen Elizabeth was fending off Spanish armadas. He couldn't afford to be impartial: Henry VII was Elizabeth's grandfather. In *Richard III*, Richard necessarily becomes the evil hunchback while all of Henry's brutal measures are tactfully left unmentioned.

Did Shakespeare draw any historical lessons from the York-Lancaster civil war? All we have (in *Richard II*) is the memorable protest in Parliament by the Bishop of Carlisle to a much earlier rebellion led by Henry Bolingbroke, Henry VII's great-grandfather. To Carlisle, this mutinous deed, which first established the royal House of Lancaster, violated the laws of God and nature. Therefore "The blood of English shall manure the ground, / And future ages groan for this foul act" and "the children yet unborn / Shall feel this day as sharp to them as thorn." Elizabethan audiences would of course have known that he was referring to the future civil war and the rise of the Tudors.

Bolingbroke's invasion and usurpation, together with Carlisle's prophecy, happened in the year 1399. That was exactly eighty-six years before Henry Tudor's own invasion and usurpation—perhaps suggesting that the old bishop (at least according to Shakespeare) could already intuit how the rhythm of that new saeculum would likely play out.

All of these civic turning points, extending across seven centuries of Anglo-American history, unfolded in an extraordinarily diverse range of social environments.

These societies were diverse in size. The United States in 1940 had a population of 132 million; the English North American colonies in 1680, about 150,000; the kingdom of England in 1485, roughly 2 million. They were diverse in living standards. The dismal English norm until the early 1700s was that most families lived in small villages, tilled the soil, and lived near subsistence—and just over half of all their children died before adulthood. By then, the typical American colonist was already healthier and more affluent. By 1860, U.S. child mortality had fallen to 33 percent; by 1940, to 6 percent; by 2020, to less than 1 percent. The average unskilled U.S. wage, in real terms, tripled from 1790 to 1860; tripled again by 1940; and doubled again by 2020.

As for technology, we may as well be describing different civilizations. How to compare the fifteenth-century manual scythe to today's self-driving, GPS-guided combine-harvester? Or the handwritten writ, delivered by a royal servant on horseback, to electronic social media connecting millions in real time?

Social and cultural standards have also shifted dramatically over time. Early in our panorama, we saw that social deference was taken for granted and that partisan fault lines were usually defined by religious as well as by national and dynastic loyalties. Since the late eighteenth century, those on the lower rungs of society have no longer regarded the high-born as their "betters." Today we take democracy mostly for granted. And we aren't motivated by religious dogma as much as we are by cultural, social, or economic dogma. Today we like to talk about our "values," our "traditions," and our sense of "fairness" in the distribution of privilege and wealth.

These differences are breathtaking indeed. Yet despite them all we witness the same recurring social dynamic—not just the same overall seasonal rhythm of the saeculum, but also the same narrative progression within the winter season. At the front end, the mood transition from Unraveling to Crisis is always marked by the *catalyst*. At the back end, the mood transition from Crisis to High is always marked by the *resolution*. In between, society is remobilized—and, by degrees, reorganized—through *regeneracy*. Regeneracies alternately divide and unite society into new tribes, but they never permit society to remain what it was before. At some point, the regenerated society experiences *consolidation* and *climax*, the culminating trial in which its most ambitious collective goals are put to the win-or-lose test.

The timing of the winter season itself is determined by the formation and aging of generations, which as we have seen have not changed much over the centuries. The progression of events within the Crisis is mostly driven by the rules of group psychology, which also have not changed much. Elias Canetti, a Jewish emigré from Austria in the late 1930s, once laid out four age-old rules about group behavior (in his book *Crowds and Power*): Crowds want to grow; crowds enjoy density; crowds foster equality; and crowds seek direction. This is a fair description of how mobilizing tribes can move almost any society from catalyst to regeneracy to consolidation. And it may not matter much whether the crowd in question is gathering in front of town guild halls or in the digital forums of Twitter and Reddit.

7

THE MILLENNIAL CRISIS

War at the beginning is better than peace at the end.

—IRANIAN PROVERB

Most Americans don't need to look at opinion surveys to know that the social mood of their country has been shifting in a more urgent direction over the last decade or so. We'll get to some of those surveys a bit later. But one quick way to assess this shift is to check out Google Ngram, a website that tracks the relative frequency of words or phrases used in a wide cross-section of U.S. books published in every year since 1800.

Each of the following phrases have hit highest-ever usage rates as of 2019 (the most recent year for which Google has data): *right-wing, left-wing, radical, racism, authoritarian, repression, inequality, cover up, populist, angry, fight, conflict, shame, politics,* and *next civil war.* The word *fascist* is at its highest since 1948; *dictator,* since 1945; *oppression,* since 1868. Other phrases of more recent origin have skyrocketed in usage since around 2008: *red zone, blue zone, false flag, deep state, social justice, national reckoning, antifa, woke, red pill,* and *false equivalency.*

Awareness of discord and conflict coincides with the coalescing of tighter communities. But, as we might expect early in a Crisis era, this has happened mainly at the "small platoon" level of personal association. Words that have risen steeply in usage include *friends, neighbors, family, clan, teamwork,* and *like-minded*—along with *lonely.* What has been falling, on the other hand, is any word that refers to large, trusted civic institutions. These include *organization, committee, citizen, member, rules, laws, official, order, procedure, connected.*

The word *insecurity* has been rising; *security* has been falling. The phrase *win the election* has been rising; *reform* has been falling. *Beat your opponent* has been rising; *persuade your opponent* has been falling. As for social priorities associated with Awakenings, those are mostly in hibernation. *Values, conscience, principle, crusade, appeal, revolt, riot,* and *anarchy* were all more used in the late 1960s than they are today. Not surprisingly, words referring to the once-powerful targets of the last Awakening—for example, *establishment, system, conformity, bourgeois, middle class*—are also in hibernation, having lost the negative valence that once made them interesting. For a growing number of younger people today, indeed, they may be acquiring a positive connotation.

Social mood is one thing. Social events are quite another. In a Fourth Turning, we expect both to shift in a characteristic direction. We expect the trajectory of key events, in particular, to follow the basic chronology of the Crisis era.

So as we turn our attention to the now-unfolding Millennial Crisis, we proceed in two steps. First, we create a schematic narrative of how far America has advanced into the Crisis Era. We find that America has already experienced the precursor, the catalyst, and the first regeneracy. Second, we speculate on the various ways the Millennial Crisis may climax and resolve in the years to come. Will America experience a second regeneracy? When is the consolidation likely to happen? And what will happen during the Ekpyrosis? These are the questions we will do our best to answer.

WHERE WE'VE COME: INTO THE CRISIS ERA

If interpreting the remote past is difficult for the historian, interpreting the recent past is downright treacherous. Every news flash—a hurricane, an election, a market dip, a scandal—warps our understanding of events and deprives us of the distance we need to see them in perspective. Even so, it should be possible to flag major events and trends that aren't likely to lose their importance with passage of years.

In this spirit, let's see if we can take the framework of the saeculum as laid out in the last chapter and use it to understand the history of the Millennial Crisis to date.

The *precursor* to the Millennial Crisis was the 9/11 attack followed by the U.S. retaliatory invasions of Afghanistan and Iraq (2001–2003). Like World War I, 9/11 struck like a bolt out of the blue, shocking a complacent public that was counting on an endless future of pacific globalism.

Like World War I, the 9/11 wars were fought with great enthusiasm but little patience—and the public soon soured on their basic objective. In 2005, two years after President G. W. Bush declared "mission accomplished," more Americans disapproved than approved of the Iraqi invasion. Soon, the lofty "nation building" goal was as widely mocked as "making the world safe for democracy" was in 1920. (As historian and journalist Robert Kagan notes, "Wilson lied, people died" is a good modern-day translation of the Harding-era mood.) Among both policymakers and the public, this post-Iraq disillusionment coincided—again, as it did after Versailles—with a long-term shift from engaging with the rest of the world to disengaging from it.

Like every precursor, the 9/11 wars offered a rising Nomad generation of diplomats and officers the opportunity to test their mettle against real-world challenges. The implications for the future are worth pondering—and we will return to them in a future chapter. Gen-Xers occupied nearly every field-grade officer rank in 2003 (major to colonel). Today, as the last Boomer officers retire, these Xers are being promoted to the highest (general officer) ranks—and will continue to dominate those ranks through the 2020s and most of the 2030s.

A precursor only temporarily interrupts the Unraveling mood of personal empowerment and civic drift, and here as well the 9/11 wars were no exception. Not long after the Twin Towers attack, Americans were following the president's advice to "go shopping" or "go to Disneyworld." The economy, already rebounding from a mild post-dotcom recession, surged ahead. A year later the stock market was rising again.

This time Americans latched on to a get-rich device even more democratically accessible than dotcom tech stocks: real estate. As home prices accelerated amid "Flip That House" shows, banks issued subprime mortgages to eager home buyers. The banks then securitized the mortgages and either held them "off the books" or sold them to voracious institutional investors. A rising flood of mortgage debt, in turn, drove home prices still higher in a circular frenzy. During the five years following 9/11, both home prices and total real estate wealth rose by nearly two-thirds, making homeowners feel $10 trillion richer than they had been before. As zeal for the War on Terror faded, entertainment once again turned back to the ennui-laden quest for brands, social status, and guilty pleasures: *Sex and the City, Desperate Housewives, American Beauty, The Sopranos, Survivor*, and the Justin Timberlake–Janet Jackson "wardrobe malfunction."

Most Americans today recall how this era ended. Early in 2006, new home building plummeted. Later that year, home prices stopped rising—and throughout 2007 they arced downward. While some banks began to sell their mortgage-backed securities, others kept buying. "As long as the music is playing, you've got to get up and dance. We're still dancing," reported Citibank CEO Charles Prince in July 2007—as if to illustrate that now-classic line from *The Big Short*: "Actually, no one can see a bubble. That's what makes it a bubble."

In 2008, it all came apart. After September, once Lehman Brothers went under, global lending froze, which in turn sent global production and stock markets into free fall. The Fed, Congress, and the U.S. Treasury eventually took unprecedented measures to cushion the blow. They cut interest rates to zero, extended unlimited credit to foreign central banks, shoveled out bailouts to nearly a thousand firms, and ran by far the largest peacetime deficit in U.S. history—nearly 10 percent of GDP.

Despite these efforts, financial markets tipped into their steepest global crash since the Great Crash of 1929. This terrifying bust, which came to be known as the Global Financial Crisis, was the *catalyst*. And it led directly to the most severe global economic contraction since the Great Depression.

The immediate peak-to-trough impact of the Great Recession (2007–2009) was certainly shallower than the Great Depression (1929–1933). But in the 1930s, while the economy plunged much faster, it also rebounded much faster. In the 2010s, by contrast, there was little rebound: Employment, productivity, and business dynamism (the rate at which the economy creates new firms and new jobs) never regained their earlier pace. As a result, the decade-over-decade slowdown in U.S. per-capita GDP growth was about the same before and after 2007 as it was before and after 1929.

America's poor economic performance since 2007 seems all the more disappointing given the massive fiscal and monetary stimulus applied by Congress and the Fed over the entire decade after the Great Recession began. Former Fed chairman Ben Bernanke may be correct that these measures averted an economic collapse worse than the Great Depression. But they worked largely by further exacerbating income and wealth inequality, something that did *not* happen in the years following 1929. And they rendered the economy dependent on ever-higher doses of stimulus—leaving it to future policymakers to wean us *off* that addiction.

Just as a crash did seventy-nine years earlier, the Global Financial Crash of 2008 marked a pivotal turning point in America's social trajectory. Where pop culture had earlier focused on glitzy cribs, cool brands, and prestige professions, it now shifted its spotlight to foreclosed homes, bartered junk, and gritty grunt jobs—not to mention the jobless and the homeless. Where policymakers once favored further deregulation of markets, now they urged sweeping public measures to punish financial misdeeds; restructure banking, housing, and monetary policy; and do something about the distribution of income and wealth. Where voters once trusted the "democratic process," now a rising share wanted to short-circuit or override anything that got in the way of delivering results.

In March 2009, President Barack Obama assumed office after an inaugural address that reminded the nation of its earlier moments of trauma. ("In the year of America's birth, in the coldest of months, a small band of patriots huddled by dying campfires on the shores of an icy river. The capital was abandoned. The enemy was advancing. The snow was stained with blood.") For a brief year, both parties united in response to the emergency. Then partisanship escalated. On the populist right, the Tea Party Movement galvanized the GOP and enabled it to take back the House during the last six years of Obama's presidency. After panicking global financial markets in the summer of 2011 by holding the debt ceiling hostage, the new Republican majority steered the nation on a dubious course of fiscal austerity amid high unemployment. On the populist left, the Occupy Movement galvanized progressives on behalf of the "99 Percent" by assailing the Democratic administration over its Wall Street bailouts and trickle-down recovery strategy.

In 2016, both parties set out to nominate a new presidential candidate. The mood was fraught. The economy had hit yet another post-recession air pocket, and public dissatisfaction with "the way things are going" remained near record highs. The Democrats narrowly missed going with their populist, Bernie Sanders, opting instead for an establishment liberal, Hillary Clinton. The Republicans went the other way. In the ensuing national election, their populist, Donald Trump, narrowly won the electoral college count, and their party managed to retain majorities in both houses.

The 2016 election constituted a clear *regeneracy* for both factions. In national politics, it mobilized party partisans to an intensity not seen since the mid-1930s if not the late 1850s. The left rallied many Democrats into a "resistance"—as if the Trump administration were an occupying army—before demanding action on various executive misdeeds by means of a special prosecutor and two successive impeachments. The right rallied around Trump, who continued while in office to behave and campaign as an outsider. He never stopped fulminating against the "deep state" throughout his own presidency. He hardly cared about the record-low approval ratings he was earning from voters for his actual governing performance.

Even during the onset of the pandemic and global recession of 2020, Trump maintained his adversarial stance. He belittled his own top health officials (as he did so many of his advisors) without, however, dismissing them. He inveighed against hapless federal bureaucrats, even while approving seven Covid-related bills authorizing those bureaucrats to spend trillions in benefit payments—easily the largest surge in federal social welfare spending in American history. And he was happy to do so, so long as the benefit checks bore his signature.

Like all genuine populists, Trump's goal was not to represent the will of a dysfunctional community. His goal was to heal and empower the community by identifying its will with his own. Anything standing in the way of that will must be challenged and overwhelmed, with violence if necessary. Populism gives life to Michel Foucault's celebrated reversal of the Clausewitz dictum: Politics is the pursuit of war by other means.

In November 2020, in an election that was mostly about whether to re-elect Trump—rather than about electing anyone else—American voters turned Trump down. Yet Trump chose to interpret this as a lost battle, not a lost war. After his defeat, it was Trump who assumed leadership of the resistance. To a crowd of Republican partisans spoiling for a fight, Trump acolyte and former New York mayor Rudy Giuliani helpfully suggested a "trial by combat." Trump, exhorting his followers to "stop the steal" and not allow an "illegitimate president" to take office, reminded them that "if you don't fight like hell, you're not going to have a country anymore." Hours later, many of them stormed the Capitol building with weapons while Congress was in session.

The next day, in the House of Representatives, 138 GOP members voted to oppose the electoral count in Pennsylvania. A year later, nearly three-quarters of Republican voters—and one-third of *all* U.S. voters—agreed that Joe Biden's victory was probably or definitely not legitimate. Nearly two years later, in the fall 2022 midterm election, more than two hundred GOP candidates running for federal or executive state offices said they at least questioned or doubted the 2020 outcome; about thirty said outright that it was "stolen." Most of these candidates won their races—although, to be sure, the most extreme MAGA deniers lost or underperformed in their elections.

Did most of these voters and candidates ever really *believe* Trump won the election? It hardly matters. Committed partisans never accept the possibility of their side losing a fair fight; they always claim the other side must have employed some sort of trickery, falsehood, or dirty dealing. And from that metaphorical understanding of "steal," it's a short distance to theories about spacecraft beaming messages to voting machines. Besides, if the other side is your enemy, you gain nothing by conceding defeat. But you may gain something if the world sees you as committed and implacable.

When Biden was inaugurated on January 20, 2021, many Americans, probably a majority, breathed a sigh of relief. At last, the nation had a consensus-minded, play-by-the-rules commander in chief who could demonstrate mere competence. Yet the weakness of the moderates' influence, this time on the Democratic side, was quickly revealed. Over the next few months, the news was monopolized by partisans on the left, who tried to redefine their party as champions of expanded and progressive government—with new entitlements for families, a "green new deal" for the world, a debt jubilee for youth, new taxes on the plutocracy, and federally regulated elections. While centrist Democrats in Congress were unwilling to help them, they were also unable to stop them.

In the end, little of the left's agenda was enacted. Of the $4.4 trillion in new spending Biden wanted during his first two years (not including the last dollop of Covid benefits approved in the spring of 2021), only one-third was approved by Congress. And most of that was achieved with rare bipartisan approval for modest spending on goals that both sides supported—like modernized infrastructure and support for threatened high-tech industries. Few new revenue measures were enacted. As a result, most of the new spending continued to be funded by higher deficits.

This underwhelming performance for the Democrats did not really hurt the left. For partisans on both sides, new policies enacted are not as important as keeping the pot boiling by galvanizing voter and donor enthusiasm. Indeed, achievements *gained* can be less helpful than achievements *thwarted*. After each Biden legislative victory, voters became more willing to blame him for all the problems he wasn't solving—until their initial support for the Democratic Party's centrist leadership team almost entirely disappeared. Biden's approval rating during 2022 was no higher than Trump's during his second year. In June 2022, it was the Republicans' turn to take a hit when the Supreme Court overturned *Roe v. Wade*, thereby fulfilling a long-sought goal of conservatives. Voter enthusiasm for the GOP duly fell during the summer and fall. Come the 2022 midterms, the two parties once again fought themselves to a virtual standoff—this time giving only a slight edge to the Republicans.

In retrospect, the evidence pointing to the 2016 election as the first regeneracy of the Millennial Crisis seems unmistakable.

Since 2016, voter participation in both presidential and midterm elections has soared to its highest rate in more than a century. Partisan emotions, as measured by voter mood thermometers, have never been hotter. Half of all voters now see politics as "a struggle between right and wrong." Nearly 90 percent expect that victory by the other party will "cause lasting harm" to the nation. By 2020, only 10 percent did *not* agree that the other party was gradually transforming America into either a "dictatorship" or a "socialist country." Canceling, shame campaigns, doxing, and personal harassment by activists make it ever-more difficult for news outlets, celebrities, and major brands to appear neutral. More than half of all Americans report suppressing their opinion over the past year because they fear retaliation—and by a large margin they report feeling "less free" to express themselves than they were a decade ago. Republican voters report the largest rise in self-suppression; Democratic voters are the most likely to report that they have retaliated against others.

Since 2016, political violence has risen, resulting in more threats, injuries, and deaths. Unlike domestic terrorism in earlier postwar decades, this new wave of violence is motivated less by single-issue convictions (like animal rights or abortion) than by the desire to intimidate or harm partisans of the "other" political party. Attacks are also rising against police, military, civil service personnel—and against legislators and judges, including high-profile members of Congress and the Supreme Court. Several Democratic and Republican senators are reportedly spending hundreds of thousands of dollars per year on personal security, in addition to what is provided by the Capitol Police. While surveys show the willingness to use violence has risen about equally on both sides, a much larger share of the actual rise in violence has been by red-zone partisans, many of them affiliated with self-designated "militia" movements.

Since 2016, as the two national parties adopt antagonistic and mutually exclusive visions of the nation's future, America's attention is increasingly fixated on who wields power, especially supreme *national* power. Any policy that would be good for one state, the new thinking goes, would be even better if it were enforced across all states. So party leaders urge partisans to vote the party ticket everywhere—that is, for the like-minded governor and senator and congressperson and president (and indirectly for like-minded Supreme Court justices) that can make it all happen. Ticket splitting by district in federal elections has declined to the lowest rate in a century. Ticket splitting in state and local elections is also getting rarer. Even school board elections are now freighted with national party issues, from mandatory vax requirements to "critical race theory" curricula. Out-of-state donors, with only national victory in mind, account for a rising share of candidates' campaign funds.

Despite all this new focus on federal elections—or perhaps, more accurately, because of it—effective governing at the national level has ground to a halt. With little or no cooperation among legislators across party lines, ordinary political process freezes. Appointees aren't confirmed, budgets aren't approved, agency recommendations are dead on arrival, and executive orders trigger automatic lawsuits. Major legislation, when it must be enacted, is either spasmodically approved as an "emergency measure" or forced through Congress by only one party with a razor-thin margin. Any bill passed is accompanied by maximum partisan signaling.

One result is little planning and wretched execution—as both Trump and Biden have demonstrated on trade, immigration, pandemic response, and foreign policy. Another is the willingness of both parties, when in power, to eke out near-term economic gains by means of fiscal and monetary stimulus—until stimulus must be withdrawn, and then everybody suffers. For now, long-term policymaking has become a deadly no-man's-land: Leaders seen there will get shot at by both sides and get rescued by neither.

Since the regeneracy, the energy and the initiative have moved to tribal partisans. Leaders of both parties know that few ordinary Americans any longer trust the status quo. Roughly two-thirds of Americans believe their political system needs "major changes" or "complete reform," even if they can't agree on what those changes should be. Leaders also know that without the energy of movement enthusiasts, their party can no longer be competitive in elections. While chronic partisan warfare may lead to governmental dysfunction, even that outcome further reinforces the partisans' dire message—that we're near the brink and that the time for compromise is over.

In this sense, both parties seek to gain by magnifying the threats facing America. For the red zone leaders, the threat is "socialism" (a word

Trump wielded repeatedly during his presidency), which allegedly enables personal lawlessness to destroy the nation through unchecked crime, illegal immigration, and government spending. For blue zone leaders, the threat is "fascism"—or "semi-fascism," according to President Biden—which allegedly enables corporate lawlessness to destroy the nation (and possibly the world) through unchecked monopoly power, social privilege, and climate change. Either way, voters are asked to grant extraordinary authority to partisan leaders so they can fend off the threat of permanent ruin posed by the other side. And voters on both sides are willing to grant it. While Republicans have a reputation for being distrustful of government, surveys show that they are even more trusting than Democrats *so long as their leaders are in power.*

Again, we may ask: Do leaders, and voters, really *believe* these dire threats? And again, we may decide that it really doesn't matter. Among social scientists, there has long been agreement that social perception creates its own reality. This bit of wisdom is encapsulated in the so-called "Thomas theorem," coined by two sociologists in 1928: "If men define situations as real, they are real in their consequences." We could just as well ask: Did American colonists in 1774 really believe that a barely perceptible (and, arguably, entirely reasonable) tax on a luxury import constituted "enslavement" by the British crown? When two tribes have lost all trust in the other, every action by one side tends to be regarded by the other as evidence of the most malign intentions. At which point, it would be irrational for you not to interpret it as a dire threat, since you know the other side shares the same perception of you.

To be sure, most Americans are often embarrassed by the extreme partisanship of their own parties' leaders and are often worried about the civic breakdown caused by partisan alarmism. And whenever voters suspect that their own side may be the worst offender, they pull back their support and weaken their own side's performance in the next election. Ordinarily, Americans prefer day-to-day competence rather than partisanship in the people they elect. Yet whenever they are reminded that the other side is pushing their country toward catastrophe, they are apt to forget about day-to-day competence. Instead of expert functionaries, they are drawn to all-in fighters.

While neither party has yet been able to gain a decisive margin in national elections, the first regeneracy of the Millennial Crisis may mark the beginning of a historic political realignment. Under Trump, the Republican Party has gone irreversibly populist. It has traded away a sizable share of its educated, higher-income, and mainly suburban base in return for non-college-educated, working-class voters, mainly outside the big metro areas, who had earlier voted for Democrats like Obama and Clinton. In 2016, for perhaps the first time since the Civil War, the highest-income voters (the top 10 percent and the top 1 percent) were more likely than less affluent Americans to vote for the Democratic Party. Since 2016, while losing share among White voters, Republicans continue to gain share among nonwhites (especially Hispanics), who are more attracted to the GOP's pragmatic and socially conservative messaging.

The Democrats, by default if not by design, are sorting themselves in the reverse direction, with increasing attention to urban and suburban professionals. Their campaign language is tailored ever more to the outlook and priorities of an educated and mainly White elite. By 2022, in another surprising historical first, Democrats were attracting a larger share of all White college graduates than of all nonwhites in pre-election surveys. Democrats now hold an unprecedented advantage in America's most affluent and educated districts, giving them a growing edge in mainstream media presence, academic credibility, and personal dollar contributions. Republicans try to make up this gap through alternative media, business PAC money, and a deeper ground game run by local volunteers.

If the altered demographic profile of the two parties in the 2016 election—almost perfectly replicated in the 2018, 2020, and 2022 elections—is signaling America's newest political realignment, it would be the first since the Nixon-Reagan elections of 1968 to 1980, roughly forty to fifty years earlier. By Walter Dean Burnham's count (as we saw in Chapter 4), that would suggest America is now moving into its *seventh* party system. Last time around, it was Southern Whites voting for Republicans rather than Democrats. This time, it's education replacing income as the key determinant of voting behavior. The current realignment has yet to confer a decisive advantage to either party. If and when it does, that election may be heralded by future historians as a memorable political turning point. In fact, the term "seventh party system" is already appearing in the latest editions of political science textbooks.

Driving today's emerging realignment is not just voters switching their party loyalties *by* demographic group. It's also the deliberate choice voters are making to live *with* that demographic group. At an accelerating rate, Americans are changing their residences in line with their partisan communities. In 2008 journalist Bill Bishop was the first to describe this dynamic. He called it *The Big Sort* in a book by that name.

Why is the "Big Sort" happening? Rising political passions, aligned as they now are with behaviors and lifestyles, are pushing like-minded tribal members to seek out geographic cohesion. Life is just easier that way. Surveys show that political differences now outrank all other differences, including those of income or religion or race, in day-to-day encounters that people wish to avoid. One way to avoid such encounters is to choose a new church, club, or employer whose views match your own. An even better way is to choose a new neighborhood. Geographic sorting, in turn, itself tends to intensify political polarization: Partisan intensity grows strongest, and voting rates and political donation rates rise fastest, in neighborhoods with the highest concentrations of people who think the same way. And, as this trend has intensified, party leaders have modified their brands in ways that appeal more to their regional voter bases. The Republican Party increasingly panders to the rural and exurban voter, the Democratic Party to the urban voter.

Politically mixed or "purple" communities are therefore getting scarcer. More and more regions are swinging all blue or all red.

Look at states. In the 1992 presidential election, there were thirty-two "battleground" or "swing" states, those considered winnable by either party. By 2000, there were twenty-two. By 2004, fourteen. And by 2020, there were only eight. In most states, presidential candidates no longer bother to campaign personally. The suspense of a presidential election now comes down to close votes in a mere handful of states; the rest are landslides. Similarly, the share of all states having "trifecta governments"—governor and both legislative houses controlled by the same party—has been rising. From 1967 until 2009, the number of trifecta states was never more than twenty-five. In 2022, the number reached thirty-nine, a seventy-year high.

Or look at counties. In 1976, only twenty-six of every one hundred voters lived in counties where the presidential margin of victory was greater than 20 percent. In 1992, thirty-eight of every one hundred voters lived in one of these "landslide counties." In 2004, it was forty-eight. In 2020, fifty-eight. In that 2020 election, Trump lost the popular vote nationally by 4 percentage points yet won in 83 percent of all U.S. counties—an unprecedented feat for any losing candidate. These were mostly big rural counties with few voters. Under Biden, meanwhile, the Democrats continued to build up ever-larger margins in crowded cities and inner suburbs.

This "de-purpling" of America generates multiple feedback effects that mostly tend to reinforce one another. Many one-party states are enacting policies almost expressly designed to offend residents of the other party—for example, bans on abortion or transgender treatments in red zone states or bans on guns and gas-powered appliances in blue zone states. States are now even billing themselves as "havens" for "refugees" from states of the other color, which further motivates voters to move to the regions that welcome them.

What's more, as the number of landslide jurisdictions climbs, so too are incumbent officeholders encouraged to adopt extreme views, since they know they will never be challenged by the other party. As a rule, moderates are most likely to be elected by districts or states in which the two parties are roughly of equal strength. But such districts and states are now dwindling in number. By fostering a sense of community solidarity, geographical polarization also promotes conspiracy thinking. If a Trump voter in 2020 does not personally know even a single Biden voter, that voter might understandably wonder how Biden could have won the election. Preliminary survey research suggests that the likelihood that a Trump voter becomes an election denier depends not just on the intensity of his or her own beliefs—but also on *how large a share of his or her congressional district voted for Trump.*

What divides blue zone America from red zone America isn't just their geographic location and voting preference, of course, but also profound differences in their core loyalties, social habits, and life goals.

Overall, America's blue zone is wealthier, healthier, more educated, more professional, more mobile, more economically unequal, and more ethnically diverse. America's red zone is more churchgoing, more neighborly, more charitable, more family oriented, more rooted, more violent, less bureaucratic, and less taxed. Surveys indicate that Americans regard blue zone cities as more entertaining, but red zone cities as more affordable. Since 2008, while the blue zone has grown steadily wealthier relative to the red zone, migration between states has flowed strongly in favor of the red zone. Higher in-migration, combined with higher fertility, transferred three congressional seats (net) from solidly Democratic states to solidly Republican states after the decennial 2020 reapportionment.

Behind all these differences in behavior lies an equally profound contrast in collective self-image. Blue zoners are more likely to self-identify as cultural creatives, skilled at high-tech, high-touch tasks that red zoners aren't smart enough to handle. Red zoners are more likely to self-identify as hardworking Americans, willing to take on strenuous tasks—like growing food, producing energy, assembling products, and fighting wars—that blue zoners aren't tough enough to handle. Marketers often quantify this divide in self-image by tracking the degree to which people choose retail brands according to their political affiliation. And they're finding that this divide has been widening in recent years. Blue zone residents increasingly "over-index" for CNN, Whole Foods, Target, Chipotle, Levi's, Starbucks, NBA, REI, Honda, and Tesla. Red zoners do likewise for Fox News, Walmart, Dollar Tree, Chick-fil-A, Wrangler, Dunkin' Donuts, NASCAR, Dollar Store, Bass Pro Shops, GMC, and Land Rover.

Whatever the issue being discussed—family, race, schools, religion, science, gender roles, manners, equality, or authority—blue and red tribes now find themselves speaking different languages. Fear of isolation and stigma drives a rising number of Americans to signal that they are members of one tribe or the other. And it persuades them to choose to live with their own kind. According to the chief economist of the national Realtor Redfin, the Big Sort has accelerated since the pandemic. "Now that workers have more control over where they live, more people . . . will vote with their feet, moving to places that align with their politics." To most Americans, the outcome feels like a dismal stalemate. We may as well be describing two societies—each having its own sectarian goals, yet both awkwardly yoked to one government.

From the onset of the Global Financial Crisis in 2008 to the ebbing of the global Covid pandemic in 2021, America's biggest challenges were twofold: dismal economic performance and paralyzing civic discord. On February 24, 2022, a great new challenge broke into the headlines: geopolitical conflict.

The Russian invasion of Ukraine shocked the world. It was the first time in seventy-seven years that one large European nation has tried to conquer another. A stunned public watched news videos re-create narratives that haven't been witnessed since World War II, when large conventional armies pounded each other's cities every night in grainy newsreels.

Once again, the long-dormant threat of war between the world's great powers has jumped back to life, only this time with nine nations already armed with nuclear weapons. Once again, the authoritarian powers are drawing together, united by their territorial ambitions and by their conviction that democracies have lost their will to resist. Once again, the democratic powers are drawing together in response—trying to overcome their own bewilderment and hoping they can respond in time to quell the strongman tide. Once again, the Crisis-era mood deepens.

In the wake of the invasion, the nation has coalesced in its support for Ukraine. A surprisingly large majority of Americans have been telling pollsters that they are willing to bear sacrifices to prevent Russian victory—from paying higher prices and higher taxes to risking a great-power war. Yet if the Ukraine invasion reminded Americans of what it feels like to be united, so too has it reminded them of the enduring depth of their political paralysis.

Since the invasion, Americans have awakened to see more clearly the consequences of America's recent disengagement from global affairs. The list of damages here is long and demoralizing. It includes all the dire presidential "red lines" against Russia, China, Iran, Syria, and North Korea that America never enforced; all the trade and defense agreements with close allies that America neglected, undermined, or scuttled; and all the commitments to governments at war against anti-American militants that America abandoned without warning—most ingloriously, in Afghanistan. Repairing this damage, if America chose to do so, would require re-engaging the world. It might also require the nation to reverse the long-term decline in its spending on defense—and become, once again, the free world's "arsenal of democracy." This would have to happen, somehow, in the face of an endless growth in future projected federal deficits—which Congress has as yet made little effort to address.

The hour may be growing late. Just before retiring at the end of 2022, Admiral Charles Richard, head of the U.S. Strategic Command, declared that "this Ukrainian crisis that we're in right now, this is just the warmup." Citing the decline in America's military capability relative to China's in the western Pacific, he added: "The big one is coming. And it isn't going to be very long before we're going to get tested in ways that we haven't been tested . . . for a long time."

Even after Ukraine, moreover, America's national government remains largely immobilized at its highest levels by party-on-party conflict. Despite brief bipartisanship during the initial U.S. response to Russia's belligerence, irreconcilable battle lines persist. Because of these divisions, Congress remains unable to deliberate on any long-term issue—a paralysis that weighs more heavily in a world where foreign policy choices grow more urgent. As of early 2023, moreover, the two major political parties remain essentially leaderless, each awaiting the next presidential primary season to see what happens. With parties leaderless, and with neither party fully in charge, the nation feels leaderless as well.

One and a half years after the Ukraine invasion, the question is worth asking: Has the first regeneracy of the Millennial Crisis come to an end? Are we now waiting for a second? Perhaps, though it's still too early to know for certain.

The first regeneracy was triggered by Donald Trump's 2016 election campaign. And there is no question that Trump's political reputation has suffered big hits ever since. The worst hit has been his record of serial failures—in 2018, 2020, 2021, and 2022—in winning elections for himself or his party. One of these failures was abject: Few Americans have forgotten his splenetic and rampaging last days in the White House. Another hit has been his fawning affection for brutal strongmen like Vladmir Putin, Xi Jinping, and Kim Jong Il—which began to play poorly even among Republicans once Russian artillery began pulverizing apartment buildings in Kharkiv and Kyiv. In this newly dangerous world, to be sure, Americans may be growing more—not less—inclined to elect a strongman of their own. By a large margin, Americans say Putin would not have invaded Ukraine had Trump been the U.S. president rather than Biden. Trump himself, however, seems unlikely to be the sort of strong personality American voters would elect a second time.

The 2016 regeneracy, however, does not depend upon any individual leader at the head of either partisan tribe. If younger versions of Trump and Biden were to rise to the top of the two parties, the same regeneracy would still be at work—so long as the same core issues and the same constituencies are shaping their agendas. A new regeneracy does not require new leaders. It requires some important shift in issues along with a rearrangement of the constituencies arrayed on either side. A new regeneracy may begin suddenly. We just have not seen it happen yet.

At this moment in the Millennial Crisis era—possibly just beyond the halfway point—it makes sense to pause and try to assess America's overall social mood. Opinion surveys suggest that the most prominent feature of that mood is almost unrelieved pessimism about the nation's future.

When Americans look forward to the year 2050, two-thirds foresee widening gaps between rich and poor, greater political division, and declining national stature. Two-thirds also see "signs of national decline," up from less than one-quarter in 1996 and less than half in 2016. Most Americans worry their leaders have neither the will nor the competence to reverse this downhill trend. Every year since 2008, well over half of Americans have believed "America is on the wrong track" or have been dissatisfied with "the way things are going in the U.S."—the first such sustained gloom since pollsters started asking these questions around the end of World War II.

Behind this palpable negativity lie three major drivers: first, worries that rising economic prosperity in America (what historian James Truslow Adams once called the American Dream) has come to an end; second, worries that civil discord may either split America into pieces or crush its democratic institutions; and third, worries that America is surrounded by aggressive global competitors eager either to challenge its dominance or hasten its decline. Let's look briefly at each of these concerns.

Dissatisfaction over America's economic performance dates to the Global Financial Crisis at the very beginning of the Millennial Crisis era. It can be summed up in the growing conviction that incomes will no longer rise for most people over the long run. By a two-to-one majority, Americans now believe the average family will see its standard of living decline over the next thirty years. Two-thirds believe their children will end up "financially worse off" than they are. (If compared to similarly worded questions asked in prior decades, this negativity has reached a postwar high.) In the past, Americans' long-term outlook closely tracked their near-term income gains. Remarkably, this is no longer true. In May 2021, when stimulus benefits prompted a forty-five-year high in the share of Americans saying they were satisfied with their "present financial situation," their assessment of their children's prospects continued to sink.

Americans also feel less secure in their living standards—in other words, they worry that they are more likely to become helpless or dependent in case of illness, unemployment, or old age. Again looking thirty years into the future, most believe people will be less prepared for retirement than they are now and be forced to work into their seventies out of financial necessity. The vast majority of Americans under fifty expect Social Security benefits to be reduced within the next thirty years—and nearly half expect no benefits at all. What's more, few Americans believe the economy works equitably for most people: Roughly three-quarters agree "our economic system is rigged in favor of the wealthiest Americans" and that "Wall Street and big business in our country often profit at the expense of ordinary Americans."

Yet if economic stagnation and unfair wealth distribution are growing long-term worries, Americans' more immediate concern is how falling civic trust threatens national cohesion if not the very possibility of democracy. That's the second driver.

By a three-to-one margin, Americans say their country is becoming *less* rather than more democratic over time. By a two-to-one margin, they say that it is likely to "cease to be a democracy in the future." Seeing partisanship rise and expecting democracy to be extinguished, they understandably worry that their country may be about to break up. Secessionist sentiment, hardly on any pollster's radar screen before 2016, is suddenly widespread. Most Americans now agree that the nation "could be on the verge of another civil war"; more say that a civil war "is likely" than "is unlikely." Nearly half of all voters and more than half of Trump voters now strongly or somewhat agree that their states should secede and "form their own separate country." Since the mid-1990s, the share of Americans who say that "violent action against the government is never justified" has fallen from 90 percent to 62 percent.

In any case, with or without civil war, a growing number of Americans believe there's a good reason why democracy in their country is weakening: It just doesn't work very well. Roughly equal shares (46 percent of Biden voters and 44 percent of Trump voters) at least somewhat agree that "it would be better for America if whoever is President could take needed actions without being constrained by Congress or the courts." Younger Americans are leading this shift: One in four voters under age thirty would prefer such a powerful leader—versus only one in ten voters age sixty-five and over. Voters today under forty are much more likely to say that democracy is "not essential"—and that it can be scrapped during an emergency—than voters over sixty today or than voters under forty twenty years ago.

Beset as they are at home, Americans are also feeling new vulnerabilities about their place in the world and new threats from abroad. That's the third driver.

Back when the U.S. War on Terror wound down just as the Great Recession emerged, Americans sensed that their nation was declining in global stature. The reason, many supposed, was that America had done too much for others and not enough for itself. And they voted for political leaders who promised to shift their focus accordingly. All three U.S. presidents since 2009 have, in their own way, practiced a style of diplomacy that reflects this attention to America's needs rather than the world's needs. Trump's foreign policy was summed up by one of his national security advisors as "We're America, Bitch." More decorously, Biden calls his own approach "a foreign policy for the middle class"—by which he means of course *America's* middle class.

Yet as Americans contemplate their relative global decline, both real and imagined, so too are they feeling more vulnerable and therefore more threatened. And threats require not less but more engagement with the world. As Frank Klingberg once hypothesized in his "foreign policy" cycle, periods of isolationism or "national introversion" contain within themselves the cyclical seed of their own termination.

Americans now support trade and industrial policies explicitly designed to strengthen America and its allies and to weaken their so-called "geopolitical competitors." They are increasingly alarmed at the behavior and aspirations of two of these competitors: China and Russia. Since around 2016, a steeply growing share of Americans have adopted a negative view of these countries—and favor using force in case a U.S. ally in their vicinity is invaded. By 2017, for the first time, a majority of Americans supported military intervention in case a NATO member or South Korea was invaded—and by 2021, for the first time, in case Taiwan was invaded. After the Ukraine invasion, this opinion shift accelerated further.

So does this grim recitation of dangers and threats accurately capture America's social mood? Not entirely. It needs to be qualified by an essential distinction. All these dangers and threats refer to the public or national realm of politics, economics, and statecraft. They don't refer to the personal or local world of values, culture, and belief.

This distinction is essential because, in their personal lives, Americans aren't feeling the dread they report in surveys about their nation. Rather, they're feeling more or less content. Families have seldom been closer. At last count, 93 percent of adults report feeling satisfied with their families. Grandparents, parents, and adult children are living together at the highest rate in decades, and they are mostly positive about the experience. More than at any time over the last fifty years, a record or near-record share report being satisfied with their job, their marriage, and (even) their child's K-12 education.

In their neighborhoods and local communities, likewise, Americans feel pretty good. According to one in-depth 2019 survey, 73 percent of Americans are satisfied about how things are going in their communities—though only 43 percent would say the same about their nation. The survey concludes, "In this time of bitter political divisions, Americans are remarkably upbeat about life close to home." According to Gallup, similarly, Americans have been reporting *record-high* satisfaction with how things are going in their personal lives since 2020 even while registering *record-low* satisfaction for how things are going in their nation. The recent gap between these two satisfaction metrics—over 80 percent for personal versus under 20 percent for national—is by far the largest since Gallup began measuring it back in the 1970s.

The direction and extreme magnitude of this gap clearly points to where the nation now finds itself in the saeculum.

Fifty years ago, recall where America found itself. With the country having entered an Awakening era, no one worried that national civic institutions were weak or ineffective. Indeed, the growing complaint was that they were doing too much all too well and oppressing everybody while doing it. Meanwhile, family life, neighborhoods, and popular culture became a roiling tempest of argument, defiance, and lifestyle experimentation—from Jimi Hendrix's subversively iconic "Star-Spangled Banner" and the trial of the "Chicago Seven" to the Black Power clenched fist and the nonstop shouting matches on Norman Lear sitcoms.

The rising generation (Boomers) diagnosed the root problem as too much civic control, which almost guaranteed that Americans would spend the rest of the Awakening pushing those strong institutions back away from their lives. At that moment, the Hero archetype was reaching its zenith of public power and the Prophet archetype was just coming on stage.

We now find ourselves at the opposite end of the Great Year. Having entered a Crisis era, Americans have few complaints that people aren't free to live according to any rules they please. Their family lives are peaceful. Their partisan tribes are tight. Their pop culture has lost much of its capacity to offend. In their growing tolerance, they no longer bother trying to change other people's opinions—so long as they don't have to interact with them. Americans now complain, instead, about something very different: the growing dysfunction of a society composed of contradictory and incompatible pieces. They worry about how, in the absence of any binding civic order, their nation can long remain secure or intact. And they fear who and what will rush in to occupy the gaping civic void at the top.

Today's rising generation (Millennials) is taking the lead in insisting on more civic control, which almost guarantees that Americans will spend the rest of the Crisis era pulling these strong institutions back into their lives. At this moment, the Prophet archetype is reaching its zenith of public power and the Hero archetype is just coming on stage.

As Americans look ahead to the future, they feel themselves entering an inflection point. They sense that a widely diverging array of possible paths are stretching out ahead of them—all of them challenging. They also sense that the path Americans ultimately travel may not feel chosen by them as much as imposed on them by events beyond their control. In the middle of a Crisis era, the social mood has reached an unstable balance of hope, fear, and dizzying uncertainty. Americans are like a compressed spring at the point of maximum potential energy. Internally secure yet externally threatened, they are ready for propulsive public action.

Back in the 1990s, during the recent Unraveling, Francis Fukuyama famously announced that America (and the world) had reached "the end of history"—in the sense that modernity's struggle for progress had finally reached its endpoint: peaceful, individualistic, and mildly governed. That announcement was premature. Over the first half of the Millennial Crisis, history has again been speeding up. Over the second half, history promises to accelerate to maximum speed.

WHERE WE'RE GOING: EKPYROSIS

Before the Millennial Crisis comes to an end, it is very likely to culminate—like all Crisis turnings—in a consolidation, climax, and resolution. This will be the Ekpyrosis. These will be the years when civic action reaches its point of maximum power and when the risk of an all-out struggle against a perceived external aggressor is highest—as will be the risk of internal political revolution or civil war. These years will also determine whether the new order does or does not prevail against its enemies and obstacles.

Before speculating on how current events may lead toward the Ekpyrosis, it's useful to construct an expectational time frame. We know when the Millennial Crisis began (2008). When is it likely to end?

One approximate way to forecast the end year is to refer back to the average length of the Anglo-American saeculum. Since the first of these saecula began, five have fully run their course. Their average length, measured from resolution to resolution, is ninety-two years. Including only the three most recent American saecula (starting in 1706), we get an average length of eighty years. Most of this shortening, as we have seen, reflects the Civil War anomaly and the recent trend toward shorter generational lengths. We shall return to anomalies and generational length shortly. Here we simply suggest that the ninety-two-year figure (using longer turnings) should bracket the maximum end of our expectation range, and eighty years (using shorter turnings) should bracket the minimum end of our range.

The last Crisis era reached its resolution in 1946. Using these two bracket points, we should expect the Millennial Crisis to reach its resolution sometime between 2026 and 2038.

That's a wide range of dates. We can refine our forecast by looking more closely at the average length of a normal turning (excluding the anomalous U.S. Civil War). Since the early fifteenth century, we have seen twenty-five turnings, with an average length of 23.8 years. Since the Puritan Awakening in the seventeenth century, we have seen seventeen turnings, with an average length of 22.4 years. Since the mid-nineteenth century, turnings have been even shorter, averaging 20.5 years. As we explained in Chapter 5, however, there are good reasons to expect that the length of a phase of life—and therefore of a generation and a turning—has been growing again since the 1960s. Four twenty-year turnings generate an eighty-year saeculum. But when turnings average twenty-one years, it's an eighty-four-year saeculum. And at twenty-two years, it's eighty-eight years. That would end the Millennial Crisis in 2030 or 2034, respectively. If, as now seems likely, we are moving back to phases of life that are at least twenty-two years in length, 2034 would be a reasonable forecast.

Still another approach would be to superimpose these twenty-two-year phases of life onto today's living generations and then calculate when each will be moving into its next phase of life. Boomers would then begin moving into late elderhood at age eighty-eight (in 2030); Gen-Xers into elderhood at age sixty-six (in 2029); Millennials into midlife at age forty-four (in 2026); and Homelanders into young adulthood at age twenty-two (in 2027). The average date here is 2028. Recall from Chapters 3 and 4 that a new turning typically arrives four years *after* each generation begins to enter a new phase of life. This would point to the Millennial Crisis ending in 2032. At eighty-six years in total length, the completed Millennial Saeculum would in this case be longer than the prior two American saecula, but shorter than the first three.

In sum, based on these approximate dates (2032 and 2034), *the early 2030s appear to be the most likely years for the resolution of the Millennial Crisis and the opening of the First Turning of the next saeculum.* Working backward from there, the most likely year for the climax would perhaps be around 2030.

Such dates of course must be regarded as probability epicenters. The resolution could arrive earlier by three or four years. Or it could arrive later—though here the margin of error is larger since we may be underestimating the dilation of turning length. Beyond these margins of error, however, we risk encountering an anomaly. If the Millennial Crisis were to end before 2029 or after 2038, the next turning would arrive either *too early* or *too late* for the phase-of-life transitions of today's living generations. In this case, we would conclude that history had broken away from the seasonal pattern.

Could the Millennial Crisis become such an anomaly? Perhaps. The historical track record is too brief to rule anything out.

In the Anglo-American lineage, the only obvious example of a turning anomaly is the Civil War Crisis, which began too early and was already over (in 1865) at about the same time that we might have expected the prior Unraveling to end. No Hero archetype emerged, and the shortened Civil War Saeculum ultimately gave rise to only three generations. This time around, clearly, we won't encounter this kind of anomaly. The Millennial Crisis began on time and thus far does not appear to be rushing toward a premature resolution.

To identify other conceivable anomalies, we need to return to our discussion in Chapter 5 and consider the experiences of other large nations. Two possibilities worth pondering are Britain from the 1850s to the 1880s and Russia from 1914 to 1946. The first example reminds us that Crisis eras can be unusually short and mild. Indeed, during the high tide of liberal reform under Palmerston, Gladstone, and Disraeli, Britain may have altogether skipped the sort of Crisis era that was afflicting so many other great powers during those decades. The second example of Russia, on the other hand, reminds us that Crisis eras can be unusually long and harsh, if not horrific—with tens of millions of what demographers call "excess deaths," most of them due to violence or starvation.

Neither case may seem especially relevant to the social experience and global situation of the United States in the early twenty-first century. But they do serve as cautionary signposts. While the saeculum prescribes a central tendency, history will always present better or worse outcomes. When nature tells the river to carve a perfect sine wave on the floodplain, the river may or may not fully comply.

One important reason America has experienced so few anomalies over its history has been its geographic remoteness. Other powerful societies subject to different saecular calendars have seldom been able to interfere with America's affairs. Clearly, America is no longer exceptional in this sense. In an age of hypersonic missiles, satellite-managed communications, and defense-in-depth strategies extending thousands of miles, no nation on earth any longer enjoys what President George Washington, in his farewell address, once called America's "detached and distant situation."

In Chapter 5, we noticed that the last two centuries have witnessed a growing convergence in the saecular timing of modern societies. Since the Great Depression and World War II, the generational experiences of much of the world have in fact merged toward archetypal synchrony. These regions include all of Europe, South Asia, China and surrounding East Asia, much of Latin America, and the United States and the rest of the anglophone world. Societies in these regions all more or less share America's current generational constellation: Prophets moving into elderhood, Nomads into midlife, Heroes into young adulthood, and Artists into childhood. As such, many already have been (or shortly will be) undergoing their own Fourth Turning, that is, their own Crisis era. A few (including Russia, once again) appear to be somewhat ahead of America's schedule. Most are probably somewhat behind.

The Millennial Crisis is therefore very likely to become a Crisis era not just for America but also for much of the world—perhaps even more than the Great Depression–World War II Crisis that preceded it. What this means, from an American perspective, is that a saecular anomaly will be less likely. Rather than interfering with or neutralizing America's saecular timing, the rest of the world will be reinforcing it.

It's time to move on to the next big question: What happens next? We know where the Millennial Crisis has taken us until now. Where does it go from here?

Let's recap: America has thus far traversed the first three stages in our Crisis era chronology. The precursor was the post-9/11 War on Terror in the very early 2000s. The catalyst was the Global Financial Crisis of 2008, which triggered the Great Recession. And the first regeneracy was the election of 2016—which essentially divided the country into two partisan and irreconcilable camps.

After its first regeneracy, our chronology suggests that a nation can only move in a limited number of directions. On the first path, the initial animosity between two factions grows until, sooner or later, a climax-defining conflict breaks out between them. This was essentially the story of the Civil War and War of Roses Crises. On the second path, one faction achieves political dominance over the other and leads a united nation into a climax-defining conflict against an external enemy. This was essentially the story of the Armada Crisis. A third and more complex path brings into play a second regeneracy, which at some point redefines the two factions—altering the key issues and constituencies—before moving on to a climax. In the American Revolution and Glorious Revolution Crises, this second regeneracy occurred after the era's largest mobilization and war. In the Great Depression–World War II Crisis, it occurred *before*.

These historical precedents imply a few obvious scenarios for the remainder of the Millennial Crisis era. Take your pick. Scenario one: The political red-versus-blue polarization of the 2016 regeneracy worsens until it ultimately culminates in a climax-defining civil conflict. Scenario two: One side, red or blue, achieves a decisive political victory over the other and leads the nation into a climax-defining conflict against an external threat. Or scenario three: The current red-blue partisan divide is redrawn by a new regeneracy—probably in an election and possibly with changes in party leadership—before pushing the nation back down paths one or two.

Some political scientists have suggested a fourth and very different scenario: America's recent fifty-fifty stasis or gridlock at the national level becomes the new normal. According to one renowned scholar, we have had such "Eras of Stalemate" before (with weak national leaders presiding over thin and unstable party majorities), and we may have to endure another such era for the indefinite future.

True enough. America has had stalemate eras before. But they have always occurred during turnings in which the public did not want more effective and decisive governance. *Lengthy stalemates have never occurred during a Crisis turning*, when one-party dominance is the norm and when national institutions are struggling to meet society's rising demand for security and order. That's why policy gridlock and paralysis during a Crisis turning is an inherently unstable equilibrium. National inaction in response to Crisis threats inevitably leads to public desperation, which in turn will ensure that one side or the other will be invited to take charge—or perhaps that the two sides separate entirely. This may happen through the regular electoral and legal process. Or it may happen after one side acquires extra-legal powers. But it will happen. This fourth scenario of indefinite stalemate would, in short, break the historical pattern and constitute a genuine anomaly.

So we return to our three original paths: We are very likely to move down one or more of them during the remainder of the Millennial Crisis era. And however much these paths may seem to differ from one another, they all move toward the same destination. They all push the nation toward a violent struggle requiring maximum mobilization. They all culminate in the Ekpyrosis, which will bring the era into a decisive consolidation, climax, and resolution. Most importantly, they all succeed in giving birth to a new and more powerful civic regime.

Looking at the end of path one and path two makes it appear that a Crisis era must culminate in—and therefore be defined by—either of two very different sorts of conflict: *either* an internal civil war *or* an external war against an outside power. But this dichotomy confuses more than clarifies. Internal and external are better seen as widely overlapping on a sort of continuum.

The American Revolution Crisis, for example, has been widely portrayed by popular historians of the victorious "Patriot" faction as an American struggle against external British oppressors. Yet observers at the time were more likely to refer to it as a "civil war" than a "revolution." This is especially true for Loyalists, who figured (no doubt correctly) that more Americans were being killed by other Americans than by the British. (Unless "private massacres" were stopped in the South, wrote General Nathanael Greene in 1780, "this country will be depopulated . . . as neither Whig nor Tory can live.")

In fact, the entire revolutionary era teemed with internal conflict. There was the genocidal scorched-earth campaign waged by the Continental Army to wipe out the Iroquois tribes which, though now allied with the British, had for generations been allied with the colonials. There was the brave effort by tens of thousands of Southern slaves to join the call from Virginia royal governor the Earl of Dunmore to flee their planter masters and join the British war against them. And of course there was the supremely consequential if nonviolent struggle in the late 1780s between Federalist and Anti-Federalist citizens over the nature and powers of the U.S. Constitution. Had the Anti-Federalists won that struggle—this is, at least, what many Federalists plausibly argued—the defenseless and strife-torn states of the newborn American confederation would have been reacquired piecemeal by Britain, Spain, and

France. In that case, the "American Revolution Crisis" would have had another outcome and name and, of course, a very different significance for subsequent generations.

Other Crisis eras present similar ambiguities. During the Glorious Revolution Crisis, the wars between native tribes and English colonials could be described as either internal or external. The various colonial rebellions in Virginia, Maryland, New York, and New England appeared to be mostly internal conflicts among factions of colonials, though the final colonial struggle on behalf of English monarchs against New France after 1689 appeared to be mostly external. The Armada Crisis, often told as the purely external struggle of a small Protestant nation against a mighty Catholic empire, could also be told as an internal struggle of resistance by a powerful Catholic faction within England. Queen Elizabeth had reason to fear rebellion and assassination by her own recusant subjects as much as she feared conquest by King Philip II's invading musketeers and pikemen.

Crisis eras we normally think of as internal civil wars, moreover, often conceal an important external dimension—because at least one faction in a civil conflict (typically the weaker faction) is always motivated to ask foreign powers to intervene on its behalf. During the War of the Roses Crisis, both houses at critical moments received vital protection and subsidies from France, Burgundy, Scotland, and the Duchy of Brittany. During the American Revolution Crisis, the Continental Congress solicited and ultimately received the decisive intervention of France. By the fall of 1862 during the Civil War Crisis, the Confederacy may have been only one major battlefield victory away from winning diplomatic recognition and assistance from Britain or France.

The external-internal distinction is therefore subtler and more mutable than it may seem at first glance. To any engaged participant, after all, conflict is always external: It's always us versus them. Yet most participants in most conflicts feel ties of loyalty to more than just one group. Events may drive die-hard supporters of a partisan faction to become ardent defenders of a united homeland. Or the reverse. Even as tribal energy grows during Crisis eras, so too can that energy swing back and forth between external and internal definitions of collective loyalties. Because these swings are difficult to predict, no one can know in advance of the Ekpyrosis what that ultimate definition of "us" will be.

To be sure, the saecular pattern tells us that America's collective loyalties will be greatly strengthened by the time the era reaches its resolution. But loyalty to what kind of nation? Or even, loyalty to how many nations? We can't yet know. The 2016 regeneracy has thus far deepened tribal cohesion across a conflict that is almost entirely internal. Yet that does not mean that the Millennial Crisis will likely be defined by internal conflict—as opposed to external conflict. Both remain possible.

In the mid-1930s, for example, the first regeneracy of the Great Depression–World War II Crisis ignited a purely internal conflict that was at least as partisan and polarizing as today's. Back then, Republicans could truthfully claim (unlike today) that the president whom they called "Stalin Delano Roosevelt" was backed by legions of young card-carrying Communists and Socialists who wanted to destroy capitalism. And back then (unlike today), that president's party was empowered for several years to reshape entirely America's domestic policy agenda. Yet by the time this era reached its climax, partisan tribal energy had been redirected into an external conflict that, surprisingly, unified the nation.

During the American Revolution Crisis era, the new nation moved fitfully in the reverse direction. The era began with the "Spirit of '76," a mood of Patriot unity in the face of British oppressors. Yet it ended with the "Spirit of '87," in which one faction of Patriots confronted and defeated another faction in order to establish a secure government. The bigger lesson here is simply this. During a Crisis era, internal and external conflict are equally capable of driving the social mood toward Ekpyrosis. Each can serve as a mood accelerator. And the early appearance of one by no means rules out the later appearance of the other.

Beyond internal and external conflicts, there is one other type of social stressor worth examining as we look ahead. It cannot itself be the focus of the Crisis climax. But it can so easily trigger an internal or external regeneracy—and has played such an important causal role in recent Crisis eras—that its presence deserves special attention.

This is the financial crash. As we have seen, financial crashes—along with the economic recessions or depressions that often follow them—constituted the initial catalysts of the last two Crisis eras: the Global Financial Crisis of 2008 and the Great Crash of 1929. Many historians have also argued that earlier financial crashes (the Panic of 1857; the London Credit Crisis of 1772; and the Great Stop of the Exchequer in 1672) contributed importantly to the catalyzing events of the three prior Crisis eras. They all triggered economic recessions that overlapped with or immediately preceded the initial year of a Crisis.

What's more, *over the entire duration of every Crisis era*, asset prices, consumer prices, and economic production rose and fell in swings of above average (and often extreme) magnitude. The recession of 1937–38, which roughly coincided with a 54 percent stock market crash, was America's second-worst economic contraction of the twentieth century—behind the "Great Depression" proper of 1929–33. The drop in real income in the 1780s, during the American Revolution Crisis, was almost certainly more severe than any subsequent depression in U.S. history, including the Great Depression. Parliament's paranoia in the 1680s over the risk of another catastrophic royal default inspired one of the most important institutional outcomes of the Glorious Revolution: the chartering of the Bank of England. As for the Civil War Crisis, while the war itself triggered a massive boom-and-bust economic cycle, that anomalous era ended just before the backwash of deflation and falling output set in.

The financial and economic turbulence of Crisis eras should be no mystery. It rides atop the eras' underlying social psychology, which as we have seen is driven by mounting waves of distrust and fear alternating with mounting counterwaves of confidence and hope. National regimentation of the economy during these eras further amplifies collective herding. Governing authorities often break the normal rules either to create new household demand for goods and services—or to crush it. In one year, vast public subsidies may be handed out, taxes cut, interest rates lowered, money created, and private debts forgiven. In the next, all the opposite measures may be necessary—along with price controls, seizure of property, and requisitioning of labor. During Crisis eras, markets respond much less faithfully to private wants—and much more faithfully to new public demands.

The impact of these shocks on the outcome of Crisis eras has likely grown more profound over the course of successive saecula. Among the long-term trends that sociologists group under the label of "modernization," the complex division of labor through commerce is paramount. As traditional agrarian communities have given way to societies of specialized wage earners and capitalists, all making life choices according to current price signals and income flows, macroeconomic performance clearly matters more to just about everybody. When it's good, people are happy in their interdependence. When it's bad, they become miserable and helpless—or worse, destitute and desperate. Leaders who manage a poor economy will be blamed for what they are doing or not doing. And factional tribes will be able to energize followers who favor radical policy alternatives.

Thus far during the Millennial Crisis, America (along with most of the rest of the world) has already encountered all these phenomena. Economic and financial volatility has clearly increased: Since the Global Financial Crisis, pundits have coined terms like the Great Austerity or the Great Uncertainty to replace the more benign labels (like the Great Moderation) popular during the Unraveling era. Public agencies have pioneered extraordinary new forms of official intervention, including monetary, regulatory, and fiscal measures of unprecedented magnitude and scope. And voters have witnessed a yawning chasm open up between the economic policy agendas of the two major parties—each promising, in radically different ways, to bring back prosperity.

The prospect of another financial crash is serious enough to place it alongside internal conflict and external conflict as a social stressor important enough to influence the outcome of the Millennial Crisis.

If we line up all three of these stressors side by side, we notice that they correspond to the three major national threats that Americans have been fearing since the era began. The first, *financial crash*, matches Americans' worries about inadequate, insecure, and unfair income growth. These first arose in the wake of the Global Financial Crisis in

2008. The second, *internal conflict*, matches their worries about violent partisanship and the failure of democracy. These came to full awareness following Trump's 2016 victory. The third, *external conflict*, matches their worries about foreign aggressor nations. These have been rising since the mid-2010s and jumped to full-threat status with Russia's invasion of Ukraine.

Now let's consider how each of these three types of social stressors may direct the future course of the Millennial Crisis. And since we are especially interested in the Ekpyrosis, we will focus on the most extreme and decisive forms of social conflict that may arise. Instead of internal conflict, we will consider the possibility of *civil war*. And instead of external conflict, we will consider some form of *great-power war*.

FINANCIAL CRASH

Thus far into the Millennial Crisis, America has experienced three financial crashes, the Global Financial Crisis (from the fall of 2007 to the winter of 2009); the Pandemic Crash (late winter of 2020); and a Post-Pandemic Crash (starting in the winter of 2022). All were global. A follow-on recession was triggered by the first two and seems likely to be triggered by the third.

In response to the first two, America led the world in an aggressive campaign of fiscal and monetary stimulus. Since 2007, the publicly held U.S. federal debt has tripled to just over 100 percent of GDP—roughly on par with its rise during World War II. Over the same period, the U.S. Federal Reserve System grew its balance sheet by 1,000 percent and the U.S. dollar money supply grew by 300 percent. In 2019, at the peak of the business cycle, a Republican president presided over the largest federal deficit in American history unprompted by either war or recession. The leaders of both parties, in a rare instance of bipartisanship, tacitly agreed that government would not stop borrowing to keep unemployment low and that the Fed would not stop buying Treasury debt to keep bond and equity prices high.

All this exceptional stimulus did have one big upside. It achieved its intended goal, which was to greatly reduce the near-term (peak-to-trough) severity of both market crashes and both recessions. This in turn mitigated the popular political reaction. Instead of new waves of polarizing populism on both the right and the left (which is what we got), we might instead have witnessed, amid great suffering, a genuinely revolutionary threat to the incumbent political establishment.

Yet the stimulus came with several downsides. It probably reduced long-term living-standard growth by remaining in place for so long after the crash threat. Chronic stimulus lowered savings, fed zombie firms, and suppressed business dynamism. Worse, it raised the risk of yet another crash by glutting Wall Street in order to feed Main Street. It habituated investors to low taxes, to guaranteed consumer demand, to narrow credit spreads, to debt pyramids built on near-zero or negative real interest rates, and to promises of Treasury bailouts and Fed backstops in case there's trouble. Only two years after the crash of March 2020, public policy had once again jacked up equity markets to valuations and multiples rivaling their all-time highs, including those of 1929.

Worst of all, it ensured that the next crash—when it came—would be one that stimulus could no longer remedy. And for this reason: Stimulus would no longer be possible. By 2022, the Fed was compelled to hike interest rates and sell Treasury debt in order to fight accelerating inflation. Congress, likewise, grew reluctant to approve another round of big deficits once it learned how the Fed's higher interest rates had exploded any pretense of long-term budget sustainability. Members of Congress may not care if their own constituents believe the federal budget is solvent. But they have to care about foreign investors, who own more than a third of all U.S. debt securities. Should foreigners lose their religion, the dollar could plummet on global exchanges.

The recovery from the Pandemic Crash, assisted by massive stimulus, was swift. The recovery from the Post-Pandemic Crash, assisted by meager stimulus, is likely to be slow and halting.

Employment will in any case struggle to expand due to historically adverse demographic headwinds. There is one thing we know for certain about the next decade: As large numbers of late-wave Boomers retire and relatively small numbers of late-wave Millennials come of age, the yearly growth of America's working-age population will slow to a virtual standstill. During the 2020s, for the first time in America's history, any positive employment growth will depend entirely on net immigration. Nor will America get much help from robust GDP growth in the rest of the world. And for a similar reason. By the late 2020s—again, for the first time ever—the total working-age population of the high-income and emerging-market economies worldwide will stop growing and begin to shrink.

A boom followed by a bust followed, in the near future, by a slow-growth recovery may serve as a Crisis-era mood accelerator in the mid-2020s. The experience would likely remind Americans of the Great Recession—only this time trigger much louder zero-sum arguments over how income gets divvied up through taxes, benefits, subsidies, and trade. Partisan tribal factions will gravitate to more radical goals and confrontational tactics. The red zone vanguard will grow more aggressively authoritarian, the blue zone vanguard more openly redistribution-ist. Threats of violence may encourage the growth of uniformed "street corps" on both sides. Centrist leaders may struggle to retain voter support for a unifying national program.

In the midst of a difficult recovery, America could experience a Crisis consolidation or a second regeneracy. A consolidation would push the current red-blue divide toward an eventual civil war showdown. A second regeneracy would redefine the partisan divide, which would lead to various alternative outcomes—including growing political unity in preparation for an external conflict. Crisis-era financial crashes nearly always occur in the years *before* or *between* regeneracies. These are years of ebbing public trust and confidence when, at some point, bubbles burst and booms collapse. Crisis-era economic recoveries, on the other hand, are typically accelerated by regeneracies and consolidations, when the nation reacquires a collective purpose.

Once America begins to enter the Ekpyrosis phases of the Millennial Crisis, perhaps sometime in the late 2020s, it will try to mobilize all available resources in order to meet extraordinary national or even global challenges. At this point, nothing like a financial crash can happen: By necessity, an expansive (and expensive) public agenda will tend to push economic production far beyond its normal limits. In order to make this possible, the nation will no longer need to get people to spend more; it will need to get them to spend less. And it will do so by employing all the usual measures for throttling private consumption—including confiscations, taxes, forced savings, rationing, and inflation.

Even more than in earlier Crisis eras, this transition from leveraged personal consumption to unleveraged national investment will require unaccustomed sacrifice and wrenching lifestyle adjustments from most Americans. Never before has America approached a major national trial with such a low rate of economic growth, with such a meager savings rate, with such heavy public and private indebtedness to the rest of the world, and with so little available fiscal room—thanks to a large public sector that is now mainly dedicated (through benefits and tax breaks) to funding the personal consumption of its eldest citizenry. This time around, in short, the very structure of the economy is tilted steeply toward the old and the past. Unless America can rapidly reverse that tilt, no ambitious investment agenda on behalf of the young and the future will be affordable.

Early in the Millennial Crisis, America's policymakers took unprecedented steps to get everyone, both individually and collectively, to buy now and pay later. Before this era is over, they will need to get everyone to do the opposite.

CIVIL WAR

Is America getting ready to engage in another civil war? The question must be taken seriously. Roughly half of all Americans think a civil war is likely. And a growing number of social scientists agree that the United States now fits the checklist profile of a country at risk. Trust in the national government is in steep decline. Check. Respect for democratic institutions is weakening. Check. A heavily armed population has polarized into two evenly divided partisan factions. Check. Each faction embodies a distinctive ethnic, cultural, and urban-versus-rural identity. Each wants its country to become something the other detests.

And each fears the prospect of the other taking power. Check, check, and check.

Most Americans, as we have seen, agree their country is becoming "less democratic" over time. Nearly all scholars agree with that assessment. According to Freedom House, America has become steadily less democratic since 2008. It currently ranks the United States sixty-first among democracies, a bit behind Argentina and Romania and a bit ahead of Poland and Panama. Global research centers that track and analyze political indicators by country now categorize the United States as something less than a full democracy. One calls it a "backsliding democracy." Another calls it an "anocracy," that is, something between democracy and autocracy.

Less democracy, it turns out, could be an indicator that civil war is on the way. When these scholars look at the historical track record, they find that a rapid shift from democracy (or from autocracy) into this anarchic middle ground sharply raises a country's likelihood of organized internal violence. High-trust democracies don't often experience civil wars. Nor do low-trust tyrannies. It's the middle ground that worries analysts. The U.S. CIA and Department of Defense borrow these researchers' methods in assessing how close countries around the world may be to outright civil war. Neither agency of the U.S. government is permitted to study or comment on domestic American politics. But that doesn't stop the outside scholars from expressing an opinion.

Barbara F. Walter, a political scientist at UC San Diego, has spent her entire career studying civil wars, from Rwanda to Myanmar. When asked about America, she says the evidence is pretty clear: "We are a factionalized anocracy that is quickly approaching the open insurgency stage, which means we are closer to civil war than any of us would like to believe." Since the end of the Cold War, the number and severity of civil wars around the world has been growing. Yet, until it happens, few people ever think it would be possible in their own country. After interviewing people who have lived through civil wars, Walter reports that none of them saw it coming. "They're all surprised."

America's track record is no different. Henry Adams was a well connected twenty-three-year-old living in the nation's capital in 1861. Nonetheless, he admits in his memoirs that he was utterly blindsided by the mobilization after the attack on Fort Sumter. "Not one man in America wanted the civil war, or expected or intended it. A small minority wanted secession. The vast majority wanted to go on with their occupations in peace. Not one, however clever or learned, guessed what happened."

If Americans are not more alarmed than they are already, it may be because most of them don't see their country fitting their image of how civil wars begin. They imagine a war between two geographically isolated factions facing an urgent political question on which neither side can back down. This is the popular image of the U.S. Civil War and the American Revolution. They happened when two isolated societies were pushed to the brink over a single existential issue: the institution of slavery or the imposition of unjust taxation.

In fact, this is *not* how most civil wars happen. Ideological separation, absolutely. But geographic separation, only to a degree. Geographic isolation played hardly any role in the War of the Roses. Nor did it prevent deadly neighbor-on-neighbor partisan warfare within the central and southern colonies during the American Revolution and within roughly a quarter of the states and territories during the Civil War. If we look at the rich track record of civil wars outside of America, we notice as well that the geographic isolation of the two factions doesn't really matter much. It played little role, for example, in the most memorably destructive civil wars of the twentieth century: Russia (1917–23), China (1927–49), and Spain (1936–39). Territorially mixed-up civil wars may be more the rule than the exception. They may also be exceptionally brutal.

Nor is the typical civil war triggered by a single urgent or "forcing" question of law or policy. Rather, it happens after one faction comes to fear that power wielded by the other will lead to the inevitable demise of its identity, its status, and its way of life—at which point the trigger could be almost anything. While slavery was indeed an essential cornerstone of the antebellum South, the abolition of slavery in the South was not on the horizon after Lincoln's election in 1860. (Ironically, as we have seen, it was secession that made emancipation possible—and total war that made it probable.) Lincoln's election did heighten Southern leaders' concern that what began as the Republican Party's commitment to limit slavery in the territories would not end there. They had long understood that the new political cohesion of the North, combined with its growing population and wealth, could over time strip their own region of status and condemn it to irrelevance. The election merely served as the tipping point.

Above all, civil wars (or, alternatively, "revolutions") begin when one or both sides are persuaded of the *irreversibility* of future events once the other side gains further advantage. This sort of alarm, bordering on paranoia, fed the zeal of the True Whigs in the early 1680s and of the Sons of Liberty in the early 1770s. And it energizes the most extreme partisans today, from red-zoners who warn of a "Flight 93 election" ("charge the cockpit or you die") to blue-zoners whose headlines declare that "Trump's next coup has already begun" or "America is now in fascism's legal phase." Such alarm is not always unjustified. During a Crisis era, the nation may indeed be open to lasting constitutional change—once a powerful new regime is able to redefine the rules. As Lincoln himself enigmatically (if presciently) prophesied in his 1858 "House Divided" speech, America was about to enter "a crisis" in which "this government . . . will become all one thing, or all the other." A civil war breaks out precisely at this point: when a critical number of people agree with this all-one-thing-or-all-the-other prognosis.

What would raise or lower the likelihood of an American civil war during the remainder of the Millennial Crisis era?

The likelihood would clearly rise in the presence of new social stressors. We've already mentioned one possible stressor: a financial crash and follow-on recession, accompanied by elevated unemployment and either deflation or "stagflation." Other stressors could also contribute, with or without recession. One would be a global supply shock in energy, food, and other commodities, which would show up in shrinking real income for most households. Another would be a new pandemic, or an abrupt sanctions-driven de-globalization (accelerating a trend already initiated by the sanctions against Russia), or a crippling cyberattack on U.S. infrastructure, or any other in a list of now-imaginable surprises.

Such stressors tend to shorten tempers, radicalize partisans, and push electorates toward more extreme policy measures. In one study of twenty advanced economies since 1870, financial crashes have been

shown to be regularly followed by more street protests, declining electoral support for incumbents, and a rising support for populism on the
left and (especially) on the right. Another global study over a shorter
time span shows that local epidemics have a similar effect: slower economic growth, higher inequality, and greater civil unrest.

On the other hand, a civil war would become less likely if a new
regeneracy redefines America's partisan divide—in a way that either allows both sides to cooperate or enables one side to dominate politically.
Whether this happens may depend upon entirely contingent events,
such as the personality of an emerging new leader or the outcome of
a close election. It always depends on the availability of an external—
rather than an internal—challenge or conflict. The Ekpyrosis must culminate in one or the other.

Social scientists quibble over what exactly constitutes a civil war.
Maybe a good working definition is this: any clash of wills between
major partisan factions resulting in organized violence that cannot be
suppressed through routine police action. A more important question
is this: If such a war breaks out, how is it likely to be resolved? Media
pundits have suggested any number of outcomes. Many say it could be
quickly settled nonviolently by peaceful secession. Others say it would
probably result in chronic low-level insurrectionary violence. Actually,
neither of these outcomes is likely.

Peaceful secession is the least probable, which is why, historically, it
hardly ever happens. To cite one group of legal scholars: "Most secessions are contested by the existing authorities. The usual result is civil
war. . . . Peaceful secessions are very rare." They are especially rare in
long-established nations like the United States in which most partisans
of at least one faction equate secession with arbitrary defiance of law. In
other words, they fear that if one faction can peacefully nullify national
authority, then why not any other faction—until all lawful authority
disintegrates? In 1861 Lincoln briefly listened to those (including some
abolitionists) who argued for letting the Confederacy secede peacefully,
before quickly dismissing the idea basically for this reason.

Any type of secession raises vast practical challenges as well. The
most obvious one: how to protect the rights of minorities within the new

majorities—in today's case, blue-zoners within red zone states or vice versa. (As the U.S. Supreme Court gives more latitude to states to choose their own social policies, it could be argued that America is already encountering this issue.) Millions of citizens may prefer to resist rather than succumb to forced migration or expropriation. Another challenge: how to divide up extensive "national" assets, everything from national parks to military bases. This was the question posed by Fort Sumter, and it turned out to be the fateful trigger of declared war. Still another: How would a seceded state ever gain global recognition (and access to international travel or finance) without the express approval of whichever faction is regarded by global institutions (like the UN) as the nominal executive of the United States?

The notion that an American civil war would primarily result in chronic disorganized terrorism—the so-called "Irish troubles" scenario—is likewise unrealistic. This typically happens when one faction is overwhelmingly more powerful than the other (so terror networks are the weaker faction's only option). Or when the society has no history of legitimate national authority. Or when, by international agreement, no national authority intervenes. In the United States, none of the above applies. Once engaged in open conflict, both American factions would grow more, not less, authoritarian—and both would do their best to suppress disorder within their own sphere of influence. Power would therefore tend to gravitate toward two foci. No nation is so brutally intolerant of splintered command as a regime struggling to prevail, especially a brand-new "revolutionary" regime.

Should it erupt, in short, an American civil war would not be quickly resolved by peaceful secession, nor would it degenerate into chronic terror. It would involve two rival regimes, each perhaps claiming lawful national leadership and each asserting a sovereignty that the other refuses to acknowledge.

The trigger that starts the conflict could be almost anything. It could start at the top with an impeachment, a contested national election, a Supreme Court decision, or a complete breakdown of House or Senate protocol. Or it could start at the bottom with several states refusing to comply with federal rules and beginning to set their own social, economic, immigration, or environmental policies. Whatever the trigger, the conflict would gradually gain momentum through a series of stand-offs, ultimatums, and shows of force. And it would likely escalate, against most leaders' original intentions, into large-scale organized violence.

As often happens in civil wars, the national government would split in two. Every federal institution—from Congress, federal courts, and the various executive departments to the armed forces, intelligence agencies, and border patrol—would abruptly and awkwardly rupture according to personal loyalties. Many people would have to choose sides overnight; families and communities would be broken; panic and confusion would be widespread. As leaders on each side issue emergency decrees, house-holds would try to cash out their investments and fortify their own local "supply chains" to the necessities of life. Markets would plunge, both in America and around the world—though very likely these negative price signals would be suppressed or overridden by government fiat. While ordinary day-to-day law enforcement would devolve to the local (mostly state) level, everyone would understand that the conflict could not have any resolution until the national or regime-level clash of wills was re-solved.

One especially unpredictable—and traumatic—dimension of any American civil war in the early twenty-first century would be its effect on the global balance of power. Even a brief civil war would likely require the United States to stand down operationally from many of its military obli-gations around the world. That would invite bold initiatives by America's global adversaries to extort or invade U.S. allies and dependents. It's also likely that one or both sides of the American war (especially the weaker or losing side) would request the assistance of foreign powers friendly to its cause. According to their own ideologies or interests, governments around the world might choose to line up on one side or the other of an internecine war on U.S. territory. An American civil war, accompanied by a sudden implosion of global U.S. power, might usher in such ghastly scenarios as a multi-sided world war in which America itself is not a major participant.

Once begun, there is no predicting how an American civil war would play out—how destructive it would be, how the world would react, how long it would last, and who would win and on what terms. We can only imagine that the range of possible outcomes would be large indeed. At best, America would emerge from a civil-war Ekpyrosis much stronger and more united as a political community than it was before—though there would inevitably be an undertow of discontent, lingering for decades, among those who committed themselves to the losing cause. The worst outcomes would be dismal indeed. Imagine, perhaps, a war which, after extensive violence, leaves the world in chaos—and leaves America riven into two or more fragments, one or more of which is directed by foreign powers.

Either way, America will once again pass through a gate of history that will forever shape the lives of everyone who can recall the experience.

GREAT-POWER WAR

Three weeks after the Russian invasion, NBC News asked Ukraine President Volodymyr Zelensky if he worried it might trigger World War III. "Nobody knows whether it may have already started," Zelensky answered, pointing out that "we've seen this eighty years ago, when the Second World War had started. . . . Nobody would be able to predict when the full-scale war would start." The "World War III" question has since reverberated in the media: Has another global war already begun?

Zelensky was correct about our very partial and limited foresight. Most people never thought about a second world war until it enveloped *them*. So Americans look back to December 7, 1941 (the Japanese attack on Pearl Harbor), and most Europeans to September 1, 1939 (the German invasion of Poland). But the Chinese look back to July 7, 1937 (the full-scale Japanese invasion of China). And other individual countries and regions look back to yet earlier dates: 1936 for the Spanish; 1935 for the Ethiopians; or 1931 for the Manchurians.

In any case, World War II did not suddenly explode out of nowhere. It gathered strength, like an avalanche starting to heave with ever-larger tremors, until whoosh—all the world gave way. The early signs during the 1930s weren't just the outright invasions, but the swelling wave of bloodless annexations, midnight coups, bribed newspapers, assassinated leaders, jailed dissidents, and rigged elections. It was the shadow of brute autocracy spreading over the world.

The same shadow is spreading today. According to one global institute (Freedom House), the share of the world's population *not* living in "free" nations has expanded over the last decade from 55 percent to 80 percent. According to another (V-Dem), the share living in "autocratic nations" has risen from 49 percent to 70 percent. Almost every year, the number of governments restricting civil liberties, criminalizing dissent, suspending due process, and manipulating elections (if they allow them at all) has greatly exceeded the number moving in a liberal direction.

The social symptoms of this trend—again, not unlike the 1930s—are broadly similar across the world: the rise of ethnocentric populism, the success of charismatic strongmen, a drift toward we-first economic autarky, a disaffection with due process and globalism, and an enthusiasm for grievance-based nationalism. Almost inevitably, such countries will try to acquire (or, in their own eyes, "re-acquire") regional spheres of influence—by diplomacy or intimidation if they can or by force if they must. Countries whose own citizens have been stripped of rights always find it easier to disregard the rights of their neighbors.

The timing of this global shift is no accident. As we have seen, it is driven by a growing generational convergence of modern societies along a similar saecular calendar. A like-minded shift can therefore be witnessed among countries that remain "free" and non-autocratic—from Japan, Argentina, and Brazil to Britain, France, Italy, and Poland. In their domestic politics, these countries too are agitated by calls from radical populists, socialists, and nationalists for stronger leadership. In their foreign affairs, they too are struggling to comply with multilateral agencies (such as NATO, WTO, IMF, and EU) that once effortlessly coordinated every member's policies. Both within and among countries, free and unfree, people are searching for more cohesive and effective civic communities than the ones they've inherited.

During the 1930s, the path toward great-power war was marked by some easily recognizable signposts: strident nationalism, shrinking global trade, accelerated displacement of unwanted populations, the fragmentation of the world into regional economic and security blocks, and a heightening rivalry between the emboldened unfree blocks and the discouraged free blocks.

Over the last ten to fifteen years, all these trends have once again been in motion. Global trade (as a share of global GDP), which had risen steeply until the Global Financial Crisis, has since been falling in a quickening arc—pulled down by recessions, rising trade barriers, a pandemic, and punitive sanctions. The flow of global refugees, put to flight by state persecution or state breakdown, is rising to a flood. And to keep them out, global walls are rising as well. By one count, the number of barrier walls between adjacent nations has quintupled, from sixteen to more than ninety, since 2000.

Ever-more countries are turning inward to celebrate their own exclusive roots in national identity movements, from the Great Han in China, 969 Buddhism in Myanmar, and Hindutva in India to renewed dreams of a "Greater Russia" or a "Greater Turkey" or even a "Greater Hungary." Fueling this new collective confidence, in many non-free countries, is the hope of regaining lost eminence by reversing some historical humiliation suffered at the hands of outsiders. As in the 1930s, the target of this ressentiment is a cabal of powerful, capitalist, godless, and technologized Western nations. And standing in as the uncontested leader of the cabal, this time around, is America.

Identifying the major participants in a coming great-power war, should it happen, is no Black Swan mystery. It's more like a Gray Rhino, to use policy analyst Michele Wucker's evocative phrase—something which, when we pause to think about it, is big, obvious, and galloping straight toward us. To list the roster on one side, we need only refer to America's four primary "adversaries" and "competitors" as they are described in recent yearbooks of the U.S. Directorate of National Intelligence. These are: China, Russia, Iran, and North Korea, in roughly that order. All four nations are growing steadily closer together in their trade and security agreements. Their policy statements are showing ever-tighter coordination, as when China now complains of Western powers orchestrating an "Indo-Pacific NATO." And all together—after adding in another couple of dozen allies, dependencies, and vassals—they dominate the vast supercontinent of Eurasia. Arrayed against them, on the other side, is America, much of the western hemisphere, most of Europe, and the high-income western Pacific Rim.

On the adversary side, virtually every member country is non-free. On the American side, most member countries are free. The adversary side is superior in land area and (assuming India remains nonaligned) in population. The American side is superior in technology, economic capacity, and projectible military strength. That's a big edge. But the adversary side believes it could prevail through technological breakthroughs combined with a greater collective willingness to plan ahead, take risks, and incur sacrifice. Once again, in all such encomia to "greater national will," we hear echoes of the 1930s.

The adversary side may have one more hope, which is that the American side disintegrates on its own. The western Pacific Rim democracies may lose confidence in American security guarantees and start cutting their own deals with China. The European Union, having already lost Britain, may lose more members as a result of economic hardship and populist party victories. Western European leaders, tiring of the war in Ukraine, may choose to come to terms with Russia over sovereignty in Eastern Europe—a tempting move that would at once gain them populist votes, pull down energy prices, and boost their economies. Xi likes to compare "China's order" with "chaos in the West." As well he might, for it's a playbook the world has seen before. Leaders of the Axis powers, after several successful invasions in the late 1930s, were themselves astonished by the disunity of their vanquished opponents.

Best of all, for the adversary side, would be for America itself to disintegrate internally. This scenario too is one that Xi no doubt takes seriously. "Time and momentum are on our side," he proclaimed after hearing of the 2021 storming of the U.S. Capitol. "America's Main Opponent is Itself," the *People's Daily* explained a few days later in a headline. Such hope is not groundless. It is possible that America's civil conflict could worsen into civil war. And if that happens, America's global security capabilities would be undermined, perhaps severely. Almost overnight, the adversary side could find itself free to realize long-sought strategic goals—starting with large regional expansions of their spheres of power—and face little possibility of an American response.

As we have seen, an American implosion is certainly possible. But its likelihood is unknowable. What we do know is this. During a Crisis era, external conflict is essentially an all-or-nothing alternative to internal conflict, and once an external conflict is fully engaged, it tends to draw most partisan tribal energy toward itself. Repeatedly over the saecula, raging partisan divisions and even near civil wars have been transformed, by unforeseen and perhaps unforeseeable events, into mobilizations for global war: against the Hapsburgs, against the Sun King, against King George III, or (most recently in World War II) against the Axis invaders.

Historians have often debated whether or how often leaders have done this deliberately—that is, launch a so-called "diversionary war" with the express purpose of distracting the public from domestic troubles. The evidence is mixed. If there are such wars, they are almost certainly minor military actions that leaders might imagine pose no real downside. (The phrase "wag the dog" was first applied to Clinton-era U.S. bombing raids on Mideast terrorist camps.) It hardly seems plausible that "diversionary" motives explain any of the Anglo-American Crisis wars thus far—if only because the costs and risks posed by entering these wars appeared at the outset so terrifyingly large.

We do know of one instance in which a Crisis-era American leader was seriously advised to instigate a diversionary war. But the advice was not followed. This was in the spring of 1861, when Secretary of State William Seward sent President Lincoln, barely inaugurated, his notorious "April First" memorandum. Seward proposed to Lincoln that he start an immediate war with Britain, France, or Spain, under flimsy pretexts, to get the Union to rally around the flag and forget about Fort Sumter. Because Lincoln understood that the sectional quarrel was far too advanced for such a bald ploy to succeed, he politely turned down Seward's counsel. (And in doing so he no doubt demonstrated the good judgment of the Republican Party in choosing him, rather than Seward, as its presidential candidate.)

The next great-power war will once again pose terrifying risks to all who enter it. The reason, of course, is the global proliferation of WMDs with rapid and effective delivery systems. Once Iran possesses nuclear weapons (which may happen at any time), there will be ten nuclear powers. Four of them will be on the adversary side—five of them if Pakistan joins.

We cannot measure the risk of such a war. All we know for certain is that each nation's perception that it must prepare for conflict itself raises the risk. "A war regarded as inevitable or even probable, and therefore much prepared for," wrote the eminent diplomat George F. Kennan, "has a very good chance of eventually being fought."

Nor can we know how such a war would begin and evolve. As Adolf Hitler reportedly observed, on the eve of Operation Barbarossa, "The beginning of every war is like opening the door into a dark room. One never knows what is hidden in the darkness." Most likely, it would begin with a proxy war that gradually draws major powers into it—or with a major power unexpectedly crossing a red line. While efforts will be made to minimize violence through cyberattacks and sweeping economic sanctions and blockades, nations will eventually resort to force on the ground. Whenever possible, they will employ asymmetric "denial" technologies (such as inexpensive drones or anti-ship missiles) to try to negate the legacy military investments of the other side.

In almost every scenario, the war is likely to escalate to the high-risk edge of nuclear terror. Some leaders, at some point, may figure they have no choice but to engage in extreme brinksmanship—the shameful art of extorting large gains by demonstrating how little they care about absorbing devastating losses. Electorates in free nations may reasonably ask their leaders why they are being asked to risk losing millions of lives to defend a territory they have barely heard of—for example, Estonia or Taiwan. It won't be the first time. Electorates in Western Europe asked similar questions eighty-four years ago. In the spring of 1939, the headline of a Parisian editorial, "Why Die for Danzig?," set off a raging debate in France.

As for possible outcomes, these would span an even vaster range for a great-power war than for a civil war.

At best, America would emerge from such an Ekpyrosis much stronger and more united domestically than it was before. It would moreover be in a position to build, together with its allies, new and effective global institutions for resolving national disputes and coordinating national economies. As Volodymyr Zelensky told the U.S. Congress as columns of Russian tanks rumbled through Ukraine: "The wars of the past have prompted our predecessors to create institutions that should protect us from war, but they, unfortunately, don't work. We see it. You see it. So we need new ones, new institutions, new alliances."

The free world would at last be in a position to build what Zelensky is asking for. Indeed, it could empower these new institutions to solve global challenges never even imagined by those they replace: how to enforce limits on the possession of WMDs; how to allocate the cost of reducing net carbon emissions; or how to manage all global-commons assets in the oceans, in the atmosphere, or in outer space. The constellation of international agencies founded nearly eighty years ago are failing in all these tasks—not so much because the agencies themselves have changed, but because the societies around them have lost their motive to cooperate. Under a new global regime, they would reacquire that motive.

At worst, should at least one desperate country resort to WMDs, the outcome of a great-power war could prove to be even more devastating than that of a civil war. The toll could be almost unimaginable—with multiple cities destroyed, many millions killed, and many tens of millions displaced—all perhaps triggered by some ill-fated combination of the wrong leader making the wrong choice at the wrong time. The most likely outcome, we hope, will be something much better than this. Balancing the losses will be, both within and between nations, a sense of collective renewal. At the end of the Fourth Turning, the vector of history will signal a reversal in social entropy.

By then, it won't be just America that has passed through another great gate of history, but much of the world—forever reshaping the lives of everyone who can recall what he or she went through.

8

HOW OUR SOCIETY
WILL CHANGE

Most people live, whether physically, intellectually or morally, in a very restricted circle of their potential being. . . . Great emergencies and crises show us how much greater our vital resources are than we had supposed.

—WILLIAM JAMES

During every Fourth Turning, especially during the climactic Ekpyrosis, America has experienced a rapid and profound social transformation—from fragmentation, sclerosis, and insecurity to a new regime of inclusive unity, collective energy, and grand expectations.

In the early 1770s, American colonists were barely governable. That's how their British governors saw them. And in truth that's how many Americans, even Benjamin Franklin in a despondent mood, came to see themselves.

By the mid-1790s, this was a different country. Having defeated the British, the colonists miraculously agreed to be ruled by a national government. Not only that, the country was to be a democratic republic—something never before attempted on this scale—with grandly named classical features like a Congress, a Senate, and a President. Federal troops proved they could suppress rebellions and win battles. The infant state even managed to appoint foreign diplomats, locate a national capital, found a national bank, assume full payment of its war debt, and levy nationwide taxes higher than its citizens had earlier paid as colonists.

Now move ahead, toward the end of the next saeculum. In the late

1850s, America was seething with discontent and division: Federal authority was vanishing; political parties were disintegrating; legislators feared violence on the floor of Congress; and local economies developed largely on their own, with little national infrastructure or standardization.

A decade later, this was a different country. Almost overnight, as an astonished Europe looked on, America mobilized for total war. Soon the U.S. president was deploying the largest army and navy in the world—while nationalizing industries to produce and transport matériel at vast scale. For the first time, the Union regulated state banks, issued paper currency, and set up an income tax, while also financing the transcontinental railway, subsidizing homesteaders, and founding a state college system. The Constitution was amended to include the first national guarantees of civic rights and due process for all persons. After the war, Americans began to look at their nation as a continental republic. Before, the United States had usually been a plural noun ("The United States are . . ."). Ever since, it has been singular.

Now move ahead again until late in the next saeculum. By the end of the 1930s, America felt "licked," to use slang common at the time. Widespread joblessness lingered, the New Deal seemed over, and an impotent America half-believed the conquering fascists and the rebuilding Communists who said *they* were the future.

A decade later, this was a different country. After outproducing Germany, Japan, and Britain combined in weaponry and infrastructure, this nation had become a "superpower," thereby redefining America's relationship with the world. Henry Stimson called the promise and peril of atomic power "a revolutionary change in the relations of man to the universe." A unionized, home-owning middle class, moving into suburbs, could purchase new mass-produced wonders, from TVs to washing machines. Meanwhile, during the war, the national government had greatly expanded its size and reach—dictating wages and prices, withholding income taxes, and regulating thousands of new activities with tens of thousands of newly hired civil servants. By 1945 it owned a staggering 40 percent of U.S. factories and capital equipment. Those years forever redefined the government's relationship with the national economy.

At the end of each of these eras, naturally enough, Americans felt relief over the end of violence, discord, and privation. Yet they also felt pride and optimism about their new sense of community and shared direction. Strikingly, most Americans at the time expressed their new confidence in language that was not intimate or personal, but expansive and collective. They wanted to celebrate their new achievement in all of its *public* dimensions—its size, power, coherence, and magnificence.

By the mid-1790s, the young poet David Humphreys had hailed the civic achievements of his rising generation in a best-selling poem entitled "Happiness of America," a Virgilian panorama of peace and plenty, from bounteous wheat fields to orderly cities bustling with commerce. ("Then wake, Columbians! . . . Awake to glory, and rapture rise . . .") Or consider this glorious vision of unity from his Federalist peer, Timothy Dwight: "One blood, one kindred, reach from sea to sea, / One language spread; one tide of manners run; / one scheme of science, and of morals one . . ." Even Jefferson, an avowed opponent of the Federalists, could not resist calling America an "Empire of Liberty," a memorable phrase shimmering with the nation's lofty civic destiny.

By the early 1870s, America had taken the central lesson of the Civil War—that size, efficiency, and planning always wins—and applied it triumphantly to national life. The integration of people into cooperative (if also competitive) civic and economic "machines" became a popular metaphor for progress. At a rate unequaled before or since, civic leaders began investing in colossal municipal waterworks and bridges, industrialists in their gigantic factories and distribution networks. Nationwide unions of farmers and workers were launched. The local family business seemed doomed. "The day of combination is here to stay," wrote John D. Rockefeller in 1880. "Individualism has gone, never to return."

By the late 1940s, similarly, the return of peace and plenty was being welcomed in words suggesting purpose, cooperation, and inclusion. The new order was planned: "National planning boards" would proliferate across the nation. It was cooperative, bringing big labor, big business, the military, and other interest groups into seamless partnerships. It was unifying: National highways and airlines and media would regularize the regional misfits. And it was broadly democratic. At home, security and affluence would be shared by the "middle class" and the "common man"; abroad, America would lead a like-minded "Pax Americana" of peaceful collaboration.

As all these examples suggest, the renewal of national community—both in spirit and in practice—is a central dynamic of the saeculum's winter season. The purpose of this chapter is to examine the primary ways Crisis eras transform society. After all, these eras aren't just a memorable cluster of spectacular events. They are a nation's searing rite of passage, reshaping the habits, expectations, dreams, and fears of the society that experiences them.

MODERNITY AND RECURRING CONFLICT

A paradox of every Crisis era is that it works toward the creation of stronger community *as an end*, yet uses conflict—typically, deadly organized conflict—*as a means*. How is this possible? Very likely, it is related to the great paradox of modernity itself, which is that progress, intended to lift us out of cyclical history, in practice pushes us back into recurring trauma.

Political historians routinely explain the order-disorder duality of great national conflicts by pointing to a social process called "modern state formation." As the name suggests, the process is unique to modernity. It is a positive feedback loop. And it works like this. Bigger state armies lead to more peace over more territory, which leads to more secure individual rights and transactions at greater scale, which leads to greater social organization and prosperity, which leads to more state revenue, which leads to bigger state armies. Looking back over this modernizing dynamic, the historian William McNeill explains how effective armies "could and did establish a superior level of public peace within all the principal European states. This allowed agricultural, commerce, and industry to flourish, and, in turn, enhanced the taxable wealth that kept the armed force in being." Sociologist Charles Tilly is pithier: "War made the state, and the state made war."

While this process may have occurred occasionally in the ancient world, it only became a regular rhythm across Western Europe after a Hero generation of worldly and ambitious princes came to power in the late fifteenth century. According to one historian, these Renaissance monarchies were essentially "machines built for the battlefield." And they set the pattern for the centuries that followed. The process was thus unidirectional and cumulative over time. Any ruler or people who failed to compete was soon swallowed up or swept aside. One by one, the multitude of outlaw duchies and independent communes succumbed to widening and strengthening national dominion.

Most modern Western thinkers have looked favorably on the net result. "As result of war, nations are strengthened," remarked Georg W. F. Hegel, who unquestionably saw stronger nations and therefore wars as drivers of progress. Thanks to modern state-making, subjects (eventually "citizens") have enjoyed greater day-to-day peace and security, more highly evolved social interdependence, spreading literacy, rising material living standards, and more secure legal rights and due process (eventually guaranteed through democratic participation). Through "internal pacification," the sinister-sounding phrase coined by sociologist Anthony Giddens, modern states empower the bureaucracies that make law, voting, representation, and public safety possible at a national level.

Even overall violence in these modern states has declined dramatically over the centuries. Any rise in casualties from major wars has been vastly outweighed by falling rates of casual violence among people able to live together peacefully in more orderly environments. (According to Steven Pinker's magisterial summary of the evidence, homicide rates in most of today's modern societies are between *ten and one hundred times lower* than the premodern norm.) People are also able to live in more affluent environments, which greatly lowers injury and mortality from accidents and disease. Among the many cumulative benefits of modernity as a long-term social process, argues sociologist Norbert Elias (in his classic, *The Civilizing Process*), is how it habituates people to self-control and "civility." It socializes and humanizes us moderns, making most of us more careful and empathic—and less volatile and impulsive.

Yet for all its benefits, modern state formation does require periodic conflict. Because these powerful civic leviathans cannot easily reform themselves, they will inevitably be regarded as less just and less secure with the passage of time. Eventually, after new institutions are created, the generations who know how to manage them competently and fairly will disappear—as will the generations who are content to be managed by them. New values and ideas will emerge, and rising generations will coalesce into factions around them. At some moment, one or more of the new factions will do everything they can to push the old regime aside and replace it with something newer and more powerful.

This entire social dynamic reflects of course the seasonal rhythm of the saeculum. The outcome, during the winter season, could be a new domestic regime (after realignment, revolution, or civil war). Or a new regime of external relationships (a new "world system"), reflecting reconfigured power relationships between nations. Typically, it will be some combination of both.

The conflict triggered by a clash of regimes, moreover, is likely to involve great violence for the simple reason that regime change, almost by definition, cannot be constrained by any established procedure. This is most obvious when one state challenges another. But it is also true within states, even within mature liberal democracies with long-honored rules for choosing new leadership. With regime change, the question always arises: What happens in a state when an important decision is properly made, but a large community within the state refuses to accept it?

American historian Carl Becker posed just this dilemma in his 1941 essay "The Dilemma of Democracy," a darkly sober meditation on the rise of dictatorships over the prior decade. Democratic governments, he observed, presuppose that "the issues to be decided do not involve those interests which men will always fight for rather than surrender." Yet in eras of distrust and upheaval these are precisely the issues that most need deciding.

> Democratic government, being government by discussion and majority vote, works best when there is nothing of profound importance to discuss, when the rival party programs involve the superficial aspects rather than the fundamental structure of the social system, and when the minority can meet defeat at the polls

in good temper, since it need not regard the decision as either a permanent or a fatal surrender of its vital interests.

For Becker, this breakdown of democratic process was a tragedy. For fascist intellectuals like Carl Schmitt or Giovanni Gentile, it was an opportunity. For all sides in the 1930s, it signaled the arrival of a new and liminal season of history. In the 2020s, with democracies again in trouble, the same signals are flashing. And for the same reason. Regimes can have lots of procedures, but there is no procedure for choosing *between* regimes. The essence is captured in the Butch Cassidy dictum: When rival rulers choose to have a knife fight, there are no rules.

In unconstrained conflict, the community that wins is typically the one that can fight the hardest and longest and with the most resources. This, in turn, is likely to be the community whose members can be rallied to become the most selflessly devoted to its success—and the most implacably opposed to surrendering to the "other." Extreme conflict thus becomes the social incubator of extreme community—a fresh new wave of what Ibn Khaldun called *'asabiyya*.

This intimate symbiosis between conflict and community is in fact an old doctrine—a cornerstone of sociology since the earliest writings of Émile Durkheim, Max Weber, and Georg Simmel. William Graham Sumner summed up the consensus over a century ago: "Loyalty to the group, sacrifice for it, hatred and contempt for outsiders, brotherhood within, warlikeness without—all grow together, common products of the same situation." According to Robert Putnam, it remains the consensus today: "It is a commonplace of sociology that external conflict increases internal cohesion." Many evolutionary biologists (for example, Mark Pagel, author of *Wired for Culture*) believe the tendency is genetically hardwired into humans. Almost all scholars agree it is deeply rooted in how humans are raised and socialized.

Today, the power of this dynamic is routinely replicated in social science experiments on subjects of any age: Just watch how any group of people interact after dividing them into groups, however arbitrary, and giving them some task to perform. They quickly forge feelings of trust toward the in-group and feelings of animosity toward the out-group. The so-called "Robbers Cave" experiment by psychologist Muzafer Sherif in 1958, involving twenty-two adolescent boys randomly separated into two teams, is regarded as one of the first and most famous of these studies. Yet long before professors ran such experiments, astute observers of humanity had no trouble understanding how easily any sort of group identity could trigger conflict. Here is James Madison's account in *Federalist No. 10*: "So strong is this propensity of mankind to fall into mutual animosities, that where no substantial occasion presents itself, the most frivolous and fanciful distinctions have been sufficient to kindle their unfriendly passions and excite their most violent conflicts."

But of course people don't always behave as selfless team partisans. Much of the time, they are just as strongly inclined to only look after their own selfish interests. So what rule determines when people are more likely to work for the group rather than for themselves? Biologists David Sloan Wilson and his coauthor E. O. Wilson have suggested the following rule of thumb: "Selfishness beats altruism within groups. Altruistic groups beat selfish groups." Brilliantly enigmatic, the Wilsons' formula throws an illuminating spotlight on the opposite solstices of the saeculum.

In an Awakening, when the old regime is strong and in charge, there is no serious conflict between regimes. In an unthreatened world, teamwork to defend the regime seems unnecessary. Society thus gravitates toward selfishness, which becomes most people's winning strategy. To be sure, acute social conflict does arise during an Awakening. But it is triggered by excessive community power and thus gives rise to decentralized protest, argument, and rule-breaking—not to organized, large-scale hostilities. During an Awakening, the rising priority of the young Prophet is that people adopt new ideals and values, which requires weakening, not strengthening, the behavioral constraints of community.

In a Crisis, on the other hand, the old regime is weak and in peril. New regimes are competing to defend, defeat, or replace it. In a threatened world, selfishness puts your own side in peril. Society thus gravitates toward altruism, which now becomes the winning strategy. The new goal is to create a more powerful civic order, making scale and commitment paramount, argument and scruple pointless. Individuals congeal into rule-following teams in order to compel the "other" to submit, likely resulting in centralized and large-scale violence. During Crises, the rising priority for the young Hero is that people adopt new civic goals and obligations, which requires strengthening the behavioral constraints of the community.

Rival communities during a Crisis, once they are fully engaged in unconstrained conflict, tend not to relent until the capitulation of the adversary. Historically, as we have seen, such struggles have been unusually destructive of lives and property. While the conflict rages, in fact, the community's willingness to sacrifice becomes itself a public rallying cry that drowns out any personal misgivings harbored by individuals. Champions who embrace sacrifice are celebrated. Shirkers who avoid it are scorned. From a group-survival perspective, indeed, shirkers and defectors must be punished as aggressively as outside enemies.

Group solidarity thus makes sacrifice more likely. Yet the causation works the other way as well: Sacrifice itself feeds back positively on solidarity. Countless studies of natural disasters show that great losses typically trigger an outpouring of community-minded behavior. In her popular book on such catastrophes, *A Paradise Built in Hell*, Rebecca Solnit concludes that, after disasters strike, "people step up—not all, but the great preponderance—to become their brothers' keeper."

The effect is greater when the catastrophe is inflicted by a hostile enemy. After the 9/11 attack, the sheer scale of the losses sent most survey measures of American patriotism and public trust soaring for nearly a year. And the effect is greatest when the losses are suffered by an entire nation in an ongoing conflict that lasts for years. In dozens of studies of wartime survivors around the world, social scientists consistently find (according to one meta-review) that afterward "in case after case, people exposed to war violence go on to behave more cooperatively and altruistically" and "tend to increase their social participation by joining more local social and civic groups or taking on more leadership roles in their communities." Most of the studies find no decline in their pro-social behavior over time.

For generations that come of age during a Crisis era, the effect of such an experience is likely to last a lifetime. The Wilsons' formula—in intergroup conflict, altruism wins—becomes an unforgettable lesson for those who understand that the fate of their nation once rode in the balance.

Evidence for the durability of this lesson dates back almost to the American republic's very founding. On September 22, 1776, just weeks after the signing of the Declaration of Independence, twenty-one-year-old Yale graduate Nathan Hale was hanged by the British in New York City as a spy. His reputed last words, "I only regret that I have but one life to lose for my country," became the first of many declarations of selfless honor to impress U.S. citizens ever afterward.

Testimonies to altruism periodically reappear during the "high community" years that follow in the aftermath of the Crisis. Even while the Civil War was still raging, American towns began to erect towering Victorian monuments to their war dead. Hundreds were in place by 1884, when Oliver Wendell Holmes, Jr., himself a thrice-wounded veteran, addressed a large Memorial Day gathering of the Grand Army of the Republic. In that speech, he drew his famous portrait of his generation: "Through our great good fortune, in our youth our hearts were touched with fire. It was given to us to learn at the outset that life is a profound and passionate thing." But then he went on to add, "It is now the moment when by common consent we pause to become conscious of our national life and to rejoice in it, to recall what our country has done for each of us, and to ask ourselves what we can do for the country in return."

Holmes's line was picked up nearly eighty years later by John F. Kennedy, in his "Ask not . . ." inaugural address. As a younger man on the campaign trail only three years after his own wartime brush with death, Kennedy recalled, "I firmly believe, that as much as I was shaped by anything, so I was shaped by the hand of fate moving in World War II." Perhaps recalling all those wartime windows showing gold stars for fallen sons, he added, "Of course, the same can be said of almost any American or British or Australian man of my generation. The war made us. It was and is our single greatest moment." Kennedy went on: "The memory of the war is a key to our characters. It serves as a breakwall between the indolence of our youths and earnestness of our manhoods. No school or parent could have shaped us the way that fight shaped us. No other experience could have brought forth in us the same fortitude and resilience."

In one of his last speeches, Kennedy declared that "in a time of domestic crisis, men of goodwill and generosity should be able to unite regardless of party or politics." Perhaps they should. But in a few years, as America entered an Awakening, it became clear that few would.

After surveying history, we may be prompted to ask: Is the experience of sacrifice through deadly conflict—that is, war—somehow *necessary* for the creation of community solidarity? The question may not have a definitive answer. All we know is that, historically, each is closely linked to the other.

This question is very different than the sorts of general questions people usually ask about war: whether it is per se immoral, whether it is worth the cost, or whether humanity could possibly create a world without it.

The morality question points to categorical beliefs and cannot be settled by evidence. The cost question is easily answered. War is rarely worth the cost, at least in terms of dollars. (In 1861, every slave family in America could have been emancipated and land purchased for it at a fraction of what both sides spent on the Civil War.) But cost has little relevance since, prior to war, parties willing and able to arrange such a transaction can seldom be found. The question of a possible world without war points to practical problems of institutional design. How would global antiwar rules be enforced? By whom? Would one nation or organization need to dominate all the others? If so, who would guard the guardians? And so on.

The question of necessity is different. It's not about ethics or institutional design. It asks whether, without war, society could still forge the community solidarity that forms the basis of modern progress itself with all its benefits.

William James, a contemporary of Holmes and a self-described "pacifist" (he declined to serve in the Civil War), understood the importance of this question. He reflected deeply on it. And in a famous 1906 speech delivered at Stanford University, he invited his audience to imagine whether it might be possible to forgo forever the horrors of war *as a social process* by instituting what he called "the moral equivalent of war."

In the speech, he acknowledges up front the fundamental role played by war in teaching society's younger members a wide range of social virtues, including toughness in adversity, obedience to command, surrender of private interest, and dedication to the commonweal. All these, he agrees, "remain the rock upon which states are built." Somehow or someday, he imagines, a nation might be able to conscript its youth into a riskless yet rigorous experience that could inculcate these attitudes and behaviors. He has no illusions that America could easily create such a "moral equivalent." Indeed, he sometimes wonders if it is possible at all. "So far, war has been the only force that can discipline a whole community, and until an equivalent discipline is organized, I believe that war must have its way."

At one point, James suggests a fascinating thought experiment. He asks hypothetically how many Americans would prefer to live in their country today (in 1906) without the Civil War ever having happened. He supposes hardly anybody would: We could hardly imagine, James explains, living in a nation lacking the sense of unity and progress won by that war. He then asks how many Americans would welcome another such cataclysm in the foreseeable future. Now he supposes, again no doubt correctly, that hardly anybody would.

James calls this attitude "highly paradoxical." And perhaps it is, though it may just reflect a difference in perspective. We never feel the same about the future as we do about the past. As individuals, we are often grateful to have grown and benefitted from a difficult rite of passage in our personal life, even if we have no wish to encounter another. As societies, most of us feel the same. At the more optimistic Awakening end of the saeculum, which is when James was delivering his speech, it may be easier to argue against the need for a strong war-making state. At the bleaker Crisis end, it may be harder.

By the time James was speaking, criticism of war was clearly more popular among the rising generation than any defense of war that Holmes's (and James's) Civil War generation might offer. In a speech Holmes made just a decade earlier, in 1895, he conceded as much.

Holmes observes that "although the generation born about 1840, and now governing the world, has fought two at least of the greatest wars in history, and has witnessed others, war is out of fashion, and the man who commands attention of his fellows is the man of wealth. . . . The aspirations of the world are those of commerce." Yet he wonders whether the new quest for personal wealth and security is not inflaming "the growing hatred of the poor for the rich." The moment will arrive, he suspects, when Americans will no longer occupy "this snug, over-safe corner of the world" and will need to overcome "this time of individualist negations." At that moment, they will rise again to war, though (Holmes predicts) they will do so no more willingly than his own generation did.

Back in the mid-1970s, Ronald Reagan famously declared that the ten most terrifying words in the English language are "I'm from the government, and I'm here to help you." Stanford historian Ian Morris, who has argued at great length (with Holmes and against James) that war is indeed inevitable, observes that Reagan's quip could only make sense at a uniquely secure moment in a uniquely comfortable corner of the world. For most of humanity and throughout most of history, writes Morris, the ten most terrifying words are "There is no government, and I'm here to kill you." War, he implies, is what happens when people are lucky enough to have an effective government willing to protect them.

Here is where the question must be left to rest. Few of us are so without hope that we insist on the strict necessity of war. At the same time, few of us are so without prudence that we insist that this time must be different.

SOCIETY IN WINTER

When summing up the significance of America's pivotal Crisis eras, historians repeatedly return to one central conclusion: These weren't simply major political or constitutional breakpoints; they were extraordinary eras of rapid social transformation that had lasting consequences.

Here's one eminent historian on the Great Depression–World War II era: "That brief span of years, it is now clear, constituted one of only a handful of episodes in American history when lasting and substantial social change occurred—when the country was, in measurable degree, remade."

Here's another on the Civil War: "The greatest consequence of the war . . . was the replacement of the awkward, unformed, immature nation of 1860 by the confident, purposeful, systematized nation of 1870."

Here's yet another on the American Revolution era: "That revolution did more than legally create the United States; it transformed American society. . . . It was as radical and social as any revolution in history."

Let's now look more closely, if also schematically, at the most important common dimensions of this social transformation. We start with the critical shift from individual to community. This is a trend that starts during the Crisis and becomes dominant in the High. But we will discuss others, five in all. Each is paired here with its saecular opposite—the trend that starts during the Awakening and becomes dominant during the Unraveling.

- from individualism to *community*
- from privilege to *equality*
- from defiance to *authority*
- from deferral to *permanence*
- from irony to *convention*

As we look ahead to the remainder of the Millennial Crisis, these shifts should provide a baseline for what to expect. All of them can be expected to accelerate during the later years of the era, especially during the Ekpyrosis, along with the pace of events themselves. When the saecular winter has come to an end, a transformed America will once again feel like a different country. Every generation, similarly, will reach an entirely new understanding of its role in history.

COMMUNITY

The society-wide impulse to re-create a strong community—often starting at a local or partisan level but inevitably ending with a unified national community—is a central driving force during the entire Crisis era.

Early in the Crisis, as we've seen in earlier chapters, a society's sense of community plunges to its nadir. Agreement on common purpose, habits, and values—already in decline during the Unraveling—is shattered entirely by the catalyst. In their public lives, people sense that civic institutions are dysfunctional (why doesn't anything work?). In their personal lives, they feel emotional distress (why do I feel so alone?).

As society moves further into a Fourth Turning, it rediscovers two remarkable truths about community in the modern world.

The first truth is that too little community, just like too much community, literally makes us sick. Loneliness and isolation are highly correlated with substance abuse, chronic disease, depression, mental illness generally, and suicide. Deaths from such causes surged during the 2010s. The evidence suggests they rose as well early in the Great Depression of the 1930s.

Now, as then, the nation's response is hindered by the bipartisan libertarianism it has inherited from the recent Unraveling: the assumption that the nation has no collective purpose other than preserving the right of each sovereign individual to live unhindered from others' claims. By the year 2008, as by the years 1929 and 1859, the national government had become a procedural "rights state" dedicated to little more than setting ground rules for personal fulfillment. Its primary goal was disconnected contentment. The only problem is that most people aren't hardwired for solitude and satiation as much as they are for loyalty, belonging, and struggle. As Sebastian Junger points out in *Tribe*, "Humans don't mind hardship, in fact they thrive on it; what they mind is not feeling necessary."

The second remarkable truth is that natural and social crises do not inhibit community creation. They facilitate it. In his encyclopedic overview of how disasters affect social cohesion (written in 1961, but not published until 1996), sociologist and World War II veteran Charles Fritz concludes that, with few exceptions, violent disasters strongly reinforce community identification and behavior.

By coining the term "community of sufferers" to describe this dynamic, Fritz by no means implies any sort of emotional suffering. To the contrary, he writes, kindness, friendliness, and cooperation flourish among these sufferers. While conceding that disasters often result in rising instances of emotional "shell shock" (what we would today refer to as PTSD), he concludes that these are more than offset by falling instances of all the neurotic and self-destructive behaviors that arise during the relative boredom of peacetime. Fritz thus begins his monograph with the provocative question "Why do large-scale disasters produce such mentally healthy conditions?"

A veritable cottage industry of social science scholarship has since emerged establishing this link. Apparently, even *the mere threat or suggestion* of disaster, disorder, epidemic disease, or economic loss fosters a spirit of solidarity. People respond by growing more judgmental in favor of in-group norms, more inclined to follow in-group rules, and more biased against out-group presence. According to other experiments, simply reminding people that they must someday die has the same effect. Thoughts of death, according to a leading "mortality salience" researcher, motivate behaviors that "contribute to nationalism, prejudice, and intergroup aggression, as well as prosocial behavior and cultural achievements." To use cultural psychologist Michele Gelfand's terminology, any perceived threat to people's personal security tends to make their society "tighter."

Early in a Crisis era, people respond to rising threats by congregating as best they can into society's little platoons—families, friends, social networks, and neighborhoods. Today, Americans are experiencing an explosive renaissance in extended-family and group living arrangements—again, with no parallel since the 1930s. But micro success cannot replace macro failure. The national civic vacuum left behind by the Crisis catalyst sucks powerful populist forces up to ever-higher levels of public policy. These forces push for a more effective national community, able to impose fairness, order, and security on the directionless chaos society is experiencing.

Once it is embodied in competing national movements, early in the Crisis, the growing quest for community *always* generates rising political engagement, activism, tribalism, and polarization—since new and competing definitions of community imply mutually exclusive national futures. This is true in the early 2020s. But it was equally true during the New Deal when the political right was calling the 1930s "the Red Decade" and the political left was calling it "the Fascist Decade." Or during the election of 1860, when Northern Radicals charged "slave oligarchs" with "crimes of blood." Or late in the reign of Charles II, when colonists traded feverish rumors that a "tyrannous popish plot" was uniting the Stuarts, Jesuits, French, and Indians to subjugate them all.

When a political regime is well established, we like to praise the ideal voter as open-minded and objective. Yet such a voter never energized a successful *new* political regime, which, at its origin, has always been fueled by committed tribal partisans. Opponents are stigmatized, wafflers are hectored, and followers are urged to action in an echo chamber of hatreds, fears, and conspiratorial threats. Intimidation, the threat of tar-and-feathering or its equivalent, is usually sufficient to bring the vacillators in line. The goal is not to persuade—belief can come later—but rather to prevail.

Either-or choices are made easy by color codes, recognizable by all. In America today, it is red and blue. In the 1930s, it was also red and blue, though the party connection was usually reversed. In the 1860s, it was blue and gray. In the 1680s, during the Anglo-American world's very first "rage of party," it was green and blue. These two colors signified "Whig" and "Tory," respectively—two simple labels that were destined to come alive again, especially in the American colonies, ninety years later.

Every successful Crisis leader has rallied followers with urgent definitions of a renewed national community. Washington presided over the founders' efforts in Philadelphia to institute a "united" government of states. Lincoln justified his demanding draft calls by repeatedly invoking the "Union," an increasingly popular synonym for the United States. In 1936, Roosevelt declared that "nationwide thinking, nationwide planning and nationwide action are the three great essentials to prevent nationwide crises for future generations to struggle through."

While national unity is the goal, how leaders try to forge such unity shifts dramatically over the course of the Crisis era. Early on, it is primarily an ideal, a slogan, a rallying cry by which new leaders try to energize supporters to create new institutions. Later, as these institutions adopt large-scale teamwork under duress, it becomes a routine by which institutions reshape individuals into citizens. At the outset of the American

Revolution and the Civil War, "militia fever" was the rule. Americans on all sides believed they could win their struggles through spontaneous local enthusiasm. Only bitter experience demonstrated that victory required (for Washington) a drilled and disciplined "continental" army or (for Lincoln and Davis) a shift from the early "improvised war" to the later so-called "organized war" requiring vast bureaucracies, standardized equipment, and ample supplies.

In each saeculum, America's spirit of community, which seems so stolid and monolithic in retrospect, typically starts out as a mere aspirational gesture. In the fall of 1933, newly elected President Roosevelt suggested that Americans wear "bright" National Recovery Administration badges like "soldiers . . . in the gloom of a night attack," so that "those who cooperate in this program . . . know each other at a glance." Critics lampooned the idea as a political gimmick, and the NRA itself was soon dismantled. But the idea lingered on in the uniformed CCC camps and among badged CIO and UAW members. A decade later, Roosevelt did in fact command roughly 16 million uniformed Americans in the armed services and millions more badged civilians at home.

After World War II was over, during the next two decades, sociologists began writing essays about America's prodigious supply of "social capital" and "habits of generalized reciprocity"—which, mysteriously, they had never noticed before. Once yet another decade had passed, they began to write about a further mystery: how these habits were beginning to weaken among youth. Mysterious? No, it's not mysterious. It's simply generations aging and the saeculum turning.

EQUALITY

"An earthquake achieves what the law promises but does not in practice maintain: The equality of all men." So wrote one survivor of the cataclysmic 1915 shock that flattened Avezzano, Italy, killing thirty thousand. We may liken a Crisis era to a social earthquake that rocks society's institutional life over an entire generation. As it renews national community, so too does it elevate social and economic equality.

The call for greater equality typically ignites shortly after the initial Crisis catalyst—by pushing the public mood in a populist direction. Facing widespread insecurity (from depression or war), people favor relief to those who suffer and support forceful leaders who ignore protocol and disregard elite opinion in order to make that relief happen. Calamities heighten the fraternal or "brotherhood" dimension of community altruism. Early in both the New Deal and the Millennial Crisis, America experienced just such trauma—along with both the populism and the unprecedented public relief measures.

But this is just the first stage. Sooner or later, more serious challenges and threats will compel the new regime to mobilize the entire community. Equality now becomes more than a policy preference. It becomes a means of collective survival. Property rights give way to enforceable new mechanisms of social sharing. Just as conscription gathers manpower as needed from the lower and middle classes, so too does taxation, rationing, inflation, or ad-hoc confiscation gather wealth as needed from the upper classes. In every Crisis era, all these methods have been employed—for the simple reason that, in times of great trial, every community socializes whatever resources are available.

Another driver of growing equality may be the sheer destruction of physical assets (significant in the South during the Civil War and the Revolution) or the devaluation of financial assets during market panics (significant during every Crisis). Still another is Crisis-era economic dislocation combined with inflation and full employment. When sclerotic incumbent producers fail to adjust to the reallocation of national spending, old wealth implodes and new enterprises rush in to create new industries. As we saw in Chapter 4, the distribution of wealth and income measurably flattens during Crisis eras, especially during their final years. Between 1939 and 1945, the share of all U.S. wealth held by the top 1 percent fell by one-quarter; the share of all income received by the top 5 percent fell by one-third.

Yet rising equality isn't just the negative outcome of wealth stripped from the privileged elite. More positively, it arises out of a new civic compact: In order to obtain the full support of marginalized classes for the new regime, elites grant them greater voice in governing it and a greater share of its future prosperity. Pushing the elites to make this offer is more than a spirit of generosity. It is also their fear of popular resistance. Even in good times, many of the marginalized feel they struggle to get by. In bad times, they may respond with fury to any new imposition.

In every Fourth Turning, the specter of such violence re-emerges. In the 1670s and 1680s, armed mobs backed insurrectionists in almost every colony, from New York to Virginia. In 1785, Shays' army of veterans so alarmed the governor of Massachusetts that he had to raise three thousand troops to thwart it—and so worried George Washington that he agreed to chair the new Constitutional Convention. During the Civil War, urban rampages (like the deadly New York City draft riot) repeatedly required Union troops to impose martial law. During the Great Depression, a rising wave of labor violence along with the growing appeal of third-party demagogues persuaded FDR to radicalize his campaign platform in 1936. Most recently, since 2008, the number of prosecutions and deaths due to "domestic terrorism" (as tallied by official agencies) has swelled.

Between suppressing episodes of popular violence, Crisis-era elites typically grow more attentive to popular grievances. In early modern England, the crown called more frequent parliaments, addressed petitions, and, at election time, handed out more money to constituents. Since 1776, the American practice has been to enlarge the electorate, guarantee new rights, and promise to expand the scope of what citizen and nation will do for each other. The most recent iteration of this civic compact was the New Deal, designed, as FDR told his advisor Frances Perkins, "to make a country in which no one is left out." He capstoned his effort with a "G.I. Bill" and a promise-laden "Economic Bill of Rights" issued at the climax of World War II.

More than economic equality, these compacts foster an ethic of social equality. Class deference weakens, and class differences in dress, language, and manners narrow. It's an old truism of sociology that a lot more people pursue money to attain status than the other way around. National emergencies open new opportunities to attain status without money—through civic achievement alone. These emergencies abruptly devalue the social clout that people may have acquired under the old regime from their wealth, credentials, or family connections.

At his first inauguration, President Washington wore only brown homespun clothing to avoid pretense (and any sign of attachment to imported British fashion). As the revolutionary era ended, Americans abandoned aristocratic wigs, hoops, and powder in favor of simpler, leaner "democratic" fashions. For decades after the Civil War, national service—not economic privilege—became the new prerequisite for entering the White House. After Lincoln's assassination, in seven of the next nine presidential elections, U.S. voters opted for celebrated combat officers of the Union Army who had worked their way up from modest social backgrounds.

During the New Deal, President Roosevelt slyly deflected attention away from his own plutocratic background by goading "economic royalists" in his fireside chats. He famously prompted one voter to say that he was "the only man we ever had in the White House who would understand that my boss is a son of a bitch." Later, during World War II, Roosevelt was proud to remind voters that all four of his sons served and risked their lives in the war. Even the biggest media superstars, like Joe DiMaggio and Clark Gable, volunteered for service without hesitation.

With labor in high demand during national emergencies, ordinary people feel freer to sever ties with old employers and neighborhoods. They negotiate new and better deals and try their hand at new careers. At the end of every Crisis era, geographic mobility surges—set in motion, in part, by the massive dislocation of wartime service. After the Civil War, veterans were much more likely to move to another state and rise to higher-status jobs. After World War II, roughly half of the returning G.I. vets enrolled in college or technical education—all costs covered by federal taxpayers. Their subsequent jobs, often in cities far north or west of where they grew up, paid better than their parents could have imagined. Compared to their prewar baseline in 1940, average employee earnings (adjusted for inflation) soared 41 percent by 1950—and 64 percent by 1955.

While society gains in economic and social equality, so too does the nation gain in the number of full citizens. In its effort to mobilize all available volunteers in wartime, the new regime is compelled to discard old social barriers and confer full citizenship on people who had earlier been denied that privilege. The logic is inescapable: Only full citizens can be motivated to fight and risk their lives for their republic. It is mainly for this reason that every Crisis era registers a successively broader definition of suffrage by wealth, religion, ethnicity, and race.

For African Americans, unhappily, many of these winter-season gains in civic and economic equality have been reversed after the Crisis era ended. Yet the lasting shifts that did occur have been dramatic indeed—and would never have happened in any other season. The rapid abolition of slavery in Northern states during and after the Revolution would not have been possible had not Black patriots composed nearly one-fifth of the Continental Army by the time of the Battle of Yorktown. Nor could President Lincoln in 1865 have mustered the supermajorities he needed in Congress to ratify the 13th Amendment had not uniformed Black soldiers by then composed fully one-tenth of the Union Army.

That same year, an event in Richmond, Virginia, offered the most extraordinary example of the power of civic necessity to break open even the strongest shackles of civic inequality. In March, just a month before the end of the war, the Confederate States Congress voted in favor of enlisting hundreds of thousands of Black slaves to help fill the decimated ranks of Rebel regiments. The vote came after months of rancorous debate, in which most of the South's top leadership (including President Davis and General Lee) supported the measure, even though they conceded it would probably lead to the general emancipation of all slaves. The measure was of course far too little and too late to change the war's outcome. But these leaders were willing to make it, even while they understood its ironic logic: In order to keep fighting the war, they were abandoning the very institution whose long-term preservation had been the primary reason they had gone to war in the first place.

"Through recorded history," concludes economic historian Walter Scheidel, "the most powerful leveling invariably resulted from the most powerful shocks." By shocks he means experiences that no society would ever choose of its own accord—total war, revolution, state failure, a lethal pandemic. Yet horrible as they are, these too serve a function. Typically arriving during Fourth Turnings, they are the social analogue to the earthquake that destroyed Avezzano. They constitute what Scheidel calls the "the great levelers" of rank and privilege and pride.

AUTHORITY

In the decades that follow a Fourth Turning, after a new regime is firmly established, political authority gradually comes to be taken for granted and is therefore less noticed. Since ever-fewer people can recall living under any other regime, most follow authority out of inertia. "Authority is by nothing so much strengthened and confirmed as by custom," observed the seventeenth-century English diplomat and historian Sir William Temple, "for no man easily distrusts the things which he and all men have been always bred up to observe and believe." During and after the Awakening, moreover, most people will perceive the burden of authority to be steadily easing—and some will suppose it must be on its way to complete irrelevance.

All this changes when the next Fourth Turning arrives and political authority leaps back to the top of the public agenda. Now that the choice of regime is in question, reliance on custom and inertia is no longer an option. As conflicts deepen, people will feel forced to choose between the authority of one or another partisan tribe. Questions about the nature of legitimate authority—who exercises it, to what extent, and to what end—again move to the center of public debate.

Crisis-era leaders do their best to reinforce their regime's legitimate authority by wielding propaganda—arguments, imagery, symbols—to galvanize their followers and fuse them into an effective community. Yet they also go further. Where they feel they must, they employ both the threat and demonstration of overwhelming force to put an end to questions about authority that cannot be resolved by argument. The purpose of such force is twofold: to persuade your own side that you are determined at all costs to win; and to persuade traitors and adversaries that they are destined in any case to lose.

Force always accompanies the creation of legitimate and durable national regimes. "Political power grows out of the barrel of a gun," declared Mao Zedong in the 1930s, long before he became the legendary founder of the People's Republic of China. In a 1786 letter to John Jay, on the prospects for a new national constitution, George Washington came to much the same conclusion: "Experience has taught us that men will not adopt and carry into execution measures the best calculated for their own good without the intervention of a coercive power." At moments of national peril, almost every successful leader acknowledges some version of this truth.

The conspicuous use of force, abundantly and often excessively applied, no doubt raises the most troubling ethical questions about how Crisis eras are typically resolved. But it must be acknowledged. It's always present.

During the Revolutionary War, General George Washington insisted he could not maintain an effective army without publicly whipping rulebreakers and executing deserters. John Adams, infuriated by the poor early performance of Patriot militias, recommended shooting deserters on the battlefield. He reasoned that such a treason law would "make whigs by the thousands. . . . It turns a man's cowardice and timidity into heroism, because it places greater danger behind his back than before his face." Once the war was over and the old (British) regime had disappeared, most Americans agreed that their greatest challenge was to empower a more authoritative political order. In the *Federalist Papers*, the word "authority" appears more than twice as often as the words "liberty" or "freedom."

During the U.S. Civil War, Radical Republican leader Thaddeus Stevens reminded President Lincoln that "instruments of war are not selected on account of their harmlessness" and later suggested that he send Union armies to "lay waste to the whole South." Lincoln eventually authorized General Sherman to do just that. "War is cruelty, and you cannot refine it," Sherman wrote to the city council of Atlanta before going on to imply that the sooner the South capitulated, the sooner it would stop. He fully conceived the doctrine of total war, even if he did not coin the term. Sherman was personally pro-Southern; he was willing to help rebuild the South after the war. But on the question of rebellion against Union authority, he was adamant. "If the United States submits to a division now, it will not stop. . . . ," he explained. "The United States does and must assert its authority, wherever it once had power; for, if it relaxes one bit to pressure, it is gone, and I believe that such is the national feeling. This feeling assumes various shapes, but always comes back to that of *Union* [emphasis in original]."

During World War II, such was the resolve of the U.S. president and Congress that perceived threats to national authority were met with crushing shows of force that seem hardly comprehensible today. At home, the nation categorically transported and interned more than one hundred thousand Japanese Americans, citizens or not, merely based on their ancestry. Abroad, the nation (and its allies) waged a months-long firebombing campaign against cities in Germany and Japan, killing perhaps a million civilians, in preparation for an invasion of both countries. Only after these enemies surrendered unconditionally did America relent. And not only relent. America used its newfound global authority to reconstruct these nations as liberal democracies—a successful exercise in "nation building" that later generations would dismiss as hopelessly beyond their power.

This conspicuous presence of coercive national authority during Crisis-era conflicts may seem to conflict with a celebrated myth: that America, during its moments of trial, has always championed freedom against tyranny. Yet the conflict is more apparent than real. Any nation, while it goes to war, becomes more authoritarian; and any democracy that intends to survive must sometimes go to war. The real question is whether, during a Crisis era, a nation permanently abandons its democratic institutions under the pressure of external or internal threats. Such a tragic outcome is possible. All we can say for sure is that America has thus far avoided it.

During Fourth Turnings, broadly speaking, Americans and their leaders have seen themselves as waging total wars on behalf of the authority of free peoples to govern themselves. And, in pursuit of that goal, they have regarded the sacrifices of individuals not as violations of their liberty, but as the price to be paid on behalf of their community's liberty. In short, authority enforced is liberty preserved. After suspending habeas corpus and arresting thousands without judicial process, Lincoln explained that, if he had not done so, the Union would have collapsed—and with it the entire Bill of Rights. Roosevelt, who often heard himself denounced as a dictator, said his critics misperceived the danger: "History proves that dictatorships do not grow out of strong and successful governments, but out of weak and helpless ones."

"*Liberté, Egalité, Fraternité ou la Mort*" was the motto popularized by the armies of the French Revolution as they braced for the invasion of the combined European monarchies in 1792. Revolutionary France was no liberal democracy. But it was a modern nation mobilizing for total war, and the slogan sums up the Crisis-era social transformations we have thus far been examining. *Fraternité* refers to community. *Egalité* refers to equality. And *Liberté*?

To be sure, liberty sounds nothing like authority. Unless, that is, we think more expansively, not about an individual—but about a people's collective determination not to be ruled by tyrants. Authority is the means by which a community enforces this determination, requiring everyone to fulfill his or her civic duty and thus *become* a free citizen. According to this concept, sometimes called "positive liberty," a free republican people must each be willing to sacrifice their own personal liberty on behalf of their community. And not just their liberty, but, if necessary, their lives. Indeed, according to the classical republican ideal as exemplified by Cato the Younger, suicide itself was preferable to submission to Caesar.

This is what the ancient Athenians had in mind when they chanted "liberty!" ("*eleutheria!*") while rowing out near the island of Salamis in their do-or-die encounter against Persian invaders. Or what Patrick Henry had in mind, after pointing out to his fellow Virginia delegates in the spring of 1775 that Britain had offered them "no retreat but in submission and slavery." He went on, according to listeners, to describe the aggressor in lurid detail: "Our chains are forged. Their clanking may be heard on the plains of Boston. . . . Is life so dear, or peace so sweet, as to be purchased at the price of chains and slavery." Then came the close. "I know not what course others may take," he declared, reportedly with a gesture that pulled an ivory letter opener near his chest. "As for me, give me liberty or give me death!"

PERMANENCE

Americans today widely agree that their nation spends too much of its public resources "buying off" special interest groups and spends too little on investments and reforms that would create permanent benefits for everyone. To be sure, people may differ over which investments or reforms deserve top priority. For some, it may be alleviating climate change or rebuilding infrastructure or improving social services; for others, it may be stopping illegal immigration or taxing the rich or overhauling health care. Even so, there's a great deal of overlap in what the public agrees needs to be done.

So why do all these things remain undone? Public policy experts offer a litany of reasons. They say that each issue is too complex. Or they say that interest group opposition is too strong. Most of all, they say that the nation must wait for just the right moment, when it is undistracted by war or recession or partisan infighting. At that moment, on that warm sunny day when we are all fulfilled and happy and can study the issue fully, only then will we be able to move ahead with these vital permanent improvements.

The views of the experts seem reasonable. They appeal to common sense. But they are totally mistaken. The sunny day theory may be how we would *like* major reforms to happen. But that is not how history says they *actually* happen.

In fact, long-term solutions to big issues happen only when the nation reinvents itself. And that happens not on a sunny summer day— but on a dark winter day when citizens' backs are against the wall and every available option points to sacrifice and danger. Paradoxically, the nation makes its most serious commitments to its long-term future *precisely when its near-term existence seems most in doubt.* These are the moments when everyone comprehends, as Benjamin Franklin allegedly quipped just after adding his signature to the Declaration of Independence, that "we must all hang together or most assuredly we will all hang separately."

Imagine the entire timeline of future-oriented institutional reconstruction in America as a punctuated equilibrium: sudden Crisis-era policy revolutions followed by decades of denial, discussion, deferral, and delay.

The ratification of the U.S. Constitution in 1788 was of course America's "founding" act of far-sighted civic statecraft. At a time when citizens had reason to fear that their republic might not last another decade, they settled on a government intended from the very beginning, declared Alexander Hamilton in *Federalist No. 34*, "to look forward to remote futurity." Henry Clay observed sixty-three years later, "The Constitution of the United States was made not merely for the generation that then existed, but for posterity—unlimited, undefined, endless, perpetual posterity." A durable accomplishment indeed it was. Yet in the decades of relative peace and prosperity that followed the founding, not even Clay's eloquence could persuade the nation to reach a lasting settlement of any of its growing disputes over tariffs, currency, national improvements, and (above all) slavery.

Ultimately, during and just after four years of total war, America settled all of them. Tariff barriers, national banks, national tax enforcement, national transportation (the "Pacific Railroad"), free land in the West (the Homestead Act), federal aid for higher education and agricultural research (the Morrill Act), the first federal act to preserve the wilderness (the Yosemite Grant), together with a constitutional ban on slavery—all these were enacted and enforced while partisanship raged, great armies clashed, and at times Washington, DC, itself was gripped by fear of capture.

In the decades following the Civil War, an entirely new set of issues arose, again demanding some sort of comprehensive national response. Among them were industrial cartels, unionization, urban squalor, consumer protection, retirement security, and financial market corruption. From the 1870s through the 1920s, all these issues were endlessly and sometimes passionately debated. But few important or lasting solutions emerged, even during the so-called "progressive" presidencies of Theodore Roosevelt, William Howard Taft, and Woodrow Wilson.

Once again, America had to wait until its next founding moment to settle nearly all of them. Specifically, it had to wait for the first and second New Deal of the mid-1930s and four years of total war in the early 1940s. In retrospect, the timing of the Social Security Act, the cornerstone of Social Security and of most of today's federal-state welfare programs, seems absurdly improbable. In 1935, U.S. GDP had shriveled, unemployment was at 20 percent, the federal government had no available revenue, families worried about their next meal, and helpless democracies around the world were being toppled by populist mobs. Yet this was the year in which America's leadership set into stone a social insurance scheme with audacious projections extending into the 1970s.

After VJ Day and demobilization, the saecular pattern resumed. During the American High, Americans began talking less about new sacrifices to attain new national goals. Instead, under the guise of what postwar political scientists called "interest-group pluralism," they began haggling over marginal gains for this group or that. Privileges multiplied, rent-seeking flourished, and once again structural solutions were deferred. During and after the Consciousness Revolution, what did pass for structural solutions were basically promises by the community to let individuals do whatever they wanted—in their families, in their life choices, and in the marketplace. Structural problems were in effect "solved" by the government disclaiming any responsibility for them. And once again, by the early twenty-first century, a dysfunctional society was limping into the next Fourth Turning.

What explains this punctuated timing? Perhaps it's the social psychology of civic crisis. Once a society is compelled to dedicate such a large share of everyone's private resources to overcome a pressing public challenge, it "resets" public thinking: So long as we're canceling private privileges to overcome *this* big challenge, why not tackle all the others at the same time? Crisis, in effect, "opens up" the realm of civic possibilities—a thesis advanced most notably by economist Mancur Olson in *The Rise and Decline of Nations*.

A complementary explanation would point to generational change. Those who came of age during the Crisis era will best understand the need for near-term private sacrifice in order to avert long-term public disaster. They have learned the hard way the truth of the old English proverb: Play in the summer, starve in the winter. In the years just following the Crisis era, thanks to the influence of this rising generation, national consensus remains solid, savings rates high, and the spirit of sacrifice strong. Only with the passage of decades does the nation succeed into the hands of those who don't recall the starving winter.

Reinforcing this shift is the generational quid pro quo that typically occurs at the climax of a Crisis era. Just as elites offer new democratic rewards to the less privileged to secure their cooperation, so too, and for the same purpose, do older generations offer new future rewards to younger generations. Often this deal is quite explicit: In return for your service, we will reward you with cash, land, education, or other in-kind transfers. Dating back to the early eighteenth century, pension payments to the veterans of America's great wars have always been a major outlay category in postwar public budgets. Over time, these outlays dwindle—until the next occasion for great public sacrifice arrives.

Over the last saeculum, this pattern has vividly repeated itself. During the New Deal and World War II, the G.I. Generation did everything older generations asked them to do and more. In return, grateful older generations—and, later, grateful younger generations—rewarded them (and the cooperative Silent who followed them) with an extraordinary growth in public benefits throughout their lives, and especially in old age. Social Security and Medicare programs have paid most G.I.s back several times what they "paid in" as contributions. But the generosity of this deal has already been cut back sharply for Boomers and Xers. And it will no doubt be cut back more in the years to come. If the pattern repeats, we can expect the next tilt toward the rising generation will be toward Millennials and perhaps by extension to Homelanders as well.

Which archetype benefits the most from this rhythm? The Artist, who comes of age early in the saeculum—when the deeds of the rewarded young Hero are still fresh in memory, when economic equality is high and rising, and when the nation is busy investing in its future. Which archetype is penalized the most? The Nomad, who comes of age late in the saeculum—when the deeds of the rewarded elderly Hero are largely forgotten, when economic equality is low and falling, and when the nation is busy mortgaging its future.

CONVENTION

It has been said a thousand times. Only adversity can build or reveal true character. Helen Keller put it best: "Character cannot be developed in ease and quiet. Only through the experience of trial and suffering can the soul be strengthened, vision cleared, ambition inspired, and success achieved." What we observe about individuals applies just as well to entire communities. Only in a crisis can a nation discover if it still *is* a community—and if so, whether it can function well enough to survive and prevail.

As a Fourth Turning moves toward its climax, citizens come to understand that their personal futures depend entirely on their collective willingness to perform their utmost on one another's behalf. This awareness coincides with a *conventional* shift in prevailing cultural norms. In its Latin etymology, the word literally means "a coming together." In popular usage, conventional implies traditional, standard, expected, sanctioned by the group.

During these urgent years, society revalorizes team players, those willing to sacrifice their own interests for their friends, neighbors, and people. Patriotism loses the ironic undertones it gained during the Awakening. The imminent prospect of losing one's country quickly rekindles attachment to it. Codes of honor, largely disregarded during eras of peace and affluence, again inspire widespread respect—once people understand that their own safety depends on those who have sworn to disregard theirs. Heroism re-emerges near the center of public awareness. Heroes are exemplars (often leaders of a group) who bestow great material benefits on their community by dint of extraordinary effort or courage—even at the cost of their own lives. In other eras, we do not need them. Now we do.

Cultural production pliably adapts to the new mood. With public attention riveted on current events, a blatantly partisan and socially constructive interpretation of events becomes a central mission for writers and artists.

During the American Revolution, virtually every Patriot could recite the fiery slogans of Thomas Paine, the best-known of dozens of pamphleteers who argued passionately about how best to build a virtuous republic. Even the most learned of them could not resist penning lyrics to the patriotic songs for the troops to march by, including John Dickinson ("The Liberty Song") and Dr. Joseph Warren ("Free America").

During the Civil War, newspapers poured out vitriol—for or against Abe Lincoln or Jeff Davis—and tony journals featured polemical essays about why the war must be won, by such literati as Ralph Waldo Emerson, Frederick Douglass, and Walt Whitman. By turns rousing and apocalyptic, the memorable songs were designed to inspire people to action: "Dixie" for the South, "Battle Hymn of the Republic" for the North, and "Many Thousand Gone" for emancipated slaves.

During World War II, nearly all of Hollywood joined the national propaganda campaign waged against the Axis enemy, from the Three Stooges to Donald Duck. George C. Marshall commissioned award-winning director Frank Capra to produce the seven-hour series *Why We Fight*. Kate Smith turned Irving Berlin's "God Bless America" into a patriotic clarion call after it became the official campaign song for both FDR and his opponent Wendell Willkie in 1940. For New Deal partisans, folk singer Woodie Guthrie countered with "This Land Is Your Land." WPA-hired virtuosos translated popular-front themes into timeless all-American art—in music (Aaron Copland), murals (Thomas Hart Benton), photography (Walker Evans), and documentaries (Pare Lorentz). For ordinary Americans at the movies, *Casablanca* (1942) and *From Here to Eternity* (1953) epitomized how World War II was able to transform life priorities almost overnight.

Near the climax of a Crisis era, norms shift further still—and in the opposite direction from what happens near the climax of an Awakening era. The demands of civic duty now crowd out opportunities for personal fulfillment. Rule-breakers face rising public stigma, even punishment. Spiritual curiosity abates: What works takes precedence over what may be ideal. Manners traditionalize, families grow closer, proper behavior is ritualized, and personal violence and risk-taking decline. Tolerance for error recedes to a minimum in a world offering few second chances— where one screw left untightened or one curtain left undrawn might cost untold lives. Demoralizing news may be subject to censorship, and displays of demoralizing affect may be frowned upon. Americans coming of age during World War II were strongly encouraged to "Whistle While You Work" and "Ac-Cent-Tchu-Ate the Positive."

Questions about who does what are resolved on grounds of efficacy and survival—not fairness. The first rule is: Put the most qualified person in charge, even if that means leveling the playing field in the search for talent in ways that previously seemed unthinkable. (Once in charge, however, that person's authority cannot easily be questioned.) Otherwise, the default choice is a traditional social division of labor by age and sex. In the realm of public activity, elders are expected to step aside for the young, women for men. When danger looms, children are expected to be protected before parents, mothers before fathers.

Are all personal desires suppressed during the Ekpyrosis? Not at all. They are merely shifted to the future or past tense. People long for a better tomorrow (Judy Garland singing "Over the Rainbow" in 1939) or ache for a nostalgic yesterday (Doris Day singing "Sentimental Journey" in 1945).

Wistful yearning for home and hearth is the natural complement to the stress of discipline and the terror of battle. During the Civil War, "Home Sweet Home" was a huge soldiers' favorite in both the Union and Confederate armies. Following the Battle of Fredericksburg, Union officers temporarily banned the song out of fear that demoralized troops would respond to its pining lyrics by deserting. On the very same December afternoon that General Burnside's troops were dying by the thousands along the Rappahannock River, many American families began celebrating their first iconic Currier and Ives Christmas, complete with ornamented pine tree. By early January, cartoonist Thomas Nast's first image of a jovial Santa Claus would appear in *Harper's Weekly*.

Exactly eighty years later, as U.S. Marines fought desperately to hold Guadalcanal in the South Pacific, Bing Crosby's sonorous recording of "White Christmas" (another Berlin tune) began airing on radio stations. It became an instant hit with U.S. troops around the world. Galvanizing a mood of sentimental belonging, the tune was later dubbed by the *Washington Post* "the song America needed to fight fascism." By the end of the war, "White Christmas" had become the bestselling single record-ing of all time and has remained so ever since.

According to every outer-world metric, history accelerates during a Fourth Turning. Populations are mobilized, economies upended, consti-tutions overhauled, cities enriched or destroyed, and nations founded or ruined. Yet according to every inner-world metric, history slows down until it comes to a complete stop. As if by a law of compensation, the culture turns toward what is traditional, timeless, eternal: at the high end, toward the classic and exemplary; at the low end, toward the corny and mawkish—devoid of cynicism or mockery. At that moment, culture becomes the stationary pole star around which the world revolves. The sounds and images are idyllic precisely because what they promise seems so very distant.

By means of such longings the community is in effect declaring: We make all these sacrifices to create a better world that will last forever. On the other side of this struggle, we will enjoy fixity of meaning. Late in the Crisis era, the nation turns its newfound collective strength toward erecting unifying public works—the harbors, canals, railroads, and high-ways (or perhaps the wireless networks and carbon-free energy plants) of a new era. By moving mountains to tame hostile nature as it had once tamed hostile people, the community reassures vulnerable citizens that their simple dream of domestic peace will always be secure.

But of course the saeculum never remains stationary. "The Best Years of Our Lives" pass quickly. Soon enough, as the pace of public events slows down, the pace of cultural change again speeds up. And not long after that, the number of those whose lives were altered by the Crisis era will dwindle and their influence will wane. Postcrisis children and grandchildren will satirize their manners, explode their single fixed meaning, and flourish among the deconstructed pieces.

Only those who were there will always remember. "When you face a crisis, you know who your true friends are," said Magic Johnson. Imagine what happens when an entire society faces a crisis: *Everybody* knows who their true friends are. Everybody feels they belong to a band of broth-ers writ large, united at least for a moment in selfless purpose. While what they do is monumentally historic, what they believe is never more than modestly conventional. They know that they will be remembered for their epic deeds alone. Twenty years afterward, the nation will grow tired of hearing those deeds recounted. But twenty years beforehand, the nation would never have believed them possible.

In 1819, "Rip Van Winkle" was published in a collection of tales by the diplomat and raconteur Washington Irving. It's a classic American short story, about a Dutch American villager living along the Hudson River in the late colonial era (the 1760s, as it turns out). One day Rip Van Winkle gets lost hunting in the nearby Catskill Mountains, encounters a mysterious band of partying dwarfs, imbibes some of their liquor, and falls asleep for twenty years.

When Rip awakes and returns to his village, he is so disoriented he fears he has lost his mind. Not only does no one any longer recognize him, but he finds that the cornerstones of his former society have been transformed beyond comprehension.

He notices in the village that images of King George have been replaced by somebody named "George Washington." He learns that some of his old friends have mysteriously gone "off to the wars." He hears people talking about the rights of citizens, the heroes of '76, members of Congress, "and other words, which were a perfect Babylonish jargon to the bewildered Van Winkle." When strangers ask him how he intends to vote, Federal or Democrat, he is so perplexed he blurts out, "I am a poor quiet man, a native of the place, and a loyal subject of the king, God bless him!" At which point, the onlookers cry, "A Tory, a spy!"

Rip's story ends well. After telling the villagers his strange tale, he is able to enjoy a peaceful old age—now that he is rid of the shrewish wife who died while he was sleeping and who (Irving tells us) once made his life miserable. Readers have since wondered if Irving was trying to draw a parallel between Rip losing his tyrant wife and America losing its tyrant king. In any event, the story captures, at a personal level, the wrenching disorientation Americans experienced as they were catapulted from the beginning to the end of their revolutionary ordeal. It's as though they had awoken to find themselves living in a new country.

Americans felt similarly transformed after the Civil War. It wasn't just the South that found its society turned upside down. In the North, Brahmin elites along with industrial workers and commercial farmers felt enmeshed in boundless global markets that no one understood. In the words of Silas Lapham, the protagonist in William Dean Howells's popular novel, "After the Civil War I found that I had got back to another world. The day of small things is past, and I don't suppose it will ever come again in this country." Retired Harvard literature professor George Ticknor likewise wrote in 1869 that the Civil War had opened "a great gulf between what happened before in our century and what has happened since, or what is likely to happen hereafter. It does not seem to me as if I were living in the country in which I was born." After World War II, many Americans once more felt lost in a new age of mass politics, mass consumption, and nuclear terror.

Today, during the Millennial Crisis, these feelings of perplexity—of disconnect from the familiar—are again on the rise. According to surveys taken between 2019 and 2022, anywhere between 40 and 60 percent of Americans agree that "things have changed so much that I often feel like a stranger in my own country." These perceptions are likely to intensify, not diminish, over the coming decade.

What gives rise in American history to this periodic Rip Van Winkle effect? We already know the answer. It's the social transformation that accompanies every Fourth Turning. It's the inexorable tide of events that moves a people toward community, equality, authority, permanence, and convention. It's the entropy reversal, arriving at the end of every saeculum, through which the civic core and the public identity of a people are reborn.

This rebirth unifies, integrates, and empowers society to a degree that people beforehand would have deemed unthinkable. It also pushes society through a relentless and deadly passage that people beforehand would have deemed unbearable. In this sense, the Fourth Turning is for a society what a rite of passage is for an individual. No society ever voluntarily chooses to enter it. And yet, as James conceded, no society ever wishes to reverse it once it is complete.

Many Americans today look forward to the rest of the Millennial

Crisis with dreadful foreboding. If this is a rite of passage, they can't imagine it ending well—perhaps because they fear their society has been corrupted beyond the possibility of rebirth.

This is to be expected. Before any rite of passage, we doubt our capacity to do what we have never done before—or, in this case, our society's capacity to achieve what almost no one alive can any longer recall achieving. Most members of John Adams's generation, entering midlife just as the American Revolution was beginning, felt the same sense of radical inadequacy. "We have not men fit for the times," wrote Adams in his diary in 1774. "We are deficient in genius, education, in travel, fortune—in everything. I feel unutterable anxiety. God grant us wisdom and fortitude." What he and his generation discovered, as they moved forward, was that they did indeed possess these talents and virtues. But they remained hidden until the force of events set them in motion.

Many Americans believe their country is lacking in leadership. Yet one lesson of Fourth Turnings is that great leaders are made, not born—and that great leaders emerge and gain renown precisely when societies need them, not before. Few of America's greatest Fourth Turning leaders (certainly not Washington, Lincoln, or Roosevelt) demonstrated outstanding leadership skills before the demanding circumstances arose that called them forth.

Many Americans suspect their country is lacking in followership. They look around and see a people so divided and fractious as to seem incapable of rallying around a single standard. Yet the turning of the saeculum is already remedying this obstacle. In fact, the young adults who are now recasting the tone of America's social and political life are an order-seeking generation fully capable of galvanizing America's civic rebirth—as soon as events and leaders unlock that potential.

Finally, many Americans despair at the wide political gulf that has emerged between tribal partisans and cannot imagine their country surviving a complete victory by the other side, red zone or blue zone. Yet here again, history suggests that their worst fears may be overdrawn.

In a democratic society, one tribe never fully dominates the other without incorporating key elements of the other's program within its own. Once the nation is fully transformed, so long as it remains one nation, both tribes will come to see at least some of their preferences reflected in the final consensus. By this time, to be sure, that consensus is likely to reflect a more powerful relationship between citizen and state. And there will still be opposing political parties. But the issues dividing the two sides won't be the same as they were before. And the conflict between them will no longer threaten to tear society apart.

This rapid, sweeping, and even bewildering redefinition of political partisanship over the course of the Fourth Turning is a pattern we see again and again. By the time President Washington delivered his farewell address, the conflict that had once raged, twenty years earlier, between Patriot and Tory, was already ancient history. By a decade after Fort Sumter, there was no longer any important debate about slavery or the supremacy of the Union. Nor, by a decade after Pearl Harbor, was any serious challenge still raised against core New Deal programs or America's new global role.

Likewise today. Americans' settled pre-Crisis understanding of the conservative-liberal divide—which began to shift during the Obama presidency and warped further and faster after the election of Trump in 2016—may become hard to recognize in the late 2020s. And by the mid-2030s, it is likely to be largely meaningless to any voter then under age fifty.

9

HOW OUR LIVES
WILL CHANGE

Keep a clean nose, watch the plainclothes
You don't need a weather man to know which way
the wind blows.

—BOB DYLAN

We have thus far examined the Millennial Crisis in all of its objective characteristics: We know its timing and its development to date. We know how such Fourth Turnings have turned out in the past. We know what sorts of social transformations to expect by the time it's finally over.

In this chapter, we flip our perspective. Instead of looking at the future from the outside-in, we look at it from the inside-out.

When the "Spirit of America" returns, after all, we want to know: *What will it feel like?*

To examine our personal experience of what still lies ahead, we need to return to the dynamic of generational change. This is the dynamic that pushes the saeculum forward—spring to summer to fall to winter. Every person belongs to a generation. Every generation belongs to one of four archetypes. And as those archetypes age into their ultimate winter or "Crisis era" constellation, each generation will participate in that future according to its own distinct life story. Each generation will have its own common narrative, its own past memories, and its own future hopes.

Since the dawn of the modern world, there has been but one Fourth Turning constellation: elder Prophets, midlife Nomads, young-adult Heroes, and child Artists. For half a millennium, that constellation has

313

recurred five times in exactly the same way, and a sixth time with a slight variation in timing and consequence. The archetypal lineup has been one of the great constants of the Anglo-American saeculum.

- The indulged *Prophet* children of the last High, born in the aftermath of the last Crisis, have always fomented the Crisis after entering elderhood.

- The abandoned *Nomad* children of an Awakening have always become the pragmatic midlife managers of the Crisis.

- The protected *Hero* children of an Unraveling have always furnished the powerful young adult team players of the Crisis.

- The suffocated *Artist* children of the Crisis have always grown up as the empathic youth who will later come of age in the next High.

In Chapters 2 through 5, we examined how turnings shape generations and how generations shape turnings. Now we focus specifically on how this pattern will play out during the remaining years of the current Fourth Turning. With the partial exception of the U.S. Civil War, every prior Crisis era witnessed each generational archetype entering a new phase of life.

Let's recall how the personalities of these four generational archetypes influence and are influenced by the Fourth Turning:

As visionary Prophets replace Artists in elderhood, they push to resolve an ever-deepening conflict over values, setting the stage for the new secular goals of the young.

As Prophet generations enter elderhood, their principled crusades acquire a last-act urgency. As the Crisis erupts, their cultural arguments coalesce around new visions of community. Within their families, they redefine elderhood as a call to spiritual stewardship. In the larger society, they begin to trade material security for moral authority and translate their life-long values into an agenda that exacts sacrifice from all generations, including their own. From the young, they seek personal loyalty and respect; to the young, they offer the opportunity for heroism and achievement unlike anything they themselves knew at a like age.

Ever since the late sixteenth century, aging Prophets have provided the torch of conviction for younger generations during times of trial. The aging Puritan Generation faced death with what historian Perry Miller describes as "cosmic optimism." Though they knew their world was heading for catastrophe, they chose to set an unyielding example—against rebels, kings, and (above all) unbelievers. As the American Revolution catalyzed, die-hard elder Awakeners briefly surged into governors' posts to inspire heroism and curse treachery. "Let us ... act like wise men," declared Sam Adams in 1772. Praying while others fought, this generation produced the first two presidents of the Continental Congress, which enacted blue laws to make "true religion and good morals" the national credo. Through the Civil War Crisis, the Transcendental Generation dominated the leadership of both the Fire-Eaters in Richmond and the Radical Unionists in Washington. Both sides believed that their war, in the words of Julia Ward Howe's famous wartime anthem, had "sounded forth the trumpet that shall never call retreat" and was "sifting out the hearts of men before His judgment seat." Afterward, the younger Henry Adams recalled those elder trumpets of war and bitterly observed, "It's always the good men who do the most harm in the world."

As pragmatic Nomads replace Prophets in midlife, they act with toughness and resolve to defend society while safeguarding the interests of the young.

Playing to win but half-expecting to lose, Nomad generations enter midlife when their nation is torn by centrifugal social forces, shadowed by looming external threats—or both. Worn out by a life of hit-or-miss risk-taking, they grow cautious in their family lives. The ablest among them emerge as cunning, pragmatic, and colorful public figures. When the Crisis hits, they find their lives painfully split between the old order and the new. But they rise fiercely (and sacrificially) to the occasion, able to make hard and fast choices without fretting much about what others think. Exalting the workable over the ideal, midlife Nomads forge an effective alliance with the elder Prophets. Whatever happens, they will find that others are quick to blame them and slow to give them credit.

Through the centuries, Nomads have starred in the role of the graying, picaresque, and (sometimes) corruptible adventurer who always finds a way to get the job done: Francis Drake and John Hawkins; Benjamin Church and Jacob Leisler; Robert Rogers and Daniel Boone; Ulysses Grant and "Boss" Tweed; Huey Long and George Patton. In the Glorious Revolution Crisis, the Cavalier Generation displayed both courage and generosity. Leaving the jeremiads to their elders, they staged the rebellions and bore the crushing war-era taxation necessary to deliver the colonies through their darkest hour. In the American Revolution, the Liberty peers of George Washington, expecting to be hanged if the rebellion failed, waged war as the canny patriots who (as the British charged of "Swamp Fox" Francis Marion) "would not fight like a Christian or a gentleman." They won the hardest victories; committed the worst war-era treacheries (Benedict Arnold); and later anchored the new nation with a prudent realism. The Gilded peers of Andrew Carnegie and George Armstrong Custer and John D. Rockefeller, who (anomalously) entered midlife just after the Civil War, proved themselves a generation of metal and muscle both during the Crisis and afterward.

As teamworking Heroes replace Nomads in young adulthood, they challenge the political failure of elder-led crusades, fueling a society-wide secular crisis.

Coming of age, Hero generations develop a strong ethic of worldly achievement, a peer-enforced code of conduct, and an overwhelming sense of generational community. Instinctive doers and builders, they gravitate toward cooperative institutions able to overcome great public dangers and bring order to social chaos. They expect to receive challenges from older generations, and they band together to meet them. At the Crisis climax, their heroism seemingly makes the difference between bright and dark futures for all of posterity. "Fire is the test of gold," Seneca once observed, "adversity, of strong men." Young Heroes enter deadly conflict because, like the rest of their society, they perceive they have no other choice.

Hero Generations provide the fulcrum for the most celebrated turning points of modern history, whether young Henry Tudor's march to Bosworth Field or the young G.I.s' charge at Omaha Beach. During the Armada Crisis, writes historian Anthony Esler, the young Elizabethan peers of Philip Sidney and Walter Raleigh advanced "ambitious projects of breathtaking scope and grandeur," distinguishing these military and colonial "overreachers" from the "burned-out generation" before them. Cotton Mather called the Glorious Revolution "a happy revolution." According to historian T. H. Breen, that colonial Crisis "released long-suppressed generational tensions" and triggered a seismic shift in political power from old to young. The American Revolution, in the eyes of posterity, cast a spotlight on the young Catos and Caesars who penned the great documents, fought the great battles, and energized the great constitutional debates. "All human greatness shall in us be found," exuded the young officer and poet David Humphreys after Yorktown. The contrast with the prior generation of youth, now their hardscrabble generals, could not have been more striking.

As Artists replace the Heroes in childhood, they are overprotected at a time of traumatic conflict and adult self-sacrifice.

Artists enter childhood enveloped by no-nonsense, fiercely protective adults at a time when mighty events are deciding the fate of nations. Children, told to stay out of harm's way, are expected to grow up compliantly. So they do, while developing a keen instinct to be helpful and kind to others in need. Though assured of their worth, they are constantly reminded that older generations are making enormous sacrifices on their behalf that they may never be able to repay—and creating expectations that they may never be able to live up to.

From the Humanist peers of Desiderius Erasmus onward, the modern generations that have added the most refinement, nuance, and openness to civilization have been those whose childhoods were most simple, basic, and closed. "You can't be too careful in these matters," said Cotton Mather of the need to "restrain your children" during a Glorious Revolution Crisis in which towns appointed tithing men "to attend to disorder of every kind in the families under their charge." An infant in the late 1770s, Henry Clay later wrote he was "rocked in the cradle of the Revolution." The young John Quincy Adams watched the Battle of Bunker Hill at a distance while holding his mother's hand. Another deferential child of the Revolution, Daniel Webster, later apologized on behalf of his peers: "We can win no laurels in a war for independence. Earlier and worthier hands have gathered them all." During the Civil War, small children were so well behaved that one foreigner remarked how—in sharp contrast to prior decades—"the most absolute obedience and the most rigid discipline prevail in all American schools." This raising of drawbridges around family life reflected what youth historian Joseph Kett calls the mid-century "desire of middle-class Americans to seal their lives off from the howling storm outside."

As these archetypes reveal, a Fourth Turning harnesses the seasons of life to prompt a renewal in the seasons of time, closing the full circle of the saeculum.

In this extended chapter, we explore these archetypes in real time by examining all of the generations that are participating in the current Millennial Crisis. For each generation, we want to know something about its identity; about its beliefs, personality, and formative events; about the role it has already played in history; and about the role it will likely play in the years to come as the Fourth Turning unfolds.

We proceed from the oldest living generation to the youngest—seven generations in all. At the older end, we start with the Lost (*Nomads*), whose last members were still alive when the Millennial Crisis began. We move on to the G.I.s (*Heroes*), many of whom are still with us today. And then to the Silent (*Artists*), who remain very much active in public life. These three generations all participated in the generational constellation of the prior Great Depression–World War II Crisis. Since 2008, they have been in or entering an extended "late elder" phase of life.

We will pay greatest attention to the four younger generations: Boomers (*Prophets*), Gen-Xers (*Nomads*), Millennials (*Heroes*), and Homelanders (*Artists*). These four fully active generations comprise the generational constellation of the Millennial Crisis.

Every reader alive since the beginning of the Millennial Crisis belongs to one of these seven generations. Few readers alive are entirely untouched by the collective life trajectories we are about to describe. In a very real sense, one of these seven is the story of *your* life.

GENERATIONS OF LATE ELDERS

Until the last decade or two of the twentieth century, only four phases of life (each at most twenty-two years in length) sufficed to locate all of the living generations that were influencing the mood and direction of their society. Once a generation moved well past elderhood (age sixty-six to eighty-eight), there weren't enough active members left to have a significant impact. Of all American males born as recently as 1900 (the last birth cohort of the Lost Generation), 45 percent reached age sixty-six, but only 7 percent reached age eighty-eight. Most of these survivors were dependents in poor health. To be sure, there have always been exceptions. Grandma Moses, born in 1860, was turning out some of her most celebrated folk art in her late nineties. Frank Lloyd Wright, born in 1867, was still working on his design of the Guggenheim Museum when he died in his early nineties. Yet this sort of golden-age efflorescence was exceptional.

For those born later in the twentieth century, it has become less exceptional. Of all American males born in 1942 (the last birth cohort of the Silent Generation), 72 percent reached sixty-six. According to projections by Social Security's Office of the Actuary, 26 percent are expected to reach eighty-eight. And a large share of these octogenarians and nonagenarians remain in good health. As of this writing, two eminent members of the G.I. Generation remain active in public life, both in their late nineties: former President Jimmy Carter and former Secretary of State Henry Kissinger. Younger members of the Silent Generation still occupy many of our nation's highest leadership posts. As of the end of 2022, these included president (Joe Biden), speaker of the House (Nancy Pelosi), Senate minority leader (Mitch McConnell), and a half dozen of Congress's party leadership posts and committee chairmanships.

The growing presence and public influence of these elder Americans—more than fifteen years after their official "retirement" age—must be recognized. So let's introduce a "late elder" phase of life for generations whose oldest members are well past age eighty-eight, the upper limit on what we have until now been calling the "elder" phase of life. We will discuss three generations whose lives in late elderhood have touched, however briefly, America in the Millennial Crisis: the Lost, G.I., and Silent Generations.

Because the active presence of late elders in politics and society is such a recent development, its effects on the saeculum are as yet unknown. Most likely, as we argued in Chapter 5, a growing role for late elders will somewhat dampen the speed of generationally driven social change. Late elders in leadership posts will delay, in musical-chairs fashion, the openings available for younger generations and therefore tend to "dilate" the length of phase-of-life roles. Also, by postponing the ascendency of the next-younger archetype to the very top leadership posts, late elders may postpone or defer new approaches to impending challenges. The nation may need to wait another several years before making a choice that it would otherwise have made right away.

There is nothing categorically good or bad about the rising influence of late elders. It all depends on the circumstances. History provides many instances in which society hugely benefits from access to a deep bench of talent and experience. History provides others in which constructive change is obstructed, at great cost, by a cadre of superannuated incumbents who have overstayed their welcome.

Valedictory: The Lost and G.I. Generations

Always with us in our memories, the Lost Generation (born 1883–1900) was still with us in person when America entered the Millennial Crisis. Back in 2008, just over five thousand members of this generation (age 108+) were celebrating their three-digit birthdays. Women outnumbered men by more than ten to one. Two of the men were World War I veterans, and the longest-lived of these (Jack Babcock, a Canadian who served in the British Army and later migrated to the United States) passed away in 2010. The very last surviving member of the Lost Generation for whom we have official records, Susannah Mushatt Jones, was born in 1899 into an African American family of Alabama sharecroppers. Before she passed away in 2016 at age 116, Jones was America's oldest living person.

Exactly a century has passed since Gertrude Stein told Ernest Hemingway that he and all his twenty-something friends living in Paris were "a lost generation." She didn't mean it as a compliment. "You have no respect for anything," she explained, and "you drink yourselves to death."

Taking pride in this putdown, Hemingway used the label a couple of years later as an epigraph for *The Sun Also Rises*, a novel about impulsive young people who drink a lot. The label stuck.

Most of today's Boomers and first-wave Xers recall as children at least one reclusive Lost grandparent, or maybe just that foreign-born "granny" down the street who scowled (with a twinkle in her eye) whenever a baseball rolled across her yard. You couldn't "pull the wool" over their eyes. Nor could you make them forget a lifetime brimming with adventure: Ellis Island and sweatshops, sleek Pierce-Arrows and the Battle of the Marne, speakeasies and hangovers, a giddy bull market and a global crash, soup lines and dust-bowl caravans. They hid their early years from those nice-looking, TV-watching youngsters they got to know in their old age—most assuredly because they didn't want any kid to try reliving them.

Late in life, Hemingway described the wisdom of old men as a "great fallacy. . . . They do not grow wise. They grow careful." Like so many of the Lost elite (especially its literary elite), Hemingway never reached old age himself. But his description was prescient for those who did—like Dwight Eisenhower, who presided over the last two terms of the Lost's brief tenure in the White House. Projecting avuncular respectability, "Ike" gave his troubled generation permission to slow down at last. He was certainly careful: He took few chances abroad, enacted few new programs, resisted deficit-financing, and famously warned against a growing "military-industrial complex."

After Eisenhower, the Lost suddenly vanished from public life. By the time a younger G.I. president was taking "longer strides" in 1961, the Lost already seemed an antediluvian embarrassment: little left to show but "old whale" mayors and tobacco-chewing "Dixiecrats," unfit for the forward-looking optimism of the times. The Lost withdrew without protest. They understood they had no place in the space-age world of better-educated young people. And unlike the G.I.s who followed them, they made few demands on the young for public benefits despite their very high rates of poverty.

Yet in later decades the aging Lost Generation continued to exert a strong influence on younger generations, mostly through their wildly original cultural artifacts—from novels, poetry, and philosophy to films, vaudeville, and jazz. Comedian George Burns, active on stage to nearly the end of his life at age one hundred, made an especially deep impression on Gen-X youth in the 1980s and 1990s. "The secret to success in life is sincerity," he used to quip, "Fake that and you've got it made."

Above all, the Lost saw life for what it was. "Our generation has seen the horrors latent in man's being rise to the surface and erupt," observed Paul Tillich after World War II. "Living is struggle," wrote Thornton Wilder in *The Skin of Our Teeth*. "Every good and excellent thing in the world stands moment by moment on the razor-edge of danger and must be fought for—whether it's a field, a home, or a country." But they also knew how to have fun. As literary critic Malcolm Cowley asked: "Did other generations ever laugh so hard together, drink and dance so hard, or do crazier things just for the hell of it?"

The G.I. Generation (born 1901–24) is still with us. There remain more than two hundred thousand G.I.s overall and tens of thousands of (mostly male) World War II veterans who saw service by the climactic summer of 1944. Yet these numbers are dwindling fast—by nearly a third with each passing year. Most of their iconic members are gone. Paul Tibbets, Jr., who piloted the *Enola Gay* over Hiroshima, died in 2007. Naomi Parker, the war assembly worker who modeled for the "Rosie the Riveter" poster, died in 2018. Dave Severance, the last survivor of the Marines who hoisted the U.S. flags atop Mount Suribachi on Iwo Jima, died in 2021. Six of their seven presidents are gone. When the Millennial Crisis comes to a close in the early 2030s, the G.I. Generation may be no more numerous than the Lost was in 2008.

The acronym "G.I." was stenciled onto soldiers' backpacks during World War II. It could mean either "general issue" or "government issue," and this generation stood squarely for both. All their lives, G.I.s have placed a high priority on being "general" or "regular" (as in "he's a regular guy"), since generality promotes effective teamwork. Likewise, their collective life story is intimately wed to the modern growth of government, which like a buddy has always catered mostly to the needs of people their own age. When they were kids, government sheltered them and invested in their future. When they were coming of age, it protected their unions and helped them get jobs and homes and an education. And ever since they started retiring, it has shifted most of its spending to pensions and health care.

Energized by teamwork and empowered by government, these G.I.s have been the confident and rational problem-solvers of twentieth-century America: victorious soldiers, WACs, and WAVEs; more than one hundred Nobel laureates; builders of Minuteman missiles, interstate highways, Apollo moon rockets, battleships, and miracle vaccines; the creators of Disney's Tomorrowland; "men's men" who knew how to get things done. Younger generations dubbed them *The Greatest Generation*. Whatever they accomplished—whether organizing "big bands," swarming ashore in Normandy, making "Bible Epic" movies, or erecting a "Great Society," they always seemed to do it big, to do it together. Among G.I.s, says the inscription on their Iwo Jima shrine, "uncommon valor was a common virtue."

For the Silent, who grew up in their shadow, the intimidating "can do" G.I. reputation fostered attitudes of caution, deference, and self-doubt. For the still younger Boomers, who had no personal memory of the G.I.s' greatest triumph, their midlife hubris triggered something quite different: a primal desire to smash and wreck all their left-brained worldly constructions. And so it happened. Not many years after the G.I.s crisply promised to "get this country moving again" under their first president, Jack Kennedy, everything they promised to make perfect began to fall apart, often under pressure from hostile youth. The evidence was there in the burning inner cities, the rebellious campuses, the defeat in Vietnam, the fragmentation of families, the humiliation of Watergate, and the ravages of "stagflation."

The high tide of G.I. optimism and power came in 1964 with their so-called "Great 89th Congress." In the next year, after the G.I.s' legislative triumphs—everything from civil rights enforcement to the founding of Medicaid and Medicare their cohesion and power seemed unstoppable. "Americans today bear themselves like victory-addicted champions," said *Look* magazine in 1965. "They've won their wars and survived their depressions. They are accustomed to meeting, and beating, tests."

Thereafter, their serried ranks were blindsided by a fifth column against which they were defenseless: their own kids. It was all over by the Watergate election of 1974, when large numbers of G.I. congressmen either resigned or were voted out of office by unhappy younger voters.

By then, the nation seemed awash with rage, violence, drugs, eroticism, and the cult of self—everything that G.I.s considered hostile to their life mission of regularizing and homogenizing the world. Many G.I.s were prepared to agree with Richard Nixon that America had become "a pitiful, helpless giant." Also by then, as they began to retire, millions migrated to age-segregated senior communities in which teamwork was still celebrated and from which every trace of the new youth culture had been expunged. A generational truce of sorts was arranged: Younger generations could take over the culture so long as G.I.s, sequestering themselves, could keep all of their newly enlarged public benefits. Thus did a world-saving generation of "junior citizens" in the early 1940s become an isolated generation of "senior citizens" by the early 1980s.

Yet so strong was the G.I. civic reputation that Americans continued to elect G.I. presidents for another four terms (Jimmy Carter, Ronald Reagan for two terms, and George H. W. Bush), even after younger generations had taken over Congress. Boomers decided they were OK with a G.I. like Reagan who shrewdly paired an insistence on national strength abroad with a laissez-faire neglect of governmental direction at home. For first-wave Gen-Xers, who began voting in the 1980s, Reagan was the first national leader they got to know well. Many young "New Right" Xers worshipped him.

When the Soviet Union crumbled to pieces in 1991, these aging G.I. commanders in chief scored yet another historic triumph. Against younger doubters, the "right stuff" generation had sworn it could bring down the Soviet Empire. Finally, it did. In that same year, as if to punctuate the moment, President Bush led a thirty-five-nation coalition to thwart Iraq's invasion of Kuwait and vindicate the global rule of law. America's worldwide reputation soared.

It was their last hurrah. In 1992, Bush lost a close election to Bill Clinton, bringing an end to thirty-two years of G.I. occupancy of the White House. In 1996, Bob Dole lost to Bill Clinton, bringing an end to fifty-two years of G.I. presidential candidacies. (The first was Republican Tom

Dewey in 1944.) By the late 1990s, America's electorate had become so de-massified, decentralized, and individualized that little the G.I.s stood for any longer had much relevance. The only Americans who might have responded positively to their invocation of "community" (which the senior President Bush still insisted was "a beautiful word with a big meaning") were the Millennials, but the oldest of these were still in grade school.

Today, not many G.Is are left. And those who are may feel that their generation has long outlasted its expiration date. Yet history is deceptive, since it is just when the "Spirit of America" seems most distant that its return may in fact be most imminent. If a time of trial must return, what would be this generation's advice? G.I.s were never very good at talking about their own lives. Recalling moments of trauma could be especially difficult.

Many G.I.s might simply point around them: Don't listen to what we say, look at what we did and what we built. So much of what our kids take for granted would not be here if (to invoke the famous hypothetical from *It's a Wonderful Life*) "George Bailey had never been born." Yet the peers of Jimmy Stewart would also add: It didn't have to be us. It could have been anyone. We just happened to be there at a moment when no other option was open to us—except to forget our personal lives for a while and do it big, and do it together, for posterity.

The Lucky Few: The Silent Generation

The Silent Generation (born 1925–42) today comprises roughly 12 million adults in their eighties and nineties. Their age location in history sandwiches them awkwardly between two better-known generations: They were born just too late to be World War II heroes and just too early to be New Age seekers. In their economic lives, that location in history has been very good to them—giving them a lifetime ride on the up escalator since the American High. But in their personal lives, it has been a source of tension. The country's top leadership posts have nearly always eluded them. And by the time the Silent were entering midlife, they were spearheading the wrenching divorce revolution and popularizing (thanks to journalist Gail Sheehy) the term "midlife crisis."

Starting out as the children of depression and war, the Silent grew up when child-rearing in America approached the point of suffocation. Just after World War II ended, they came of age tiptoeing cautiously into a post-crisis social order that no one wanted to disturb. Unlike G.I. youth, they rarely talked about "changing the system," but instead, more blandly, about "working within the system." In job interviews, their first questions were about pensions. Not wanting anything to go on their "permanent records," they kept their heads down during the Korean War and the McCarthy era.

In 1951, *Time* published an in-depth essay that ticked down the cardinal traits of these youth. The "younger generation" had no militant beliefs. It hungered for a planned future within big organizations. It trusted "sociability" and liked to do everything in groups. Then came the passage that christened them: "Youth today is . . . working fairly hard and saying almost nothing. The most startling fact about the young generation is its silence. . . . It does not issue manifestoes, make speeches or carry posters. It has been called the 'Silent Generation.'"

The Silent's plans for a secure and prosperous future worked—spectacularly. Unlike older generations, they didn't have to wait to start their careers: They joined the postwar boom in their early twenties just as it was taking off. What's more, because these baby-bust Silent were few in number, employers bid up the wages of entry-level workers. In the Sputnik era, notes demographer Richard Easterlin, the typical young man could earn more at age thirty than the average wage for men of all ages in his profession—and could certainly live better than most "retired" elders. Without delay, the Silent bought homes and cars and moved into suburbs. They emulated older G.I.s by marrying and having babies, and they did so at very young ages—younger on average, in fact, than any other generation in U.S. history.

Easterlin famously called them "the fortunate generation." More recently, sociologist Elwood Carlson has called them "the lucky few" in a book by that name. That economic good fortune stuck with them as they grew older. By the mid-1960s, most Silent couples had obtained fixed thirty-year mortgages at under 5 percent interest—just in time for the raging inflation of the next twenty years, which means the Silent paid negative real rates on their homes. Their next lucky stroke happened in the early 1980s, when most Silent were starting to save seriously for retirement. At just that moment, both bond and equity prices began their steepest-ever twenty-five-year climb. The Silent prospered, often benefitting from veteran's benefits and defined-benefit company pensions on top of Social Security and their own personal savings. Luckier still, the last Silent birth cohort reached age sixty-five in 2007: the perfect moment to cash out of the market.

This is without doubt the wealthiest—as well as the healthiest and most educated—generation of late elders America has ever seen. And not just in absolute terms, but relative to the young. After coming of age in the 1950s, they quickly amassed more wealth than the seniors of that era. (In the early 1960s, the elderly were much poorer than young adults by most measures.) By 2010, for the first time, the median net worth of households aged seventy-five-plus surged higher than that of *any* nonelderly age bracket, and today it remains multiples higher than that of households age thirty-five to forty-four.

Yet in other, more personal areas of their lives, the Silent have felt less lucky. So eager to follow the rules when they were young, they sense that they never grasped an authentic identity—leaving them frustrated that they've never quite lived up to their promise.

Early in life, *Esquire* essayist Frank Conroy admitted, the Silent's "clothing, manners, and lifestyle were . . . scaled-down versions of what we saw in the adults." They crowded into the so-called "helping professions." According to historian William Manchester, "they sought not fame but the approval of others" and thereby "became a generation of technicians, of interchangeable parts. Its members knew it—and for the most part they liked it." Without hesitation, they followed *The Tender Trap* date-and-mate path: pairing off quickly, "tying the knot" after high school graduation, moving to the suburbs, and then blending in. Even their best-known cultural artifacts seemed hobbled and derivative: "doo-wop" pop songs, "cool" jazz, "sophisticated" essays, and "beat" poetry.

Then came the Awakening of the late sixties and the seventies, which awkwardly washed over them just as they were entering midlife. A new crop of youth was calling their bluff by voicing questions they never dared to ask. The effect was paralyzing. If the Silent joined the radical youth, they risked ending their careers and breaking up their young families. If they didn't, they shamed themselves as hypocrites by failing to live up to their earnest ideals. By waffling, they struck other generations as terminally indecisive. The Silent ended up following all three paths. "During the ferment of the '60s, a period of the famous Generation Gap, we occupied, unnoticed as usual, the gap itself," journalist Wade Greene recalled.

Not trusting its own voice, the Silent Generation adopted the moral relativism of the arbitrator, mediating arguments between others and reaching out to people of all cultures, races, incomes, ages, and disabilities. Their inner tension helped them become America's greatest generation of songwriters, comedians, and therapists. It pushed the likes of Bob Dylan, Abbie Hoffman, and Ken Kesey to become lone pied pipers for a younger generation willing to follow their call to nonconformity. It persuaded Ralph Nader and Daniel Ellsberg to push to get more secrets out, and Phil Donahue and Ted Koppel to get more talk going—all in the hope that airing more points of view would somehow build a better society.

Accordingly, as the Silent ascended to national leadership roles in the 1980s and 1990s—America's Unraveling—they strove to break America out of the brutal survivalism and simplicity of their youth by adding refinement and complexity to every institution they touched. As legislators, they created flowcharts and added subcommittees and replaced gutsy choices with anonymous "processes"—as in, a budget *process* or a war powers *process*. As CEOs, they hired economists and shuffled financial assets. As regulators, they opened everything to (endless) expert debate. *How* things got done mattered more than *whether* they got done.

Where the G.I.s had reached the brink of elderhood pursuing a small number of large missions, the Silent reached theirs pursuing a vast number of tiny missions. Where the word "liberal" once referred to a G.I.-style energizer with a unifying national agenda that called for hiring bulldozers, the Silent transformed liberals into enervators who argued on behalf of every interest group and called for hiring lawyers. America's style of elder leadership (in media adjectives describing the Fed's transition from Chairman Paul Volcker to Chairman Alan Greenspan) went from "macho" to "maestro." Like Michael Dukakis's 1988 party convention lectern, the Silent recast G.I. red-white-and-blue as salmon, azure, and eggshell.

Since the Silent showed little apparent interest in national unity, other generations have seldom looked to this generation to fill top national leadership posts. Remarkably, a Silent has been nominated as a major-party presidential candidate only four times (Walter Mondale in 1984, Michael Dukakis in 1988, John McCain in 2008, and Joe Biden in 2020) and has been elected as president only once. Early on, candidates like Dukakis were considered "dwarfs" who suffered from a "stature gap" compared to older G.I. candidates. Later on, candidates like Senator Richard Lugar (once described by the *Washington Post* as "a resume in search of rhetoric") suffered from a "passion gap" compared to younger Boomer candidates.

Today, as the Silent look back, they can take pride in their many accomplishments. Thanks to their efforts, America is surely a kinder and more tolerant country than it otherwise would have been.

Indeed, these peers of Martin Luther King, Jr., Ralph Abernathy, Medgar Evers, Cesar Chavez, James Meredith, Russell Means, and John Lewis may justly be called America's "civil rights generation." They were the young freedom riders and sit-in demonstrators who appealed to the nation's conscience on equal rights—and won. Their leading feminists—including Maya Angelou, Ruth Bader Ginsburg, Kate Millett, Gloria Steinem, and Susan Brownmiller—likewise awakened the nation's conscience to the rights of women. On issues of race and gender, the Silent have been a generation of equipoise. Unlike the G.I.s who came before them, they believed that accommodating diversity would enhance social harmony. Unlike the Boomers who came after them, they still valued social harmony.

In an era when crude passions are running high, this generation's personal habits of civility and good manners also set a high bar for younger generations. Even in President Joe Biden, for all of his propensity to tie himself (and others) into complicated knots, younger voters recognize a fundamental decency they may miss when his generation has passed on.

Yet there's also the negative side of the ledger. Under the Silent watch, America has grown more commercial, litigious, credentialed, and bureaucratic. By tearing down national barriers and taboos, they made American society feel more open yet also less like a community. "To tear down the walls of the state," observed progressive social critic Michael Walzer, commenting on his generation's openness to more immigration, "is not to create a world without walls, but rather to create a thousand petty fortresses." With some reason, the Silent often worry that their efforts to guarantee a more open and tolerant society may have ended up doing just the opposite.

Most regret their role in ushering in the R-rated decade of the 1970s, along with Hugh Hefner's alluring *Playboy* ethic and the sudden flood of no-fault divorce laws (which they voted for as young state legislators). In retrospect, they mostly agree, they rushed into marriage too young. And their marriage breakups, in an era when divorce was still heavily stigmatized, wreaked lasting damage on their families and traumatized their Xer children.

More broadly, they regret that all their efforts to improve social fairness have left younger generations so much worse off materially, and so much less hopeful of progress, than themselves. Generous grandparents, most of today's late elder Silent do what they can personally to provide for their offspring. They are also quick to disavow most special age privileges. Unlike the G.I. Generation, most don't feel they've really earned the "senior citizen" label. Still, they cannot help but sense that there is something fundamental they failed to pass on.

The late sociologist Charles Tilly said of his generation that "we are the last suckers." He and his peers learned young always to trust the system and always to play by the rules. The irony is: That strategy actually worked out well for Tilly's generation as a whole. "Eighty percent of life is just showing up" observed Woody Allen, in a joke that leaves younger generations gasping with incomprehension. John Updike's old prediction (made by Harry Angstrom in *Rabbit Is Rich*) that "These kids coming up, they'll be living on table scraps. We had the meal," now pains the Silent because it turned out to be so accurate. What the Silent cannot understand is: Why did following the rules stop working for those who came after us?

Having witnessed so many older people sacrifice for them as children, the Silent will always feel burdened by high expectations. And they will always be haunted by their inability to meet them, especially when they see mounting discord push their country to the brink of another great crisis. Every Artist archetype asks itself the same question late in life—whether it will become the only generation that can both recall America's triumph in one great trial and also watch its disintegration in the next. The (Artist) peers of statesmen Winfield Scott and John Crittenden had similar worries in their seventies and eighties after the secession of the Confederacy in 1861: Would they number among the few Americans to witness both the birth and death of the United States?

Survivors' guilt can be both a burden and a blessing. In the first and last scene of *Saving Private Ryan*, Ryan as an old man grieves at the grave of the older captain who died trying to save Ryan's life when he was a green private. He then asks his family plaintively, "Am I a good man? Am I worthy of these people's sacrifice?" The answer must be yes: These are good people. The Silent never wanted to be the *greatest* generation, but they may be the *nicest* generation of leaders that younger Americans will encounter for a long time to come.

These three late elder generations—Lost, G.I., and Silent—represent a living connection between two Crisis eras, one happening now and the other happening at the end of the prior saeculum. As collective life stories, they are of course very different. More than that, they are *archetypically* different: Each bears testimony to life lessons with special relevance to today's younger counterpart: Lost for Gen-Xers, G.I.s for Millennials, and Silent for Homelanders.

We should also pay attention to the growing longevity of these late elder generations, which strongly suggests that the saecular timetable may today be growing a bit longer—after centuries of growing shorter. One comparative metric may suffice to illustrate this point: At any point more than seventy years after their first birth year (that is, since 1995), the Silent have maintained a greater share of national leaders than the Lost did when the Lost were *five years younger* in age. As the peak age of leadership drifts older, the year at which successive generations can expect to acquire influence will likewise be delayed.

To delay, however, is not to stop. The seasons of the saeculum, pushed forward by generational aging, are still following one another in their expected order. Now we turn to the active constellation of the current season, the Millennial Crisis—and to the four generations that will determine how it ends.

BOOMER ELDERS

The Boom Generation (born 1943–60) today comprises 57 million Americans mostly in their sixties and seventies. As a social generation, Boomers are a bit older than the oft-cited Census Bureau definition (born 1946–64). The Census Bureau picked these dates as an approximate shorthand for the "baby boom" fertility bulge after World War II—nothing more. But to define a social generation, we must think about age location in history. If you remember World War II as a child, were out of college when JFK was shot, or learned about Woodstock as something "kids" were doing, you're too old to be a Boomer—you belong to the Silent. But if you can't recall the moment JFK was shot, nor recall Jim, Jimi, and Janis when they were still alive, you're too young—you belong to X.

Prequel: What a Long Strange Trip

However the Boom Generation is dated, the Boomer life story is known to all. They started out as feed-on-demand Dr. Spock babies, then grew into the indulged Beaver Cleavers of the fifties, then into the college and inner-city rioters of the late sixties, then into the young family-values moms and dads of the eighties and nineties, and finally into the still-questing new retirees of the post-pandemic era. The way Boomers sometimes imagine it, their collective story is iconic: No phase of life really meant anything until they experienced it and could tell other generations all about it.

Along the way—somewhere between LBJ and Reagan, between the Summer of Love and the Big Chill—Boomers shook the windows and rattled the walls (to paraphrase Bob Dylan) of everything the G.I. Generation, their archetypal nemesis, had built. "You go on build it up, mother, we gonna burn it down!" was songwriter Jacob Brackman's message to the powers that be in his 1968 *Esquire* essay, "My Generation," amid the countless demonstrations, protests, sit-ins, teach-ins, love-ins, and riots spreading across the country. The best and brightest youth refused to be "folded, spindled, or mutilated" in the gears of their parents' military-industrial complex. Thus did young Boomers, to the astonishment of older Americans, touch off the most passionate and violent youth up-heaval of the twentieth century.

In so doing, this "generation" (a word Boomers re-popularized in a profusion of variants—as in "Pepsi," "Rock," "Now," "Sixties," "Love," "Pro-test," "Woodstock," and "Me" Generation, just to name a few) became fa-mous for its cultivation of self and its carelessness about material wealth. Even after they found steady jobs and moved from hippie to yuppie—or, according to Todd Gitlin, from *J'accuse* to Jaccuzi—most Boomers cared more that their careers were meaningful than that they led anywhere.

It's no coincidence that Boomers mark first the apogee, and then the rapid decline, in generational progress as measured by real-dollar in-comes. First-wave Boomers, born mainly in the mid-to-late 1940s, have done best, even exceeding the Silent Generation. But late-wave Boom-ers, born mainly in the mid- to late 1950s, have substantially underper-formed first-wavers at every age. First-wave Boomers in their forties and fifties, for example, had a median family income nearly $10,000 higher (adjusted for inflation) than late-wave Boomers later had at the same age. Ninety percent of Boomers born in 1943 outearned their parents at age thirty or forty; only 60 percent of Boomers born in 1960 did so.

One explanation for this turnaround is simple age location. First-wave Boomers started out more like the Silent: They followed the rules more carefully, studied harder, went to school longer, and got married earlier. Late-wave Boomers—who hit the social and family turmoil of the sixties at progressively younger ages—got into more trouble, graduated less often from college, and married much later (if at all). The difference in age location also extends to the economy. Most first-wavers launched careers (before 1973) during the revved-up go-go years. Most late-wavers launched careers (in 1973 or after) when the economy was stagflating.

A fuller explanation requires exploring three collective personality traits that define Boomers as a generation—and that gathered force moving from first wave to last.

The first Boomer trait is their individualism, what the demographer Cheryl Russell once called "the Boomer master trend." From the very beginning, Boomers behaved as if they didn't really need institutions, their families, or one another. This is the first generation of women in history to regard themselves as "economically alone," a fact that Hillary Clinton hammered home in her 2016 campaign. In their housing, Boomers pioneered the *Going Solo* "art of living alone." Their marriages have been fragile, fraught with he-sheds and she-sheds and parallel life paths, and often ending in divorce. In their work lives, a growing share pursued build-it-and-they-will-come dreams—like Steve Jobs and Kevin Costner, though rarely with their success. In religion, they became a *Generation of Seekers*, always moving on to the next orthodoxy offering enlightenment.

As we have seen, Robert Putnam explains most of the growing shift away from civic and group participation in postwar America as a Boomer-driven phenomenon. It started early. Among first-wave Boomer youth in the late sixties, this individualism inspired a cultural rebellion—against conventional views of authority, marriage, gender roles, and race. Among late-wave Boomer youth in the late seventies, it inspired an economic rebellion—against taxes, regulation, and "big government."

As voters, both the older (more humanist, Democratic-leaning) and younger (more born-again, Republican-leaning) Boomers have been generally tolerant of the growing rich-versus-poor spread in America's income distribution. Herding everyone into a powerful middle class—a fixation of their parents—always seemed oppressive: Why not different strokes for different folks? In their life choices, Boomers have tended to avoid the group security offered by close neighborhoods or unions or paternalistic benefit plans.

The second Boomer trait is their attraction to personal risk-taking. As youth, Boomers pushed the envelope on danger, propelling rates of accidents, suicide, crime, drug use, and STDs to levels never witnessed by their parents. By the 1990s, many of those indicators rose swiftly for midlife Americans, even as they fell for youth, indicating that risk proneness followed Boomers as they grew older. By the late 1970s, five times as many Americans under age thirty died in motorcycle accidents as Americans over age fifty; since the early 2010s, motorcycle fatalities over age fifty have regularly *exceeded* those under age thirty. Elder Boomers now show higher rates of lifestyle-related chronic disease than the previous generation at the same age. This marks a reversal of many of the health gains achieved by the G.I.s and Silent as elders.

Risky marriage choices have also taken their toll and have become a major cause of "solo living." So have risky financial choices. Boomers opted for defined-contribution pensions, and then chose not to contribute—or not to roll their pension over, or to borrow again from their pension (or from their home). Despite their ample average lifetime earnings, roughly one-third of Boomers, especially late-wavers, are reaching age sixty-five with virtually no savings and no pension.

Finally, there is the Boomers' values orientation. Boomers have always preferred dividing the world into right versus wrong, good versus bad. They came of age creating the "counterculture," whose purpose was to judge their parents. In the 1990s and 2000s, they led the "culture wars," whose purpose was to excoriate one another. More recently, they have focused on issuing unyielding standards of social rectitude to the rising Millennial Generation—aging progressives doing this mostly in colleges, aging evangelicals mostly in churches.

Values-oriented Boomers are suspicious of purely material measures of life success. While the G.I. Generation invented "Gross National Product," Boomers have experimented with more meaningful alternatives—like "Leading Cultural Indicators" or "Gross National Happiness." Surveys show that Boomers are less likely than other generations to agree that the American Dream requires marriage or wealth. Even high-end Boomers are a lot more likely than prior generations to say that giving their kids "good values" is more important than providing them with a material inheritance.

Measured by years of tenure, Boomers have proven to be a dominant generation of political and business leaders. They've held the White House for twenty years and could be in line for more. They've enjoyed a twenty-four-year generational plurality in the U.S. House and are on track to exceed that in the Senate. They still dominate corporate boards.

Yet their governing style has been one of ironic detachment, in which institutions are allowed to run themselves with little accountability. On their watch, "visionary" CEOs have pocketed trillions through debt-financed LBOs, stock buybacks, and various mark-to-market repackagings. With even Democratic leaders like President Bill Clinton agreeing that "the era of big government is over," few Boomer political leaders have bothered themselves much with managing the big government that remains in operation. Liabilities grow, regulations multiply, programs overlap, and infrastructure crumbles.

Meanwhile, Boomer leaders remain vastly more interested in rightness and wrongness. Clinton's 1992 vow to run "the most ethical administration in history" was widely mocked. Yet Boomer Republicans are no less fixated on the idea that values take precedence over laws—or that "politics is downstream from culture," to use the CPAC dictum. Even Boomer centrists tend to be communitarians who argue that a workable society requires more than a mere Silent-style agglomeration of personal rights. It must be more, argues political philosopher Michael Sandel, than a "procedural republic." It must be committed to a common vision of the good life.

Thus do we hear an echo of that periodic Awakening refrain going back to Luther and Calvin: Only by changing the human heart on a large scale, only by a "reformation of manners and morals," can a people enter the "city on a hill" and again inspire the world.

Along the road toward this reformation, Boomers have intensified the nation's ideological polarization in every age bracket they have entered. They started young. In the late sixties and early seventies, they earned early notoriety for radicalizing the political left and badgering its moderate Silent leaders into militancy. They steered civil rights groups toward confrontation and the clenched fist. They force-marched the moderate Students for a Democratic Society toward "New Left" doctrines of personal liberation. They fueled terrorist splinter groups like the Symbionese Liberation Army and the Weather Underground, which in 1970 officially declared war on the United States government.

Boomers were no less active on the political right. Swelling the ranks of Young Americans for Freedom, young conservatives attacked "liberal" Republicans and fought to roll back the "totalitarian state" in all of its regulatory guises. By the late seventies, they had fueled the rise of the "New Right," ensuring that Reagan Republicans would triumph over all the moderate clones of Richard Nixon and Gerald Ford. And at the race-tinged populist fringe, young Boomer voters were starting to energize the South's eventual split from the Democratic Party. In the 1968 election, non-college-educated White Boomer youth were twice as likely as their older counterparts to vote for George Wallace, the segregationist third-party candidate.

As Boomers matured, scorched-earth politics matured along with them. It entered the U.S. House of Representatives in the early nineties—when Boomers took charge. (In his leadership of the GOP's historic takeover of the House in 1994, Newt Gingrich made good his freshman promise: "I intend to go up there and kick the system over, not try to change it.") Likewise for the Senate in the late nineties—when Boomers took charge. Likewise for national cable news in the early 2000s, with Bill O'Reilly gaining market share for Fox News and Keith Olbermann for MSNBC.

As civic leaders, Boomers have pushed public discourse toward the language of ultimatums and catastrophe. There was drug czar Bill Bennett defining his mission as "Consequence and Confrontation"; ex-VP Al Gore predicting a "true planetary emergency"; Navy Secretary Jim Webb summoning "ruthless and overpowering" retaliation against foreign enemies; journalist James Fallows rooting for a "7.0 magnitude diplo-economic shock"; and "Default Newt" and "Cookie-Monster" Richard Darman with their budgetary "train wrecks." As Tea Party founder Rick Santelli admitted, "There's so much compromise in politics. I'm not a good compromiser."

By 2014, with the passing of former Senate Majority Leader Howard Baker (known as the "Great Conciliator"), tributes from politicians of both parties acknowledged that the gentler leadership style of the Silent Generation was fading from memory.

For some, righteous fury had to go beyond words. It demanded action. There was David Koresh, leading his Branch Davidians to fiery deaths near Waco, Texas; Terry Nichols, mastermind of the Oklahoma City bombing, the deadliest domestic terror attack in U.S. history; Randy Weaver, going down with his family in a hail of bullets at Ruby

Ridge; and Cliven Bundy, leading armed cattle ranchers against federal Bureau of Land Management agents. As they get older, many Boomers are settling in as iconic elder leaders of antigovernment militias, inspiring younger Xers and Millennials with age-worn martial slogans ("Don't Tread on Me," "*Molon Labe*").

Boomers have never stopped vying with one another in hyperbolic metaphor, inflating perceived flaws or slights into the metaphysical equivalent of abuse, exploitation, oppression, rape, terrorism, tyranny, or genocide. For Boomers, truth is absolute only when it grows out of inner conviction, in which case it creates its own social reality and *may as well be true*. For many, the starting point for every inquiry is that organized social life is a conspiracy and that the self is the victim. According to critical theorist Kimberlé Crenshaw, truth can be ascertained only by the "lived experience" of the victimized perceiver. Or, in the words of America's first postmodern president, Donald Trump: "It's true because many people feel the same way that I do."

Understandably, for such an inner-focused generation, culture has always mattered more than politics. And here is where Boomers have left their deepest mark. Let other generations work at rewriting the Constitution or overhauling government. Boomers effected their own revolution by following the Beatles' White Album advice: "Better free your mind instead." Since World War II, no generation has done so much to change the way we talk, the way we dress, the way we recreate, and the way we relate to nature, to God, and to each other.

From pop music, movies, and TV to slang, advertising, and humor, Boomers mark a continental divide in mindset. Before they arrived, the perfect life was all about looking proper, seeming affable, and fitting in. Afterward, it was all about looking cool, showing conviction, and standing out. Weird and cultish youth fads from the 1970s—like health foods, alternative medicine, yoga, and self-empowerment—are now multibillion-dollar industries serving all age groups. Young Boomers cared next to nothing about the G.I.s' cultural contributions: Bob Hope? *The Lawrence Welk Show*? Are you serious? Like young Ralph Waldo Emerson, they assumed that during their childhood "there was not a book, a speech, a conversation, or a thought" worth noticing. By contrast, most young Millennials, however objectionable they may find Boomers' political views, have respectfully memorized the Boomer culturama: everything from Mom's *Whole Earth* maxims to Dad's Beatles-to-Eagles discography.

Such lifelong cultural dominance has shielded Boomers from the criticism they hear from younger generations that they are hypocrites—who want others to do as they say, not as they do. Boomers just shrug it off. They may even feel the charge does them honor, since they like to think they invented the very moral standards by which they are being judged. They also find it easy to apologize for any role they played in the unraveling of America's institutions. And that's because they have never really tried to assume leadership or control of those institutions, tasks that had always been carried out so vigorously by their parents. Older generations were the "power elite," a phrase that gained popularity in the 1950s. Boomers always wanted to lead the "cultural elite," a phrase that gained popularity in the 1990s. Their role would be all about ideals and aspirations, not about mere behavior and compliance.

Since the Global Financial Crisis, as they've begun to move past age sixty-five, Boomers have been redefining elderhood. And once again, they are choosing a very different path than the one chosen by their parents.

Starting around 1970, G.I.s began retiring earlier and, in an era of expanding public benefits, with more money than they had expected. Starting around 2010, Boomers began retiring later and, in an era of retracting public benefits, with less money than they had expected. G.I.s wanted to be away from their kids and near their peers—which led to the construction of vast age-restricted desert communities with names like Sun City and Leisure World. Boomers want to be away from their peers and near their kids—persuading a growing share to "age in place" as the mater or pater familiae who presides over a multigenerational home. Indeed, today's renaissance in extended-family households is every bit as dramatic as the collapse of household size during the Awakening. G.I.s, having grown up close to their parents, were later often surprised to be so distant from their grown-up kids. Boomers, having grown up distant from their parents, are today surprised to be so close to their kids.

Of the growing share of Boomers who are childless and spouseless, relatively few join "senior communities." Though some home-share with younger people or live intentionally with friends, most do what they have always done—live solo. This choice is certain to take a toll on their health as they grow older. According to Laura Carstensen, director of the Stanford Center for Longevity, "patterns of social disengagement reflect the price that Boomers will pay for having rejected family values and traditions many years ago."

With so many Boomers working later in life, the very concept of a busy and leisured "retirement" is fading in popularity in favor of something more passive yet also more serious. Rather than trying to impress the young with G.I.-style energy or Silent-style nice, aging Boomers are assuming an inwardly focused persona. Many are still trying to climb that Maslovian pyramid of values. Teaching, learning, or experiencing is more their style than mere serving or playing.

Those who age in place are retrofitting their lifelong homes with Wi-Fi pipelines to give them 24/7 access to culture. Those who move are opting more for college communities, small towns, or wilderness isolation, making new elder enclaves resemble rural hamlets more than condo mini-cities, Taos or Bozeman more than Sun City West or the Villages. The new septuagenarian elite is clustering in areas long associated with their generation: the West Coast, Mountain States, New Mexico, New England. Those who travel are fueling a boom in eco- and heritage tourism, in monastic retreats, and in philanthropic or "immersion" challenges.

To refer to their new phase of life, Boomers are shifting their vocabulary. "Senior," along with such adjoining adjectives as "active" and "entitled," is declining rapidly in usage. "Elder" is rising in its stead, now often accompanied by "wise" or "spiritual." For the aging Esalen set, the "Conscious Aging" movement has founded "spiritual eldering institutes" teaching Boomers (says one guide) to engage in "vision quests" and to become "seers who feed wisdom back into society." Among graying feminists, "crone" and "witch" are now words of high esteem for all the Grandmother Willows who can (in the words of anthropologist Joan Halifax) "function like old cobblers and dressmakers, sewing us back into the fabric of creation." Graying evangelicals, Rick Warren teaches, should find solace, through faith, in a transition beyond "this broken planet" which God "did not intend as our final destination."

Toward the Climax: Gray Champions

"This generation has a rendezvous with destiny," announced Franklin Roosevelt just three years into the Great Depression, when the leading edge of his own generation was in its seventies. As the Missionary Generation supplanted Progressives in old age, the persona of American old age shifted from friendly and accommodating to judgmental and argumentative. Some Missionaries celebrated the New Deal; many loathed it. Nearly all believed that what ailed America was less an affliction of the body than of the spirit. The incoming president remarked of "our common difficulties" that "they concern, thank God, only material things." Several years later, he repeated "the belief I have already affirmed many times that there is not a problem, social, political, or economic, that would not find full solution in the fire of a religious awakening."

The Missionaries had come of age just before and after the turn of the century—an era whose thunder American novelist Winston Churchill attributed to "the springing of a generation of ideals from a generation of commerce." Their social causes (populism, modernism, women's suffrage, fundamentalism, labor anarchism, prohibition) projected what Jane Addams called a "higher social morality."

According to Frederic Howe, in *Confessions of a Reformer*, "Early assumptions as to virtue and vice, goodness and evil" were "the most characteristic influence of my generation. It explains the nature of our reforms . . . our belief in men rather than institutions and our messages to other people. Missionaries and battleships, anti-saloon leagues and Ku Klux Klan . . . are all a part of that evangelistic psychology . . . that seeks a moralistic explanation of social problems and a religious solution to most of them." George Santayana described his generation as "prophets" who "apply morals to public affairs."

Following World War I, their emerging midlife leadership cared little about managing economic or military affairs—but cared very much about managing America's morals. "The great political questions are in their final analysis great moral questions," insisted William Jennings Bryan, once the populist "Boy Orator of the Platte," who now urged his generation to enact Prohibition. At last taking over the very institutions they had attacked in their youth, Missionaries now wanted to infuse them with ideals. After banning alcohol, giving the vote to women, and closing the immigration door, they went on to become the great scolds of the Roaring Twenties. Whether lauded as Puritans in Babylon (President Calvin Coolidge) or ridiculed as hypocritical Babbitts (by a younger novelist), this generation always demanded the nation's attention.

During the 1930s and '40s, many of these elders suffered terrible privation. Public agencies offered only meager allowances to those who were "superannuated" out of their jobs or, after the banks collapsed, lost their life savings. Yet few Missionaries complained. They took too much pride in directing the sacrifices of others. During fifteen crisis-laden years, they consolidated their social authority—over ineffective opposition from the Lost and often with the encouragement of G.I.s. In religion and education, old Missionaries continued to monopolize the pulpits and lecterns. In politics, they remained in control of now-graying presidential cabinets, congressional committees, and state assemblies. In war, they became guiding patriarchs, often with legendary egos (Secretaries Henry Stimson and Cordell Hull; Admirals William "Bull" Halsey, Jr., and Ernest King; Generals MacArthur and Marshall; industrialists Henry Kaiser and Bernard Baruch; physicist Albert Einstein).

Young people began looking to elders not for warmth and understanding, but for wisdom and guidance. Thanks to his indomitable personality, which more than compensated for his disabled body, Franklin Roosevelt became the leader whom "young men followed," writes historian Arthur M. Schlesinger, Jr., "as they had followed no American since Lincoln." As the Crisis climaxed, this generation tried to deliver what the octogenarian art critic Bernard Berenson described, just after World War II, as "that humanistic society which under the name of Paradise, Elysium, Heaven, City of God, Millennium, has been the craving of all good men these last four thousand years or more."

This was the last time the Prophet archetype entered a Fourth Turning.

Fast forward to April 13, 2029. This is the day (according to NASA) that the large asteroid Apophis, named after the Egyptian demon serpent of darkness, is expected to pass so perilously close to earth as to be easily visible to the naked eye. Imagine millions of Boomers, now mostly in their seventies and early eighties, watching the live videos or even flying to Asia to see it in person. At their age, G.I.s would have been telling their adult children that maybe we should destroy the asteroid just to be safe—and the Silent would have been marveling at our high-tech ability to predict its exact approach.

But the Boomers' head will be in a very different place. Easily accepting that the science may be wrong and that a catastrophe may occur, they will contemplate the passing of all things, the feebleness of all human efforts, and the transcendence of the spirit.

Their religious right, quoting Daniel and Ezekiel, will think back to Hal Lindsey's seventies-era mega-seller *The Late Great Planet Earth*, along with all the subsequent dispensational sermons and novels looking forward to the "end times." Their New Age left may be holding an old copy of *Chariots of the Gods?* or talking with their friends about Atlantis. A few will be fumbling for their notes on the Mayan calendar, figuring that maybe the scholars were just a few years too early when they dated the end of the world to 2012. *The Celestine Prophecy* author James Redfield describes his peers as "a generation whose intuitions would help lead humanity toward a . . . great transformation." Like so many Boomers, he effortlessly mingles images of perfection and apocalypse.

As the Crisis era reaches its climax, Boomers will bring their redefinition of elderhood to full culmination. Their late-life cultural questing will no longer evoke juvenescence, as it still sometimes does today, but rather the championing of values that seem "old," even remotely ancient, to younger generations. Slow eating, slow talking, slow walking, and slow driving will become badges of contemplation, not decline. Boomers will flaunt, not avoid, the natural imprints of time—many finding a peace and satisfaction that eluded them when their bodies were stronger. As Henry Wadsworth Longfellow observed at age ninety in "Morituri Salutamus,"

> For age is opportunity no less
> Than youth itself, though in another dress,

And as the evening twilight fades away
The sky is filled with stars, invisible by day.

With the nation mobilized and history accelerating, Boomers will at last confront the end result of their lifelong absorption with values. All their lives, surveys show, Boomers have been gloomier than other generations about America's direction. Having blazed a decades-long trail of scorched-earth rhetoric, now at last they will find their words gaining traction on actual events. The fate of civilization, humanity, religion, or the planet will seem to be at stake. Finally comes the opportunity to rectify, to purify, to transform. Boomers are likely to urge one another to stay resolute and not to back down. And they will worry that younger generations may shirk from the gathering threats to America's principles and integrity—and will settle for something meaner, smaller, more slavish and materialistic.

Many indeed will find catharsis in a historic rupture that clarifies basic national choices. So has every Prophet archetype in a Fourth Turning. After Britain's punitive measures against Boston in 1774, Princeton president John Witherspoon vowed "to prefer war with all its horrors, and even extermination, to slavery." Emerson, after hearing of the bombardment of Fort Sumter, confessed he felt relief in a "war" which "shatters everything flimsy, sets aside all false issues, and breaks through all that is not real as itself. . . . Let it search, let it grind, let it overturn." This time around, leaders of the aging Boomer clerisy are likely to react in a similar fashion.

With the Crisis itself placing new burdens on the lives of younger generations, Boomers will choose to retain their moral authority by arguing—uncharacteristically—to impose sacrifices on themselves and other older Americans for the sake of their community. This will seem less surprising in the context of their own families: Most Boomers today are already providing generously, sometimes more generously than they can afford, for their own children and grandchildren. But it will seem more surprising when they do so in the context of the national community and support tax and benefit changes that hit their own ranks the hardest. But the logic will be inexorable. The young, acting on behalf of the community at a time of peril, will now have a much better claim on resources than they do. So Boomers will let go.

Everything will be on the table. A persuasive case will be made for taxing consumption and assets along with meaningful inheritance taxes, since these draw the most revenue out of affluent elderly age brackets. Perhaps some version of all three will be legislated. Stricter tax compliance measures will flush assets out of the tax havens of Boomer plutocrats. Rationing of high-end luxury services and goods may be instituted to save resources, if such opulence has not already been driven into the shadows by social stigma. Surging inflation, likely during the Crisis climax in any case, may be welcomed by policymakers as a means of devaluing fixed-income debt. Government and young people (debtors) will benefit the most; high-net-worth Boomers (creditors) will be penalized the most. Regulations may thwart attempts by firms to sell this debt. Financial repression—forcing savers and fixed-income creditors to swallow their losses—is standard practice by governments during wartime.

Public benefits will also be overhauled. Entering prior Crisis eras, government spending on benefits to the nonindigent was minimal. This time, it is massive—and it flows mostly to the elderly. What's more, due to the rapid growth in the number of retiring Boomers relative to younger taxpayers, that flow is due to grow rapidly in the years to come. In 2005, when the oldest Boomers were eligible for early retirement, total Social Security and federal health benefit spending was 7.8 percent of GDP. By 2045, when the youngest Boomers will be in their mid-eighties, the CBO projects it will have reached 14.7 percent of GDP. By then, incredibly, these benefits, plus interest payable on the national debt, are expected to consume more than all federal revenue.

If Boomers were to wage a successful fight to defend all this spending, younger generations would find the cupboard bare. They would be unable to meet the demands of current emergencies much less build a fresh future for a new regime. But most Boomers won't have their heart in this fight. Here too they will make large concessions and even rationalize them as participation in a larger cause. Retirement ages will be raised, and benefits may get fully taxed or means tested. Most importantly, health benefits will be subjected to radical changes—possibly converting today's extravagant and dysfunctional fee-for-service labyrinth into a simple capitated allowance. Doctors and hospitals, for the first time, will work within fixed budgets.

By such means, aging Boomers will construct a new ethic of decline and death, much like they did in youth with sex and procreation. Where their youthful ethos hinged on self-indulgence, their elder ethos will hinge on self-denial. As they experience their own bodies coping naturally with physical decline, many will be cared for by families at home—and increasingly in their own homes. Informal "Eden Alternative" modes of long-term care will also be popular; the institutional nursing-home model, already in steep decline today, will continue to atrophy. Rather than surround themselves in technology, aging Boomers will prefer to explore their own spiritual interior, sometimes with the aid of psychedelics.

With the same psychic energy with which they once probed *eros*, Boomers will now explore *thanatos*, the end-time. Their final preparation for what they leave behind will focus less on things than on thoughts. Their bodies they can quickly relegate to personalized cardboard eco-coffins, but their insights for family and friends will be carefully recorded and stored, enabling them to communicate with heirs in perpetuity.

While Boomer elders will still make heavy demands on the young, the nature of those demands will differ greatly from those imposed by "senior citizens" when they were coming of age. Where the Awakening-era G.I.s burdened the young fiscally, Crisis-era Boomers will burden the young culturally. They will reverse the coin of elderhood from what they will remember of the Awakening: Where G.I. elders once obtained a secular reward in return for ceding moral authority, Boomers will seek the reverse.

"You and I are on our way to an unexpected harvest festival," announced Craig Karpel to his fellow Boomers in *The Retirement Myth*, his prescient forecast of a retirement more materially constrained than most of his peers ever imagined. He likened his generation's approaching elderhood to a journey to "Owl Mountain," a "primordial sanctuary . . . preserved since the most ancient times," sustaining wisdom passed down from "villages in the middle of nowhere speaking to us across the millennia." As they feel the transformative dimension of time, Boomers will struggle to craft myths and models that can re-sacralize the national community, heal its dysfunctions, and lead the nation into its next Golden Age.

To be sure, the very otherworldliness that Boomers will regard so highly in themselves will strike many Gen-Xers and Millennials as evidence of incompetence, even delusion. Their contempt for this world will strike them as possibly dangerous. Yet regardless of what youth think of these old messengers, they will respect their message and march to their banner. At a moment of national peril, they will need fearless leaders in whom they can see an aspirational vision of what they could collectively become.

Thus will the Gray Champion ride once more.

Eight or nine decades after his last appearance, as Nathaniel Hawthorne foresaw, America will be visited by the "figure of an ancient man . . . combining the leader and the saint [to] show the spirit of their sires." Again there will appear the heir to the righteous Puritan who stood his ground against Governor Andros, to the old colonial governors of the American Revolution who broke from England, to the aging radicals of the Civil War who pitted brother against brother with a "fiery gospel writ in burnished rows of steel," and to "the New Deal Isaiahs" who achieved their "rendezvous with destiny."

What are the typical attributes of the Gray Champion? Boundless self-confidence. Uncompromising principle. Contempt for the status quo. Inability to back down or give up. Yet also a simplicity of manner and a serenity of soul. And the charismatic ability to reconnect the rising generation with its cultural heritage. Oriented toward final ends, the Gray Champion can be careless about the human or material cost of attaining them. While a Gray Champion can come from any generation, he (or she) has often come from the Prophet archetype, for reasons of both age and personality.

Once the Crisis moves into its consolidation phase, probably late in the 2020s, the emergence of a Gray Champion, who may today still be unknown to most of the public, will be a practical necessity. Boomer or not, this figure will help galvanize the nation and will represent, for younger generations, the translation of old Boomer arguments during the Culture Wars into a new Crisis-era context of community needs. By now, Boomers will be entirely unchecked by the moderating influence of older Silent leaders.

They will redefine and reauthenticate a civic expansion—crafted from some mix of Unraveling-era cultural conservatism and public-sector liberalism. The same generation that once railed against the "Establishment" will help the young build a new fail-safe Leviathan. In foreign affairs, they will narrowly define the acceptable behavior of other nations—and broadly define the appropriate use of American arms. The same generation that once chanted "Hell No, We Won't Go!" could emerge as America's most martial elder generation since World War II.

Elder Boomers will find transcendence in the Crisis climax. As they battle time and nature to win their release from history, they will feel themselves in a position to help steward the nation, and perhaps the world, across several painful thresholds. It is easy to envision old Aquarians as pillars of fire leading to the Promised Land—but just as easy to see them as unhinged Ahabs determined to wreck the ship and take everyone down with them. Either is possible.

As the Crisis resolves, elder Boomers will not have the last word, but the deep word. If they triumph, they will collectively deserve the eulogy Winston Churchill offered to Franklin Roosevelt: to die "an enviable death." If they fail, their misdeeds, like those decried by Elijah, could cast a dark shadow that endures for centuries. Whatever the outcome, posterity will remember the Boomers' Gray Champion persona long after the hippie and yuppie images have been forgotten to all but the historian.

GEN X IN MIDLIFE

Generation X (born 1961–81) today comprises roughly 85 million adults mainly in their forties and fifties.

Their first wave, born in the early 1960s, debuted to the public in the mid-eighties as a hardened, throwaway Brat Pack of youth stars in such films as *The Breakfast Club* and *St. Elmo's Fire*. A bit later, they appeared as a new breed of post-Boomer celebrity—all-action, no-nonsense, bottom-line-focused—like Michael Jordan, Michael Dell, Michael J. Fox, and Tom Cruise. In the early nineties, they got their name from a 1961-born British Columbian Doug Coupland, who wrote a sardonic novel drawing a deep divide between his own circle of friends and the Boomers who had come along just before them. The Xers' last wave, born in 1980 and 1981, were the last teens to graduate from high school before the bursting of the dotcom bubble.

Prequel: Keeping It Real

The iconic *Time* cover image (July 16, 1990) evokes what older Americans first thought about this "next generation" and more importantly what Xers thought about themselves: Unsmiling black-clad youths in a dimly lit room, maybe a prison cell, are gazing without expression in different directions, apparently unaware of each other's presence. "Overshadowed by the baby boomers," the tagline asks, are these kids "laid back, late blooming, or just lost?"

Twenty years earlier, the media liked to show ebullient youth standing on a hillside teaching the world to sing (so went the Coca-Cola ad). No longer. These "baby busters" were typically shown as tough, wary, untrusting, maybe a bit traumatized.

Gen-Xers first arrived as toddlers in the early 1960s, when the watchful if increasingly indulgent parenting style enjoyed by Boomer kids transitioned into something approaching hands-off neglect. As the Awakening exploded and adults of all ages sought to "find themselves," institutions that once protected kids no longer seemed to work. Schools were breaking down, families were breaking up, and a new invention, "no-fault" divorce, proved spectacularly popular. What's more, starting in the early sixties, adults no longer wanted more kids—making Xers the first babies people took pills not to have and signaling a sudden end of the postwar demographic "baby boom." By the early seventies, total fertility had plunged beneath its previous Depression-era low.

Teachers and parents were widely urged, Pink Floyd–style, to give up trying to protect or structure children's lives. The Bill Cosby parent-as-fallible-pal model prevailed, G-rated films nearly disappeared, and the Brooke Shields and Jodie Foster tween sexploitation film was born. Educator Neil Postman, alarmed by the emergence of these "proto-adults," called it *The Disappearance of Childhood*. Meanwhile, the overall media portrayal of children turned unremittingly negative—with child-as-devil horror movies (from *Rosemary's Baby* and *The Exorcist* to *It's Alive* and *Children of the Corn*) playing to packed theaters throughout the entire Xer childhood.

The portrayal didn't improve much as these children got older. Even at their best, they were, like the Tatum O'Neal adolescent, hard before their time. Words like "latchkey," "abused," "abandoned," "throwaway," and "runaway" for the first time became commonly attached to children. And the word "dumb." The 1983 *Nation at Risk* report decried the "rising tide of mediocrity" that America's educators claimed was graduating from high school, students whose "educational skills . . . will not surpass, will not equal, will not even approach, those of their parents."

Young Xers thus acquired the child-of-divorce syndrome on a grand scale: the feeling that *they* were the reason why no one thought much of them and why everyone was so unhappy—after all, America was doing great until *they* came along. Low collective self-esteem became one of their primary peer personality traits. "We're rotten to the core," sang the thug-boys in *Bugsy Malone*. "We're the very worst—each of us contemptible, criticized, and cursed." Sixteen years later, from their dingy basement, Wayne and Garth famously chanted, "We're not worthy!" As novelist David Leavitt observed, "Mine is a generation perfectly willing to admit its contemptible qualities."

Xers learned early—indeed, were deliberately taught—not to trust older people and institutions to look after their best interests. They grew up instead trusting their own instincts and serving themselves. Out of this understanding grew strong peer personality strengths: self-sufficiency, resilience, keen survival instincts, and the power to distinguish reality from illusion. Not coincidentally, words like "survivor" and "reality" soon attached themselves, permanently, to media by and about Gen-Xers. While older people put them down as a "low-sweat," "slacker," or "why bother?" generation, Xers took pride in their own indifference—which is, after all, the finely honed skill of not wasting energy on stuff that just doesn't matter.

Entering the labor market in the 1980s and '90s, young Xers encountered an economy increasingly tilted toward affluent older generations who had already purchased their high rung on the ladder—on Wall Street, in the professions, in academia—and who no longer felt much obligation to keep the lower rungs in place. At the low-skill end, entry-level union jobs began instituting two-tier wage scales and legislators began scrapping the job training programs and welfare benefits that had remained in place during the Boomer youth era. Globalizing trade and a historic new surge in immigration pulled down wages in just the age and skill brackets in which young Xers found themselves. Budding careerists with credentials did better, but the share of young men with college degrees actually retrogressed from Boomers to Xers.

Raised to take care of themselves, most Xers welcomed a less regulated economy, figuring that—since the rules were rigged against them—fewer rules were better. They embraced a high-turnover, low-trust, free-agency lifestyle, hoping that by moving quickly they could always find a market break. Many gladly cashed out their workplace benefits, triggering the trend toward opt-in "cafeteria" and "total rewards" pay packages. At an early age, they gravitated to temp work—a sector which suited their grab-and-go instincts and which today is aging with them. By the 1990s, Xers were dissolving the old A-frame corporate pyramid—and replacing it with splintery M-frame or matrix substitutes, crowded with individual incentives and "deals" and unburdened by much sense of common mission.

While Boomer youth had focused on their inner lives, Xer youth tended to focus on bottom-line outcomes. For the last several decades, the UCLA college freshman survey has been asking students what life goals they consider important. In the 1960s and early 1970s (when Boomers were college freshmen), a three-to-one majority said "developing a meaningful philosophy in life" rather than "being very well off financially." In the late 1970s (when Xers were entering college), those priorities reversed. Why waste time on meaningful? By the early nineties, "It's It and That's That" and "Why Ask Why" had become notorious X-targeting beer ads.

Individualism, for Boomer youth, was a great discovery and achievement. For Xer youth, it was merely the new reality—without the transcendence. Unlike Boomer youth culture, which celebrated meaningful rural settings, Xer youth culture—from hip-hop and thrash metal to alt-rock and grunge—flourished in anonymous and hardscrabble urban settings. "On the streets" was where markets flourished, risk-takers ventured, winners were sorted out from losers, and losers learned to start all over again.

"Generation X," originally coined as a mock anti-label joke on Boomer yuppies, assumed a deeper meaning as Xers grew older. It suggested the absence of any generational center of gravity. Xers are, per capita, the most immigrant and diverse American generation born in the twentieth century. Entering midlife, they have also become the most spread out in terms of income and wealth, with little discernible middle class. Their social loyalties are splintered into countless regional, occupational, and ethnic pieces. Because Xers assumed (and certainly were told) that collectively they had no future, each figured his or her only chance was to take risks and be different. Lucky niches were prized, mainstream brands were shunned.

Generation X has had a profound and positive impact on institutions that reward initiative and derring-do—and that insist on bottom-line results no matter what the cost.

In the 1980s, a new wave of Xer recruits rescued America's military from its Boomer-era demoralization and pulled its reputation back to a lofty "Top Gun" level of public esteem. After America's surprisingly swift Gulf War victory in 1991, the first large-scale action fought with mostly Xer enlistees, President H. W. Bush declared the Boomer-era "Vietnam Syndrome" to be over: "The ghosts of Vietnam have been laid to rest beneath the sands of the Arabian desert."

In commerce, Xers have matured into one of the most innovative generations of entrepreneurs in American history. Boomers like Al Gore may have "invented" the Internet. But surely it's Xers like Marc Andreessen, Larry Page, Sergey Brin, Jeff Bezos, Peter Thiel, Elon Musk, Travis Kalanick, Sheryl Sandberg, Dick Costolo, and Brian Chesky who figured out how to make fortunes from the Internet and, more importantly, how digital technologies would elevate productivity and revolutionize the global economy. Thanks to Xers, U.S. corporations have returned to dominance among high-income economies (by market cap) and small business has joined the military in high public esteem.

In the culture, the Xer impact has been more mixed. Their music, shows, and novels have been out-of-the-box creative, to be sure. But much of it has been too raw, violent, or transgressive to win a large following with other generations. In religion, Xers have backed away from Boomer spiritual pretensions—preferring strictly personal credos without much need for community or public ritual. In 1985, Robert Bellah gave this belief a name, "Sheilaism," after a young nurse named Sheila: "I believe in God. I'm not a religious fanatic. I can't remember the last time I went to church. My faith has carried me a long way. It's Sheilaism. Just my own little voice."

In politics, Xers have been conspicuous mainly by their absence. In their twenties, relatively few of them voted. In their thirties and forties, they were very late in running for any political office, especially for the presidency. Today, with their leading edge now passing age sixty, they have only recently attained a plurality in the House of Representatives. They remain years away from dominance in the Senate or in state governorships. No prior generation at this age has been so weakly represented in civic leadership. In part, this disinterest in politics reflects Xers' instinctive libertarianism: They have always believed society works better bottom-up than top-down.

When they do vote, Xers have tended to favor the party of less government—the GOP. This habit was acquired early, back in the 1980s, when young voters surprised older liberals by voting for Reagan. The first big Xer TV star (Michael J. Fox) was shown as a plucky, tie-wearing teen capitalist who stunned his hippie parents with anti-Streisand one-liners like "People who have money don't need people." Ever since, at every age and in every presidential election, Xers have repeatedly voted more Republican than the nation as a whole. The same tilt appears among all Xers who have successfully run for office. Elected Xers represent the most Republican-leaning generation of congresspeople and state governors since the Lost.

Redefining midlife in the long grinding aftermath of the GFC, Xers have found economic solvency to be their overriding preoccupation. Like partygoers waking up after a wild night at the casino, Xers show a wide disparity in wealth outcomes—wider than any midlife generation since (again) the Lost.

A few have become fabulously wealthy, some are comfortable, many are struggling, and a large number are desperate. The latter include an aging wave of front-end Xers born in the early 1960s who are now homeless, unattached, or underemployed—and passing age 60. Their suffering has contributed to an astonishing recent rise in midlife mortality rates, inspiring economists Anne Case and Angus Deaton's term "midlife deaths of despair." Of all employed Xers, nearly one in ten continues to rely on gig work as their sole source of household income. This leaves millions of midlife Americans without job security, health insurance, or pensions—and starring as the gritty protagonists of *Deadliest Catch* and *Ice Road Truckers* reality shows. Two-thirds of these "gig" Xers say they are struggling financially.

Overall, Gen X has experienced somewhat less upward family mobility than late-wave Boomers: Per person, barely half of all Xers earned more than their parents by age thirty or forty, and *less than half* of Xer men earned more than their fathers. Per household, the median income of Xers has been slightly lower than that of Boomers at the same age—an extraordinary generational backstep. Gen-Xers have struggled even more to build up household net worth in order to provide for their future. Gen X currently owns 30 percent of all U.S. real and financial assets; back when Boomers were the age of Gen-Xers, they owned 49 percent. In surveys, Gen-Xers report being "more worried" than other generations about their finances. When asked how they're preparing for retirement, nearly half say they'll "just figure it out when they get there."

In surveys, Xers (women especially) are more likely than today's older or younger generations to agree that *their* generation is worse off than their parents. They are also the most likely to call themselves "lower class" and the least likely to call themselves "upper class." This is grim payback for a generation that has always valued material success. Unlike Boomers, they can't easily take refuge in spiritual transcendence. Ironically, the generation of avid *Rich Dad Poor Dad* readers, who once idolized the wheeler-dealer "rich dad" and ridiculed the wage-slave "poor dad," is now the *least* likely to agree that "becoming wealthy is an achievable goal."

As young adults, the early and late waves of this generation seemed to be a study in contrasts. Most first-wavers (born in the 1960s, "Atari" or "New Wave" Xers) started out at a tougher time, in the grim shadow of the double Volcker recessions or the long Bush, Sr., recession. As young voters, they gravitated to Ronald Reagan and leaned most heavily to the GOP. Most last wavers (born in the 1970s, "Nintendo" or "Clinton" Xers) entered the workforce during the Roaring Nineties. In politics, they were OK with a cool Boomer Democrat who could play the sax—so long as he governed lightly. At age thirty-five, the best most first-wavers could hope for was that maybe the future wouldn't totally suck. At age twenty-five, many last-wavers were daydreaming about seven-figure stock options.

Yet since the dotcom bust, and especially since the GFC, those contrasts have faded. Younger last wavers were hit even harder by the Great Recession than older first-wavers—and are today the most pessimistic about their economic prospects. As voters in 2020, last wavers remained a bit more moderate than first-wavers, but their nineties reputation as progressive has been eclipsed by younger Millennials.

Overall, midlife for Xers has been a transition from Generation Xtreme to Generation Xhausted: a time to take stock, slow down, batten hatches, hedge risks, grow roots, and show true grit. They're playing and experimenting less. They're paying off debt and saving more. They're focusing harder on the tasks and relationships that really matter and ignoring the rest. Often for the first time, they're assuming responsibilities in their communities.

Most of all, they've matured into the most protective parental generation in living memory—obsessed with providing their own kids with the hands-on care and structure they never had. For Xers, parenting means always being there, always knowing where your child is, always watching out for danger. Once their child leaves for grade school or college, they become every teacher's or professor's worst nightmare: the not-with-my-child-you-don't mom or dad, unafraid to sue the school principal or shout at school board members. Next to their own child, what happens to everyone else's child means little.

Along the way, Xers are becoming a generation of midlife fogeys. Seeking protection (but no handouts) for themselves and their families in a dangerous, pitiless world, many are drawn to strongmen who can smash a few heads and make things happen. Since 2016, Xers have proven decisive in tipping the Republican Party toward populism. Less religious and less trusting than Boomer conservatives, they are more likely to figure that rules may have to be broken to make the system work again. Xers composed the clear majority of the elected politicians who supported Donald Trump's "steal" claim in 2020—and of the Capitol Hill arrestees in 2021. In 2022, for the first time, many surveys showed Americans age forty-five to sixty-five (Whites especially) more likely to vote for the GOP than either younger *or older* voters.

"Gen X's greatest gift to society: Grouchiness," proclaimed a recent *Washington Post* headline. This generation's most celebrated humorists (from Conan O'Brien and Tina Fey to Louis C.K., Chris Rock, and Dave Chappelle) come across as rough-edged and grumpy, full of snark and vitriol. They roll their eyes at PC complaints and feel a special bond with the unlettered "deplorables" in their audience. According to Pew Research, Xers are "savvy, skeptical and self-reliant; they're not into preening or pampering, and they just might not give much of a hoot what others think of them."

Accustomed to lurking, this neglected "middle-child" generation doesn't mind watching Boomers and Millennials arguing with each other and getting most of the media attention. They're content not to get involved. "Withdrawing in disgust is not the same thing as apathy," goes the famous line in *Slacker*. Yet as they grow older, Xers wonder if their strategy of withdrawal may have contributed to trends that worry all Americans: the growing dominance of self-interest (especially profit) in how we behave; the coarser, ruder, brassier tone of our daily lives; and the collapse of national civic life—including the glaring fact that nobody even pretends to be in charge. Slogans like "works for me" and "move fast and break things" may make sense at age twenty-five. They make less sense at age fifty-five, when people shift their focus to the kind of country their kids are about to inherit.

All their lives, maybe as early as disco in the late seventies, Xers have blamed Boomers for ruining America just before they got here. Most recently, tech billionaire Bruce Gibney called Boomers a *Generation of Sociopaths*, guilty of "generational plunder"—always tearing down and borrowing, never building up and investing. Yet if Xers want to identify the generation least like their own, they should look not to Boomers (with whom they share more than they would like to admit) but to the Silent, their archetypal opposite, who were the parents of most early wave Xers and did the most to shape the Xers' upbringing.

Who were the Silent? They were sheltered and trusting children, cautious and conformist youth, empathic young adults, and newly experimental as they entered midlife. How does the Xer life story compare? At every phase of life, Xers have been just the opposite.

Toward the Climax: Winner Take All

"Now once more the belt is tight and we summon the proper expression of horror as we look back at our wasted youth," F. Scott Fitzgerald said after the crash that hit his peers at the start of what should have been their highest-earning years. "A generation with no second acts," he called his Lost peers—but they proved him wrong. They ended their frenzy and settled down, helping to unjangle the American mood. Where their Missionary predecessors joined moralistic crusades in midlife, the post-Crash Lost returned without fanfare to the basics of life. "What is moral is what you feel good after," declared Ernest Hemingway, "what is immoral is what you feel bad after."

They never thought much of themselves. "Mama, I have been a bad boy. All my life I have been a bad boy," murmured author Thomas Wolfe just before his death from tuberculosis, a burned-out wreck at age thirty-eight after a lifetime of wildness. On the eve of World War I, the *Atlantic Monthly* accused the "rising generation" of "mental rickets and curvature of the soul." During the war, the alleged stupidity of American youth became a raging issue when IQ tests indicated that half of all draftees (a large number of them recent immigrants) had a "mental age" of under twelve.

After the war, their morals were assailed by aging Missionaries. In the dark days of the Depression, when FDR blasted "a generation of self-seekers" for wrecking "the temple of our civilization," he clearly meant the middle-aged Lost—who throughout the 1930s were attacked as "Copperheads," "nay-sayers," "Irresponsibles," and (as war approached) isolationists. FDR led crowds in thunderous chants against "Martin, Barton, and Fish," three prominent Lost Republicans who opposed him in Congress.

The Great Depression brought them a midlife hangover. According to Malcolm Cowley, it was a time of "doubt and even defeat" for his peers. But as life went on, they lent the 1930s much of that decade's gutsy-but-solid reputation. With FDR winning term after term, the Republican-leaning Lost did not attain a majority of congressional seats and governorships until 1941, later in their life cycle than any other generation in U.S. history—until Generation X.

When World War II hit, the Lost shed their isolationism and provided the war-winning generals whose daring (Patton), warmth (Bradley), and persistence (Eisenhower) energized younger troops. At home, they mastered deadly new technologies—from radar and sonar to proximity fuses and nuclear fission—and managed the world's most efficient war machine. With little philosophizing, their first president dropped two atom bombs and then arranged a peace that was less vengeful and more secure than the one he recalled from his own soldier days.

This "no second act" generation lent America the grit to survive dark global emergencies and, in the end, to triumph over them. During the Great Depression, the Lost were hard hit but refused to ask for public favors. In World War II, they manned the draft boards, handed out the ration coupons, mapped the invasions, and dispatched the bomber fleets. They gave the orders that killed thousands but saved millions. From "Blood and Guts" generals to "Give 'Em Hell" presidents, the Lost knew how to take "the heat," and prevail.

This was the last time the Nomad archetype entered a Fourth Turning.

Imagine, sometime in the late 2020s, that the United States is plunged into sudden hostilities with a major-power adversary. Only this war will seem to break all the rules. It will begin with a massive cyberattack of unknown origin, intended to cripple America's energy, transportation, and communications infrastructure. It will be followed by an anti-satellite barrage, in order to render America blind as well as dumb. Then come the AI-guided drone swarms, perhaps synchronized with an invasion of U.S.-allied nations by unidentifiable hybrid troops who quickly mix with the civilian population.

The war will manifest itself as a gigantic puzzle full of ruses and feints, decoys and dead ends, destruction and denial. Nothing will be clear, yet everything will be at stake. Whichever officers are in charge of the American response, they will need to be cool under fire, willing to call a bluff, and unfazed by extreme risk. They must act alone. There will be no time to convene meetings. They must be resilient problem-solvers, accustomed to thinking fast outside the box and kludging together high-tech solutions on the fly.

Now picture the fifty- and sixty-somethings who will preside over U.S. military forces, from the Marines to the Space Force, as well as U.S. corporate cyber-strategy offices.

From childhood on, nearly all of them will have shared an immersion in certain standard pop-culture themes—from D&D to *The Legend of Zelda*; from *Twin Peaks* to *The X-Files*; from *WarGames* and *The Last Starfighter* to *The Dark Knight Rises* and *World War Z*; from *Mad Max* to *I Am Legend*. Standard plotline: a lone protagonist—unassisted, unprepared, from whom nothing is expected—is chosen at random to decide the fate of humanity. The situation looks dicey. Motives are hidden. Few can be trusted. The world may hardly seem worth saving. But at a pivotal moment, this wayfarer shrugs off the stress, arranges priorities, does what it takes, and saves the kingdom.

Generation X, America's rising cadre of hands-on military chieftains and business bosses, does in fact possess the temperament and skills for America's next unexpected challenge. Player One—or Rogue One, take your pick—will be ready.

Whether Xers look forward to such a role is another question altogether.

"I've glimpsed our future," warns the high-school valedictorian in the 1989 film *Say Anything...*, "and all I can say is—go back!" Decades later, many of her classmates have reflected on that message. And for good reason: They may suspect their own collective story will not have a comfortable ending. Nomad generations—what Christian Slater once referred to as "a long list of dead, famous wild people"—have always been the ones that lose ground in wealth, education, security, longevity, and other measures of progress. Yet they have also been the generations that lie at the fulcrum between triumph and tragedy, the ones who hoist their society through its darkest trials.

As the Crisis era deepens, even the youngest Gen-Xers will be reaching their late forties and their generation as a whole will have moved fully into midlife.

By now, it will become obvious that the oldest Xers will be, on the cusp of elderhood, significantly worse off economically than Boomers were at the same age. They will continue to fan out across an unusually wide range of money and career outcomes. The entire distribution, moreover, will be pulled down by the Crisis-era growth in public spending. The Xers at the high end will find their income and wealth shaved away by emergency tax measures, Xers at the low end by falling real wages and eroding public safety nets. While reductions in old-age benefits will start affecting Boomers already well into retirement (and many, inevitably, will be "grandfathered" out of the new austerity), such reductions will hit most Xers full force on day one.

Xers will say to themselves, Sure, we always knew it was going to turn out like this.

The Crisis-era image of a middle-aged worker will be a modest-wage job-hopper who retains the flexibility to change life directions at a snap. The prototype midlife success story will be the entrepreneur who excels at deal-making, leverage, and high-tech problem solving. The prototype failure will be the ruined gambler, broke but still trying. Rivaling them at the affluent-but-not-rich edge of their generation, in a sort of *Revenge of the Nerds*, will be the slow-but-steady plodders (many of them immigrants and from diverse ethnic backgrounds). They will overtake many quick strikers who took one risk too many.

With Xers, midlife will lose moral authority and gain toughness. Their mindset will be hardboiled and hands-on, their risk-taking now mellowed by a Crisis-era need for security. Middle-aged people will mentor youth movements, lend an easygoing class to hard times, and contribute nuts-and-bolts workmanship to whatever the nation needs to accomplish. Millennials will admire them for their gutsy resolve, wild humor, and seeming indifference to the approval of others. Throughout the economy, Xers will be associated with risk and dirty jobs. They will seek workable outcomes more than inner truths. "We won't have a bad backlash against our lost idealism," predicted *Slacker* filmmaker Richard Linklater, since his generation "never had that to begin with."

Most of the bleeding-edge musical and media innovations of the Xers' earlier years will be ignored—or overhauled—by younger Americans whose pop culture will be tuned into a more upbeat and politically correct vibe. Even Xers themselves who want to revisit their profanity-laced youth in the manner of *Hot Tub Time Machine* will make sure their own kids or grandkids are not in the same room. A few aging cultural renegades, refusing to back down in the face of younger media Bolsheviks, will scatter around the world, feeling like those whom Doug Coupland calls "a White Russian aristocracy, exiled in Paris cafes, never to get what is due to us."

As they confront their life problems, Xers will prioritize their efforts according to their attachments. First priority will be their families. They will continue to take pride in their ability to "have a life" and wall off their families from financial woes. Their divorce rate will remain well below that of midlife Boomers. As the Crisis-era mood deepens, they will grow even more protective of their children. Their next priority will be the schools and local youth and community activities that most affect their families and where they figure their contributions can make the most difference. Their last priority will be national public leadership.

Inevitably, as Boomer and Silent leaders retire, the Xer share of national leaders will rise. But this share will remain much lower than for earlier generations at their age—and by the late 2020s they will see the Millennial share rising rapidly in their rearview mirror. Few of their classmates and friends will have built civilian public-sector careers. When Xers do run for national office—as happened in the 2020 Democratic presidential primary—most will strike voters as fringy and uncredentialed and thus will struggle to be taken seriously.

They will be more successful in local politics, where they have real skin in the game. By the end of the decade, Xers will constitute a decisive majority of governors and mayors, a growing share of whom will be former entrepreneurs, CEOs, and housewives who will brag about their political inexperience. A growing share too will be immigrants or come from immigrant families.

As the Crisis era moves toward its climax, government at every level will be called upon to mobilize people and resources—to build new infrastructure, to enlarge production capacity, to care for the suffering, to transport military personnel, or to provide civil defense. All this will put the rough-and-ready Xer leadership style to the extreme test. And, by and large, that style will prove to be effective.

Xers in charge will be masters of triage: They won't worry about the unsolvable and won't fuss over the merely annoying. As elected leaders, they will speak plainly to voters and respond flexibly to constituent requests. They will focus doggedly on bottom-line results and won't mind bribing, threatening, or cutting corners to get them. Their hand strengthened by the emergency, they will sweep aside procedural legalisms, much to the anguish of many older Boomers and Silent. As military commanders and as chiefs of protective services, Xers will release their inner warrior. They will demonstrate deft timing, tactical creativity, an instinctive sense of what counts and what doesn't, and an ability to move on quickly from one problem to the next.

Where this generation will take the nation, however, remains unknowable. Gen-X voters and leaders at the zenith of midlife power will introduce dizzying volatility to the nation's political direction—and, perhaps, even uncertainty about what sort of nation, or nations, America will become. While middle age is ordinarily regarded as the most rooted phase of life, middle-aged Xers will sense they have little stake in the old order, as though their names and signatures are missing from the social contract. From childhood into midlife, they will have heard only one message: What you do with your life is up to you; and if you get in trouble, well, better fix it on your own. They will not recall a time when most of their peers felt strong bonds of obligation and reward connecting them to the republic.

The historical track record of the Nomad archetype is encouraging.

For the sake of their families and children, these generations typically choose to build where others have destroyed, to give back what they were never given. Having grown up in a time when walls were dismantled, families dissolved, and loyalties discarded, Xers in the heat of emergency will likely seek to defend a powerful and newly energized republic as a means of securing the kind of well-anchored institutional world that was denied to them earlier in life. Their weak ("We're not worthy!") collective self-esteem will enhance their new civic role. Since they are unlikely to ask much personally in return for sacrificing their "lives, fortunes, and sacred honor," other generations will, if grudgingly, go along with their directives.

Yet other, darker trajectories are possible. Should a critical mass of Xers decide that a single American nation is hopelessly fractured, they may opt to break it up into a multitude of "Don't Tread on Me" pieces. Another possibility is that populist Xer firebrands act to "save" the republic by taking direct action now and justifying it later. Disillusioned libertarians funded by tech tycoons could decide to repurpose the winning commercial slogans they recall from the late 1990s—*No Excuses, Just Do It, No Rules Just Right*—into the winning political slogans of the late 2020s. Start with a winner-take-all ethos that valorizes action for action's sake, exalts strength and impulse, and holds compassion in contempt. Add class desperation, anti-rationalism, and perceptions of national decline. The product, at its most extreme, could be a new American fascism.

Whatever happens, the Ekpyrosis—the culmination of the Crisis era—will lend new meaning to Xers' lives and highlight the core strengths of their peer personality. Many of the traits they will have heard criticized for decades—their toughness, realism, lack of affect—will now be recognized as vital national resources. If they succeed in saving the republic, they will hear less dismay about their political incorrectness. Fewer Americans will any longer complain about how their soldiers act too much like gladiators, their entrepreneurs too much like robber barons, their politicians too much like bosses. A strong new regime will in any case render those talents less necessary with the passage of time. Middle-aged Hispanic, Asian, and Arab Americans (among others), while not hiding their racial or ethnic identities, will join in building the new mainstream—no doubt aware that they have much to gain from a system that works.

During the Crisis era, Xers will provide the on-site tacticians and behind-the-scenes managers whose decisions will determine day-to-day outcomes. If one or more Boomers occupy the Gray Champion role, Xers won't be in charge of the grand strategy. In that case, Xers may be the only ones capable of deflecting the more dangerous Boomer tendencies. Millennials won't check Boomers, nor will Boomers check themselves. Only Xers will be in the position to force Boomer priest-warriors to "get real" when the sacrifice they ask for vastly outweighs the future reward. It may indeed be some middle-aged statesman, general, or presidential advisor who, acting alone, prevents some righteous old Aquarian from "loosing the fateful lightnings" (to quote again "The Battle Hymn of the Republic") and turning the world's lights out.

Yet the Gray Champion may not be a Boomer. It may be an Xer, especially if the Crisis climax arrives late. We have certainly witnessed Nomad Gray Champions before—George Washington and Queen Elizabeth, for example. Here the danger will be different: that this Nomad leader will exercise too much prudence and seek to cut a deal too soon before the final goal has been achieved. Security will be procured, but at the cost of stunting the new regime's future after the resolution is reached.

However the Crisis turns out, Xers can count on getting less than their fair share of the credit and more than their fair share of the blame. Now entering elderhood, Xers won't be at all surprised. All their lives, Xers have suffered a blighted reputation in the eyes of other generations. Even Xers themselves half-accept the judgment, which is why they don't think the world owes them much. As national leaders, their crowning achievement may be to use that collective humility about their own deserts in order to provide a better world for their children and grandchildren.

MILLENNIAL RISING ADULTS

The Millennial Generation (born 1982–2005?) today comprises roughly 102 million people mostly in their twenties and thirties. They became the most mentioned generation in the media in the mid-2010s, when they surpassed "Boomers." (Gen-Xers never came close to dominance.) They have been variously described as "Generation Nice," the "We Generation," and the "Me Generation." *Me* is an odd name since, after all, Boomers originally got that label from Tom Wolfe in the 1970s. Maybe *Mini-Me* is more appropriate. The oldest Millennials, Boomer-parented trophy kids conceived soon after Reagan's first inauguration, began graduating from high school in 2000 and earned their college degrees just in time for the Great Recession. The last birth cohort of the Millennial Generation cannot yet be precisely identified. But it is likely that the youngest Millennials, children of Xers, were entering high school during the Covid pandemic—and that many are now preparing to graduate.

Prequel: Yes We Can

Arriving as infants in the early 1980s, first-wave Millennials have no memory of the Consciousness Revolution that was so defining for coming-of-age Boomers or of the parental neglect that was so defining for Gen-X children. What shaped them, instead, was the older generations' backlash against the social and family experimentation of that era. Rates of divorce, abortion, and per-capita alcohol consumption all began a sustained fall from their early eighties high. Books and articles appeared describing how badly kids had been treated in the seventies— and arguing that the next generation needed a new sense of protection, mission, and collective purpose.

With "family values" ascendant, young children began to receive more time and more sheltering from adults.

The phrase "kids are special," hardly ever appearing in the mid-seventies according to Ngram, became commonplace by the mid-eighties. Fathers present at the birth of their children, still rare in the late 1970s, became the norm by the late 1980s thanks to the Boomer-friendly Lamaze movement. The evil-child movie, so popular when Xers were small, began bombing at the box office. Suddenly adorable-child movies became in vogue—starting with *Baby Boom*, *Three Men and a Baby*, and *Parenthood*. A decade later, Hollywood featured Boomer soccer moms and dads striving to become better people for the sake of their kids. Gold stars and "bring your parent to school day" ("Hi, I'm Keisha's mom") became staples of the much-lampooned self-esteem movement. And a decade or so after that, "bring your parent to work day" moved into companies, much to the incomprehension of older employees.

When the first Millennials appeared, child safety became an obsession. "Baby on Board" signs proliferated in the windows of early-eighties minivans, now featuring multiple ways to buckle toddlers securely in place. Over the next two decades, the child-safety gadget industry (guards for plugs, stoves, doors, stairs) enjoyed double-digit growth.

The Millennial childhood era signaled the arrival of America's fourth great episode of moral panic over children, in a post-Awakening rhythm dating all the way back to the mid-eighteenth century. From rubber-padded playgrounds, school metal detectors, and drug-free zones to Amber alerts, Megan laws, and Code Adams, a new wall of adult vigilance began to arise around the childhood world. Law enforcement and public stigma turned with a frenzy against child abuse. By the late nineties, most measures showed that the incidence of child abandonment, runaways, and parental violence had dramatically improved.

Millennial kids did not resist the sheltering. They welcomed it. They understood the logic: They were special and therefore worthy of protection.

Being worthy explains another contrast with Gen-X children: the Millennials' growing desire to protect themselves, that is, their own aversion to risk. The CDC tracks more than one hundred "youth risk surveillance indicators" for grades eight, ten, and twelve—everything from buckling seatbelts, smoking cigarettes, and taking drugs to having sex, drinking while driving, and fighting in school. Nearly all these indicators dropped from the mid-1990s to the mid-2010s, most of them dramatically. Likewise, rates of violent crime (mostly committed by people in their late teens to early thirties) fell steeply precisely when Millennials replaced Xers in those age brackets. From 2001 to 2016, the incarceration rate for males under age thirty *fell by half*—even as prisons built new geriatric wings for Xer and Boomer inmates over age forty.

Teen attitudes toward parents and authorities have shifted in a parallel direction—toward agreeable convention and away from alienation (Xers) or protest (Boomers). By 2003, only 15 percent of teens reported having a "serious" or "major" problem with any family member. That was down from 25 percent in 1983 and 50 percent in 1974, when a staggering 40 percent of Watergate-era teens agreed they would be "better off not living with their parents." A growing share of Millennial teens chose a parent rather than a celebrity as a role model. And after leaving home for work or college, Millennials have remained closer to their parents. Recent surveys show that adults in their early twenties talk and spend time with their parents much more often than their parents ever did with *their* parents.

Did parents and teachers want more achievement from young people? Well, fine, Millennials could oblige. No youth generation in American history has willingly subjected itself to so many tests and exams—nor has any trusted in the ethic of meritocracy so utterly. In grade school, without complaint, Millennial high-school students by the mid-2010s were bearing roughly twice the average daily homework load as late-wave Xers were in the mid-1990s. During the first decade of the 2000s, the number of high-school AP test takers doubled. Extracurricular activities, from drama to club sports, have turned practically professional, draining families of both time and money. While teen interest in most party drugs has ebbed, their reliance on "smart drug" stimulants has soared.

In the end, their quest for more gold stars has been successful. Millennial rates of educational attainment have leapt ahead of prior generations at every level, especially in college and graduate degrees—despite exorbitant higher-ed tuition hikes that threaten to mortgage their futures (and strip their parents of savings).

If Millennial youth valued being closer to their parents, so too did they value being closer to one another and their community. When they were in grade school, civics lessons were newly emphasized. By high school, rates of "volunteering" had soared. By the early 2010s, Millennials were flocking to Mark Zuckerberg's novel "social media" brand. Soon they migrated en masse to multiple digital fishbowl environments in which everybody keeps track of everybody in real time. After leaving home, they championed the "sharing" economy, not caring (as young Xers would have cared) that trading, renting, borrowing, and thrifting rendered them perilously dependent on other people. Preparing for careers, Millennials labored earnestly to domesticate callings that their parents had brutalized; they often did so by adding the mild "social" prefix, as in *social* marketing, *social* investing, or *social* entrepreneuring.

Where young Boomers and Xers so often fled the influence or surveillance of the community, Millennial youth embraced it, their most dreaded fear being rejection, isolation, and loneliness—that is, "FOMO."

Over the last twenty years, Millennials have certainly shifted the youth culture in a sunnier if blander direction. A key leading indicator appeared back when their first wave was still in grammar school—and (recall Mentré's tiles on a roof) when Gen-X teens were just discovering Nirvana and Pearl Jam, Dr. Dre and Tupac. That was the spectacular early-nineties revival in family-friendly Disney animation, starting with *The Lion King* and extending over the next decade to *Finding Nemo*. TV kid programming meanwhile joined in as well, with year after year of cheerful, clubby, and didactic shows—like *Barney & Friends*, *Blue's Clues*, *SpongeBob SquarePants*, and *Dora the Explorer*.

By the time first-wavers reached their late teens and twenties, the new mood had begun flowing into older youth genres. It hit music in the late nineties with the rise of poppy, choreographed boy bands—and later with the mainstream collaborative sound of such big Millennial brands as Taylor Swift, Drake, Ariana Grande, and Bruno Mars.

It hit network TV and movies starting in the mid-2000s, shifting programming toward shows with closer and more supportive families, more superheroes banding together to save the world, and greater sharing across diverse ethnicities and gender roles. As Millennials age into the prime viewership demo, the contest shows are growing kinder and less competitive, more like *Nailed It!* than *The Apprentice*. The celebrity talk shows cast warmer, happier hosts, more like Jimmy Fallon than Conan O'Brien. Sitcoms feature smarter and higher-achieving young adults, more like *The Big Bang Theory* than *Seinfeld*. And workplace comedies are increasingly crowded with young people who really want to contribute, more like *Parks and Recreation* than *The Office*.

For Millennials, as for older generations, the dominant challenge of the last fifteen years has been coping with economic duress. Only for them, wall-to-wall retrenchment has literally defined their entry into the adult workplace. Millennial first-wavers came of age with the dotcom bust and 9/11 and were just settling into budding careers when the Great Recession altered their life trajectories. For the last wave, youth hiring improved for two or three years in the late-2010s, but that respite too was upended by the pandemic lockdown of 2020.

Like Xers, Millennials have fallen behind their parents in real earnings at the same age—and, by some measures, they have even fallen behind Xers alone. They're also lagging in wealth accumulation. Young couples have the lowest homeownership rate since their Silent grandparents in the early 1950s (though at that time, unlike today, the rate was rising rapidly). Today's gap in self-reported "economic satisfaction" between thirty-somethings (low) and all their elder family relatives receiving Social Security (high) is the widest ever measured.

These are frustrating results for a generation which, unlike Boomers or Xers, worked hard to make themselves "career ready": following the rules, staying safe, remaining upbeat, and earning so many credentials. Their parents expected so much of them, and they of themselves. So confident have Millennials been in their bright collective outlook that many are haunted by the fear that this inadequacy is personal and doesn't affect their peers. Surveys show that, when adults are asked why they're reluctant to talk about their personal finances, 55 percent of Millennials cite shame over perceptions of failure—versus only 28 percent of Xers and 13 percent of Boomers.

Millennials are responding by doubling down on all the signature strategies that already define their peer personality. They are trying harder to achieve—earning another degree or outworking their rivals in the Xers' "hustle economy." Averse to "vacation shame," they are more likely than older generations *not* to take earned days off. They are pooling tasks and expenses with their friends. Group living, rare among their parents after college, has become almost the rule for young urban workers.

A rising share of Millennials—roughly one-half of all adults under thirty since the pandemic—are living with their parents. That's roughly the same percentage as young G.I.s living at home near the end of the Great Depression in 1940. Millennials are less likely than Xers to "boomerang" reluctantly back home, since a growing number never really left home in the first place. Even away from home, they remain close to parents and older relatives, from whom they receive advice and support. In 2018, 37 percent of twenty-one- to thirty-seven-year-olds reported getting monthly financial assistance from an older family member.

Most of all, this generation continues to obsess over risk avoidance. They search eagerly for "job stability" with big organizations—and look at no-frills contract "jobs" as a desperate last recourse that threatens to turn them into permatemps. Once employed, they're much more likely than their parents at the same age to snatch up insurance benefits, max out on regular pension contributions, and strategize formal "advancement" options. Fewer young Millennials dare start their own businesses. Many regard the unbridled marketplace as a child-devouring Moloch, evoked in their imaginations by *The Hunger Games*, *Divergent*, or *Squid Game*.

When investing, they're nervous about "risky" stocks or real estate and prefer passive, market-wide ETFs—essentially, crowd investing—so that, if there's a crash, at least they go down with all their friends. Aside from heavy borrowing to pay for college, which they figure they cannot rationally avoid, Millennials are incurring less debt. They're replacing credit cards with cash cards and taking out fewer mortgages, mostly by buying "tiny houses" or just by renting rather than owning.

Sheer precarity has persuaded Millennials to defer or avoid rites of passage that earlier generations took for granted: moving, getting married, having children. Among young adults, rates for all these activities have sunk to historic lows. Millennials bring an unromantic prudence to such choices that often surprises their parents. Young women are more likely to insist on partners who can be providers. Marriage comes after the achievement of economic security, not before, and a low credit score can be a relationship ender. Homogamy—marriage within the same socioeconomic class—has soared to levels not seen since the pre–World War I Edwardian era. Prenups and separate bank accounts are becoming more common among newlyweds.

For their Boomer or Xer parents, "cool" once meant being a rebel, nonconformist, or risk-taker. For today's young adults, it means honest, friendly, or competent.

The struggle to achieve, behave, fit in, risk-manage, and please others—all at the same time—is pushing Millennials toward an optimizing, menu-driven, even perfectionist approach to life that often leaves them chronically stressed: every aspect of "adulting" must be step-by-step learned and mastered. Young women, excelling at this play-by-the-rules game plan, have surged ahead of young men in higher-ed degrees and in preparation for professional careers. In pursuit of greater focus, they have fueled the last decade's largest increase in Adderall and Ritalin prescriptions. They also increasingly complain of burnout. Generalized anxiety disorder is by far the fastest-growing psychiatric complaint among both the men and women of this generation, the result of rarely being able to let go.

Anxiety may help explain the remarkable decline in courtship and sexual activity among Millennials, first among teens and later among single young adults. Few are fully comfortable with the rituals of dating, and many fear the risks of casual sex. Young men feel threatened by their inability to provide, young women by their inability to be provided for. Most struggle to find a place for dependence and intimacy in a world that prizes independence and invulnerability. Compared to their moms and dads, they tend to regard the weakening of established gender roles as more a burden than a triumph. They are much likelier to agree—both men and women, and across the political spectrum—that "feminism has done more harm than good."

Millennials also express surprisingly traditional views about marriage. They regard married family life as such an important bulwark of social health that they believe it ought to be available to everyone, including gay men and women. Yet here again Millennials in their late twenties and thirties have trouble making it work in their own lives. A record share of them continue to avoid marriage because they feel they aren't prepared for it, can't afford it, don't dare risk it, can't find a reliable partner—or all of the above.

Millennials often hear Boomers (and many Xers) complain about their "can't even" fragility. "Teacup syndrome," they call it: Lacking resilience, today's youth break rather than bend under pressure. Millennials respond that their challenges are greater, their standards are higher, and their time horizons are longer than those of their parents, whose wacko, what-me-worry life story should hardly be regarded as a standard worth following. Back in his day, "Old Economy Steve" could stumble his way into a comfy middle-class salary and benefits with a college degree that cost him almost nothing (or with no degree at all). But who wants to argue with Boomers, a generation better known for talking than listening? "OK, Boomer" became the Millennials' dismissive signal that they wish to cut the conversation short.

As they mature, Millennials are shifting America's culture in a left-brained direction: toward rationalism, objectivity, and top-down systemizing. Moving into universities as students (and now as teachers), they have triggered a vast expansion of STEM curricula and professional prep—and a massive exodus away from the liberal arts and humanities that were once so attractive to young Boomers. The former, they believe, help us cooperate and build a better world; the latter merely foment argument between incomparable and subjective "perspectives." Millennials are spearheading the steep recent growth in the share of all Americans who identify with "no religion." Many suspect that godly dogma has helped to splinter public truth and breed rabbit-hole conspiracy thinking, benefitting no one.

Where Boomer young adults once prioritized, in popular culture, the individual and the interior, Millennials are prioritizing the opposite— the collective and the exterior. In dress, Millennials prefer "normcore." In music, they express every emotion—except rage or confrontation. A large share of their movies are formulaic sequels in which the naughty or nihilistic edges are smoothed over. Unlike Xers, they value fitting in and dread being alone. Unlike Boomers, they prize facts about the world and shun metaphors about its meaning. In a society in which conservatives are rule-breakers, Millennials are the progressives. With cancel culture, Millennials celebrate *silencing* the transgressors.

In politics, Millennials have become the most Democratic-leaning generation of young-adult voters since the G.I.s during the New Deal. Ever since the 2006 midterms—and, more notably, since Obama's first election in 2008—roughly 60 percent of Millennials have voted Democratic. Driving this partisan age tilt, survey evidence suggests, is the contrasting emphasis each party gives to empowering "the community" (overwhelmingly favored by Millennials) rather than "the individual" (much more favored by Xers and Boomers). Even *within* each party, the generational contrast is stark. Compared to their party's leaders, Millennial Democrats talk less about rights and due process; Millennial Republicans talk less about tax cutting and deregulation. What both groups talk more about is how their side can build an entirely new kind of community structured around new rules.

Among Millennials, notoriously, "socialism" is almost as popular as "capitalism." In the 2020 election, more than half said they would support or be open to supporting a "Democratic Socialist" for national office. Yet waving this red flag is a surprisingly even-tempered generation of young voters—more likely than older voters to call themselves "moderate" and less likely to call themselves angry or extreme. Against the libertarian distrustfulness of their parents, Millennials believe that the nation needs a comprehensive system. With leadership, cooperation, talent, and expertise, they believe this system can be made to work. And until it does, there will be no secure framework within which they can build a better future for themselves, their country, and the world.

While Millennials have been around for a while—their first wave is now reaching forty—they remain a study in unfamiliar contrasts.

In their aspirations for the nation, they've staked out a political agenda that borders on the revolutionary. While all generations express rising discontent about America's current direction, Millennials are the most likely (on both the left and the right) to believe that the current regime is fundamentally broken and needs to be overhauled if not replaced. More than older generations, they think the solution may require granting extraordinary powers to one side and discarding precedents and procedures that impede the establishment of a new regime.

In their cultural norms, on the other hand, Millennials don't seem revolutionary at all. They get along swell with their parents. They shun risk and disorder. They prefer entertainment that affirms more than shocks. They apply cost-benefit algorithms to solving any sort of problem—including saving the world, an approach they call "effective altruism." They work tirelessly to make big organizations run efficiently.

And as they grow older, they often find themselves attracted to traditional social roles (in marriage, family, or church) simply because life is more functional and cooperative that way.

A decade ago, former Yale professor William Deresiewicz wrote a book about first-wave Millennial college grads and called them "Excellent Sheep" in a book with that name. (Their idea of diversity, he mordantly observed, is like "thirty-two flavors of vanilla.") A decade earlier, after interviewing incoming college students, columnist David Brooks called them "Organization Kids." That label marks a fitting contrast to their archetypal opposites, first-wave Boomers, whose college grads gained an early reputation as Up-the-Organization Kids.

From first-born to last-born, Boomers and Millennials are both generations of trends—but in contrary directions. For Boomers, the protection, rules, and pressure of childhood gradually eased with each successive cohort. For Millennials, they gradually strengthened. First-born Millennials sometimes think of themselves as "Xennials," the youngest Americans who can still recall vestiges of an Xer-like free-range childhood. For later-born Millennials, especially the tightly tethered "attachment babies" arriving after the early nineties, the childhood perimeter was smaller, tighter, and better guarded.

The two generations are also filling two very different roles in history. Boomers served as a youth bridge for a society moving into an Awakening. Millennials serve as a youth bridge for a society moving into a Crisis. The history of the former has been endlessly retold. The history of the latter is still missing its climax—and thus has not yet been written.

Toward the Climax: Powers Unite

"I promise as a good American to do my part," one hundred thousand young people chanted on Boston Commons in 1933. "I will help President Roosevelt bring back good times." These young G.I.s were touted by Malcolm Cowley as "brilliant college graduates" who "pictured a future in which everyone would be made secure by collective planning and social discipline"—whereas at the same age, reported Cowley, his own Lost peers had grown "disillusioned and weary" and "skeptical and afraid of bigness."

During their childhood, G.I.s had been fussed over by protective parents determined to raise up kids as good as the Lost Generation had been bad. Youth clubs, vitamins, safe playgrounds, pasteurized milk, child labor laws, even Prohibition: All were efforts to keep these kids away from the danger and depravity of the prior generation. Rates of crime, accidental death, suicide, and alcoholism among youth declined from their high levels during Teddy Roosevelt's presidency. Thanks to a nationwide movement to start new public schools, the share of kids with high-school diplomas climbed from barely 10 percent (for first-wave G.I.s) to more than 50 percent (for the last wave). This was the largest one-generation gain in educational attainment in American history.

G.I.s responded by growing up as the straight-arrow achievers that adults had been praying for—as the first Boy Scouts, the first Miss Americas, and (with Charles Lindbergh in 1927) the first All-American Heroes. "There's no such thing as a bad boy," Father Flanagan had declared when G.I.s were little, distinguishing them from the "bad kids" which until then had been a media obsession.

By the mid-1920s, cynicism and individualism were out on college campuses; optimism and cooperation were in. Students learned to police themselves through what social historian Paula Fass describes as a "peer society" of strict collegial standards. A new youth vernacular spoke of trust and geometric order, of "levelheaded" and "regular guys" who were "on the square," "fit in," and could be "counted on."

When the Great Depression struck, young people came to be known not as alienated youths, but as the "Locked-Out Generation" of America's "submerged middle class." Realizing that the Missionary-imposed New Deal restacked the deck in their favor, they came to regard federal authority as a trusted friend who would always be there to help them. Thanks to government, uniformed young adults planted trees, cut trails, and built dams that brought power and water to their communities. Clean-cut "apple-pie socialists" argued about which system "worked best." Demonstration banners defended the dictatorship of the proletariat as patriotic—as in "Communism is Twentieth Century Americanism." Their most radical folk poets wrote encomia to massive concrete public works: "Your power is turning our darkness to dawn," sang Woody Guthrie, "so roll on Columbia, roll on."

While the souring economy dampened many a career and marriage plan, young G.I.s were determined to act on the 4-H motto and "Make the Best Better." Older people lent them direction and help. America "cannot always build the future for our youth," said FDR on the eve of World War II, "but we can build our youth for the future." Young people cast a reported 80 percent of their first-time votes for FDR in 1932 and 89 percent in 1936—by far the largest youth mandates ever recorded. Roosevelt thereupon proclaimed that "the very objectives of young people have changed," away from "the dream of the golden ladder—each individual for himself" and toward the dream of "a broad highway on which thousands of your fellow men and women are advancing with you." Before long, these young people, now fully in uniform, crowded onto roads and seaways in order to save the nation.

Wartime service did indeed become a "broad highway" of advancement for this generation. All races, ethnicities, genders, and regions contributed. And all ages. During the war, the military draft required every man age eighteen to forty-five to show up for service, sweeping almost every G.I. birth cohort into its net. To be sure, late-wave G.I.s bore most of the combat: The median age of service was twenty-six. Yet one in twelve who served was thirty-eight or older. And those who were ineligible for combat service often served in a myriad of supporting roles, from civil defense to public health. All were told that their service would not end until the war was over.

General Marshall heralded them all as "the best damn kids in the world"—a world they proceeded to conquer. To cite the motto of their Seabees (naval construction crews who built airfields overnight on Pacific islands): "The difficult we do at once. The impossible takes a little longer."

This was the last time the Hero archetype entered a Fourth Turning.

From early childhood on, Millennials have been saturated with pop-culture superheroes as no other youth generation since the G.I.s in the

1930s. For young G.I.s, the heroes included the Shadow, Buck Rogers, Flash Gordon, the Phantom, and eventually, by the eve of World War II, Superman, Batman, and Captain America. For young Millennials, they now include many of the same characters, profitably reimagined by the DC and Marvel Comics franchises.

Perhaps the earliest and most iconic of these superhero brands was Power Rangers, which has remained a bestseller for kids ever since the early 1990s. These are wholesome kid soldiers in bright, primary-color uniforms—no relation to the junk-fed mutant turtles of the Xer child era. When summoned, these ordinary youths transform themselves into thunderbolting evil-fighters. Cheerful, confident, and energetic, Power Rangers are nurtured to succeed in the face of great odds. Whatever they do—from displaying martial arts to piloting high-tech weaponry—they choreograph as a group. Their very mottos, "Powers Unite" and "The Power of Teamwork Overcomes All," speak of strength in cooperation and energy in conformity. Their missions are not chosen by themselves, but by an immaterial elder wizard in whose wisdom they have total trust.

Imagine, sometime in the late 2020s, that federal and state governments are commandeering a comprehensive makeover of America's public infrastructure. While the trigger may be some near-term emergency (mobilization for national defense, stimulus response to an economic crash), the goals will include long-term payoffs (higher economic productivity, less carbon emissions, better schools, more livable public spaces). If executed on the same scale as the New Deal, such an effort would employ perhaps 15 million Americans, both in the public and private sectors. A nationwide rebuild on this scale would require planners and communities to reimagine how we want to live and work—the first such national reimagining in eighty or ninety years.

The vast majority of these workers will be Millennials. They will be happy to find a stable job and to contribute (at last) to something enduring that benefits everybody. Most of the techies, designers, and supervisors will also be Millennials. By now the last big bulge of government workers, first-wave Xers hired in the early eighties, will be hitting age sixty-two and retiring. This will leave thirty-something team leaders entirely in charge of ambitious new billion-dollar projects, from smart highways, transit loops, and universal IoT Wi-Fi to urban reconstruction, modular housing, and solar and geothermal power farms.

Millennials will be the ideal generation to carry out this mission. Many grew up volunteering for public causes and designing communities in dozens of popular video games like *SimCity*, *Civilization*, *Age of Empires*, *Tropico*, and *FarmVille*. They have always excelled at large projects that require working in teams, minimizing defects, meeting measurable goals, and integrating diverse pieces into a workable whole. Imagine the next wave of forty-year-old tech-engineers creating networked systems that transform our community lives—our neighborhoods, our commutes, our parks, our malls, our civic centers—just as thoroughly as the last two generations of forty-year-olds created networked devices that transformed our personal lives.

Emerging Millennial leaders will also become the most effective public face for this national makeover. Unlike older leaders, they will be able to make the case soberly, citing cost-benefit numbers and disclaiming any partisan rancor. What's more, older Americans will by now recognize that any new material framework for community life will necessarily matter less to them than to the young. Millennials will mostly be building it, mostly living in it, mostly benefitting from it, and mostly paying off the debt incurred to finance it—on top of the trillions in other liabilities they will be inheriting.

The Millennial perspective on the Crisis era will be very different from that of older Americans. For Boomers, the Crisis will mark a transcendent culmination; for Xers, a brutal midlife course correction. But for Millennials, it will be a launching pad for adult lives that will still lie largely ahead of them: They will have yet to set the national agenda, assume power as national political leaders, or see their children come of age. Unlike their parents, Millennials will not be able to recall, even in childhood, a moment when anything built or done by "we, the people" wasn't broken, decrepit, or distrusted. This will be their opportunity to construct a new and modern national community that works—and that they will be able to enjoy and take pride in as they grow older.

Today, to be sure, all this remains an opportunity waiting to be seized. The way forward will be difficult. At every step, this generation's trademark confidence will be threatened by adversity.

The Millennials' most pressing challenge in the 2020s will be getting themselves off the ground economically—a project initially delayed by the Great Recession and delayed again by the pandemic. Until recently, most of this generation could figure they still had plenty of time. During the 2020s, a growing share will realize they're running out of time to catch up on marriages, children, and real careers.

Once fully expecting to surpass their parents' living standards while ushering in more equitable outcomes, Millennials may sense impending failure on both counts. More than ever, young households will fear that they will never match the net worth of their parents, young men that they will never outearn their fathers, and young contractors that "middle-class" job security will forever remain out of their grasp. Within their own ranks, Millennials will see a hardening of class and income hierarchy—reinforced by privileged family backgrounds and bequests, by expensive credentials, by selective marriages, and by slowing business dynamism.

Surveys already show that Millennial stress is overwhelmingly driven by economic worries. Among first-wavers in their late thirties, the toll is appearing in rising opioid death rates; among late-wavers in their early twenties, in rising suicide rates. In the next few years, the realization will hit Millennials: Rather than reverse the social disintegration of America propelled by their Boomer and Xer parents, their generation is coming to embody its most extreme manifestation.

History suggests that Millennials will resist this prospect, as will most of their aging parents, who will still regard this generation as "special." A growing number of young adults in both political parties will seize opportunities to re-establish a republic with rules designed to benefit all members, to strengthen cooperative behavior, and to define and safeguard a common future. Unlike young Boomers, they won't try to tear the system down (clearly, it's already in shambles), but rather to build up something new that functions.

As young public leaders, Millennials will be helped by the vacuum left behind by Xers and late-wave Boomers, who are poorly represented in elected offices. As young voters, they will gain clout by organizing and going to the polls in higher numbers. The Millennial engagement surge is already underway. Since 2016, the voting participation rate among youth has risen even faster than among older Americans. In 2020 53 percent of eligible Americans under thirty voted, the highest share since the voting age was lowered to eighteen in 1971.

Over the coming decade, Millennials will flock toward older leaders who hold out the promise of national salvation through collective action. They will enlist in crusades urging immediate action to avert catastrophes: climate-change disaster, economic ruin, dictatorial rule, end-stage plutocracy, or global subjugation by hostile foreign powers. A "big brand" generation, Millennials will gravitate toward only one or two such Gray Champions. For Millennials, irresistible scale will be essential: Doing something big, *anything big*, will be more important than doing *nothing*. Regardless of what urgent agenda is prescribed, that agenda will empower the community to bulldoze over entrenched private interests and to establish new public goals—establish, in effect, a new constitution that again prioritizes the republic's future. Representing this future, of course, Millennials will see themselves.

Of all generations pushing society through the Crisis era, Millennials will thereby become the most propulsive. Let elder Boomers conceive the visionary ends. Let midlife Xers furnish the practical means. But then let young-adult Millennials, working together, furnish the critical mass that moves their entire society rapidly in one direction.

Despite the growing level of partisan stress in national public life, Millennials will continue to have close personal relationships with older generations. No "generation gap" will arise with Boomers or Xers over personal values. Rather than argue with elders, Millennials will join them when possible to achieve common goals and, as always, to seek out their personal advice—about the "ought-to-dos" from Boomers and about the "want-to-dos" from Xers. But Millennials will always see their own peer personality as corrective to the shortcomings of their elders—to the impracticality of most Boomers and to the indiscipline of most Xers.

The deepening Crisis-era mood will push the pop culture further in the direction that Millennials have already moved it—toward lower-stress moods, less original branding, and more conventional plotlines. In the cheerful spirit of giving no offense, stricter guardrails will be placed around acceptable language and manners. Many Gen-X comedians, now unwelcome in college towns, will find themselves banned from a broadening swath of mainstream networks. In Millennial hands, entire Xer genres, like hip-hop, will continue to grow more wholesome. Pointing the way is Millennial rapper Kendrick Lamar: "My new meaning for 'keepin' it gangsta' is . . . really about takin' care of your family, handlin' your business and puttin' positive energy out there where everybody can benefit from it, not just yourself."

Millennials will also remain surprisingly active, especially on social media, in policing acceptable behavior *within* their generation. They will steadily raise the politeness bar, and they will stigmatize those who don't meet it. High-achieving young adults, underneath their inclusive veneer, are turning out to be strict meritocrats, perfectly willing to exclude those who lack the ability or desire to earn a credential. More than Xers, they trust experts. Millennials will be especially harsh toward the rapidly rising number of their trust-fund peers who inherit wealth, most of whom (unlike high-end Xers) already feel guilty about their own good fortune. This new "social ethic"—based on the Millennial premise that social inhibitions can enhance the power of the group—will grow vastly more influential during the coming decade.

Most Millennials will continue to adhere to low-risk lifestyles. Yet as the Crisis era moves toward its climax, growing numbers will be drawn to participation in high-risk political movements and, ultimately, in an emergency mobilization of civic life. Slowly at first, and then in a rush, millions of life trajectories will suddenly change course. The first to welcome this shift will be those young adults who feel the least attachment to the old regime and care the least about its survival. Some may be idealistic optimists who carefully prepped themselves to serve defunct institutions they now realize have betrayed them. More may be quarter-life-crisis dead-enders: single, bored, and stuck in futureless jobs.

Inevitably, the majority of these life switchers will be male. They will include young men who see no useful role for their toxic gender in the old regime. Or who are unmarriageable due to their lack of prosocial skills. Or who find disintegrated America so uninspiring that they immerse themselves in alternative fantasy worlds—commanding troll armies, winning swag in VR sim arenas, trading all day in crypto and NFTs. Imagine a whole generation of distracted men suddenly contributing their energy and talents to real-world activities that can engage their imagination: joining teams that matter, winning conflicts, exercising power, building big new things, and changing how the world works. At the end of the Unraveling era, government had become the soft "mommy" sector and commerce the hard "daddy" sector. By the end of the Crisis era, those identities may be reversed.

As the Crisis deepens, the re-engagement of young men will mark a saecular inflection in the social mood every bit as important as the re-valuation of young women nearly a half century earlier during the Awakening. And it will clarify the archetypal contrast between Boomer and Millennial life stories. The Prophet, raised during an era of strong social order and a wide gender-role divide, ultimately weakens the social order and narrows the gender-role gap. The Hero follows a reversed narrative and ultimately strengthens the social order and widens the gender-role gap. The Prophet compensates for a riskier personal life by opting for fewer risks in public life. For the Hero, the compensation works in the other direction.

Millennials will approach the Crisis climax showcasing many of the peer traits for which they are already well known: compliance with authority, desire to contribute, instinct for teamwork, and patience in the pursuit of long-term goals. Yet with so much at stake, Millennials will also display further traits that hardly anyone (yet) associates with them. Even in the face of devastating setbacks and extreme privation, they will be able to maintain their cohesion and optimism. In time, after gaining confidence in attaining modest public goals, they will happily embrace even the most Promethean challenges—from overhauling the economy and rebuilding infrastructure at home to joining in grand alliances and rebuilding nations abroad.

If their mobilization includes service in war, which seems probable, Millennials will cast aside any earlier pacifism and rally to take on adversaries in deadly struggles that they know will require their utmost exertion and (perhaps) sacrifice. At some discrete moment in the Crisis era, every young-adult generation follows this abrupt rite-of-passage script. One year, they are agreeable, well-socialized young people averse to violence following a long era of peace. The next, they face the likelihood of conflict on an unimaginable scale. This moment happened in the fall of 1941, in the winter of 1861, in the spring of 1775, and in the summer of 1675.

The Hero archetype will not be averse to militarized mass violence, just to uncontrolled *personal* violence—quite the opposite of Boomer youth back in the Awakening. Where Boomer youth once screamed against duty and discipline, Boomers and Xers will demand and receive both from Millennial enlistees. While Millennials of all ages may have to put their personal lives on hold for some period of time, late-wave Millennials (especially those born soon after 9/11) are likely to participate most fully—and bear the greatest sacrifice—in any military campaigns. As was true for the G.I. Generation, national recruitment in response to a national emergency could prove to be an especially powerful coming-of-age slingshot for the Millennials' youngest birth cohorts. And, as was true for late-wave G.I.s, after the Ekpyrosis is over they will likely be collectively unrecognizable to anyone who knew them beforehand.

Near the climax of the Crisis, the full power of this rising generation will assert itself, providing the nation with a highly effective instrument for imposing order on an ungovernable society or an unruly world. Once a Crisis-era leader commits the nation to clear a path for a bright future, the Millennial-propelled juggernaut will appear unstoppable.

As the Crisis era enters its culminating Ekpyrosis and public activity reaches its moment of maximum fury and consequence, the future of America and every generation will hang on the outcome. Yet the outcome will matter to Millennials most of all. Older Americans, no matter how sympathetic to the goals of the new regime, will always be bound by earlier habits of thought and behavior. Only Millennials will be able to imagine that the fate of the nation will rest mostly on their success or failure and that the Crisis outcome will likely define the rest of their collective life story.

Looking ahead from today's vantage point, most Millennials might doubt America's ability to pull together in the face of adversity or their own generation's willingness to pull together around any common public goal. Yet one lesson of history is that the real danger may be quite the opposite—that the nation pulls together all too brutally or recklessly. The young-adult hunger for social discipline and centralized authority could take an ominous turn in the 2020s and enable Millennial brigades to put their energy and mass behind the agendas of older demagogues. Whatever startling new type of regime arises to compete with the old regime over the next decade—this may include a right- or left-leaning autocracy animated by class or ethnic or sectional antagonism—we can be sure that Millennials will be doing most of the heavy lifting.

In his 1935 novel *It Can't Happen Here*, fifty-year-old Sinclair Lewis warned that the rising G.I. Generation might choose to follow anyone, even a revolutionary populist, who promised to restore order, equality, and prosperity. So may many older Americans be warning, once again, ninety years later. To be sure, no generation looks forward to a dark and dictatorial future, least of all Millennials themselves. Unless pushed in that direction by sheer desperation, they will struggle to establish a new regime that offers better lives to most citizens while also revitalizing the best ideals of liberal democracy.

But whatever happens, there will be a new regime—and this regime will collectively define the Millennials for the rest of their lives. Its new constitution and infrastructure will be built largely with their hands and perhaps purchased with their lives. Its achievements will be exaggerated, and its weaknesses concealed, by their later retelling of how it all came to be.

To Millennials themselves, the new regime will always seem glorious—a happy marriage of left-brain planning and collective effort. No other generation will view it so benignly, least of all the first future crop of children who grow up with no memory of how it came to be.

HOMELANDER YOUTH

The Homeland Generation (2006?–?) today comprises 75 million children whose oldest members are now in high school. History suggests that its name will remain in flux until its leading edge is nearing thirty. For now, the most popular label is Generation Z. Alternative labels include Zoomers (a play off "Gen Z" and "Boomers"), iGen (a reference to the impact of mobile digital tech), and Plurals (an allusion to this generation's tolerance of racial, ethnic, and gender-role diversity).

Our tentative label, "Homelanders," was chosen by our readers in an online survey we conducted in 2006. Several different names were suggested and voted on. Homeland Generation was the winner, apparently because the decade of the 2000s was marked by 9/11, the War on Terror, the creation of the Department of Homeland Security, and a sense that the "homeland" was no longer safe. Readers also noted a worldwide shift toward nationalism and a rising identification with one's roots. A few mentioned that this generation of children is literally kept more at "home" than any earlier generation of kids, thanks to the protective child-raising style of Gen-X parents.

The first Homelander birth cohort was born around 2006, shortly before the onset of the Great Recession. On schedule, the first cohort of a likely Artist archetype will have no memory of life before the Crisis era. The last cohort will be born sometime in the late 2020s.

Prequel: Safe Spaces

What's most striking about America's newest generation of children is that, well, there's nothing very striking about them.

To begin with, they're not very visible to most adults, in part because they're relatively small in number and also because they are seldom seen unsupervised outside of their homes or classrooms. When adults talk to them (better get permission first!), most seem well-rounded, earnest, respectful of achievers, and—though a bit awkward and self-conscious, as kids always are—agreeable. Look at their best-known actors (Jacob Tremblay, Iain Armitage), actresses (Aubrey Anderson-Emmons, Mckenna Grace), and athletes (Katie Grimes), and you notice many of the same traits in exaggerated form. They are super-coached by a tight crew of family and trainers. They are super-focused on meeting the highest professional standards. Interacting with adult fans, they are often super-nice, apologetically going out of their way to make *their adult interviewers* feel at ease.

Today's Homelander kids are still perhaps a decade or more away from a public moment that will define them as a generation in the eyes of older Americans. Yet even now we see hints that such an event will likely have a subtler, gentler feel than the events that have defined other recent youth generations. As teen comedian Dylan Roche puts it, "Older people always ask me, why can't kids today be more like they were. Well, the answer's simple: Most of the wild crap you did is now illegal." This deadpan joke reinforces an old truth: One generation's punch line is the next generation's *set-up* line.

In broad brush, the Homelanders' emerging peer personality can be regarded as the culminating endpoint of major Millennial trends. Special, close to parents, sheltered, risk-averse, compliant, cooperative, agreeable: All the traits that were steadily more pronounced during the Millennial youth era are now maxing out in the Homelander childhood era—even to a degree that many older Americans suspect may not be functional. At what point, they wonder, does sheltered become *oversheltered*, agreeableness *docility*, and risk-aversion *disabling anxiety*?

Like all generations in childhood, Homelanders are being shaped by their location in history and by the peer personality of their parents.

Let's look first at location in history. Homelander kids have no memory of a prosperous or confident America—that is, of living in a country that isn't either plunging into a recession or struggling to get out of one. Or of a country that isn't riven by partisan rancor and despondent about its long-term prospects. While children don't always understand the issues, they understand the adult mood perfectly: It's a dangerous world out there, beset by sudden poverty, homelessness, armed violence, and rage in high places. The lessons? Stay close to home, follow the rules, and don't upset older people who are doing their best to take care of you.

One obvious and measurable impact of hard times on Homelanders is the sheer reduction in their number. Would-be parents, especially Millennials, are deciding they can't afford to have kids. Since 2007, the U.S. total fertility rate has fallen almost every year. In 2018, the total fertility rate fell below its earlier low point (in 1976), permitting Gen-Xers to pass the "unprecedented baby bust" label from themselves to Homelanders. In 2021, during the pandemic, 3.6 million Homelanders were born, which is *nearly one million less* than would have been born at the 2007 rate. Public schools are emptying. Many second- and third-tier liberal arts colleges, looking down the road, are preparing to downsize or close their doors.

Immigration has also fallen sharply since the GFC, which translates into fewer children arriving in young immigrant families. While the fraction of all U.S. children who live in Xer- and Millennial-led immigrant families remains substantial (roughly one-quarter), a growing share of these children are themselves born in America—making them a growing "second generation" generation of Americans. They are increasingly Asian rather than Hispanic. They are more spread out geographically across America. And a growing share speak English at home as a first language.

As for their parents, while both Gen-Xers and Millennials are now raising children, Generation X is still firmly in charge of the Homelander world. Gen-Xers are the parents of most Homelanders born through 2011, which means they will remain the parents of most Homelander kids in K-12 schools until the mid-2020s. Being the older parental generation, moreover, they will continue to have a dominant influence on most of the institutions that shape children's lives, like school boards, PTAs/PTOs, curriculum task forces, and state legislatures.

What do Xers want for their Homelander kids? "Being there for them" pretty much sums it up. No matter how chaotic and dangerous their own lives, Xers take pride in providing their kids with the stability, shelter, and reassurance that they themselves never had. Years before the pandemic transformed the oldest Homelanders into lockdown "quaran-teens," this grown-up home-alone generation of parents was doing its best to raise never-alone offspring, kids who have trouble recalling even one moment when some trusted adult did not know exactly where they were.

Unlike Boomers raising Millennials thirty years ago, Xers today don't view child-rearing as a way to save the world, make a perfect child, or self-actualize the parent. It's just a practical means of making your child totally safe, never afraid, decently behaved, and sensitive to the needs of others. Forget the Boomer "supermom" who strives to realize her true potential. Now it's the Xer "good enough mom" who just tries to roll with life the best she can.

Boomer parents once read aspirational childcare manuals with New Agey advice about how to spend quality time with their children—that is, how to deepen their relationship with children and teach them better values. Being a good parent was to be a good person. By contrast, Xers read manuals that are more behavioral and prescriptive—full of dos and don'ts—with less emphasis on how the parent should feel about it. Child-rearing is explained like any other practical skill: There are more and less effective ways to get the job done. Xer parents read tip books by hired "super-nannies" and cull secrets from animal trainers like "dog whisperer" Cesar Millan. You don't have to worry about being a good person. And quality time? No, in the Xer parental code, that's Boomer hypocrisy. You've got to give children *quantity time*. You've got to put in your hours and *be there*.

Committed to hands-on presence, Xers are making it happen: For parents of all educational levels, average parental time spent with children has continued to rise since 2000. To make time for kids, Xer parents are cutting back on time for every other purpose—paid work, household chores, nights out with the spouse, and (since the pandemic) commuting. Dual-working parents are tag-teaming to make sure someone is at home. Single parents are getting their own parents to help out. And divorce rates among Xers continue to decline. During the Homelander child era, the share of children being raised in two-parent families has been growing for the first time in at least fifty years.

Also boosting parental presence is the rapid growth of multigenerational households, which makes more adults available to fill the in-loco-parentis role. Vacation? There's always the "grand-travel" option (Homelander child with Boomer grandparent). For Homelander kids, entertainment is increasingly enjoyed at home with other family members. In the 2010s, "co-viewing" and "family TV" became media industry bywords for profitability, along with the now-ubiquitous PG-13 rating (safe enough for the kids, yet interesting enough for the adults). Three-quarters of parents say they watch videos with their kids several times a week or more. Though parents do worry about kids spending too much time on mobile phones, they hesitate to take phones away from their kids because phones are also their means of supervising them.

When they cannot be physically with their kids, these parents are all about 24/7 oversight and control. They make sure there are baby monitors and videocams in bedrooms, GPS trackers in their kids' backpacks, strict ID screening at school, text check-ins during the day, and wristbands at every public event. They install "guardian" cyberfilters on their kids' devices, and (in many states) mandate that high schools install keystroke trackers on every school-issued laptop. Thanks to Xer parents and voters, malls enforce teen curfews; teachers ban rough-and-tumble recess activities; schools stage SWAT-style "active shooter" drills with kids present; and passers-by are encouraged to call 911 if they spot an unaccompanied ten-year-old walking alone in a public place.

Xer parents are instinctively distrustful of K-12 schools, where they can't observe directly what is going on—and where Xers themselves know that they received a notoriously poor education. In thousands of school districts, parents are battling school boards and state educators over curriculum, grading systems, and book censorship. Continuing a trend pioneered by some Boomer parents, a growing share of Xer parents are opting out of public schools in favor of local private schools or homeschooling.

Yet whatever the school, public or private, these parents are insisting on more and stricter rules governing behavior and the curriculum. Indeed, Homelander kids encounter a veritable floodtide of rules as soon as they set foot on school property: rules on talking, on touching, on playing, on running; rules on what you may and may not say; jot-and-tittle rules about how assignments must be completed; draconian regulations on scanning for personal possessions (omg, don't get caught with an aspirin or butter knife!). Oh yes, and rules about how to dress: One-fifth of public schools now require students to wear uniforms; one-half enforce a strict dress code. In some cases, rules for prom night run over ten single-space pages.

Wouldn't just a bit of common-sense discretion make more sense? Of course. But few Xer parents trust the teachers' discretion, and few teachers trust the parents not to sue them.

Underlying this embrace of rules is a newly ascendent educational competency, "social and emotional learning" (SEL), which is now woven into most curricula. The warm and fuzzy label is a bit misleading. Yes, SEL does teach kids to be empathic and helpful to others. But more fundamentally, it teaches them to exercise self-control—that is, to follow a rule—which SEL defines as the ability to "manage emotions" and "resist an impulse for the sake of someone else's priorities." Homelanders need to be well trained in SEL in order to study for multiple-choice quizzes in kindergarten. Or to decipher complex "expectations matrices" of dos and don'ts on the classroom wall by the third grade. Or to win today's staggeringly difficult national Spelling Bee by the eighth grade (recent winning words include "erysipelas," "cernuous," and "murraya").

Back in the days of *Ferris Bueller's Day Off*, teens learned that rules didn't matter much: Xer teens could always figure out how to duck and feint and work their way around them. Today's Homelander teens are encountering a much less forgiving world. The meritocracy offers fewer top openings—and, for these, fewer young people who don't possess perfect qualifications can hope to apply. "Permanent records," meanwhile, are a lot more permanent in a searchable, digital universe: Youthful indiscretions are never forgotten or erased. For Homelanders, society is organized into discrete Dantean tiers. They extend from the top, where kids win awards and earn A-averages, to the bottom, where they are subject to suspensions, expulsions, courts, and social services.

So how are Homelanders turning out? What kind of emerging youth generation is being shaped by this tightening, even hothouse style of parental upbringing?

There is a great deal that should please older Americans. This is, for example, the most *wanted* generation of children in living memory—in the sense that a smaller share of pregnancies now end in abortions than in any year since *Roe v. Wade*, and possibly (though illegal abortions before 1973 can only be estimated) since the 1950s or 1960s. Much of this progress has been achieved through a dramatic reduction in teen pregnancies, which have always been the pregnancies most likely to be aborted.

These children are also growing up safer and healthier. During the Homelander era, mortality rates in infancy and childhood continue to decline. (The same cannot be said about their parents' age brackets.) The child poverty rate in 2019, measured so that it takes into account all government benefits, sank to the lowest ever in American history— 11 percent, less than half of what it had been twenty-five years earlier. It sank even lower during the pandemic.

According to our best estimates, most forms of bullying, fighting, and victimization of school-age children are also continuing to decline, along with teen pregnancy and alcohol and drug abuse. The pregnancy rate for Homelander teens is now barely a quarter of what it was for Gen-X teens in the early 1990s. The only drugs showing steady or rising prevalence among teens are those that adults have de facto legalized: cannabis and (nicotine) vaping. The opioid epidemic, a scourge among older Americans, has mercifully left teenagers largely untouched.

Beyond these positive behavioral indicators, the emerging Home-lander peer personality bears watching as well. In an adult world wracked by competitive egos, rising tribalism, and unleashed rage, here comes a new generation cultivating gentler virtues: tolerance, self-control, and sensitivity to the needs of others. At home, they are emotionally support-ive of their parents. Surveys show their biggest worries are about academic performance—not so much because they care themselves, but because they don't want to upset their parents. At school, they often ostracize peers who pick on the disabled or disadvantaged. They form support groups for one another. And they are more open about their own vulnerabilities ("tw" is online code for "trigger warning"; "cw" for "content warning"). All this may help explain the decline in fighting and bullying.

For Homelanders, as their "SEL" competency suggests, life is about controlling emotions to keep others happy. An astonishing number of recent blockbuster animated movies for Homelander kids—including *Frozen*, *Inside Out*, and *Encanto*—revolve around precisely this theme: emotional management. Recent re-enactments of the famous Stanford "marshmallow test" (measuring how long unsupervised four year olds can refrain from eating a marshmallow) confirm that today's Homeland children do indeed perform much better at tasks requiring self-control than their parents did at the same age. With their well-honed skill at working within the rules, Homelander youth mobilize for political change (on such mainstream issues as gun control, climate change, and racial tolerance) in the most earnest and unthreatening ways imaginable. They ally with parents and credentialed leaders, don't break laws, and speak deferentially about the experience of older people.

This emphasis on emotional management does have one obvious downside: unremitting stress. As they age into their teen years, a growing share of Homelanders are visiting counselors and psychiatrists, reporting suicidal thoughts, and going on meds—mainly amphetamine boosters for boys to calm them down, serotonin boosters for girls to cheer them up.

Here we see evidence that their parents' snowplow parenting style may have been excessive after all, by robbing kids of their need to experience agency, risk, and failure on their own.

All those "unboxing" videos, nonstop crib monitors, scheduled play-dates, overcoached ball games, homework tutors, and deluxe fidget toys (even "fidgeting" now needs a dedicated device) come at a psychic cost. These kids grow up in homes so well scrubbed that they develop asthma and other immune disorders. They do homework so attentively that they are reading more but enjoying reading less—and suffering chronic sleep deprivation. Among friends or in the classroom, they worry a lot about being judged or saying something "wrong." Most are so well provided for at home that inactivity and obesity are a growing emotional burden (and long-term health threat). An athletic few train in club sports so compliantly that repetitive stress injuries are now epidemic.

Unlike young Millennials, Homelander kids have been growing up in a nation whose prospects are obviously darkening—and with parents who are repeatedly cautioning them against risk. Unlike young Xers, young Homelanders don't want to grow up faster. They want to grow up *slower*. After all, why be in a rush to leave home for a life that adults so clearly find miserable?

While some find it easier (as kids) to attain transient celebrity on social media, most find it harder to imagine themselves (as adults) attaining enduring fame or fortune. According to surveys, fewer teens are daydreaming about becoming another Neil Armstrong or Oprah Winfrey or Steve Jobs. With their parents' encouragement, they are prepping for safer futures—career paths with better-defined stepping stones. More than ever, parents are pushing training in STEM fields (often in high-school "career academies") that have definable credentials. They're no longer hoping that their kid starts the next Apple. They're just hoping, at best, that he or she may someday get a secure job working there.

Less focused on grand public outcomes, Homelanders are paying more attention to the interior world of personal emotions.

This shift is starting to redirect the popular culture. In music, teens are now favoring a moodier, lower-energy, more disco-pop style, often performed by late-wave Millennials in their twenties. In their choice of TV shows and movies, Homelanders are turning away from such favorite Millennial genres as superheroes and high-school championships. They are turning instead toward nuanced story lines about close family relationships and conflicting social roles. They are fascinated more by inner tension than by outer action.

The new youth look points to softness and childlike vulnerability ("softgirl" or even "softboy"), which sometimes veers into pastoral escapism ("cottagecore"). This could be interpreted as a widening of gender-role differences. Equally, it could be interpreted as a search for some ageless and epicene alternative to any gender roles at all. The latter makes sense for a generation experiencing rising gender dysphoria along with a growing support for LGBTQ+ movements and the gender-effacing they/them pronoun. Many Homelanders look at adults' hyper-sexualized relationship culture and say, No, I would rather not grow up into all that. Among these Homelanders are the "e-girls" and "e-boys" who explore the gothier, edgier side of their generation's persona, though their rebel attitude is, for the most part, safely confined to their bedrooms as recorded on TikTok videos.

David Brooks, that veteran observer of generational trends, recently remarked of today's teens that, for them, "everything feels personalized and miniaturized." They believe that "the awfulness of the larger society is a given. The best you can do is find a small haven in a heartless world." Homelanders may sense that it is their role, like the Polynesian princess in *Moana*, to give the world back its heart. Unlike young Millennials, they define their challenges in terms of small acts of altruism. And very unlike young Xers, they are gently challenging adult norms in the name of fairness, sensitivity, and responsibility. *Time*'s 2022 "Kid of the Year" cover featured Orion Jean, age eleven, whom it dubbed "Ambassador for Kindness."

The British journalist Katie Agnew, a self-confessed "wild child" of the nineties, "drawn to short skirts, bad boys, and fast cars," confesses that her own kids ("born in the Noughties") could not be more different. They're sober and responsible. Seemingly small moral dilemmas bother them. When she wants a cigarette, she's the one who goes out on the porch hoping her kids don't notice. She wonders, "Why are today's children such boring goody-goodies?"

Toward the Climax: Caring and Connected

"Overprotective was a word first used to describe our parents," biographer Benita Eisler recalls of her Silent peers' Depression-era youth, when the Lost Generation ruled the child's world with a firm hand. A decade earlier, no one talked about "overprotection" because drawing tighter boundaries around children was still a gathering national crusade. After the *Literary Digest* demanded in the early 1920s a "reassertion of parental authority," a growing share of parents called for what historian Daniel Rodgers describes as "a new, explicit insistence on conformity into child life." Thus raised, G.I.s passed through childhood showing America's largest measurable one-generation improvement in health, size, education, and behavior.

By the time the Silent entered school, the mood had shifted. As the nation's economy shut down and parents worried about bigger problems like finding a job and putting food on the table, compliant child behavior was simply taken for granted. Children who complained about their dinners were told to recall various horrors around the world (like "the starving Armenians"). Leading parenting books spelled out a no-nonsense "total situation" style of parenting. Among these was a 1928 bestseller by behavioral psychologist John B. Watson, whose rules critics likened to the housebreaking of puppies. Favorite children's stories were about anthropomorphic animals, locomotives, and boats that were eager to please and that helped adults get big tasks done.

Whenever movie kids like Alfalfa or Shirley Temple encountered adults, they would "mind their manners." Yet also, through their guileless innocence, these same kids could pull on the heartstrings of the most hard-bitten parent. Audiences watching *Gone with the Wind* openly sobbed at a child's fatal fall from a pony, which no doubt reminded them all to keep a watchful eye over their own charges. Norman Rockwell's enduring image of Roosevelt's fourth freedom, "Freedom from Fear," showed a sleeping child lovingly guarded by Mother and Father.

When the Crisis era reached its climax, during World War II, America had perhaps the best-behaved teenagers in its history, but controversy simmered about whether the long absence of soldiering fathers (and the employment of mothers) would cause them to grow up emotionally handicapped. Government did its best to fill the parental gap: Having just created aid to families with dependent and disabled children during the Great Depression (these benefits are today covered by TANF and SSI), Congress went on to organize and pay for daycare, after-school care, and pregnancy benefits to all families that needed them for as long as the war lasted.

Times were indeed fearful for children who saw the world in black-and-white simplicity: There was our nation in uniform (good) and everybody else (bad). Any day could bring devastating news about the fate of their fathers. Author Frank Conroy recalls asking, as a boy, "what was in the newspapers when there wasn't a war going on." As they reached their teens, they did their best to contribute, hoarding ration stamps or saving dimes to buy war bonds. They had no energy left for defiance or crusades. The main issues they reported caring about were "race relations" and "world government," but even here their aspirations were lukewarm and abstract.

In its 1951 look at how Silent youth were behaving in the classroom, *Time* observed, "Educators across the U.S. complain that young people seem to have no militant beliefs. They do not speak out for anything. Professors who used to enjoy baiting students . . . now find that they cannot get a rise out of the docile notetakers in their classes. . . . Today's generation, either through fear, passivity or conviction, is ready to conform."

This was the last time the Artist archetype entered a Fourth Turning.

• • •

The oldest Xers, following Boomers, recall the experience of reaching their late teens forty years ago as something akin to arriving at a beach at the end of a long summer of wild goings-on. The beach crowd is exhausted, the sand is hot and full of debris—no place for walking barefoot. You step on a bottle and, if you don't you cut yourself, some cop yells at you for littering. You can't recall how you got here or if anyone knows where you are. The sun is directly overhead, beating down without mercy. There's no shelter in sight, or any patch of shade that hasn't already been taken by the entitled hordes who arrived before you.

Today, the experience of the oldest Homelanders reaching their late teens is very different—indeed, nearly the opposite. Imagine waking up in a clean, safe apartment with your family. It is equipped with every amenity, including climate control, but you realize, on further inspection, that it's actually a fortified bunker. Thanks to monitors, everyone knows exactly where you are. After leaving the apartment, possible only after complying with some burdensome protocol, you will be tracked and allowed only to enter other similar apartments, most of them also occupied by friends, family, or credentialed adults.

The Xer teens were lost and couldn't be found. Everything that sheltered or tracked them was torn down when the prior generation reached its teens, though Xers weren't sure why. They looked in vain for structure or rules that mattered. The early life experience for the Nomad archetype resembles agoraphobia. It is the feeling of wandering alone toward borderless horizons.

The Homelander teens are found and can't be lost. All the concrete barriers and monitors were installed when the prior generation reached its teens, though Homelanders aren't sure why. They look in vain for autonomy and independence. The early life experience for the Artist archetype resembles claustrophobia. It is the feeling of encountering, on all sides, a world crowded with the close and familiar.

History suggests that the Homelander youth experience will not change much during the rest of the 2020s.

Indeed, during the regulatory shutdowns of the recent global pandemic, the bunker analogy came almost literally to life. For months at a time, children of all ages were eating, playing, and schooling at home, always under close 24/7 surveillance, even while their parents (though more at risk from Covid-19) occasionally traveled out to accomplish necessary tasks. While parents and their kids were able to bond even more closely, most children, teens especially, fretted that their social and educational development had essentially been put on hold. After the pandemic, more parents are *choosing* to work or school their kids at home simply because it's cheaper or more convenient. That's how child-rearing works during the Homelander era: Each ratchet up in protectiveness becomes more or less permanent.

In the years to come, as the Crisis era moves toward its climax, this pattern of convulsive sheltering in the face of perceived danger is likely to continue. And the cumulative closing down of the childhood world is likely to intensify. The purpose will not only be to make the child's world safer. It will also be to make it easier for adults, especially parents, to get other things done in their lives *while* their children are safe.

During the Crisis climax itself, both purposes will loom large. On the one hand, the scale and ferocity of civic action will likely raise new perceived risks to families and children. On the other, the new regime will likely call many parents away from home for long periods of time. The parenting role of extended families will grow still larger. And to fill in the gaps, voters will deputize the broader community to do what parents alone cannot. By the late 2020s, the needs of Homelanders may motivate government to offer universal childcare and pediatric medicine (basic, standardized, yet effective) for the first time.

The overprotection of youth will continue to have its detractors. Lenore Skenazy, author of *Free-Range Kids*, regularly and eloquently lampoons its excesses. America infantilizes its youth, she insists, by criminalizing moms and dads for allowing their child to do things on their own outside the home. She blames the trend on America's new "worst-first" or "crisis" approach to parenting. Her words are well chosen, since they illustrate just why this approach has become so deeply rooted. Adjectives like "worst-first" and "crisis" no longer come across as hyperbole to most parents. Over the rest of this decade, they will instead be mere descriptors of the world parents see around them.

As time passes, Homelanders will continue to change the youth pop culture—by making it seem safer, more formulaic, and (probably) less interesting to older generations. Uncontroversial and blandly PC plot-lines will migrate from Disney to mainstream networks and streaming services. During their teens, Homelanders' political advocacy has tended to support the sober and risk-assessed consensus of experts—on issues ranging from school safety to the enforcement of mask and vaccine rules during the pandemic. As leading-edge Homelanders graduate from high school and move into college, youth political movements will continue to be broadly supportive of the views of their parents and their parents' communities. (To be sure, whether their parents continue to belong to a single political community remains an open question.)

When Homelanders do criticize older people, they will typically see themselves as speaking on behalf of the community against mavericks who fail to abide by the rules. "Karen" is the online meme they have already invented to tag such people—those who are selfish, rude, aggres-sive, and disputatious. Mindful of their rights, Karens always know why they don't need to be polite. "Generation Karen," by implication, mostly refers to Gen-Xers, people their parents' age.

Any response from Xers is likely to be reciprocal, and the one that seems to be emerging is the charge that Homelanders' very docility and amiability are threats to America's future. Declares one Bloomberg col-umnist, "What worries me is the complacency—the lack of question-ing or healthy acts of rebellion." She goes on: "What happened to youth pushing back against authority and being a little selfish? Instead, we have rule followers afraid to upset their communities. And it seems when they do push back against their elders it's to shame them for not following the rules."

During the 2020s, as the Crisis-era challenges intensify, Homeland-ers will have less interest in pursuing this argument with Xers—since they will feel that events have basically settled it in their favor. If Xers feel shamed by young people who behave better than they do, so be it. More readily than their parents, Homelanders will understand that a community in crisis almost always improves its odds of survival by fol-lowing *some* rule, even an imperfect rule, rather than following none. Coming-of-age youth will be noticed—or, perhaps, *not* noticed—for following such rules. Violent crime committed by youth may drop to multi-decade lows.

During the Crisis climax, younger Homelanders will become the fearful watchers and tiny assistants. Tethered close to home, they will do helpful little deeds like recycling, keyboarding, or tending to elders, the early twenty-first-century equivalents of planting World War II victory gardens or collecting scrap metal.

The older Homelanders, meanwhile, will be busy with their secondary and post-secondary education and training, readying themselves for adult careers pending critical events whose outcome will seem utterly uncertain. While studying, they will be keeping a close eye on fast-changing news reports and hoping that the next headline will tell them how breaking history will shape their future. They will also be getting to know Millennials just a few years older than they are. And they will be wondering if they will join them in their collective effort—or not.

These coming-of-age youth won't have any advance knowledge of who exactly will be asked to serve in the Millennial Crisis climax. Nor do we. This is why we must await the outcome of particular events before we can determine for certain the birth year boundary between Millennials and Homelanders. Two questions will be critical. First, at what age will Americans be asked to serve in the conflict? Second, when will the Crisis climax occur?

Age of service matters. During World War II, twenty was the youngest age at which large numbers of soldiers were fully engaged in front-line fighting. This age threshold was a bit older than in earlier wars of comparable scale. And given the modern military's growing preference for experience and training, this threshold is likely to rise still further during the next Crisis climax. During the recent 9/11 wars in Afghanistan and Iraq, for example, the *average* age of military service was thirty-three. Of those who served, nearly twice as many were forty or older as were under twenty-five. In a larger-scale conflict, this age mix would undoubtedly get a lot younger. Still, participation may be minimal under age twenty-two or twenty-three.

Timing also matters. History shows that what sorts birth cohorts into separate generations is participation in the Crisis climax. If the Crisis climax comes early enough—and if the threshold age for participation in the conflict is old enough—the Millennial-Homeland dividing line could be moved a year or two *earlier*. In this case, the Millennial generation would be slightly shorter. If it's the other way around, the line would be moved a year or two *later* and the Millennial generation would be slightly longer. As always, contingent events play a critical role in drawing lines between generations.

To illustrate, consider the Silent Generation. Its first birth year (1925) could not be identified with any certainty until we knew the outcome of events—in this case, that Americans born in 1924 constituted the last cohort that was old enough to experience active duty in significant numbers by the combat climax of World War II (in 1944).

But of course events could have turned out differently. If the A-bomb had not been available and the United States had had to invade the main Japanese islands with massive casualties extending through 1947 (as military planners had expected), younger-born Americans might well have regarded themselves as belonging to the G.I. Generation, which would have been longer as a result. The late columnist Russell Baker (born in 1925) was among the hundreds of thousands of younger U.S. servicemen training in California in August 1945, nervously awaiting the invasion order. While jubilant upon hearing about Japan's surrender, he also recognized that it forever separated him from those who had actively taken part in the war. "I hated the war ending," he sheepishly confessed many years later. "I wanted glory."

Whenever it happens, the resolution of the Millennial Crisis will draw a firm line between the beginning of full adulthood for one generation and the end of youth for the next. Everyone on the older, Millennial side of that line will feel they belong to the cadre that fully came of age during the Crisis era. Everyone on the younger, Homelander side will understand that they don't belong. Homelanders will have to search for a different generational rite of passage. The quest to find their own collective catharsis may grow into one of the great questions, and perhaps frustrations, of the rest of their lives.

Part Three

COMING OF SPRING

10

A NEW SAECULUM
IS BORN

No winter lasts forever; no spring skips its turn.

—HAL BORLAND

On VJ Day, August 15, 1945, peace had been declared, but America remained mobilized for total war. Harbors were jammed with warships, highways with convoys, depots with war matériel, bureaucracies with war planners, factories with war workers. Still geared for military production, assembly lines were expected to shut down just as millions of veterans came home looking for work. A return to prewar class conflict seemed likely. The eminent sociologist Gunnar Myrdal warned of a coming "radicalization of labor" and an "epidemic of violence." The first threat of this came a few months after VJ Day, when auto workers went on strike against General Motors.

The strike fizzled. In what came to be known as "the Treaty of Detroit," GM and the auto workers worked out an amicable deal. "At no other time in U.S. history have labor's demands been so plausible," cheered *Fortune*'s editors. There was no going back to the 1930s. These were new times, times for teamwork and trust.

Through the ecstatic victories and heartrending reversals of global war, Americans had wavered between a bright ideal of social unity and a dark recollection of social conflict. They yearned to belong to something strong and universal and unquestioned. While statesmen laid plans for global governments, politicians talked of "collective action" for the "common man." At the height of the war, in an "Open Letter to Japan," the

Saturday Evening Post declared in defiant amazement that "Your people are giving their lives in useless sacrifice, while ours are fighting for a glorious future of mass employment, mass production, and mass distribution, and mass ownership."

As the war neared its foreseeable triumph, Americans worried that such hopes might never be attained. Looking forward to the future, people did then what they still do today: They assumed it would resemble the recent past. Their most recent frames of reference—the hardbitten thirties and the cynical twenties—were not remembered favorably. *Fortune* feared a resumption of "rude pushing ways" and "ill temper." Republishing an old 1932 photo of police routing World War I veterans petitioning for their benefits, the editors warned that "a slice of blueberry pie" would not satisfy "the veteran's gripe."

Many economists saw a new depression ahead. Harvard economist Sumner Slichter warned of "the greatest and swiftest disappearance of markets in all history." The Research Institute of America's Leo Cherne predicted "insecurity, instability, and maladjustment" for "middle-class families . . . susceptible to the infections of a postwar disillusionment." A month after VJ Day, *Life* magazine forecast a sharp further decline in the U.S. birthrate. Fearing depopulation and economic collapse, the federal government planned a massive campaign, involving some two hundred organizations, to provide work relief on the scale of the original New Deal.

It wasn't necessary. Upbeat America confounded the pessimists. Veterans mustered out without any hint of riot, cheered by hometown welcomes that didn't stop when the parades were over. As the triumphant mood lingered, few tried to restart old political or cultural arguments. Instead, returning vets wanted to get married, have kids, and move into nice homes and good jobs. By the first peacetime Christmas, after the actual number of unemployed reached barely one-tenth of what labor officials had predicted, the buoyant mood persisted. Finally even the cautionaries relented. Joining the "many prophets of hope," *Fortune* exuded that "We would seem to have it in our power to have a standard of living far beyond anything in recorded history." World War II had marked "the supreme triumph of man in his long battle with the scarcities in nature."

By June 1946, the nation realized that the postwar mood shift was permanent. "The Great American Boom is on," *Fortune* proclaimed, "and there is no measuring it! The old yardsticks won't do.... The spectacle is so vast and confusing it is hard to understand.... There is a rich queerness to the U.S. scene in this summer of 1946.... Parallels with 1929 or 1939 or any other period break down quickly."

Quoting Walt Whitman just after the Civil War, the editors invited America to "Open up all your valves and let her go—swing, whirl with the rest—you will soon get under such momentum you can't stop if you would." The new boom was not just in economic activity, but also in fertility. Babies conceived in the ecstasy of VJ night were born in mid-April 1946, launching a procreative birth bulge that lasted until a tragedy in late 1963 altered the national mood in a different way.

Those two markers—VJ Day and the Kennedy Assassination—bracket an era variously known as "Pax Americana," "Good Times," the "Best Years," "Happy Days," and the "American High." Between those two dates, national confidence grew in a sort of slow crescendo.

During the early years of the Berlin blockade, the McCarthy hearings, and the Korean War, the mood still often reverted to the survivalist paranoia of the recent world war. Wagons were still circled, guns were still drawn. During the Eisenhower presidency, the sense of alarm gave way to a new complacency. And once national prosperity and power had grown to commanding global dominance, the mood grew expansive, even extravagant. At the inauguration of John F. Kennedy, the aging poet Robert Frost announced "The glory of a next Augustan age ... A golden age of poetry and power." Two years later, the first lady compared her husband's administration to Camelot, almost as if she knew that their "one brief shining moment" (to quote from the popular musical then running on Broadway) was about to come to an end.

The American High constituted the spring season of a new Great Year. The Fourth Turning of the Great Power Saeculum had ended. The First Turning of the Millennial Saeculum had been born.

In this chapter, we intend to look beyond the Fourth Turning of the Millennial Saeculum—and to the First Turning that will follow. We first examine the common characteristics of prior First Turnings, earlier facsimiles of the post–World War II American High. We then imagine possible scenarios, some better than others, of how another such era could play out through the midpoint of the twenty-first century. Finally, we project today's generations into these scenarios. As always, we want to know what the next First Turning will feel like and how it may shape our lives.

FIRST TURNINGS IN HISTORY

Thanks to vintage TV and nostalgia movies, memories of the American High remain deeply etched decades later. Today's seniors widely remember it as an era in which laws were seen as effective, large organizations as efficient, science as benign, public schools as excellent, careers as reliable, families as strong, and crime as under control. Government could afford to do almost anything it wanted, while still balancing its budget.

From year to year, the middle class swelled and the gap between rich and poor narrowed. Worker productivity and worker pay grew at a fast pace—faster than anyone recalled before the Great Depression and faster in fact than in any decade since. Economist John Kenneth Galbraith wrote, in *The Affluent Society*, of a nation in which poverty was no longer "a major problem" but "more nearly an afterthought." "The frontiers of our economic system are formed by our mental attitude and our unity," said the prominent liberal Republican Harold Stassen in 1946, "rather than by any limitation of science or of productivity." Indeed, U.S. farmers had become so productive that the federal government could afford to take their surplus, in a "Food for Peace" program, and use it to feed tens of millions of starving people abroad.

On the world stage, Americans saw themselves bearing a new imperial role—believing, with physicist J. Robert Oppenheimer, that "the world alters as we walk in it." According to the nation's preeminent political columnist, Walter Lippmann, "What Rome was to the ancient world, what Great Britain has been to the modern world, America is to be to the world of tomorrow." Americans understood they had no rival. Upon Japan's surrender, Churchill had declared, "America at this moment stands at the summit of the world." A few years later, British historian Robert Payne described America as "a Colossus" with "half the wealth of the world, more than half of the productivity, nearly two-thirds of the world's machines."

Yet even as America grew grander and wealthier, so too did it seem to grow nicer and more community-minded—if also blander. Churches and charities again became fashionable. Crime and divorce rates declined, ushering in an era of unlocked front doors, of nicely groomed youth, of President Eisenhower celebrating the "well-being" of the American family. A popular TV sitcom, *The Andy Griffith Show*, featured a small-town sheriff and deputy who seldom wore firearms but rather traded folksy jokes all day since there was no crime—not even many family quarrels.

An affluent, orderly, familial America needed appropriate living quarters. Enter suburbia, the American High's most enduring monument. The suburb's inventor was William Levitt, whose wartime stint in the Seabees familiarized him with his peers' taste for general-issue housing. Postwar "Levittowns" were soon emulated everywhere. Through the 1950s, more than four of every five new houses were built in one of the "New Suburbia" developments that *Fortune* lauded as "big and lush and uniform—a combination made to order for the comprehending marketer." Compared to the toilet-less farmhouses and dank urban tenements many Americans had called home before the war, suburbia was nothing less than a middle-class miracle.

The planned orderliness of suburbia was a fitting lifestyle for a nation entering what one contemporary writer called an "age of security." With the horrors of Hitler and Stalin fresh in everybody's mind, the nation's confidence was buttressed by a vigilant Cold War realism. "When World War II ended in 1945, no one dared to predict that no others would follow," explains historian Paul Johnson. "There was a general, despondent assumption that . . . future conflicts would stretch on endlessly." To guard against this threat, many of the American High's grandest federally funded edifices (interstate highways, basic research institutes, higher-ed expansion, new math and science curricula) were built explicitly in the name of national defense.

Mass consumption reflected this preoccupation with security. Following advertising cues, most consumers were content with just a few basic styles of home, car, appliance, or dress. Standardized tastes facil-

itated mass production, which met private needs so efficiently that resources could be set aside for large survival-oriented civic tasks, such as
maintaining a powerful military (which cost three times more as a share
of GDP during that era than it does today). Uniform lifestyles helped
foster social equality by limiting differences in consumption. They also
provided the cultural underpinnings for thrift and teamwork, with everybody "pitching in" like good neighbors who share lawnmowers. Universal peacetime conscription triggered virtually no youth opposition.

As most Americans began championing a single common national
purpose, political partisanship declined. By the late 1950s, voters frequently complained that they could no longer tell the difference between
the two parties. After the young union radicals in the thirties matured
into the Big Labor bureaucrats of the fifties, the Democrats learned to
"get along" with Big Business. Republicans, meanwhile, reconciled themselves to the New Deal. President Eisenhower delivered a clear warning
to any remaining GOP free-market purists. "Should any political party
attempt to abolish Social Security, unemployment insurance, and eliminate labor laws and farm programs," he wrote, "you would not hear of
that party again in our political history."

Political theorist James Burnham announced the triumph of
"managerialism"—a new political economy which erased the dividing
lines between capitalists, workers, and government. When every group
submitted to regulation and long-term planning, consensually agreed
upon in periodic "deals," every group benefitted and common national
goals were attained.

To make all this agreeableness work during the American High, a
special suite of personality skills was required. In *The Organization Man*,
sociologist William H. Whyte gave it a name: "the social ethic." It was
the ready ability to "adapt" yourself easily and effortlessly to the needs of
your firm, family, or community. Self-help books emphasized "fitting in."
School councilors tutored students to "adjust" to stereotypical gender
roles: breadwinner for boys, homemaker for girls. Soft drink ads in the
late 1950s and early 1960s did not appeal to self-emancipation or rule-
breaking. Instead, with slogans like "Be sociable, have a Pepsi" or "Say
Pepsi, please," they appealed to friendliness and civility. In *The Quest for*

Community, sociologist Robert Nisbet observed that "the social group has replaced the individual" as the key focus of social science research: "social *order* has replaced social *change* as the key problem."

Nisbet was astonished by how swiftly, following World War II, America had been gripped by "the obsessive craving of men for tranquility and belonging." "Man's integration with fellow man, his identification with race, culture, religion, and family . . . these are rich themes at the present time." He pointed out, in particular, "the almost complete collapse of that literary revolt against the village, church, class, and community so spectacular in American writing a generation or two ago." Whereas young writers and intellectuals after World War I sought to flee "Main Street," the newest crop of young writers were surprising older generations by searching earnestly to rediscover it.

To be sure, that wasn't the whole story. Even as it was happening, the American High drew plenty of criticism for its materialism, complaisance, conformity, and shallowness.

Whyte and Nisbet themselves by no means approved of the trends they identified. And many others piled on. David Riesman described postwar Americans as *The Lonely Crowd*, a pitiable herd of "outer-directed" adults who constructed their sense of self to fit the approval of others. To Daniel Bell, the era represented *The End of Ideology*, so bereft of inspiring ideals that politicians merely haggled over means and never questioned ends. To Alan Valentine, it was *The Age of Conformity*, in which the citizen was "satisfied with not less than the best in airplanes and plumbing but accepts the second rate in politics and culture." Higher critics from Europe were especially scathing. According to Erich Fromm, in *The Sane Society*, America suffered from "an epidemic of normalcy." According to Herbert Marcuse, in *Eros and Civilization*, America utterly repressed the former and, as a result, barely attained the latter.

Some of the attacks were unforgettable. The 1956 film *Invasion of the Body Snatchers* satirized citizens so robotic that nobody noticed when they were taken over by aliens. Several years later, *The Manchurian Candidate* prompted audiences to worry about how easily young people could be "brainwashed" into complying with arbitrary commands. FCC Chairman Newton Minow assaulted television as a "vast wasteland" of vapid, albeit wholesome programming. When the young socialist Michael Harrington wrote *The Other America*, his implicit message was that mainstream (middle-class) America was hobbled by a blinkered conscience.

Mind-numbing uniformity was always a target. Folksinger Malvina Reynolds sang of "little boxes made of ticky tacky" which "all look just the same." Philosopher and art critic Lewis Mumford despaired of the "multitude of uniform, unidentifiable houses, lined up inflexibly, at uniform distances on uniform roads, in a treeless communal waste, inhabited by people of the same class, the same income, the same age group, witnessing the same television performances, eating the same tasteless prefabricated foods, from the same freezers."

The critics are well remembered because their remarks evoke what many later Americans would find so baffling about the High mindset. During that era, apparently, people had no problem with casual racism and sexism, rampant groupthink, stifling formality, and a kitschy pop culture. How could they feel so triumphant about a nation so stunted in its sensibilities?

By the 1990s, at the other end of the saeculum, this incomprehension was well rendered in the film *Pleasantville*, about two Xer teens who get transported back in time to a 1950s community whose inhabitants live unfeeling, black-and-white lives. By exposing these automatons to anger, transgressive art, and (especially) sex, the Xers teach the inhabitants how to awaken themselves and live lives in full color. By the end of the movie, young audiences couldn't help but wonder how Americans ever agreed to submit to such a collective lobotomy.

At the time, of course, most Americans felt very differently. To those who lived through it, the American High was no creaking anachronism. It felt extremely "modern"—a wedding of optimism, technology, and prosperity to a crisp (if unreflective) sense of collective purpose.

Today, during a Crisis era, it may indeed be getting easier than it was back in the 1990s for Americans to appreciate the upside of the American High. Conservatives, to be sure, have always had a fondness for the 1950s. Now more than ever they can appreciate its virtues—low crime, stable families, conventional values, and full (if not always inspirational) churches. Yet even progressives have reasons to view the era in a more favorable light. Imagine a world in which unions are strong, wages are rising, the middle class is large, voters are personally engaged at every level of civic life, families expect the future to be better than the present, and citizens not only trust big government but *actually do* what "the experts" tell them to do.

And while the American High gets a bad rap for regressive racial attitudes, not all of it is deserved. During that era, after all, the nation did enable Black Americans to enjoy spectacular gains in living standards (in both absolute terms and relative to Whites); and, just as the era was ending, voters overwhelmingly supported federal laws guaranteeing civil rights that had been promised, but never enforced on a national scale, by the outcome of the Civil War. Would Americans do as much today? Progressives may even have to relent in their attack on the prevailing sexual prudery of the grainy Ed Sullivan years. Back then, teens were certainly more enthusiastic about sex—and young adults were doing a lot more of it—than either group is today. Who deserves to call whose world a "wasteland"?

In the early 2020s, all Americans—and especially the rising generation of young Americans—are better able than they once were to appreciate what the High achieved. It had little to do with inner-world personal gratification. It had everything to do with what Americans find so difficult today: outer-world community performance.

That rising appreciation is probably a good thing. And it's probably only natural. Because the nation is likely to enter a similar era in the not-so-distant future.

Anglo-American history has experienced six First Turning Highs, dating back to the fifteenth century:

- Tudor Renaissance, 1487–1525 (Tudor Saeculum)

- Merrie England, 1597–1621 (New World Saeculum)

- Augustan Age of Empire, 1706–1727 (Revolutionary Saeculum)

- Era of Good Feelings, 1794–1822 (Civil War Saeculum)

- Reconstruction and Gilded Age, 1865–1886 (Great Power Saeculum)

- American High 1946–1964 (Millennial Saeculum)

All six eras have been regarded, in their own time and after, as "postwar." The epic Crisis has been settled, the promised land delivered, and society gathers around a newfound sense of solidarity and direction. It is time to reconstruct and savor victory (or recover from defeat). People want to gather, nest, plan, procreate, and build. The mood is dynamic: Each new exercise of social cooperation builds on the success of the last, until—near the end of the High—the trend toward greater order and cohesion becomes something close to herd instinct.

The High moves toward the summer solstice. It is an era of transition toward longer days and shorter nights, in which both the demand and supply of social order are high and rising. It is the season of hope and innocent joy. "April . . . hath put a spirit of youth in everything," wrote William Shakespeare. After a winter of war and death, the world is primed for procreation. Indeed, observed John Greenleaf Whittier, it is death that makes new life possible: "The Night is the mother of the Day, / The Winter of the Spring, / And ever upon old Decay, / The greenest mosses cling." Amid the budding leaves and flowers, future aspirations multiply. "Spring," according to Leo Tolstoy, "is the time of plans and projects." During the saeculum's First Turning, soldiers are knighted, kings crowned, empires proclaimed, city walls enlarged, academies founded, and children indulged.

In the overall rhythm of the saeculum, First Turnings mark the culmination of the five social trends we examined in Chapter 8—toward *community, equality, authority, permanence,* and *convention.* During the Fourth Turning, these trends make their initial appearance as direction-of-change reversals and are conspicuous for that reason. Yet even by the Crisis's resolution their institutional presence remains makeshift and hastily constructed. Only during the subsequent First Turning do these trends reach their full consummation in a seemingly permanent social order. Like a tree evolving from its first budding branches to its densest plenitude of leaves, the First Turning High completes what the Fourth Turning only initiates.

All Highs witness a rising mood of national unity. Civic celebrations are popular, and participation in government (as seen in voting rates, for example, in the last three Highs) is high and rising. The public supports an ambitious agenda for national improvement and, most of the time, comes to entrust a single party to carry it out. Over the last four Highs, respectively, these single parties were the trans-Atlantic Whigs, the Democratic-Republicans, the Republicans, and the Democrats. These become *dominant* parties. Competitor parties, which tend to be associated with one class or region, lose favor—especially if they have become tainted with the crime of treason or secession (the fate of the Tories not long after the Glorious Revolution, the Federalists after the War of 1812, and the Democrats after the Civil War).

What political competition remains becomes less partisan in the sense that it no longer reflects fundamental differences in national goals. James Monroe, in his first inaugural address in 1817, was gratified "to witness the increased harmony of opinion which pervades our Union. Discord does not belong to our system." The British diplomat and historian James Bryce, after traveling extensively in America in the 1870s and early 1880s (and comparing it with Europe), was most impressed by "the unity of the nation. . . . The people are homogeneous: a feeling which stirs them stirs alike rich and poor, farmers and traders, Eastern men and Western men—one may now add, Southern men also."

Political debate tends to be constructive and dispassionate—even decorous much of the time. Leaders and organizations at least pretend to work in everyone's interest. None of this was true during the Crisis that preceded the High, nor will it remain true during the Awakening that will follow.

With renewed consensus on the ends of government, public trust in political leadership is strong. And because families and local communities are supportive, new laws gain greater compliance with less enforcement. Governments and markets work together with relative ease. During Highs, personal rights tend to be narrowly defined—which leads to more decisions being made by local authorities or by community sentiment, and fewer by courts and lawyers.

As a rule, Highs are eras of robust economic and demographic expansion. Upon resolution of the Crisis-era conflict, people discover that most prior barriers to growth have been removed. They have guaranteed public access to new territories for their homes and farms and new markets for their trade. And, with government help (including favorable subsidies, tariffs, regulations, and powers of eminent domain), they can scale up new technologies seemingly without limit. Also helping to boost living standards are national policies that prioritize creditors, saving, and broader and deeper capital investment. Fiscal and monetary policies are often explicitly disinflationary. These have included paying off all war debt at par (at the insistence of Treasury Secretary Alexander Hamilton); returning the nation to the gold standard (what Rutherford B. Hayes called "honest money"), or putting tax cuts on hold until budget balance had been achieved (a priority of President Eisenhower's that would astonish modern-day conservatives).

During Highs, immense waves of publicly subsidized infrastructure redefine public space, shrink distance, homogenize manners, and unify markets. After the Revolution came the turnpike, steamboat, and canal waves, culminating in the Erie Canal, a 363-mile engineering miracle that transformed New York City into the nation's commercial capital. After the Civil War came the railroad and municipal utility waves, epitomized by such landmarks as the Donner Summit railway tunnel through the Sierra Nevada and the Brooklyn Bridge over the East River. After World War II came the sweeping waves of highway building, river damming, university expanding, and downtown bulldozing most seniors today can still recall from their childhood.

Amid this climb in living standards, remarkably, economic inequality continues to decline even after the Crisis is over—or, at least, rises much more modestly than in subsequent Awakenings and Unravelings. Emerging from the Crisis with a new social contract, people feel they have a "fresh start" on more equal terms. Among the prime-age adults who recently struggled and suffered together as a team, few wish to flaunt their wealth and many recall how close they were to having all their privileges stripped away.

In a High, moreover, the importance of "fitting in" means that social reputation often matters more than money. Both community spirit and civic engagement are robust, making America in the 1720s, 1810s, 1880s, or 1950s a nation of joiners. During the Era of Good Feelings, the number of charitable organizations in New England multiplied more than sixfold. Membership rises as well in national fraternal organizations that extend across many social classes. The Masons, Oddfellows, Knights of Pythias, Grand Army of the Republic, Elks, Grange, Knights of Labor, Shriners, Knights of Columbus, Congress of Industrial Organizations, March of Dimes, AARP—all these monuments of civic engagement were founded near the end of a Crisis era or during a High. Often linked to wartime service, these groups promote brotherly friendship and community service on a grand scale. They foster an abundance of trust both between and within social classes, what sociologist Robert Putnam calls "bridging" as well as "bonding" social capital.

So focused on sociability, both men and women take a special interest in what they imagine to be the source of sociability: strong families and separate gender roles. In this very conventional sense, Highs are always family-oriented eras.

After the Revolution had been won, both Federalists and Republicans stressed the right ordering of family life (on what Jefferson hoped would be an endless vista of family farms) for the shaping of republican virtue. Men would bring order to public life. Women would bring order to family life and, as "Republican Mothers," ensure the raising of patriotic children. After the Civil War, writes historian Richard White, Victorian America became nothing less than "a home-ordered society," in which "home sweet homes" would be protected by husbands and managed by pious and submissive wives. According to the "cult of true womanhood," females became repositories of virtue empowered to "domesticate" the vice-ridden world of men. Frances Willard, perhaps America's most powerful woman in the 1880s, declared that the purpose of her organization, the Women's Christian Temperance Union, was "to make the whole world more HOMELIKE."

Some of her causes, like temperance (she called it "home protection") and women's suffrage, would not be enacted in her lifetime. Others, like the suppression of "immodesty" (federal Comstock laws), would be.

The public world, managed according to conventionally masculine values, exudes top-down control and Apollonian rationality. Public works show off the nation's newfound unity. Designed to reassure individuals that their community is both supreme and law-abiding, these works have inspired the monumental yet orderly architectural styles of Highs since the late seventeenth century: Baroque, Palladian, Georgian, Neoclassical, Federal, Greek Revival, Empire, High Victorian, Beaux Arts, WPA, Modern, and International.

The triumph of mankind over nature—the conquest of ignorance and poverty through reason and technology—becomes a new focus of prestige and celebration.

In the colonial Augustan Age, every gentleman of letters, from William Brattle in Boston to William Byrd in Westover, Virginia, proudly appended the initials "FRS" to their names. This meant they were "Friends" of the Royal Society of London for Improving Natural Knowledge and therefore "natural philosophers" who took a keen interest in science. In 1807, the public jubilation that greeted the success of Lewis and Clark's eight-thousand-mile "Corps of Discovery Expedition" bolstered the reputation of President Jefferson, America's natural-philosopher-in-chief, during an otherwise troubled second term.

In an 1876 opening ceremony, President Grant and Emperor Pedro II of Brazil together pulled the handle that started the stupendous 650-ton Corliss steam engine at the 1876 Philadelphia Centennial Exhibition. This popular display of America's machine-age power attracted 10 million visitors (at a time when the U.S. population was only 46 million). In 1961, President Kennedy excited America's imagination by pledging "before this decade is out" to land "a man on the moon." The nation ultimately met that goal by means of a 3,200-ton, three-stage Saturn V space vehicle overseen and monitored by hundreds of thousands of civil servants.

Society's newfound obsession with cooperation, scale, and material progress tends to push the broader intellectual climate in a compatible direction. The classic is now favored over the romantic, the public over

the personal, the universal over the singular. Rules become more important, spontaneity less.

In the late 1940s and 1950s, America witnessed a revival of "formal-
ism" not only in architecture, but in music, literature, visual arts, and the
social sciences. America experienced something similar in every earlier
High, going back to the early 1700s, when colonials were delighted to
read Alexander Pope's "Augustan" couplets, hear Henry Purcell's martial trumpets, and copy as best they could the balanced and harmonious
Palladian spaces of Inigo Jones and Christopher Wren. During that era,
a happy society was often analogized to a colony of eusocial insects like
ants or bees. "All nature is industrious and every creature about us is dili-
gent in their proper work," preached Boston minister Benjamin Colman
in 1717. "Diligence is the universal example. Look through the whole
creation, and every part of it has a work and service assigned to it."

The popular culture tends to dwell on the conventional and sentimental. Themes and plotlines reinforce social stereotypes. Happy,
family-friendly endings are standard. Good news about mainstream success is played up; bad news about the marginalized and the oppressed is
played down. Religion is encouraged, so long as it promotes outer-world
"works" (collaborative, moderate, probably useful) more than inner-
world "faith" (sectarian, extreme, possibly destructive).

Looking back from today's vantage point, Highs provide relatively
few memories of heroic deeds or fiery crusades or zany celebrities. Their
political debates (the Missouri Compromise? Bimetallism?) are mostly
forgotten. Instead, Highs bring to mind eras of optimism and social solidarity: long on earnest cooperation, short on creative originality. They
evoke seemingly timeless images of stable communities and families—
whether in the fresh rectangles of Philadelphia and Williamsburg; the
six-mile-square log-built townships of Tennessee; the garish Queen
Anne trolley suburbs of Buffalo; or the ticky-tacky houses of Levittown.

What did Americans think of these eras while they were living in
them? Naturally, many heaped lavish and hyperbolic praise on them—as
we might expect from people thinking, or at least hoping, that they were
living in a new golden age.

Americans in the years just after World War II liked to describe themselves as exceptional. So did Americans in the years just after the nation's founding. To the end of his life, Jefferson believed that "there is not a country on earth where there is greater tranquility, where the laws are milder, or better obeyed . . . , where strangers are better received, more hospitably treated, and with a more sacred respect." A multitude of Jefferson's peers wrote soaring panegyrics to "The Rising Glory of America," which almost became its own poetic genre. One ardent Jeffersonian, Joel Barlow, labored for twenty years on a six-thousand-line patriotic epic entitled "The Columbiad," which was greeted with much praise and (alas) with at least as much ridicule.

Yet along with all the praise, as the sorry example of Barlow might suggest, came the inevitable lampooning and fault-finding. The unique vulnerability of any era in which people think very highly of themselves should be obvious: Nothing tempts critics so much as collective pride. The American High attracted plenty of criticism. So did earlier Highs, and usually for many of the same reasons—that, for all their worldly achievements, these eras were corrupted by complacent materialism, herdlike conformity, and the vulgar collapse of high culture and high ideals.

After the Civil War, these complaints were attached to the very label we still use to describe the era, "The Gilded Age." This was the title of an 1873 novel by Mark Twain and Charles Dudley Warner, whose scandalous plotline implied that most of what their readers thought golden about their age was in fact mere gloss. Many other famous novelists and scholars echoed their disapproval—including Walt Whitman, William Dean Howells, both Henry and Charles Francis Adams, Jr., and most of the other genteel "mugwumps" who may have felt left behind by the surging prosperity of the postwar middle class. During the Era of Good Feelings, similar themes were echoed by the high-born clerisy of those years (most often, New England Federalists). They lamented a cheap commercialism "widely and thinly spread" (according to one divine) and of a democracy that "corrodes everything elegant in art" (according to another).

Few of these contemporary protests, whatever their merits, ever seriously impeded the forward momentum of the High. For the most part, they were issued by dissidents who belonged to minority parties or by cultural elites perched outside society's cohesive mainstream. In time, however, a more powerful protest would arise—so powerful it would bring the High crashing to a close. This would mark the beginning of the Second Turning, the Awakening. Leading this protest would be the children of the High, the Prophet archetype, now coming of age.

But looking beyond the High takes us ahead of our story. Let's linger in the High a bit longer. Using history as our guide, let's now turn to what America may be like after the Millennial Crisis comes to a close.

THE NEXT FIRST TURNING: SCENARIOS

The next First Turning will begin when the current Fourth Turning reaches its resolution, which as we have seen is most likely to happen in the early 2030s. To make the future tangible, let's choose a date: 2033. Let's also assume that the recent trend toward somewhat longer generations and turnings continues. We therefore project that this turning will last twenty-three years. So we're looking at 2033 to 2056 as suggestive start and stop dates.

What can we say concretely about an era that won't start for another ten years and won't stop until almost another thirty-five?

Ask most futurists this question, and they will give you a narrow answer, consisting mostly of new technological capabilities superimposed on new quantitative (economic, demographic, environmental) constraints. That's pretty much it. It's as though we could foresee the future by visualizing all of us today suddenly transported into a different world and then pondering how we would cope with such a world. The shortcoming of the standard futurist approach should be obvious: It superimposes a future world on a society that itself remains unchanged, or at best on a society that will keep changing as it has in the recent past.

But society is never static, nor does it keep changing in the same direction for long. This explains the repeated failure of the standard capabilities-and-constraints approach. When it was used in the 1950s in order to look ahead twenty years, it failed to point out nearly everything that was so strikingly new about the 1970s. When it was used again in the 1970s, it said little about what America would become in the 1990s. Needless to say, no futurologist twenty years ago told us where America would find itself today.

For anyone looking twenty or thirty years into the future, the first key insight should be this: *The adults of that future world will mainly be all of us, only older.* The first key puzzle will therefore be to figure out how today's generations, as they grow older, are likely to transform the attitudes and behaviors of every age bracket. The next puzzle, perhaps, will be to figure out how the next generation of children is likely to be raised differently by tomorrow's adults. Solving these puzzles requires in turn some historical understanding of how such changes have occurred in the past, which changes recur in a predictable rhythm, and how this rhythm translates into new social moods. It requires, in short, some understanding of how the saeculum works.

With that understanding, we know something even more important than what sort of future world society will be facing—namely, *what sort of society will be facing that world.* To state this another way: It is more helpful to foresee how *we* will change than to foresee how the world around us will change.

Will America be facing a very different world by the year 2040 or 2050 than it faces today? No doubt. Perhaps different beyond recognition.

Indeed, one great and unavoidable source of uncertainty about the next First Turning must be acknowledged up front. Beyond the early 2030s, everything about America's role in the world—politically, economically, and technologically—will be radically dependent on how the Crisis era is resolved. While the Ekpyrosis is always history's pivotal moment of entropy reversal, it can also catapult a society in very unexpected directions before it's over. When we examined (in Chapter 7) the sorts of civil or great-power conflicts that may come to define the Fourth Turning's culmination, we acknowledged that these conflicts could end in a very broad spectrum of possible outcomes, ranging from the most uplifting and triumphant to the most ruinous and tragic.

The historical track record, over the last six Fourth Turnings of the Anglo-American saeculum, points to largely successful resolutions in every instance. And in most of the following discussion, we will assume a similarly successful resolution for the current Fourth Turning. Even so, the risk of catastrophe cannot be dismissed. Six is a small sample size, the tail risk is large, and we know several examples (in other countries) of saecula that ended badly. A Fourth Turning failure is a distinct possibility, and we will return to it later on.

In short, while any prediction about the future state of the world may seem especially uncertain from today's vantage point, predictions about America's basic social mood may be more reliable. We must therefore let the rhythm of the saeculum be the final guide.

Now let's take that look. Let's try to imagine what life in America may look and feel like during its coming spring season.

Favorable Scenarios

From the outset, the most striking feature of this new era will be an overwhelming sense of national unity—a sense unfamiliar to most Americans today. The memory of the Crisis climax will still be fresh in everyone's mind, along with the lives and fortunes sacrificed in order to ensure that the nation would prevail. Symbols and uniforms of national membership will be regularly celebrated and widely seen. National news will be closely followed. Voting rates will remain at their high 2020s levels. At every level of community, from the U.S. Congress to local neighborhoods, people will be expected, even in peacetime, to continue to prioritize some definition of group purpose above their own private interest.

Following the Crisis, loyalty to the new national regime will become the first organizing principle in party politics. Should the Fourth Turning culminate in civil war, First Turning electorates will cast into the wilderness whichever faction led the losing side—in this case, perhaps, leading red zone Republicans or leading blue zone Democrats. Should there be a great-power war, the faction which most opposed the war or maintained the closest ties with the enemy could remain under a dark cloud of suspicion.

The range of acceptable debate, already narrowed during the recent Crisis climax, will remain narrow in peacetime. All legitimate political factions, certainly both major parties, will agree on the paramount need to defend and strengthen the new regime—not just to rebuild whatever may have been physically destroyed, but to redesign and modernize public institutions across the board. Political discussion will focus on means, not ends.

Following almost any Crisis climax scenario, it won't just be America that will require rebuilding and redesigning. It will be much of the rest of the world as well in what may be a global First Turning. Once again, following the precedent of the Truman Doctrine and the Marshall Plan, America will likely be called upon to provide leadership and assistance to that effort. Once again, America will be motivated by enlightened self-interest: By investing heavily in a peaceful, prosperous, and democratic post-Crisis world, America will be able to secure the long-term "freedom from fear" its citizens will be yearning for.

As the next global First Turning opens, the most desperate need will be to calm a world in turmoil—enforcing new peace agreements, setting up provisional governments, resettling refugees, rebuilding destroyed cities, formalizing alliances, and possibly redrawing national boundaries. America will necessarily play a large role in all such activities, including (perhaps) aggressive nation building. America will feel compelled to carry out such tasks mostly because leaving them undone will jeopardize everything else it has achieved.

However carefully the global victors manage the post-Crisis settlement, history suggests that they will need to stay vigilant in order to counter ongoing threats to peace—perhaps from defeated adversaries that haven't given up their ambitions or from former allies who now want to exert an independent sway over world affairs. Should a new conflict arise, America will likely lead the coalition that reconfirms the rules or boundaries of the new world order. Such reconfirming wars, as we have seen, tend to be stand-offs. Patience will be high, enthusiasm low. Long-cycle theorists Modelski and Thompson write that a new world power can "set the rules." True enough. But it must also bear the costs.

As they contemplate the world's longer-term future—along with the possible causes of future wars—America and its allies will likely heed Ukraine President Zelensky's bold plea back in 2022. They will create "new alliances" and "new institutions" able to guarantee collective security, perhaps by means of unprecedented powers of intrusive enforcement. These powers may include rigorous surveillance to prevent nuclear proliferation, quotas or taxes on emissions or resource extractions that damage the global commons, and refashioned monetary, taxation, and trade agreements able to handle an era of instant and decentralized commercial transactions.

Today, most of these goals—the banning of rogue nuclear states, for example, or an enforceable global budget for atmospheric carbon—seem like hopeless one-world dreams. Come the next First Turning, they could become reality. All that is necessary is for a few great powers to take the lead in proposing these rules and to persuade most countries that they will be enforced. In the 2030s, America and its strongest allies may possess the opportunity and the will to do both.

American voters will go along with this expanded global role so long as it serves their long-term interests and does not relinquish their national sovereignty. Even so, global collective security will be a tough sell to many voters, some of whom will denounce it as the corrupt embrace of empire. Americans in the late 2030s, intensely focused on restarting normal lives close to home, will be in no mood to expand their definition of community any further than they must. Psychologically still geared up for conflict, yet now demobilized, Americans may find it even harder to trust the diplomats who want peace than the warriors who want to keep fighting.

In this fraught atmosphere, passionate displays of patriotic rootedness may trigger a climate of paranoia and xenophobia. Government regulation of news and social media, already imposed during the Crisis climax to thwart deep fakes and hacking, could give way to outright censorship. Data on personal behavior and communication, gathered in near-infinite abundance by surveillance tech, will enable authorities to peer into almost anyone's private life. State interrogators will grill tycoons with global financial interests and celebrities with deviant political loyalties. Whether or not the inquisition results in many adverse judgments, it will certainly make ordinary people careful about straying from community norms.

This seems to be an early First Turning pattern. Just as strength of community loyalty reaches its saecular flood tide, the reach of community authority surges over its usual boundaries. Soon after the Armada Crisis came the anti-Catholic reaction to Guy Fawkes's "demonic" Gunpowder Plot. Soon after the Glorious Revolution came the Salem witchcraft hysteria. Soon after the American Revolution Crisis came the anti-French "Alien and Sedition" furor (which Jefferson described as "the reign of witches"). And soon after World War II came the public alarm touched off by the anti-Communist hearings led by Senator Joseph Mc-Carthy and the House Committee on Un-American Activities (which playwright Arthur Miller again likened to the Salem inquisition). "There is a prodigious fear of this court in the country," cautions one Salem minister to the chief witch-trial judge in Miller's *The Crucible*. "Then there is a prodigious guilt in the country," the judge responds. "Are *you* afraid to be questioned here?"

By the 2040s, later in the First Turning, the national mood will shift by degrees toward greater confidence and optimism. By then, the new regime will have proved itself by delivering what most Americans long for. They will desire more social stability and will get it—with low rates of crime and social disorder. They will desire more affluence and will get it—with high rates of real wage growth. They will desire more time for family and community and will get both—with resurgent birth rates and proliferating ties to local civic groups.

In national politics, the growing sense of achievement both at home and abroad will push confidence toward complacency, even triumphalism. Partisan differences between parties will continue to narrow. Neither party will express any fundamental dissatisfaction with America's direction, each disagreeing with the other only on how to push the nation ahead faster. By the early 2050s, for the first time in living memory, the nation will take progress for granted.

Americans will take special pride in the much faster growth rate of its economy—which may have been catapulted forward, as so often happens in First Turnings, by the clearing away of economic obstacles during the preceding Fourth Turning.

During the Millennial Crisis climax, acting out of necessity, America's political leaders will have overhauled major parts of the economy that are today encumbered with decades of dysfunctional subsidies, NIMBY regulations, and barriers to competition that favor incumbents.

These large "social" sectors—including education, health care, communications, finance, and construction—today amount to roughly half of GDP. They constitute a major roadblock to rising living standards because they currently experience *negative* productivity growth during a typical year, which means that their prices rise faster than average workers' income. All this will change in the next First Turning. From banking, colleges, and home building to hospitals, big pharma, and social media, countless industries will be jolted back to life during the years of emergency. With a fresh policy framework in place, take-home wages will jump, public budgets will find welcome relief, and a vast economic frontier will again be open to innovation.

The construction sector in particular will be both transformed and enlarged. Builders will need to satisfy the pent-up demand from a rising generation of parents for affordable homes. Creating those residential communities near bustling urban job centers—the first surge in suburban living since the 1950s and (before that) the 1870s—will in turn require assertive land use management, which may be no problem for a nation full of veterans who recently served as national war planners. It will also require the first massive surge in infrastructure spending in eighty years, amping up the public works recovery that began during the Millennial Crisis. Working together, engineers, city managers, and contractors will figure out how to provide modern yet bucolic neighborhoods with easy access to schools and transportation—all at an affordable cost.

The U.S economy, restructured by the 2040s to produce more efficiently what the typical family wants, will deliver dramatically higher living standards. Compared to today, this typical family will be better housed, better educated, and healthier; have more disposable income; and live in safer and cleaner neighborhoods. Total national investment—in housing, community infrastructure, defense, and the environment—will also be higher. But this larger investment expense will be covered by higher rates of household saving, as well as by federal surpluses favored at the national level by "Victorian" fiscal hawks. Americans won't feel burdened, but rather buoyed, by knowing they belong to a nation that is once again investing in its future.

What's more, this greater affluence will mainly benefit an enlarged middle class. By the 2040s, measures of wealth and income inequality will have declined from the historically exceptional levels of the late 2010s.

This decline in inequality will likely happen in two stages. The first stage will be sudden and will accompany the inflation, mobilization, and economic regimentation triggered by the Crisis climax. The second, more gradual stage will be set in motion by the First Turning's transformed economic and policy environment. Full employment with rapid earnings growth, augmented by a higher minimum wage, will expand workers' share of national income. Immigration rates will remain well below what they were before the Crisis era began in 2008—and reduced immigration will effectively bid up low-skilled wages. Comprehensive taxation of capital income and bequests will lighten the middle-class tax burden. Social welfare programs will become relatively less generous for the nonpoor elderly and relatively more generous for young working families.

In the next First Turning, America's middle class will be further strengthened by the twenty-first-century return of the "social ethic." Compared to today, individuals will be judged less by how much money or power they possess than by how well they fit in with their family and community and serve their friends and coworkers. There will be a renaissance in volunteering and charitable giving. Participation in local civic organizations will again be fashionable. Many churches will reverse their declining membership by shifting their focus from liturgy to community uplift. In the workplace, firms will turn away from the hustle economy of lone contractors—and embrace the collaborative economy of workplace teams. The open office and the sticky paternalism of generous benefit plans will at last complete its triumph over the solo cubicle and the at-will, cash-only job model. Private-sector unions, once given up for dead, will make a comeback.

The restrengthening of America's middle class won't therefore be simply the outcome of economic forces. It will be the outcome of social forces as well. It will reflect America's newfound obsession with community, with belonging, and (to put it in less flattering terms) with harmonious sameness. Robert Putnam has for years insisted that America is poised to experience a revival of civic trust, a return from "I" to "We."

In the 2030s and 2040s, his long-predicted "Upswing" will at last come to pass.

A stronger social ethic will also encourage a renewed emphasis on conventional family roles—making the next First Turning, like all First Turnings, an era that celebrates family life.

Over the last fifteen years, at least since the beginning of today's Crisis era, families have already been experiencing their own upswing. Happy families are now lionized by pop culture and idealized by teens; and extended families today do more to support young adults than at any earlier time in American history. In the next First Turning, family life will become even more central to American social life—with this important difference. Until the Millennial Crisis is resolved, the extended family will continue to serve as the indispensable substitute for all the nuclear families young people would like to form but cannot. After the resolution, young people will start forming those nuclear families. And after years—decades even—of delay, they may start forming them in flood-tide numbers.

A postwar baby boom is a familiar event to most demographers. It arises after a long deferral of family formation and babies—not only during the years of the crisis itself, but also during the pre-crisis years of regime instability and uncertainty about the future. When the boom happens, therefore, it may be fueled by vast numbers of young adults all at once. The post–World War II U.S. baby boom was the product of two generations rushing simultaneously to have children at just about every possible age: from first-wave G.I. moms catching up by giving birth at record fertility rates for women in their mid-forties, all the way to young Silent newlyweds eager to start families just out of high school. At the outset of the next First Turning, we may see much the same across-the-board rush of family formation among Millennials and Homelanders.

As happens after every Fourth Turning, the baby boom of the late 2030s and 2040s will likely get an extra boost from public policy. This time around, access to cheap new land won't be on the table. But a fresh round of veterans' benefits may again make household formation more affordable, along with renewed support for the idea—last popular during the American High—of ensuring a "living wage" to young workers. Pronatalist incentives, like the refundable childcare tax credit now supported in some form by both Democrats and Republicans, may at last find widespread voter support.

The Millennial Crisis is the first Fourth Turning in Anglo-American history in which the nation's total fertility rate has fallen below the replacement rate. Indeed, it is the first era ever in which most of the nations of the world have begun to register below-replacement fertility. A rising number of these nations are offering generous "baby bonuses" to encourage more births. In the next First Turning, it is easy to imagine America participating in a global pronatalist makeover of social democracy. In this new "sustainable" welfare state, citizens will find themselves somewhat worse off for choosing to remain childless, and somewhat better off for choosing to raise future taxpaying citizens.

In earlier First Turnings, a renewed focus on family life and children has always widened the gap between gender roles. Almost certainly, that gap will widen again. Through the rest of the Fourth Turning, a growing share of young adults will be denied the opportunity to assume age-old gender roles that most of their parents took for granted: for women, to make a home; for men, to afford a home. As soon as the First Turning arrives and that opportunity returns, young adults will re-embrace these roles. And as they do so they will feel—much as young adults felt in the late 1860s and the late 1940s—that they are helping to define a hopeful new era. Already today, amid discussions of a "stalled" gender revolution, some sociologists suggest that Millennials may ultimately favor "egalitarian essentialism"—which means ensuring equal rights in the public sphere but making room for separate roles in the private sphere. When they set social policy, Millennials may get to see how these new-fangled "trad" roles work out on a national scale.

Let's now look at where all these trends may lead. What kind of America will emerge by the time the next First Turning culminates, say by the mid-2050s?

Everything by then will seem transformed—and, to most Americans then alive, transformed for the better.

The change will be seen most clearly in the nation's outward appearance, in cityscapes and neighborhoods redesigned for order and sociability. New infrastructure will make communities more livable, workplaces safer, transportation quicker, public spaces cleaner, and schools better administered. Sustainability will be managed on a heroic scale. Engineers and architects may have succeeded in integrating trees, water, and greenery into a redesigned suburbia or onto urban plazas and rooftops. Ubiquitous sensors linked to AI will smoothly orchestrate flows of people and vehicles.

The human landscape, as well, will evoke consensus and social discipline. In legislatures, partisan anger will be subdued, politeness high. In neighborhoods, families will "look out for" one another. On the streets, crime rates will be low and rebellion rare—or at least well hidden from surveillance. In universities, classrooms will buzz with students working to acquire skills helpful to the new regime. At home, comfortably raised children will idly daydream about crusaders, rebels, and saints—figures utterly out of place in the well-governed secular world they see around them.

Taking over America's top leadership spots will be a new generation of rational optimists. Unlike the older retiring generation, which will have been motivated since the Crisis climax mainly by backward-looking worries about what could go wrong, these new leaders will be driven by forward-looking ambitions of greatness yet to come. They will already have overcome a multitude of national challenges. So why stop now? They will share the hope that stirs excitement and celebration during every First Turning—the hope of humanity's mastery of nature itself.

Led by a generation of confident technocrats now mostly in their sixties and assisted by a younger generation of obliging specialists now mostly in their forties, the nation by the end of the next First Turning will have created a world full of marvels.

We can only wonder what they might be. Perhaps they include affordable medical breakthroughs, which extend health spans even more than life spans by curing the most common chronic diseases of aging. Or free global access to high-speed Wi-Fi and online training, which could lift developing countries out of poverty through basic manufacturing and higher-yielding agriculture. Or stunning progress in global climate control—in the near term with climate engineering and in the long term with zero-carbon energy production on a massive scale, perhaps through nuclear, geothermal, ocean thermal, or space-based solar power. Of the wide range of tech visions that today remain mere buzzwords, many by then will likely have become reality, from gene engineering, hyperloops, and bioprinting to smart dust, nanobots, and quantum computing.

In the next First Turning, even more exciting than mastering nature will be satisfying humanity's ancient desire to comprehend nature. Here too we may imagine America exploring new frontiers by 2050—perhaps, it now seems, in competition with China. These frontiers may include the founding of permanent settlements on Mars, or underground factories on Mercury, or communities floating above the clouds on Venus, or perhaps manned flights to explore the outer-planet moons.

As Americans survey achievements of such magnitude, we can easily imagine them acquiring a collective hubris about their role in world history. They may dare to ask a question that recurs at some point during every First Turning: Hasn't their nation—and perhaps the world as well—entered a new golden age? A new age of Augustus?

Roman citizens, during Augustus's reign (conventionally dated as 27 BCE to 14 CE), took pride in having brought closure to an era of decline, strife, and total war—and in having inaugurated a new era of peace abroad, harmony at home, and unprecedented affluence and civility throughout their empire. So may Americans by the mid-twenty-first century. As were the Augustans, they may be obsessed with the construction of gigantic public works. They may be drawn to architectural styles that elevate the community over the individual. They may write histories that place their own nation at the apex of progress. They may prefer cultural expression that respects conventional norms—and writers and artists who dwell on the ideal and universal more than the fallen and the particular. They may regard human suffering as mostly a problem to be solved. And they may not enjoy stories that don't have happy endings.

Yet just as worldly satisfaction begins to swell, as we have seen, so too will the tide of criticism mount. That is the pattern of all First Turnings.

Yes, some will say, we all know what we've gained, but shouldn't we look at what we've lost? Behind the gleaming public works, they will see neighborhoods displaced. Behind the crisp public order, they will see civil liberties violated and privacy invaded. Behind the powerful global alliances, they will see foreign peoples oppressed. Behind the aggressive mastery of nature, they will see natural catastrophes lurking. Parting ways with the golden age triumphalists, these critics will notice a dark underside to every achievement. Instead of optimism, community, and Promethean heroics, they will detect complacency, conformity, and Faustian blindness.

By this time, we can be sure that the First Turning will be nearing an end. Once Americans no longer fear relapse into the winter season, the spring season itself will be nearly over. The same is true for any turning in the saeculum: As soon as we fully understand we're in it, we're about to move on to what comes after. Alternatively: Each season is driven forward, at least in part, by the misapprehension that we're still living in the prior season. "The owl of Minerva," wrote Hegel in perhaps his most famous metaphor, "spreads its wings only with the falling of the dusk."

Unfavorable Scenarios

To be sure, the foregoing sketch of the next First Turning is merely thematic. It is intended to provide an impression. The actual history of this era, as it is experienced and recorded, will necessarily be crowded with the sorts of tangible randomness—the unique scandals, wars, celebrities, and inventions—for which no forecast is possible.

More fundamentally, even as a thematic outline, this sketch could well be mistaken in its optimism. Our look into the future rests on a few basic assumptions about the future resembling the past. The most important assumptions are that—following the pattern of earlier Fourth Turnings—the Crisis will climax in a serious national challenge and that the climax will come to a largely successful resolution.

In the Anglo-American saeculum, all Fourth Turning challenges have registered high on the seriousness scale: They have been, at a minimum, nation threatening. This is important. The more serious is the national challenge, the more altered the world will be once the First Turning opens. Should the challenge this time be milder, we should imagine a world relatively less altered compared to the one we live in now. We may consider this to be a good or bad outcome depending on what we think of today's world. There will be less downside risk of things being much worse, at least right away; but also less upside opportunity—for rejuvenating community life and for healing institutional dysfunction.

The more disturbing question, raised earlier in this chapter, is what happens if the challenge is indeed serious—but this time around it is *not* successfully resolved. We can conjure up many scenarios here, some of which are sobering indeed.

At the darkest end of the possibility spectrum, we can imagine a war that triggers the unconstrained use of WMDs, most likely an exchange of nuclear warheads. To be sure, this scenario is possible in any turning. Since 1945, by some counts, the world has experienced sixteen "near miss" nuclear war incidents—roughly one every five years. During a Crisis era climax, these odds will certainly grow. Wars will be undertaken for greater stakes. Nations will be more likely to perceive that their survival is in jeopardy. Tensions will rise, along with the possibility of misperception and miscalculation. Leaders may try to "out-crazy" each other to force the other to back down. In the very worst nuclear outcome, the catastrophic loss of life, of industry, and of public services—to say nothing of the damage to the natural environment—would generate misery on a global scale. While both humanity and civilization would survive, the world might require decades, perhaps an entire saeculum, to regain most of what had been lost.

Even the small risk of such a dreadful outcome, some might argue, is a good reason for *all* political leaders to do everything they can to avoid a Fourth Turning climax. The problem is: This small risk won't persuade *every* leader to do so, especially if he or she now understands that every other leader is prepared to back down in a confrontation.

More to the point, the world may in fact require a global Fourth Turning climax to put an end to the possibility of general nuclear war, most likely (as we have imagined) through instituting some sort of post-Crisis global enforcement agency. On our current course, absent such a global regime, the yearly likelihood of a nuclear war has been estimated at around 1 percent per year. And this yearly risk is due to rise as more nations gain nukes and possibly other types of WMDs (say, bioweapons or predatory nanobots). As the years go by, the cumulative odds inevitably mount. By the end of another saeculum (ninety years), the odds of it happening may easily exceed three out of four.

Accepting the risk of a Fourth Turning, therefore, *may be humanity's least risky course.* Short term, to be sure, the odds of catastrophe rise. Yet longer term the odds decline. The Fourth Turning serves to reverse institutional entropy, not just at the national but also at the global level. Accepting the risk of a Fourth Turning now, in this sense, may be regarded as an investment in a less risky global saeculum to follow.

Another unsuccessful Fourth Turning outcome would be one that doesn't result in large-scale WMD destruction but does result in America emerging as a damaged and diminished nation. Several scenarios could lead to this outcome. America could be clearly defeated in a great-power conflict. America could be exhausted or fragmented after a self-destructive civil conflict. Or America could emerge unvanquished and intact, but drastically degraded in its political constitution—for example, by losing free elections, by losing basic civil liberties, or by losing all barriers against central government control over state and local governance.

Most likely, in an unsuccessful outcome, America would suffer an overlapping of all three scenarios. We might imagine, for example, a great-power war in which America's performance is fatally undermined by political divisions at home. Or a civil war in which other great powers intervene and overwhelm. Or, in any Crisis climax that does not go well, a desperate citizenry submitting to authoritarian rule in order to stop what they fear is a descent into anarchy. In the worst of these scenarios, America would emerge torn into pieces or occupied. In the best, America would emerge intact and functional, but also weakened and demoralized.

Should any of these scenarios happen, it would constitute the first Anglo-American Fourth Turning that ends in failure—or, at the very least, that compels America during the subsequent First Turning to dedicate itself entirely to regaining some measure of what it has lost. The only historical analogue would be to imagine, on a national scale, the outcome for the losing faction in a civil conflict, for example, the South after the U.S. Civil War.

Such an outcome would surely be unfortunate for Americans. Yet in today's world it would be unfortunate for other peoples as well. A suddenly weaker and less functional America would pull down the entire world. It would reduce the global rate of tech innovation and economic growth; undermine the enforcement of global rules for trade and legal disputes; leave air and sea lanes less protected; embolden global terrorists and pirates; enfeeble any backstop against global financial, economic, or energy emergencies. Most importantly, it would strip the world's democracies of the strong security guarantees they now depend on and render many of them defenseless against powerful regional autocrats.

This is not to say that America is indispensable to the future of the world. Other democracies could develop the global rulemaking and rule-enforcing capabilities that America currently provides. But they could not develop them quickly. At best, before that happens, the world would need to survive decades of relative anarchy. For the foreseeable future, then, the seasons for America and for the rest of the world are closely linked. It's hard to imagine an upbeat global First Turning after a Crisis outcome failure for America. Nor, perhaps, vice versa.

Let's return now to our imagined First Turning scenario. How would it differ if it were to follow an unsuccessful, rather than a successful, Crisis outcome?

Clearly, it would change the state of the world—and the challenges facing America in that world—a great deal. Rather than investing the surplus of unprecedented prosperity, Americans may be struggling to raise living standards back to where they were before the Crisis era began. Rather than leading a coalition of victorious allies, the nation may be struggling to mount a resistance to a coalition of victorious adversaries. In the very worst scenario, if we dare to go that far, rather than erecting gleaming green communities or sending manned missions to other planets, Americans could be choosing hardy crops that survive in radioactive soil and building insulated shelters to survive a nuclear winter.

So yes, success or failure matters. Depending on which way it goes, Americans in the next First Turning would be living very different lives and working toward very different national goals. No question about that.

In most of these scenarios, however, the social mood would be similar. Like all First Turnings, the era following failure would still prioritize community, cooperation, political unity, and conventional norms. The focus on building—or perhaps now, rebuilding—cities and economic infrastructure is likely to be especially strong, along with the desire to start new families. All this seems to be the clear pattern in modern nations that have suffered Crisis-era defeat—for example, during World War II.

The generational dynamics following failure would also be broadly the same. Even after defeat, the Hero archetype goes on to play a relatively large role in post-Crisis national politics. The Artist archetype goes on to play the constructive understudy role. And the Prophet archetype, born after the Crisis, goes on as always to trigger the next Awakening, which (if anything) may be even more intense in societies after defeats than after victories. In the 1970s, for example, the youth protest movements in Germany and Italy were among the most radical and violent in Europe. One reason, perhaps, was that history in both countries had already discredited the ruling Hero archetype—which made it more likely that youth would treat this generation with unusual defiance and contempt.

The seasons of the saeculum are durable. Across a wide range of outcomes, the rhythm persists: Winter keeps following fall, and spring keeps following winter. In the language of complexity theory, it is a system with a wide attractor basin: No matter how contingent events change real-world outcomes, the social cycle tends to reassert itself over time.

What keeps driving the social mood forward in approximately the same pattern? As always, it is the momentum of generational aging. Looking ahead to the next First Turning, we return to our original insight: The adults of that future world will mainly be all of us, only older.

It's time we meet our older selves.

THE NEXT FIRST TURNING: GENERATIONS

From the end of the Fourth Turning to the end of the next First Turning, the generational constellation will turn another quarter-rotation. One late elder generation will disappear, and another will emerge. The same will occur in the four active phases of life: The lineup will move forward one notch. Contemplating this changing mix of active archetypes, we can appreciate how and why the world of the 2040s will feel different from the world of the 2020s.

As in earlier chapters, we'll proceed from the oldest generation to the youngest. We start first with three late elder generations: G.I.s (*Heroes*), Silent (*Artists*), and Boomers (*Prophets*).

We then move on to the four younger generations: Gen-Xers (*Nomads*), Millennials (*Heroes*), Homelanders (*Artists*), and New Prophets (*Prophets*). These four fully active generations comprise the generational constellation of the next First Turning or High. Each will be entering a new phase of life: Xers into elderhood, Millennials into midlife, Homelanders into young adulthood, and New Prophets into childhood.

We assume the First Turning will begin in 2033 and end, twenty-three years later, in 2056. Population figures in those years are derived from the latest official United Nations projection (medium variant) for the United States.

Late Elder Generations: G.I.s, Silent, and Boom

At the beginning of the next First Turning in 2033, the G.I. Generation (age 109+) will number only a few thousand. But with the outcome of yet another Crisis now fresh in their memory, Americans will respectfully stop to salute their living connection to an earlier moment of national trial. It has happened before. After World War II, James Hard, the last confirmed Civil War combat veteran (who claimed to have shaken Abraham Lincoln's hand), was interviewed frequently in newspapers until his death in 1953 at age 109. After the very last confirmed Civil War veteran, Albert Woolson, died in 1956 at age 106, President Eisenhower released a written obituary expressing the American people's "sorrow" at having "lost the last personal link to the Union Army."

When surviving G.I. veterans are questioned about current events, they may be less surprised than younger generations that America was able to pull itself together during the Crisis climax. (Hard, similarly, claimed he never doubted that America would "whip the Japs.") Other G.I.s may simply marvel at all the history they have witnessed. This will be our last chance to hear their voices. By the late 2030s, they will all be gone.

The Silent Generation (age 91–108), meanwhile, will enter the next First Turning with about 3 million members. Just as the nation is entering its next High, the media will be memorializing the departure of many of this generation's top musical and cinematic celebrities, whose earnest yet stylish mien during the American High could now be enjoying a comeback. Museums and the fine arts, on the other hand, will suffer now that the generation of philanthropists that always supported them so generously is at last running out of donors.

Already seared by their childhood memory of global war and depression, the Silent will recall the recent Crisis climax with a profound sense of disappointment, even anguish. Like the aging members of the Compromise Generation who encountered the Civil War—or of the Enlightenment Generation who encountered the Stamp Act Crisis—they may have had children or grandchildren on both sides of the conflict. And they may have dedicated their entire careers to serving and improving an old regime that no longer exists. Many will feel, with some distress, that national life has assumed a more regimented flavor since the recent Crisis. They will sympathize with the mounting pressures brought to bear on the new era's young-adult Homelanders, who will be their grandchildren and great-grandchildren.

Only a handful of Silent, maybe one or two hundred, will witness the end of the next First Turning in the mid-2050s.

In 2033, the Boom Generation (age 73–90) will still be a substantial presence—all 42 million of them. Their convictions will burn bright as ever, and Boomers will continue to voice them often. As senior legislators, academics, and media guest stars, many will remain, in their seventies and eighties, among the most quotable Americans, always quick to take a stand—and always ready to take listeners on long and solipsistic voyages into their own heads.

Entering the next First Turning, America could well have a Boomer president. But as the nation moves even a few years into the new High, voters will no longer be in the mood for a Gray Champion. If they haven't done so already, they will opt for a lower-key pragmatist as national leader—in other words, for an Xer.

Very likely, this Nomad chief executive will need to remind older Prophets that the Crisis era is over and that the time for showdowns is past. This is how President Truman prevailed against two grandiloquent elder Missionaries during the American High. In November 1946, when the president of the United Mineworkers Union, John L. Lewis, dared Truman to stop his coal miners from striking, Truman did just that—and the old crusader backed down. "Well, John L. had to fold up," Truman later recounted. "He couldn't take the gaff. No bully can." Six years later, Truman showed similar guts in firing Douglas MacArthur ("Mr. Prima Donna, Brass Hat, Five Star MacArthur," Truman called him), even while younger congressmen were likening the general's preachings to "the words of god himself." In the mid-2030s, a handful of eminent Boomers may wake up to find that their long careers have been terminated by a similar slap down—delivered by an Xer who refuses to be intimidated.

As the next First Turning opens, to be sure, Boomer opinions will still matter. But with each passing year, as Boomers age and their numbers thin, they will matter less. Indeed, this rate-of-change *subtraction* is a useful way to think about how the nation will feel as it shifts from a Fourth Turning into a First Turning. Let's take everything salient about the Boomers' peer personality—their individualism, their crusading zeal, their obsession with values and culture, their otherworldliness—and then let's steadily subtract all of that from America's current social mood. While most younger Americans will embrace the shift, most surviving Boomers won't. What's left, in their eyes, will be a nation that is blander, shallower, and more herdlike than the one they will recall from their younger years—bustling with plans and optimism, to be sure, but woefully deficient in character and wisdom.

While Boomers will appreciate that their generation's New Age cultural landmarks will by now be venerated in grand fashion, many will be chilled—if they aren't already—to see them turned into soulless memes and commercial brands. It's a lesson that comes hard to every generation, and it will come especially hard to the 2.5 million Boomers who will live to see the end of the next First Turning. The lesson is this: If society is to change, something old must be taken away to make room for something new. And in the era to come, it's Boomers whose influence must diminish.

Gen-X Elders

At the opening of the next First Turning, Generation X (age 52–72) will remain America's second-largest generation of adults, at 84 million. By the end, Gen X (age 75–95) will shrink to third place, at 47 million. In between, Xers will almost certainly comprise the era's dominant generation of senior national leaders—presidents, supreme court justices, congressional committee chairpersons, large-cap CEOs, and big-dollar political donors and philanthropists.

As a "recessive" political generation, however, Gen-Xers are not likely to occupy the highest public offices for long. Early in the era, they may have to beat back the leadership aspirations of contentious older Boomers who can't accept that the recent Crisis is over. Later in the era, they may be eclipsed by ambitious younger Millennials who want to construct another Empire of Liberty or Great Society. In between, Gen-X national leaders—at least one of whom is likely to be an acclaimed military commander—will give America vital time to heal, rebuild, and recover.

Unlike the Boomer leaders who came before them, Xer leaders won't argue about symbols or beliefs. They will be content if society basically *works* again, even if they need to leverage imperfect or immoral means to make that happen. Senior Xers will galvanize the era's bottom-line focus on tangible community objectives—like national security, infrastructure, wages, and public health. Then, for each one, they will negotiate a plan that puts everybody into motion. From foreign alliances to urban reconstruction, they will evaluate projects by results, not by motives. While Xer leaders may justify their deeds in the name of patriotism or humanity, they will never forget that success depends on particular people getting the job done. For them, loyalty and honor will matter more than conviction or principle.

Unlike the Millennial leaders who will come after them, few Xers will imagine that the nation (or the world) can ever be made secure against

existential risk. Xers will be aware of—and may even admire—their juniors' plans for bigger and more powerful civic institutions. But they will
not trust them. Hypervigilant since childhood, Xers will never commit
their welfare to some fallible technology or Borg-like system. For them,
individuals must retain agency and choice in order to stay alive. To quote
the fictional aging fighter ace Maverick (played by Tom Cruise) lecturing his young students: "It's not the plane, it's the pilot." In an era that
trusts the growing power of technology and community, Xers know that
their views may brand them as retrograde and roguish, adherents of
some bygone warrior creed. They'll insist on them anyway.

Both as elders and as national leaders, perhaps the Xers' most important contribution will be the demands they *don't* make for themselves. Xers will have already agreed, during the Crisis climax, to pay
higher taxes, to accept public benefit cuts, and to invest in bonds that
were likely to get inflated away. Now, during the next First Turning, that
diminished expectation of public reward will continue, making possible
the enlarged share of public and private spending flowing to young people and to the future. Wherever great public works appear in the 2030s
and 2040s, not many Americans will be asking who is *not* getting paid
in order to afford them. Old Xers will know. But they will probably keep
that secret to themselves.

Gen-Xers in the next First Turning can be expected to follow the
historical script for Nomads entering elderhood.

**As seasoned Nomads replace Prophets in elderhood, they slow the
pace of social change, shunning the old crusades in favor of simplicity and survivalism.**

Uninspired by grand causes and ideologies, elder Nomads calm society,
accept the outcome of the Crisis, and build a workable civic order out
of its glory (or ashes). Believers in functional social rituals, they become
old-fashioned elders who practice thrift and caution and try to safeguard
family life. They are less impressed than their juniors by promises of rapid
progress—and more fearful of where institutional hubris may lead. The
twilight years of Queen Elizabeth I and George Washington, though separated by two saecula, exemplify the elder Nomad style. Still the canny

and picaresque warrior, each had become risk averse, worn from care, protective of a hard-won peace, graciously "old regime" in manner, not too proud to show occasional vanity or cupidity, and resistant yet kind to pushier and more confident juniors.

Still stigmatized, Nomad elders strike other generations as burnt out, corruptible, even reactionary. They ask little for themselves at a time when the public mood is focused less on rewarding the old than investing in the young.

During the Augustan Age, the elder Cavalier Generation stood accused of "a sad degeneracy" in an era, write historians John Demos and Serane Boocock, that sermonized on old age with "a note of distaste . . . almost of repulsion." After the American Revolution, according to historian David Hackett Fischer, Washington's Liberty peers had the "unhappy fate . . . to be young in an era when age was respected, and old in a time when youth took the palm." In their last years, many became self-doubting pessimists who (like John Adams) knew for certain that "mausoleums, statues, monuments will never be erected to me."

Nearly a century later, around 1900, Gilded Generation "geezers" and "fogies" were greeted by what historian Andrew Achenbaum calls "an unprecedented devaluation of the elderly." Few Gilded protested after a celebrated (younger) doctor, William Osler, publicly and only half-facetiously recommended "peaceful departure by chloroform" for men over sixty in order to speed social progress. Likewise, during the American High, the retirees of the Lost Generation made few claims on America's buoyant economic growth—despite their high rate of poverty. In 1964, remarkably, they were more likely than any younger generation to vote for Barry Goldwater even after he had promised to slash their Social Security benefits.

Millennials in Midlife

At the opening of the next First Turning, Millennials (age 28–51) will remain America's largest generation of adults, at 113 million. By the end, Millennials (age 51–74) will shrink to second place, at 107 million. During most of the years in between, Millennials will be the largest generation of voters and the dominant generation of midlife parents. For nearly the entire era, they will possess the largest generational share of governors and members of Congress. In the latter half of the era, after the mid-2040s, they will also show the fastest growth in senior leadership positions—including, most likely, the presidency.

We earlier described the social mood of the next First Turning, from beginning to end, as the steady subtraction of Boomer peer personality traits. That's just half the story. We can also describe it as the steady *addition* of Millennial traits—their sociability, aptitude for teamwork and consensus, belief in secular progress, trust in technology and scale, and optimism about human nature. During the next First Turning, the Millennial influence will be rising just as its archetypal opposite, the Boomer influence, will be falling. By the early 2050s, in Jungian terms, inner-world idealism will remain weak, and individualism will be reaching its nadir. Meanwhile, outer-world materialism will remain strong, and community will be reaching its zenith.

As a "dominant" political generation, Millennials' rise to senior leadership roles may come early. When will the first Millennial president take office? It could happen soon, late in the current Fourth Turning, especially if the two parties continue to field unimpressive older candidates. Ordinarily, however, voters turn to older leaders during emergencies— and America may be facing many of these during the rest of the 2020s. Early in the First Turning, Millennial candidates may have to defer to any Xers or Boomers who distinguished themselves as leaders or commanders late in the Crisis era. Only by the early 2040s, as the oldest Millennials are reaching sixty, will the odds of a Millennial president begin to rise rapidly.

Already by the early 2030s, plenty of Millennials will be winning elections by impressing voters with their energy and civic spirit. If the First Turning begins in 2033, first-wave Millennials will be the same age as G.I.s were in 1953, when G.I.s first captured a generational plurality in the House of Representatives. (That plurality lasted until 1975, well into the subsequent Awakening.)

When the incoming Millennial tide ultimately displaces the Xer incumbents, the collision will feel like Thomas Jefferson attacking the record of John Adams in 1800 or John Kennedy attacking the record of

Dwight Eisenhower in 1960. The cause of the younger Hero will appear confident, rational, optimistic, and grandly ambitious. The cause of the older Nomad will appear anxious, small-minded, and uncertain. The prudent survivalism that served Nomad leaders well early in the era will by now be out of favor. As the First Turning wears on, Americans will grow more collectively assertive. They will want a nation that doesn't merely hoard its growing power, but employs it to rid society of poverty, misery, and ignorance; to heal the global environment; and perhaps (to paraphrase *Star Trek*) "to boldly go where no nation has gone before." They will want a Millennial-led America.

With Millennials in charge, community will become no mere aspiration. It will become an all-encompassing lifestyle. The same adults who today, in their late twenties, fret over FOMO will by then, in their late fifties, preside over wall-to-wall AI algorithms designed to ensure that no one feels disconnected or alone. With continuous guidance from peer feedback, each individual's aspirations, opinions, and tastes will be nudged gently toward the constructive median. Marketing and entertainment—by then, these industries will have fully merged—will propagate messages that have all the edge of a Disney cartoon sequel. Their main function will be to remind people of what their friends (and the experts) already recommend.

Yet the flip side of a society that bends individual lives into bland synergy is a society capable of stunning collective achievement.

By the early 2050s, an impressive share of the Millennials' secular visions will have been translated into digital blueprints, and those in turn will have been welded and molded into the networked tubes, towers, and terraces that will by now define twenty-first-century civilization. Millennials will take great pride in all their wonders of technology and social organization—everything from productivity-enhancing bots to communal memory stations; from behavior-optimizing psychotropics to algorithmic crowd control; from global government planning boards to mammoth engines of global climate control. Yet even now, as the next First Turning draws to a close, few of these fifty- and sixty-somethings will consider slowing down. Most will feel they have so much building still to do, so many space-age ziggurats yet to erect.

Millennials in the next First Turning can be expected to follow the historical script for Heroes entering midlife.

As confident Heroes replace Nomads in midlife, they establish an upbeat, constructive ethic of social discipline.

Their ears ringing with post-Crisis accolades, midlife Heroes become the High's optimistic public planners and institution builders. During the Crisis, they saved the nation. Now they set out to strengthen, enrich, and glorify the nation—and perhaps even the world. They organize and rationalize every sphere of life, from science to religion, statecraft to the arts. They deploy technology to reach their goals and trust quantitative yardsticks to measure their progress. At their peak of power, they expect to propel civilization over a new threshold of progress. Older and younger people regard them as the most competent, if least reflective, generation of their time.

Admired for their powerful ethic of achievement, midlife Heroes are often promoted early to national leadership roles. They are confident they can make big institutions work better than their Prophet and Nomad predecessors—and they take for granted the support of younger Artists.

Not surprisingly, midlife Heroes have provided Highs with most of their public energy. The Arthurians founded a new dynasty, the Elizabethans adorned a new empire, and the Glorious laid the foundation of an affluent and enlightened New World civilization. "Be up and doing. Activity. Activity," Benjamin Colman preached to his Glorious peers during the Augustan Age. "Be fruitful: This is the way to be joyful." His generation established the colonies' first stable and prosperous ruling class, albeit at the cost of chiseling slavery into law.

In the Era of Good Feelings, while Jefferson asked the nation to "unite in common efforts for the common good," his midlife Republican peers called for "energy in government," "usefulness and reason" in science, and "abundance" in commerce. During the American High, John Kennedy spoke for the grander ambitions of "a new generation" of midlife G.I.s ("born in this century") who wanted to join "a struggle against the common enemies of man: tyranny, poverty, disease and war itself."

Homelanders in Rising Adulthood

At the opening of the next First Turning, Homelanders (age 4–27) will number about 99 million, most of them still children. By the end, Homelanders (age 27–50) will emerge as America's largest generation of adults, at 107 million. In between, they will be earning most of the high-school and college diplomas, starting most of the new careers and households, and giving birth to most of the babies. As the era draws to a close, they will become the dominant generation of parents in K-12 schools; the newest generation of freshly minted CEOs, legislators, generals, and admirals; and the largest generation of voters.

Early in the next First Turning, Homelanders will largely play a bystander role in national life. Many of course will be too young to play anything else. In 2033, 60 percent of Homelanders will still be children. Even a decade later, the oldest will be in their mid-thirties and roughly half will not yet be fully degreed or launched into careers. Yet even as full-fledged young adults, most Homelanders will prefer not to call attention to themselves. Silence may be a prudent habit they will have developed growing up—and also a sensible response to the strict rules still enforced by older generations. In the early post-Crisis world, young people will be anxious not to appear selfish, make foolish mistakes, or let others down.

Early in life, Homelanders will embrace the conventional. Most will try to stay safe and avoid scandal, work for mainstream credentials, take an interest in family life, and strive to be model citizens, employees, spouses, and neighbors. As youth celebrities and media stars, most will take care not to offend. As young political leaders, most will support the public consensus—and even those who don't will try to remain polite, informed, and constructive. In their choice of careers, they will seek out secure employers that are helping to build out the new regime—and master new specialties where their contributions will be well rewarded.

As America's new civic order acquires a new infrastructure during the next First Turning, Millennials will likely assume a proprietary interest in what they will deem to be "their" expansive vision. Homelanders, working as the Millennials' understudies, will by contrast see themselves as the experts, technicians, and specialists who make sure that the whole system works. For every broad civic or economic goal proposed by older leaders, Homelanders will need to labor in largely anonymous teams to work out all the details—from the materials, engineering, programming, and costs to the ultimate satisfaction it brings to the people who use it.

More than other generations, these young adults will excel at communicating with other people (including other age groups) who hold different points of view. It's a talent that will make them fresh, powerful, and elegant new contributors to the arts and entertainment. At home, Homelanders will come to define, without knowing it, their era's paradigmatic image of everyday life—what future generations will regard as the "timeless" image of 2040s-era America.

Late in the era, as they begin to enter middle age, Homelanders are likely to sense a growing frustration about where their lives have taken them. Even while older Millennials tirelessly press for still larger public undertakings, Homelanders will begin to harbor doubts. With their narrow-gauge awareness of how big plans can go awry, they will raise new questions about the human cost of civic gigantism. Many may also come to regret the unqualified trust they once placed in their youthful commitments—and the personal risks they never took. Homelanders won't feel the same solidarity that motivates Millennials, the reigning generation of leaders. As they prepare to assume top leadership positions themselves, they may feel something different: a profound sense of uncertainty.

Homelanders in the next First Turning can be expected to follow the historical script for Artists entering young adulthood.

As sensitive Artists replace Heroes in young adulthood, they become trusting helpmates, lending their expertise and cooperation to an era of growing social calm.

An Artist generation comes of age just as the post-Crisis social order is solidifying. With little room to maneuver, this "inheritor generation" embarks early on approved life paths. Adept since childhood at satisfying social expectations, they now seek to assist the Heroes in their grand constructions—hoping they can thereby merit some of the reflected glory that comes with founding a new regime. Yet even as they eagerly collaborate, Artists probe cautiously for a more authentic personal role. This effort leads to a cult of expertise (refining the Heroes' outer-world achievements) and to critical gestures of conscience and feeling (exposing the Heroes' inner-world limitations).

In the first two "Renaissance" Highs, young adults were regarded as the most educated and least adventuresome adults of their era. During the colonial Augustan Age, the rococo college graduates of the Enlightenment Generation praised themselves as "docile and tutorable" and thereafter became America's first true professionals in medicine, law, and politics. During the Era of Good Feelings, (Compromise) youths came of age with what John Quincy Adams confessed was "our duty to remain the peaceable and silent." Their new frontier folk felt less like adventurers than like settlers or, as with Lewis and Clark, like civil servants.

In the Gilded Age, the Progressive Generation started out as famously mild-mannered young adults, collectively described by one admirer as "a harmonious blending, a delightful symmetry, formed of fitting proportions of every high quality." In the American High, the Silent Generation kept out of trouble and joked nervously about their "gray flannel suits." Proudly calling themselves "technocrats," they crowded into government and big corporations.

New Prophet Youth

New Prophets (born 2030–2052) are a conjectural generation. None of them are yet born, and they don't yet have a generational name. Following the recent saecular pattern, their first birth year should fall about four years before the end of the Fourth Turning, and their last birth year about three years before the end of the next First Turning. By then, in the year 2056, they will range in age from four to twenty-six and will number roughly 105 million.

New Prophets will constitute the new post-Crisis generation of children. The older half will be parented mostly by Millennials, the younger half mostly by Homelanders. By the end of the era, they will include all children in grade school plus youth both in and out of college.

All New Prophet children will have this much in common: They will not recall a moment in which imminent national threats still hung unresolved over their parents and families. Instead, these children will bask in the security of a world at peace—a world fiercely protective of its newfound order and able to lavish fresh attention on its newest members. Much of the social energy that was directed against adversaries before the early 2030s will later be redirected, after the early 2030s, toward home and hearth and the first living fruits of the new regime.

It will be a profound shift in nurture. But it won't happen all at once. In the early years of the next First Turning, child-raising is likely to remain protective, much like it is for today's Homelander kids. In later years, as the overall social mood grows more expansive, child-raising will gradually become more relaxed and easygoing. Late-wave Millennials, who will parent mainly first-wave New Prophets, will be stricter, especially when their children are young. First-wave Homelanders, who will parent mainly late-wave New Prophets, will be more permissive, especially as their children reach their teens. Homelander parents will be relieved to raise their children *unlike* the way they were raised.

New Prophets will be seen, and will see themselves, as the children of the generation that was formatively shaped by the Millennial Crisis. By the end of the next First Turning, older people will view them as healthy, brilliant, creative, and strong-willed—full of limitless potential. New Prophets will have been raised to want nothing. For as long as they can remember, their nation has been working with great success (and few complaints) to pacify the world, fabricate abundance, harmonize social factions, manage nature, and push back the frontier on disease, ignorance, and aggression. And their parents, as they remind their children of these accomplishments, will tell them something else: that all this progress you see is not quite enough, that we raised you to sanctify and adorn what we have built—to hoist into place the glorious capstone on what we began.

Contemplating all this, New Prophets will be wondering: What should we do with our lives?

New Prophets in the next First Turning can be expected to follow the historical script for Prophets entering childhood.

As indulged Prophets replace Artists in childhood, they are nurtured with growing freedom in a fail-safe world designed by powerful adults.

The upbeat First Turning social mood projects its optimism onto children, giving rise to a fertility bulge, a preoccupation with family life, and long investment horizons. In the orderly post-Crisis world, parents can safely devote more time to child-raising and offer new freedoms to a new generation. Yet First-Turning adults, however effective they may be as material providers, are less effective as moral exemplars. Raised in a well-ordered but spiritually apathetic society, children cultivate intense inner lives. They tend to form stronger bonds with mothers (their links to personal values) than with fathers (their links to civic deeds). Presumed to have a bright future, children are encouraged to demand much of life.

The Puritan children of the Elizabethan Renaissance, heirs to national victory and a new commercial empire, were parented by what historian David Leverenz describes as a "mixture of relatively good mothering" and "distant . . . repressive fathers." The Augustan Age's Awakener children, raised in an era of relative affluence, cultivated what historian Gary Nash describes as an "antirational, antiscientific . . . and moralistic" attitude toward their parents' world. The Transcendental children of the Era of Good Feelings, according to a British visitor, showed "prominent boldness and forwardness." "The elements added after 1790" to the child's world, notes historian Joseph Kett, "were increasingly on the side of freedom."

The Gilded Age's Missionary kids grew up in a "long children's picnic," says historian Mary Cable, "a controlled but pleasantly free atmosphere." Middle-class mothers dressed their little boys in luxurious "Lord Fauntleroy" suits. Jane Addams recalled how her peers had been "sickened with advantages." Boomer children, raised during the American High in stable, affluent families, grew up with few duties and much free time. No generation of kids before or after was so likely to have a mom at home to tend to their needs. Their more troubled relationships with their dads were described in the 1960s by on-campus academics as "ambivalent" (Kenneth Keniston), "Oedipal hostility" (Lewis Feuer), or an attitude of "parricide" (Henry Malcolm). Young Boomers looked with boredom toward a future that promised to be (in the words of late-waver Cheryl Merser) "the way life was on *The Jetsons*—happy, easy, uncomplicated, prosperous."

Now, at last, the next First Turning is over. The archetypal constellation has moved into a new alignment. As the Second Turning begins, Millennials will now be moving into elderhood, Homelanders into midlife, New Prophets into young adulthood, and yet another batch of newborns into childhood.

Yet the generational forces unleashed by the next First Turning will by no means be over. As the Second Turning begins, indeed, these forces will just be getting underway.

Let's return to the question that New Prophets will be asking as they begin coming of age sometime in the mid-2050s: What should we do with our lives?

Millennial parents of New Prophets will suppose the answer is self-evident. And so has every earlier generation of leaders at the end of a First Turning. They have all supposed that the rising Prophet archetype will follow dutifully in their footsteps.

In the 1730s, they supposed the rising Awakeners would follow their parents' vision of commerce, slavery, and empire. They paid no attention to teenagers like Jonathan Edwards who walked in the woods to "solitary places, for meditation" where he could reflect on "the divine glory in almost everything." Or the young John Woolman, who imagined "past ages" in which people "walked in uprightness before God in a degree exceeding any that I knew, or heard of, now living."

In the 1820s, they supposed the rising Transcendentals would follow their parents' vision of orderly Republican rationalism. Thomas Jefferson went so far as to predict, in 1822, that "there is not a young man now living in the U.S. who will not die a Unitarian." They had no inkling of the born-again evangelical tidal wave that was about to sweep across

America. And they would have been stunned to learn about teenagers like William Lloyd Garrison, who would soon call the Founders' Constitution "a Covenant with Death, an Agreement with Hell."

In the 1890s, they supposed the rising Missionaries would become civic-minded industrialists. When they built the Chicago World's Fair—featuring an electrified Neoclassical "White City," a moving sidewalk, and Krupp artillery—they imagined youth would find it irresistible. They weren't listening to George Cabot Lodge, age twenty at the time, who recoiled at this "world of machine-guns and machine-everything-else." Or Ida B. Wells, thirty-one, who protested that to Negro Americans the White City was a "whited sepulcher." Or Frank Lloyd Wright, twenty-six, who later attributed its ugliness to an "overwhelming rise of grandomania."

In the early 1960s, similarly, the now-in-charge G.I. Generation supposed the rising Boomers would be eager to design bigger Pontiacs, work for the Pentagon, and colonize the planets. In 1965, *Time* magazine declared teenagers to be "on the fringe of a golden era"—and two years later described collegians as cheerful builders who would "lay out blight-proof, smog-free cities, enrich the underdeveloped world, and, no doubt, write finis to poverty and war." Even the G.I.s' "best and brightest" journalists had no clue of what lay in store for them.

By this time there can be no doubt: The saecular summer will be nigh. The Second Turning will be ready to ignite.

From the late 2050s into the 2070s, we can imagine America engulfed in the next Awakening, initially triggered by the New Prophets' youthful defiance and soon finding plenty of mentors and allies among the older Homelanders. Universities may be rocked by protest, cities by riot, the military by noncompliance, families by argument. Youthful rule-breaking may become widespread. Utopian lifestyle experiments may proliferate. Vast numbers of youth, invoking higher values, may choose to unplug themselves entirely from their parents' cyber-age crystal palace. However it plays out, social comity will be shattered.

Eventually even Millennials, now retiring from national leadership roles, perhaps not always willingly, will have to admit defeat. By now their left-brained vision of a harmonious networked utopia will have fallen into disrepute. They will have spent a lifetime building a broad highway that leads to ever-greater felicity and cooperation. And by now they will see large pieces of it in ruins.

Their children will have preferred something else. Not works, but faith. Not mastery for all, but salvation for each. Not the broad highway, but the small gate and the narrow path. Millennials won't understand this path—nor the young people who choose it. They will wonder why, as kids, they were so much closer to their Boomer parents than their own kids are to them. They will stare at their data and their models, now displayed holographically before them, and wonder what went wrong. And their data and their models will stare back at them.

Later, by the 2080s and 2090s, perhaps we can imagine America entering another Third Turning, a new Unraveling marked by fragmentation and drift. As senior leaders, Homelanders will preside uncertainly over this era, lamenting that the civic cohesion they recall from the 2040s has mysteriously disappeared. And then, perhaps around the year 2100, we can imagine the beginning of the next Fourth Turning. Coming of age will be another Hero generation. And beginning to assume national leadership will be the New Prophets, whose first wave will now be entering their early seventies. We can hardly imagine what this Crisis climax might be about—nor can we guess the likelihood that America, if America still matters, will come out on top.

By this time, indeed, so much will be beyond our imagining.

Beyond our imagining will be all the nations, empires, and alliances yet to rise and fall; all the economies yet to prosper or decay; and all the celebrities, politicians, and preachers yet to make their audiences roar with approval and then disappear.

Beyond our imagining as well will be all the technologies yet to reshape how we are linked to machines, how we are linked to one another, and, for better or worse, how machines are linked to one another.

Yet perhaps we can imagine one reality that won't change. The nature of the archetypes. The rhythm of generations. And the turning of history through four seasons.

Perhaps, even then, the saeculum will abide.

Epilogue

The past isn't dead. It's not even past.

—WILLIAM FAULKNER

On the flat earthen floors of their rounded hogans, Navajo shamans or chanters (called *hatalii*) sift colored sand in intricate patterns across a giant circular area, perhaps ten feet across. As the image materializes, it gradually reveals four quadrants. Each quadrant represents a season of life and a season of time, each embellished by its own associated bird or plant or spirit deity (called *yei*). The shamans complete the painting by encompassing it with a circle. But as they do so, they always leave a gap in the fourth quadrant. This signifies the moment of death and rebirth, what the ancient Greeks called Ekpyrosis. According to Navajo lore, this moment can be completed (and the circle closed) only by the gods, never by mortal man.

The shamans learned these images from their Navajo ancestors, who have been painting them for centuries. Like most traditional peoples, they accept not just the circularity of life, but also the need to ensure its proper reenactment. Each generation knows its ancestors have drawn similar circles and expects its heirs to keep drawing them. The Navajos ritually reenact the past while anticipating the future. Thus do they transcend time.

What purpose does the sand painting serve? Not to be preserved or admired. In fact, the shamans start working at sunup because the painting must be erased and all the sand removed from the hogan by sundown. The painting, rather, is the central focus of a purification ritual. It serves to heal a person who is sick—or, by extension, to restore the pow-

453

ers of a tribal leader whose people are demoralized or confused. After communing with the spirit world, the head shaman identifies just the right painting that will propitiate any offended force of nature and will enable the seasons of time to resume their proper rhythm for that person or that community.

The Navajo are not alone in this practice. Four-sided sand paintings of surprisingly similar design are also crafted in brilliant colors by Buddhist monks in Tibet, as part of a curative ritual that they too have received from many centuries of ancestors. The healing arts of the Navajos and the Tibetans, like those of most traditional peoples, are based on the principles of complementarity, balance, and the restoration of natural energy.

Today, the need for healing has never been greater. America, along with most of the rest of the modern world, is demoralized and confused. Multiple indexes of global unhappiness have surged over the last fifteen years. It is not hardship that causes this misery, but hardship without purpose. We feel disconnected in space from our broader communities. We also feel disconnected in time from our parents and our children. Linear history, which ties us to an incessant desire for novelty and progress, destroys the bond between us and those who came before us. And we fully expect it must do the same between us and those who will come after us.

If only the *hatalii* could invite the entire modern world, like a sick Navajo child, to sit in the middle of the sand painting until our balance and our connections were restored.

We are distressed because we have entered a season of history that we dread completing. We understand that the Fourth Turning is a season of crisis likely to bring wrenching and unwanted changes to our lives. Yet on reflection we dread even more a future that is a linear extension of the past. This linear future is guaranteed to make us even less happy and is in any case unsustainable. In short, we know that there is nothing worse than a Fourth Turning—except *not* having a Fourth Turning.

But if avoiding the Fourth Turning is not possible or even desirable, what then should we do?

We should follow ancient wisdom and conform our behavior to the season. If it's winter, we should act like it's winter. We should help our community prepare to be strong in the coming spring while allowing the least possible suffering so long as the storms rage. Though we may not be able to prevent the winter from happening, we *are* able to make the winter turn out better or worse. But we can't help at all unless we first acknowledge that winter has indeed arrived. Only then we can see clearly, plan responsibly, and act effectively.

Knowing the season, we can decide how we can best assist those around us. We may be a mother, a teenager, or a grandfather. We may be a CEO, a mechanic, a congressperson, an officer, or a nurse. Whatever our personal role, we want to ask ourselves: How should we perform that role so that the winter season turns out well?

Think also of our generational role. The generation we belong to may not define us as individuals. But it is likely to define most of our friends and acquaintances who are roughly our own age. So even if we don't feel we are like the rest of our peer group, we had better understand our collective life trajectory. After all, we are fated to live with and among them for the rest of our lives.

In these pages, we have suggested that every generation belongs to one of four basic archetypes, each playing a distinctive role in history according to a basic life-cycle script. Each of us belongs to a generation and therefore to one of these archetypes. As we reflect on what the coming seasons of history imply for our personal future, we should also reflect on what they imply for the future of our generation. What is expected from our generation? If our generation has weaknesses, how can these best be avoided? If it has strengths, how can these best be harnessed?

As we look ahead into the distant future, it's helpful to recall the positive endowments that each archetype ultimately leaves to posterity. These give us an aspirational view of what each can accomplish when it lives up to its potential. For the Hero archetype, these legacies are mostly in the realm of community, affluence, and technology. For the Artist: arts and letters, expertise, and due process. For the Prophet: values, vision, and religion. And for the Nomad: survival, honor, and liberty.

As we have seen, there is a natural, cross-cycle complementarity among these four archetypes. Without the Hero, a civilization would never cohere as a community or enjoy material progress; without the Prophet, it would be dead in spirit and morally blind. Without the Artist, a civilization would never flourish at its highest level of expression; without the Nomad, it would not survive at all.

To a modern audience, any sort of prescriptive role is a tough sell. Just as we don't like to think about seasons of history, so too do we resist anything that bars us from being whatever we want to be. We fear that roles inhibit creativity. The ancients had a different view. They believed that a social role, whether we choose it or not, offers us a standard to live up to. We then become creative by trying to meet that standard. Without roles, and left only to our own personal impulses, we can be neither creative nor authentic—nor, the ancients thought, can we even know our essence, who we really are.

Nowhere is this ancient understanding more eloquently expressed than in the *Bhagavad Gita*. To the sage Vyasa, who by tradition originally composed this poem (as part of a much larger epic) sometime late in the first millennium BCE, time is both seasonal and cyclical, each cycle part of a larger cycle. The ruling principle underlying all these circles of time, as well as everything that happens within them, is *dharma*. Hindu ancients believed *dharma* was both descriptive and prescriptive throughout the universe. For humans, *dharma* informs us of both our essence and our purpose; it tells us both who we are and who we ought to be.

The *Gita* sets the stage by introducing a noble young warrior, Arjuna, who is about to lead a giant army into a great battle. After looking across at the leaders of the enemy, many of whom are members of his own family, Arjuna is seized by what appears to be a very modern anxiety. As he contemplates all the carnage about to happen, he is overwhelmed by self-loathing and despair. He turns to ask his charioteer (who just happens to be Krishna) how—despite the merit and justice of his cause—any of the gods could approve of his desire to slay his enemies so that his side will prevail.

The answer to Arjuna's question composes most of the rest of the *Gita*, which Krishna delivers in a poetic discourse that ranges widely across a multitude of ethical and spiritual problems. Along the way he delivers a clear message about social roles and their connection to the seasons of history.

Krishna tells Arjuna that no one should forsake his *dharma*, which for him includes his role as warrior. He must fulfill that role, and do so with as much proficiency, honor, and humanity as he can muster. If Arjuna refuses, nothing good will come of it. Someone else will fill the role less well. Injustice will prevail. And Arjuna will be rightly scorned for not living up to his obligations. As for life and death, Krishna says, don't worry about these. Only worry about your soul. Life and death will come endlessly in any case to you humans, for you are all mortal.

What's more, Krishna assures Arjuna that each person's *dharma* is connected to the order of history and to the order of the cosmos in ways that exceed human comprehension. Each person has a role, chosen or not, that he or she should strive to fulfill as perfectly and as selflessly as possible. Confusion arises when people try to fill someone else's role, or when people neglect their role in the pursuit of some tangible result. Pay no attention to result, advises Krishna, for you humans are in no position to know the ultimate result of your actions, either for yourselves or for others. Instead, be mindful of the infinitely complex web that connects all events through all time. And focus instead on how performing your own role well can bring balance and completion to the purpose of every other being.

We don't have to be a warrior like Arjuna to understand that life is filled with excruciating choices. All people, modern and ancient, face them. Though we peer as hard as we can into the future, we can never be certain which choice is best. Where we moderns differ from the ancients is that we try to figure everything out ourselves, from scratch. For us, believers in linear progress, the past is obsolete and therefore unhelpful, and the future is a blank mystery in which anything could happen.

The ancients did not have modern analytical tools. But they did possess a profound understanding of the natural rhythms of time. They sensed that events worked themselves out in seasonal patterns and that all events, past and future, were interwoven in ways that could be intuited but not explained. They derived this understanding from their gods, their shamans, and their families. They derived it as well from the social roles they filled, which were designed to preserve the community by informing each person how he or she ought to behave in all circumstances. Invariably, everyone knew, circumstances would change. The circle would turn. What was happening now would stop, and what had happened before would start again.

We moderns have lost much of this perspective. Our gods and shamans no longer inspire the same reverence. Our families, while still strong in many ways, are no longer certain what wisdom they should pass on to children. As for our social roles—the roles we play in our families, workplaces, and neighborhoods—these no longer exert the same formative influence that they did for the ancients. Our roles no longer shape or define us; we reshape and redefine them as we see fit. As such, our roles no longer prepare us for a future different from the present.

All these changes proceed from modernity's apparent success. Because we assume that the modern world has forever liberated us from cycles of nature and time, we conclude that it has placed history on a straight line of our choosing. We are therefore free to dispense with all the ancients' lore and ritual.

But has modernity succeeded? Has it liberated us?

In some obvious ways, it has. In many other ways, it has not. And among modernity's failures, surely the most historically consequential is the rise of the saeculum. This seasonal cadence of social time, beating to the rhythm of a long human life, lay largely dormant in the ancient world. Paradoxically, it was roused and awakened by the very birth of modernity—which, in the societies of Western Europe, happened nearly six centuries ago. Unlike other ancient cycles, the saeculum did not weaken as modernity grew stronger. Instead, the saeculum and modernity grew stronger together. And the saeculum grew strongest in America, precisely where modernity took its earliest and firmest grip.

Driving the seasons of the saeculum forward are social generations, which, like the saeculum itself, lay largely dormant until modernity arrived. These generations, each striving to reform and improve their societies in a modern manner, give rise to the solstices and equinoxes of the saeculum and to the periodic recurrence of spring, summer, fall, and winter.

The rhythm of generational change has also grown more powerful over the centuries. And along the way, social generations themselves have become more self-conscious. Over the last century, they have begun to talk and write about themselves, to give themselves names, to attract marketing brands, to assess their collective opinion in regular surveys, and to speculate on how they intend to change society and politics.

The ancients were very familiar with phases of life. But they were only dimly aware of social generations. Here we find one rhythm of social life that has run counter to the prevailing modern trend. The ancients didn't know much about generations. We moderns do.

Social generations and their archetypes, as they continue to gain strength, may provide the modern world a unique opportunity to do what traditional roles no longer can—to reestablish our ties to both our history and our ancestors.

Generations connect us to history because they remind us that ours is not the first or only peer group to encounter *this* season of history at *this* phase of life. We know that others have done so before us. Perhaps we can learn from them. We also know that others will do so after us. Perhaps we can help them prepare.

Generations also connect us to our families because they remind us that we all have forebearers who encountered *this* season of history at *some* phase of their lives. We may wonder how their location in history affected what happened to them as children, what happened to the children they raised, or what happened to alter the direction of their lives at a critical moment. We may be able to draw parallels between them and ourselves, our children, or our parents.

In truth, most of us possess first-person personal contact, through our families, to an impressive span of historical time. The challenge, for most of us, is to appreciate just how impressive it is.

To illustrate, consider a Gen-X woman born in 1965. Let's first ask her who was the oldest person she personally got to know as a young child. Very likely, this was a Lost Generation grandparent (or great-grandparent) born in the mid-1890s. Let's then imagine how long this Xer will live. Suppose we project that she lives to at least age ninety (in 2055), when she gets to know a grandchild (or great-grandchild) who in turn could be expected to live to the year 2130.

Now let's measure this total span of time—from the first moment in the life of the oldest person this Xer got to know personally as a child to the last moment in the life of the youngest person she will know personally before passing away. In her case, this stretch of years—let's call it her *personal history span*—stretches from 1895 to 2130, or 235 years. We invite you, the reader, to perform the same calculation with your own life. Chances are, you will come to a similar figure.

Two hundred and thirty-five years is a long time. For most of us, our personal history span is about as long as the United States has yet been in existence. We are staggered to reflect on all the seasonal solstices—all the Awakening eras and Crisis eras—those within our personal history span *have* lived through and *will* live through. As we contemplate the full range of these experiences—in the lives of those who once cared for us and in the lives of those whom we will someday care for—we can't help but look for structure, parallels, and lessons.

Following the example of the Navajo shamans, perhaps we will begin to pay attention to the seasons of history. From the lives of our elders, we may try to derive healing powers, not just to help us with our own lives but to pass those powers on to our young.

Like the young warrior Arjuna, enlightened by Krishna, perhaps we will appreciate how the interdependence of people and events across space and time exceeds all understanding. At that point, we may turn from endless analysis to deep intuition. We may then ask simply: In everything that happens, what are the most important and enduring patterns? And what role can I serve within them?

Today, during the winter season, such clarity is likely to be obscured by the storms and passions of day-to-day events. They fill our headlines, crowd our social media, invade our conversations, and distract our attention. Only when the next season arrives will we be able to grasp the full significance of what we are experiencing now. And only with the passage of many more seasons of history will time strip away everything ephemeral, leaving behind only the bare and archetypal pattern of seasonality itself.

At that moment, looking back, we will finally recognize what Ibn Khaldun observed at the very dawn of modernity: "The past resembles the future more than one drop of water resembles another."

Acknowledgments

This book is not the outcome of a one-shot project. It is rather the latest tier in many layers of thinking and discussion that go back well over thirty years and include many earlier books. The first debt I must acknowledge in writing this book, therefore, is to everything that went into these earlier projects. Foremost, I am grateful for the opportunity to collaborate for so many years with Bill Strauss, coauthor of many of the books that proved to be the forerunners of this one, especially *Generations* (1991), *13th Gen* (1993), *The Fourth Turning* (1997), and *Millennials Rising* (2000). I am also indebted to all the scholars, editors, and friends who proved instrumental in creating those works.

My second debt of thanks goes to our readers—vast numbers of whom have contacted me over the years to share their insights and observations.

Thinking about history archetypically, as the product of overlapping generational scripts, is an acquired taste, like the habit of closely observing how people dress or talk. It starts with a glance here and a comparison there, and then it draws you in, until you can't help but notice significant patterns in everything you see changing around you, from politics to pop culture. For me, the greatest blessing derived from the books and articles that I have written on generations and history, both alone and with Bill Strauss, has been the enthusiastic feedback of readers who have acquired this taste. These readers' feedback has inspired me and kept me motivated. I hope I may be forgiven for not having time to respond to many of them.

Among these longtime readers, a few deserve special mention. I want to thank Steve Barrera and Aileen Lynch-McCulloch for their extreme diligence in helping me to source the citations in this book. I want to thank Pete Markiewicz and John Rundle for the advice they offered on technology and complexity theory; and Taylor Mann and Jim Goulding for assisting me in the initial research. I owe much as well to the many years of correspondence with email forum members, including David Kaiser, Marc Antony, Dave Sohigian, and Jennifer McCollum.

Special thanks goes to my friend and longtime reader Glenn Horton, who generously made his Florida home available to me so that I could write undisturbed for weeks at a time. While Franklin Roosevelt may have had his Shangri-La, I had Glenn's isolated asylum in the Keys.

Every author relies, more than he ever wants to admit, on the advice and wisdom of old friends. Here let me acknowledge three: Richard Jackson, Gerald Koenig, and John Mauldin. The combined depth of knowledge of these individuals—in demography, history, law, the military, economics, and markets—made this book better than it otherwise would have been.

I must express special gratitude to the organization I work for, Hedgeye Risk Management. I thank Keith McCullough and Michael Blum, Hedgeye's leaders, for their unstinting support of all the time and effort I needed to complete this book. I thank the intellectually stimulating environment provided by my sector-head colleagues. And I thank all my clients, many of whom end up instructing me about how the world works as much as I instruct them.

I also thank the members of my own Hedgeye "Demography" team, with whom I work every day: Victoria Hays, Jennifer Shen, Christian Ford, and Matthew Ahern. Their efforts improved the book by keeping me better informed day to day about breaking attitudinal and behavioral trends. At critical moments during the book's completion, they also stepped up and helped me get my facts right.

This book benefitted greatly from the superb editorial team at Simon & Schuster, in particular Priscilla Painton and Megan Hogan. Quite simply, the book would not read as well without their expert guidance. I must also thank my longtime agent (the only agent I have ever had or wanted to have), Rafe Sagalyn. Without his gentle yet persistent urging and guidance, this book never would have happened.

And of course I am grateful for my family, who at every turn has proven to be warmly supportive of this effort. I extend a special thanks to my cousins Margot Garcia and Kirk Weaver for inviting me to work in their cabin in the Sierras—my second Shangri-la. Most of all, I thank my immediate family for their support—and for tolerating without complaint all the missing evenings and weekends while this book was coming together. This includes my wife Gisella, who made sure everything functioned in my absence, and all of our kids, Giorgia, Nathaniel, Destiny, Faith, Megan, and Eva.

Notes

Notes include references for quotations, surveys, and the titles of books, movies, and songs; they also include sources for important facts. Full reference information for books and journal articles mentioned in the Notes can be found in the Bibliography.

1. WINTER IS HERE

1 **that "America is falling apart":** Results of Axios poll (conducted January 11–13, 2021); discussed in "4 in 5 Say US Is Falling Apart," *The Hill*, January 14, 2021.

1 **"losing American democracy":** Results of survey by the New York Times-Siena College Research Institute (conducted October 15–18, 2020); discussed in "Americans Are Afraid. Not for Themselves, but for the Country," *New York Times*, November 1, 2020.

1 **"the country is in a crisis":** Results of survey by Global Strategy Group (conducted June 24–28, 2021); see *GBAO Navigator*, June 2021.

1 **"proud to be an American":** "Record-Low 38% Extremely Proud to Be American," Gallup, June 29, 2022.

2 **U.S. life expectancy . . . fell further in 2020:** For U.S. life expectancy at birth for 2021, see *Mortality in the United States, 2021,* Report No. 456, NCHS Data Brief, U.S. Centers for Disease Control and Prevention, December 2022, p. 2. For all earlier years since 1900, see *United States Life Tables, 2020* 71, no. 1 (National Vital Statistics Report, U.S. Centers for Disease Control and Prevention, August 8, 2022), pp. 51–53.

2 **"truthiness":** Coined and defined by Stephen Colbert on *The Colbert Report*, October 17, 2005.

2 **the biblical story of the tower of Babel:** Jonathan Haidt, "Why the Past 10 Years of American Life Have Been Uniquely Stupid," *Atlantic*, April 11, 2022.

3 **"How Dumb Can a Nation Get":** Eugene Robinson, "How Dumb Can a Nation Get and Still Survive?" *Washington Post*, October 7, 2021.

3 **"Past the Point of No Return":** Thomas B. Edsall, "How to Tell When Your Country Is Past the Point of No Return," *New York Times*, December 15, 2021.

3 **"negative experience" or sadness index:** See Clifton, *Blind Spot.*

3 **the share of popular song lyrics:** See Brand, Acerbi, and Mesoudi, "Cultural Evolution of Emotional Expression in 50 Years of Song Lyrics."

3 **the share of all newspaper headlines:** See Rozado, Hughes, and Halberstadt, "Longitudinal Analysis of Sentiment and Emotion in New Media Headlines Using Automated Labeling with Transformer Language Models."

4 **"deaths of despair":** See Case and Deaton, *Deaths of Despair and the Future of Capitalism.*

4 **out-earning their parents at age thirty or age forty:** See Chetty et al., "The Fading American Dream."

4 **Less than half of young men are out-earning their fathers:** Ibid.

4 ***think* they are doing as well:** "Generation X Is the Least Likely to Believe They'll Get Rich One Day," *Fast Company*, July 21, 2021; includes discussion of Fast-Company-Harris survey (2021). Author analyzed unpublished cross-tabbed survey data.

4 **"it is essential to live in a democracy":** Mounk, *The People vs. Democracy* (2018), p. 105.

4 **a "bad" or "very bad" way to run the country:** Ibid., pp. 107, 110.

5 **one word they have heard frequently:** See Google Ngram usage history on these two words; "precarity" has grown from almost no usage at all before 2008 to now nearly half of that of "affluence."

5 **global trade has been shrinking:** See "Trade (% of GDP)" or "Exports of Goods and Services (% of GDP)," World Bank online; annual data series for "World" since 1970 peaked in 2008 by both measures.

5 **trade barriers have proliferated:** See *Report on G20 Trade Measures*, World Trade Organization, November 14, 2022, Chart 3.6, "Cumulative trade coverage of G20 import-restrictive measures on goods in force since 2009," p. 25.

5 **the number of democracies . . . the number of autocracies:** See *Democracy Report 2022: Autocratization Changing Nature?*, V-Dem Institute, 2022, Figure 3, p. 13; Figure 4, p. 14; and Figure 8, p. 18. See also *Freedom in the World 2022*, Freedom House, 2022, p. 4.

5 **move less:** See William Frey, "Despite the Pandemic Narrative, Americans Are Moving at Historically Low Rate," Brookings Institution, November 30, 2021, Figure 5.

5 **stay closer to their families:** See "A Majority of Young Adults in the U.S. Live with Their Parents for the First Time since the Great Depression," Pew Research Center, September 4, 2020.

5 **buy a credential rather than a home:** On young adults' growing post-secondary educational attainment, see Table 104-20, "Percentage of persons 25 to 29 years old with selected levels of educational attainment, by race/ethnicity and sex: Selected years, 1920 through 2017," Digest of Educational Statistics online, National Center for Education Statistics, U.S. Department of Education, https://nces.ed.gov/programs/digest/d17/tables/dt17_104.20.asp, accessed November 2022. On young adults' declining home ownership, see Acolin, Goodman, and Wachter, "A Renter or Homeowner Nation?," Exhibit 2, "Homeownership Rate by Age Group, U.S. Decennial Census and American Community Survey (1900–2014)," p. 147.

5 **increasingly marry . . . later in life:** See Figure MS-2, "Median age at first marriage: 1890 to present," Marital Status Visualizations, Historical Marital Status Tables, U.S. Census Bureau, November 2022.

5 **only within their own class:** See Mare, "Educational Homogamy in Two Gilded

Ages"; see also "Equality in Marriages Grows, and So Does Class Divide," *New York Times*, February 27, 2016.

6 **more correlated with education (though less with race or ethnicity):** See Jackson and Holzman, "A Century of Educational Inequality in the United States."

6 **more correlated with health and longevity:** See Case and Deaton, "Life Expectancy in Adulthood Is Falling for Those Without a BA Degree, But as Educational Gaps Have Widened, Racial Gaps Have Narrowed."

6 **Americans born in 1930 . . . born in 1960:** See National Academy of Sciences, *The Growing Gap in Life Expectancy by Income.*

6 **declining birth rate:** See annual total fertility rate (TFR) data since 1960 on FRED online (economic data from the St. Louis Federal Reserve Bank).

6 **falling home ownership:** See Acolin, Goodman, and Wachter, "A Renter or Home-owner Nation?"

6 **fewer business start-ups:** On business start-ups by young adults, see Table 3, "Share of New Entrepreneurs by Age Group," in "Who Is the New Entrepreneur? New Entrepreneurs in the United States, 1996–2021," Kauffman Foundation, October 2022. On declining share of all jobs available in start-up firms or small firms, see Akbar Sadeghi, "Business Employment Dynamics by Age and Size of Firms," U.S. Bureau of Labor Statistics, January 2022, slides 3 and 11.

6 **"castles protected by unbreachable moats":** Buffett, full quote: "In business, I look for economic castles protected by unbreachable 'moats,'" in Chairman's annual let-ter to Shareholders, 1995, available at https://www.berkshirehathaway.com/.

6 **"competition is for losers":** Thiel, "Competition Is for Losers," *Wall Street Journal*, September 12, 2014.

6 **"the news they *wanted* to hear":** Will Farrell as Ron Burgundy, in *Anchorman 2*, movie, directed by Judd Apatow (2013).

7 **"megaparties":** Mason, *Uncivil Agreement*, pp. 15, 23.

7 **lasting damage to the country:** "Amid Campaign Turmoil, Biden Holds Wide Leads on Coronavirus, Unifying the Country," Pew Research Center, October 9, 2020.

7 **a struggle between right and wrong:** Ibid.

7 **violence may be justified:** See the Washington Post-University of Maryland poll (conducted online, December 17–19, 2021), question 12; poll discussed in "1 in 3 Americans Say Violence Against Government Can Be Justified, Citing Fears of Political Schism, Pandemic," *Washington Post*, January 1, 2022.

7 **two-thirds *expect* violence:** See CBS News Poll (conducted August 29–31, 2022), question 29; see also discussion in "Rising Numbers of Americans Concerned About Political Violence: Poll," *The Hill*, September 5, 2022.

8 **"global democratic recession":** See Diamond, "Facing Up to the Democratic Reces-sion"; see also Larry Diamond, "We Have Entered a New Historical Era," address to the Freeman Spogli Institute for International Studies, April 11, 2022.

8 **"steadily more dissatisfied with democracy":** Foa, Klassen, Wenger, Rand, and Slade, *Youth and Satisfaction with Democracy: Reversing the Democratic Discon-nect?*, p. 1.

8 **especially anglophone affluent nations:** Ibid., p. 12.

8   **their country is heading in the right direction:** See NBC News Survey (conducted by Hart Research Associates-Public Opinion Strategies, August 12–16, 2022), question 4, p. 3; survey discussed in "Record Percentage Says US Headed in Wrong Direction: NBC Poll," *The Hill*, August 21, 2022.

8   **its best years are still ahead:** Ibid., question 16b, p. 15.

8   **financially "worse off" than they are:** "Economic Attitudes Improve in Many Nations Even as Pandemic Endures," Pew Research Center, July 21, 2021, p. 4. See also the record-high share responding "do not feel confident" to the question "Do you feel confident that life for our children's generation will be better than it has been for us?," in WSJ/NORC poll, reported in Janet Adamy, "Most Americans Doubt Their Children Will Be Better Off, WSJ-NORC Poll Finds," *Wall Street Journal*, March 24, 2023.

8   **"signs of national decline":** Hunter, Bowman, and Puetz, *Democracy in Dark Times*, p 18.

9   **U.S. voter turnout rates:** See "National Turnout Rates 1789–Present," US Elections Project, https://www.electproject.org/national-1789-present, accessed November 2022.

9   **Individual donations and volunteering for political campaigns:** See data on trends from 1990 to 2022 in "Cost of Election" and "Large Versus Small Individual Donations" at Open Secrets, www.opensecrets.org.

9   **Civic literacy . . . has been climbing steeply:** See results of annual Annenberg Civics Knowledge Survey, in "Americans' Civics Knowledge Increases During a Stress-Filled Year," Annenberg Public Policy Center, September 14, 2021.

9   **Measures of partisanship . . . and sorting:** See Druckman and Levy, "Affective Polarization in the American Public." See also Mason, "'I Disrespectfully Disagree,'" and Mason, *Uncivil Agreement*.

9   **"this government . . . will become all one thing, or all the other":** Lincoln, "A House Divided," Speech at Springfield, Illinois (June 16, 1858), in Basler (ed.), *The Collected Works of Abraham Lincoln*, vol. 2, pp. 461–69.

9   **"democracy is under threat":** See the New York Times-Siena College poll (conducted October 9–12, 2022); poll discussed in "Voters See Democracy in Peril, but Saving It Isn't a Priority," *New York Times*, October 18, 2022.

11 **close to half of Americans . . . believe a civil war is imminent:** Garen J. Wintemute et al., "Views of American Democracy and Society and Support for Political Violence: First Report from a Nationwide Population-Representative Survey," medRxiv preprint submission; survey discussed in "Half of Americans Anticipate a U.S. Civil War Soon, Survey Finds," *Science*, July 19, 2022. See also Economist-YouGov poll (conducted August 20–23, 2022); poll discussed in "Two in Five Americans Say a Civil War Is At Least Somewhat Likely in the Next Decade," *YouGovAmerica*, August 26, 2022.

11 **"heading toward a waterfall":** Strauss and Howe, *The Fourth Turning*, p. 2.

15 *The Big Chill:* movie, directed by Lawrence Kasdan (Carson, 1983).

15 **"The era of big government is over":** Clinton, Address Before a Joint Session of the Congress on the State of the Union, January 23, 1996; text archived in the American Presidency Project (UC Santa Barbara).

16 *Megatrends:* Naisbitt, *Megatrends*.

16 *Powershift*: Toffler, *Powershift*.

17 **"Sex O'Clock in America"**: Term first made widely known in magazine story: "Sex O'Clock in America," *Current Opinion*, August 1913, though the unnamed author attributes journalist William Marion Reedy (1862–1920). The story begins: "A wave of sex hysteria and sex discussion seems to have invaded this country."

17 **"Almighty Dollar"**: First use of this phrase is usually attributed to Washington Irving in "The Creole Village" (1837); it certainly became very popular in the 1840s and 1850s (see Google Ngram).

18 **"white savagery"**: The Paxton Boys were called "white savages" by Benjamin Franklin, cited in Hindle, "The March of the Paxton Boys."

20 **he would likely "be beaten badly" at the polls**: See Lincoln quoted in Joel Achenbach, "The Election of 1864 and the Last Temptation of Abraham Lincoln," *Washington Post*, September 11, 2014; see also White, *Emancipation, the Union Army, and the Reelection of Abraham Lincoln*.

21 **"secular stagnation"**: Term introduced by Hansen in presidential address to the annual meeting of the American Economic Association (December 28, 1938); text of speech printed in Hansen, "Economic Progress and Declining Population Growth."

21 **"debt deflation"**: Term introduced in Fisher, "The Debt-Deflation Theory of Great Depressions."

22 **Political parties worldwide issued ever more slogans**: Data on over one thousand parties in over fifty countries since 1945, collected by the Manifesto Project; analyzed by the *Economist*, in "How the West Fell Out of Love with Economic Growth," *Economist*, December 11, 2022.

22 **governments in thirty nations were paying troll armies**: See "Thirty Countries Use 'Armies of Opinion Shapers' to Manipulate Democracy—Report," *Guardian*, November 14, 2017.

22 *Wolf Warrior 2*: movie, directed by Wu Jing (Wu Jing, 2017).

22 **"Anyone who offends China"**: Marketing tagline cited in "Disney's Troubles Show How Technology Has Changed the Business of Culture," *Economist*, January 19, 2023.

25 **"There is a mysterious cycle in human events"**: Roosevelt, Acceptance Speech for the Renomination for the Presidency, Philadelphia, Pennsylvania, June 27, 1936; text archived in the American Presidency Project (UC Santa Barbara).

25 **"The farther backward you look"**: Churchill, quoted in Kegley, "Neo-Idealist Moment in International Studies?"

28 **"Time and his aging"**: Aeschylus, *The Eumenides*, line 286.

29 **"participation mystique"**: Cited throughout (as "mystic participation" in English) in Lévy-Bruhl, *Primitive Mentality*.

30 **"were revealed *ab origine* by gods or heroes"**: Eliade, *The Myth of the Eternal Return*, p. 34.

31 **"the heavenly city of the 18th-century philosophers"**: See Becker, *The Heavenly City of the Eighteenth-Century Philosophers*.

31 **"This progress must inevitably be towards some end"**: Acton, Ward, Prothero, and Leathes (eds.), *The Cambridge Modern History*, editors' introduction.

31 **"Providence was progress"**: Lord Acton, cited in Butterfield, *Man on His Past*, pp. 137–38.

31 **"Not to believe in progress"**: Ibid., p. 338, ff. 1.

32 **Only "the wicked walk in a circle"**: Augustine of Hippo, *The City of God*, book 12, chapter 13, p. 355.

33 **"end of history"**: See Fukuyama, *The End of History and the Last Man*.

33 **"Homo Deus"**: See Harari, *Homo Deus*.

33 **the transhuman "singularity"**: See Kurzweil, *The Singularity Is Near*.

36 **"A true cycle . . . is self-generating"**: Schlesinger, Jr., *The Cycles of American History*, p. 27.

2. SEASONS OF TIME

40 **"the longest human life between birth and death"**: Censorinus, *De Die Natale*, chapter 17: "*Saeculum est spatium vitae humanae longissimum partu et morte definitum.*" *De Die Natale Liber*, sometimes translated as "The Birthday Book," was presented by Censorinus to his patron Quintus Caerellius on his birthday.

41 **"age of gold"**: Publius Virgilius Maro, *Aeneid*, Book VI, lines 792–93. See also Reckford, "Some Appearances of the Golden Age," pp. 79–87.

41 **Rome's eighth saeculum . . . living in the ninth**: Rose, "World Ages and the Body Politique," p. 138.

41 **and a "natural" saeculum**: See Censorinus, *De Die Natale*, chapter 17.

42 **The ritual was never renewed**: See Zosimus, *New History (Historia Nova)*, Book 2.

43 **"what a century I see opening up before us!"**: Erasmus in letter to Budaeus, February 21, 1517, cited in Jean Lafond, "*Réflexions sur deux fins de siècle: les seizième et dix-septième siècles*," in Citti, *Fins de Siècle*, p. 128.

44 **"And time to begin a new"**: John Dryden, "The Secular Masque" (1700).

44 **a new age of "perpetual improvement"**: Godwin, *Enquiry Concerning Political Justice*, book I, chapter VIII, "Human Inventions Susceptible of Perpetual Improvement."

44 **eventual attainment of human immortality**: See discussion in Chonaill, "'Why may not man one day be immortal?'"

44 **"formidable distances of years"**: Rümelin, *Reden und Aufsätze*.

44 **"loaded, fragrant"**: Ralph Waldo Emerson, "Considerations by the Way," in Emerson, *The Conduct of Life* (1860). See *The Collected Works of Ralph Waldo Emerson*, p. 195.

44 **"not with centuries"**: Cournot, *Considérations sur la marche des idées et des événements dans les temps modernes*, p. 105.

44 **"cease to think by reigns"**: Gourmont, cited in Maurice Penaud, "*Rémy de Gourmont et la notion de fin de siècle*," in Citti, *Fins de Siècle*, p. 307.

44 **"century of fascism"**: Benito Mussolini, "Fascism" ("*Fascismo*") article published in the first edition of the Italian Encyclopedia, vol. 14, in 1932; it is reputed to have been ghostwritten, at least in part, by Giovanni Gentile.

45 **"American Century"**: Henry Luce, "The American Century," *Life*, February 17, 1941.

45 **"century of the common man"**: Henry Wallace, "The Price of Free World Victory,"

speech before the Free World Association, New York City, May 8, 1942. Recording available at American Rhetoric Online Speech Bank.

45 **undertook his epic *Study of War*:** See Wright, *Study of War.*

45 **"to think of war as romantic":** Ibid., p. 230.

46 **an "alternating rhythm":** Toynbee lays out this war-and-peace cycle in all eras of history in Toynbee, *A Study of History*, vol. 9 (1954), pp. 234–87; he focuses on the modern West on pp. 234–60.

46 **five repetitions of this cycle:** Ibid., Table I, p. 255.

47 **"knows war only by hearsay":** Ibid., p. 322.

47 **"probing wars":** Farrar, "Cycles of War," pp. 161–79.

47 **Historian Richard Rosecrance:** See Rosecrance, "Long Cycle Theory and International Relations."

47 **"cycle has been repeated time and time again":** Rosecrance, *International Relations: Peace or War?*, p. 302.

47 **developed after the fifteenth century:** Hopkins and Wallerstein, "Cyclical Rhythms and Secular Trends of the Capitalist World Economy: Some Premises, Hypotheses, and Questions," in Hopkins and Wallerstein (eds.), *World-Systems Analysis.*

48 **"regularities and repetitions":** Modelski, *Long Cycles in World Politics*, p. 34.

48 **calls this property "closure":** Ibid., pp. 112–13.

48 **"a concatenation of four generations":** Ibid., p. 116.

48 **"They are the key markers of world time":** Ibid., p. 34.

48 **"respect, acclaim, and imitation":** Ibid., p. 153.

48 **"economies, culture, and geopolitics at the same time":** Thompson, *Power Concentration in World Politics*, p. 76.

50 **"express trains of history":** Marx, quoted by Gerhard Masur in "Crisis in History," in Wiener (ed.), *Dictionary of the History of Ideas*, vol. 1, p. 594.

50 **"return to the status quo impossible":** Ibid., p. 594.

50 **"revitalization of the system's normative foundations":** Modelski, *Long Cycles in World Politics*, p. 119.

51 **"an instance of the revitalization process":** Wallace, "Revitalization Movements," p. 267.

51 **"random in space and time":** Wuthnow, "World Order and Religious Movements," in Bergesen (ed.), *Studies of the Modern World-System*, p. 57.

52 **"at least since Herodotus":** Ibid., p. 73.

55 **"history will reveal itself":** Hegel, *Philosophy of History*, p. 86.

56 **"our fearful trip is done":** Walt Whitman, "O Captain! My Captain!" (1865).

56 **declared the Civil War to be the "Second American Revolution":** Beard and Beard, *The Rise of American Civilization*, vol. II, chapter XVIII, p. 52.

56 **reused countless times, most recently by:** McPherson, *Battle Cry of Freedom*, p. ii.

56 **called the New Deal "The Third American Revolution":** Degler, *Out of Our Past.*

56 **"the late 1780s, the late 1860s, and the mid-1930s":** Ackerman, *We the People: Foundations*, p. 44.

56 **"may lead to a fourth American republic":** Walter Dean Burnham, "The Fourth American Republic?," *Wall Street Journal*, October 16, 1995.

56 echoed this "fourth republic" prediction: See for example James V. DeLong, "The Coming of the Fourth American Republic," AEI, April 21, 2009.

58 "1670 to 1700 the first American revolutionary period": Richard Maxwell Brown, "Violence and the American Revolution," in Kurtz and Hutson (eds.), *Essays on the American Revolution*, p. 87.

58 greater casualties than all other U.S. wars combined: See estimate of casualties in Hacker, "A Census-Based Count of the Civil War Dead."

59 "not many northerners doubted the answer": McPherson, *Battle Cry of Freedom*, p. 854.

60 "riots of the 1960s combined": Bushman, *From Puritan to Yankee*, p. 187.

60 "good and bad, right and wrong": Bellah, *The Broken Covenant*, p. xvi.

60 "reorientation in beliefs and values": McLoughlin, *Revivals, Awakenings, and Reform*, p. xiii.

61 "new order" was founded: Ibid., p. viii.

61 in support of McLoughlin's four-awakenings thesis: Fogel, *The Fourth Great Awakening & the Future of Egalitarianism*.

61 "Fourth Great Awakening": Ibid., pp. 9–10.

61 "Few would doubt that the piety of the Awakening": Hatch, "The Origins of Civil Millennialism in America."

62 several decades of "social reconstruction": Fukuyama, *The Great Disruption*, chapter 16, "Reconstructions Past, Present, and Future."

64 calls a "cultural watershed": Commager, *The American Mind*, p. 42.

64 describes as a "searing experience": Hofstadter, *Age of Reform*, p. 166.

67 closing "global war" phase in 2030: Thompson, *Power Concentration in World Politics*, table 10.1, p. 232.

67 great-power war "in the late 2020s": Goldstein, "The Predictive Power of Long Wave Theory, 1989–2004."

67 "History is the memory of states": Kissinger, *A World Restored*, p. 331.

3. SEASONS OF LIFE

68 "group feeling" or "social cohesion": Khaldun, *The Muqaddimah*, p. 123.

68 compares its life cycle to that of a person: Ibid., pp. 141–42.

69 predictable succession of generations: Ibid., pp. 105–6.

69 "the greatest work of its kind": Toynbee, cited by Dhaouadi in "The *Ibar*."

71 "divisible into four parts": Jung, "The Stages of Life" ("*Die Lebenswende*," first published in 1931), in Jung, *Modern Man in Search of a Soul*.

71 "the seasons of the year and the seasons of the human life": Levinson, *The Seasons of a Man's Life*, p. 7.

71 a "crystallizing moment": Mannheim, "The Problem of Generations," in *Essays on the Sociology of Knowledge*, p. 310.

76 "If you aren't a liberal . . . you have no head": This saying has appeared in many versions, with some (in the early nineteenth century) referring to being a republican in your youth and others (later in the century) referring to being a socialist in your youth. The exact origin is disputed. See Garson O'Toole, "If You Are Not a Liberal

at 25, You Have No Heart. If You Are Not a Conservative at 35 You Have No Brain," Quote Investigator website.

77 **master regulator of the pace of social change:** Comte, *The Positive Philosophy of Auguste Comte.*

78 **"and have taken possession of society":** Mill, *A System of Logic, Ratiocinative and Inductive* (1843), vol. II, p. 589.

78 **"years of greatest vigor partially overlap":** Wilhelm Dilthey, cited in Marías, *Generations*, p. 55.

78 **an extraordinary body of generations theory:** For Mannheim see "The Problem of Generations," in *Essays on the Sociology of Knowledge*; for Ortega y Gasset see *Man and Crisis*; for Mentré see *Les Générations Sociales.*

79 **"Who controls the past controls the future":** Orwell, *1984*, p. 30.

79 **"the royal roads to total history":** Esler, *Generations in History*, p. 152.

79 **"whether you want to be or not":** Wolfe, *You Can't Go Home Again*, chapter 45, pp. 758–59.

80 **"If there is such a thing as a Lost Generation in this country":** Ibid.

80 **every generation "is born, lives, and dies":** Ferrari, *Teoria dei periodi politici* ("Theory of Political Periods"), p. 7.

81 **"the same concrete historical problems":** Mannheim, "The Problem of Generations," in *Essays on the Sociology of Knowledge*, p. 304.

81 **"the same age vitally and historically":** Ortega y Gasset, in Marías, *Generations*, p. 98.

81 **their "sixties took place in the seventies":** Merser, *Grown Ups*, p. 98.

81 **"necessary to know the relief":** Marías, *Generations*, p. 102.

82 **"unanimous adherence to certain fundamental notions":** Comte, *The Positive Philosophy of Auguste Comte.*

82 **"generational *Weltanschauung*":** See discussion of Wilhelm Dilthey in Marías, *Generations*, especially p. 52.

82 **when they reached their late teens and early twenties:** See, for example, "How Birth Year Influences Political Views," *New York Times*, July 7, 2014; "The Politics of American Generations: How Age Affects Attitudes and Voting Behavior," Pew Research Center, July 9, 2014. See also Ghitza, Gelman, and Auerbach, "The Great Society, Reagan's Revolution, and Generations of Presidential Voting."

82 **two-to-one majority *the other way*:** Percentages of freshmen checking "objectives considered to be essential or very important" for each item can be tracked annually starting with the fall class of 1967. See *The Freshman Survey*, conducted annually by the Higher Education Research Institute, based at UCLA, https://heri.ucla.edu /cirp-freshman-survey/.

83 **"in large measure, to ask who we are":** Marías, *Generations*, p. 106.

83 **"directed," and "suppressed" members:** Peterson, in *"Die Literarischen Generationen"* ("Literary Generations") (1930), cited by Marías, *Generations*, p. 106.

83 **"preestablished vital trajectory":** Ortega y Gasset, in Marías, *Generations,* p. 94.

83 **each generation's sense of "essential destiny":** Mannheim, "The Problem of Generations," in *Essays on the Sociology of Knowledge*, p. 306.

84 **"completes the drama of human existence":** Heidegger, *Being and Time*, p. 366. Full

translated sentence: "The fateful destiny of Dasein in and with its 'generation' constitutes the complete, authentic occurrence of Dasein."

84 **Millennial generation on its cover:** "The Me, Me, Me Generation," *Time* cover, May 20, 2013.

84 **Generation X on its cover:** "Twentysomething," *Time* cover, July 16, 1990.

84 **Boomers on its cover:** "Twenty-five and Under," *Time* cover, January 6, 1967.

85 **"I prefer to starve where the food is good":** Thomson, quoted by Tim Page, in "Virgil Thomson: the Composer in Review," *Washington Post*, April 7, 1996.

86 **Most have identified a similar sequence of generations:** See Strauss and Howe, *The Fourth Turning*, pp. 69–72.

89 **(thinking, intuition, feeling, sensation):** Carl Gustav Jung, "A Psychological Theory of Types" (*"Psychologische Typen,"* first published in 1921), in Jung, *Modern Man in Search of a Soul.* Jung concludes by supposing that this quaternity of four can be doubled to eight by imagining an "introvert" and "extravert" version of each; this forms the basis for the Myers-Briggs paradigm.

89 **Myers-Briggs "personality type indicator":** Myers, *The Myers-Briggs Type Indicator.*

89 *King, Warrior, Magician, Lover*: Moore and Gillette, *King, Warrior, Magician Lover.*

89 *Awakening the Heroes Within*: Pearson, *Awakening the Heroes Within.*

89 **headman, clown, shaman, hunter:** Thompson, *At the Edge of History*, p. 108.

91 **"and then comes back with the message":** Campbell, *The Power of Myth*, p. 123.

94 **"The commonest axiom of history":** Mumford, *The Brown Decades*, p. 3.

95 **"we need idealistic children":** Spock, *The Common Sense Book of Baby and Child Care*, p. 321.

95 **"I hate the idea that you should always protect children":** Blume, *Letters to Judy*, p. 273.

96 **"good values and good citizenship":** Bill Clinton, State of the Union Address, January 23, 1996; text archived in the American Presidency Project (UC Santa Barbara).

97 **likened generational succession to "tiles on a roof":** François Mentré, cited in Marías, *Generations*, p. 155.

98 **"most often carries its value commitments into the grave":** Namenwirth and Bibbee, "Change Within or of the System: An Example from the History of American Values."

100 **political regime change regularly triggered by generational succession:** See Book VI, chapters 5–9, of Polybius, *The Histories.*

100 **driven by a four-generation rhythm:** Ibn Khaldun, *The Muqaddimah*, pp. 105–6.

100 **created one in 1859:** Littré, *Paroles de Philosophie Positive* ("Words of Positive Philosophy").

100 **laid out another in 1874:** Ferrari, *Teoria dei periodi politici* ("Theory of Political Periods").

100 **applied it to generational succession in 1930:** Wechssler, *Die Generation als Jugendreihe und ihr Kampf um die Denkform* ("Generations as a Succession of Youth Groups and Their Conflict Over Forms of Thinking").

100 **four-stage "Physical Generation Cycle":** Toynbee, *A Study of History*, vol. 9 (1954), pp. 234–87.

100 **distilled them into a four-part theory**: Marías, *Generations*. For the four-generations theory, see pp. 177–79.

100 **widely known as the "AGIL" theory**: AGIL is an acronym for the following four functional stages: adaptation; goal attainment; integration; and latency. See Parsons, *The Social System*, chapters 2–3. For more brevity and clarity, especially in the contributions of Robert Bales to the AGIL model, see Swanson, "Review of *Working Papers in the Theory of Action*."

100 **(Institutions versus Ideals)**: Huntington, "American Ideals versus American Institutions."

101 **What Modelski calls the "generational mechanism"**: Modelski, *Long Cycles in World Politics*, p. 116.

102 **"might therefore well delineate our wheel of time"**: Namenwirth, "Wheels of Time and the Interdependence of Value Change in America."

4. SEASONS OF AMERICAN HISTORY

103 **"the rediscovery of the world and of man"**: See Michelet, *History of France*, vol. VII; Burckhardt, *The Civilization of the Renaissance in Italy*.

107 **almost entirely Northern European and Protestant**: For estimates of the ethnic ancestry of free residents in British mainland colonies in 1700 and 1755, see Boyer, Clark, Jr., Halttunen, Kett, Salisbury, Sitkoff, and Woloch, *The Enduring Vision*, Figure 4.1, p. 99. For estimates in the United States upon its first census enumeration in 1790, see Purvis, "The European Ancestry of the United States Population, 1790."

107 **more standard in America than in England itself**: Boorstin, *The Americans: The Colonial Experience*, part 10, "The New Uniformity," p. 269.

112 **like "tiles on a roof"**: Mentré, cited in Marías, *Generations*, p. 155.

117 **Then it started moving**: *2001: A Space Odyssey*, movie, directed by Stanley Kubrick (Kubrick, 1968); *A Clockwork Orange*, movie, directed by Stanley Kubrick (Kubrick, 1971); *Sleeper*, movie, directed by Woody Allen (United Artists, 1973); *Star Wars*, movie, directed by George Lucas (Lucasfilm, 1977); *Close Encounters of the Third Kind*, movie, directed by Steven Spielberg (Columbia and EMI, 1977); and *E.T.*, movie, directed by Steven Spielberg (Amblin Entertainment, 1982).

117 **"all government in America was at a low point"**: Donald, "An Excess of Democracy."

118 **The future teemed with images**: *Mad Max* movie franchise (1979–present); *Blade Runner*, movie, directed by Ridley Scott (The Ladd Company et al., 1982); *Terminator* movie franchise (1984–present); *The Matrix* movie franchise (1999–present).

118 **the three "most effective" presidents in U.S. history**: For a rankable list of surveys and results, see "Historical rankings of presidents of the United States," Wikipedia.

119 **often had a dystopian dark side**: Huxley, *Brave New World*; Orwell, *Animal Farm*; Orwell, *1984*.

119 **oppressive communities portrayed in novels and movies**: *The Hunger Games* movie franchise (2012–present); *Elysium*, movie, directed by Neill Blomkamp (Tristar Pictures et al., 2013); and *The Circle*, movie, directed by James Ponsoldt (EuropaCorp et al., 2017).

121 **"ebb and of flow, in human history":** Schlesinger, Jr., *The Cycles of American History*, p. 23.

122 **"liberal" versus "conservative" eras:** Schlesinger, Sr., *Paths to the Present*.

122 **"public energy" versus "private interest":** Schlesinger, Jr., *The Cycles of American History*, p. 25.

122 **about fifteen years per era:** Ibid., p. 30.

123 **"we are en route to a sixth party system":** Burnham, *Critical Elections and the Mainsprings of American Politics*, p. 135.

123 **"each realignment cycle has run about forty years":** Schlesinger, Jr., *The Cycles of American History*, p. 35.

123 *one* **realignment every** *two* **phases of life:** Paul Allen Beck, "A Socialization Theory of Partisan Realignment," in Niemi, *The Politics of Future Citizens*. See also Beck, "Young vs. Old in 1984: Generations and Life Stages in Presidential Nomination Politics."

124 **similar decline between 1900 and 1920:** Richard L. McCormick, "Political Parties," in Greene (ed.), *Encyclopedia of American Political History*, p. 20.

125 **minority party merely reflects the sun's light:** Lubell, *The Future of American Politics*, pp. 191–92.

125 **rates not seen in over a century:** See "National Turnout Rates 1789–Present," US Elections Project, https://www.electproject.org/national-1789-present, accessed November 2022.

125 **national party partisanship is off the charts:** See Druckman and Levy, "Affective Polarization in the American Public." See also Mason, "'I Disrespectfully Disagree,'" and Mason, *Uncivil Agreement*.

125 **discovered a "historical alternation of moods":** Klingberg, "The Historical Alternation of Moods in American Foreign Policy."

126 **Klingberg explains his cycle:** Ibid.; see also Klingberg, *Cyclical Trends in American Foreign Policy Moods*.

128 **two-stroke economic "K-Cycles":** Described in Kondratieff, *The Long Waves in Economic Life*.

128 **According to Toynbee, Modelski, and Thompson:** See Toynbee, *A Study of History*, vol. 9 (1954), p. 322; and see Modelski and Thompson, *Leading Sectors and World Powers*, p. 67.

129 **S-curve plays out over two consecutive K waves:** Perez, *Technological Revolutions and Financial Capital* (2002), ch. 5, "The Four Basic Phases of Each Surge of Development."

130 **capitalism tends to raise inequality over time:** Piketty, *Capital in the Twenty-First Century*, p. 34.

131 **historical taxonomy of equalizers:** Categorized in Parts II–V of Scheidel, *The Great Leveler*.

131 **"during the revolution and early nation-building":** Lindert and Williamson, *Unequal Gains*, p. 90.

132 **have pushed the nation's poverty rate . . . to an all-time low:** See "Poverty Rates Using the Official and Supplemental Poverty Measures: 2009 to 2021," in *Poverty*

in the United States: 2021, Current Population Reports (September 2022), U.S. Bureau of the Census, Figure 4, p. 7.

132 **"wars, social strife, and revolutions, that lower it"**: Milanovic, *Global Inequality*, p. 98.

132 ***Bowling Alone***: Putnam, *Bowling Alone: The Collapse and Revival of American Community*.

132 **reached its all-time peak**: See Putnam, *The Upswing*, Figure 1.1 on p. 10 and Figure 1.2 on p. 13.

133 **"largest ever recorded in opinion surveys"**: Burnham, *The Current Crisis in American Politics*, p. 295.

133 **variety of the indicators he tracks**: See Putnam, *Bowling Alone*, Section II, "Trends in Civic Engagement and Social Capital."

133 **According to one 1987 survey**: Cited in ibid., p. 25.

133 **"a story of collapse *and* renewal"**: Ibid.

133 **born roughly between 1910 and 1940**: Ibid., p. 254.

134 **"second consecutive generation of 'free agents'"**: Ibid., p. 259.

134 **"The wartime Zeitgeist of national unity and patriotism"**: Ibid., p. 267.

134 **just after the American Revolution and the Civil War**: See Skocpol, "How Americans Became Civic," in Skocpol and Fiorina (eds.), *Civic Engagement in American Democracy*, especially p. 33.

136 **Voting rates and political participation . . . are surging**: See "National Turnout Rates 1789–Present," US Elections Project, https://www.electproject.org/national-1789-present, accessed November 2022.

136 **"longtime *incivisme* of their parents' generation"**: Putnam, *Bowling Alone*, p. 133.

137 **fictionalized in Samuel Hopkins Adams's novel *Flaming Youth***: Adams, *Flaming Youth*.

137 **fictionalized in *Peyton Place***: Metalious, *Peyton Place*.

137 **steered out of public vocations**: Friedan, *The Feminine Mystique*.

137 **likens to the "Dr. Spock 1950s"**: Cable, *The Little Darlings*, p. 105.

137 **"extremely important" in high school senior surveys**: See Figure 19 in Hawkins et al., *State of our unions: 2022*.

137 **several years later than they "ideally" would like**: See Figure 3 in *Shifting Life Milestones Across Ages: A Matter of Preference or Circumstance?* (Stanford Center on Longevity, 2018).

137 **"family and children" as giving them "meaning in life"**: *What Makes Life Meaningful? Views from 17 Advanced Economies* (Pew Research Center, November 18, 2021), p. 16.

138 **than Xers and Boomers were at the same age**: See Pepin and Cotter, "Separating Spheres? Diverging Trends in Youth's Gender Attitudes About Work and Family." See also "Young Men Embrace Gender Equality, but They Still Don't Vacuum," *New York Times*, February 11, 2020.

138 **lowest fertility rate in American history**: In 2018, the U.S. total fertility rate (TFR) dropped to 1.730, beneath its earlier low point of 1.738 (in 1976). See annual TFR data (since 1960) on FRED online (economic data from the St. Louis Federal Reserve Bank).

138 **fertility rebounded sharply in the early 1980s:** For trends in total fertility rates since 1800, see Coale and Zelnick, *New Estimates of Fertility and Population in the United States*, p. 73.

139 **Immigration to America has also followed a saecular rhythm:** For trends in immigration and for trends in total fertility rates prior to 1800, see Strauss and Howe, *Generations*, appendix B.

139 **the only decade in American history:** See National Academy of Sciences, Engineering, and Medicine, *The Economic and Fiscal Consequences of Immigration* (2017), Table 2-2, p. 48.

139 **the U.S. net immigration rate has fallen sharply:** The average net immigration rate (per 100 U.S. capita) from 1990 to 2007 was 4.5; since 2008, it has been 2.7. See "Data That Supplement Information" (Excel files) for *The Demographic Outlook: 2022 to 2052* (U.S. Congressional Budget Office, July 27, 2022) or earlier years of this volume.

140 **"without being sufficiently well armed":** *New York Gazette* in 1749, in Bridenbaugh, *Cities in Revolt*, p. 113.

140 **over the centuries the general trend in criminal violence:** Roth, *American Homicide*.

141 **inversely correlated with basic indicators of social trust:** Ibid., Introduction.

141 **followed by a further decline during Prohibition:** Available data on per-capita U.S. alcohol consumption indicate that cyclical peaks were reached in 1980–81, in 1906–10, and in 1830–40; see the *First Statistical Compendium on Alcohol and Health* (National Institute on Alcohol Abuse and Alcoholism, February 1981); *NIAAA Quick Facts* (CSR, Inc., periodic); Burnham, "New Perspectives on the Prohibition 'Experiment' of the 1920s"; Blocker, Jr., *American Temperance Movements*; and the statistical appendix to Rorabaugh, *The Alcoholic Republic*. For evidence that the late 1740s and 1750s may have been another peak era of alcohol consumption, see Rorabaugh, *The Alcoholic Republic*, and Bridenbaugh, *Cities in Revolt*, ch. 3.

141 **For other mind-altering substances . . . the trends are similar:** For trends in narcotics consumption, see Morgan, *Drugs in America: A Social History, 1800–1980* (1981) and Courtwright, *Dark Paradise: Opiate Addiction in America before 1940* (1982).

142 **"nation that firmly rejects narcotics":** David Musto in "Drug Use? America Can't Seem to Remember When," *Washington Post*, August 27, 1990.

142 **"they were statesmen and thought about politics":** Edmund Morgan, "The American Revolution Considered as an Intellectual Movement," in Schlesinger, Jr., and White (eds.), *Paths of American Thought*, p. 11.

143 **"religious depression of the '30s":** Handy, "The American Religious Depression, 1925–1935."

143 **"than at any other time in the country's religious history":** Ahlstrom, *A Religious History of the American People*, vol. 1, p. 442.

143 **the first step toward a "Higher Consciousness":** Ferguson, *The Aquarian Conspiracy*.

143 **pounding it to pieces with sledgehammers:** See Kate Wheeling, "When Michigan Students Put the Car on Trial," *Smithsonian Magazine*, April 2020.

143 **"the core of rebellion":** Hobbes, *Behemoth or The Long Parliament*, p. 58.

143 **campus unrest later in the 1740s, 1830s, 1880s, and 1960s:** See citations in col-

lective biographies of Awakeners, Transcendentals, Missionaries, and Boomers in Strauss and Howe, *Generations*.

143 **"moderately predictable rhythm"**: Barkun, "Communal Societies as Cyclical Phenomena."

144 **"young men born with knives in their brain . . .":** Emerson, *Historic Notes of Life and Letters in New England* (1883), in Emerson, *The Collected Works of Ralph Waldo Emerson*.

144 **"to chide, or pray, or preach, or protest":** Emerson, "The Chardon Street Convention" (1884), in Emerson, *The Collected Works of Ralph Waldo Emerson*.

144 **"a cycle of clean-living movements":** Engs, *Clean Living Movements*, p. 267.

145 **"a philosophy of the well-fed":** Cao Yu, quoted in *The Observer*, April 13, 1980.

146 **by some measures, an unprecedented decline:** See Public Religion Policy Institute (PRRI), *The 2020 Census of American Religion* (2021).

147 **between the personal "conversion" and the public "covenant":** Bellah, *The Broken Covenant*, pp. 31–32.

5. COMPLEXITY, ANOMALIES, AND GLOBAL HISTORY

148 **"The fox knows many things, but the hedgehog knows one big thing":** Berlin, *The Hedgehog and the Fox*, p. 91.

148 **that this cycle is powered by "generations" and that it is "mysterious":** Roosevelt, in Acceptance Speech for the Renomination for the Presidency, June 27, 1936; text archived in the American Presidency Project (UC Santa Barbara).

150 **rewards and punishments in a predictable manner:** See Hume, *An Enquiry Concerning Human Understanding*, section VIII, "Of Liberty and Necessity," Part II.

151 **As Frank Klingberg noticed:** Klingberg, "The Historical Alternation of Moods in American Foreign Policy."

155 **let's use the following analogy:** This analogy appears in Lewis, *Flash Boys*, p. 198.

156 **George Modelski likened:** George Modelski, "The Study of Long Cycles," in Modelski (ed.), *Exploring Long Cycles*, pp. 1–2.

157 **"at the edge of chaos":** Packard, *Adaptation Toward the Edge of Chaos*.

158 **Giambattista Vico . . . Georg W. F. Hegel:** See Vico, *Principi di Scienza Nuova* (*"Principles of New Science"*), and see Hegel, *Phänomenologie des Geistes* (*"The Phenomenology of Spirit"*) (1807).

160 **An estimated two-thirds of all mammalian species:** Kendall, Prendergast, and Bjørnstadt, "The Macroecology of Population Dynamics: Taxonomic and Biogeographic Patterns in Population Cycles."

161 **synchronized by pheromones and behavioral cues:** Miettinen, "Cyclical Metapopulation Mechanism Hypothesis: Animal Population Cycles Are Generated and Driven by a Population-Wide Hormone Cycle."

161 **"you go over a bridge of your peers":** Schowalter, "Childhood Circa 1995," *Wall Street Journal*, February 9, 1995.

163 **relatively high, around twenty-seven or twenty-eight:** See Wrigley et al., *English Population from Family Reconstitution*, p. 135.

163 **did not complete puberty until their late teens:** See Wood, *Dynamics of Human Reproduction*, pp. 416–17 and p. 437, Figures 9.18, 9.19.

163 **two years younger than in Europe:** See Haines, "Long Term Marriage Patterns in the United States from Colonial Times to the Present."

163 **popularized the word "adolescence":** Hall, *Adolescence*.

164 **marriage ages for both men and women also sank:** U.S. Census Bureau, "Figure MS-2 Median age at first marriage: 1890 to present" (2022).

164 **age of first marriage for both men and women has climbed steeply:** Ibid.

165 **a historic high of twenty-seven today:** See Figure 3 in Mathews, "Mean Age of Mother, 1970–2000," and Osterman et al., "Births: Final Data for 2020," p. 4.

165 **living with older family members (usually parents):** See chart in "Financial Issues Top the List of Reasons U.S. Adults Live in Multigenerational Homes," Pew Research Center, March 24, 2022, p. 12.

165 **age eighteen to twenty-four: "emerging adulthood":** Arnett, "Emerging Adulthood."

165 **has risen by about six years, from fifty-three to fifty-nine:** See "Generations of American Leaders," https://www.fourthturning.com/goal/overview.php.

166 **as anyone born in 1974 or after:** See "Generation Y" (editorial), *Advertising Age*, August 30, 1993, in which the term "Generation Y" was defined as everyone who was, at that time, a teenager—that is, born from 1974 to 1980.

167 **"Generation Y was a placeholder":** The writer is Matt Carmichael, quoted in "From GIs to Gen Z (Or is it iGen?): How Generations Get Nicknames," NPR, October 6, 2014.

169 **back up to a mere two-thirds of the national average:** See Lindert, *Unequal Gains*, pp. 203–4.

170 **In the four elections from 1866 to 1872:** See Leadership Shares at the Generations of American Leaders interactive database at https://www.fourthturning.com/goal /overview.php.

170 **they were "pragmatists":** See James's lectures, eventually published in James, *Pragmatism*.

170 **"the law of competition":** Carnegie, *The "Gospel of Wealth" Essays and Other Writings*, pp. 2–3.

170 **"let the chips fall where they may":** Conkling, in speech nominating Ulysses Grant for a third term as president, June 5, 1880.

170 **"gelded men of the Gilded Age":** Geoffrey Blodgett, "Reform Thought and the Genteel Tradition," in Morgan (ed.), *The Gilded Age*, p. 56

172 **"Among democratic nations each new generation is a new people":** Tocqueville, *Democracy in America*, p. 448.

172 **"the earth belongs to the living generation":** Letter of Thomas Jefferson to James Madison, September 6, 1789, available at the Papers of Thomas Jefferson at Princeton University.

172 **"one generation is to another as one independent nation to another":** Ibid.

174 **"generation of 1820":** See Spitzer, *The French Generation of 1820*.

174 **"generation of 1871" in Germany:** See Krol, *Germany's Conscience*, p. 77.

174 **as well as in France:** Kalman, "*Faisceau* Visions of Physical and Moral Transformation and the Cult of Youth in Inter-war France."

174 **"the hungry forties":** Hamerow, *Restoration, Revolution, Reaction*, p. 75.

175 **"blood and iron":** Bismarck, in a speech at a meeting of the budget commission of the Prussian Parliament, September 30, 1862, quoted in Greusel, *Blood and Iron*, p. 159.

175 **nineteenth century's most sexually repressed generation:** See Hale, Jr., *Freud and the Americans*, p. 29.

175 **"the generation of 1914":** See Wohl, *The Generation of 1914*.

6. A WINTER CHRONOLOGY

185 **"Something happened to America at that time":** Senator Daniel K. Inouye, speech to a joint meeting of Congress, excerpted in the *Congressional Record*, vol. 141, no. 157 (October 11, 1995).

185 **in surveys taken after the war:** Settersten et al., "Two Faces of Wartime Experience: Collective Memories and Veterans' Appraisals in Later Life."

186 **a Roper poll found that a plurality of Americans:** Gelernter, *1939: The Lost World of the World's Fair*, p. 27.

187 **"The melancholy days are come":** William Cullen Bryant, "The Death of the Flowers," 1825.

187 **"changes into stone the water of heaven":** Victor Hugo, *Les Misérables*, p. 158.

187 **"The light that loses, the night that wins":** Algernon Charles Swinburne, *Atalanta in Calydon* (1865), chorus, stanza 1.

192 **Americans wanted summary punishment meted out:** Berinsky, *In Time of War*, p. 38.

192 **showed no decline at all in support:** Kalmoe, *With Ballots and Bullets*, chapter 6, "Weighing the Dead."

194 **"movable feast":** Hemingway, *A Movable Feast*.

194 **"the shows were broader, the buildings were higher":** Fitzgerald quoted in Turnbull, *Scott Fitzgerald*, p. 183.

194 **having reached a low ebb:** Allen, *Only Yesterday*, chapter 12.

194 **more than a million Americans owned stock on margin:** Ibid., p. 260.

195 **"aching disillusionment of the hard-boiled era":** Ibid., pp. 296–97.

195 **"the only thing we have to fear is fear itself":** Roosevelt, in first Inaugural Address, March 4, 1933; text archived in the American Presidency Project (UC Santa Barbara).

196 **not always disapprovingly:** see Katznelson, *Fear Itself*, chapter 7.

196 **"avarice" of "economic royalists":** Roosevelt, in renomination acceptance speech, June 27, 1936; text archived in the American Presidency Project (UC Santa Barbara).

196 **"I welcome their hatred!":** Roosevelt, in address at Madison Square Garden, New York City, October 31, 1936; text archived in the American Presidency Project (UC Santa Barbara).

197 **"I see one-third of a nation":** Roosevelt, in address at Madison Square Garden, New York City, January 20, 1937; text archived in the American Presidency Project (UC Santa Barbara).

197 **"All about us rage undeclared wars":** Roosevelt, in 1939 Annual Message to Con-

gress, January 4, 1939; text archived in the American Presidency Project (UC Santa Barbara).

198　"as a united nation, our democracy has gone into action": Roosevelt, March 15, 1941, cited in Katznelson, *Fear Itself*, p. 306.

199　"Overnight we have become . . . at long last a united people": Walter Lippmann, December 9, 1941, cited in ibid., p. 316.

200　included the acquisition of full citizenship rights: See Euell A. Nielsen, "The Double-V Campaign (1942–1945)," blackpast.org, July 1, 2020.

200　"present at the creation": Acheson, *Present at the Creation*.

200　"four freedoms . . . everywhere in the world": Roosevelt, in 1941 State of the Union address, January 6, 1941; text archived in the American Presidency Project (UC Santa Barbara).

201　"This war must be waged": Roosevelt, in 1945 State of the Union address, January 6, 1945; text archived in the American Presidency Project (UC Santa Barbara).

201　the term "manifest destiny": John L. O'Sullivan, editor of the *Democratic Review*, in the journal (April 1859). See Pratt, "The Origin of 'Manifest Destiny.'"

202　historian Joanne Freeman reports: Freeman, *The Field of Blood*.

202　According to two North Carolina Whigs: They were Willie Mangum and David Outlaw, in ibid., pp. 158–59.

202　"The age is dull and mean": John Greenleaf Whittier, "For Righteousness' Sake (Lines Inscribed to Friends Under Arrest for Treason Against the Slave Power)" (1856).

202　Harriet Beecher Stowe's *Uncle Tom's Cabin*: Stowe, *Uncle Tom's Cabin*.

203　"because we have hated each other so": Chesnut, *A Diary from Dixie*, entry for March 12, 1861, pp. 18–20.

204　"There are but two parties now, Traitors and Patriots": Grant, in letter to his father in 1861, quoted in Kalmoe, *With Ballots and Bullets*, p. 75.

204　"savage and brutal policy": Lee, in letter to James A. Seddon, CSA Secretary of War, January 10, 1863, archived at the Lee Family Digital Archive, located at Stratford Hall, Stratford, Virginia.

206　"a new nation, conceived in Liberty": Lincoln, in Gettysburg Address, November 19, 1863, text archived in the American Presidency Project (UC Santa Barbara).

206　"every drop of blood drawn with the lash": Lincoln, in second Inaugural Address, March 4, 1865; text archived in the American Presidency Project (UC Santa Barbara).

207　"us Democrats to claim Lincoln": Roosevelt, in letter to historian and journalist Claude Bowers, April 3, 1929, quoted in Rietveld, "Franklin D. Roosevelt's Abraham Lincoln," p. 13.

207　"fight to the death between the free world and the slave world": Vice President Henry A. Wallace, "Century of the Common Man" speech, New York City, May 8, 1942, in American Rhetoric, online speech bank, https://www.americanrhetoric .com, accessed November 2022.

207　"Ladies and Gentlemen: This Nation in the past two years": Roosevelt, in 1944 State of the Union address, January 11, 1944; text archived in the American Presidency Project (UC Santa Barbara).

208 **"redress by the Sword"**: Abigail Adams, quoted in Yazawa, *From Colonies to Commonwealth*, pp. 90–91.

209 **"blows must decide"**: "George III's Official Correspondence 1772–1780," in Georgian Papers Programme (partnership of the Royal Collection Trust and King's College London), https://georgianpapers.com, accessed November 2022.

209 **"Tyranny, oppression and Murder"**. Abigail Adams, quoted in Yazawa, *From Colonies to Commonwealth*, pp. 90–91.

209 **"These are the times that try men's souls"**: Paine, *The American Crisis*, no. 1 (December 19, 1776), first line.

210 **Nineteen slaves escaped**: "The Practice of Slavery at Monticello," the Jefferson Monticello website (Thomas Jefferson Foundation), https://www.monticello.org, accessed November 2022.

210 **It was the war's largest all-American fight**: See Hoock, *Scars of Independence*, p. 316.

210 **seventy-five thousand White and Black American Loyalists**: See Jasanoff, *Liberty's Exiles*, p. 6 and appendix.

211 **"The war ended but the misery continued"**: Kulikoff, "'Such Things Ought Not to Be.'"

211 **American per-capita incomes had dropped an estimated 20 to 30 percent since 1774**: See Lindert and Williamson, *Unequal Gains*, chapter 3, "When Did Colonial America Get Rich."

211 **"The Congress is abused, laughed at and cursed"**: Rush, quoted in Taylor, *American Revolutions*, p. 319.

211 **few delegates to the Congress even bothered to show up**: Ibid.

211 **"for the sole and express purpose"**: Endorsement by the Continental Congress, according to Larson and Winship, *The Constitutional Convention*.

211 **"A republic," he replied, "if you can keep it"**: Franklin, quote heard by fellow Constitutional Convention delegate (and signer) James McHenry and entered into his diary, September 18, 1787; see Josh Levy, "'A republic if you can keep it': Elizabeth Willing Powel, Benjamin Franklin, and the James McHenry Journal," *Unfolding History*, blog of the U.S. Library of Congress on its manuscript holdings, January 6, 2022.

212 **They also tended to be young**: Elkins and McKitrick look at nine Federalist leaders and nine Anti-Federalist leaders identified by Merrill Jensen. They find that, of the first group, six were born in 1742 or later (average birth year: 1744.0), and of the second group, two were born in 1742 or later (average birth year: 1734.8). Elkins and McKitrick, "The Founding Fathers: Young Men of the Revolution," pp. 202–3.

212 **local leaders with backcountry ties**: In his examination of state delegate voting in 1784–88, Jackson Turner Main divided delegates into "cosmopolitan" and "localist" parties. Of the former, 47 percent were under age forty, versus only 32 percent of the latter. Main, *Political Parties Before the Constitution*, p. 377.

212 **"Indeed, Doctor, we forgot it"**: This version of Hamilton's remark is from Duffield, *The God of Our Fathers*, p. 15; see also Chernow, *Alexander Hamilton*, p. 236.

213 **"I must study politics and war"**: Letter from John Adams to Abigail Adams, May 12,

1780; text archived in the Adams Family Papers (An Electronic Archive), Massachusetts Historical Society.

213 **nearly nine in ten colonists in British North America:** See Galenson, "The Settlement and Growth of the Colonies," tables 4.1 and 4.2, pp. 170–71.

214 **a stunning 10 percent of the regional population:** See Mandell, *King Philip's War*, p. 164.

214 **were not resettled for another thirty years:** Ibid., pp. 167–68. Not until 1697 was Cotton Mather able to report, in *Magnalia Christi Americana*, that most of the towns destroyed in King Philip's War had been resettled.

214 **"Declaration of the People of Virginia":** See preserved image of Nathaniel Bacon's Declaration of Grievances, care of the Colonial Williamsburg Foundation, at the Encyclopedia Virginia, online at https://encyclopediavirginia.org/, accessed November 2022.

216 **the Black share of the Southern colonial population:** See Galenson, "The Settlement and Growth of the Colonies," tables 4.1, 4.2, 4.3, and 4.4, pp. 170–73.

217 **"one hundred years exactly" before the heroes of 1776:** See Jefferson's introduction to newly discovered manuscript by Thomas Mathew, in Mathew, *The Beginning, Progress and Conclusion of Bacon's Rebellion in Virginia in the Years 1675 and 1676*, first page.

217 **"The Gray Champion":** Title of short story in Hawthorne, *Twice-Told Tales*.

218 **"I will not make windows into men's souls":** Widely attributed to Elizabeth by Sir Francis Walsingham. See "Quotes in Context: Elizabeth I," in "History in the (Re)Making," https://thehistoricalnovel.com/2018/04/10/quotes-in-context -elizabeth-i/, accessed November 2022. Another version credited to Francis Bacon is that Elizabeth was "not liking to make windows into men's hearts and secret thoughts"; see Bucholz and Key, *Early Modern England 1485–1714*, p. 126.

219 **"He blew, and they were scattered":** Translated from Latin inscription: "1588. *Flavit Jehovah et Dissipati Sunt.*"

219 **over one in ten combat-age men for service:** See Bucholz and Key, *Early Modern England 1485–1714*, p. 150.

219 **"I know I have the body but of a weak and feeble woman":** See Bucholz and Key, *Early Modern England 1485–1714*, p. 146. There are several recorded versions of this speech. See "Quotes in Context: Elizabeth I," in "History in the (Re)Making," https://thehistoricalnovel.com/2018/04/10/quotes-in-context-elizabeth-i/, accessed November 2022.

220 **radical Whigs were the first to use the term:** See Hertzler, "Who Dubbed It 'The Glorious Revolution'?"

220 **"she-wolf of France":** Epithet by Richard Plantagenet Duke of York ("She-wolf of France, but worse than wolves of France"), in Shakespeare, *Henry VI, Part 3*, Act I, Scene 4.

221 **killing at least ten thousand soldiers:** The number of deaths most often cited by chroniclers is twenty-nine thousand; the smallest number cited is nine thousand for the Lancastrian side (which bore most of the casualties). A conservative estimate is ten thousand, total deaths out of two armies that together totaled between fifty and sixty thousand. See James Ross, "The Battle of Towton (1461): a 550-year

retrospective" (2011), lecture at the UK National Archives, or essay at https://cdn
.nationalarchives.gov.uk/documents/towton.pdf, accessed Nov 2022.

221 **one in every fifty English males:** The estimated population of England in 1460 was
2 million. (See estimate of 2.096 million in 1500, by Maddison in *The World Economy*, Table B-13, p. 247.) Half were male, and roughly half of these were age fifteen
to fifty. Thus, ten thousand deaths represented about 2 percent of these males.

221 **the deadliest single day of combat:** One possible competitor would be the first day
of the Battle of the Somme (July 1, 1916), with fatalities often estimated at about
twenty thousand. While this is twice as large as the Battle of Towton figure, the
population of Britain in 1916 was twenty times larger.

222 **what historians call the "new monarch":** See Gunn, "Politic History, New Monarchy and State Formation."

223 **"The blood of English shall manure the ground":** Bishop of Carlisle, in Shakespeare, *Richard II*, Act IV, Scene 1.

223 **These societies were diverse in size:** For the U.S. population in 1940, see decennial
resident population totals, U.S. Census Bureau. For population of English colonies
in mainland North America in 1680, see Gelenson, "The Settlement and Growth of
the Colonies: Population, Labor, and Economic Development," Table 4.1, p. 170. For
population of England in 1500, see Maddison, *The World Economy*, Table B-13, p. 247.

223 **half of all children died before adulthood:** Survival to age fifteen of about 50 percent was an approximate norm in most early modern societies. See "Mortality rates
of children over the last two millennia," in Our World in Data, https://ourworldin
data.org, accessed November 2022.

223 **already healthier and more affluent:** In 1774, average household incomes in the
American colonies may have been roughly 50 percent higher than the average in
England and Wales—and they were more equally distributed. See Lindert and Wil-
liamson, *Unequal Gains*, p. 37.

223 **By 1860 U.S. child mortality:** Survivor rate to age fifteen in 1860 (Whites only) derived from Hacker, "Decennial Life Tables for the White Population of the United
States, 1790–1900"; in 1940 (Whites only), derived from U.S. Public Health Service, *United States Life Table and Actuarial Tables: 1939–1941* (1947); in 2020,
derived from U.S. Centers for Disease Control and Prevention, *United States Life
Tables, 2020* (National Vital Statistics Report, U.S. Centers for Disease Control and
Prevention, August 8, 2022).

223 **The average unskilled U.S. wage, in real terms:** Yearly unskilled wage series deflated
by yearly CPI index, from 1790 to 2020. Both series derived from linked series provided by MeasuringWorth, https://www.measuringworth.com; accessed Nov 2022.

224 **Elias Canetti . . . laid out four age-old rules:** Canetti, *Crowds and Power*, part 1,
"The Crowd."

7. THE MILLENNIAL CRISIS

227 **"Wilson lied, people died":** Kagan, *The Jungle Grows Back*, p. 19.
228 **"We're still dancing":** "Prince Finally Explains His Dancing Comment," *New York
Times*, April 8, 2010.

228 **"That's what makes it a bubble"**: An investor says this to Michael Burry (Christian Bale) in *The Big Short*, movie, directed by Adam McKay (Regency Enterprises and Plan B, 2015).

229 **"The snow was stained with blood"**: Obama, in first inaugural address, January 20, 2009; text archived in the American Presidency Project (UC Santa Barbara).

230 **dissatisfaction with "the way things are going" remained near record highs**: See "Satisfaction with the United States," Gallup, 2022.

231 **Politics is the pursuit of war by other means**: Foucault, *"Society Must Be Defended,"* p. 16.

231 **"trial by combat"**: "Rudy Giuliani Says 'Trial By Combat' Remark Before Capitol Violence Was 'Game of Thrones' Reference," *Deadline*, January 14, 2021.

231 **"if you don't fight like hell"**: Trump, quoted in "Incitement to Riot? What Trump Told Supporters Before Mob Stormed Capitol," *New York Times*, January 10, 2021.

231 **voted to oppose the electoral count in Pennsylvania**: See "How Members of Congress Voted on Counting the Electoral College Vote," *Washington Post*, January 7, 2021.

231 **victory was probably or definitely not legitimate**: See "Toplines and Crosstabs December 2021 National Poll: Presidential Election & Jan 6th Insurrection at the US Capitol," University of Massachusetts Amherst Poll, December 28, 2021.

231 **about thirty said outright that it was "stolen"**: See "See Which 2020 Election Deniers and Skeptics Won in the Midterm Elections," *New York Times*, November 9, 2022.

232 **only one-third was approved by Congress**: See "See Everything the White House Wanted, and Everything It Got," *New York Times*, October 20, 2022.

233 **soared to its highest rate in more than a century**: See "National Turnout Rates 1789–Present," US Elections Project, https://www.electproject.org/national-1789-present, accessed December 2022.

233 **see politics as "a struggle between right and wrong"**: See "Amid Campaign Turmoil, Biden Holds Wide Leads on Coronavirus, Unifying the Country," Pew Research Center, October 9, 2020.

233 **victory by the other party will "cause lasting harm"**: Ibid.

233 **either a "dictatorship" or a "socialist country"**: Hunter, Bowman, and Puetz, *Democracy in Dark Times*, p. 18.

233 **"less free" to express themselves than a decade ago**: See "America Has a Free Speech Problem," *New York Times*, March 18, 2022.

233 **harm partisans of the "other" political party**: See Rachel Kleinfeld, "The Rise in Political Violence in the United States and Damage to Our Democracy," testimony to Select Committee to Investigate the January 6th Attack on the United States Capitol, March 31, 2022; available at the Carnegie Endowment for International Peace website. Also see Kleinfeld, "The Rise of Political Violence in the United States."

233 **Attacks are also rising against**: Ibid.

233 **hundreds of thousands of dollars per year on personal security**: See "Lawmakers Confront a Rise in Threats and Intimidation, and Fear Worse," *New York Times*, October 1, 2022.

233 **affiliated with self-designated "militia" movements**: See Kleinfeld, "The Rise of Political Violence in the United States."

234 **Ticket splitting . . . in federal elections has declined to the lowest rate in a century:** See "Vital Statistics on Congress," Brookings Institution, February 8, 2021.

234 **Ticket splitting in state and local elections is also getting rarer:** See "Decline in Ticket-Splitting Reaches Beyond Congress," *Roll Call*, May 26, 2021.

234 **system needs "major changes" or "complete reform":** See "Many in U.S., Western Europe Say Their Political System Needs Major Reform," Pew Research Center, March 31, 2021.

235 **"semi-fascism," according to President Biden:** "Biden Says 'Extreme MAGA Philosophy' Is Like 'Semi-Fascism,'" *The Hill*, August 25, 2022.

235 *so long as their leaders are in power:* See Davide Morisi, "Republicans Trust the Government More Than Democrats Do Under Their Own Presidents," LSE Phelan United States policy blog hub, October 31, 2019.

235 **"they are real in their consequences":** Thomas and Thomas, *The Child in America*, p. 572.

236 **than less affluent Americans to vote for the Democratic Party:** See Thomas Piketty, "Brahmin Left vs Merchant Right: Rising Inequality & the Changing Structure of Political Conflict," in Gethin, Martínez-Toledano, and Piketty (eds.), *Political Cleavages and Social Inequalities*, p. 35.

236 **Republicans continue to gain share among nonwhites:** See Bowman and Goldstein, *The Exit Polls*, p. 7; see also "Voters Of Color Are Backing the GOP at Historic Levels," CNN, July 17, 2022.

236 **larger share of all White college graduates than of all nonwhites:** See "The Key Insights from Our First Poll of the 2022 Midterms," *New York Times*, July 16, 2022.

237 **the term "seventh party system" is already appearing:** See Brewer and Maisel, *Parties and Elections in America*, 9th ed., p. 42.

237 **in a book by that name:** Bishop, *The Big Sort*.

237 **political differences now outrank all other differences:** See "American Democracy in Crisis: The Fate of Pluralism in a Divided Nation," Public Religion Research Institute, February 19, 2019.

237 **"battleground" or "swing" states . . . by 2020, there were only eight:** See Dr. Randal S. Olson, "The Shrinking Battleground: Every 4 Years, Fewer States Determine the Outcome of the Presidential Election," January 13, 2015, https://randalolson .com/2015/01/12/the-shrinking-battleground-presidential-elections/, and "What Are Battleground States?," at Taegan Goddard's Electoral Vote Map, https://elector alvotemap.com/what-are-the-battleground-states/, both accessed December 2022.

237 **"trifecta governments" . . . a seventy-year high:** See "State government trifectas," Ballotpedia (online, regularly updated), and Karl Kurtz, "A Significant Decline in Divided Government," *The Thicket at State Legislatures*, National Conference of State Legislatures blog, November 7, 2012.

238 **"landslide counties." . . . In 2020, fifty-eight:** See "For Most Americans, the Local Presidential Vote Was a Landslide," *Daily Yonder*, December 17, 2020.

238 **yet won in 83 percent of all U.S. counties:** See "How Democrats Are Losing the War for Counties," UVA Center for Politics, October 13, 2021.

238 **the likelihood a Trump voter becomes an election denier:** See Blake Hounshell, "Was Election Denial Just a Passing Threat," *New York Times*, November 28, 2022.

239 **voting preference, of course, but profound differences:** See "America Has Two Economies—and They're Diverging Fast," Brookings Institution, September 19, 2019.

239 **America's blue zone is wealthier, healthier:** See Case and Deaton, "The Great Divide: Education, Despair, and Death."

239 **more economically unequal:** See "Blue Districts Have More Income Inequality Than Red Ones," *Axios*, June 6, 2018.

239 **more neighborly:** See Brueckner and Largey, "Social Interaction and Urban Sprawl"; see also "Where to Hear 'Hi, neighbor!': in the Suburbs," *Los Angeles Times*, November 27, 2006.

239 **more charitable:** See "The Most And Least Charitable States In The U.S. In 2017," *Forbes* (December 4, 2017).

239 **more entertaining:** See Bishop, *The Big Sort*, pp. 152–55.

239 **more affordable:** See Ronald Brownstein, "America Is Growing Apart, Possibly for Good," *Atlantic*, June 24, 2022.

239 **transferred three congressional seats (net):** See "Redistricting 2021: Red States, Blue Voters," Brookings Institution, September 30, 2021.

239 **people choose retail brands according to their political affiliation:** See "Trader Joe's Democrats and Walmart Republicans: Modeling US Elections Using Chain Stores," *Towards Data Science*, a Medium publication, September 28, 2020.

240 **"moving to places that align with their politics":** See "Redfin Predicts a More Balanced Housing Market in 2022," Redfin, November 18, 2021.

241 **"the big one is coming":** See "'The Big One Is Coming' and the U.S. Military Isn't Ready," *Wall Street Journal*, November 4, 2022.

242 **Putin would not have invaded Ukraine:** Sixty-two percent of American voters said that Putin would not have invaded Ukraine had former President Trump still been in office, according to the Harvard Center for American Political Studies (CAPS)–Harris Poll conducted February 23–24, 2022; see "62 Percent of Voters Say Putin Wouldn't Have Invaded Ukraine If Trump Were President: Poll," *The Hill*, February 25, 2022.

242 **greater political division, and declining national stature:** See "Looking to the Future, Public Sees an America in Decline on Many Fronts," Pew Research Center, March 21, 2019.

242 **Two-thirds also see "signs of national decline":** Hunter, Bowman, and Puetz, *Democracy in Dark Times*, p. 18.

242 **Americans have believed "America is on the wrong track":** See "Our Nation, Diverse and Divided," *Wall Street Journal*, December 27, 2019.

242 **dissatisfied with "the way things are going in the U.S.":** See "Satisfaction with the United States," Gallup, 2022.

243 **once called the American Dream:** Adams, *The Epic of America*, p. 195.

243 **standard of living decline over the next thirty years:** See "Looking to the Future, Public Sees an America in Decline on Many Fronts," Pew Research Center, March 21, 2019.

243 **children will end up "financially worse off" than they are:** See "Economic Attitudes Improve in Many Nations Even as Pandemic Endures," Pew Research Center,

July 21, 2021. See also the record-high share responding "do not feel confident" to the question "Do you feel confident that life for our children's generation will be better than it has been for us?," in WSJ/NORC poll, reported in Janet Adamy, "Most Americans Doubt Their Children Will Be Better Off, WSJ-NORC Poll Finds," *Wall Street Journal*, March 24, 2023.

243 **satisfied with their "present financial situation":** See "Historic Shift in Americans' Happiness Amid Pandemic," NORC at the University of Chicago, June 2020.

243 **into their seventies out of financial necessity:** See "Looking to the Future, Public Sees an America in Decline on Many Fronts," Pew Research Center, March 21, 2019.

243 **nearly half expect no benefits at all:** Ibid.

243 **"rigged in favor of the wealthiest Americans":** Hunter, Bowman, and Puetz, *Democracy in Dark Times*, p. 11.

243 **"often profit at the expense of ordinary Americans":** Ibid., p. 12.

244 *less* **rather than more democratic over time:** See "Yahoo! News Survey—January 6th," YouGov, June 10–13, 2022.

244 **likely to "cease to be a democracy in the future":** Ibid.

244 **the nation "could be on the verge of another civil war":** See "New Poll Shows Majority of Americans Worried About Another U.S. Civil War," Engagious, October 1, 2020.

244 **more say that a civil war "is likely" than "is unlikely":** See "Will the U.S. Have Another Civil War?" Zogby, February 4, 2021.

244 **secede and "form their own separate country":** See "New Initiative Explores Deep, Persistent Divides Between Biden and Trump Voters," UVA Center for Politics, September 30, 2021.

244 **"never justified" has fallen from 90 percent to 62 percent:** See Washington Post–University of Maryland poll, December 17–19, 2021.

244 **"constrained by Congress or the courts":** See "New Initiative Explores Deep, Persistent Divides Between Biden and Trump Voters," UVA Center for Politics, September 30, 2021.

244 **versus only one in ten voters age sixty-five and over:** See "Yahoo! News Survey—January 6th," YouGov, June 10–13, 2022.

244 **than voters under forty twenty years ago:** Mounk, *The People Vs. Democracy*, pp. 105–10.

245 **"We're America, Bitch":** "A Senior White House Official Defines the Trump Doctrine," *Atlantic*, June 11, 2018.

245 **"a foreign policy for the middle class":** "Real Talk About a Foreign Policy for the Middle Class," *Washington Post*, May 20, 2021.

245 **the cyclical seed of their own termination:** Klingberg, "The Historical Alternation of Moods in American Foreign Policy."

245 **a negative view of these countries:** See "Views of Russia and Putin Remain Negative Across 14 Nations," Pew Research Center, December 16, 2020; "Unfavorable Views of China Reach Historic Highs in Many Countries," Pew Research Center, October 6, 2020.

245 **in case Taiwan were invaded:** Smeltz et al., *A Foreign Policy for the Middle Class*, p. 31.

245 **93 percent of adults report feeling satisfied with their families:** See "Americans Largely Satisfied with 10 Personal Life Aspects," Gallup (April 8, 2019).

245 **Grandparents, parents, and adult children are living together at the highest rate in decades:** See Pew Research Center, "Financial Issues Top the List of Reasons U.S. Adults Live in Multigenerational Homes" (March 24, 2022).

245 **near-record share report being satisfied with their job:** See "Satisfaction with job or housework," GSS Data Explorer (2022), https://gssdataexplorer.norc.org /trends, accessed November 2022.

245 **their marriage:** See "Happiness of marriage," GSS Data Explorer (2022).

245 **their child's K-12 education:** See "K-12 Parents Remain Largely Satisfied with Child's Education," Gallup (August 26, 2021).

246 **"Americans are remarkably upbeat about life close to home":** See "AEI Survey on Community and Society," American Enterprise Institute (February 2019).

246 **largest since Gallup began measuring it back in the 1970s:** See "Satisfaction with Own Life Five Times Higher Than with U.S.," Gallup (January 31, 2022).

247 **had reached "the end of history":** Fukuyama, *The End of History and the Last Man.*

250 **America's "detached and distant situation":** Washington, in Washington and Rogers, *Washington's Farewell Address to the People of the United States, 1796*, p. 22.

252 **we have had such "Eras of Stalemate" before:** See Fiorina, *Unstable Majorities*, chapter 9.

253 **"as neither Whig nor Tory can live":** Greene, quoted in Hoock, *Scars of Independence*, p. 319.

255 **"Stalin Delano Roosevelt":** Arch-Republican William Randolph Hearst, quoted in Kennedy, *Freedom from Fear*, p. 277.

256 **the Panic of 1857:** Huston, *The Panic of 1857 and the Coming of the Civil War.*

256 **the London Credit Crisis of 1772:** Sheridan, "The British Credit Crisis of 1772 and The American Colonies."

256 **the Great Stop of the Exchequer in 1672:** Li, "The Stop of the Exchequer and the Secondary Market for English Sovereign Debt, 1677–1705."

258 **largest federal deficit in American history unprompted by either war or recession:** On growth in publicly held U.S. federal debt since 2007, see "Historical Tables," U.S. Office of Management and Budget (online). On growth in Federal Reserve balance sheet assets since 2002, see FRED online (economic data from the St. Louis Federal Reserve Bank). On historical total FY federal budget balances, see OMB "Historical Tables."

260 **will stop growing and begin to shrink:** Trends in total population aged twenty to sixty-four in all "more developed" countries, as projected for 2020 to 2040 according to "World Population Prospects 2022" (medium fertility variant), United Nations Population Division.

262 **ranks the United States sixty-first among democracies:** This is according to Freedom House's "Total Global Freedom Score" as of November 2022, https://freedom house.org/.

262 **One calls it a "backsliding democracy":** See "Global State of Democracy Report 2021," International IDEA, 2021.

262 **Another calls it an "anocracy":** See "Polity Project," Center for Systemic Peace, https://www.systemicpeace.org/polityproject.html, accessed November 2022.

262 **"we are closer to civil war than any of us would like to believe":** Walter, in "Is Civil War Coming to America?" *New York Times* (Jan 18, 2022).

262 **none of them saw it coming. "They're all surprised":** See "Are We Really Facing a Second Civil War?," *New York Times*, January 6, 2022.

263 **"Not one, however clever or learned, guessed what happened":** Adams, *The Education of Henry Adams*, p. 42.

264 **"Flight 93 election":** Publius Decius Mus, "The Flight 93 Election," *Claremont Review of Books*, September 5, 2016.

264 **"Trump's next coup has already begun":** "Trump's Next Coup Has Already Begun," *Atlantic*, December 6, 2021.

264 **"America is now in fascism's legal phase":** "America Is Now in Fascism's Legal Phase," *Guardian*, December 22, 2021.

264 **"all one thing, or all the other":** Lincoln, "A House Divided" speech at Springfield, Illinois, June 16, 1858, in Basler (ed.), *The Collected Works of Abraham Lincoln*, vol. 2, pp. 461–69.

264 **one study of twenty advanced economies since 1870:** Funke, "Going to Extremes: Politics After Financial Crises, 1870–2014."

265 **higher inequality, and greater civil unrest:** See "A Vicious Cycle: How Pandemics Lead to Economic Despair and Social Unrest," International Monetary Fund, October 16, 2020.

265 **"Peaceful secessions are very rare":** See "Secession," Centre for Constitutional Studies, July 4, 2019, https://www.constitutionalstudies.ca/2019/07/secession/, accessed December 2022.

268 **"Nobody knows whether it may have already started":** "World War III 'May Have Already Started' with Russian Invasion, Zelenskyy Says," NBC News, March 16, 2022.

269 **expanded over the last decade from 55 percent to 80 percent:** See "The Global Expansion of Authoritarian Rule," Freedom House, February 2022, p. 4.

269 **living in "autocratic nations" has risen from 49 percent to 70 percent:** See "Democracy Report 2022," V-Dem Institute, March 2022, p. 6.

270 **falling in a quickening arc:** In terms of "Trade (% of GDP)" or "Exports of Goods and Services (% of GDP)," World Bank online, the annual data series for "World" since 1970 peaked in 2008 by both measures.

270 **number of barrier walls between adjacent nations has quintupled:** See "As Migration Is Rising, So Are Border Barriers," *Deutsche Welle*, August 13, 2021.

270 **Michele Wucker's evocative phrase:** Wucker, *The Gray Rhino*.

270 **four primary "adversaries" and "competitors":** See "Annual Threat Assessment of the US Intelligence Community," Office of the Director of National Intelligence, April 9, 2021.

270 **"Indo-Pacific NATO":** "Spectre of 'Indo-Pacific NATO' accelerates China's Decoupling from the West," *Financial Times*, March 26, 2022.

271 **compare "China's order" with "chaos in the West":** See "Xi's New Slogan for China's Trajectory: 'Time and Momentum Are on Our Side,'" Mercatus Institute for China Studies, July 9, 2021.

271 **"Time and momentum are on our side"**: See "The Long Game: China's Grand Strategy to Displace American Order," Brookings Institution, August 2, 2021.

271 **"America's Main Opponent is Itself"**: See "Beijing's Visions of American Decline," *Politico*, March 11, 2021.

272 **proposed to Lincoln that he start an immediate war**: See "The 'Foreign War Panacea,'" *New York Times*, March 17, 2011.

273 **"A war regarded as inevitable or even probable"**: Kennan, *The Cloud of Danger* (1977), p. 202.

273 **"One never knows what is hidden in the darkness"**: Lukacs, *The Duel*, p. 214.

273 **"Why Die for Danzig?"**: *"Mourir pour Danzig?," L'Oeuvre*, May 4, 1939.

274 **"new institutions, new alliances"**: "Text of Zelensky Virtual Address to Congress," *Washington Post*, March 16, 2022.

8. HOW OUR SOCIETY WILL CHANGE

276 **Ever since, it has been singular**: Based on a comparison of Google Ngram results for searches (case-sensitive, smoothing of zero) of "The United States is" versus "The United States are"; the "is" phrase rises rapidly after 1865 and surpasses "are" permanently by 1874.

276 **"a revolutionary change in the relations of man to the universe"**: Stimson, diary entry, May 31, 1945, recounting his message to the Interim Committee and invited scientists; see authorized online copy of Stimson diary, available at http://www .doug-long.com/stimson.htm.

276 **By 1945 it owned a staggering 40 percent**: See Hooks, "The Weakness of Strong Theories," pp. 37–38.

277 **"Then wake, Columbians!"**: Colonel David Humphreys, *A poem, on the happiness of America: addressed to the citizens of the United States* (1786).

277 **"one scheme of science, and of morals one . . ."**: Timothy Dwight, *Greenfield Hill: a poem, in seven parts* (1794).

277 **"Empire of Liberty"**: Jefferson used this phrase frequently. See, for example, Jefferson, in letter to George Rogers Clark, December 25, 1780, available at Founder Online, U.S. National Archives.

277 **"Individualism has gone, never to return"**: Rockefeller, quoted in Topik, *Global Markets Transformed*, p. 102.

278 **"a superior level of public peace"**: McNeill, *The Pursuit of Power*, p. 117.

278 **"War made the state, and the state made war"**: Tilly, "Reflections on the History of European State-Making," p. 42.

279 **"machines built for the battlefield"**: Ellis and Maginn, *The Making of the British Isles*, title of chapter 4.

279 **"As result of war, nations are strengthened"**: Hegel, cited in Porter, *War and the Rise of the State*, p. xvi.

279 **"internal pacification"**: Giddens, *The Nation-State and Violence*, chapter 7, p. 181.

279 *ten and one hundred times lower* **than the premodern norm**: See Pinker, *The Better Angels of Our Nature*, chapters 2 and 3; see also Morris, *War! What Is It Good For?*, pp. 177 and 397.

279 habituates people to self-control and "civility": Elias, *The Civilizing Process*.

280 "interests which men will always fight for rather than surrender": Becker, "The Dilemma of Modern Democracy," p. 19.

281 a permanent or a fatal surrender of its vital interests: Ibid.

281 "common products of the same situation": Sumner, *A Study of the Sociological Importance of Usages, Manners, Customs, Mores and Morals*, p. 13.

281 "that external conflict increases internal cohesion": Putnam, *Bowling Alone*, p. 267.

281 the tendency is genetically hardwired into humans: Pagel, *Wired for Culture*; see particularly argument at end of chapter 6.

282 "Robbers Cave" experiment: Sherif, "Experiments in Group Conflict" in *Scientific American*, November 1956. See also article by psychologist Elizabeth Hopper, "What Was the Robbers Cave Experiment in Psychology?," ThoughtCo, November 21, 2019, https://www.thoughtco.com/robbers-cave-experiment-4774987, accessed November 2022.

282 "excite their most violent conflicts": In Madison, *The Federalist Papers* (1787–88), no. 10; text archived online at U.S. Library of Congress.

282 "Altruistic groups beat selfish groups": Wilson and Wilson, "Rethinking the Theoretical Foundation of Sociobiology," p. 345.

283 "to become their brothers' keeper": Solnit, *A Paradise Built in Hell*, p. 3.

283 "taking on more leadership roles in their communities": Bauer et al., "Can War Foster Cooperation?," p. 250.

284 "I only regret that I have but one life to lose for my country": Seymour, *Documentary Life of Nathan Hale*, p. 310.

284 "and to ask ourselves what we can do for the country in return": Holmes, Jr., in speech delivered on Memorial Day, May 30, 1884, at Keene, New Hampshire, before John Sedgwick Post No. 4, Grand Army of the Republic, in Holmes, *The Occasional Speeches of Justice Oliver Wendell Holmes*.

284 "Ask not . . . " inaugural address: The famous quote is "Ask not what your country can do for you—ask what you can do for your country." John F. Kennedy, inaugural address, January 20, 1961; text archived in the American Presidency Project (UC Santa Barbara).

284 "It was and is our single greatest moment": Kennedy, quoted in Renehan, *The Kennedys at War*, chapter 1.

285 "brought forth in us the same fortitude and resilience": Ibid.

285 "should be able to unite regardless of party or politics": Kennedy, Report to the American People on Civil Rights, from the White House, June 11, 1963; text archived in John F. Kennedy Presidential Library and Museum (Boston, Massachusetts).

285 what he called "the moral equivalent of war": James, "The Moral Equivalent of War."

286 "remain the rock upon which states are built": Ibid.

286 "I believe that war must have its way": Ibid.

286 James calls this attitude "highly paradoxical": Ibid.

287 no more willingly than his own generation did: Oliver Wendell Holmes, "The Soldier's Faith," speech given at Harvard University on Memorial Day, May 30, 1895, in Holmes, *The Occasional Speeches of Justice Oliver Wendell Holmes*.

287 **"I'm from the government, and I'm here to help you"**: Widely attributed to Ronald Reagan since the 1970s. Video clip of President Reagan saying this during a press conference, August 12, 1986, available at Ronald Reagan Presidential Foundation & Institute (online).

287 **"There is no government, and I'm here to kill you"**: Ian Morris, "In the Long Run, Wars Make Us Safer and Richer," *Washington Post*, April 25, 2014; see also Morris, *War! What Is It Good For?*, p. 26.

287 **"when the country was, in measurable degree, remade"**: Kennedy, *Freedom from Fear*, p. 377.

288 **"the confident, purposeful, systematized nation of 1870"**: Nevins, "A Major Result of the Civil War."

288 **"It was as radical and social as any revolution in history"**: Wood, *Radicalism of the American Revolution*, pp. 5–6.

289 **Deaths from such causes surged during the 2010s**: See Case and Deaton, *Deaths of Despair and the Future of Capitalism*. See also Case and Deaton, "Rising Morbidity and Mortality in Midlife Among White Non-Hispanic Americans in the 21st Century."

289 **they rose as well early in the Great Depression of the 1930s**: See "Long-Term Trends in Deaths of Despair, from the Long-Term Capital Project," Joint Economic Committee of the U.S. Congress, September 2019.

289 **"what they mind is not feeling necessary"**: Junger, *Tribe*, p. xxi.

289 **kindness, friendliness, and cooperation flourish among these sufferers**: See Fritz, *Disasters and Mental Health*; pp. 28–44 introduce the phrase "community of sufferers" and describe the formation of community bonds, as well as the remission of neurotic behavior.

290 **"Why do large-scale disasters produce such mentally healthy conditions?"**: Ibid., p. 1.

290 **scholarship has since emerged establishing this link**: See Gelfand, *Rule Makers, Rule Breakers*, for references to many studies, especially in chapter 4.

290 **"prosocial behavior and cultural achievements"**: Jeff Greenberg in "Mortality Salience," article entry in Baumeister and Vohs, *Encyclopedia of Social Psychology*, pp. 592–93.

290 **threat to people's personal security tends to make their society "tighter"**: See Gelfand, *Rule Makers, Rule Breakers*, chapter 4.

290 **explosive renaissance in extended-family and group living arrangements**: See Pew Research Center, "Financial Issues Top the List of Reasons U.S. Adults Live in Multigenerational Homes" (March 24, 2022).

291 **it was green and blue**: See Melleuish, "Of 'Rage of Party' and the Coming of Civility."

291 **"for future generations to struggle through"**: Roosevelt, address at the Thomas Jefferson Dinner, New York City, April 25, 1936; text archived in the American Presidency Project (UC Santa Barbara).

292 **"militia fever" was the rule**: Royster, *A Revolutionary People at War*, chapter 1, "*Rage Militaire.*"

292 **to the later so-called "organized war"**: Nevins, "A Major Result of the Civil War."

292 "those who cooperate in this program . . . know each other at a glance": Roosevelt, quoted in Katznelson, *Fear Itself*, p. 229.

292 "but does not in practice maintain: The equality of all men": Survivor cited by Junger, *Tribe*, pp. 43–44.

293 the share of all income received by the top 5 percent fell by one-third: See Putnam, *Bowling Alone*, p. 271.

294 deaths due to "domestic terrorism" . . . has swelled: See Seth G. Jones, "The Evolution of Domestic Terrorism," statement before House Judiciary Subcommittee on Crime, Terrorism, and Homeland Security, February 17, 2022; also see "Terrorism in America 18 Years After 9/11," *New America*, September 2019.

294 "to make a country in which no one is left out": Roosevelt, quoted in Perkins, *The Roosevelt I Knew*, p. 109.

294 more people pursue money to attain status than the other way around: See Ridgeway, "Why Status Matters for Inequality," especially p. 2.

295 "who would understand that my boss is a son of a bitch": North Carolina mill worker, quoted in Kennedy, *Freedom from Fear*, p. 297.

295 more likely to move to another state and rise to higher-status jobs: See Lee, "Military Service and Economic Mobility." See tables on pp. 373 and 375 for statistics.

295 G.I. vets enrolled in college or technical education: See *75 Years of the GI Bill: How Transformative It's Been* (U.S. Department of Defense, January 9, 2019).

295 soared 41 percent by 1950—and 64 percent by 1955: See United States Bureau of the Census, "Series D 722–727. Average Annual Earnings of Employees: 1900 to 1970," *Historical Statistics of the United States, Colonial Times to 1970, Part 1* (1975), p. 164.

296 one-fifth of the Continental Army by the time of the Battle of Yorktown: See Lanning, *Defenders of Liberty*, chapter 15, "The Assessment: Numbers, Influence, Results."

296 composed fully one-tenth of the Union Army: See "Black Soldiers in the U.S. Military During the Civil War," Educator Resources, U.S. National Archives.

296 to help fill the decimated ranks of Rebel regiments: See Levine, *Confederate Emancipation*, p. 4.

296 "invariably resulted from the most powerful shocks": Scheidel, *The Great Leveler*, p. 6.

297 "always bred up to observe and believe": Temple, in "An Essay Upon the Original and Nature of Government" (written in 1671), included in Temple, *The Works of Sir William Temple*, p. 98; edited for stylistic clarity.

298 "Political power grows out of the barrel of a gun": Mao Zedong in 1938, in Mao Zedong, *The Little Red Book*, p. 36. Some suggest Mao may have first said this in 1927.

298 "for their own good without the intervention of a coercive power": Washington, in letter to John Jay, August 1, 1786. Available in the Web edition of Philip B. Kurland and Ralph Lerner (eds.), *The Founders' Constitution*, a joint venture of the University of Chicago Press and the Liberty Fund, https://press-pubs.uchicago.edu /founders/, accessed Nov 2022.

298 **"greater danger behind his back than before his face"**: Adams, quoted in Hoock, *Scars of Independence*, p. 188.

298 **the word "authority" appears more than twice as often**: Based on word count in *The Federalist Papers* (1787–88); text archived online at U.S. Library of Congress. Variants of "authority" appear 373 times; variants of "freedom," 7 times; variants of "liberty," 168 times.

298 **"on account of their harmlessness"**: Stevens, quoted in Miller, *Thaddeus Stevens*, p. 182.

298 **"lay waste to the whole South"**: Ibid.

298 **"War is cruelty, and you cannot refine it"**: Sherman, in a letter to the mayor and councilmen of Atlanta, Georgia, September 12, 1864, in Sherman, *Sherman's Civil War*, pp. 707–9.

299 **"always comes back to that of *Union*"**: Ibid.

300 **if he had not done so, the Union would have collapsed**: Lincoln, in letter to Matthew Birchard and others, June 29, 1863, in Smith, *The Writings of Abraham Lincoln*, pp. 406–10.

300 **"but out of weak and helpless ones"**: Roosevelt, Fireside Chat, April 14, 1938; text archived in the American Presidency Project (UC Santa Barbara).

300 **"As for me, give me liberty or give me death!"**: Henry, in speech to the Second Virginia Convention, March 23, 1775, as reported many years later in Wirt, *Sketches of the Life and Character of Patrick Henry*, p. 123.

301 **"most assuredly we will all hang separately"**: Quote attributed as an "anecdote" about Franklin on signing of Declaration, July 4, 1776, in Sparks, *The Works of Benjamin Franklin*, vol. I, p. 408.

302 **"to look forward to remote futurity"**: Hamilton, in *The Federalist Papers* (1787–88), no. 34; text archived online at U.S. Library of Congress.

302 **"unlimited, undefined, endless, perpetual posterity"**: Clay, speech before U.S Senate, February 5–6, 1850, in Colton (ed.), *The Works of Henry Clay*, p. 844.

303 **"opens up" the realm of civic possibilities**: See Olson, *The Rise and Decline of Nations*, especially chapter 7.

305 **"vision cleared, ambition inspired, and success achieved"**: Keller, *Helen Keller's Journal, 1936–1937*, entry for December 11, 1937.

306 **"The Liberty Song"**: Song by John Dickinson, 1768. See history of the song at Dickinson College Archives & Special Collections.

306 **"Free America"**: Song by Joseph Warren, 1774. Lyrics available at Song of America, https://songofamerica.net/.

306 **"Dixie"**: Song by Daniel Decatur Emmett, 1859. Lyrics available at Song of America, https://songofamerica.net/.

306 **"Battle Hymn of the Republic"**: Music by William Steffe, 1850s, lyrics by Julia Ward Howe, 1861, and published by Howe in *The Atlantic*, February 1862.

306 **"Many Thousand Gone"**: Author unknown. See Ballad of America for background, lyrics, and a sample recording, https://balladofamerica.org/many-thousand-gone/, accessed November 2022.

306 *Why We Fight*: Seven films total were produced by the US Department of War, directed by Frank Capra and Anatole Litvak (1942–1945).

NOTES   499

306 **"God Bless America"**: Song by Irving Berlin, 1918, revised in 1938.

306 **"This Land Is Your Land"**: Song by Woody Guthrie, 1940.

306 *Casablanca*: Movie, directed by Michael Curtiz (Warner Bros., 1942).

306 *From Here to Eternity*: Movie, directed by Fred Zinneman (Columbia Pictures, 1953).

307 **"Whistle While You Work"**: Music by Frank Churchill, lyrics by Larry Morey, written for the movie *Snow White and the Seven Dwarfs* (Walt Disney Productions, 1937). Lyrics available on lyrics.com.

307 **"Ac-Cent-Tchu-Ate the Positive"**: Music by Harold Arlen, lyrics by Johnny Mercer, sung by Bing Crosby (1944). Lyrics available on lyrics.com.

307 **"Over the Rainbow"**: "Over the Rainbow," music by Harold Arlen, lyrics by Yip Harburg, sung by Judy Garland, written for the film *The Wizard of Oz*, directed by Mervyn LeRoy (1939). Lyrics available on lyrics.com.

307 **"Sentimental Journey"**: Music by Les Brown and Ben Homer, lyrics by Bud Green, sung by Doris Day, 1944. Lyrics available on lyrics.com.

307 **"Home Sweet Home"**: Composed by Sir Henry Bishop, adapted from John Howard Payne's 1823 opera *Clari, or the Maid of Milan*. Became popular hit after publication in 1852.

307 **Thomas Nast's first image of a jovial Santa Claus**: "Santa Claus in Camp," cover illustration in *Harper's Weekly*, January 3, 1863.

307 **"White Christmas"**: Song by Irving Berlin, sung by Bing Crosby; written for the movie *Holiday Inn*, directed by Mark Sandrich and Robert Allen (Paramount Pictures, 1942).

307 **"the song America needed to fight fascism"**: "'White Christmas' Was the Song America Needed to Fight Fascism," *Washington Post*, December 25, 2021.

308 **"The Best Years of Our Lives"**: Movie, directed by William Wyler (Samuel Goldwyn Productions, 1946).

308 **"When you face a crisis, you know who your true friends are"**: Attributed to Magic Johnson.

309 **"Rip Van Winkle"**: The story originally appeared in Washington Irving's *The Sketch Book of Geoffrey Crayon, Gent*, published serially throughout 1819 and 1820.

310 **"I don't suppose it will ever come again in this country"**: Silas Lapham, in Howells, *The Rise of Silas Lapham*, p. 20.

310 **"living in the country in which I was born"**: Ticknor, *Life, Letters, and Journals of George Ticknor*, p. 397.

310 **"I often feel like a stranger in my own country"**: For a 2019 survey, see "Anger at the News," Axios Survey Monkey poll (October 17–20, 2019). For 2021, see "Competing Visions of America: An Evolving Identity or a Culture Under Attack?," Public Religion Research Institute. For 2022, see "Our Precarious Democracy: Extreme Polarization and Alienation in Our Politics," University of Chicago Institute of Politics.

311 **"I feel unutterable anxiety. God grant us wisdom and fortitude"**: Adams, *The Works of John Adams: Volume 2*, p. 338.

9. HOW OUR LIVES WILL CHANGE

315 "cosmic optimism": Miller, *The New England Mind: The Seventeenth Century*, pp 37–38.

315 "Let us . . . act like wise men": Adams, quoted in Maier, "Coming to Terms with Samuel Adams."

315 make "true religion and good morals" the national credo: See Strout, *The New Heavens and New Earth*, pp. 67–68.

315 "before His judgment seat": Lyrics, by Julia Ward Howe, to "The Battle Hymn of the Republic"; published by Howe in *The Atlantic*, February 1862.

315 "who do the most harm in the world": Adams, quoted by Frederic Bancroft in a diary, of which excerpts are published in Jacob E. Cooke, "Chats with Henry Adams," *American Heritage*, December 1955.

316 "fight like a Christian or a gentleman": British officer on Marion, quoted in Whitney, *The Colonial Spirit of '76*, p. 296.

316 "Fire is the test of gold": Seneca the Younger, *De Providentia* (*"Ignis aurum probat, miseria fortes viros"*).

317 "projects of breathtaking scope and grandeur": Esler, *The Aspiring Mind of the Elizabethan Younger Generation*, p. 165.

317 "a happy revolution": Mather, cited in Miller, *The New England Mind: From Colony to Province*, p. 159.

317 "long-suppressed generational tensions": T. H. Breen, "Transfer of Culture: Chance and Design in Shaping Massachusetts Bay, 1630–1660," in Breen, *Puritans and Adventurers*.

317 "All human greatness shall in us be found": Colonel David Humphreys, *The Glory of America; or Peace Triumphant over War* (1783).

317 "restrain your children": Cotton Mather, *The Young Man's Preservative* (1701).

317 "attend to disorder of every kind": See Edmund Morgan in "Puritan Tribalism," in Morgan, *The Puritan Family*.

317 "rocked in the cradle of the Revolution": Clay, cited in Peterson, *The Great Triumvirate*, pp. 8–9.

318 "We can win no laurels": Webster, Dedication Speech for the Unveiling of the Bunker Hill Monument, June 17, 1843; for text, see American Battlefield Trust (online).

318 "the most absolute obedience": Foreigner was French visitor Georges Fisch, cited in Smith and Judah, *Life in the North During the Civil War*, pp. 309–11.

318 "from the howling storm outside": Kett, *Rites of Passage*, p. 116.

319 only 7 percent reached age eighty-eight: All estimates of survivorship by year of birth are derived from "The Longevity Visualizer," a downloadable analytic tool, based on life tables, published by and available from the Office of the Chief Actuary, U.S. Social Security Administration.

320 "a lost generation": Hemingway, *A Movable Feast*, p. 74.

320 "you drink yourselves to death": Ibid.

321 *The Sun Also Rises*: Hemingway, *The Sun Also Rises*, 1926.

321 "They do not grow wise. They grow careful": Hemingway, *A Farewell to Arms*, chapter 35.

321 "military-industrial complex": Eisenhower, Farewell Radio and Television Address to the American People, January 17, 1961; text archived in the American Presidency Project (UC Santa Barbara).

321 "longer strides": Kennedy ("Now it is time to take longer strides") in Special Message to the Congress on Urgent National Needs, May 25, 1961; text archived in the American Presidency Project (UC Santa Barbara).

322 "rise to the surface and erupt": Tillich, interviewed by Huston Smith, in Smith, *Search for America* (Season 2, 1959) video series, episode 16 ("Human Fulfillment"). See Huston Smith archives, http://hustonsmith.org/SfA.htm.

322 "a field, a home, or a country": "Antrobus," speaking in Act III, Wilder, *The Skin of Our Teeth*.

322 "crazier things just for the hell of it?": Cowley, *A Second Flowering*, p. 248.

323 *The Greatest Generation*: Brokaw, *The Greatest Generation*.

323 "get this country moving again": Senator John F. Kennedy, Remarks at Salem, Ohio, Stadium, October 9, 1960; text archived in the American Presidency Project (UC Santa Barbara).

323 "They are accustomed to meeting, and beating, tests": See "America's Mood Today," *Look*, June 29, 1965.

324 either resigned or were voted out of office: In the House, the G.I. Generation share dropped more than 10 percentage points, from 58.5 percent in 1973 to 46.8 percent in 1975—and lost its plurality to the younger Silent; see "Generations of American Leaders," https://www.fourthturning.com/goal/overview.php.

324 "a pitiful, helpless giant": Nixon, Address to the Nation on the Situation in Southeast Asia, April 30, 1970; text archived in the American Presidency Project (UC Santa Barbara).

325 "a beautiful word with a big meaning": Bush, Address Accepting the Presidential Nomination at the Republican National Convention in New Orleans, August 18, 1988; text archived in the American Presidency Project (UC Santa Barbara). Full quote: "And that's the idea of community—a beautiful word with a big meaning."

325 "George Bailey had never been born": Angel "Clarence," in *It's a Wonderful Life*, movie, directed by Frank Capra (Liberty Films, 1946).

325 thanks to journalist Gail Sheehy: Sheehy, *Passages*.

326 *Time* published an in-depth essay: "The Younger Generation," *Time*, November 5, 1951.

326 the typical young man could earn more at age thirty: See Easterlin, *Birth and Fortune*, Chapter 2, "The Economic Fortunes of Young Adults."

326 live better than most "retired" elders: In 1959, among families, median income for those aged 25–34 was about two times higher than that for those aged 65+; among unrelated individuals, it was three times higher. See "Income of Families and Persons in the United States: 1959," *Current Population Reports: Consumer Income*, Series P-60, no. 35 (U.S. Bureau of the Census, January 5, 1961), p. 25.

326 than any other generation in U.S. history: See Strauss and Howe, *Generations*, p. 284.

326 **"the fortunate generation"**: See Easterlin, *Birth and Fortune*, Chapter 1, "Accident of Birth: Generation Size and Personal Welfare."

326 **"the lucky few"**: Carlson, *The Lucky Few*.

327 **the elderly were much poorer than young adults**: In 1959, the official poverty rate for people aged 18–64 was 17.0 percent; for people aged 65+ it was 35.2 percent. See "Historical Poverty Tables: People and Families—1959 to 2021," Current Population Survey (2022), U.S. Census Bureau.

327 **surged higher than that of *any* non-elderly age bracket**: See "Changes in U.S. Family Finances from 2007 to 2010: Evidence from the Survey of Consumer Finances," *Federal Reserve Bulletin* 98, no. 2 (June 2021): 17.

327 **"were . . . scaled-down versions"**: Frank Conroy, "My Generation," *Esquire*, October 1968.

327 **"but the approval of others"**: Manchester, *The Glory and the Dream*, p. 578.

327 **"became of a generation of technicians"**: Ibid., pp. 778–79.

327 *The Tender Trap*: movie, directed by Charles Walters (Metro-Goldwyn-Mayer, 1955). Also, "(Love Is) The Tender Trap," song written for the movie (1955).

328 **"we occupied, unnoticed as usual, the gap itself"**: Wade Greene, "Fiftysomething—and in Charge," *New York Times*, January 2, 1990.

329 **"dwarfs" . . . "stature gap"**: See "Will Hart's Demise Give Us the Late, Late Mario Scenario?," *Washington Post*, May 24, 1987.

329 **"a resume in search of rhetoric"**: "Richard Lugar: A Resume in Search of Rhetoric," *Washington Post*, February 3, 1996.

330 **"to create a thousand petty fortresses"**: Walzer, *Spheres of Justice*, p. 39.

330 **voted for as young state legislators**: See Strauss and Howe, *Generations*, p. 284.

330 **"we are the last suckers"**: Tilly, quoted in Putnam, *Bowling Alone*, 2020, p. 255.

330 **"Eighty percent of life is just showing up"**: Allen, quoted in "He's Woody Allen's 1-1-Silent Partner," *New York Times*, August 21, 1977.

330 **"We had the meal"**: Harry "Rabbit" Angstrom, in Updike, *Rabbit Is Rich*, p. 629.

331 **"Am I a good man?"**: Ryan, in *Saving Private Ryan*, movie, directed by Steven Spielberg (Dreamworks, Paramount, Amblin Entertainment, and Mutual Film, 1998).

332 **"You go on build it up, mother, we gonna burn it down!"**: Jacob Brackman, "My Generation," *Esquire*, October 1968.

333 **"folded, spindled, or mutilated"**: Popular placard in Berkeley's 1964 Free Speech Movement ("I will not be folded, spindled, or mutilated"), cited in Gerstle, *The Rise and Fall of the Neoliberal Order*, p. 100.

333 *J'accuse* **to Jaccuzi**: Gitlin, *The Sixties*, p. 433.

333 **Boomers mark first the apogee, and then the rapid decline**: See CPS (Census) median household income data analyzed by birth cohort group, in Howe and Elliott, "A Generational Perspective on Living Standards," Figure 2, p. 102.

333 **Ninety percent of Boomers born in 1943**: See Chetty et al., "The Fading American Dream."

334 **"the Boomer master trend"**: Russell, *The Master Trend*.

334 **"art of living alone"**: Klinenberg, *Going Solo*.

334 *Generation of Seekers*: Roof, *A Generation of Seekers*.

334 **rose swiftly for midlife Americans, even as they fell for youth:** From 1990 to 2020, the 45–54 age bracket showed by far the greatest rise in rates of "deaths of despair" (total of suicides, alcohol-related deaths, and drug-related deaths), in both percentage terms and in percentage-point terms; the second-highest increase was in the 54–64 age bracket. See *Long-Term Trends in Deaths of Despair*, Social Capital Project, Report No. 4-19, Joint Economic Committee of the U.S. Congress (September 2019), data supplement tables (Excel file).

334 **five times as many Americans under age thirty died in motorcycle accidents:** See U.S. Department of Transportation's Fatality Analysis Reporting System (FARS) data, summarized over time in "Fatality Facts: Motorcycles and ATVs" (Age and Sex), as compiled online by the Insurance Institute for Highway Safety and the Highway Loss Data Institute, https://www.iihs.org/topics/fatality-statistics/detail /motorcycles-and-atvs#age-and-sex.

335 **higher rates of lifestyle-related chronic disease:** For an excellent recent overview of cohort drivers of rising chronic disease prevalence over age sixty-five, see Zheng, "A New Look at Cohort Trend and Underlying Mechanisms in Cognitive Functioning."

335 **roughly one-third of Boomers:** See "Millions of Baby Boomers Are Getting Caught in the Country's Broken Retirement System," *Washington Post*, May 4, 2020. See also results of GOBankingRates survey, tabulated by age in Sean Dennison, "64% of Americans Aren't Prepared for Retirement—and 48% Don't Care," Yahoo! News, September 23, 2019.

335 **Boomers are less likely than other generations to agree:** See Metlife, *2011 Metlife Study of the American Dream* (survey conducted in 2011 by Strategy First Partners and Penn Schoen Berland).

335 **giving their kids "good values":** See Allianz, The Allianz American Legacies Pulse Survey (survey conducted in 2012 by Research Now), https://www.allianzlife .com/-/media/files/allianz/documents/ent_1371_n.pdf, accessed November 2022.

335 **They've enjoyed a twenty-four-year generational plurality:** See "Generations of American Leaders," https://www.fourthturning.com/goal/overview.php.

336 **"the most ethical administration in history":** Clinton as president-elect in 1992, quoted in "Ethical Issues Facing the White House," *New York Times*, November 3, 1996.

336 **"procedural republic":** Sandel, "The Procedural Republic and the Unencumbered Self."

336 **officially declared war on the United States government:** Declaration was taped by Bernardine Dohrn and sent anonymously to a radio station; see "The Americans Who Declared War on Their Country," *Guardian*, September 20, 2003.

337 **twice as likely as their older counterparts to vote for George Wallace:** See Lipset and Ladd, Jr., "The Political Future of Activist Generations."

337 **"kick the system over, not try to change it":** Gingrich, quoted in "Adding Aye of Newt," *New York Times*, March 23, 1989.

337 **Boomers took charge:** Boom Generation attained a plurality in the House in the 1994 election and in the Senate in the 2000 election; see "Generations of American Leaders," https://www.fourthturning.com/goal/overview.php.

337 was fading from memory: See "As Leaders, Boomers Are a Bust," *New York Times*, June 27, 2014.

338 the "lived experience" of the victimized perceiver: Crenshaw, quoted in "Intersectionality at 30: A Celebration Hosted by the Department of Gender Studies," London School of Economics and Political Science, https://www.lse.ac.uk/gen der/events/2018-19/lt/Intersectionality-at-30-A-Celebration, accessed November 2022.

338 "many people feel the same way that I do": Trump, quoted by Kurt Andersen, "How America Lost Its Mind," *Atlantic*, September 2017.

338 "there was not a book, a speech, a conversation, or a thought": Emerson; full quote is: "From 1790 to 1820, there was not a book, a speech, a conversation, or thought in the State." Cited in Wood, *Empire of Liberty*, p. 543.

339 "power elite" . . . "cultural elite": See Google Ngram usage history on these two phrases. "Power elite" rises fastest in 1950s and peaks in 1970; "cultural elite" rises fastest in 1990s and peaks in 2004.

339 today's renaissance in extended-family households: See Pew Research Center, "Financial Issues Top the List of Reasons U.S. Adults Live in Multigenerational Homes" (March 24, 2022).

340 "the price that Boomers will pay": Carstensen, "Baby Boomers Are Isolating Themselves as They Age," *Time*, May 12, 2016.

340 "Senior" . . . "Elder": See Google Ngram history on these two phrases. Usage of "senior" has declined by one-quarter since 2002; usage of "elder" has meanwhile risen by more than one-third.

340 "seers who feed wisdom back into society": Schachter-Shalomi and Miller, *From Age-ing to Sage-ing*, p. 20.

340 "crone" and "witch": See Google Ngram history on these two phrases. Both have approximately quadrupled in usage since 1980.

340 "sewing us back into the fabric of creation": Halifax, quoted in Schachter-Shalomi and Miller, *From Age-ing to Sage-ing* (2008), p. 83.

340 "this broken planet": Warren, "Why Be Concerned About Hell?," PastorRick.com, accessed November 2022.

341 "This generation of Americans has a rendezvous with destiny": Roosevelt, Acceptance Speech for the Renomination for the Presidency, Philadelphia, Pennsylvania, June 27, 1936; text archived in the American Presidency Project (UC Santa Barbara).

341 "they concern, thank God, only material things": Roosevelt, Inaugural Address, March 4, 1933; text archived in the American Presidency Project (UC Santa Barbara).

341 "full solution in the fire of a religious awakening": Roosevelt, Letter of Greeting to the United Methodist Council, January 17, 1938; text archived in the American Presidency Project (UC Santa Barbara).

341 "generation of ideals from a generation of commerce": Churchill, *Mr. Crewe's Career*, p. 53.

341 "higher social morality": Addams, *Democracy and Social Ethics*, p. 70.

341 "Early assumptions as to virtue and vice": Howe, *Confessions of a Reformer*, p. 17.

341 "apply morals to public affairs": Santayana, *Character and Opinion in the United States*, pp. 4–5.

341 "are in their final analysis great moral questions": Bryan, *The First Battle*, p. 344.

342 "followed no American since Lincoln": Schlesinger, Jr., *The Crisis of the Old Order*, p 19.

342 "Elysium, Heaven, City of God, Millennium": Berenson, *Aesthetics and History*, p. 137.

343 Hal Lindsey's seventies-era mega-seller: Lindsey and Carlson, *The Late Great Planet Earth*.

343 *Chariots of the Gods?*: Däniken, *Chariots of the Gods?*

343 "lead humanity toward a . . . great transformation": Redfield, quoted in "Prophecy Fulfilled: The Celestine Sequel," *Newsweek*, June 23, 1996.

344 "as the evening twilight fades away": Longfellow, "Morituri Salutamus," a poem he read in 1875 at the fiftieth anniversary of his class at Bowdoin College.

344 Boomers have been gloomier than other generations: See "Baby Boomers: The Gloomiest Generation," Pew Research Center (June 25, 2008).

344 "to prefer war with all its horrors": Witherspoon, quoted in Roche, *The Colonial Colleges in the War for American Independence*, p. 29.

344 "Let it search, let it grind, let it overturn": Emerson in his journal during 1862, excerpted in Masur (ed.), *The Real War Will Never Get in the Books*, pp. 133–34.

345 are expected to consume more than all federal revenue: In 2045, as a share of GDP, CBO projects Social Security and federal health programs outlays at 14.7 percent, net interest outlays at 5.5 percent, and total federal revenues at 18.7 percent. See *The 2022 Long-Term Budget Outlook* (U.S. Congressional Budget Office, July 27, 2022).

346 "an unexpected harvest festival": Karpel, *The Retirement Myth*, chapter 16, "Owl Mountain," pp. 229–44.

347 "figure of an ancient man": In "The Gray Champion," short story in Hawthorne, *Twice-Told Tales* (1837).

347 "fiery gospel writ in burnished rows of steel": Lyrics, by Julia Ward Howe, to "The Battle Hymn of the Republic"; published by Howe in *The Atlantic*, February 1862.

347 "the New Deal Isaiahs": Term coined by H. L. Mencken, in "The New Deal Mentality," *American Mercury* 36 (May 1936).

348 "an enviable death": Churchill's eulogy before the House of Commons (April 17, 1945); see "What Mackenzie King's Diaries Reveal About the Day Franklin Delano Roosevelt Died," *Maclean's*, April 21, 2020.

348 *The Breakfast Club*: movie, directed by John Hughes (A&M Films, 1985).

348 *St. Elmo's Fire*: movie, directed by Joel Schumacher (Channel-Lauren Shuler, 1985).

349 Doug Coupland, who wrote a sardonic novel: Coupland, *Generation X*.

349 The iconic *Time* cover image: "Twentysomething," *Time* cover, July 16, 1990.

349 total fertility had plunged: In 1971, the U.S. total fertility rate (TFR) dropped to 2.01, beneath its earlier estimated low of 2.12 (in 1936); by 1976, it had dropped

to 1.74, which remained its lowest level until 2018. See annual TFR data (since 1960) on FRED online (economic data from the St. Louis Federal Reserve Bank) and (partially estimated, from 1917 to 1959) in "Natality Statistics Analysis: United States, 1963," Vital and Health Statistics, NVSS, series 21, no. 8, U.S. Department of Health, Education, and Welfare (March 1966), Table 1.

350 *The Disappearance of Childhood*: Postman, *The Disappearance of Childhood*.

350 *Rosemary's Baby*: movie, directed by Roman Polanski (William Castle Enterprises, 1968).

350 *The Exorcist*: movie, directed by William Friedkin (Hoya Productions, 1973).

350 *It's Alive*: movie, directed by Larry Cohen (Larco Productions, 1974).

350 *Children of the Corn*: movie, directed by Fritz Kiersch (Los Angeles Entertainment Group et al., 1984).

350 "rising tide of mediocrity": National Commission on Excellence in Education, *A Nation at Risk: The Imperative for Educational Reform* (April 1983).

350 *Bugsy Malone*: movie, directed by Alan Parker (Goodtimes Enterprises and Robert Stigwood Organization, 1976).

350 "We're not worthy!": Quote from Wayne Campbell (Mike Myers) and Garth Algar (Dana Carvey) in unison, in *Wayne's World*, movie, directed by Penelope Spheeris (Lorne Michaels, 1992).

350 "willing to admit its contemptible qualities": Leavitt, quoted in Kanter and Mirvis, *The Cynical Americans*.

351 the share of young men with college degrees: See Kurt Bauman, "College Completion by Cohort, Age and Gender, 1967 to 2015," U.S. Census Bureau Working Paper 2016-04 (March 4, 2016), Figure 1.

351 "meaningful philosophy . . . well off financially": Percentages of freshmen checking "objectives considered to be essential or very important" for each item can be tracked annually starting with the fall class of 1967. See *The Freshman Survey*, conducted annually by the Higher Education Research Institute, based at UCLA, https://heri.ucla.edu/cirp-freshman-survey/.

352 "The ghosts of Vietnam have been laid to rest": Bush, quoted in "Has America Had Enough of War?" *Financial Times*, May 7, 2021.

353 U.S. corporations have returned to dominance: See "Market capitalization of listed domestic companies (% of GDP)," World Bank online; annual data by county and country group since 1975. Since 2018, the U.S. share of total "high income" market cap has been 55 percent or higher, which is higher than any prior year dating back to 1983.

353 small business has joined the military in high public esteem: See "Confidence in Institutions," Gallup online, with annual public "confidence" scores on over a dozen institutions since the 1970s; "the military" and "small business" in 2022 scored 64 percent and 68 percent, respectively, in the share of the public saying they have a "great deal" or "quite of lot" of confidence in them. They are the only two institutions whose score has risen since the late 1970s or early 1980s, and the only two whose current score is well over 50 percent.

353 Robert Bellah gave this belief a name, "Sheilaism": Bellah et al., *Habits of the Heart*, chapter 9, "Religion."

353 **They remain years away from dominance:** See "Generations of American Leaders,"
https://www.fourthturning.com/goal/overview.php.

353 **The first big Xer TV star:** Fox, in *Family Ties* (NBC sitcom, 1982–89).

353 **voted more Republican than the nation as a whole:** See, for example, "How Birth
Year Influences Political Views," *New York Times,* July 7, 2014, and Pew Research
Center, "The politics of American generations: How age affects attitudes and voting
behavior" (July 9, 2014). See also Ghitza, Gelman, and Auerbach, "The Great Society, Reagan's Revolution, and Generations of Presidential Voting," Figure 11, p. 19.

353 **most Republican-leaning generation of congresspeople and state governors:** See
"Generations of American Leaders," https://www.fourthturning.com/goal/over
view.php.

354 **an aging wave of front-end Xers:** See Culhane et al., "The Emerging Crisis of Aged
Homelessness."

354 **"midlife deaths of despair":** Case and Deaton, *Deaths of Despair and the Future of
Capitalism.*

354 **nearly one in ten continues to rely on gig work:** See Prudential, "Gig Economy
Impact by Generation" (survey conducted in 2017 by Harris Poll Online).

354 **Two-thirds of these "gig" Xers:** See ibid.

354 **barely half of all Xers earned more than their parents:** See Chetty et al., "The Fading American Dream."

354 **Per household, the median income of Xers has been slightly lower:** See CPS (Census) median household income data analyzed by birth cohort group, in Howe and
Elliott, "A Generational Perspective on Living Standards," Figure 2, p. 102.

354 **Gen X currently owns 30 percent of all U.S. real and financial assets:** See "Distribution of Household Wealth in the U.S. since 1989," in Distributional Financial
Accounts (online), Board of Governors of the U.S. Federal Reserve System.

354 **Gen-Xers report being "more worried":** See "5 Generations' Financial Priorities
During COVID-19," *The Ascent,* April 14, 2020, a Motley Fool publication, survey
conducted in 2020 by Pollfish.

354 **"just figure it out when they get there":** When asked if they are preparing for retirement, 46 percent gave this answer. See Allianz, "Generations Apart: How Boomer
and Generation Xers Are Facing Their Financial Futures" (survey conducted in
2015 by Larson Research and Strategy Consulting), https://www.allianzlife.com
/-/media/files/global/documents/2016/06/16/20/50/ent-1743-n.pdf, accessed November 2022.

354 **agree that *their* generation is worse off than their parents:** "Generation X Is the
Least Likely to Believe They'll Get Rich One Day," *Fast Company,* July 21, 2021;
includes discussion of Fast-Company-Harris survey (2021); author analyzed unpublished cross-tabbed survey data.

354 **"lower class" . . . "upper class":** Ibid.

354 ***Rich Dad Poor Dad:*** Kiyosaki and Lechter, *Rich Dad Poor Dad.*

355 **"becoming wealthy is an achievable goal":** "Generation X Is the Least Likely to Believe They'll Get Rich One Day," *Fast Company,* July 21, 2021.

356 **Xers composed the clear majority:** For age composition of Capitol Hill insurrec-

tionists, see Robert A. Pape and Keven Ruby, "The Capitol Rioters Aren't Like Other Extremists," *Atlantic*, February 2, 2021.

356 **more likely to vote for the GOP:** See NPR/PBS NewsHour/Marist Poll of intentions to vote in 2022 election (April 26, 2022); also age breakdown in AP Votecast online for 2022 election, in "How different groups voted according to exit polls and AP VoteCast" (November 10, 2022).

356 **"Gen X's greatest gift to society":** "These TV Shows Have Figured Out Gen X's Greatest Gift to Society: Grouchiness," *Washington Post*, October 16, 2017.

356 **"they just might not give much of a hoot":** "Generation X: America's neglected 'middle child,'" Pew Research Center (June 5, 2014).

356 **"Withdrawing in disgust":** Message on an "oblique strategy" card, in *Slacker*, movie, directed by Richard Linklater (Detour Filmproduction, Orion Classics, 1990).

357 *Generation of Sociopaths*: Gibney, *A Generation of Sociopaths*.

357 **"we look back at our wasted youth . . . no second acts":** Fitzgerald in 1931, quoted in Frederick J. Hoffman, "Some Perspectives on the 1920s," in Fine and Brown (eds.), *The American Past*.

357 **"What is immoral is what you feel bad after":** Hemingway, *Death in the Afternoon*, p. 13.

357 **"All my life I have been a bad boy":** Last words of Wolfe according to Max Perkins, in Cowley, *A Second Flowering*, p. 185.

357 **"mental rickets and curvature of the soul":** Cornelia Comer, in "A Letter to the Rising Generation," to which Randolph Bourne responded, in "The Two Generations," *Atlantic*, February and May 1911.

357 **a "mental age" of under twelve:** See Boorstin, *The Americans: The Democratic Experience*, pp. 220–23.

357 **"a generation of self-seekers":** Roosevelt, Inaugural Address, March 4, 1933; text archived in the American Presidency Project (UC Santa Barbara).

358 **"Martin, Barton, and Fish":** Congressmen Joseph W. Martin (1884–1968), Bruce Fairchild Barton (1886–1967), and Hamilton Fish III (1888–1991).

358 **"doubt and even defeat":** Cowley, *Exile's Return*, p. 306.

358 **the Republican-leaning Lost did not attain a majority:** See "Generations of American Leaders," https://www.fourthturning.com/goal/overview.php.

359 **From childhood on:** Movies: *WarGames*, directed by John Badham (United Artists, 1983); *The Last Starfighter*, directed by Nick Castle (Lorimar, 1984); *The Dark Knight Rises*, directed by Christopher Nolan (Warner Bros. et al., 2012); *World War Z*, directed by Marc Forster (Skydance et al., 2013); *Mad Max*, directed by George Miller (Kennedy Miller, 1979); and *I Am Legend*, directed by Francis Lawrence (Village Roadshow et al., 2007).

359 **"I've glimpsed our future":** Valedictorian (Ione Skye Lee), in *Say Anything . . .* , movie, directed by Cameron Crowe (Gracie Films, 1989).

360 **"a long list of dead, famous wild people":** Slater, quoted in Howe and Strauss, *13th Gen*, p. 206.

360 *Revenge of the Nerds*: movie, directed by Jeff Kanew (Interscope Communications, 1984).

361 **"We won't have a bad backlash":** Linklater, quoted in "Slackers," *Boston Phoenix*, October 11, 1991.

361 *Hot Tub Time Machine*: movie, directed by Steve Pink (New Crime Productions, Metro-Goldwyn Mayer, United Artists, 2010).

361 **"a White Russian aristocracy":** Coupland, quoted in Strauss and Howe, *The Fourth Turning*, p. 289.

365 **receive more time and more sheltering from adults:** On growing parental time spent with children, see Sandberg and Hofferth, "Changes in Children's Time with Parents."

365 **The phrase "kids are special":** See Google Ngram usage history on this phrase since 1970.

365 **Fathers present at the birth of their children:** See Leavitt, *Make Room for Daddy*.

365 **adorable-child movies became in vogue:** *Baby Boom*, movie, directed by Charles Shyer (Metro-Goldwyn-Mayer and United Artists, 1987); *Three Men and a Baby*, movie, directed by Leonard Nimoy (Touchstone et al., 1987); and *Parenthood*, movie, directed by Ron Howard (Universal, 1989).

366 **the incidence of child abandonment, runaways, and parental violence:** See Finkelhor and Jones, "Why Have Child Maltreatment and Child Victimization Declined?"

366 **Nearly all these indicators dropped:** See trends, 1991 to 2019, in "Youth Risk Behavior Surveillance System (YRBSS online)," U.S. Centers for Disease Control and Prevention.

366 **rates of violent crime . . . fell steeply:** See overview of trends from 1993 to 2021 in "Violent crime is a key midterm voting issue, but what does the data say?," Pew Research Center (October 31, 2022).

366 **the incarceration rate for males under age thirty *fell by half*:** For trends in male incarceration rates by age bracket, see *Prisoners in 2001* (and in subsequent years), an annual publication from the Bureau of Justice Statistics, U.S. Department of Justice.

367 **That was down from 25 percent in 1983:** See 1974, 1983, and 2003 editions of the annual survey of high-school seniors, "The Mood of American Youth," published by the National Association of Secondary School Principals (NASSP).

367 **much more often than their parents ever did:** See analysis of Morning Consult survey in "Young Adulthood in America: Children Are Grown, but Parenting Doesn't Stop," *New York Times*, March 13, 2019. See also analysis of AARP survey of young adults and Boomers in "AARP The Magazine Generations Study," AARP (January 2013).

367 **bearing roughly twice the average daily homework load:** See Pew analysis of American Time Use Survey data for teens aged 15–17 in 2014–17 versus 2003–2006 and mid-1990s; it shows average homework durations of one hour, forty-four minutes, and thirty minutes, respectively. See "The way U.S. teens spend their time is changing, but differences between boys and girls persist," Pew Research Center (February 20, 2019).

367 **the number of high-school AP test takers:** See *The 7th Annual AP Report to the Nation* (CollegeBoard, February 9, 2011); accessible online at www.collegeboard.org.

367 **Millennial rates of educational attainment:** On growing educational attainment, see "Table 104-20. Percentage of persons 25 to 29 years old with selected levels of educational attainment, by race/ethnicity and sex: Selected years, 1920 through 2017," Digest of Educational Statistics online, National Center for Education Statistics, U.S. Department of Education, https://nces.ed.gov/programs/digest/d17/tables/dt17_104.20.asp, accessed November 2022.

367 **rates of "volunteering" had soared:** See percent of college freshmen saying "volunteering" as something they did "frequently" or "occasionally" during the past year, in *The Freshman Survey*, conducted annually by the Higher Education Research Institute, based at UCLA, https://heri.ucla.edu/cirp-freshman-survey/.

368 **family-friendly Disney animation:** *The Lion King*, movie (Walt Disney, 1994) and *Finding Nemo*, movie (Walt Disney, 2003).

369 **fallen behind their parents in real earnings:** Early data for cohorts born in the early 1980s indicate that a slightly smaller share are outearning their parents than cohorts born in the 1960s and 1970s. See Chetty et al., "The Fading American Dream: Trends in Absolute Income Mobility since 1940."

369 **even fallen behind Xers alone:** See CPS (Census) median household income data analyzed by birth cohort group, in Howe and Elliott, "A Generational Perspective on Living Standards," Figure 2, p. 102.

369 **lagging in wealth accumulation:** As a share of all household wealth, Millennials in 2022 are roughly on par with Gen-Xers at the same age (in 2003). See "Distribution of Household Wealth in the U.S. since 1989," in Distributional Financial Accounts (online), Board of Governors of the U.S. Federal Reserve System.

369 **the lowest homeownership rate:** For homeownership rates by age bracket from 1900 to 2014, see Acolin, Goodman, and Wachter, "A Renter or Homeowner Nation?," Exhibit 2, "Homeownership Rate by Age Group, U.S. Decennial Census and American Community Survey (1900–2014)," p. 147.

369 **why they're reluctant to talk about their personal finances:** "Financial Taboo Survey," TD Ameritrade (July 2019); discussion of survey conducted February 13–20, 2019, by Harris.

369 **more likely . . . *not* to take earned days off:** See "Vacation Shaming in the Workplace: Millennials Most Likely to Feel Guilt for Taking Time Off Work," Enterprise Holdings (March 4, 2016); discussion of survey data from 2016 Alamo Family Vacation Survey (conducted January 2016 by Research Now).

369 **same percentage as young G.I.s living at home:** "A majority of young adults in the U.S. live with their parents for the first time since the Great Depression," Pew Research Center (September 4, 2020).

370 **reported getting monthly financial assistance:** "Failure to Launch: Americans Still Rely on Parents to Help with Mobile Phones, Gas, Groceries and Health Insurance," Cision Newswire, June 20, 2018; discussion of survey responses from the COUNTRY Financial Security Index, compiled by GfK from randomly sampled panel.

370 **They search eagerly for "job stability" with big organizations:** In a survey (conducted in September 2022) of college-grad job seekers, the top response (82 per-

cent) to the question "What motivates you most to apply for a job?" was "job stability"; see "Enter Your Pay Transparency Era," by Handshake (2023).

370 **evoked in their imaginations:** *The Hunger Games*, movie series (Color Force, Studio Babelsberg, and Good Universe, 2012–); *Divergent*, movie, directed by Neil Burger (Red Wagon Entertainment and Summit Entertainment, 2014); *Squid Game*, Netflix TV series (2021–).

370 **Millennials are incurring less debt:** See analysis of data from Census Bureau and Equifax in "The Graying of American Debt," Research and Statistics Group, Microeconomic Studies, Federal Reserve Bank of New York (February 12, 2016), p. 10.

370 **Homogamy . . . has soared to levels:** See Mare, "Educational Homogamy in Two Gilded Ages: Evidence from Intergenerational Social Mobility Data"; see also "Equality in Marriages Grows, and So Does Class Divide," *New York Times*, February 27, 2016).

371 **largest increase in Adderall and Ritalin prescriptions:** "Attention-Deficit/Hyperactivity Disorder Medication Prescription Claims Among Privately Insured Women Age 15–44 Years: United States, 2003–2015," Morbidity and Mortality Weekly Report, 67(2), U.S. Centers for Disease Control and Prevention (January 19, 2018).

371 **decline in courtship and sexual activity among Millennials:** See Kate Julian, "Why Are Young People Having So Little Sex?," *Atlantic*, December 2018; see also "'There isn't really anything magical about it': Why More Millennials Are Avoiding Sex," *Washington Post*, August 2, 2016.

371 **likelier to agree . . . that "feminism has done more harm than good":** "SPLC Poll Finds Substantial Support for 'Great Replacement' Theory and Other Hard-Right Ideas," Southern Poverty Law Center (June 1, 2022), Section 2; survey conducted in 2022 by SPLC and Tulchin Research.

372 **a vast expansion of STEM curricula:** See "The Most-Regretted (and Lowest-Paying) College Majors," *Washington Post*, September 2, 2022); see also Ben Schmidt, "College Majors 2019 Update" (August 28, 2020), available at http://benschmidt.org /post/2020-08-25-college-majors-2019-update/, accessed November 2022.

372 **the steep recent growth in the share of all Americans who identify with "no religion":** Trends in religious affiliation by age bracket analyzed in "In U.S., Decline of Christianity Continues at a Rapid Pace," Pew Research Center (October 17, 2019).

372 **the most Democratic-leaning generation of young-adult voters since the G.I.s:** See, for example, "How Birth Year Influences Political Views," *New York Times*, July 7, 2014, and Pew Research Center, "The politics of American generations: How age affects attitudes and voting behavior" (July 9, 2014). See also Ghitza et al., "The Great Society, Reagan's Revolution, and Generations of Presidential Voting," Figure 11, p. 19.

372 **roughly 60 percent of Millennials have voted Democratic:** See Edison exit polls for national and midterm elections since 2006, broken down by age, available online at various CNN websites.

373 **"the community" . . . rather than "the individual":** See survey in "The Millennial Generation: Who They Are & How the GOP Can Connect with Them," LifeCourse

Associates and the Congressional Institute (2015), Figure 4, p. 11; survey conducted in November 2014 by LifeCourse Associates.

373 **"socialism" is almost as popular as "capitalism":** "Socialism as Popular as Capitalism Among Young Adults in U.S.," Gallup (November 25, 2019).

373 **a "Democratic Socialist" for national office:** See *US Attitudes Toward Socialism, Communism, and Collectivism*, Victims of Communism Memorial Foundation (October 2019); results and discussion of survey conducted in 2019 by YouGov.

373 **more likely than older voters to call themselves "moderate":** "A wider partisan and ideological gap between younger, older generations," Pew Research Center (March 20, 2017).

373 **the most likely . . . to believe that the current regime is fundamentally broken:** See poll by the New York Times/Siena College Research Institute (conducted July 5–7, 2022), question 23, "Do you think America's system of government needs to be completely replaced, needs major reforms, needs minor changes, or doesn't need change?"

373 **the solution may require granting extraordinary powers to one side:** See Yahoo! News Survey (conducted by YouGov, June 10–13, 2022), question 24, "Would America be better or worse off with more powerful political leaders who could enact policies with less involvement from the other branches of government?"

374 **"Excellent Sheep":** Deresiewicz, *Excellent Sheep.*

374 **"Organization Kids":** David Brooks, "The Organization Kid," *Atlantic*, April 2001.

374 **"I promise as a good American to do my part":** Chant by children led by Boston mayor James Michael Curley, described in Manchester, *The Glory and the Dream*, p. 89.

374 **"brilliant college graduates":** Cowley, *Exile's Return*, p. 276.

375 **declined from their high levels during Teddy Roosevelt's presidency:** See Strauss and Howe, *Generations*, pp. 266–67.

375 **largest one-generation gain in educational attainment:** See Goldin and Katz, "Human Capital and Social Capital: The Rise of Secondary Schooling in America: 1910–1940"; see also Strauss and Howe, *Generations*, p. 267.

375 **"peer society":** Fass, *The Damned and the Beautiful*, chapter 3, "The World of Youth: The Peer Society."

375 **"Locked-Out Generation":** See Geoffrey Helman, "The Trotskyists," *New Yorker*, December 16, 1939.

375 **"Communism is Twentieth Century Americanism":** Cited in Cohen, *When the Old Left Was Young*, p. 142.

376 **"so roll on Columbia, roll on":** "Roll On, Columbia, Roll On," song, by Woody Guthrie (1941).

376 **"but we can build our youth for the future":** Roosevelt, Address at University of Pennsylvania, September 20, 1940; text archived in the American Presidency Project (UC Santa Barbara).

376 **a reported 80 percent of their first-time votes for FDR:** See Campbell, Converse, Miller, and Stokes, *The American Voter*, p. 155.

376 **"the very objectives of young people have changed":** Roosevelt, Radio Address

to the Young Democratic Clubs of America, August 24, 1935; text archived in the American Presidency Project (UC Santa Barbara).

376 **median age of service was twenty-six:** See Smith, "Populational Characteristics of American Servicemen in World War II."

376 **"the best damn kids in the world":** Marshall, quoted by Ronald Reagan, speech to Republican National Convention, September 15, 1988.

380 **the highest share since the voting age was lowered to eighteen in 1971:** See U.S. voter participation rates by age (as a share of all eligible voters) by year, tabulated by the US Elections Project, https://www.electproject.org/home.

381 **"My new meaning for 'keepin' it gangsta'":** See "The Story Behind How Kendrick Lamar Became the King of West Coast Rap," *Mic*, May 27, 2015.

384 *It Can't Happen Here:* Lewis, *It Can't Happen Here.*

386 **"Most of the wild crap you did is now illegal":** Dylan Roche, at the Helium Comedy Club, September 10, 2016, archived at https://www.youtube.com/watch?v=X-JJWku8_6Q, accessed November 2020.

386 **In 2018, the total fertility rate fell below its earlier low point:** In 2018, the U.S. total fertility rate (TFR) dropped to 1.730, beneath its earlier low point of 1.738 (in 1976). See annual TFR data (since 1960) on FRED online (economic data from the St. Louis Federal Reserve Bank).

386 **Immigration has also fallen sharply:** For the net immigration rate (per 100 U.S. capita) since 2000, see "Data Underlying Figures" (Excel file) for *The Demographic Outlook: 2022 to 2052,* U.S. Congressional Budget Office (July 27, 2022).

387 **Asian rather than Hispanic:** See "Key findings about U.S. immigrants," Pew Research Center (August 20, 2020).

387 **speak English at home as a first language:** Ibid.

388 **average parental time spent with children:** For evidence on the continuing rise in parental time with children since the early 2000s, especially among mothers with less education, see Prickett and Augustine, "Trends in Mothers' Parenting Time by Education and Work from 2003 to 2017."

388 **cutting back on time for every other purpose:** See data sources cited in Claire Cain Miller, "The Relentlessness of Modern Parenting," *New York Times*, December 25, 2018.

388 **divorce rates among Xers:** On decline in Xer divorce rates, see Cohen, "The Coming Divorce Decline."

388 **growing for the first time in at least fifty years:** According to CPS (Census) data on "Living Arrangements of Children Under 18 Years," the share of children living with two parents was 87.7 percent in 1960, dropped at every five-year interval until reaching a low of 67.3 percent in 2005, and has since risen to 70.4 percent in 2020. See discussion in Nicholas Zill, "Growing Up with Mom and Dad: New Data Confirm the Tide Is Turning," Institute for Family Studies, June 18, 2021.

388 **they watch videos with their kids:** See "Making Screen Time Family Time," Screen-Media (Q4, 2020), Chart 3.1, "Frequency of co-viewing sessions," p. 6.

389 **one-half enforce a strict dress code:** See "Table 233.50, 'Percentage of public schools with various safety and security measures: Selected years, 1999–2000 through 2017–18,'" Digest of Educational Statistics online, National Center for

Education Statistics, U.S. Department of Education, https://nces.ed.gov/programs
/digest/d19/tables/dt19_233.50.asp, accessed November 2022.

390 *Ferris Bueller's Day Off*: movie, directed by John Hughes (Paramount, 1986).

390 **a smaller share of pregnancies now end in abortions:** The abortion ratio (abortions
per pregnancies) had declined to a low of 18.3 percent in 2016 before rising to
20.6 percent in 2020—both figures much lower than in any prior year from 1974
to 2011; using annual Guttmacher Institute data compiled annually on Wikipedia
("abortion statistics in the United States"). In 1973 and earlier years, the effect of
illegal abortions on this rate, which can only be estimated, may have been substantial. See Krannich, "Abortion in the United States: Past, Present, and Future
Trends."

390 **a dramatic reduction in teen pregnancies:** For the ongoing decline in birth rates in
every teen age bracket, see *Births: Final Data for 2020*, vol. 70, no. 17, National Vital
Statistics Report, U.S. Centers for Disease Control and Prevention (February 7,
2022), p. 13.

390 **mortality rates in infancy and childhood:** For the ongoing decline in the infant
mortality rate and in mortality rates in child age brackets, see *Deaths: Final Data
for 2019*, vol. 70, no. 8, National Vital Statistics Report, U.S. Centers for Disease
Control and Prevention (July 26, 2021), Figure 2, p. 7, Table 5, p. 31.

391 **The child poverty rate in 2019:** See "Expanded Safety Net Drives Sharp Drop in
Child Poverty," *Washington Post*, September 11, 2022.

391 **most forms of bullying, fighting, and victimization:** See dramatic declines from
1995 to 2015, in *Indicators of School Crime and Safety: 2017*, National Center for
Education Statistics, U.S. Department of Education (March 2018).

391 **their biggest worries are about academic performance:** See "Most U.S. Teens See
Anxiety and Depression as a Major Problem Among Their Peers," Pew Research
Center (February 20, 2019), p. 8, "About six-in-ten teens say they feel a lot of pres-
sure to get good grades."

391 **recent blockbuster animated shows:** *Frozen*, movie (Walt Disney, 2013); *Inside
Out*, movie (Walt Disney, 2015); *Encanto*, movie (Walt Disney, 2021).

391 **Recent re-enactments of the famous Stanford "marshmallow test":** See Carlson
et al., "Cohort Effects in Children's Delay of Gratification."

392 **reporting suicidal thoughts, and going on meds:** See *Protecting Youth Mental
Health: The U.S. Surgeon General's Advisory*, U.S. Surgeon General, U.S. Public
Health Service (2021), pp. 8–10.

392 **asthma and other immune disorders:** See "Trends in Allergic Conditions Among
Children: United States, 1997–2011," NCHS Data Brief, no. 121, U.S. Centers for
Disease Control and Prevention (May 2013).

392 **reading more but enjoying reading less:** On nine- and thirteen-year-olds reading
less for fun, see "Among many U.S. children, reading for fun has become less common, federal data show," Pew Research Center (November 12, 2021); on teens aged
15–17 doing more homework, see "The way U.S. teens spend their time is changing, but differences between boys and girls persist," Pew Research Center (February 20, 2019).

392 **suffering chronic sleep deprivation:** See "Why Teens Need More Sleep, and How We Can Help Them Get It," *Washington Post*, January 18, 2022.

392 **fewer teens are daydreaming:** See Mann et al., *Dream Jobs? Teenagers' Career Aspirations and the Future of Work.*

393 **"everything feels personalized and miniaturized":** David Brooks, "Will Gen-Z Save the World?," *New York Times*, July 4, 2019.

393 **like the Polynesian princess:** *Moana*, movie (Walt Disney, 2016).

394 **"Ambassador for Kindness":** "Kid of the Year" *Time* cover, March 7, 2022, "Ambassador for Kindness: Orion Jean, 11."

394 **"Why are today's children such boring goody-goodies?":** Katie Agnew, "Why Are Today's Children Such Boring Goody Goodies?" *Daily Mail*, January 11, 2016.

394 **"a word first used to describe our parents":** Eisler, *Private Lives*, p. 29.

394 **"reassertion of parental authority":** *Literary Digest*, cited in Fass, *The Damned and the Beautiful*, p. 37.

394 **"explicit insistence on conformity":** Rodgers, in Hiner and Hawes (eds.), *Growing Up in America*, p. 130.

394 **"total situation" style of parenting:** See ibid., p. 130.

394 **a 1928 bestseller by behavioral psychologist John B. Watson:** Watson, *Psychological Care of Infant and Child.*

395 **a child's fatal fall from a pony:** In *Gone With the Wind*, movie, directed by Victor Fleming (Selznick International Pictures and Metro-Goldwyn Mayer, 1939).

395 **"when there wasn't a war going on":** Frank Conroy, "My Generation," *Esquire*, October 1968.

395 **"Today's generation . . . is ready to conform":** "The Younger Generation," *Time*, November 5, 1951.

397 **regularly and eloquently lampoons its excesses:** Skenazy, *Free-Range Kids.*

398 **"we have rule followers afraid to upset their communities":** Allison Schrager, "Gen Z Is Too Compliant to Achieve Greatness," *Bloomberg Businessweek*, February 14, 2022.

399 **the *average* age of military service was thirty-three:** See Committee on the Assessment of Readjustment Needs of Military Personnel, Veterans, and Their Families, *Returning Home from Iraq and Afghanistan: Assessment of Readjustment Needs of Veterans, Service Members, and Their Families* (Institute of Medicine of the National Academies, the National Academy Press, 2013).

400 **"I hated the war ending":** Baker, *Growing Up*, pp. 228, 230.

10. A NEW SAECULUM IS BORN

403 **"epidemic of violence":** Gunnar Myrdal, "Is American Business Deluding Itself?" *Atlantic*, November 1944.

403 **"have labor's demands been so plausible":** *Fortune*; all *Fortune* citations in this chapter are from July, August, or December of 1945 or from January and June of 1946.

404 **"mass production, and mass distribution, and mass ownership":** *Saturday Evening*

Post, cited in Alan Brinkley, "For America, It Truly Was a Great War," *New York Times Magazine*, May 7, 1995.

404 **"rude pushing ways" and "ill temper"**: "The Job Before Us," *Fortune*, July 1945, p. 111.

404 **"the veteran's gripe"**: *Fortune*, 1945–46.

404 **"swiftest disappearance of markets in all history"**: Sumner H. Slichter, "Jobs After the War," *Atlantic*, October 1944, p. 87.

404 **"the infections of a postwar disillusionment"**: Leo Cherne, "The Future of the Middle Class," *Atlantic*, June 1944, p. 79.

404 **a sharp further decline in the U.S. birthrate**: *Life* forecast cited in Jones, *Great Expectations*, pp. 18–19.

404 **"a standard of living far beyond anything in recorded history"**: "Not Peace But a Sword," *Fortune*, January 1946, p. 97.

404 **"long battle with the scarcities in nature"**: Ibid.

405 **"any other period break down quickly"**: "The Boom," *Fortune*, June 1946, pp. 97–99.

405 **"under such momentum you can't stop if you would"**: Ibid., p. 262.

405 **"golden age of poetry and power"**: Robert Frost, "The Gift Outright." Poem (not all of which was delivered in person at the inauguration) is available online at the John F. Kennedy Presidential Library and Museum.

405 **"one brief shining moment"**: Jacqueline Kennedy, interviewed by Theodore H. White in "For President Kennedy an Epilogue," *Life*, December 6, 1963.

406 **"more nearly an afterthought"**: Galbraith, *The Affluent Society*, p. 323.

406 **"limitation of science or of productivity"**: Harold E. Stassen, "Jobs and Freedom," *Atlantic*, March 1946, p. 49.

406 **"the world alters as we walk in it"**: J. Robert Oppenheimer, "Prospects in the Arts and Sciences," *Bulletin of the Atomic Scientists* 11, no. 2 (February 1955): 44. The essay was delivered as a speech at the closing of the Columbia University Bicentennial Anniversary celebration, December 26, 1954.

406 **"America is to be to the world of tomorrow"**: Walter Lippmann, quoted in Alan Brinkley, "For America, It Truly Was a Great War," *New York Times Magazine*, May 7, 1995.

406 **"stands at the summit of the world"**: Winston Churchill, speech in the House of Commons, August 16, 1945; text of speech available online at the UK Parliament Hansard.

407 **"two-thirds of the world's machines"**: Robert Payne, quoted in Halberstam, *The Fifties*, p. 116.

407 **"made to order for the comprehending marketer"**: *Fortune*, 1945–46.

407 **"future conflicts would stretch on endlessly"**: Paul Johnson, "Another 50 Years of Peace?," *Wall Street Journal*, May 5, 1995.

408 **"again in our political history"**: Dwight D. Eisenhower, in letter to Edgar Newton Eisenhower, November 8, 1954; document #1147, archived at the Presidential Papers of Dwight David Eisenhower, available online at the Dwight D. Eisenhower Memorial Commission.

408 "managerialism": Burnham, *The Managerial Revolution.*

408 "the social ethic": Whyte, *The Organization Man*, p. 6.

409 "social *change* as the key problem": Nisbet, *The Quest for Community*, p. 24.

409 "tranquility and belonging": Ibid., p. 25.

409 "writing a generation or two ago": Ibid., p. 22.

409 to fit the approval of others: Riesman, *The Lonely Crowd.*

409 haggled over means and never questioned ends: Bell, *The End of Ideology.*

409 "the second rate in politics and culture": Valentine, *The Age of Conformity*, p. 83.

409 "an epidemic of normalcy": Fromm, *The Sane Society*, chapter 2, "The Pathology of Normalcy."

409 as a result, barely attained the latter: Marcuse, *Eros and Civilization.*

409 nobody noticed when they were taken over by aliens: *Invasion of the Body Snatchers*, movie, directed by Don Siegel (Walter Wanger Productions, 1956).

409 "brainwashed" into complying with arbitrary commands: *The Manchurian Candidate*, movie, directed by John Frankenheimer (M.C. Productions, 1962).

409 "vast wasteland": Newton Minow, in speech to National Association of Broadcasters, May 6, 1961; text of the speech is available at American Rhetoric Online Speech Bank.

410 hobbled by a blinkered conscience: Harrington, *The Other America.*

410 "all look just the same": "Little Boxes," song, by Malvina Reynolds (1962); recorded by Pete Seeger (1963). Lyrics available on lyrics.com.

410 "prefabricated foods, from the same freezers": Lewis Mumford in 1961, cited in Halberstam, *The Fifties*, p. 140.

410 *Pleasantville*: Movie, directed by Gary Ross (New Line Cinema, 1998).

412 "a spirit of youth in everything": William Shakespeare, "Sonnet 98."

412 "The greenest mosses cling": John Greenleaf Whittier, "A Dream of Summer" (1847).

412 "the time of plans and projects": Leo Tolstoy, *Anna Karenina* (1878), part II, chapter 13.

413 "Discord does not belong to our system": James Monroe, first inaugural address, March 4, 1817; text archived in the American Presidency Project (UC Santa Barbara).

413 "one may now add, Southern men also": Bryce, *The American Commonwealth*, vol. 3, part 5, "Illustrations and Reflections," chapter 96, "The Strength of American Democracy," p. 349.

414 "honest money": "Our motto is honest money for all and free schools for all. There should be no inflation which will destroy the one, and no sectarian interference which will destroy the other." Hayes, "Speech delivered at Marion, Lawrence County, Ohio, July 31, 1875," in Howard, *The Life, Public Services, and Select Speeches of Rutherford B. Hayes*, p. 256.

414 a priority of President Eisenhower's: See Eisenhower, Annual Message for the Congress on the State of the Union, February 2, 1953; text archived in the American Presidency Project (UC Santa Barbara).

415 **multiplied more than sixfold:** See Wood, *Empire of Liberty*, p. 486.

415 **founded near the end of a Crisis era or during a High:** For list of national political and fraternal organizations with founding dates, see Skocpol, *Diminished Democracy*, Table 2.1, pp. 26–28.

415 **"bridging" as well as "bonding" social capital:** See Putnam, *Bowling Alone*, pp. 22–24.

415 **"Republican Mothers":** See Kerber, "The Republican Mother," and Reinier, "Rearing the Republican Child."

415 **"a home-ordered society":** White, *The Republic for Which It Stands*, p. 139.

415 **"to make the whole world more HOMELIKE":** Francis Willard, quoted in ibid., p. 165.

416 **appended the initials "FRS" to their names:** For a list of names, see "Colonial fellows of the Royal Society of London, 1661–1788" in *Notes and Records of the Royal Society of London*, vol. 8, no. 2 (April 1951).

416 **to land "a man on the moon":** Kennedy, Address to Joint Session of Congress, May 25, 1961; text available online at the John F. Kennedy Presidential Library and Museum.

417 **"a work and service assigned to it":** Benjamin Colman in *A Sermon at the Lecture in Boston After the Funerals of those Excellent & Learned Divines*, published by Samuel Gerrish & Daniel Henchman in 1717.

418 **"and with a more sacred respect":** Thomas Jefferson, cited in Wood, *Empire of Liberty*, p. 485.

418 **a six-thousand-line patriotic epic:** Barlow, "The Columbiad" (1807).

418 **an 1873 novel:** Twain and Warner, *The Gilded Age*.

418 **"widely and thinly spread":** William Dunlap, cited in Wood, *Empire of Liberty*, p. 572.

418 **"corrodes everything elegant in art":** Andrews Norton, cited in ibid., p. 573.

424 **"the reign of witches":** Jefferson, letter to John Taylor, June 4, 1798, cited in "Jefferson on the Reign of Witches," *Harper's*, July 4, 2007.

424 **"Are *you* afraid to be questioned here?":** Miller, *The Crucible*, p. 62.

427 **his long-predicted "Upswing":** Putnam, *The Upswing*. See chapter 1, "What's Past is Prologue."

431 **"only with the falling of the dusk":** Hegel, *Elements of the Philosophy of Right*, p. 14.

432 **estimated at around 1 percent per year:** On the yearly risk of nuclear war, see Martin Hellman in "An Existential Discussion: What Is the Probability of Nuclear War?," *Bulletin of the Atomic Scientists*, March 18, 2021.

436 **death in 1953 at age 109:** James Albert Hard (July 15, 1843–March 12, 1953).

436 **died in 1956 at age 106:** Albert Henry Woolson (February 11, 1850–August 2, 1956).

436 **"lost the last personal link to the Union Army":** Eisenhower, quoted in "Last Union Army Veteran Dies," *New York Times*, August 3, 1956.

436 **that America would "whip the Japs":** See archive of press clippings on James Hard at the Monroe County Library System website, https://www.libraryweb.org/~digitized/scrapbooks/James_Hard_scrapbook.pdf, accessed November 2022.

438 **"He couldn't take the gaff. No bully can"**: Truman, quoted in O'Neill, *American High*, p. 89.

438 **"Five Star MacArthur," Truman called him**: Truman, quoted in "This Day in History: Truman Dismisses MacArthur," Truman Library Institute (April 11, 2016).

438 **"the words of god himself"**: Dewey Jackson Short (R-MO), quoted in Patterson, *Grand Expectations*, p. 230.

440 **"It's not the plane, it's the pilot"**: Maverick (Tom Cruise) in *Top Gun: Maverick*, movie, directed by Josef Kosinski (Skydance et al., 2022).

441 **"a sad degeneracy"**: Full quote from Increase Mather: "If the body of the present standing *Generation*, be compared with what was here forty years ago, What a sad Degeneracy is evident to the view of every man," in Mather, "Returning unto God the great concernment of a covenant people. Or A sermon preached to the Second Church in Boston in New-England," March 17, 1679.

441 **"a note of distaste ... almost of repulsion"**: Demos and Boocock, "Old Age in Early New England."

441 **"old in a time when youth took the palm"**: Fischer, *Growing Old in America*, p. 88.

441 **"monuments will never be erected to me"**: Adams, in letter to Benjamin Rush, 1809, quoted in Haraszti, *John Adams & the Prophets of Progress*.

441 **"devaluation of the elderly"**: Achenbaum, *Old Age in the New Land*, p. 54.

441 **"peaceful departure by chloroform"**: Osler, "Valedictory Address at Johns Hopkins University," February 22, 1905, in Roland (ed.), *Sir William Osler, 1849–1919*, pp. 11–30.

441 **to vote for Barry Goldwater**: "Election Polls—Vote by Groups, 1960–1964," Gallup (archived July 26, 2011).

442 **captured a generational plurality in the House of Representatives**: G.I.s captured a plurality of governors in 1951, of House members in 1953, and of senators in 1959. See "Generations of American Leaders," https://www.fourthturning.com/goal /overview.php.

444 **"Be up and doing. Activity. Activity"**: Colman, cited in Miller, *The New England Mind: From Colony to Province*, p. 414.

444 **"unite in common efforts for the common good"**: Thomas Jefferson, first inaugural address, March 4, 1801; text archived in the American Presidency Project (UC Santa Barbara).

444 **"tyranny, poverty, disease and war itself"**: John F. Kennedy, inaugural address, January 20, 1961; text archived in the American Presidency Project (UC Santa Barbara).

447 **"docile and tutorable"**: See "Speeches of Students of the College of William and Mary Delivered May 1, 1699," *William and Mary Quarterly* 10, no. 4 (October 1930); end of the fifth speech, p. 337.

447 **"our duty to remain the peaceable and silent"**: John Adams, in letter to *Columbian Centinel* (1793), in Bemis, *John Quincy Adams and the Foundations of American Foreign Policy*, p. 36.

447 **"formed of fitting proportions of every high quality"**: Sunday school spokesman Daniel Wise, in Kett, *Rites of Passage*, p. 120.

449 "distant . . . repressive fathers": Leverenz, *The Language of Puritan Feeling*, p. 3.

449 "antirational, antiscientific . . . and moralistic": Nash, *The Urban Crucible*, p. 133.

449 "prominent boldness and forwardness": British visitor was William Faux, cited in Furnas, *The Americans*, p. 591.

449 "were increasingly on the side of freedom": Kett, *Rites of Passage*, p. 60.

449 "a controlled but pleasantly free atmosphere": Cable, *The Little Darlings*, p. 105.

449 "sickened with advantages": Addams, *Twenty Years at Hull-house*, p. 73.

450 "ambivalent": Keniston, *Young Radicals*, p. 55.

450 "Oedipal hostility": Feuer, *The Conflict of Generations*, p. 470.

450 attitude of "parricide": Malcolm, *Generation of Narcissus*, p. 56.

450 "happy, easy, uncomplicated, prosperous": Merser, *Grown Ups*, p. 88.

450 "the divine glory in almost everything": Edwards, quoted in Richard L. Bushman, "Jonathan Edwards as Great Man: Identity, Conversion, and Leadership in the Great Awakening" in Brugger (ed.), *Our Selves/Our Past*.

450 "that I knew, or heard of, now living": Woolman, quoted in Cady, *John Woolman*, p. 27.

450 "who will not die a Unitarian": Jefferson, in letter to Benjamin Waterhouse, June 26, 1822, available online at the National Archives.

451 "an Agreement with Hell": Garrison, "Address of the Executive Committee of the American Anti-Slavery Society," *Anti-Slavery Examiner*, no. 12 (1845).

451 "machine-guns and machine-everything-else": Lodge, in letter to his mother in 1896, quoted in Lears, *No Place of Grace*, p. 239.

451 "whited sepulcher": Ida B. Wells in Wells et al., *The Reason Why the Colored American Is Not in the World's Columbian Exposition*, p. 9.

451 "overwhelming rise of grandomania": Wright, *A Testament*, p. 57.

451 "on the fringe of a golden era": "Students: On the Fringe of a Golden Era," *Time*, January 29, 1965.

451 "finis to poverty and war": "Man of the Year: The Inheritor," *Time*, January 6, 1967.

EPILOGUE

461 "one drop of water resembles another": Ibn Khaldun. *The Muqaddimah*, p. 12.

Bibliography

For foreign texts, standard English translations were used except where texts have not been translated or where text titles have only been mentioned in passing.

All references to any generation's share of representatives in the U.S. House or Senate, or of U.S. state governorships, are to numbers derived from the author's "Generations of American Leaders" interactive database. This database tracks more than thirty-five thousand U.S. leaders, including the names, birth and death dates, terms served, and party memberships of every House and Senate member, every state governor, president, vice president, and Supreme Court justice since 1789. "Generations of American Leaders" may be publicly accessed at: https://www.fourthturning.com/goal/overview.php.

Unless otherwise indicated, all figures for the number of members in a generation in any given year since 1950 are derived from the most recent estimates of total U.S. resident population, by single year of age and sex, available online at the U.S. Census Bureau. In Chapter 10, all estimates of the number of members in a generation in future years are derived from the "World Population Prospects 2022" projections (both sexes combined by single age in the medium fertility variant for the United States), available online at the Population Division of the United Nations.

Achenbaum, W. Andrew. *Old Age in the New Land: The American Experience Since 1790.* Johns Hopkins University, 1978.

Acheson, Dean. *Present at the Creation: My Years in the State Department.* W. W. Norton, 1969.

Ackerman, Bruce. *We the People: Foundations.* Harvard University, 1991.

Acolin, Arthur, Laurie S. Goodman, and Susan M. Wachter. "A Renter or Homeowner Nation?" *Cityscape* 18, no. 1 (2016): 145–157.

Acton, Lord J. D., A. W. Ward, G. W. Prothero, and Stanley Leathes, eds. *The Cambridge Modern History.* Macmillan, 1905.

Adams, Henry. *The Education of Henry Adams.* Ignacio Hills, 2009. First published 1918.

Adams, James Truslow. *The Epic of America.* Little, Brown and Company, 1931.

Adams, John. *The Works of John Adams, Second President of the United States, With a Life of the Author, Notes and Illustrations: Volume 2.* Charles C. Little and James Brown, 1850.

Adams, Samuel Hopkins. *Flaming Youth.* Boni & Liveright, 1923.

Addams, Jane. *Democracy and Social Ethics.* Macmillan, 1902.

Addams, Jane. *Twenty Years at Hull-house, with Autobiographical Notes.* Macmillan, 1910.

Ahlstrom, Sydney E. *A Religious History of the American People*. 2 vols. Yale University, 1972.

Allen, Frederick Lewis. *Only Yesterday: An Informal History of the 1920s*. Harper and Row, 1931.

Arnett, Jeffrey Jensen. "Emerging Adulthood: A Theory of Development from the Late Teens Through the Twenties." *American Psychologist* 55, no. 5 (May 2000): 469–80.

Augustine of Hippo (Saint Augustine). *The City of God* (translated by Marcus Dods). Hendrickson, 2009.

Baker, Russell. *Growing Up*. Memoir, 1982.

Barkun, Michael. "Communal Societies as Cyclical Phenomena." *Communal Societies* 4 (Fall 1984): 35–48.

Basler, Roy P., ed. *The Collected Works of Abraham Lincoln*. 8 vols. Rutgers University, 1953.

Bauer, Michal, Christopher Blattman, Julie Chytilová, Joseph Henrich, Edward Miguel, and Tamar Mitts. "Can War Foster Cooperation?" *Journal of Economic Perspectives* 30, no. 3 (Summer 2016): 249–74.

Baumeister, Roy F., and Kathleen D. Vohs, eds. *Encyclopedia of Social Psychology*. Sage Publications, 2007.

Beard, Charles, and Mary Beard. *The Rise of American Civilization*. The MacMillan Company, 1927.

Beck, Paul Allen. "Young vs. Old in 1984: Generations and Life Stages in Presidential Nomination Politics." *PS: Political Science and Politics* 17, no. 3 (Summer 1984): 515–24.

Becker, Carl. "The Dilemma of Modern Democracy." *The Virginia Quarterly Review* 17, no. 1 (Winter 1941): 11–27.

Becker, Carl L. *The Heavenly City of the Eighteenth-Century Philosophers*. Yale University, 1932.

Bell, Daniel. *The End of Ideology: On the Exhaustion of Political Ideas in the Fifties*. Free Press, 1960.

Bellah, Robert N. *The Broken Covenant: American Civil Religion in Time of Trial*. University of Chicago, 1992.

Bellah, Robert N., Richard Madsen, William M. Sullivan, Ann Swidler, and Steven M. Tipton. *Habits of the Heart: Individualism and Commitment in American Life*. Harpercollins, 1985.

Bemis, Samuel Flagg. *John Quincy Adams and the Foundations of American Foreign Policy*. A. A. Knopf, 1949.

Berenson, Bernard. *Aesthetics and History*. Pantheon, 1948.

Bergesen, Albert, ed. *Studies of the Modern World-System*. Academic Press, 1980.

Berinsky, Adam J. *In Time of War: Understanding American Public Opinion from World War II to Iraq*. University of Chicago, 2009.

Berlin, Isaiah. *The Hedgehog and the Fox*. Princeton University, 2013. First published 1953.

Bishop, Bill. *The Big Sort: Why the Clustering of Like-Minded America Is Tearing Us Apart*. Mariner Books, 2009.

Blocker, Jack S. *American Temperance Movements: Cycles of Reform*. Twayne, 1989.

Blume, Judy. *Letters to Judy: What Your Kids Wish They Could Tell You.* Putnam, 1986.

Boorstin, Daniel J. *The Americans: The Colonial Experience.* Vintage, 1958.

Boorstin, Daniel J. *The Americans: The Democratic Experience.* Random House, 1973.

Bowman, Karlyn, and Samantha Goldstein. *The Exit Polls: A History and Trends over Time, 1972–2020.* American Enterprise Institute, 2022.

Boyer, Paul S., Clifford E. Clark, Jr., Karen Halttunen, Joseph F. Kett, Neal Salisbury, Harvard Sitkoff, and Nancy Woloch. *The Enduring Vision: A History of the American People* (eighth edition). Cengage Learning, 2013.

Brand, Charlotte O., Alberto Acerbi, and Alex Mesoudi. "Cultural Evolution of Emotional Expression in 50 Years of Song Lyrics." *Evolutionary Human Sciences* 1, e11 (2019).

Breen, T. H. *Puritans and Adventurers: Change and Persistence in Early America.* Oxford University, 1980.

Brewer, Mark D., and L. Sandy Maisel. *Parties and Elections in America.* 9th ed. Rowman & Littlefield, 2021.

Bridenbaugh, Carl. *Cities in Revolt: Urban Life in America, 1743–1776.* Oxford University, 1955.

Brokaw, Tom. *The Greatest Generation.* Random House, 2000.

Brueckner, Jan K., and Ann G. Largey. "Social Interaction and Urban Sprawl." *Journal of Urban Economics* 64, no. 1 (July 2008): 18–34.

Brugger, Robert J., ed. *Our Selves/Our Past: Psychological Approaches to American History.* Johns Hopkins University, 1981.

Bryan, William J. *The First Battle: A Story of the Campaign of 1896.* W. B. Conkey, 1896.

Bryce, James (Viscount). *The American Commonwealth.* 3 vols. Macmillan, 1888.

Bucholz, Robert, and Newton Key. *Early Modern England 1485–1714* (3rd edition). John Wiley & Sons, 2020.

Burckhardt, Jacob. *The Civilization of the Renaissance in Italy.* First published in 1860 as *Die Kultur der Renaissance in Italien.*

Burnham, James. *The Managerial Revolution.* John Day Company, 1941.

Burnham, J. C. "New Perspectives on the Prohibition 'Experiment' of the 1920s." *Journal of Social History* 2, no. 1 (Fall 1968): 51–68.

Burnham, Walter Dean. *Critical Elections and the Mainsprings of American Politics.* W. W. Norton, 1970.

Burnham, Walter Dean. *The Current Crisis in American Politics.* Oxford University, 1982.

Bushman, Richard L. *From Puritan to Yankee: Character and the Social Order in Connecticut, 1690–1765.* W. W. Norton, 1970.

Butterfield, Herbert. *Man on His Past.* Cambridge University, 1969.

Cable, Mary. *The Little Darlings: A History of Child Rearing in America.* Scribner, 1975.

Cady, Edwin Harrison. *John Woolman.* Washington Square Press, 1965.

Campbell, Angus, Philip E. Converse, Warren E. Miller, and Donald E. Stokes. *The American Voter.* John Wiley & Sons, 1960.

Campbell, Joseph. *The Power of Myth.* Doubleday, 1988.

Canetti, Elias. *Crowds and Power* (translated from the German by Carol Stewart). Farrar, Straus and Giroux, 2021. Originally published as *Masse und Macht* in 1960.

Carlson, Elwood. *The Lucky Few: Between the Greatest Generation and the Baby Boom.* Springer, 2008.

Carlson, Stephanie M., Ozlem Ayduk, Catherine Schaefer, Nicole Wilson, Yuichi Shoda, Lawrence Aber, Anita Sethi, Philip K. Peake, and Walter Mischel. "Cohort Effects in Children's Delay of Gratification." *Developmental Psychology* (2018).

Carnegie, Andrew. *The "Gospel of Wealth" Essays and Other Writings.* Penguin, 2006. "The Gospel of Wealth" essay originally published in 1901.

Case, Anne, and Angus Deaton. *Deaths of Despair and the Future of Capitalism.* Princeton University, 2020.

Case, Anne, and Angus Deaton. "The Great Divide: Education, Despair, and Death." *Annual Review of Economics* 14, (2022): 1–21.

Case, Anne, and Angus Deaton. "Life Expectancy in Adulthood Is Falling for Those Without a BA Degree, but as Educational Gaps Have Widened, Racial Gaps Have Narrowed." *PNAS* 118, no. 11 (2021).

Case, Anne, and Angus Deaton. "Rising Morbidity and Mortality in Midlife among White Non-Hispanic Americans in the 21st Century." *Proceedings of the National Academy of Sciences* (November 2, 2015).

Censorinus. *De die natali liber ad Q. Caerellium ("The Birthday Book Dedicated to Quintus Caerellium").* 238 AD. Passages translated by the author from the Latin text edited by Nicolaus Sallmann, 1983.

Chernow, Ron. *Alexander Hamilton.* Penguin Random House, 2004.

Chesnut, Mary Boykin (ed. by Isabella D. Martin and Myrta Lockett Avery). *A Diary from Dixie.* D. Appleton and Company, 1905.

Chetty, Raj, David Grusky, Maximilian Hell, Nathaniel Hendren, Robert Manduca, and Jimmy Narang. "The Fading American Dream: Trends in Absolute Income Mobility since 1940." *Science* 356, no. 6336 (April 28, 2017): 398–406.

Chonaill, Siobhan Ni. "'Why May Not Man One Day Be Immortal?': Population, Perfectibility, and the Immortality Question in Godwin's Political Justice." *History of European Ideas* 33, no. 1 (2007).

Churchill, Winston. *Mr. Crewe's Career.* Macmillan, 1908.

Citti, Pierre, ed. *Fins de Siècle ("Ends of the Century").* Université de Bourdeaux, 1990.

Clifton, Jon. *Blind Spot: The Global Rise of Unhappiness and How Leaders Missed It.* Gallup, 2022.

Coale, Ansley J., and Melvin Zelnick. *New Estimates of Fertility and Population in the United States: A Study of Annual White Births from 1855 to 1960 and of Completeness of Enumeration in the Censuses from 1880 to 1960.* Princeton University, 1963.

Cohen, Philip N. "The Coming Divorce Decline." *Socius: Sociological Research for a Dynamic World* 5 (2019): 1–6.

Cohen, Robert. *When the Old Left Was Young: Student Radicals and America's First Mass Student Movement, 1929–1941.* Oxford University, 1993.

Colton, Calvin, ed. *The Works of Henry Clay: Comprising His Life, Correspondence and Speeches*, Volume 3. G. P. Putnam's Sons, 1904.

Commager, Henry Steele. *The American Mind: An Interpretation of American Thought and Character Since the 1880s.* Yale University, 1950.

Comte, Auguste. *The Positive Philosophy of Auguste Comte* (edited and translated from the French by Harriet Martineau). 2 vols. John Chapman, 142, Strand, 1853.

Coupland, Douglas. *Generation X: Tales for an Accelerated Culture.* St. Martin's, 1991.

Cournot, Antoine Augustin. *Considérations sur la marche des idées et des événements dans les temps modernes ("Considerations on the Advance of Ideas and Events in Modern Times").* Hachette, 1872.

Courtwright, David T. *Dark Paradise: Opiate Addiction in America Before 1940.* Harvard University, 1982.

Cowley, Malcolm. *Exile's Return.* W. W. Norton, 1934.

Cowley, Malcolm. *A Second Flowering: Works and Days of the Lost Generation.* Viking, 1973.

Culhane, Dennis, Dan Treglia, Thomas Byrne, Stephen Metraux, Randall Kuhn, Kelly Doran, Eileen Johns, and Maryanne Schretzman. "The Emerging Crisis of Aged Homelessness." Available on Actionable Intelligence for Social Policy: AISP online, University of Pennsylvania (2019).

Däniken, Erich von. *Chariots of the Gods?* Putnam, 1968.

Degler, Carl. *Out of Our Past: The Forces That Shaped Modern America.* Harper & Row, 1970.

Demos, John, and Sarane Spence Boocock. "Old Age in Early New England," in Demos and Boocock (eds.), *Turning Points: Historical and Sociological Essays on the Family.* University of Chicago, 1978.

Deresiewicz, William. *Excellent Sheep: The Miseducation of the American Elite and the Way to a Meaningful Life.* Free Press, 2014.

Dhaouadi, Mahmoud. "The *Ibar*: Lessons of Ibn Khaldun's Umran Mind," *Contemporary Sociology* 34, no. 6 (2015).

Diamond, Larry. "Facing Up to the Democratic Recession." *Journal of Democracy* 26, no. 1 (January 2015): 141–55.

Donald, David. "An Excess of Democracy: The American Civil War and the Social Process." *The Centennial Review* 5, no. 1 (Winter 1961): 21–39.

Druckman, James, and Jeremy Levy. "Affective Polarization in the American Public." Northwestern IPR Working Paper Series, WP-21-27 (May 17, 2021).

Duffield, George, Jr. *The God of Our Fathers: An Historical Sermon.* T. B. Pugh, 1861.

Easterlin, Richard A. *Birth and Fortune: The Impact of Numbers on Personal Welfare* (second edition). University of Chicago, 1980.

Eisler, Benita. *Private Lives: Men and Women of the Fifties.* Franklin Watts, 1986.

Eliade, Mircea. *The Myth of the Eternal Return* (translated from the French by Willard R. Trask). Princeton University, 1954.

Elias, Norbert. *The Civilizing Process: Sociogenetic and Psychogenetic Investigations* (translated from the German by Edmund Jephcott). Blackwell, 1982. Originally published in 1939.

Elkins, Stanley, and Eric McKitrick. "The Founding Fathers: Young Men of the Revolution." *Political Science Quarterly* 76, no. 2 (June 1961): 181–216.

Ellis, Steven G., and Christopher Maginn. *The Making of the British Isles: The State of Britain and Ireland, 1450–1660.* Routledge, 2013.

Emerson, Ralph Waldo. *The Collected Works of Ralph Waldo Emerson*. Bybliotech, 2014.

Engs, Ruth Clifford. *Clean Living Movements: American Cycles of Health Reform*. Praeger, 2000.

Esler, Anthony. *The Aspiring Mind of the Elizabethan Younger Generation*. Duke University, 1966.

Esler, Anthony. *Generations in History: An Introduction to the Concept*. William and Mary College, 1982.

Farrar, Jr., L. L. "Cycles of War: Historical Speculations on Future International Violence." *International Interactions* 3, no. 2 (1977): 161–79.

Fass, Paula S. *The Damned and the Beautiful: American Youth in the 1920s*. Oxford University, 1977.

Ferguson, Marilyn. *The Aquarian Conspiracy: Personal and Social Transformation in the 1980s*. J. P. Tarcher, 1980.

Ferrari, Giuseppe. *Teoria dei periodi politici ("Theory of Political Periods")*. G. Bernardoni, 1874.

Feuer, Lewis. *The Conflict of Generations: The Character and Significance of Student Movements*. Basic Books, 1969.

Fine, Sidney, and Gerald S. Brown, eds. *The American Past: Conflicting Interpretations of the Great Issues*. Macmillan, 1970.

Finkelhor, David, and Lisa Jones. "Why Have Child Maltreatment and Child Victimization Declined?" *Journal of Social Issues* 62, no. 4 (2006): 685–716.

Fiorina, Morris P. *Unstable Majorities: Polarization, Party Sorting, and Political Stalemate*. Hoover Institution, 2017.

Fischer, David Hackett. *Growing Old in America*. Oxford University, 1977.

Fisher, Irving. "The Debt-Deflation Theory of Great Depressions." *Econometrica* 1, no. 4 (October 1933): 337–57.

Foa, R. S., A. Klassen, D. Wenger, A. Rand, and M. Slade. *Youth and Satisfaction with Democracy: Reversing the Democratic Disconnect?* Centre for the Future of Democracy, Cambridge University, November 2020.

Fogel, Robert William. *The Fourth Great Awakening & the Future of Egalitarianism*. University of Chicago, 2000.

Foucault, Michel. *"Society Must Be Defended": Lectures at the Collège de France, 1975–1976*. Picador, 2003.

Freeman, Joanne B. *The Field of Blood: Violence in Congress and the Road to the Civil War*. Farrar, Straus and Giroux, 2018.

Friedan, Betty. *The Feminine Mystique*. W. W. Norton, 1963.

Fritz, Charles E. *Disasters and Mental Health: Therapeutic Principles Drawn from Disaster Studies*. University of Delaware Disaster Research Center, 1996.

Fromm, Erich. *The Sane Society*. Fawcett Publications, 1955.

Fukuyama, Francis. *The End of History and the Last Man*. Free Press, 1992.

Fukuyama, Francis. *The Great Disruption: Human Nature and the Reconstitution of Social Order*. Free Press, 2000.

Funke, Manuel, Moritz Schularick, and Christoph Trebesch. "Going to Extremes: Politics After Financial Crises, 1870–2014." *European Economic Review* 88 (September 2016): 227–60.

Furnas, J. C. *The Americans: A Social History of the United States, 1587–1914*. G. P. Putnam's Sons, 1969.

Galbraith, John Kenneth. *The Affluent Society*. Houghton Mifflin, 1958.

Galenson, David W. "The Settlement and Growth of the Colonies: Population, Labor, and Economic Development," in Stanley L. Engerman and Robert E. Gallman, *The Cambridge Economic History of the United States*, Volume I, The Colonial Era. Cambridge University, 1996.

Gelernter, David. *1939: The Lost World of the Fair*. Free Press, 1995.

Gelfand, Michele. *Rule Makers, Rule Breakers: How Tight and Loose Cultures Wire Our World*. Scribner, 2018.

Gerstle, Gary. *The Rise and Fall of the Neoliberal Order: America and the World in the Free Market Era*. Oxford University, 2022.

Gethin, Amory, Clara Martínez-Toledano, and Thomas Piketty. *Political Cleavages and Social Inequalities: A Study of Fifty Democracies, 1948–2020*. Harvard University, 2021.

Ghitza, Yair, A. Gelman, and Jonathan Auerbach. "The Great Society, Reagan's Revolution, and Generations of Presidential Voting," *American Journal of Political Science* (September 1, 2022).

Gibney, Bruce Cannon. *A Generation of Sociopaths: How the Baby Boomers Betrayed America*. Hachette, 2017.

Giddens, Anthony. *The Nation-State and Violence*. University of California, 1985.

Gitlin, Todd. *The Sixties: Years of Hope, Days of Rage*. Bantam, 1987.

Godwin, William. *Enquiry Concerning Political Justice*. Oxford University, 2013. Originally published 1793.

Goldin, Claudia, and Lawrence F. Katz. "Human Capital and Social Capital: The Rise of Secondary Schooling in America: 1910–1940." *The Journal of Interdisciplinary History* 29, no. 4 (Spring 1999): 683–723.

Goldstein, Joshua S. "The Predictive Power of Long Wave Theory, 1989–2004," in T. C. Devezas (ed.), *Kondratieff Waves, Warfare and World Security*. IOS, 2006.

Greene, Jack P., ed. *Encyclopedia of American Political History*. Scribner, 1984.

Greusel, John Hubert. *Blood and Iron: Origin of German Empire as Revealed by the Character of Its Founder, Bismarck*. Shakespeare Press, 1915.

Gunn, S. "Politic History, New Monarchy and State Formation: Henry VII in European Perspective." *Historical Research* 82, no. 217 (August 2009): 380–92.

Hacker, J. David. "A Census-Based Count of the Civil War Dead." *Civil War History* 57, no. 4 (December 2011): 307–48.

Hacker, J. David. "Decennial Life Tables for the White Population of the United States, 1790–1900." *Historical Methods: A Journal of Quantitative and Interdisciplinary History* 43, no. 2 (April 2010): 45–79.

Haines, Michael R. "Long Term Marriage Patterns in the United States from Colonial Times to the Present." Historical Paper 80, National Bureau of Economic Research, 1996.

Halberstam, David. *The Fifties*. Villard Books, 1993.

Hale, Nathan G., Jr. *Freud and the Americans: The Beginnings of Psychoanalysis in the United States, 1876–1917*. Oxford University, 1971.

Hall, Stanley G. *Adolescence: Its Psychology and Its Relations to Physiology, Anthropology, Sociology, Sex, Crime, Religion and Education.* D. Appleton and Company, 1904.

Hamerow, Theodore S. *Restoration, Revolution, Reaction: Economics and Politics in Germany, 1815–1871.* Princeton University, 1967.

Handy, Robert T. "The American Religious Depression, 1925–1935." *Church History* 29, no. 1 (March 1960): 3–16.

Hansen, Alvin H. "Economic Progress and Declining Population Growth." *The American Economic Review* 29, no. 1 (March 1939).

Harari, Yuval Noah. *Homo Deus: A Brief History of Tomorrow.* HarperCollins, 2017.

Haraszti, Zoltán. *John Adams & the Prophets of Progress.* Harvard University, 1952.

Harrington, Michael. *The Other America: Poverty in the United States.* Macmillan, 1962.

Hatch, Nathan O. "The Origins of Civil Millennialism in America: New England Clergymen, War with France, and the Revolution." *William and Mary Quarterly*, 31, no. 3 (July, 1974), 407–30.

Hawkins, Alan J., Jason S. Carroll, Anne Marie Wright Jones, and Spencer L. James. *State of Our Unions: 2022. Capstones Vs. Cornerstones: Is Marrying Later Always Better?* The National Marriage Project. 2022.

Hawthorne, Nathaniel. *Twice-Told Tales.* 1837.

Hegel, Georg Wilhelm Friedrich. *Elements of the Philosophy of Right* (translated from the German by Tim Newcomb). Newcomb Livraria, 2020. Originally published as *Grundlinien der Philosophie des Rechts* in 1820.

Hegel, Georg Wilhelm Friedrich. *The Phenomenology of Mind* (translated from the German by J. B. Baillie). Andesite Press, 2017. Originally published as *Phänomenologie des Geistes* in 1807.

Hegel, Georg Wilhelm Friedrich. *Philosophy of History* (translated from the German by J. Sibree). Cosimo, 2007. Originally published as *Vorlesungen über die Philosophie der Weltgeschichte* in 1837.

Heidegger, Martin. *Being and Time* (translated from the German by Joan Stambaugh). State University of New York, 2010. Originally published as *Sein und Zeit* in 1927.

Hemingway, Ernest. *Death in the Afternoon.* Charles Scribner's Sons, 1932.

Hemingway, Ernest. *A Farewell to Arms.* Scribner, 1929.

Hemingway, Ernest. *A Movable Feast.* Scribner, 1964.

Hemingway, Ernest. *The Sun Also Rises.* Scribner, 1926.

Hertzler, James R. "Who Dubbed It 'The Glorious Revolution?'" *Albion: A Quarterly Journal Concerned with British Studies* 19, no. 4 (Winter 1987): 579–85.

Hindle, Brooke. "The March of the Paxton Boys." *William and Mary Quarterly* 3, no. 4 (October 1946).

Hiner, N. Ray, and Joseph M. Hawes, eds. *Growing Up in America: Children in Historical Perspective.* University of Illinois, 1985.

Hobbes, Thomas. *Behemoth or The Long Parliament.* The University of Chicago, 2014. Originally published in 1681.

Hofstadter, Richard. *Age of Reform.* Vintage, 1955.

Holmes, Oliver Wendell, Jr. *The Occasional Speeches of Justice Oliver Wendell Holmes* (ed. by Mark DeWolfe Howe). Harvard University, 1962.

Hoock, Holger. *Scars of Independence: America's Violent Birth.* Broadway Books, 2017.

Hooks, Gregory. "The Weakness of Strong Theories: The U.S. State's Dominance of the World War II Investment Process." *American Sociological Review* 58, no. 1 (February 1993): 37–53.

Hopkins, Terrence, and Immanuel Wallerstein, eds. *World-Systems Analysis: Theory and Methodology.* SAGE Publications, 1982.

Howard, J. Q. *The Life, Public Services, and Select Speeches of Rutherford B. Hayes.* Robert Clarke & Co., 1876.

Howe, Frederic. *Confessions of a Reformer.* Charles Scribner's Sons, 1925.

Howe, Neil, and Bill Strauss. *13th Gen: Abort, Retry, Ignore, Fail?* Vintage, 1993.

Howe, Neil, and Diana Elliott. "A Generational Perspective on Living Standards: Where We've Been and Prospects for the Future," in Federal Reserve Bank of St. Louis and the Board of Governors of the Federal Reserve System (ed.), *Economic Mobility: Research and Ideas on Strengthening Families, Communities, and the Economy* (2016).

Howells, William Dean. *The Rise of Silas Lapham.* Houghton Mifflin, 1884.

Hugo, Victor. *Les Misérables* (translated by Charles E. Wilbour). Random House, 1992. Originally published in 1862.

Hume, David. *An Enquiry Concerning Human Understanding.* Dover, 2004. Originally published in 1748.

Hunter, James Davison, Carl Desportes Bowman, and Kyle Puetz. *Democracy in Dark Times: The 2020 IASC Survey of American Political Culture.* Finstock & Tew, 2020.

Huntington, Samuel P. "American Ideals Versus American Institutions." *Political Science Quarterly* 97, no. 1 (Spring 1982): 1–37.

Huston, James L. *The Panic of 1857 and the Coming of the Civil War.* Louisiana State University, 1987.

Huxley, Aldous. *Brave New World.* Chatto & Windus, 1932.

Ibn Khaldun. *The Muqaddimah: An Introduction to History* (abridged; introduced and translated from the Arabic by Franz Rosenthal). Princeton University, 2005. Text first written in 1377.

Jackson, Michelle, and Brian Holzman. "A Century of Educational Inequality in the United States." *Proceedings of the National Academy of Sciences,* July 27, 2020.

James, William, "The Moral Equivalent of War." Lecture 11 in William James, *Memories and Studies.* Longman Green and Co., 1911; pp. 267–96.

James, William. *Pragmatism: A New Name for Some Old Ways of Thinking.* Longmans, Green, 1907.

Jasanoff, Maya. *Liberty's Exiles: American Loyalists in the Revolutionary World.* Alfred A. Knopf, 2011.

Jones, Landon Y. *Great Expectations: America and the Baby Boom Generation.* Coward, McCann & Geoghegan, 1980.

Jung, Carl Gustav. *Modern Man in Search of a Soul.* Translated by William Stanley Dell and Cary F. Baynes. K. Paul, Trench, Trubner & Co., 1933. Facsimile. Martino Fine Books, 2017.

Junger, Sebastian. *Tribe: On Homecoming and Belonging.* HarperCollins, 2016.

Kagan, Robert. *The Jungle Grows Back: America and Our Imperiled World.* Vintage, 2019.

Kalman, Samuel. "*Faisceau* Visions of Physical and Moral Transformation and the Cult of Youth in Inter-war France." *European History Quarterly* 33, no. 3 (July 2003): 343–66.

Kalmoe, Nathan P. *With Ballots and Bullets: Partisanship and Violence in the American Civil War.* Cambridge University, 2020.

Kanter, Donald L., and Philip H. Mirvis. *The Cynical Americans: Living and Working in an Age of Discontent and Disillusion.* Jossey-Bass, 1991.

Karpel, Craig S. *The Retirement Myth: What You Must Know to Prosper in the Coming Meltdown.* HarperCollins, 1995.

Katznelson, Ira. *Fear Itself: The New Deal and the Origins of Our Time.* Liveright, 2013.

Kegley, Charles W., Jr. "Neo-Idealist Moment in International Studies? Realist Myths and the New International Realities." *International Studies Quarterly* 37 (1993).

Keller, Helen. *Helen Keller's Journal, 1936–1937.* Doubleday, Doran, 1938.

Kendall, Bruce E., John Prendergast, and Ottar N. Bjørnstadt. "The Macroecology of Population Dynamics: Taxonomic and Biogeographic Patterns in Population Cycles." *Ecology Letters* 1, no. 3 (November 1998): 160–64.

Keniston, Kenneth. *Young Radicals: Notes on Committed Youth.* Harcourt, Brace & World, 1968.

Kennedy, David M. *Freedom from Fear: The American People in Depression and War, 1929–1945.* Oxford University, 1999.

Kerber, Linda. "The Republican Mother: Women and the Enlightenment: An American Perspective." *American Quarterly* 28, no. 2 (Summer 1976): 187–205.

Kett, Joseph F. *Rites of Passage: Adolescence in America, 1790 to the Present.* Basic Books, 1977.

Kissinger, Henry. *A World Restored: Metternich, Castlereagh and the Problems of Peace 1812–1822.* Weidenfeld & Nicolson, 1957.

Kiyosaki, Robert, and Sharon L. Lechter. *Rich Dad Poor Dad.* Warner, 2000.

Kleinfeld, Rachel. "The Rise of Political Violence in the United States." *Journal of Democracy* 32, no. 4 (October 2021): 160–76.

Klinenberg, Eric. *Going Solo: The Extraordinary Rise and Surprising Appeal of Living Alone.* Penguin, 2012.

Klingberg, Frank L. *Cyclical Trends in American Foreign Policy Moods: The Unfolding of America's World Role.* University Press of America, 1983.

Klingberg, Frank L. "The Historical Alternation of Moods in American Foreign Policy." *World Politics* 4, no. 2 (January 1952): 239–73.

Kondratieff, Nikolai D. *The Long Waves in Economic Life.* Translated by W. F. Stolper. *Review of Economics and Statistics* 17, no. 6 (November 1935): 105–15. Facsimile. Martino Fine Books, 2014.

Krannich, Richard S. "Abortion in the United States: Past, Present, and Future Trends." *Family Relations* 29, no. 3 (July 1980): 365–74.

Krol, Reinbert. *Germany's Conscience: Friedrich Meinecke: Champion of German Historicism.* Transcript, 2021.

Kulikoff, Allan. "'Such Things Ought Not to Be': The American Revolution and the First National Great Depression," in Andrew Shankman (ed.), *The World of the Ameri-*

can Revolution and Republic: Land, Labor, and the Conflict for a Continent. Routledge, 2014, pp. 134–64.

Kurtz, Stephen G., and James H. Hutson, eds. *Essays on the American Revolution*. Institute of Early American History and Culture, 1973.

Kurzweil, Ray. *The Singularity Is Near*. Viking, 2005.

Lanning, Michael Lee. *African Americans in the Revolutionary War*. Citadel Press, 2021. Originally published in 2000.

Larson, Edward J., and Michael P. Winship. *The Constitutional Convention: A Narrative History from the Notes of James Madison*. Random House, 2005.

Lears, T. J. Jackson. *No Place of Grace: Antimodernism and the Transformation of American Culture, 1880–1920*. University of Chicago, 2021. Originally published in 1981.

Leavitt, Judith Walzer. *Make Room for Daddy: The Journey from Waiting Room to Birthing Room*. University of North Carolina, 2009.

Lee, Chulhee. "Military Service and Economic Mobility: Evidence from the American Civil War." *Explorations in Economic History* 49 (2012): 367–79.

Leverenz, David. *The Language of Puritan Feeling: An Exploration in Literature, Psychology, and Social History*. Rutgers University, 1979.

Levine, Bruce. *Confederate Emancipation: Southern Plans to Free and Arm Slaves During the Civil War*. Oxford University, 2006.

Levinson, Daniel J. *The Seasons of a Man's Life*. Ballantine Books, 1978.

Lévy-Bruhl, Lucien. *Primitive Mentality* (translated from the French by Lilian A Clare). Macmillan, 1923.

Lewis, Michael. *Flash Boys: A Wall Street Revolt*. W. W. Norton, 2014.

Lewis, Sinclair. *It Can't Happen Here: What Will Happen When America Has a Dictator?* Doubleday, Doran, and Company, 1935.

Li, Ling-Fan. "The Stop of the Exchequer and the Secondary Market for English Sovereign Debt, 1677–1705." *The Journal of Economic History* 79, no. 1 (March 2019): 176–200.

Lindert, Peter H., and Jeffrey G. Williamson. *Unequal Gains: American Growth and Inequality Since 1700*. Princeton University, 2016.

Lindsey, Hal, and Carole C. Carlson. *The Late Great Planet Earth*. Zondervan, 1970.

Lipset, Seymour Martin, and Everett C. Ladd, Jr. "The Political Future of Activist Generations," in Philip G. Altbach and Robert S. Laufer (eds.), *The New Pilgrims: Youth Protest in Transition*. David McKay, 1972.

Littré, Émile. *Paroles de Philosophie Positive ("Words of Positivist Philosophy")*. A. Delahays, 1859.

Lubell, Samuel. *The Future of American Politics*. Doubleday, 1952.

Lukacs, John. *The Duel: The Eighty-Day Struggle Between Churchill and Hitler*. Yale University, 2001.

Maddison, Angus. *The World Economy*, Development Centre Studies: Organisation for Cooperation and Development, 2006.

Maier, Pauline. "Coming to Terms with Samuel Adams." *The American Historical Review* 81, no. 1 (February 1976): 12–37.

Main, Jackson Turner. *Political Parties Before the Constitution*. W. W. Norton & Company, 1974.

Malcolm, Henry. *Generation of Narcissus*. Little, Brown and Co., 1971.

Manchester, William. *The Glory and the Dream: A Narrative History of America, 1932–1972*. Little Brown, 1974.

Mandell, Daniel R. *King Philip's War: Colonial Expansion, Native Resistance, and the End of Indian Sovereignty*. Johns Hopkins University, 2010.

Mann, Anthony, Venessa Denis, Andreas Schleicher, Hamoon Ekhtiari, Terralynn Forsyth, Elvin Liu, and Nick Chambers. *Dream Jobs? Teenagers' Career Aspirations and the Future of Work*. Organisation for Economic Cooperation and Development, 2020.

Mannheim, Karl. *Essays on the Sociology of Knowledge* (edited and translated by Paul Kecskemeti). Routledge, 1952.

Mao Zedong. *The Little Red Book: Quotations from Mao Tse-Tung*. Foreign Language Press, 2012. First published in 1966, with forward by Lin Piao.

Marcuse, Herbert. *Eros and Civilization: A Philosophical Inquiry Into Freud*. Beacon Press, 1955.

Mare, Robert D. "Educational Homogamy in Two Gilded Ages: Evidence from Intergenerational Social Mobility Data." *Annals: AAPSS* (January 2016): 117–39.

Marías, Julián. *Generations: A Historical Method* (translated from the Spanish by Harold C. Raley). University of Alabama, 1970. Originally published as *El método histórico de las generaciones* in 1967.

Mason, Lilliana. "'I Disrespectfully Disagree': The Differential Effects of Partisan Sorting on Social and Issue Polarization." *American Journal of Political Science* 59, no. 1 (January 2015): 128–45.

Mason, Lilliana. *Uncivil Agreement: How Politics Became Our Identity*. University of Chicago, 2018.

Masur, Louis P., ed. *The Real War Will Never Get in the Books: Selection from Writers During the Civil War*. Oxford University, 1993.

Mathew, Thomas. *The Beginning, Progress and Conclusion of Bacon's Rebellion in Virginia in the Years 1675 and 1676* (1705). Reprinted with an introduction by Thomas Jefferson in the Richmond (VA) *Inquirer* in 1804; published in *American Colonial Tracts Monthly*, no. 8 (December 1897).

Mathews, T. J., and Brady E. Hamilton. "Mean Age of Mother, 1970–2000." *National Vital Statistics Reports* 51, no. 1 (December 11, 2002).

McLoughlin, William G. *Revivals, Awakenings, and Reform*. University of Chicago, 1978.

McNeill, William H. *The Pursuit of Power: Technology, Armed Force, and Society since A.D. 1000*. University of Chicago, 1982.

McPherson, James M. *Battle Cry of Freedom: The Civil War Era*. Oxford University, 1988.

Melleuish, Greg. "Of 'Rage of Party' and the Coming of Civility." *M/C Journal* 22, no. 1 (2019).

Mentré, François. *Les Générations Sociales ("Social Generations")*. P. Mersch, L. Seitz & Cie., 1920.

Merser, Cheryl. *Grown Ups: A Generation in Search of Adulthood*. New American Library, 1987.

Metalious, Grace. *Peyton Place*. Julian Messner, 1956.

Michelet, Jules. *History of France*. 19 vols. First published in 1867 as *Histoire de France*.

Miettinen, Janne. "Cyclical Metapopulation Mechanism Hypothesis: Animal population cycles are generated & driven by a population-wide hormone cycle." ResearchGate Project Page (update: June 22, 2022).

Milanovic, Branko. *Global Inequality: A New Approach for the Age of Globalization*. Harvard University, 2016.

Mill, John Stuart. *A System of Logic, Ratiocinative and Inductive*. John W. Parker, West Strand, 1843.

Miller, Alphonse B. *Thaddeus Stevens*. Harper and Brothers, 1939.

Miller, Arthur. *The Crucible*. Penguin, 1976.

Miller, Perry. *The New England Mind: From Colony to Province*. Harvard University, 1953.

Miller, Perry. *The New England Mind: The Seventeenth Century*. Harvard University, 1939.

Modelski, George, ed. *Exploring Long Cycles*. Lynne Rienner, 1987.

Modelski, George. *Long Cycles in World Politics*. Macmillan, 1987.

Modelski, George, and William R. Thompson. *Leading Sectors and World Powers: The Coevolution of Global Politics and Economics*. University of South Carolina, 1996.

Moore, Robert, and Douglas Gillette. *King, Warrior, Magician, Lover*. HarperCollins, 1990.

Morgan, Edmund. *The Puritan Family: Religion and Domestic Relations in Seventeenth-Century New England*. Harper & Row; 1944, 1966.

Morgan, H. Wayne. *Drugs in America: A Social History, 1800–1980*. Syracuse University, 1981.

Morgan, Howard Wayne, ed. *The Gilded Age*. Syracuse University, 1970.

Morris, Ian. *War! What Is It Good For?: Conflict and the Progress of Civilization from Primates to Robots*. Farrar, Straus and Giroux, 2014.

Mounk, Yascha. *The People vs. Democracy: Why Our Freedom Is in Danger and How to Save It*. Harvard University, 2018.

Mumford, Lewis. *The Brown Decades: A Study of the Arts in America, 1865–1895*. Harcourt Brace & Co., 1931.

Myers, Isabel. *The Myers-Briggs Type Indicator*. Consulting Psychologists Press, 1962.

Naisbitt, John. *Megatrends: Ten New Directions Transforming Our Lives*. Warner Books, 1982.

Namenwirth, J. Zvi. "Wheels of Time and the Interdependence of Value Change in America." *Journal of Interdisciplinary History* 3, no. 4 (Spring 1973): 649–84.

Namenwirth, J. Zvi, and Richard C. Bibbee. "Change Within or of the System: An Example from the History of American Values." *Quality and Quantity* 10 (1976): 145–64.

Nash, Gary B. *The Urban Crucible: Social Change, Political Consciousness, and the Origins of the American Revolution*. Harvard University, 1979.

National Academy of Sciences. *The Growing Gap in Life Expectancy by Income: Implications for Federal Programs and Policy Responses*. National Academies Press, 2015.

National Academy of Sciences, Engineering, and Medicine. *The Economic and Fiscal Consequences of Immigration*. National Academies Press, 2017.

Nevins, Allan. "A Major Result of the Civil War." *Civil War History* 5, no. 3 (September 1959): 237–50.

Niemi, Richard G., and Associates. *The Politics of Future Citizens.* Jossey-Bass, 1974.

Nisbet, Robert. *The Quest for Community: A Study in the Ethics of Order and Freedom.* ISI Books, 2010. Originally published in 1953.

Olson, Mancur. *The Rise and Decline of Nations: Economic Growth, Stagflation, and Social Rigidities.* Yale University, 1982.

O'Neill, William L. *American High: The Years of Confidence, 1945–1960.* Free Press, 1986.

Ortega y Gasset, José. *Man and Crisis* (translated from the Spanish by Mildred Adams). W. W. Norton & Company, 1962. Originally published as *En Torno a Galileo* in 1942.

Orwell, George. *Animal Farm.* Secker and Warburg, 1945.

Orwell, George. *1984.* Secker and Warburg, 1949.

Osterman, Michelle J. K., Brady E. Hamilton, Joyce A. Martin, Anne K. Driscoll, and Claudia P. Valenzuela. "Births: Final Data for 2020." *National Vital Statistics Reports* 70, no. 17 (February 7, 2022).

Packard, Norman H. *Adaptation Toward the Edge of Chaos.* University of Illinois at Urbana-Champaign, Center for Complex Systems Research, 1988.

Pagel, Mark. *Wired for Culture: Origins of the Human Social Mind.* W. W. Norton, 2012.

Paine, Thomas. *The American Crisis.* Sixteen numbered pamphlets (various printers), published from 1776 through 1783.

Parsons, Talcott. *The Social System.* Free Press, 1951.

Patterson, James T. *Grand Expectations: The United States, 1945–1974.* Oxford University, 1996.

Pearson, Carol S. *Awakening the Heroes Within.* HarperCollins, 1991.

Pepin, Joanna R., and David A. Cotter. "Separating Spheres? Diverging Trends in Youth's Gender Attitudes About Work and Family." *Journal of Family and Marriage* (2017).

Perez, Carlotta. *Technological Revolutions and Financial Capital: The Dynamics of Bubbles and Golden Ages.* Edward Elgar Publishing, 2002.

Perkins, Frances. *The Roosevelt I Knew.* Penguin, 2011. Originally published in 1946.

Peterson, Julius. *"Die Literarischen Generationen"* ("Literary Generations"), in Emil Ermatinger (ed.), *Philosophie der Literaturwissenschaft.* Junker & Dünnhaupt, 1930.

Peterson, Merrill D. *The Great Triumvirate: Webster, Clay, and Calhoun.* Oxford University, 1987.

Piketty, Thomas. *Capital in the Twenty-First Century.* Harvard University, 2017.

Pinker, Steven. *The Better Angels of Our Nature: Why Violence Has Declined.* Penguin, 2012.

Polybius. *The Histories* (translated by Brian McGing and Robin Waterfield). Oxford University, 2010.

Porter, Bruce D. *War and the Rise of the State: The Military Foundations of Modern Politics.* Free Press, 1994.

Postman, Neil. *The Disappearance of Childhood.* Delacorte, 1982.

Pratt, Julius W. "The Origin of 'Manifest Destiny.'" *The American Historical Review* 32, no. 4 (July 1927): 795–98.

Prickett, Kate C., and Jennifer March Augustine. "Trends in Mothers' Parenting Time by Education and Work from 2003 to 2017." *Demography* 58, no. 3 (April 2021).

Purvis, Thomas L. "The European Ancestry of the United States Population, 1790: A Symposium." *The William and Mary Quarterly* 41, no. 1 (January 1984): 85–101.

Putnam, Robert. *Bowling Alone: The Collapse and Revival of American Community* (revised and updated). Simon & Schuster; 2000, 2020.

Putnam, Robert D. *The Upswing: How America Came Together a Century Ago and How We Can Do It Again.* Simon & Schuster, 2020.

Reckford, Kenneth J. "Some Appearances of the Golden Age." *The Classical Journal* 54, no. 2 (November 1958): 79–87.

Reinier, Jacqueline S. "Rearing the Republican Child: Attitudes and Practices in Post-Revolutionary Philadelphia." *William and Mary Quarterly* 39, no. 1 (January 1982): 150–63.

Renehan, Edward J. *The Kennedys at War: 1937–1945.* Doubleday, 2002.

Ridgeway, Cecilia L. "Why Status Matters for Inequality." *American Sociological Review* 79, no. 1 (2014): 1–16.

Riesman, David. *The Lonely Crowd: A Study of the Changing American Character.* Yale University, 1950.

Rietveld, Ronald D. "Franklin D. Roosevelt's Abraham Lincoln," in William D. Pederson and Frank J. Williams (eds.), *Franklin D. Roosevelt and Abraham Lincoln: Competing Perspectives on Two Great Presidencies.* M. E. Sharpe, 2003.

Roche, John F. *The Colonial Colleges in the War for American Independence.* Associated Faculty Press, 1986.

Roland, Charles G., ed. *Sir William Osler, 1849–1919: A Selection for Medical Students.* Hannah Institute, 1999.

Roof, Wade Clark. *A Generation of Seekers: The Spiritual Journeys of the Baby Boom Generation.* HarperCollins, 1993.

Rorabaugh, W. J. *The Alcoholic Republic: An American Tradition.* Oxford University, 1979.

Rose, H. J. "World Ages and the Body Politique." *Harvard Theological Review* 54, no. 3 (July 1961): 131–40.

Rosecrance, Richard. *International Relations: Peace or War?* McGraw-Hill, 1973.

Rosecrance, Richard. "Long Cycle Theory and International Relations." *International Organization* 41, no. 2 (Spring 1987): 283–301.

Roth, Randolph. *American Homicide.* Harvard University, 2009.

Royster, Charles. *A Revolutionary People at War: The Continental Army and American Character, 1775–1783.* University of North Carolina, 1979.

Rozado, David, Ruth Hughes, and Jamin Halberstadt. "Longitudinal Analysis of Sentiment and Emotion in New Media Headlines Using Automated Labeling with Transformer Language Models." *Plos One*, October 18, 2022.

Rümelin, Gustav. *Reden und Aufsätze ("Speeches and Essays").* Laupp, 1875.

Russell, Cheryl. *The Master Trend: How the Baby Boom Generation Is Remaking America.* Springer, 1993.

Sandberg, John F., and Sandra L. Hofferth. "Changes in Children's Time with Parents: United States, 1981–1997." *Demography* 38, no. 3 (August 2001): 423–36.

Sandel, Michael J. "The Procedural Republic and the Unencumbered Self." *Political Theory* 12, no. 1 (February 1987): 81–96.

Santayana, George. *Character and Opinion in the United States: With Reminiscences of William James and Josiah Royce and Academic Life in America.* Charles Scribner's Sons, 1920.

Schachter-Shalomi, Zalman, and Ronald S. Miller. *From Age-ing to Sage-ing: A Revolutionary Approach to Growing Older.* Balance, 2008.

Scheidel, Walter. *The Great Leveler: Violence and the History of Inequality from the Stone Age to the Twenty-First Century.* Princeton University, 2017.

Schlesinger, Arthur M., Jr. *The Crisis of the Old Order, 1919–1933.* Houghton Mifflin, 1957.

Schlesinger, Arthur M., Jr. *The Cycles of American History.* Houghton Mifflin, 1986.

Schlesinger, Arthur M., Jr., and Morton White, eds. *Paths of American Thought.* Houghton Mifflin, 1963.

Schlesinger, Arthur M., Sr. *Paths to the Present.* Macmillan Company, 1949.

Settersten, R. A., Jr., C. Recksiedler, B. Godlewski, and G. H. Elder, Jr. "Two Faces of Wartime Experience: Collective Memories and Veterans' Appraisals in Later Life," in A. Spiro III, R. A. Settersten, Jr., and C. M. Aldwin (eds.), *Long-Term Outcomes of Military Service: The Health and Well-Being of Aging Veterans.* American Psychological Association, 2018, pp. 19–36.

Seymour, George Dudley. *Documentary Life of Nathan Hale: Comprising All Available Official and Private Documents Bearing on the Life of the Patriot.* New Haven, 1941.

Sheehy, Gail. *Passages: Predictable Crises of Adult Life.* E. P. Dutton, 1976.

Sheridan, Richard B. "The British Credit Crisis of 1772 and The American Colonies." *The Journal of Economic History* 20, no. 2 (June 1960): 161–86.

Sherif, Muzafer. "Experiments in Group Conflict." *Scientific American* 195 (November 1956): 54–58.

Sherman, William T. *Sherman's Civil War: Selected Correspondence of William T. Sherman, 1860–1865* (ed. by Jean V. Berlin and Brooks D. Simpson). University of North Carolina, 1999.

Skenazy, Lenore. *Free-Range Kids.* John Wiley & Sons, 2009.

Skocpol, Theda. *Diminished Democracy: From Membership to Management in American Civic Life.* University of Oklahoma, 2003.

Skocpol, Theda, and Morris P. Fiorina, eds. *Civic Engagement in American Democracy.* Brookings Institution, 1999.

Smeltz, Dina, Ivo Daalder, Karl Friedhoff, Craig Kafura, and Emily Sullivan. *A Foreign Policy for the Middle Class—What Americans Think.* The Chicago Council on Global Affairs, 2021.

Smith, George Winston, and Charles Judah. *Life in the North During the Civil War.* University of New Mexico, 1966.

Smith, Mapheus. "Populational Characteristics of American Servicemen in World War II." *The Scientific Monthly* 65, no. 3 (September 1947): 246–52.

Smith, Steven B. *The Writings of Abraham Lincoln.* Yale University, 2012.

Solnit, Rebecca. *A Paradise Built in Hell: The Extraordinary Communities That Arise in Disaster.* Penguin, 2010.

Sparks, Jared. *The Works of Benjamin Franklin: With Notes and a Life of the Author.* 10 vols. Oxford University, 1840.

Spitzer, Alan Barrie. *The French Generation of 1820*. Princeton University, 1987.

Spock, Benjamin. *The Common Sense Book of Baby and Child Care*. Duell, Sloan and Pearce, 1946.

Stowe, Harriet Beecher. *Uncle Tom's Cabin; or, Life Among the Lowly*. John P. Jewett and Company, 1852.

Strauss, William, and Neil Howe. *The Fourth Turning: An American Prophecy*. Broadway, 1997.

Strauss, William, and Neil Howe. *Generations: The History of America's Future, 1584 to 2064*. Morrow, 1991.

Strout, Cushing. *The New Heavens and New Earth: Political Religion in America*. Harper & Row, 1973.

Sumner, William Graham. *A Study of the Sociological Importance of Usages, Manners, Customs, Mores and Morals*. Ginn and Company, 1906.

Swanson, G. E. "Review of *Working Papers in the Theory of Action*: by Talcott Parsons; Robert F. Bales; Edward A Shils." *American Sociological Review* 19, no. 1 (February 1954): 95–97.

Taylor, Alan. *American Revolutions: A Continental History, 1750–1804*. W. W. Norton, 2016.

Temple, Sir William. *The Works of Sir William Temple: In Two Volumes*. London, 1720.

Thomas, W. I., and D. S. Thomas. *The Child in America*. A. A. Knopf, 1928.

Thompson, William Irwin. *At the Edge of History: Speculations on the Transformation of Culture*. Harper & Row, 1972.

Thompson, William R. *Power Concentration in World Politics: The Political Economy of Systemic Leadership, Growth, and Conflict*. Springer International, 2020.

Ticknor, George. *Life, Letters, and Journals of George Ticknor: Volume 2*. S. Low, 1876.

Tilly, Charles. "Reflections on the History of European State-Making," in Tilly (ed.), *The Formation of National States in Western Europe*. Princeton University, 1975.

Tocqueville, Alexis de. *Democracy in America* (edited and translated from the French by Harvey C. Mansfield and Delba Winthrop). University of Chicago, 2000. Originally published as *De la Démocratie en Amérique* in 1835 (vol. 1) and 1840 (vol. 2).

Toffler, Alvin. *Powershift: Knowledge, Wealth, and Violence at the Edge of the 21st Century*. Bantam Books, 1990.

Tolstoy, Leo. *Anna Karenina*. Originally published serially in 1878.

Topik, Steven C., and Allen Wells. *Global Markets Transformed: 1870–1945*. Harvard University, 2012.

Toynbee, Arnold J. *A Study of History*. 12 vols. Oxford University, 1934–1961.

Turnbull, Andrew. *Scott Fitzgerald*. Grove Press, 1962.

Twain, Mark, and Charles Dudley Warner. *The Gilded Age: A Tale of Today*. American Publishing Company, 1873.

Updike, John. *Rabbit Is Rich*. Alfred A. Knopf, 1981.

Valentine, Alan Chester. *The Age of Conformity*. H. Regnery Company, 1954.

Vico, Giambattista. *Principi di Scienza Nuova ("Principles of New Science")*. Stamperia Muziana, 1744.

Wallace, Anthony F. C. "Revitalization Movements." *American Anthropologist* 58, no. 2 (April 1956): 264–81.

Walzer, Michael. *Spheres of Justice: A Defense of Pluralism and Equality.* Basic Books, 1983.

Washington, George, and Bruce Rogers. *Washington's Farewell Address to the People of the United States, 1796.* Houghton Mifflin, 1913.

Watson, John B. *Psychological Care of Infant and Child.* W. W. Norton, 1928.

Wechssler, Eduard. *Die Generation als Jugendreihe und ihr Kampf um die Denkform ("Generations as a Succession of Youth Groups and Their Conflict Over Forms of Thinking").* Quelle & Meyer, 1930.

Wells, Ida B., Frederick Douglass, Irvine Garland Penn, and Ferdinand L. Barnett. *The Reason Why the Colored American Is Not in the World's Columbian Exposition.* University of Illinois, 1999. Originally published by Ida B. Wells in 1893.

White, Jonathan W. *Emancipation, the Union Army, and the Reelection of Abraham Lincoln.* Louisiana State, 2014.

White, Richard. *The Republic for Which It Stands: The United States During Reconstruction and the Gilded Age, 1865–1896.* Oxford University, 2017.

Whitney, David C. *The Colonial Spirit of '76: The People of the Revolution.* Encyclopedia Britannica, 1974.

Whyte, William H. *The Organization Man.* Simon and Schuster, 1956.

Wiener, Philip P., ed. *Dictionary of the History of Ideas.* 4 vols. Charles Scribner's Sons, 1968.

Wilder, Thornton. *The Skin of Our Teeth.* Harper & Brothers, 1942.

Wilson, David Sloan, and Edward O. Wilson. "Rethinking the Theoretical Foundation of Sociobiology." *The Quarterly Review of Biology* 82, no. 4 (December 2007): 327–48.

Wirt, William. *Sketches of the Life and Character of Patrick Henry.* James Webster, 1817.

Wohl, Robert. *The Generation of 1914.* Harvard University, 1979.

Wolfe, Thomas. *You Can't Go Home Again.* Tingle, 2022. Originally published by Harper & Row in 1940.

Wood, Gordon S. *Empire of Liberty: A History of the Early Republic, 1789–1815.* Oxford, 2009.

Wood, Gordon S. *The Radicalism of the American Revolution.* Knopf Doubleday, 1993.

Wood, James W. *Dynamics of Human Reproduction: Biology, Biometry, and Demography.* Aldine de Gruyter, 1994.

Wright, Frank Lloyd. *A Testament.* Horizon Press, 1957.

Wright, Quincy. *Study of War.* University of Chicago, 1942.

Wrigley, E. A., R. S. Davies, J. E. Oeppen, and R. S. Schofield. *English Population History from Family Reconstitution 1580–1837.* Cambridge University, 1997.

Wucker, Michele. *The Gray Rhino: How to Recognize and Act on the Obvious Dangers We Ignore.* St. Martin's, 2016.

Yazawa, Melvin. *From Colonies to Commonwealth: Familial Ideology and the Beginnings of the American Republic.* Johns Hopkins University, 1985.

Zheng, Hui. "A New Look at Cohort Trend and Underlying Mechanisms in Cognitive Functioning." *The Journals of Gerontology: Series B* 76, no. 8 (October 2021): 1652–63.

Zosimus (fl. 490–520 CE). *New History (Historia Nova).* Green and Chaplin, 1814.

Index

Note: Page numbers in italics indicate charts.

due process, 269
Duff, Hilary, *75*
Dukakis, Michael, *73*, 329
Durkheim, Émile, 281
Dustin, Hannah, *87*
Dwight, Timothy, 277
Dylan, Bob, 313, 328
dynasties, 68–69

East Asia, 177, 178, 251. *See also specific countries*
Easterlin, Richard, 326
Eastern Europe, 271. *See also specific countries*
economy, 2–3, 224
  American Revolution Crisis and, 256
  central-bank policy and, 21
  Civil War Crisis and, 256
  Crises and, 255–58
  dissatisfaction with, 243
  economic capacity, 271
  economic change, 5, 18, 21
  economic globalism, 22
  economic inequality, 8
  economic insecurity, 243
  economic privilege, 21
  First Turning and, 424–26
  fiscal policy, 21
  gig economy, 4
  Glorious Revolution Crisis and, 256
  during Highs, 414–15
  Millennial Crisis and, 240, 257, 424–26
  Millennial Generation and, 368–70, 379
  parallel rhythms and, 128–30
  "sharing economy," 367
Edison, Thomas, *85*
education, 6
  G.I. Generation and, 375
  health and, 6
  Homeland Generation and, 387, 389–90, 391, 392–93, 398, 399
  income and, 6
  longevity and, 6
  Silent Generation and, 395
  "social and emotional learning" (SEL), 390
  voting behavior and, 236–37
Edwardian era, 175
Edward IV, 221, 222
Edwards, Jonathan, *87*, 105, 109, 450
Edward VI, 62
Einstein, Albert, 72, 342
Eisenhower, Dwight D., 12, *73*, *75*, 84, 109, 124, 321, 358, 405, 407–8, 414, 436, 443
Eisler, Benita, 394
Ekpyrosis, 26, 49, 187–88, 191–92, 247–58, 307, 453
  civil war and, 268
  Fourth Turning and, 192, 275
  Generation X and, 363–64
  G.I. Generation and, 383
  Great Depression-World War II Crisis and, 192
  Millennial Crisis and, 226, 247–58, 260–61, 265, 273–74, 288, 383
  social mood and, 255
élan vital, 44
elderhood, 70–71. *See also under specific generations*
  late, 319–32
  leadership roles and, 165
elections, 7
  1974, 324
  1992, 237–38, 324
  1996, 324
  2000, 237–38
  2004, 237
  2016, 230, 241, 251
  2018, 241
  2020, 11, 231, 237, 241
  2021, 241
  2022, 9, 231, 241
  electoral college and, 230

About the Author

Neil Howe is a historian, economist, and demographer who writes and speaks frequently on generational change, American history, and long-term fiscal policy. He has coauthored seven books with William Strauss, including *Generations* (1991), *13th Gen* (1993), *The Fourth Turning* (1997), and *Millennials Rising* (2000). His other books include *On Borrowed Time* (with Peter G. Peterson, 1988) and *The Graying of the Great Powers* (with Richard Jackson, 2008). He is managing director of demography for Hedgeye, an investment advisory firm. He is also a senior associate at the Center for Strategic and International Studies and at the Global Aging Institute. He grew up in California and holds graduate degrees in history and economics from Yale University. He lives in Great Falls, Virginia.